To my good friend,
Chris Barker
With sincere appreciation
for our friendship.

Roy Honeycutt
Kansas City, Mo.
December 21, 1971

Volume 1

The Broadman Bible Commentary

EDITORIAL BOARD

General Editor
Clifton J. Allen

Old Testament Consulting Editors
John I Durham
Roy L. Honeycutt, Jr.

New Testament Consulting Editors
John William MacGorman
Frank Stagg

Associate Editors
William J. Fallis
Joseph F. Green

Editorial Consultant
Howard P. Colson

BROADMAN PRESS · Nashville, Tennessee

The
Broadman
Bible
Commentary

Volume 1

General Articles
Genesis · Exodus

Dewey Decimal classification: 220.7
Library of Congress catalog card number: 78–93918
Printed in the United States of America
20.JY69KSP

Advisory Board

Clifton J. Allen, Formerly Editorial Secretary, Baptist Sunday School Board

J. P. Allen, Pastor, Broadway Baptist Church, Fort Worth

John E. Barnes, Jr., Pastor, Main Street Baptist Church, Hattiesburg

Olin T. Binkley, President, Southeastern Baptist Theological Seminary

William J. Brown, Manager, Eastern Department, Baptist Book Stores, Baptist Sunday School Board

John R. Claypool, Pastor, Crescent Hill Baptist Church, Louisville

Howard P. Colson, Editorial Secretary, Baptist Sunday School Board

Chauncey R. Daley, Jr., Editor, *Western Recorder*, Middletown, Kentucky

Joseph R. Estes, Secretary, Department of Work Related to Non-Evangelicals, Baptist Home Mission Board

William J. Fallis, Senior Editor, General Religious Books, Broadman Press

Allen W. Graves, Dean, School of Religious Education, Southern Baptist Theological Seminary

Joseph F. Green, Editor, Bible Study Books, Broadman Press

Ralph A. Herring, Formerly Director, Seminary Extension Department, Southern Baptist Convention

Herschel H. Hobbs, Pastor, First Baptist Church, Oklahoma City

Warren C. Hultgren, Pastor, First Baptist Church, Tulsa

Lamar Jackson, Pastor, Southside Baptist Church, Birmingham

L. D. Johnson, Chaplain, Furman University

J. Hardee Kennedy, Professor of Old Testament and Hebrew, New Orleans Baptist Theological Seminary

Herman L. King, Director, Publishing Division, Baptist Sunday School Board

William W. Lancaster, Pastor, First Baptist Church, Decatur, Georgia

Randall Lolley, Pastor, First Baptist Church, Winston-Salem

C. DeWitt Matthews, Professor of Preaching, Midwestern Baptist Theological Seminary

John P. Newport, Professor of Philosophy of Religion, Southwestern Baptist Theological Seminary

Lucius M. Polhill, Formerly Executive Secretary, Baptist General Association of Virginia

Porter Routh, Executive Secretary-Treasurer, Executive Committee, Southern Baptist Convention

John L. Slaughter, Formerly Pastor, First Baptist Church, Spartanburg

R. Houston Smith, Pastor, First Baptist Church, Pineville, Louisiana

James L. Sullivan, Executive Secretary, Baptist Sunday School Board

Ray Summers, Chairman, Department of Religion, Baylor University

Charles A. Trentham, Pastor, First Baptist Church, Knoxville

Keith Von Hagen, Director, Book Store Division, Baptist Sunday School Board

J. R. White, Pastor, First Baptist Church, Montgomery

Conrad Willard, Pastor, Central Baptist Church, Miami

Kyle M. Yates, Jr., Professor of Religion, Oklahoma State University

Contributors

Clifton J. Allen, Baptist Sunday School Board (retired): *General Article*

Morris Ashcraft, Midwestern Baptist Theological Seminary: *Revelation*

G. R. Beasley-Murray, Spurgeon's College, London: *2 Corinthians*

T. Miles Bennett, Southwestern Baptist Theological Seminary: *Malachi*

Reidar B. Bjornard, Northern Baptist Theological Seminary: *Esther*

Robert G. Bratcher, American Bible Society: *General Article*

James A. Brooks, New Orleans Baptist Theological Seminary: *General Article*

Raymond Bryan Brown, Southeastern Baptist Theological Seminary: *1 Corinthians*

John T. Bunn, Campbell College: *Song of Solomon; Nahum*

Joseph A. Callaway, Southern Baptist Theological Seminary: *General Article*

Ronald E. Clements, University of Cambridge: *Leviticus*

E. Luther Copeland, Southeastern Baptist Theological Seminary: *General Article*

Bruce C. Cresson, Baylor University: *Obadiah*

Edward R. Dalglish, Baylor University: *Judges; Ezekiel*

G. Henton Davies, Regent's Park College, Oxford: *Genesis*

John I Durham, Southeastern Baptist Theological Seminary: *Psalms; General Article*

Frank E. Eakin, Jr., University of Richmond: *Zephaniah*

Clyde T. Francisco, Southern Baptist Theological Seminary: *1, 2 Chronicles; General Article*

D. David Garland, Southwestern Baptist Theological Seminary: *Habakkuk*

A. J. Glaze, Jr., Seminario Internacional Teologico Bautista, Buenos Aires: *Jonah*

James Leo Green, Southeastern Baptist Theological Seminary: *Jeremiah*

Emmett Willard Hamrick, Wake Forest University: *Ezra; Nehemiah*

William L. Hendricks, Southwestern Baptist Theological Seminary: *General Article*

E. Glenn Hinson, Southern Baptist Theological Seminary: *1, 2 Timothy; Titus; General Article*

Herschel H. Hobbs, First Baptist Church, Oklahoma City: *1, 2 Thessalonians*

Roy L. Honeycutt, Jr., Midwestern Baptist Theological Seminary: *Exodus; Hosea*

William E. Hull, Southern Baptist Theological Seminary: *John*

Page H. Kelley, Southern Baptist Theological Seminary: *Isaiah*

J. Hardee Kennedy, New Orleans Baptist Theological Seminary: *Ruth; Joel*

Robert B. Laurin, American Baptist Seminary of the West; *Lamentations*

John William MacGorman, Southwestern Baptist Theological Seminary: *Galatians*

Edward A. McDowell, Southeastern Baptist Theological Seminary (retired): *1, 2, 3 John*

Ralph P. Martin, Fuller Theological Seminary: *Ephesians*

M. Pierce Matheney, Jr., Midwestern Baptist Theological Seminary: *1, 2 Kings*

Dale Moody, Southern Baptist Theological Seminary: *Romans*

William H. Morton, Midwestern Baptist Theological Seminary: *Joshua*

John P. Newport, Southwestern Baptist Theological Seminary: *General Article*

John Joseph Owens, Southern Baptist Theological Seminary: *Numbers; Daniel*

Wayne H. Peterson, Golden Gate Baptist Theological Seminary: *Ecclesiastes*

Ben F. Philbeck, Jr., Carson-Newman College: *1, 2 Samuel*

William M. Pinson, Jr., Southwestern Baptist Theological Seminary: *General Article*

Ray F. Robbins, New Orleans Baptist Theological Seminary: *Philemon*

Eric C. Rust, Southern Baptist Theological Seminary: *General Article*

B. Elmo Scoggin, Southeastern Baptist Theological Seminary: *Micah; General Article*

Burlan A. Sizemore, Jr., Midwestern Baptist Theological Seminary: *General Article*

David A. Smith, Furman University: *Haggai*

Ralph L. Smith, Southwestern Baptist Theological Seminary: *Amos*

T. C. Smith, Furman University: *Acts; General Article*

Harold S. Songer, Southern Baptist Theological Seminary: *James*

Frank Stagg, Southern Baptist Theological Seminary: *Matthew*

Ray Summers, Baylor University: *1, 2 Peter; Jude; General Article*

Marvin E. Tate, Jr., Southern Baptist Theological Seminary: *Proverbs*

Malcolm O. Tolbert, New Orleans Baptist Theological Seminary: *Luke*

Charles A. Trentham, First Baptist Church, Knoxville: *Hebrews; General Article*

Henry E. Turlington, University Baptist Church, Chapel Hill, North Carolina: *Mark*

W. Curtis Vaughan, Southwestern Baptist Theological Seminary: *Philippians*

John D. W. Watts, Baptist Theological Seminary, Zurich: *Deuteronomy; Zechariah*

R. E. O. White, Baptist Theological College, Glasgow: *Colossians*

Kyle M. Yates, Jr., Oklahoma State University: *Job*

Preface

THE BROADMAN BIBLE COMMENTARY presents current biblical study within the context of strong faith in the authority, adequacy, and reliability of the Bible as the Word of God. It seeks to offer help and guidance to the Christian who is willing to undertake Bible study as a serious, rewarding pursuit. The publisher thus has defined the scope and purpose of the COMMENTARY to produce a work suited to the Bible study needs of both ministers and laymen. The findings of biblical scholarship are presented so that readers without formal theological education can use them in their own Bible study. Footnotes and technical words are limited to essential information.

Writers have been carefully selected for their reverent Christian faith and their knowledge of Bible truth. Keeping in mind the needs of a general readership, the writers present special information about language and history where it helps to clarify the meaning of the text. They face Bible problems—not only in language but in doctrine and ethics—but avoid fine points that have little bearing on how we should understand and apply the Bible. They express their own views and convictions. At the same time, they present alternative views when such are advocated by other serious, well-informed students of the Bible. The views presented, therefore, cannot be regarded as the official position of the publisher.

This COMMENTARY is the result of many years' planning and preparation. Broadman Press began in 1958 to explore needs and possibilities for the present work. In this year and again in 1959, Christian leaders—particularly pastors and seminary professors—were brought together to consider whether a new commentary was needed and what shape it might take. Growing out

of these deliberations in 1961, the board of trustees governing the Press authorized the publication of a multivolume commentary. Further planning led in 1966 to the selection of a general editor and an Advisory Board. This board of pastors, professors, and denominational leaders met in September, 1966, reviewing preliminary plans and making definite recommendations which have been carried out as the COMMENTARY has been developed.

Early in 1967, four consulting editors were selected, two for the Old Testament and two for the New. Under the leadership of the general editor, these men have worked with the Broadman Press personnel to plan the COMMENTARY in detail. They have participated fully in the selection of the writers and the evaluation of manuscripts. They have given generously of time and effort, earning the highest esteem and gratitude of Press employees who have worked with them.

The selection of the Revised Standard Version as the Bible text for the COMMENTARY was made in 1967 also. This grew out of careful consideration of possible alternatives, which were fully discussed in the meeting of the Advisory Board. The adoption of an English version as a standard text was recognized as desirable, meaning that only the King James, American Standard, and Revised Standard Versions were available for consideration.

The King James Version was recognized as holding first place in the hearts of many Christians but as suffering from inaccuracies in translation and obscurities in phrasing. The American Standard was seen as free from these two problems but deficient in an attractive English style and wide current use. The Revised Standard retains the accuracy and clarity of the American Standard and has a pleasing style and a growing use. It thus enjoys a strong advantage over each of the others, making it by far the most desirable choice.

Throughout the COMMENTARY the treatment of the biblical text aims at a balanced combination of exegesis and exposition, admittedly recognizing that the nature of the various books and the space assigned will properly modify the application of this approach.

The general articles appearing in Volumes 1, 8, and 12 are designed to provide background material to enrich one's understanding of the nature of the Bible and the distinctive aspects of each Testament. Those in Volume 12 focus on the implications of biblical teaching in the areas of worship, ethical duty, and the world mission of the church.

The COMMENTARY avoids current theological fads and changing theories. It concerns itself with the deep realities of God's dealings with men, his revelation in Christ, his eternal gospel, and his purpose for the redemption of the world. It seeks to relate the word of God in Scripture and in the living Word to the deep needs of persons and to mankind in God's world.

Through faithful interpretation of God's message in the Scriptures, therefore, the COMMENTARY seeks to reflect the inseparable relation of truth to life, of meaning to experience. Its aim is to breathe the atmosphere of life-relatedness. It seeks to express the dynamic relation between redemptive truth and living persons. May it serve as a means whereby God's children hear with greater clarity what God the Father is saying to them.

Contents

General Articles

The Book of the Christian Faith

CLIFTON J. ALLEN

We begin with the affirmation—the Bible is the Word of God. But we must not stop at this point. Christians must do more than praise the Bible. They must be prepared to grapple with serious questions about the Bible. These questions are raised not by cynics and skeptics only; they are raised also by devout and searching students of the Bible. To engage in such searching study involves the necessity for facing all valid questions about the nature and authority of the Bible and openmindedness in evaluating the validity of its claims and the integrity of its witness. We have no reason to avoid these questions. The Bible is in no danger of embarrassment or liquidation!

Christians must also become more aware of the realistic, but often hostile and skeptical, questions of the unbelieving and secular world about the Bible. These questions call for answers which come from accurate and thorough knowledge and from reverent faith nurtured by intelligent understanding of the Bible. A view of the Bible which has not encountered attack from ignorance, prejudice, unbelief, or humanistic pride may be unreliable because it has not been tested. A faith that asks no questions is scarcely faith because it seeks no meanings.

We properly ask about the Bible: What is its nature? How did it come to us? What is the basis of its authority? What is its relevance and significance? As we consider these questions it is essential to keep in mind what the Bible is about. More than anything else, it is a record and an interpretation of God's self-disclosure to man: it is the authentic account of the revelation of God in Jesus Christ for the redemption of man. It is the story of salvation:[1] the saving purpose, the saving acts, the saving grace, and the saving power of the Lord; the

saving mission of the people of God; and the consummation of God's saving work through the lordship of Christ. This concept as to what the Bible is about is the basic perspective from which this article will seek to explore important questions about the Bible.

I. The Nature of the Bible

It is in order now to ask, What is the nature of the Bible? In what sense is the Bible the Word of God? Why is it so difficult to understand? How can such an ancient book have timeless relevance? Answers to these questions—and others of like importance—call for a mature understanding of what the Bible is and penetrating insight as to its background, its characteristics, and its central purpose.

1. Origin, Setting, and Culture

First of all, let it be observed that the Bible is of ancient origin. The first chapters tell about the creation of the universe and of man, of God and his dealings with men from the beginning of the world, and of events which antedate exact historical identification. And then the narrative begins to tell the story of Abraham and his descendants, the era involved beginning about 2000 B.C. The written account of the continuing story of God and his people extends on to cover the first century of the Christian era. Thus the Bible must be understood as a very ancient book.

Further, the Bible has come to us out of a Semitic setting, that is, the setting of the ancient Near East. The Bible has to do primarily with the descendants of Abraham, God's chosen people, who inhabited the land of Canaan, a narrow strip along the eastern shore of the Mediterranean. This small area was a sort of bridge or connecting route between the people of the Tigris-Euphrates

---

[1] Cf. A. M. Hunter, *The Message of the New Testament*, particularly pp. 11–12.

Valley in the east and the people in the Nile Valley to the southwest. Abraham himself was representative of the Semitic people who lived in southwest Asia—Babylonians, Assyrians, Aramaeans, Canaanites, and Phoenicians.

We recognize also that the people of the Bible reflected the culture which was their heritage and their setting. The Old Testament reflects the agricultural background and experience of the people of Israel; but it reveals also the growing influence of urban development. The way the people thought about God in anthropomorphic terms, as intimately associated with the things of nature, as vindictive, and as being partial toward the people of Israel reflected the impact of their cultural heritage. The way the people thought of the family—of the authority figure in the husband and the father, of the subservience and inferiority of women, and of the importance of having children—was also affected by their culture. Their concept of the material order as the immediate expression of the presence and power of God and their strong leaning toward idolatry showed the impact of cultural concept and practice. The thought forms and concepts which appear throughout the Bible are the natural expression of the experience of the people.

By the time of the New Testament, Jews in Palestine felt strong antipathy, even bitter hostility in many cases, toward Gentiles. Throughout the Roman world, involvement in commerce and trade in the great cities of the empire contributed to communication, understanding, and in some cases a degree of goodwill. The New Testament itself, however, with its dynamic gospel of God's redemption in Christ, reflects its origin and cultural setting in the Judeo-Christian heritage of the Graeco-Roman civilization. The New Testament has come to us out of a Jewish background, through the Greek language, from life under the control of Rome, and out of a divine intention that the gospel knows no difference of race or language or culture and is meant for all peoples, all cultures, and all generations.

2. Literature of Many Kinds and Forms

The Bible is much more than a collection of religious writings. To be understood adequately, it must be seen as literature of different kinds and forms. If one analyzes the Bible carefully to distinguish varying literary forms he will find examples of the following: history, law, poetry, drama, prophecy, wisdom literature, apocalyptic literature, hymns, anthems, sermons, addresses, letters, epics, acrostics, genealogies, statistical lists, parables, allegories, and stories. For practical purposes, a knowledge of the more refined distinctions of literary forms is not essential; but for a mature understanding of the Bible, a recognition that it is literature of varying kinds is imperative.

The first five books of the Bible came to be called the Law. But the Pentateuch is much more than law, as a literary form. The book of Genesis is historical, biographical, and theological. There is like material in the next four books. But in these four books we have the laws which became the mandate and guide for the worship of God, for man's moral conduct, and for man's living in community and in interpersonal relationships. Inevitably, many of the laws reflected the impact of Israel's cultural situation, the immaturity of the people in their spiritual and moral development, and the effort of divinely called leaders to cultivate faithfulness to God and righteousness and justice among the people.

The next part of the Old Testament is usually thought of as a section of historical books. In the Hebrew Bible, the books from Joshua to 2 Kings were known as the Former Prophets. The Latter Prophets included Isaiah and Jeremiah and the last twelve books of the Old Testament. These two groups, regularly called the Prophets as a section of the Hebrew Scriptures, thus included most of the historical material in the Old Testament and nearly all of the prophetic materials—a combination of history and prophecy.

History—and this would include books

other than the ones named above—tells the story of people and events: of suffering, struggle, success, failure, apostasy, repentance and renewal, fidelity, and rebellion. The facts of history were recorded with realism, showing the people at their worst and their best, showing how the people misunderstood the purposes of God and at times acted in ways utterly foreign to the nature of God though they claimed to be doing the will of God, and showing how God acted to reveal himself, to execute judgment, to bestow mercy and blessings, to overrule the ignorance and perversity of his people, and to carry forward his purpose in Israel.

The history of Israel cannot be understood apart from prophecy. And let it be remembered that the prophets declared the word of God to the people of their respective generations. Prophecy is not primarily a prediction of future events, but a proclamation of judgment or consolation or duty or purpose in relation to the people at the point of their need. We understand the prophetic writings best not as mystical foretellings of future events but as fearless declarations of the purpose of God for his people in their immediate situation. Granting this, however, we must not overlook that many of the prophets declared the word of God with application to the future, pointing out the directions of God's purpose for his people, the sure promise of his redemption for all people, and the certain consummation of his kingdom of righteousness and peace.

Much of the Old Testament is poetry. Aside from the strictly poetical books, poetry is found in books of law, books of history, and books of prophecy. It is important to realize that poetry must be understood as poetry, though it be a medium of divine revelation. It depends on images and figures of speech. The element of feeling and emotion is dominant. Truth is expressed imaginatively and must be understood through imagination. An effort to understand poetry on the basis of the literal phrasing ignores the nature of poetry and leads to sure mis-

understanding of meaning.

The poetry of the Bible, in keeping with the nature of real poetry, is the expression of intense feeling, which will include fear as well as trust, wrath as well as kindness, lust as well as purity, hate as well as love, self-pity as well as self-confidence, and despair as well as hope. The clue to interpretation will call for the application of poetic insight.

The book of Job is almost entirely poetry. But it is also an example of drama. Hence another literary form is utilized to teach the need for a true understanding of the problem of human suffering. The intensity of Job's suffering and the nature of the problem faced made drama all the more effective as the medium of truth, the truth finally revealed to Job through God's self-revelation of his sovereignty, his righteousness, and his greatness.

Another kind of literature is known as wisdom literature. It is represented particularly by Proverbs and Ecclesiastes in the Old Testament and the letter of James in the New Testament. The book of Job may also be identified as wisdom literature. The wisdom writings, though adopting various literary forms, represent the distilled wisdom of human experience and set forth the values and virtues, the principles and insights, that may well make up one's philosophy of life, particularly in terms of choosing goals and following patterns that contribute to integrity, harmony, reverence, chastity, diligence, self-confidence, and achievement.

When we turn to the New Testament we are immediately confronted by the Gospels. As to the literary form, they combine history, biography, parable, extended discourse, dialogue, and prayer. But the Gospels are unique. They are documents of faith. They tell about one central figure, Jesus Christ. They are the dramatic record of Jesus in action, of what he said and did, of the impact of his personality on other persons, of what other persons thought about him and how they reacted to him, and, finally, of Jesus' self-giving on the cross and his resurrection from the dead. The

Gospels as literature can never be separated from the living reality and dynamic impact of the Son of man.

The book of Acts is the second part of the Luke-Acts story. It, therefore, sustains the closest possible relation to the Gospels—and is almost a series of feature stories. It tells of what the followers of Jesus did and taught in the consciousness of his living presence with them and through the power of his Spirit.

The letters in the New Testament have much in common as a literary form, but they vary greatly in length and purpose and style of writing and intended audience. Some were addressed to churches, some to individuals, some to scattered groups of Christians, and some to unidentified recipients. These letters, including those to the seven churches in the book of Revelation, constitute an interpretation of the gospel of Christ, a portrayal of New Testament church life and practice, and a record of ministry and fidelity and persecution and struggle and hope on the part of persons engaged in service to Jesus Christ. A characteristic of these letters, naturally, is the personal element, the relation of the writer to his readers (in some cases, to one person). He wrote to share his experience and concern, conscious of the bond of Christian fellowship.

The Bible includes still another kind of literature known as apocalyptic. The two principal books of apocalyptic literature are the book of Daniel and the Revelation. This kind of literature was the product of times of intense crisis for the people of God. It was marked by a strong eschatological concern and expectation and a focus on the dynamic manifestation of God in judgment. The style of apocalyptic literature was the presentation of truth by means of images and symbols which represented evil forces, the sufferings and rewards of God's people, and the mighty acts of God in judgment and deliverance and victory. One should come to it with intelligent awareness that the framework of symbols and images points to persons and events and forces in the long distant past. Even so, the truth about the complete sovereignty and eternal purpose of God which gave encouragement and consolation to his people in the past is equally relevant for God's people through the unfolding centuries.

We will therefore understand that the Bible is an example of varying literary forms. God used the skills and interests of many writers as the medium of his self-revelation. The many kinds of writing contribute to richness of meaning and diversity and depth of human interest. Awareness of characteristic elements of literary style and form will provide clues to a fuller understanding of the message of truth.

3. Divine Revelation Through Human Media

The Bible is a divine revelation. This is indeed the most significant aspect of its nature, the explanation of its significance, and the ground of its authority. We must not stop, however, with these affirmations. We must explore in depth what is meant by revelation, what is meant by inspiration, how these are related, and how they are to be understood in the light of all we can know about the nature of the Bible and how it has come to us in the providence of God.

What is revelation?—Revelation is the truth which has come to us from God. God has spoken to man in many ways—through the world of nature, through judgments in human history, through providences in personal experience, and through the inner voice of conscience. But the Bible is the unique account of God's self-disclosure. It is the written record of his words and acts.

From the beginning to the end, the Bible declares that God has revealed himself to man and that the Bible is itself a trustworthy account of this revelation. Such phrases as the following occur repeatedly throughout the Old Testament: "God said"; "the Lord spoke"; "God commanded"; "the word of God came"; "God made known"; "the Lord appeared." These are representative of a much larger number of revelation formulae. The Bible also tells again and again of what God did, of his acts of creation, of judgment, of deliverance, of election, of guidance, of consolation, of destruction, of manifestation, of healing, and of overruling sovereignty. God acted to make himself known to his people and to accomplish his purpose through them.

But the supreme act of God's self-revelation about which the Bible tells was his coming in Jesus Christ. "The Word became flesh and dwelt among us, full of grace and truth; we have beheld his glory, glory as of the only Son from the Father" (John 1:14). The word of God was spoken to man by the living Word. "In many and various ways God spoke of old to our fathers by the prophets; but in these last days he has spoken to us by a Son" (Heb. 1:1–2). This sublime statement from the letter to the Hebrews gathers up the full truth about revelation and gives us the clue to the Bible as the revelation of God. The Old Testament pointed to the coming of One who would be the agent of God's redemption. The New Testament tells of his coming, of his sinless life and self-giving ministry, of his death, of his resurrection, of his saviourhood, and of his lordship; and it declares that in him the whole fulness of deity dwelt bodily (Col. 2:9).

We are now prepared to look at the Bible as a whole. It is to be seen in the light of God's perfect revelation in Jesus Christ. The supreme revelation of God is a Person. All that the Bible tells us about God and his nature and his acts and what various persons understood about him or attributed to him must be interpreted and brought into harmony with the nature and truth and love and purpose of God in Christ. This recognizes that many persons to whom God spoke "in many and various ways" before the coming of Christ did not understand God perfectly, did not apprehend his purposes fully, and could not know his will clearly.

Old Testament examples of seeming conflict with the fact that God is love, it is claimed by many persons, are simply mysteries of omniscience and therefore should not be questioned. Such persons will approach any number of baffling mysteries in the Scriptures in this way and be satisfied. On the other hand, many other persons will insist that the Bible, though the completely authoritative revelation of God, can be rightly understood, rightly interpreted, only in the full light of the truth of Jesus Christ, the living Word, the complete and perfect revelation of God. Such persons will hold that this is in harmony with the eternal purpose of God that all things in heaven and on earth and under the earth shall come under the lordship of Christ. The Holy Scriptures are to be best understood in the light of what he taught and what he did and who he is as the Word of God.

Inspiration and revelation.—Two Scripture passages immediately come to mind: first, Paul's word to Timothy, "All Scripture is inspired by God and profitable for teaching, for reproof, for correction, and for training in righteousness, that the man of God may be complete, equipped for every good work" (2 Tim. 3:16–17); second, from 2 Peter, "No prophecy of Scripture is a matter of one's own interpretation, because no prophecy ever came by the impulse of man, but men moved by the Holy Spirit spoke from God" (1:20–21). These passages, and others either directly or indirectly, affirm that the Bible is an inspired revelation.

Such terms as the following are usually applied to inspiration: verbal inspiration, plenary inspiration, and dynamic inspiration. The connotation or meaning attached to these words varies widely. The question revolves largely around the degree of inerrancy in the words of the Scriptures and the concept of unity in the message of the Scriptures.

The view of verbal inspiration is usually applied to the Scriptures in the original languages rather than to subsequent translations, though actually this view is often understood and championed chiefly on the basis of the King James Version. While again there are variations in the meaning attached to verbal inspiration, the supporters of this view would claim that the writers of the Scriptures were inspired to the degree of using the very words given by God as the medium for his truth. The Scriptures therefore are inerrant and infallible.

This obviously reduces the writer almost to the equivalent of a tool in the hands of God and makes him virtually the completely controlled agent of God. While few thinking persons would agree that verbal inspiration is essentially divine dictation, written down almost mechanically, the process leaves almost no room for responsible action or personal involvement on the part of the writer. There are many persons who hold this view of inspiration and find it fully satisfying in keeping with their concept of God's sovereignty and wisdom and God's initiative in revelation. They feel that any compromise of this position leads to an undermining of biblical authority.

Another view of the Bible may be described as plenary inspiration. The term has varying connotations. The heart of this view is that the Bible is fully inspired but not verbally inspired. The writers were not controlled agents to the extent that they did not utilize their background of experience and knowledge. But they were all so completely enlightened and guided and empowered by God's Spirit that they were preserved from any error in transmitting the divine revelation. Hence the Bible is fully inspired and the revelation inerrant as to fact and event and doctrine. Such a view of inspiration, satisfying and acceptable to a great number of sincere and thoughtful Christians, including competent scholars, seeks to avoid something of the extreme literalism and rigidly controlled elements of verbal inspiration while at the same time maintaining a concept of practical inerrancy of the whole Bible and its several parts.

Still another concept of inspiration may be identified as dynamic. Admittedly, the term lacks preciseness because the reality which it identifies is marked by mystery and complexity. Essentially, however, this view holds that the Holy Scriptures came into being and derived their character as the authoritative revelation of God through the activity of God's Spirit whose quickening and enlightening and guiding power made chosen men the medium of God's purpose. The Scriptures are indeed inspired ("God-breathed") because their truth is from God and about God. "Men moved by the Holy Spirit spoke from God" (2 Peter 1:21). In ways which we cannot understand and through processes which we cannot identify, God chose and equipped many persons to record his acts, to interpret his purposes, and to declare his word.

According to this view, the inspiration of the Bible is much more its completeness and adequacy as the written record of God's self-revelation and as the guide for man in all matters of faith and practice than it is a matter of inerrancy in wording and analogy and certain details about persons and events. Inspiration is more a matter of the message of God's salvation than the method or process by which it was reduced to written form. The authority of the Bible is in its wholeness and unity in the light of the truth of God in Christ.

The view of dynamic inspiration rests solidly on the repeated declaration in the Scriptures that through them God speaks to man. This view rests again on the inherent nature of the Scriptures as a unique treasure of divine wisdom which fits the totality of human experience as to religious faith, moral duty, and ethical responsibility. The Bible continues to speak in basic principle to every generation with relevance and currency: it continues to declare the word of the living God to living man in the contemporary human situation.

This view rests further on the fact that the Scriptures are effective in human experience for the purposes of God. Relevant examples of this truth are found in the following passages: Psalm 119:9,11; John 5:39; 20:31; Romans 15:4; Hebrews 4:12; 2 Peter 1:16–19; and Romans 1:16. The evidence and proof of the inspiration of the Scriptures is that they are indeed "profitable for teaching, for reproof, for correction, and for training in righteousness, that the man of God may be complete, equipped for every good work" (2 Tim. 3:16–17).

The truth of the biblical revelation is God-breathed. It is indwelt by the living Spirit of God. It is effective for regeneration and sanctification. It is redemptive and reconciling. Consequently, a dynamic view of inspiration focuses on the truth which has its essence and purpose and authority in Jesus Christ.

Therefore, a dynamic view of inspiration is not dependent on a mystical, inexplicable, and unverifiable inerrancy in every word of Scripture or on the concept that inspiration can allow no error of fact or substance. Rather, it accepts the Bible in wholeness and unity as inspired: inerrant as the only completely authentic witness to God's self-revelation in Christ and his salvation through Christ; inerrant because its truth is the perfect instrument of the Spirit to bring men to faith and righteousness and hope; and inerrant because its teaching, interpreted by the life and work of Christ, is the infallible guide as to how the people of God ought to live and what they can surely believe under the leading of the Spirit of Christ.

There is perhaps need at this point to stress the fact that the different views of inspiration are not without problems, not without unanswered questions. These should be faced with honesty and objectivity.

The following problems are inherent in a view of verbal inspiration: (1) Since fallible persons copied the original manuscripts over hundreds of years, with meticulous accuracy but not without mistakes, and since other fallible persons translated the original Scriptures into different languages, and since there are textual variations in the most trustworthy manuscripts extant, the value of an infallible verbal original is lost to the present and future generations, no copies of the original writings now being available.

(2) A careful reading and examination of the Scriptures discloses some obvious contradictions or discrepancies, not involving any major doctrine or issue but quite sufficient to raise a problem as to the validity of verbal inspiration. Two examples serve to illustrate the point: The reference to Abiathar (Mark 2:26) and Ahimelech (1 Sam. 21:1) is inconsistent. In one case the Lord is said to incite David to take a census, in another case, Satan (2 Sam. 24:1; 1 Chron. 21:1).

(3) Verbal inspiration seems to submerge human instrumentality to the point that writers of the Scriptures were less than free in their response to the will of God's Spirit.

(4) Verbal inspiration tends to place all of the Bible on the same level of divine revelation.

(5) Verbal inspiration involves serious difficulties in interpretation in that the wording of various passages, directly or indirectly, seems to attribute to God acts and attitudes out of harmony with his nature as holy love and clearly in conflict with the example and teaching of Jesus (cf. Deut. 17:2–7; 2 Sam. 21:1–9 in relation to Deut. 24:16; Psalms 69:22–28; 109:6–19; 137:7–9; 1 Chron. 13:9–10).

(6) Verbal inspiration seems to require explanations which make verbal inspiration unreal. For example, Mary refers to Joseph as the father of Jesus (Luke 2:48). What Mary meant is easily explained, unless one is restricted to verbal inerrancy.

(7) Verbal inspiration appears irreconcilable with what seem to be facts growing out of objective research into and serious study of the Bible. Evidence supports a multiple authorship of the Pentateuch, drawing on oral and written sources and ultimately involving collating and editing, all of which seems to strain the view of verbal inspiration to the point of unreality. Much of the Old Testament would involve a similar problem. Luke explains with care (1:1–4) his method of research and sources of information, which would have little relevance if every word he wrote was virtually dictated by the Spirit. Paul admits that some of his utterances are his, not God's (1 Cor. 7:12,25; cf. vv. 8–10,40). Of course, many of the conclusions of critical study cannot be dogmatically proved, but established and identifiable facts serve to bring in question the feasibility of verbal inspiration more

than to undergird it as an acceptable view.

A view of plenary inspiration involves most of the problems already mentioned with respect to verbal inspiration, the differences being chiefly a matter of degree. Particularly, this view involves the problems of a divine will virtually imposed on the writers of the Scriptures, the submergence of the findings of critical studies as controverting full inspiration, and attributing to God attitudes and actions seemingly out of harmony with his revelation in Christ. It legitimizes many statements of Scripture as revelation, though they seem to be the result of human weakness and a misunderstanding of God. This view gives little recognition to the progressive aspect of revelation.

The view of dynamic inspiration likewise involves problems—problems peculiar to itself. (1) It faces the necessity to recognize and to give due weight to many biblical statements which seem to imply or emphasize the element of full if not verbal inspiration. Also, it must explain these without the bias of presupposition and interpret such statements without losing the thrust of their supernatural implication. (2) This view involves the temptation to depend too strongly on human criteria and wisdom to distinguish between the clearly spoken word of the Lord and the misunderstanding of men about the purpose and will of the Lord. (3) This view involves the tendency—which becomes real in all too many cases—to minimize the element of divine inspiration and to give more attention to the human medium of inspiration. (4) This view involves the obligation—often overlooked by critical scholars—to recognize the element of reverent faith as the clue to the understanding of the Scriptures and to recognize that many difficult questions about the nature of the Bible are not answerable by the resources of critical research but by trust in God with humility. (5) The supporters of this view are under obligation to bring to the Bible a greater degree of disciplined study to find the deeper levels of truth and a greater degree of sensitivity to the dynamic of the living Spirit to hear the

word of the Lord through the Spirit.

To the writer of this article, the problems of the dynamic view of inspiration, though real, do not invalidate this view of the Scriptures. The problems are resolved by reverent faith in the Lord of the Scriptures and in the Scriptures themselves as the Word of God, in wholeness and unity in Christ. They are resolved by openmindedness to truth and the fruits of objective research. And they are further resolved by submission to the Holy Spirit who interprets the Word of God in Christ to all persons who desire to know the mind of Christ and to do the will of the Lord.

Persons of earnest purpose toward God and of strong conviction about his revelation in the Scriptures will have different views about inspiration. Each person may well seek for fuller understandings about the Bible as the basis for the view that makes the Bible more meaningful in his own experience.

Some summary statements relative to revelation and inspiration are now in order. (1) One's view of revelation and inspiration should not ignore the findings of objective research and critical examination. (2) An acceptable view of revelation and inspiration must allow for the translation of the original languages of the Scriptures and the variations in the available texts of the Hebrew and Greek Scriptures and their implications based on irrefutable knowledge. (3) Many questions have no prospect of being answered. "Proof" in any exact or dogmatic sense is hardly appropriate to one's view of revelation and inspiration. Belief in the fact of inspiration is crucial; a view of the method of inspiration is secondary in importance. (4) It should be remembered that titles and inscriptions and matters of this kind in the Bible are editorial additions, not parts of the original texts of the Scriptures. (5) Some statements about revelation are the result of the Hebrew affinity for anthropomorphism—as the statement that God gave to Moses two tables of stone written by the finger of God (Ex. 31:18). (6) Proof texts are often applied to a view of revelation and inspiration to support questionable conclusions. For example, Jesus said that not an iota or a dot will pass from the law—evidently the Mosaic law—until all is accomplished (Matt. 5:18); and this is said by some to establish inerrancy and infallibility. Surely Jesus with infinite wisdom used a figure of speech to emphasize a truth. He could hardly have meant a literal reference to tiny particles of writing—else how could he set aside explicit words of the Law (Matt. 5:33–34,38–39; cf. Ex. 21:24; Lev. 19:12; Num. 30:2; Deut. 19:21; 23:21)? (7) The Scriptures are an unfolding revelation of God and hence a progressive revelation with their perfect and absolute culmination in the Word made flesh in Christ. (8) The fact of divine revelation and inspiration is in no sense dependent on a particular view of inspiration and is in no jeopardy from critical research and scholarly study.

God's use of human media.—Through these means the inspired revelation is given to men. The Bible is a divine-human book. God revealed himself to living persons. God spoke to men, and they reported what he said: they told of what he did. They passed the record on to the next generation, and the next, and the next, and so on. For an unknown period of time revelation was communicated almost wholly by oral tradition. In the course of time oral tradition became written accounts of the words and acts of the Lord. When this first transpired and to what extent, no one knows. Moses wrote the words of the Lord (Ex. 24:4). How much Moses wrote cannot be determined with any exactness, but references to his part in communicating God's revelation—particularly commandments and statutes—justify the conclusion that what he wrote was an important source on which many years later the writers of the Pentateuch drew for a trustworthy account of God's revelation to and dealings with the children of Israel.

The point of emphasis here is that God ordained human media as the means of a written revelation. How many writers? We do not know. Who were they? We do not know. Moses, Samuel, David, Solomon, and Ezra—God used them. Amos, Isaiah, Jeremiah, and Ezekiel—God used them. But there were others, many others, known and unknown, extending over a period of several centuries, who were moved by the Holy Spirit to put in writing the word of God. And along with writers there should be remembered those who copied and collated the writings and finally gave to them the form in which they ultimately became the Hebrew Scriptures.

Likewise the New Testament. How many writers and who they were—we cannot be certain. We call the familiar names—Paul, Luke, Mark, Matthew, John, James, Jude, and Peter—and evidence is strong to confirm their contributions. But evidence likewise raises questions at least about some of them. The identity of other writers is even more a mystery.

The fact that the revelation of God came through human media explains much about the Bible. It explains to a large degree its variety of literary form and quality, aspects of its human interest and varying moods, and varying levels of spiritual insight and ethical witness.

Let this principle of revelation be stressed. The treasure of inspired revelation, the truth of the biblical revelation, has come to us in "earthen vessels." The writers were men. They were finite and fallible. They were human, and hence subject to limitations of knowledge and understanding. But they were persons through whom the transcendent power of God operated—quickening, illuminating, guiding, and enabling them to be the media of the saving message of God in Christ. The Holy Scriptures have their essential character in their nature as the inspired revelation of God. Pointing to Christ and finding their meaning and unity in Christ, they are the Word of God.

II. From the Revelation to the Book

Another needful question for consideration is: How did the revelation of God become the Book of Holy Scripture? The developments are not traceable by objective evidence, cataloged and verified. They are arrived at by implications and deductions from the internal witness of the Scriptures and what one believes about the way God accomplishes his purpose to reveal himself.

At first revelation was preserved and communicated by oral transmission, which became in the course of time oral tradition. Tradition here in no way implies unreality or something unreliable. From the time of the creation of man, God revealed himself to man; and man began to pass on to succeeding generations the account of experience and the deposit of truth growing out of God's dealings with him and his understanding of the purposes of God.

The Hebrew mind seems to have had a peculiar capacity for memory. Hence the varied cultural experience of people and places, of geography and history, of ritual and worship, of laws and customs, was committed to memory. Leaders of tribes and families assumed a responsible role in passing on these traditions, the most important being those having to do with the words and acts of the Lord.

The developing religious experience of the people who worshiped God became another medium of receiving, interpreting, and communicating revelation. God dealt with his people—disciplined them, gave commandments to them, manifested his glory to them, executed judgment on them, delivered them, blessed them, entered into covenant with them, and called leaders and prophets to declare his words to them. Years became decades and decades centuries. All the while the religious experience of the children of Israel, enriched at times by the observance of the feasts and fidelity in worship and perverted at other times by idolatry and iniquity and hypocrisy, became a medium for revelation.

The events of history involving the people of Israel were still another medium for revelation. God placed his people in the land of Canaan, surrounded by the nations of the ancient Near East. They were on the highway of the nations and inevitably in the current of history. What happened within and without Israel, never apart from God's sovereign purpose and power, furnished a medium of revelation events.

In this same context of religious experience and historic events, God called prophets to declare his word to his people. The word of God came to the prophets, and they declared it faithfully. The prophetic ministry became the climactic medium in the life of Israel for the deposit of revelation. It was the prophetic message, both spoken and written, that enunciated most fully and interpreted most clearly the truth about God, his purpose for his people, and his will and way for all men.

All these were sources, both direct and indirect, from which priests and scribes and kings and prophets drew to write the Old Testament Scriptures. In many cases God spoke directly to chosen individuals who wrote the truth revealed to them. In many other cases, the evidence strongly suggests, writers reported the events and commandments and experiences of earlier traditions and records. And thus the oracles of God became the written revelation of the Old Testament.

Exactly when the several parts, the many books, of the Old Testament were written cannot be determined. The writing covered hundreds of years. There is a rather general consensus among scholars that editors collated written material, produced out of the sources described above, and gave it permanent form. Trustworthy biblical study shows that the Pentateuch existed essentially in its present form by 400 B.C. The books of Joshua, Judges, 1 and 2 Samuel, and 1 and 2 Kings were known by the Jews as the "Former Prophets" and likely came largely into their present form between 650 and 550 B.C. The "Latter Prophets"—the books of Isaiah, Jeremiah, and Ezekiel and from Hosea to Malachi—were likely in their present form by 200 B.C. The "Writings"—the poetical books along with Ruth, Esther, Daniel, Ecclesiastes, Ezra, Nehemiah, and 1 and 2 Chronicles—were written over a long period of time and became a collection by 132 B.C. A council of Jewish rabbis about A.D. 90 accepted the 39 books of the

Old Testament as the Hebrew Canon of the Scriptures. The same 39 books have been likewise accepted in Christian tradition.

Something of the same kind of development took place—in principle but not in pattern—relative to New Testament writings. The supreme difference was that Jesus Christ came, the living Word among men. Some of the writers saw him in the flesh, heard him, saw him, felt him, and knew the magnetism of his physical presence as well as the power of his living Spirit within them. The apostles were persons who companied with Jesus from the baptism of John until the time of Jesus' ascension (Acts 1:21-22). The other writers, we may safely assume, like Luke, knew and talked with some "who from the beginning were eyewitnesses and ministers of the word" (Luke 1:2). Thus the New Testament came out of the face-to-face acquaintance of the apostles with Jesus and their face-to-face conversations with him after his resurrection, out of the oral traditions of eyewitnesses of the Lord, out of the redemptive experience of believing followers, out of the historic events of apostolic witness, out of the koinonia of the living church, out of trials and sufferings and persecution for the name of Christ, and out of the vision of the living Christ and the direct communication of his word of truth and grace and victory.

As with the Old Testament, the time of writing of the 27 New Testament books cannot be fixed definitely. Each book, in some sense, stands alone. Scholars have varying views, and these will be dealt with in the introductions of the book treatments. Evidence generally accepted places the actual writing from A.D. 50 to 100, though some evidence supports a later date for some books, for example, some of the general letters. During the same period many Christian books were written. The question arose as to which of all the writings should be acknowledged as authoritative and counted as part of the Scriptures. The test of their acceptance and worth for more than three centuries—guided, we may be certain, by the Holy Spirit—led to the acceptance of the 27 books which became the New Testament. By the end of the fourth century these books had won their acceptance as being God-given revelation for Christians throughout the ages to come. "The canon was determined by usage, by the common consent of the Christian community, testing the books in its daily life over centuries; not by formal authority" (F. W. Beare, IDB, I, 531).

One word must summarize the truth and give the key to the mystery and the reality of inspired revelation becoming the Holy Scriptures—the sovereign Spirit of God. He called and enlightened, guided and enabled, and moved men to speak from God and for God.

III. The Significance of the Bible

The significance of the Bible rests on obvious and important characteristics, namely, its authority and its relevance.

1. Authority of the Bible

The authority of the Bible of course grows out of its being the inspired revelation of God. Looked at in wholeness and unity, it is the Word of God. Hence it has the authority of God behind it. It is the divine mandate for the religious faith and moral duty of mankind.

But much more needs to be said. How is the authority of the Bible related to Jesus Christ? He claimed all authority in heaven and on earth. He exercised authority over nature and sickness and demons and death. God "made him both Lord and Christ" (Acts 2:36). The final and ultimate authority over all persons and all things is the living Christ. It follows, therefore, that the authority of the Bible must always be seen in the light of the lordship of Christ. Its authority is not in inerrancy of word and phrase or perfect consistency of all numbers and events or perfect understanding of God by his chosen servants. Instead, its authority is in its authentic witness to Jesus Christ as the Word of God. And let it be emphasized that one's understanding of who Christ is as the Son of God and the Word made flesh, of his saving work through his death and resurrection, and of his eternal lordship must be tested by the New Testament. A true understanding of Christ and what his authority means cannot be determined by subjective judgment and experience alone. The authority of the written Word is found in the authority of the living Word through the guidance of the Spirit. On this basis the New Testament is to be accepted by Christians as the authoritative guide for all matters of faith and practice.

The authority of the Bible, therefore, is not something legal and judicial, not the compulsion of literalism or the obligation of proof, but the freedom of the lordship of Christ and the voice of his Spirit. The authority is confirmed by inward acceptance instead of outward declaration. Therefore, to conclude, "the authority of Scripture is found in the power of the living Lord to authenticate himself as he speaks to the human heart through the words and Scripture" (Rolston, *The Bible and Christian Teaching*, p. 34).

2. Relevance of the Bible

Again, the significance of the Bible is due to its relevance. It speaks to every generation. This is true because it is the Word of God, who is eternal and unchangeable. Also, it speaks to persons at the deepest levels of human experience, to their needs and aspirations and possibilities and responsibilities as persons in the image of God. The Bible is always contemporary because it is the word of life from the Lord of life.

The relevance of the Scriptures is seen also in their universal dimension. They declare God's message to man as man—hence to all cultural groups, to all races, to all nations, and to all persons irrespective of social or economic status, whatever their human situation.

The Bible is relevant for all mankind because it declares the message of salvation. It tells the good news of God's love for a sinful race, of God's redemption through Jesus Christ, of his desire that all persons should come to repentance, and of the riches of grace in Christ whereby whoever will call on the name of the Lord shall be saved (Rom. 10:13). At no point is the Bible more relevant than when it declares the fact of man's universal guilt for sin, the fact that Jesus died for the sins of the world, the fact that Jesus arose from the dead, and the assurance that Jesus Christ "is able for all time to save those who draw near to God through him, since he always lives to make intercession for them" (Heb. 7:25). For this reason, above all, the Bible is the Book of the Christian faith.

The Bible is relevant because it confronts Christians with the meaning and demands of Christian discipleship. For them the Bible is the authoritative guide for doctrine and practice, for worship and ministry, for fellowship and witness, for assurance and hope. Since Jesus is Lord, the teachings of Jesus in the New Testament and the example of his life in the flesh must be the criteria for living the Christian life in the world.

The relevance of the Bible is reflected by the compassionate concern of God for the well-being of all men. Hence it declares the dignity and worth of every man, whatever his race or situation, as a person in God's image. It declares also the judgment of God on persons who by pride and greed and lust exploit other persons and rob them of rightful opportunities to realize the highest potential of personhood. The Word of God rings out against oppression and injustice and corruption and pleads for the hungry and sick and helpless. The Bible declares the lordship of Christ over the totality of life, over the social order and all persons in it. Man is to love his neighbor as himself. The Book of the Christian faith is a charter for justice and peace on earth and a commission for ministry to persons in need everywhere.

The relevance of the Bible derives from the fact that it speaks meaningfully and confidently to the issues of mankind in a dynamic universe. Science, technology, cybernetics, research, space exploration, atomic energy, and social change reflect the laws of the universe. We find in the Bible the word that gives us a Christian perspective: God in Christ is the creator of all things (John 1:3); "in him all things hold together" (Col. 1:17). The God who created and controls the material universe is fully capable with infinite wisdom and power to control the moral universe. With Job we can say, "I know that thou canst do all things, and that no purpose of thine can be thwarted" (42:2).

The Bible is relevant because it confronts honestly the searching questions of mankind: Who is God? What is God like? What is man? What is man's destiny? How can man know God? If a man dies, will he live again? What is the meaning of existence? What is the meaning of history? What is life for? Answers are to be found not in logic or dogmatics or scientific proof but in man's experience of God through faith in Jesus Christ and in trustful communion with him through the Spirit.

The Bible is relevant because it encourages hope in Jesus Christ. His resurrection from the grave declared his victory over sin and death. His kingdom is everlasting. He will come again in glory and triumph. "According to his promise we wait for new heavens and a new earth in which righteousness dwells" (2 Peter 3:13). The eternal purpose of God for the redemption of man will come to fulfilment in Christ (Eph. 1:9–10).

IV. How to Come to the Bible

Since the Bible is the Word of God for the life of man, and since it is the authoritative guide for all areas of moral and spiritual experience and for all matters of religious faith and moral conduct, what is the proper approach to the Bible? With what attitude and objectives should Christians read and study the Bible?

1. The approach to the Bible calls for recognition of its nature and purpose, also for awareness of the attributes of the Bible that affect the understanding of its message and relevance to life in our time. The Bible is not magic. It is revelation. It is a divine-

human book. It had many writers. It came into being through a long period covering some twelve or more centuries. It was first written in Hebrew, Aramaic, and Greek. The clue to its message and significance is Jesus Christ, the living Word.

2. The approach to the Bible should be one of reverence and faith. It is about God. The energy and wisdom and guidance of the Holy Spirit are in it. The purpose of God is accomplished by it. The redemptive and reconciling and sanctifying truth of God is its content and dynamic. It breathes the loving concern of the gracious God. It declares the moral judgment of the righteous God. It speaks with the authority of the sovereign God. It witnesses to the saving grace of God in Christ. How can any person dare to handle the sacred Book other than with reverence toward God and reverence for the truth and power of God in Christ? This book calls for faith—not unthinking or unquestioning faith but intelligent and trusting faith. It is the one completely trustworthy account of God's full revelation in Christ and his salvation through Christ. For the person willing to believe the Bible, while he searches for truth about the Bible and from the Bible, the Bible will come alive with meaning and certainty.

3. The approach to the Bible calls for openness of mind, a teachable spirit, and an eagerness to learn. Laborious research and critical study by linguists, archaeologists, historians, and biblical scholars have provided a vast store of knowledge and insight to enrich Bible study. The serious student of the Scriptures must be willing to engage in disciplined study to learn from the labors of others. But with an openness of mind to truth whatever its sources, he must himself develop critical faculties to test the concepts and viewpoints of others, always testing new ideas and concepts by the Bible itself and in the laboratory of obedient discipleship. He must further test these concepts and viewpoints by reading widely from many writers and from the laboratory of experience involving

mature Christians. The test, finally, of all truth about the Bible is whether it contributes to a more vital faith in the Bible, fuller obedience to its teaching, and a more meaningful commitment to Christ as Lord.

4. The approach to the Bible properly requires readiness for obedience to its commandments and disciplined practice of its teaching. It is the voice of divine authority. It is the prescription for harmonious relationships. It is the directive for moral excellence in personal living, righteous principles and Christian love in social relationships, and Christlike self-giving and ministry to the needs of other persons. Above all, it is a divine call to voluntary faith in Jesus Christ as Saviour and full commitment to him as Lord. God's word gets through to the obedient heart. His word must be translated into experience. "The key to the understanding of the Scriptures of both the Old and New Testaments is the acknowledgment of Jesus as Lord" (Rolston, *ibid.*, p. 33).

5. The approach to the Bible calls for a sense of dependence on and dynamic communion with the Holy Spirit. Men moved by the Spirit spoke from God. Hence persons attentive to the Spirit, guided by the Spirit, empowered by the Spirit, and eager to do the will of the Spirit hear best the word from God. He is the divine Counselor, the supreme Interpreter. He knows the will of God. He makes the written Word a living word, written on the heart, "to be known and read of all men" (2 Cor. 3:2).

For Further Reading

Cartledge, Samuel A. *The Bible: God's Word to Man.* Philadelphia: Westminster Press, 1961.

Dodd, C. H. *The Authority of the Bible.* London: Collins Clear Type Press, Revised Edition, 1960.

Henry, Carl F. H. *Revelation and the Bible.* Grand Rapids: Baker Book House, 1958.

Hunter, A. M. *The Message of the New Testament.* Philadelphia: Westminster Press, 1944.

Huxtable, John. *The Bible Says.* Richmond: John Knox Press, 1962.

Interpreter's Dictionary of the Bible. Nashville: Abingdon, 1962. See articles: "Canon of the Old Testament," R. H. Pfeiffer, Vol. A–D; "Canon of the New Testament," F. W. Beare, Vol. A–D; "Inspiration and Revelation," G. W. H. Lampe, Vol. E–J; "Scripture, Authority of," Alan Richardson, Vol. R–Z.

Kelly, Balmer H., Editor. *Introduction to the Bible.* "The Layman's Bible Commentary," Volume 1. Richard: John Knox Press, 1959.

Rolston, Holmes. *The Bible in Christian Teaching.* Richmond: John Knox Press, 1962.

Rowley, H. H. *The Relevance of the Bible.* Carter Lane, England: James Clarke and Co., 1941.

Smart, James D. *The Interpretation of Scripture.* Philadelphia: Westminster Press, 1961.

The Scriptures in Translation

From its very beginning the Christian church has known that its message is for all men. Consequently, it has the duty of proclaiming this message in the languages that men speak. Pentecost was the symbol and evidence of this basic truth. All men everywhere should hear in their own language the great things that God has done in Christ.

Even before the New Testament canon was fixed (in the fourth century), the books of the New Testament were being translated from the original Greek into other languages: Syriac and Latin, in the second century; and the languages of Egypt, in the third century. The first translator known by name appears in the fourth century: Ulfilas, who at the age of thirty was consecrated bishop of the Christians in Gothia. He devised the Gothic alphabet and translated most of the Bible into that language.

By 1452, when printing was invented, the Bible had been translated in whole or in part into 33 languages (22 in Europe, 7 in Asia, and 4 in Africa). By the end of 1968 the total was 1392: 242 complete Bibles, 320 additional New Testaments, and 830 other languages with at least one complete book of the Bible.

I. The Bible in English

The first Bible in English is associated with John Wycliffe (*ca.* 1330–1384), "the morning star of the Reformation." It was his belief that "no man was so rude a scholar but that he might learn the Gospel according to its simplicity." The New Testament appeared in 1380, and the whole Bible in 1382. There are two distinct Wycliffe versions, and it is uncertain how much of either is the work of Wycliffe himself. Associated with him were John Purvey and Nicholas of Hereford.

The Wycliffe Bible, which was almost a word-for-word equivalent of the Latin Vulgate, was the only Bible in English for nearly 150 years. It is reported that the equivalent of $175 was paid for a copy, and George Foxe wrote that "some gave a load of hay for a few chapters of St. James or of St. Paul in English." In 1415 the Wycliffe Bible was condemned and burned, and in 1428 Wycliffe's body was exhumed and burned.

William Tyndale (*ca.* 1494–1536), "the Father of the English Bible," was a graduate of Oxford and proficient in Latin, Greek, Hebrew, French, Italian, and Spanish. His interest in Bible translation arose from his conviction that all should be able to read and understand for themselves the Word of God: "I had perceived by experience how that it was impossible to establish the lay-people in any truth, except the scriptures were plainly laid before their eyes in their mother tongue, that they might see the process, order, and meaning of the text . . . which thing only moved me to translate the New Testament."

Unable to find the support he needed in England, and faced with the Constitutions of Oxford, which prohibited the unauthorized translation of the Scriptures, Tyndale went to the Continent. After spending some time in Wittenberg, he moved on to Hamburg and Cologne, where he turned his translation over to a printer. The city senate, however, forbade the printing. Tyndale went on to Worms, and toward the end of February, 1526, the first printed New Testament in English was completed. About a month later copies began to appear in England. Of the nearly 18,000 copies of his printed New Testament only 2 now survive.

Tyndale translated from the Greek, and was influenced by Luther's translation of the New Testament (1522). He began translating the Old Testament from Hebrew, and published the Pentateuch in 1530. He was then living in Antwerp, a free city; but on May 21, 1535, he was betrayed and arrested by order of Charles V, the Holy Roman Emperor. He was imprisoned in a fortress in Vilvorde, six miles north of Brussels. In a letter to a friend he asked for warm clothing, a lamp, and most especially for a Hebrew Bible, grammar, and dictionary, "that I may pass the time in that study." In August, 1536, he was tried and found guilty of heresy, and on October 6 he was strangled and burned at the stake. "Lord, open the King of England's eyes!" were his last words.

His influence on the Bible continues to this day. Eighty percent of the King James Version New Testament is his, and his influence was also felt in the Old Testament (through the Great Bible of 1539). Readers of the English Bible owe more to Tyndale than to any other single translator.

Within one year of his death two complete Bibles were circulating in England with Henry VIII's permission and approval: the Miles Coverdale Bible (1535), printed on the Continent, and the so-called "Thomas Matthew" Bible (1537), edited by John Rogers, a friend of Tyndale's. Published with "the kinges most gracyous lycence," it was printed in England, and was the first authorized English Bible.

The Great Bible of 1539 (so called because of its oversize pages, 15 by 9 inches) was Coverdale's revision of the Matthew Bible, and was "appointed to the use of the churches" by Archbishop Cranmer.

With the ascendance of Mary Tudor ("Bloody Mary") to the throne in 1553, many Protestants sought refuge on the Continent. Many of them went to Geneva, where William Whittingham, who was married to the sister (or sister-in-law) of John Calvin, translated the New Testament (1557) and served as editor of the whole Bible (1560). Printed in Roman type, in small octavo size, and with verse divisions, the Geneva Bible (known also as the "Breeches" Bible because of the use of the word "breeches" in Gen. 3:7) became

the Bible of the English people: it was the Bible of Shakespeare and of Bunyan; of the Pilgrims who came to the New World, and of the Mayflower Compact; of Oliver Cromwell and his army (the "Soldier's Pocket Bible" of 1643). In Scotland it was appointed to be read in the churches. It ran through 140 editions and remained popular for nearly 100 years.

Its success caused Archbishop Matthew Parker to call for a revision of the Great Bible; and in 1568 the Bishops' Bible (so called because of the great number of bishops on the committee) was published, the second authorized version.

In 1603 James VI of Scotland succeeded Queen Elizabeth I as James I of England, and at a meeting in Hampton Court in January, 1604, the Puritan leader, John Reynolds, president of Corpus Christi College of Oxford, suggested that a new translation be made. This met with the King's approval, and in 1611 the King James Version of the Bible was published. It took some 40 years for it to displace the Geneva Bible in the affection of the English people, but once established it became the Bible of English-speaking peoples all over the world, and has so continued to recent times. It was not a fresh translation; the first of the 15 rules adopted by the committee stated: "The ordinary Bible read in the Church, commonly called the *Bishops Bible,* to be followed, and as little altered as the truth of the original will permit." It was never formally authorized by King or Parliament, but the name "Authorized Version" became attached to it, and that is how it is known in England.

The revision of this Bible (English Revised, 1885; American Standard, 1901) did not displace the KJV in the esteem of the people or the use of the churches. The latest revision, the Revised Standard Version of 1952, has achieved great popularity and rivals the use of the KJV in the churches, even if it has not won the universal acclaim of English-speaking Protestants. Six publishers are now producing the RSV in various formats.

II. *The Reason for Newer Translations*

Bible translation is not confined to committees appointed by churches or monarchs; many translations are the work of individuals. In 1755 John Wesley published his translation of the New Testament, and it is estimated that over 200 translations of the New Testament have appeared since the KJV of 1611.

To mention only a few that appeared in this century: In 1901 the Twentieth Century New Testament was produced by a group of laymen helped by a few scholars. This translation still reads with surprising freshness and clarity. The Scottish scholar, James Moffatt, translated the New Testament in 1913, and the whole Bible in 1924. Edgar J. Goodspeed, an American scholar, brought out a translation of the New Testament in 1923. The British Roman Catholic, Monsignor Ronald Knox, translated the whole Bible in 1950; and J. B. Phillips published *Letters to Young Churches* in 1947, and finished the New Testament in 1957. In 1966 the American Bible Society published its first translation of the New Testament in English, *Good News for Modern Man,* also called Today's English Version.

New translations continue to appear. Various reasons for these translations merit consideration.

Language Changes. This applies in some degree to all languages but is especially evident in English. The average Bible reader is perhaps not aware of how antiquated, obsolete, and archaic is much of the language of the KJV. What does "We fetched a compass, and came to Rhegium" (Acts 28:13) mean? It means "We sailed around and put in at Rhegium," or in nautical terms, "We tacked around to Rhegium." "Compass" here is not the directional instrument, and "fetched" does not mean "procured." In 1 Peter 3:1 "the conversation of the wives" does not refer to their talking but to their conduct; in 2 Peter 2:7 "the filthy conversation" of the wicked is their immoral conduct. In Romans 1:13,

"let" means prevented; in 1 Thessalonians 4:15, "prevent" means precede; in Mark 1:30, "anon" means immediately, and in Mark 6:25, "by and by" means at once. "The feebleminded" in 1 Thessalonians 5:14 has nothing to do with intelligence quotient; it refers to timid, fainthearted people. The widow's "nephews" in 1 Timothy 5:4 are her grandchildren, and "the chief estates of Galilee" in Mark 6:21 are the leading men of that province.

The Scriptures must be read in the language that people speak today, not in the language of their forefathers. The United Bible Societies are of the opinion that Bibles in major modern languages must be revised at least every 40 to 50 years, so that the language may be kept up-to-date and intelligible.

Older and Better Biblical Manuscripts. When the King James revisers did their work on the New Testament they used the Greek New Testament of Theodore Beza, whose edition was based on Erasmus' Greek New Testament of 1516. The *Textus Receptus,* as it became known, was based on late and inferior manuscripts. Erasmus used very few Greek manuscripts, none older than the tenth century, and some as late as the sixteenth century. For the book of Revelation he had one twelfth-century manuscript from which the last six verses were missing: Erasmus supplied these by translating the verses from the Latin version into Greek.

When the English revisers in 1881 published the ERV New Testament, they found over five thousand places in the text that needed correcting in the light of older and better manuscripts; and since that time other discoveries have brought to light even older manuscripts.

Inasmuch as no original copy of any of the biblical books has survived, textual scholars must reconstruct the text from existing copies of the originals. The number and age of biblical manuscripts, and the care with which the copyists did their work, enable modern textual scholars to determine the original text with much greater certainty than any other comparable work of ancient literature. Modern translations, therefore, are much nearer the original text than ancient translations.

In Matthew 5:22, "Whosoever is angry with his brother without a cause shall be in danger of the judgment" (KJV), the Greek word translated "without a cause" was added by later scribes; it was no part of the original text. In Matthew 6:4,6,18 the scribes added "openly" to the statement, "thy Father . . . shall reward you." In Colossians 1:14 copyists added the phrase "through his blood" from the similar passage in Ephesians 1:7; the words do not belong to the original text of Colossians. The explanation of the moving of the water in the pool of Bethzatha, in John 5:3*b*-4, is a later addition, as is the whole of Acts 8:37, the Ethiopian eunuch's confession of faith. "Fasting" was added to prayer in Matthew 17:21, Mark 9:29, Acts 10:30, and 1 Corinthians 7:5.

Perhaps the most notable scribal addition in the New Testament is found in 1 John 5:7-8: "There are three that bear record in heaven, the Father, the Word, and the Holy Ghost: and these three are one." No early Greek manuscript has these words; and when Erasmus first edited his Greek New Testament he omitted them. When challenged by Stunica, the editor of the Complutensian Polyglot Bible, Erasmus promised to include the words if they were found in any Greek manuscript. Not long afterward, a sixteenth-century Greek manuscript "conveniently" appeared and Erasmus, true to his promise, included the words in his third edition of 1522. They thus became part of the *Textus Receptus,* the text from which the translations of the New Testament were made until the latter part of the last century.

The sensational manuscript discoveries in the Essene community of the Dead Sea have in some instances pushed back scholars' knowledge of the Hebrew Old Testament text by as much as one thousand years. Two nearly complete copies of the book of Isaiah were discovered, over one

thousand years older than the standard text. With this evidence the RSV was able to correct places in the translation of Isaiah, where the Masoretic Text (of the ninth and tenth centuries A.D.) was clearly faulty. In Isaiah 33:8 the KJV has "he despised *cities,*" translating the Masoretic Text '*arim;* the Dead Sea copy has '*adim,* "witnesses": the only difference between the two Hebrew words is the middle consonant, *resh* 'r' and *daleth* 'd'—the two are almost exactly alike.

Although they made occasional mistakes, the Jewish scribes were scrupulously careful and took great pains to insure that their copy was an exact replica of the manuscript they were copying. They went as far as to add up all the words, and even all the letters, in a book, and then determine the middle word and the middle letter, counting and recounting before discarding the old manuscript.

Although the changes made by them were for the most part accidental, in places they deliberately changed the text—but then recorded the change! There are some 18 such intentional scribal changes in the Old Testament (called *tiqqune soferim*), and most of them were made in order to safeguard, as they thought, the dignity of God. In Genesis 18:22, for example, the original text had, "The Lord continued to stand before Abraham." But since this places the Lord in an inferior position (since it is the lesser who attends on the greater), the scribes changed this to "Abraham still stood before the Lord"—and thus it stands in the Masoretic Text. In Job 32:3 the original text had "they had condemned God." This was felt to be offensive, so it was changed in the Masoretic Text to "they condemned Job."

Better Knowledge of the Cultural, Historical, and Literary Milieu of the Scriptures. Archaeological and manuscript discoveries constantly enlarge our knowledge of biblical times and allow us more accurately to understand the text. In 1 Samuel 13:21 the KJV has "Yet they had a file," thus contradicting the preceding verse which declares that the Israelites had to go to the Philistines in order to sharpen their tools. The Hebrew word *pim* was understood to be "edges" (lit., mouths), and the phrase *happesira pim* was taken to mean sharpener of edges, that is, "a file." A small weight was discovered inscribed *pim* (or *payim*), and on the basis of this evidence the correct meaning of the text has been ascertained: "the charge was a pim," about two-thirds of a shekel.

Another example is in 1 Kings 10:28: the reference to "linen yarn" (KJV) is puzzling; but inscriptions of the Assyrian king Shalmaneser III (858–824 B.C.) show that the Hebrew word *miqweh* is really a place name, meaning "from Que (or Kue)," the territory known later as Cilicia. An altar of incense inscribed with the word *hamman* proved that the word, occurring eight times in the Old Testament (Lev. 26:30; 2 Chron. 14:5; 34:4, 7; Isa. 17:8, 27:9, Ezek. 6:4,6), means incense altar, not "images," as the KJV has it.

A better knowledge of Semitic psychology, reflected both in the Old and the New Testaments, enables us to understand the language better. The owner of the vineyard replies to the man who was protesting his wage, "Is your eye evil because I am good?" (Matt. 20:15, RSVmg). The "evil eye" is a symbol of jealousy, not of sorcery. A "hard heart" was not a figure of insensitivity or lack of pity, but of stupidity or obstinacy (cf. Matt. 13:15; Mark 8:17; John 12:40). When we read that the angels took Lazarus "into Abraham's bosom" (Luke 16:22–23), we know that this is a way of describing the great messianic feast, with Abraham, the father of the chosen people, serving as host: Lazarus was given the place of honor next to the host himself.

Figurative and symbolic language always reflects the culture of the people, and a knowledge of the culture enables the reader to understand the language. For the Hebrews the horn was a figure of strength and power; in 1 Samuel 2:10, "The Lord shall . . . exalt the horn of his anointed" means that the Lord will endue him with strength. The phrase "the horn of salvation" may be taken abstractly to mean a great salvation, or concretely a great Saviour (cf. 2 Sam. 22:3; Psalm 18:2; Luke 1:69).

Better Knowledge of* the *Biblical Languages. The many literary works that have been discovered in Hebrew, Aramaic, Greek, and cognate languages give us a much better understanding of the languages of the Bible. In the case of the New Testament, one needs only mention the thousands of letters, bills, receipts, court orders, and so forth, which show that the Greek of the New Testament was, by and large, the common Greek spoken in the Mediterranean world of the first century, not the ancient classical Greek, nor yet a "Holy Spirit Greek," as some formerly styled it.

The word which in the KJV is translated "earnest" (Eph. 1:14; 2 Cor. 1:22; 5:5) is used regularly in contracts for the initial down payment which validated and guaranteed the contract. In all three passages the Holy Spirit is said to be the *arrabōn*, God's "down payment" which guarantees all the other blessings he still has in store for his people. In Luke 15:13 we read that the younger son "gathered all together" and left home for the distant country. The verb *sunagō* is shown to mean "turn into cash"—that is, the younger son sold his part of the estate and took the money with him. In 1 Corinthians 13:5 the verb *logizomai*, which is translated by the KJV "thinketh" (no evil) and by the RSV "is not . . . resentful," is a regular financial term, meaning "to keep an account"; what Paul means is that love "does not keep a record of wrongs" (TEV).

Idiomatic language must be recognized and understood, for a literal rendition will be inaccurate. The Italians have a saying, *Traduttori, traditori,* meaning "translators are traitors"—and so they are whenever they translate idioms in a literal fashion. "The children of the bridechamber" (Mark 2:19) is a verbal equivalent of the Greek, but it is not a faithful translation: the expression means friends of the bridegroom. "Sons of disobedience" (Eph. 2:2) are people who disobey God, and "children of wrath" (Eph. 2:3) are people who are the object of God's wrath. A "child of hell" (Matt. 23:15) is a man destined to hell.

Certain idiosyncrasies of the language must be recognized. The use of the passive voice of the verb in the Gospels often reflects the Semitic tendency to avoid naming God as the subject of an action. In "Blessed are those who mourn, for they shall be comforted" (Matt. 5:4), the implied subject of the verb "comfort" is God, and the meaning is "God will comfort them." The same applies to other Beatitudes: "They shall be satisfied . . . they shall obtain mercy . . . they shall be called sons of God" (Matt. 5:6,7,9) mean "God will satisfy them . . . God will be merciful to them . . . God will call them his sons." Luke 6:37–38 means: "Do not judge others, and God will not judge you; do not condemn others, and God will not condemn you; forgive others, and God will forgive you. Give to others, and God will give to you: you will receive a full measure, a generous helping, poured into your hands—all that you can hold. The measure you use for others is the one God will use for you" (cf. also Matt. 7:1–2; Mark 4:24).

Better Understanding of the Translator's Task. This factor, above all others, requires that fresh translations and revisions be undertaken in order to convey the meaning of the Scriptures to readers today. The final test of faithfulness is the degree to which the readers of the translated text understand the meaning of the text as well as the readers of the original. This means that a translator has failed if all he does is to supply a verbal equivalent of the original. Rather, he must express the meaning of the text as clearly, naturally, and idiomatically as possible, in terms of the language into which he translates.

Ronald Knox has stated the matter well: "Any translation is a good one in proportion as you can forget, while reading it, that it is

a translation at all." The English man of letters, Hilaire Belloc, said that translation is "the resurrection of an alien thing in a native body; not the dressing up of it in native clothes, but the giving to it of native flesh and blood." And Martin Luther put it more vividly: "I endeavored to make Moses so German that no one would suspect he was a Jew." It is the needs of the readers that will determine the form of the translation.

III. The Translator's Task

Determine the Text He Is to Translate. Modern translators have at their disposal the best critical texts available, the result of the learning and dedication of textual scholars. The by now venerable edition of the Hebrew Masoretic Text (Rudolph Kittel's *Biblia Hebraica*) serves as the standard Old Testament text; the widely used Nestle editions of the Greek New Testament are being replaced by the United Bible Societies' Greek New Testament of 1966, edited by Kurt Aland, Matthew Black, Bruce Metzger, and Allen Wikgren.

These authoritative editions, however, do not exempt the translator from making textual choices. In the Old Testament he will often need to depart from the Masoretic Text, where it is clear that the original text is preserved by one of the ancient versions (Greek, Syriac, Latin, Samaritan, or the Targums), or may be restored by a revocalization of the Hebrew consonants or by an emendation of the text. In Genesis 4:8, for example, the Masoretic Text has simply, "Cain said to Abel," with the implication that what he said follows. But the Hebrew text does not supply this. On the basis of the Septuagint, the Samaritan, and the Syriac, a modern translation may add the words, "Let us go out to the field." In Genesis 21:9 the Masoretic Text states that Sarah saw Ishamel "playing"; on the basis of the Greek and Latin versions, some translations will add "with her son Isaac."

In Genesis 24:67 the Hebrew text reports that Isaac took his bride Rebekah into the tent of his mother Sarah; some translators will omit "of his mother Sarah" and read "Isaac took her into his tent." In Ruth 3:15 the Masoretic Text has "he went back to town"; but some Hebrew manuscripts, as well as some of the ancient versions, read, "she went back to town," which makes more sense in the context.

In the New Testament the evidence is sometimes almost evenly divided between two or more readings, and the editors cannot be dogmatic about the original text. In John 7:8 some manuscripts report Jesus as saying, "I am not (*ouk*) going up to this feast," while others have, "I am not yet (*oupō*) going up to this feast." Later on, after his brothers had gone, Jesus went to the feast in Jerusalem. So the reading "not" seems clearly ruled out by the facts; but many manuscripts, ancient versions, and Church Fathers have the more difficult reading "not," which is followed by many translations.

Sometimes the better attested text does not make sense, and the translator follows a variant reading. In 2 Peter 3:10 the last part of the verse reads "and the earth and its works will be found." The sense of this is doubtful; and most translations prefer the variant reading "will disappear" or "will burn up," both of which have less support than the more difficult reading. In Jude 5 the older Greek manuscripts have "Jesus" (or Joshua) as the subject of the verb "saved." This is very difficult to understand, and translators as a whole prefer the variant "the Lord," or else (as the RSV) the conjectural "he who saved," with the subject unspecified.

Determine the Meaning of the Text. This is not always possible, since all the information which elucidates the meaning of the text may not be available to him. All the cultural, historical, literary, linguistic, grammatical, or lexical data may not be ascertainable.

The very first two verses of the Bible illustrate the translator's difficulties. Do the first words of Genesis mean "In the beginning God created" or do they mean "When God began to create"? In the next verse does the phrase *ruach 'elohim* mean the Spirit of God, a spirit of God, a wind from God, or an awesome wind? All these are possible translations of the two Hebrew words, and no final certainty is possible.

No exegete is certain about the meaning of the verb *apechei* used absolutely in Mark 14:41 (usually translated "It is enough"). What does the dative of *pugmē* (fist) in Mark 7:3 mean? Problems are caused not only by linguistic or lexical factors; the greatest difficulties result from insufficient knowledge of the cultural or historical circumstances. In 1 Corinthians 7:36–38 the exegete does not know for sure whether Paul is speaking about a man and his unmarried daughter, or about a man and his fiancée; the words are easy enough (*parthenos* means simply virgin), but the historical context is unknown.

In 1 Corinthians 11:10 Paul says that a woman speaking or praying in church should have a covering over her head "because of the angels." To what belief does this qualifying clause refer? And what is meant in 1 Timothy 2:15 by the statement that a woman will be saved "through child-bearing" (*dia tēs teknogonias*)?

In these and other places a complete and absolute determination of the meaning of the text is impossible. In order to understand the meaning of a written text, the translator should learn as much as possible of the culture, history, and language of the people and reconstruct as fully as possible the original communicative event of which the written document is a product.

Transfer the Meaning into the Target Language. Faithfulness to the original, of course, is paramount. The ultimate test of faithfulness is the degree to which the readers of the translated text will understand as much and as well as did the readers of the original. This, of course, can never be finally established; and that is one reason why translation is not simply a science but also an art. The translator, then, must do his work in terms of the capacity and needs of his readers. The translation may make perfect sense to him, but if it does not to his readers, then he has not done his work adequately.

Cultural equivalents.—There are many differences between the culture of biblical times and the culture of many of the peoples receiving the Scriptures for the first time. The translator must find in the target language an equivalent item or function that will convey the same meaning in terms of the culture of his readers. It is obviously impossible to translate "your sins . . . will be white as snow" (Isa. 1:18) in cultures which know nothing of snow. The translator must find an equivalent which represents the ultimate in whiteness, or purity. It may be the egret, a very white bird, and the translation may read "your sins . . . will be white as an egret's feather." In the Kissi language of the Republic of Guinea, James 3:12 is difficult because it speaks of fig trees, olives, grapevine, and figs, all of which are unknown in that culture. So the translation substitutes, as follows: "Can the mango tree bear oranges? Can the kola tree bear mangoes?"

In the South Toradja language of Indonesia "grapes gathered from thorns, or figs from thistles" (Matt. 7:16) becomes "bananas from thorn trees, guavas from cane," and wolves "in sheep's clothing" (Matt. 7:15) becomes "crocodiles in human form." The Mossi people, whose landlocked tribe is on the edge of the Sahara Desert, know nothing of ships. The translation of Hebrews 6:18–19, which speaks of hope "as a sure and steadfast anchor of the soul," required a cultural equivalent. This was found in the picketing-peg, to which the Mossi tie their valuable cattle and horses; its function in relation to animals is the same as that of an anchor in relation to a ship.

A recent check of a translation in a tribal language of the Philippines revealed that the reader did not know, any more than the average American reader, what is meant by "a sabbath day's journey," the distance between the Mount of Olives and the city of Jerusalem (Acts 1:12). How is

distance measured in that society? By the time it takes a pot of bananas to boil! And so the readers of Acts in that tribe will learn that it takes less time to go from the Mount of Olives to Jerusalem than for a pot of bananas to boil—a perfectly natural way to speak of distances.

Connotative values.—Sometimes the target language will have the same word as the biblical language, denoting the same object or event but connoting a different value. The Chol tribe in Mexico has bread, but it is an expensive item and is used only for dessert or special occasions. If "I am the bread of life" (John 6:35) were translated literally, the meaning would be distorted, for Jesus was claiming to be the indispensable sustenance for man's life, not a dispensable luxury. The functional equivalent of the biblical bread in Chol society is the thin corn cake eaten daily, the *waj*, and this is what faithfully conveys to the Chol people the meaning of the verse. A translator in the rain jungles of the Peruvian Amazon found it difficult to translate Matthew 5:45, God "sends rain on the just and on the unjust." In semiarid Palestine rain is a precious commodity and represents God's impartial goodness in giving it to all; but in the tribe in which the translator works, rain is a curse, since it falls so often and so heavily.

Grammatical differences.—These cause the most difficulty. Languages which belong to the same family as the biblical languages (the Indo-European) normally follow the same rules, and the translator does not have to solve the problems caused by languages governed by different rules.

Honorifics is one example of this. Where a society has a rigid class or caste system a speaker will use different forms of address in talking to a superior, to an inferior, or to an equal. Everyone knows his place in the system and knows what form to use. This may prove especially difficult in translating dialogues in the Gospels when Jesus is one of the speakers. Would he address Nicodemus as an equal or as a superior? How would Nicodemus address Jesus? How would Jesus speak to Pilate? How would the Pharisees speak to Jesus? How would the Samaritan woman address him? The translator must have a highly developed historical sensitivity in order to represent the way in which people in Palestine would address one another if they had the same system of honorifics.

In many languages the words for brother or sister always specify whether he or she is younger or older, and whether he or she is the son or daughter of the same father and/or mother. These specific relationships must be clearly defined in speaking of Lazarus, Martha, and Mary, of Peter and Andrew, of James and John, and of others.

Many languages have a different form for the inclusive and the exclusive use of the first person plural pronouns—we, us, and our—depending on whether the speaker includes or excludes the person, or persons, to whom he is talking. This distinction is not optional but obligatory. In Luke 7:5 the Jewish elders in Capernaum speak to Jesus on behalf of the Roman centurion, whose servant was sick, and say: "He loves *our* people and he himself built *our* synagogue." The first "our" is obviously inclusive, since Jesus was also a Jew; the second "our" is exclusive, since he was not a resident of Capernaum. During the storm on Lake Galilee the disciples wake Jesus, who was asleep in the boat, with the question: "Teacher, don't you care that *we* are about to die?" (Mark 4:38). Were the disciples speaking of themselves only (exclusive), or did they include Jesus also (inclusive)?

Many languages are much more precise in some particulars than the biblical languages. The Guaicas of Venezuela attach to the principal verb in a statement of fact one of three suffixes to specify whether (1) the speaker himself knows the truth of what he is saying; or (2) he has heard it on what he considers to be good authority; or (3) he is simply reporting what is being said without being able to vouch for its truth.

The Zapotecs of South Mexico have four

mutually exclusive ways of framing a question, depending on whether (1) the question is purely rhetorical, not a request for information; or (2) the question is a demand for information not known to the speaker; or (3) it is a demand for information previously known but now forgotten; or (4) it requests information on matters previously known but partly forgotten. The translator of Mark 6:38 must determine into which category belongs Jesus' question to his disciples, "How many loaves do you have?"

In translating John 19:17 some languages cannot say simply, "Jesus went out carrying his cross." They must specify whether he carried it in his arms, on his shoulder, across his back, or on his head. When the translators working in the Akha language of North Burma came to "they were sawn in two" (Heb. 11:37), they had to settle the question, "Which way? Lengthwise or across?"

In all such matters the translator has to solve problems which ordinarily do not arise in languages belonging to the same family of languages as Hebrew or Greek.

IV. *The Task Ahead*

Some three thousand people all over the world give most or all of their time to Bible translation. Many of them, especially those with the Wycliffe Bible Translators, work in languages into which no part of the Bible has ever been translated. But a greater number of translation projects has to do with completing either the New Testament or the whole Bible in languages which have only a part of the Scriptures, or in revising older translations. Many of the Bibles now in use in what are called the younger churches were translated by foreigners (missionaries, mostly) many years ago, in some instances over one hundred years ago. They are clearly inadequate today: the vocabulary is obsolescent or archaic, and the language is unnatural. These Bibles clearly reveal their foreign origin. Native speakers of these languages are now engaged in a complete revision of these Bibles to meet the needs of people today.

More than ever it is recognized that one Bible is not enough in languages which have a large number of Christians. In many languages at least three different types of translations are needed: (1) a traditional translation, with which most Bible readers are acquainted (such as the RSV in English); (2) a more specialized translation, embodying the latest results of textual, historical, literary, and anthropological findings, and equipped with variant readings, alternative renderings, notes, and introductions which situate the biblical books in their historical and cultural milieu (such as the *Jerusalem Bible* in French and in English); (3) a common-language translation, which purposely avoids traditional theological terms and religious vocabulary in favor of a more natural and idiomatic rendering, using a limited vocabulary, in order to make the text intelligible to readers who have little if any knowledge of the Scriptures (such as *Dios Llega al Hombre* in Spanish, and *Good News for Modern Man* in English). While the first two types of translation have been fairly common in the past, only recently have the Bible societies recognized the urgent need for common-language translations, and work is going on in the production of such translations in French, Arabic, Portuguese, Swahili, Chinese, Thai, and other major languages.

Increasing cooperation between Roman Catholics and Protestants has resulted in the formation of translation committees, representing all branches of the Christian church, which aim at producing a Bible acceptable to all Christians. In French the *Traduction Oecumenique de la Bible* is under way, and similar projects in nearly one hundred other languages are going forward.

For Further Reading

BEEGLE, DEWEY M. *God's Word into English.* New York: Harper & Brothers, 1960.

BRATCHER, ROBERT G. *Why So Many Bibles?* Philadelphia: The Evangelical Foundation, 1961.

BRUCE, F. F. *The English Bible.* New York: Oxford University Press, 1961.

GRANT, FREDERICK C. *Translating the Bible.* Greenwich, Conn.: Seabury Press, 1961.

GREENSLADE, F. B. A. (ed.) *The West from the Reformation to the Present Day.* ("The Cambridge History of the Bible.") Cambridge: University Press, 1963.

METZGER, BRUCE M. "Ancient Versions," IDB, IV, 749–60.

————. "Medieval and Modern (Non-English) Versions," IDB, IV, 771–82.

NIDA, EUGENE A. *Bible Translating.* London: United Bible Societies, 1961.

————. *God's Word in Man's Language.* New York: Harper & Brothers, 1952.

————. *Toward a Science of Translation.* Leiden: E. J. Brill, 1964.

REUMANN, JOHN H. P. *The Romance of Biblical Scripts and Scholars.* Englewood Cliffs, N. J.: Prentice-Hall, 1965.

ROBERTSON, E. H. *The New Translations of the Bible.* London: SCM Press, 1959.

ROBINSON, H. WHEELER, ed. *The Bible in Its Ancient and English Versions.* Oxford: Clarendon Press, 1940.

SCHWARZ, W. *Principles and Problems of Biblical Translation.* Cambridge: University Press, 1955.

Interpreting the Bible

Granted that the Bible is the divinely inspired rule of faith and practice, how is it to be interpreted? It is not enough to accept the authority of the Bible—it must be properly utilized and appropriated.

The goal of interpretation is to find out the thought process and the meaning of the writer or writers of the book or passage to be studied. The interpreter is then to convey that meaning to a contemporary person. Are there principles which will provide guidelines for this interpretation? Are there warnings and guidelines to be learned from the history of biblical interpretation?

Interpretation is especially important in relation to a book such as the Bible. For a Christian the Bible demands accurate and adequate interpretation because of its place of authority. It also needs interpretation because it contains ideas and thoughts written between two thousand and thirty-five hundred years ago. It was formulated in an environment and in languages different from those of the Western world.

I. Lessons from the History of Interpretation

A historical perspective provides the contemporary interpreter with warnings and guidelines. During the past two thousand years, numerous examples of the misuse and distortion of the Bible have occurred. In other cases, helpful insights have been achieved.

1. Seeking a Hidden Meaning—Allegorizing

Allegory teaches that beneath the ordinary and obvious meaning of a passage the real or spiritual meaning is found. The chief goal of the allegorical interpreter is to seek to decipher these so-called spiritual and hidden meanings. Although developed by the Greeks, this system of interpretation was being used by Jewish interpreters in the first century A.D. Ignoring Jesus' example, this method was then adopted by most of the Christian interpreters; it dominated exegesis until the Protestant Reformation.

Bible verses were said to have two, three, and four meanings. Mickelsen points out that "Jerusalem," for the medieval interpreters, could have reference to the literal city in Palestine. Allegorically it could mean the church. Morally it could refer to the soul. From a future perspective, it refers to the heavenly city. The historical interpretation—the plain, evident meaning—was described as milk, while the allegorical interpretation was described as exhilarating wine.

The Bible was made to mean what it plainly did not say. It became a magician's bag from which interpreters drew forth mysteries and truths to decorate their own imaginative worlds. This pursuit of multiple meanings is really a magical approach to language and literary works. It removes any certainty of meaning.

The search for hidden meanings became so extreme that a premium was placed on the unusual. Augustine, in the fifth century A.D., found interpretations fruitful in proportion to their difficulty. For example, the ark represented the church which is rescued by the wood on which Christ hung. Its very dimensions stand for the human body of Christ, and the door in its side signifies the wound in Christ's side.

In more modern times men like Emanuel Swedenborg of Sweden and groups like Unity and Christian Science have utilized allegorical interpretation. In both Unity and Christian Science, grammar, context, and history are ignored. The important meanings are the hidden or spiritual meanings.

It is obvious that when the grammatical-historical approach is abandoned there is no way to control or govern exegesis.

2. Extreme Literalism

Some sound principles of interpretation were developed by rabbinical interpreters such as Hillel and Eliezer. An unfortunate emphasis on "letterism" or hyperliteralism, however, developed among the majority of Jewish interpreters. They bogged down in the trivialities and the incidental and missed the meaning of a given passage.

In the period after the Reformation, seventeenth-century Protestants tended, in many instances, to idolize the Bible to such an extent as to miss its essential meaning. The Bible was not seen as a historical and literary book but simply as dogma. In more recent times, Jehovah's Witnesses, other cultic groups, and fundamentalists have tended toward hyperliteralism. Grammar, historical and literary content, and central biblical motifs are largely ignored.

3. Church-controlled Interpretation

It is generally conceded that the turning point in interpretation in the Middle Ages was the work of Augustine. In his writing entitled *The Christian Doctrine,* he outlined principles for the interpretation of the Bible. In this same work he established the doctrine that the church and church tradition are the bases for interpretation. Throughout the Middle Ages interpretation was thus bound by a dull conformity. Church tradition was supreme.

This type of interpretation was used by church authorities to establish ecclesiastical power. Although only a small portion of the Bible was officially interpreted, many official doctrines involved the interpretation of certain verses which became binding.

In reaction to the Protestant Reformation, the Roman Catholic Council of Trent met from 1545 until 1563. The Latin Vulgate was declared the authentic version for expositions. Interpretation was not to be contrary to the teaching of the Catholic Church. This meant that no discussion of alternative interpretations was possible.

To counteract church-controlled interpretation, Calvin called for religious discussion of obscure and difficult passages among Christian scholars. Lacking this, said Calvin, there would be no liberty or opportunity for new light to break forth from the Bible.

The dogmatic approach is frequently called the "crystallization of doctrine" view. Lip service is paid to the idea that doctrine is to be subordinate to the Bible. As a matter of fact, however, the church as embodied in the church hierarchy is seen as the infallible teacher and interpreter.

The "crystallization of doctrine" view is also found in some forms of Protestant orthodoxy. For example, many denominations and confessional groups affirm that interpretations taught by the founder or early leaders of that group are semisacred. In the second generation of the Protestant Reformation there was a tendency to accept the sixteenth-century creedal statements as completely true and scriptural in content. In the present era, however, new understandings of biblical languages, biblical history, and scientific research have revealed the historical conditioning of many traditional interpretations.

Critical scholarship, combined with a devout Christian faith, is the answer to a dogmatic church-controlled interpretation. Such scholarship should reverence the Bible and never sanction irresponsible criticism that undermines positive faith.

4. Attempts to Establish Grammatical-Historical-Theological Principles of Interpretation

The Protestant Reformers. While some efforts were made in earlier centuries, the major attempt to establish grammatical-historical-theological principles came with the Protestant Reformation in the sixteenth century. In opposition to the elaborate and complicated interpretation of patristic and medieval scholasticism, the Reformers emphasized the literal sense of the Bible as the only source of authority. The Bible was to have priority over tradition and was to be tradition's judge instead of its servant.

Martin Luther abandoned the fourfold

interpretation of the medieval period and stressed the inherent and fundamental meaning. Allegory, said Luther, consisted of "monkey tricks" to show the cleverness of the exegete. The text was to be understood in terms of its plain meaning and within the total biblical context. As Mays has pointed out, this was to insure that the text should guide the understanding rather than an unproved theology.

The Reformers' view was not the extreme literalism of the rabbinical biblicism. Christ and the New Testament were central. Principles of interpretation were to be derived from the Bible. Luther stressed the grammatical sense and emphasized the need of diligent study of languages and history. John Calvin, undoubtedly the greatest interpreter of the Reformation, likewise interpreted the Scriptures grammatically and historically.

The Nineteenth-Century Historical Critics. The next attempt to establish grammatical-historical (if not theological) principles of interpretation was the rise of historical criticism. Reacting against the Protestant scholasticism of the seventeenth century, Herder and Semler in the eighteenth century began treating the Bible as literature. In the nineteenth century, the historical critics affirmed that historical setting and development were indispensable in understanding the meaning of the Bible. Many helpful results came out of this study. The humanity of Jesus was taken seriously, and the literary nature of the Bible was fully recognized.

Unfortunately, in most cases, non-biblical philosophical presuppositions guided the historical investigation and criticism of the Bible. Naturalistic presuppositions were generally accepted. Theoretical reconstructions of the Old and New Testaments were based on the dialectical philosophy of Hegel and the evolutionary thought of Spencer.

The critical scholars had rejected the dogmatic presuppositions of the Protestant Scholastics. In turn, however, as Mays has indicated, they replaced them with the new dogmatic premises of a theology determined by idealism, romanticism, and the Enlightenment.

The historical critics succeeded in textual work, grammar, literary history, and archaeology; but they missed the theological meaning of the Bible. A great assortment of facts and data was analyzed and classified. The interest of the trained interpreter was focused on historical reconstruction. The meaning or frame of reference, however, was lacking. The theological and practical principles were largely ignored.

The Theological Interpreters. Since World War I biblical interpretation has refashioned itself in significant theological circles in a way which places more emphasis on the theological and practical principles of biblical interpretation. Theological word books are furnishing tools for this approach. Commentaries emphasize the underlying structural unity of the Bible.

In much current exegetical work, the interpreters are once again seeking to be faithful to the nature of the Bible. The historical question and the theological question are both asked in approaching the Bible. What happened in the Bible and the interpretation of these happenings is being seen as one inseparable event.

II. Principles of Biblical Interpretation

The theory behind biblical interpretation is called hermeneutics. Interpretation or exegesis is the actual explanation of the text utilizing principles or theory. There are numerous ways in which the generally accepted and basic principles of biblical interpretation could be presented. One convenient and widely used approach is to consider the principles under the designations of grammatical, historical, theological, and practical. Some writers will suggest variations of arrangement, wording, and order, but the principles will be essentially the same.

The advantages of utilizing these principles are many. This approach exercises some control over interpretation. A check is placed on the temptation of interpreters to seek out hidden meanings in the Bible. Scholars and laymen who follow these principles have made constructive and abiding contributions to Bible knowledge and understanding.

1. Grammatical or Linguistic Principle

From general interpretation arises the first basic principle—the grammatical or linguistic principle. The Bible is a historical product. However divine it may be according to its final origin and essential contents, it was written by men in human languages and under human conditions. It is to be interpreted, therefore, with similar helps and with the utilization of some of the same principles as other books of antiquity.

In the Reformation period, John Calvin was the man who did the most to restore the linguistic principle. In more modern times, Ernesti, an eighteenth-century German scholar, was a pioneer in restoring this principle to its rightful place. His work placed the grammatical principle in such a position before the world that it has ever since maintained its fundamental importance. He published his *Principles of Interpretation* in 1761.

Meaning of Words—Etymology. One facet of the grammatical principle is etymology. This is the study of the roots from which words are derived. In most cases the interpreter will obtain material concerning etymology from specialists and commentaries. In Galatians 3:24 the KJV suggests that "the law was our school-master to bring us unto Christ." According to etymology, this is not an accurate translation. The word translated school-master is derived from two Greek words which mean a child leader. The word evidently refers to the household servant who led the child to school and back again. He did not as much teach as maintain discipline. The RSV has a more accurate translation, "The law was our custodian until Christ came."

Current Usage—Idioms. Another part of the grammatical principle involves current usage and idioms. First-century usage suggests, according to Stibbs, that when Luke 15:13 states that "the younger son gathered all he had" it means that he realized his estate and turned it into ready money.

Relationship of Words—Syntax. Still another point to be considered under the linguistic or grammatical principle is syntax or the relation or order of words in a sentence. In John 1:1 it is affirmed that "the Word was God." The meaning is made plain by the article before "Word" and the omission of the article before the predicate "God." The syntax will not allow the translation "God was the Word." Theologically, the latter translation, which is not allowed by the grammatical construction, would mean that all of God is expressed in the "Word."

Good translations and commentaries make much of the delicate meanings of verbs, nouns, and clauses and their relationships. The verb is especially important in Greek. In Hebrew the verb system is less complex but important nevertheless.

Method of Thought—Logical Principle. Closely related to the linguistic principle, and for the purposes of this study considered under the linguistic principle, is the logical principle or method of thought of an author. An interpreter must seek to understand the biblical author's method of reasoning. The people of the Bible lived in a thought world more accustomed to paradox than precision. They expressed themselves in ways that cannot be forced into the rigid and exact categories of modern Western thought and logic.

Traditional interpretations may need revising in the light of present knowledge of Hebrew ways of thinking and speaking. Stibbs points out that the phrase, "I loved Jacob, and I hated Esau" (Mal. 1:2-3 KJV), is the way the Hebrew states a comparison rather than a direct opposite. It might better be translated, "I loved Jacob more than Esau."

Literary Style—Rhetorical Principle. Closely related to this emphasis upon the method of reasoning is the rhetorical principle. Each type of literature in the Bible should be understood in the light of its own literary style. In straightforward narrative, words are taken at face value. In poetic sections a different approach is needed. Fortunately the RSV and certain other modern translations indicate in the printing that which is the formally poetic.

Jesus said, "If your right eye causes you to sin, pluck it out" (Matt. 5:29). Is he suggesting self-mutilation? Obviously this verse must not be interpreted in a literalistic way. Jesus often used hyperbole and figurative language to stress truth. Herod was called the "fox" (Luke 13:32). Paul referred to James and Cephas as "pillars" in the Jerusalem church (Gal. 2:9). The word pillar must not be taken to refer to a shaft of masonry work. The literary context makes clear its meaning. Peter describes the devil as a roaring lion (1 Peter 5:8). Metaphoric language must be recognized as such.

The statement, "Let us make man in our image, after our likeness" (Gen. 1:26), is not to be taken as describing different parts of man. If an interpreter understands Hebrew parallelism, he will see that both image and likeness have exactly the same meaning. The repetition is for emphasis.

Context—Immediate and General. Basic to any understanding of a word or verse in the Bible is the context, both immediate and general.

If verses are seen in context, states Mounce, difficulties in interpretation have a way of solving themselves. The "work out your own salvation" phrase of Philippians 2:12 makes sense if seen in its context. It is a call to concern for the welfare of others as God's design for the deliverance of the Philippian church from a threatening disunity (cf. Phil. 2:1–5; 4:2–3). This phrase may challenge the individual with a sense of responsibility to make salvation meaningful in terms of personal commitment and growth. The context indicates, however, that this is a secondary meaning.

Although the grammatical or linguistic principle is basic, the discovery of the grammatical sense by no means exhausts interpretation. The historical, theological, and practical principles must also be brought to bear upon a particular verse or passage in the Bible if it is to be properly interpreted.

2. The Historical Principle

The second basic principle for biblical interpretation is usually designated as the historical principle. Since the mid-nineteenth century this principle has been a basic premise of all serious interpreters. It includes a consideration of the geographical (spatial background), historical (temporal background), and cultural (material and social background) materials. Since the Bible originated in a historical context, it can only be understood accurately and completely when this context has been studied. In some way the interpreter must creep out of his twentieth-century skin and identify himself with the life and feelings of biblical times.

It must be remembered, however, that the study of the historical background and culture is not to overshadow the actual content being considered. For an evangelical interpreter, the biblical writers are considered to be men of their times and yet men above their times.

Luke 9:62 suggests that "no one who puts his hand to the plow and looks back is fit for the kingdom of God." An understanding of this teaching of Jesus is heightened by knowledge of the agricultural implements of first-century Palestine. The plow was a one-handled tool. If the farmer did not give close attention the plow would jump out of control. The teaching is clear. The kingdom demands immediate attention and wholehearted consideration.

In 1 Corinthians 9:27 Paul uses a figure taken from athletic games. He states that he pommels his body and subdues it. A study of historical background informs the interpreter that the Greeks used boxing gloves made of a piece of hard wood or metal strapped on the fist with leather. A characteristic of the Corinthians was that their eyes tended to protrude. The word translated as "pommel" by the RSV means hitting under the eye and giving oneself a knockout blow. This is an idiom. The principle is obvious. Paul takes his body as his opponent and affirms that he gives it a knockout blow and leads it into slavery. This is done so that he would not disqualify himself as a preacher and missionary.

According to 1 Corinthians 11:5, the women of Corinth were to keep their heads veiled when they prayed. Cartledge suggests that the historical context helps to illuminate this statement. In ancient Corinth women of chaste character wore their veils in public. Some of the Corinthian Christian women decided to throw off that restriction. Paul protested, for he did not want the Christian women to be mistaken for the sacred prostitutes of the Aphrodite cult of Corinth.

Knowledge of the political administration of the Roman empire in the first century A.D. illuminates numerous passages such as Philippians 1:27. The KJV states, "Only let your conversation be as it becometh the gospel of Christ." The word conversation means "citizen life" or "manner of life." Philippi was a Roman colony (Acts 16:12). Philippians 3:20 states that the Christian's citizenship is in heaven. With a knowledge of historical background the interpreter can understand what these verses meant to first-century readers. They would understand that they were to live their lives under the constitution and obligations of heaven, even as the political citizen lived his life under the constitution and obligations of Rome.

Fortunately, there is ample material available today to study history and culture. The interpreter should avail himself of Bible histories, atlases, and studies of the biblical people and their cultures.

3. The Theological Principle

The Bible is only incidentally language and history. It was not written just for historical or aesthetic ends. Essentially it was written as a book of faith. The primary conviction of the Bible writers is that a gracious God has acted in history in order to create in Christ a people for himself. Interpretation must seek to understand these theological insights.

Fortunately, since World War II, new tools such as theological word books are being produced. These studies indicate, for example, that Jesus was not simply the refined teacher of the Golden Rule and of the general fatherhood of God. Rather he was accepted as the Messiah who fulfilled in his life, death, and resurrection the promises of the Old Testament prophets that God in the fulness of time would act redemptively in history.

The biblical accounts do not describe objective external events presented in terms satisfactory to the classification methods of natural sciences. The writers and reporters were involved in the events and both remembered and interpreted. What happened and the interpretation are fused together. The New Testament writers were confronted and overwhelmed by the reality of encounter with God in Jesus Christ. They found new life in that encounter. It follows, therefore, that Jesus is described in the Bible by men who believed in him as the Messiah. The same principle applies to the account of the escape of the Hebrews across the Red Sea: it is reported by men who remembered, were caught up in the deliverance, and saw it as God's action.

In many cases there is an interval between the biblical events and the literary fixation of the witness. As Mays has pointed out, the Bible is the result of a complex process of forming, shaping, and growth. This interval of time between events and text is not neutral and vacant. As they were told and perhaps retold, the events gained a new dynamic contemporaneity. The witnesses themselves confirmed and deepened their understanding and insight concerning the original event.

The interpreter also contributes to the character of the interpretation. He is not like an experimenter in chemistry; he has presuppositions of which he must be aware. They must be tested in his confrontation with the Bible; he must admit biases and prejudices.

In one sense a fully adequate theological interpreter must be related to a Christian group of which, by faith, he is a member. The Bible cannot be fully understood from the outside by grammar, logic, rhetoric, and history alone. It must be understood from its center. The Bible's center yields itself best to men who have a personal relation with God through Jesus Christ and who are indwelt by the Spirit of God.

The theological principle also includes what is called doctrinal interpretation. Interpretation is to be in accord with the central emphases of the Bible. This idea or approach was strongly urged by Luther, Calvin, and the other Protestant Reformers in the sixteenth century. The Reformers contended that there was a central truth in the Bible which acted as a base or touchstone for interpretation.

Luther found this touchstone in the Pauline concept of justification by faith, especially as it is presented in Romans and Galatians. It is obvious that Luther overemphasized the theme of justification by faith because of his struggle against medieval Roman Catholic legalism and sacramentalism.

In the nineteenth century the Pauline concept of "in Christ" was thought by many to be the key to Paul's thinking. This divergence from the Reformation view has led in recent years to a reopening of the question of what really is the central interpretative key of the Bible. Scholars have turned again to ask the Bible itself to disclose its own theological center.

It is generally agreed that Luther had a valid insight in seeking an interpretative touchstone when he started with Paul. It is held by many scholars now, however, that the doctrine of justification by faith and the concept of being in Christ are both inadequate and lack comprehensiveness. The theme of holy history, redemptive history, or salvation history seems for many theologians to be the more adequate key to Paul's life and thought and also of the central message of the Bible. This redemptive-historical perspective embraces both the concept of justification by faith and being in Christ and adds additional dimensions.

Other competent scholars would add a qualifying word to the term redemptive history. This word is eschatological (last things). In the early years of this century Albert Schweitzer pointed out that eschatology is the dominant motif of the Bible. Since that time no thoughtful interpreter has been able to eliminate from his thinking the centrality of future orientation in the biblical world view.

The Old Testament tells of God's continuing activity in history, and yet for the Old Testament writers the fulness of God's purposes is always in the future. In the New Testament it was recognized that Christ brought the first installment of the realities of redemption. And yet the completion of these realities and the fulness of their power remain for the future. In Christ the future (the age to come) has moved back into the present (1 Cor. 10:11).

It would seem that the most fruitful way in which to state the key to the interpretation of the Bible would be in terms of a combination of the eschatological and the holy history emphases. This approach could be designated as "eschatological-holy history."

An interpreter should go beyond the precise verbal and historical meaning of the text to understand the theology that informs the text. This means that the interpreter seeks to discover, for example, not merely what directives Paul gave to the Corinthians, but also the theology that moved him to give the directives. Behind the parables of Jesus are the affirmations about God's kingdom coming in Christ's person and the challenge of radical response to him. Bright insists that such a theological approach is not a violation of sound principles of interpretation. To expound the theological content of the text is included in the task of grammatical-historical-theological interpretation.

In addition to the central theological

touchstone of eschatological-holy history, subordinate emphases should be noted.

The New Testament is the norm for interpreting the Old Testament. Prophecy is not self-interpretive but should follow New Testament insights. This does not mean that the New Testament rejects the Old Testament—it fulfils it.

Systematic passages should have priority over incidental passages. For example, justification is treated in a systematic form in Romans and Galatians. These books should be the primary guides for discussion of this doctrine. Incidental and ambiguous verses should be subordinated or looked at in the light of the larger and clearer emphases. This approach is actually the kind of procedure which educated people follow when any body of material or system of thought is under examination.

Universal principles are to be sought in the midst of local ceremonies. It was through foot washing that Jesus Christ taught the principle of love and humility. Paul's command to "greet one another with a holy kiss" (Rom. 16:16) should be seen as teaching the principle of Christian fraternity through the vehicle of the first-century ceremony.

Doctrines should not be based simply on one verse or a few miscellaneous verses. Rather, the general tenor of the Bible should be sought. Inevitably there will be aspects of biblical truth that appear to finite minds to be contradictory. A reverent Bible student, recognizing his finiteness, will live with these apparently contradictory truths.

Basic to all these subordinate emphases is the overarching emphasis of the Bible on God's saving purpose in history. Each part of the Bible must be seen in relation to this organic and teleological purpose. In Christ's public ministry, God is seen in the process of acting. A greater and more decisive coming of the kingdom was seen in the cross and resurrection. The fulness of the kingdom, however, will only come at the Parousia.

Seen from the eschatological-holy history perspective, the mystery concept discussed in the parables of Matthew 13 is better understood. The mystery is that the kingdom which is to come in apocalyptic power has entered into the world in advance, to work in a less overt and dramatic form among men. The kingdom at the time of Jesus' ministry might have looked like leaven or a small mustard seed, but it will yet come in power and glory.

The eschatological-holy history emphasis provides a framework for the proper kind of typology. The Old Testament has many types which have a real existence and significance of their own but represent a permanent and greater thing or event whose full embodiment or antitype is found in the New Testament. Some interpreters see too much as typical. Others are too skeptical toward typology. Moderate and constructive interpreters take the New Testament as their point of departure in typological studies. The meaning thrown back upon Old Testament types by the New Testament is of central importance.

The theological principle also includes a consideration of the literature of interpretation. The Bible was written hundreds of years ago. Many devout scholars have studied the Bible. By seeing how others have interpreted it, the contemporary interpreter benefits from the wisdom and the errors of the past.

4. The Practical Principle

The fourth principle of biblical exegesis is the practical principle. The culmination of biblical interpretation is the application of the biblical message to the modern world. Having found out what it *did* mean, the interpreter must ask, What *does* it mean?

Some interpreters are adept at making clear what the biblical writers meant in their time. They are aware of the theological convictions which guided the prophets and the apostles. They have less ability, however, to relate this meaning to the contemporary world. Other interpreters conduct contemporary discussions which have little relationship to the biblical meaning and message. An adequate interpreter will seek to present the biblical word as the address of God to men in specific situations today. Such interpretation will result in translation into contemporary idiom. Furthermore, he will seek to guide his hearers or readers to a responsible implementation of Bible truth in action.

The creation account in Genesis 1:1—2:4 portrays the cosmos in terms of a world picture understandable in the ancient world. A skilful interpreter will point out that God is not interested in giving man the details of cosmology or the detailed methodology of his creative activity. There is found, however, in the Genesis account a world view which places the living Lord as the Creator and end of all things. The interpreter is to apply this central emphasis of the ancient story to the needs of people who are living in an age of emptiness, boredom, and nihilism.

Isaiah 6:1 describes God with throne, robe, and bodily appearance. Utilizing the doctrine of accommodation suggested by John Calvin four centuries ago, a contemporary interpreter realizes that this was the way God was represented to Isaiah. The truth for then, expressed in eighth century B.C. categories, and for today is that there is a personal God of holiness and transcendence behind the dramatic language. For Isaiah, Calvin, and contemporary men of faith, the use of the upward metaphors to describe God preserves the otherness and transcendence of God. Isaiah's statement will forever refute any monist or mystical identification of God and man such as some Hindus and Buddhists teach today.

The test of a practical application is whether or not it communicates the intention implied in the biblical text. For example, in the first century the resurrection of Christ meant that the new age had begun, Christ had been enthroned, and man could live by the power of the new age here and now. This principle is applicable today, as much as ever before.

After the original meaning of a passage has been learned, the interpreter is in a position to apply it to life today. But the emphasis should be on principles and not on specific details. The New Testament writers constantly moved through specifics to principles. It is obvious that no one should try to dress as first-century people did or follow their hair styles. Yet the principle of propriety or quiet modesty is involved in the biblical materials which deal with dress and appearance (1 Peter 3:3; 1 Tim. 2:9).

The principles outlined above should not be looked at as rigid and mechanical rules. They should be helpful guidelines, however, as the Christian seeks to improve his biblical understanding and appropriate the resources and guidance which God has given to man in and through the Bible. Improper habits of biblical interpretation should be frankly admitted and rejected. Constant practice and dialogue with other interpreters should be encouraged. In a culture in which dozens of radical cults claim to interpret the Bible properly, it is imperative that attention be given to understanding and putting into practice these generally accepted principles.

For Further Reading

BLACKMAN, M. C. *Biblical Interpretation.* Philadelphia: Westminster Press, 1957.

BRIGHT, JOHN. *The Authority of the Old Testament.* Nashville: Abingdon Press, 1967.

CARTLEDGE, SAMUEL A. *The Bible: God's Word to Man.* Philadelphia: Westminster Press, 1961.

DENBEAUX, FRED J. *Understanding the Bible.* Philadelphia: Westminster Press, 1958.

MAYS, JAMES LUTHER. *Exegesis as a Theological Discipline.* Richmond: Union Theological Seminary, 1960.

MICKELSEN, A. BERKELEY. *Interpreting the Bible.* Grand Rapids: Wm. B. Eerdmans Publishing Co., 1963.

RAMM, BERNARD. *Protestant Biblical Interpretation.* Boston: W. A. Wilde Co., 1956.

STIBBS, ALAN M. *Understanding God's Word.* Chicago: Inter-Varsity Press, 1950.

WOOD, JAMES D. *The Interpretation of the Bible: An Historical Introduction.* London: Duckworth Press, 1958.

The Geography of the Bible

B. ELMO SCOGGIN

Throughout history, Palestine had an importance far out of proportion to its size. It is the bridge that connects the earth's two greatest land masses, Eurasia and Africa. It is so situated that all the great land routes between these two continents and also major eastern and western sea routes converge upon it. As a result, there has been constant movement of peoples across the "Land of the Bible" for purposes of migration, commerce, and war.

I. The Old Testament World

Never more than a few hundred miles long and probably one hundred miles in width, the Old Testament world was constituted primarily of three parts: Palestine in the center, Egypt to the west-southwest, and Mesopotamia to the east-northeast. These, with smaller areas between them, make up what came to be known as the "Fertile Crescent."

Palestine. This part of the Old Testament world was much the smallest but most important of the three parts. The traditional north and south boundaries of Palestine, Dan to Beersheba, are about 150 miles apart. Although there were brief periods when the southern boundary extended to the Gulf of Aqabah and the city of Ezion-Geber, 300 miles distant from Dan, for the most part the Hebrews were thought of as possessing only the land from Dan to Beersheba. The edge of the desert was at the most no more than 75 miles east of the Mediterranean coast.

The heart of the Old Testament world, then, is roughly a 75 by 150-mile rectangle of mountains, deserts, gorges, and plains.

The eastern and western neighbors of Palestine, Mesopotamia, and Egypt were the "river lands." Each of them is characterized by a massive river system running its full length, and each is separated from Palestine by strips of desert. The Sinai Desert, between Palestine and Egypt, is particularly severe and served as a buffer between the two countries.

Egypt. This southwestern neighbor of Palestine often sent her armies northward. On occasion they marched against the great powers of the East—Syria, Babylon, Assyria, and Persia. Frequently, the Egyptians fought the inhabitants of Palestine.

The southern mineral deposits of Palestine and its northern forests also attracted Egyptian traders and soldiers.

The economy of Egypt is tied inseparably to the Nile River. It has desert sections east and west of the river but is centered around the long, narrow strip of alluvial soil deposits on both sides of the Nile. These deposits broaden into the rich delta on the north where the river joins the Mediterranean Sea. The Palestinians sent to the fertile Nile Valley to buy grain when their own country could not produce it.

Mesopotamia and Syria. The northeastern neighbors of Palestine constitute the eastern arm of the "Fertile Crescent" and, like Egypt to the southwest, are characterized by very important river systems, the Tigris and Euphrates. Both of these rivers rise in the mountains south of the Caspian Sea and are subject to seasonal floods. Canals, dykes, and dams were used to control these floods to some extent and to irrigate the fields. The remains of these irrigation systems are still visible in many places.

Life was harsher and less stable in Mesopotamia than in the Nile Valley. It lay north of Egypt and had colder winters. The deserts and other boundaries that separated it from its neighbors were less restrictive, so that successive invaders conquered the land and established their dynasties. Palestine was often the victim of the conflicts between Egypt and Mesopotamia, who fought their wars on Palestine's soil.

Syria has no fixed geographical lines in

the Bible and at various times includes the area from Sinai to Mesopotamia. The Hebrew Bible used the name Aram to designate it as the country of the Aramaeans, who settled the area with Damascus as their capital about the thirteenth century B.C. They came to the height of their power almost simultaneously with the Hebrews in Palestine.

The Phoenician coast, parts of the Euphrates Valley, and parts of Palestine were little more than Syrian provinces at one time or another in Syrian history.

II. The New Testament World

Soon after the resurrection of Jesus, Christians began to travel far beyond the limits of the Old Testament world. Persecutions, missionary travels, and commerce sent followers of the Christ throughout the Mediterranean lands. There they preached their new faith, joined together in worshiping communities, and eventually established churches.

Luke 2:1 says that Augustus Caesar ruled the "entire" inhabited world. This Roman Empire extended roughly from the Atlantic to the Euphrates and from the Rhine and Danube rivers to the Arabian and Sahara deserts.

Asia Minor. This subdivision is bounded on the south by the Mediterranean Sea and Mesopotamia; on the north, by the Black Sea and the Caspian Sea; on the east, by Armenia and Media; and on the west, by the Greek Islands and the narrow Bosphorus and Hellespont Strait.

Asia Minor was of considerable importance during the New Testament period. Paul's missionary journeys here proved fruitful and resulted in churches at many places. It was from Asia Minor that the Spirit called Paul to Macedonia in Greece.

Greece. The westward spread of the gospel was soon well under way as a result of the "Macedonian call." Major Greek cities—Corinth, Philippi, and Thessalonica among them—became the sites of strong Christian communities and contributed to the growth and spread of the new faith.

Italy. Westward from Greece across the Adriatic Sea lies the Italian peninsula with the islands of Sicily, Sardinia, and Corsica to the west. The gospel was well established in Rome within a generation after the resurrection of Jesus.

Egypt and North Africa. The major cities of the Mediterranean world had well established Jewish communities within them long before the time of Christ. It was to these communities that news of the gospel first came. The large city of Alexandria became a strong center of the new Christian faith and even competed with Rome and Jerusalem for dominance. From Alexandria the faith spread westward along the north African coast to Cyrene, Carthage, and possibly as far as Gibraltar.

The Western Mediterranean. There are those who think that Tarshish, the place to which Jonah fled (Jonah 1:3), may have been in Spain, and that the contact between Palestine and Spain goes well back into Old Testament times. We know from Romans 15:28 that Paul intended to go to Spain. Either Paul or someone in the western communities influenced by him may well have taken the gospel on to Britain, invaded by the Romans in A.D. 43.

III. Palestine

Palestine is the land to which biblical history and geography are tied. Although the country is small, its position is very important.

1. Boundaries

Palestine is bounded by the Mediterranean Sea on the west; by the desert on the east; by Syria on the north; and by Egypt on the south. The northern border shifted often because of the changing fortunes of Syria or some other neighbor. The southern border was rather fixed by the desert, which served as a natural boundary between Palestine and Egypt.

2. Subdivisions

There are at least four distinct zones in Palestine running north to south.

The Coastal Plain. This area extends in varying widths from the "Ladder of Tyre" to the "Brook of Egypt." The coastal plain falls rather naturally into three subdivisions. The first of these was *Zebulon.* The plain ranges up to five miles in width in the north around the Bay of Acco, but at the tip of Mount Carmel it is no wider than a few hundred feet. Mount Carmel almost juts into the sea at this point and forms the beautiful Bay of Acco at the north side of which was the harbor of Acco (Judg. 1:31).

The second division was *Sharon.* From the tip of Carmel southward the plain begins to broaden again, reaching a width of 15 miles or more at some points. That section of the plain lying between Mount Carmel and the Yarkon River is usually referred to as Sharon. In biblical times it was heavily forested and had swampy areas.

The third division was *Philistia,* the name given to the coastal plain from the Yarkon southward. The Philistines not only had their five major cities in this area—Ashdod, Ashkelon, Ekron, Gath, and Gaza—but also gave their name to the whole country.

The Philistine Plain was more hilly than Sharon. It did not receive as much rain as the northern area and was therefore neither swampy nor heavily forested. These gentle lowlands were suitable for grain crops, olive trees, and grapes, though toward the southern end water was indeed scarce. Gaza was the last flourishing city before the desert.

The Western Mountain Range. Variously known as the Lebanon Range, the Western Plateau, or the Judean Highlands, this range begins high in Lebanon and continues southward to the region of Sinai. Cracks in the earth's surface, running east and west, have caused these mountains to descend in a series of steps.

From Esdraelon northward the region is identified as *Galilee.* The northern end of the range lies near the coast. It is known today as Lebanon, but in biblical times it was known as Phoenicia. It was distinguished by its large forests of huge cedars

which added to the difficulty of passage over the mountains. There were many excellent harbors on Phoenicia's rocky coasts and her forests provided abundant timber for Phoenician ships.

The first step down from the heights of Lebanon is the plateau of upper Galilee. The most prominent mountain of this area is Mount Canaan, over 3000 feet in elevation, the highest mountain in Palestine west of the Jordan Valley. The whole of northern Palestine is visible from the top of Canaan. Lower Galilee lies south of a line running eastward from Acco toward the northern end of the Sea of Galilee. It is a plateau but is lower than upper Galilee. Its dominant feature is that it is made up of hills and valleys or small plains. It is the area allotted to Zebulon and Naphtali in the conquest of Canaan (Josh. 19:10,32).

This section is comparatively well watered and is important for the production of grapes, olives, grains, and vegetables.

The Plain of Esdraelon lies between the plateau of lower Galilee and the mountains of Samaria. This triangular shaped plain is connected by the Kishon brook to the Mediterranean in the Bay of Acco and to the Jordan Valley by the Valley of Jezreel. Esdraelon was poorly drained in biblical times and trapped many ancient armies in its marshy bogs.

Mount Tabor, at the northeastern corner of the plain, is one of the traditional sites of the transfiguration of Jesus (Matt. 17).

The Central Mountains rise from the Plain of Esdraelon to form, to the south, the region known as Samaria and made up of the territories of Manasseh and Ephraim.

The Carmel Range is under 2000 feet in elevation, even at its highest points in the northwest and southeast, and is much lower in the middle near Meggido where it is crossed by the Meggido Pass.

Manasseh is a large basin surrounding Shechem. It has a saucer-like appearance because of the higher land around its edges. Ephraim, southward from Manasseh, has the shape of a great dome. It is a limestone formation approximately 3000 feet high in places and is therefore one of the best watered areas of Palestine. Its soil is fertile and excellent for olives, grapes, and other crops.

The area of Benjamin lies between Ephraim and Judah. Perhaps its most distinctive feature is relatively easy access from the west by the Valley of Ajalon and from the east by the valley leading up from Jericho. The Benjaminite territory was bordered on the north by Bethel, and on the south by Jerusalem.

Judah and the Shephelah were the territory of the highlands of Judah. This area begins just north of Jerusalem and extends to the point where the mountains drop away north of the ancient city of Arad. The Shephelah is the name given by the ancient Hebrews to the limestone hills that lie between the Philistine Plain and the Judean Mountains. The term means "lowlands" and was the area immediately below the mountain regions inhabited by the Hebrews. It was a "no man's land" between the Hebrews and the Philistines, and they fought often to control it.

The Negev lies past the southern end of the Judean highlands. It actually includes the area from just west of the southern end of the Dead Sea all the way to the coast of the Mediterranean south of Gaza. Beersheba is on the northern edge of the Negev. On the south it fades into the wilderness wastes of Sinai. There are a few springs and wells within this area and limited farming can be done in some low places.

The Jordan Valley. More accurately known as the Great Rift Valley, the Jordan is a depression of varying depths that runs through the whole length of Palestine. Its average width is ten miles. The Jordan River is wholly contained within it. In its northern extreme, the valley is 1800 feet above sea level, though it has already fallen 1500 feet when it comes into Palestine in the Huleh swamps. It is 630 feet below sea level at the Sea of Galilee and about 1300 feet below at the Dead Sea shore. From here it rises to 750 feet above

sea level in the Arabah before sloping to sea level again on the Red Sea at Elath.

Because of the depth of the valley, there are many steep slopes and precipices. The mountains on the west are 3000 feet or more above the valley in places and much higher than that on the east.

The valley has a climate all its own. It is warm the year round, even in the north, and has desert conditions in the south. Where watered by springs or streams, tropical vegetation is plentiful. The valley may be subdivided as follows:

Huleh Valley, sometimes called Waters of Merom. This swampy, marshy area is about 210 feet above sea level and is the meeting place of the various branches of the River Jordan. In biblical times it was a large marshy flat grown up in reeds and bushes.

The Sea of Galilee in the Old Testament (Num. 34:11) was called Sea of Chinnereth. The New Testament (Luke 5:1) calls it Lake of Gennesaret. The sea lies only 10 miles south of Huleh, in which short distance the valley drops 840 feet, making Galilee's shoreline 630 feet below that of the Mediterranean. It is the only sweetwater lake in Palestine. It is 13 miles long and 7 to 9 miles wide. The cold, clear, dark blue water teems with fish life. From the mountain rim above, it appears as a beautiful, calm jewel. Yet, it is capable of violent storms.

The small valleys and plains about the sea are fertile and well watered. The tropical climate makes them productive of a wide variety of fruits and vegetables throughout the year. Important towns, Magdala and Capernaum among them, were on its shores in biblical times. The city of Tiberias survives even today.

The Jordan Valley, between the Sea of Galilee and the Dead Sea is less than 70 miles long. In its northern reaches, this valley is fertile and lush with growth, especially above the confluence of the Jordan and the Yarmuk. Further south the Jordan has cut a bed through gray-blue marl, and the riverbanks are full of flora and fauna.

Approximately 15 miles south of the Sea of Galilee, the valley of Jezreel comes in from the west. The Jordan Valley narrows here for about 25 miles where the *Wadi Far'ah* joins again from the west. The west bank from *Wadi Far'ah* to the Jericho Oasis is a desert wasteland with few springs and brooks. East of the river there are many more springs and streams. The two largest are the Yarmuk, mentioned above, and the Jabbok. The eastern bank developed more cities than the western bank because of the superior water supply.

The Dead Sea was known in biblical times as the Salt Sea. It is in the deepest fissure on the earth outside the ocean floors. The shoreline is 1300 feet below sea level, and the sea is 1200 feet deep in the northern half. El-Lisan, "the tongue," is the boot-shaped peninsula running out from the eastern side. Above it the sea is 30 miles long. About 15 miles of the sea lie south of el-Lisan and there it is no more than 35 feet deep. The sea width ranges from two and a half miles at el-Lisan to 8 to 10 miles just above it. The land around the sea is salty marl. The shores are mostly narrow. Around the sea the heat is almost unbearable for most of the year.

The famous "Dead Sea Scrolls" were discovered in 1947 in a cave on the northwestern side of the Dead Sea. Further explorations and excavations have revealed also a cemetery and the remains of a library workshop and living quarters which belonged to the scribes who copied and preserved these ancient documents.

The Arabah is the name usually given to that section of the Great Rift Valley running the 110 miles from the Dead Sea to the Red Sea. This desolate wasteland rises from 1300 feet below sea level to 750 feet above, then slopes down again to sea level at Elath. Rainfall is very sporadic, yet the valley is sometimes a raging flood because of the runoff from rains in the nearby hills.

Copper deposits on both sides of the southern Arabah have been exploited since pre-Solomonic times. The copper mines and the road connecting Elath and the Red Sea to points north are the most important features of the Arabah.

The Eastern Plateau. The mountains of this area are generally higher than those to the west. Steep descents toward the Jordan characterize the western side of the plateau. There is no clearly marked line of demarcation between the plateau and the Syrian and Arabian deserts to the east.

Comparatively heavy amounts of rainfall result from the lifting and cooling of the air by the high plateau.

The desert has a powerful influence on the region east of the Jordan. Hot winds blow in during the spring and fall. Freezing winds whip in from the desert in winter.

The plateau is characterized by four rivers: Yarmuk, Jabbok, Arnon, and Zered. They begin near the eastern desert and flow in a northerly direction before turning west. There are also many smaller streams that flow in the same direction. Thus most of the rainfall on the plateau eventually flows to the Jordan.

Transjordan is divided into four subdivisions:

The northernmost section is *Bashan.* It is generally north of the Yarmuk River. It is famous for its fertility and productivity. In the days of Amos it was a fabled land of richness and ease whose women he could call "cows of Bashan" (4:1).

Gilead includes on the southeast the Ammonite territory. It encompasses the central section of the region east of the Jordan. It is higher and more rugged than other areas, rising occasionally to over 3000 feet. The desert is only 25 miles from the Jordan in some places. The terrain is difficult to traverse, especially the western, forested portion. The tribes of Reuben and Gad occupied the southern part of Gilead where Reuben continued his nomadic existence (1 Chron. 5:9).

Northern Gilead became a center of Israelite population east of the Jordan when western Palestine became crowded. The tribe of Mannasseh was the dominant presence.

The western border of *Moab* is formed

by the eastern shoreline of the Dead Sea. No clear line divides it from Gilead on the north. It is high tableland running the length of the Dead Sea. The River Arnon divides Moab into two parts. The River Zered divides it from Edom on the south.

The tablelands range from 2000 feet in height north of the Arnon to more than 4000 feet on the south. According to 2 Kings 3:4, the culture was pastoral.

Edom begins about the southern end of the Dead Sea and continues southward. It consists of high granite and sandstone mountains rising to the east of the Arabah. In some places these mountains are over 5000 feet high. On the western slopes they have adequate rainfall. The area is rough and was difficult to conquer.

3. Mountains

Mountains served as barriers to easy passage through Palestine. The passes between them were guarded by strategic cities. The valleys and narrow plains served the agricultural economy of Palestine.

The mountains and hills provided protection from intruders, sites for the cities, and soil for the fields of the plains. They also trapped the warm air during rainy seasons, causing it to rise and cool, then dump its moisture in the form of rain.

4. Climate

Two primary seasons characterize the climate of Palestine, the dry summer from about mid-May to mid-October, and the rainy season during the months from November through April. The rainy season varies from year to year. It is seldom longer than described here though it is sometimes much shorter. The long, dry summer is relieved by the heavy dews so characteristic of the area. The story of Gideon's fleece in Judges 6:38 and the references to the "morning mist" in Hosea 6:4 and 13:3 illustrate its appearance.

The rainy season is much less regular than the summer drought. A typical winter is about equally divided between rainy days and days with little or no rain. There are seasons, however, when rain begins as late as January and others when it comes abundantly as early as October. Hail and snow are not unheard of, but they do not come with any regularity.

To the people of the Bible the weather was entirely in God's hands, and he used it at will to bless and punish his children and their neighbors (Isa. 5:6; 1 Kings 17:1–7).

5. Rivers and Valleys

The Jordan Valley is by all means the most important valley in Palestine. It has its own river and receives the brooks that flow from the various oases along its length in addition to those rivers that flow to it from the mountains.

The Valley of Jezreel runs from the west through the Esdraelon plain and comes eastward to the Jordan at ancient Bethshean. It is actually a lowland route from the Mediterranean at Acco to the Jordan Valley. Ajalon, Sorek, and Elah are smaller and narrower valleys in the highlands of Judah running from the plain of Philistia up to the mountaintops.

These and other valleys and plains served not only to carry the waters of winter and the perennial streams such as the Jordan, but also as agricultural centers, as passes through the mountains, and as routes for major roads and highways. The great armies of history moved over Palestine through these valleys.

6. Roads and Highways

Palestine is the land bridge between the two "river-lands," Egypt and Mesopotamia, across which bridge commercial and military traffic has traveled since long before the time of the Hebrews.

The geographical structure of the country, the distribution of plains, valleys, and mountains was such that various cultures and peoples could live side by side in semi-isolation. This same geography, however, dictated the location of major international routes which have remained virtually unchanged until today. These strategic routes also made it possible for this fragmented country to be unified at various times, often under foreign control.

There were four major routes through Palestine:

The most important was the coastal highway, known by geographers as the *Via Maris,* the "way of the sea" (Isa. 9:1). It goes from Egypt northward, moving inland through the Meggido Pass, with a lesser route continuing up the coast. At Meggido the route forks with one prong skirting Esdraelon on the west, then passing through Jezreel to Acco on its way up the Phoenician coast. The second fork passes through Esdraelon to the northeast by Mount Tabor and follows the Rift Valley past the Sea of Galilee and Hazor toward Damascus. The mighty armies of Egypt, Assyria, Babylon, and Palestine moved over this route.

The King's Highway is the biblical term used (Num. 20:17) to designate the route running from beyond Damascus southward along the Transjordan Plateau to Elath and points beyond. At least the south-central part of this route was used by the children of Israel during the Exodus.

The mountain route west of the Jordan was less important though not insignificant. It began at Meggido and went southward by Shechem, Bethel, Jerusalem, and Hebron to Beersheba, where it intersected other routes.

The Jordan Valley also provided terrain suitable for travel. There were two routes, one on either side of the river. These routes lay primarily between Bethshean and Jericho at which two junctures they were met by other roads.

These four longitudinal routes were connected by many lesser latitudinal roads.

Conclusion

The physical geography of Palestine left its indelible stamp on the "people of the book." Its very smallness contributed to their being welded into a community. Its rugged, mountainous terrain helped to form their spirit and influenced their language (Isa. 5:1-7; 44:3; 51:1). Its rocky roughness forced them to toil unusually hard and long for the "fruit of the vine" and "bread from the ground." Its alternate seasons of rain and drought, dew and dryness, heat and cold, plenty and famine affected not only the routine of their daily existence but had much to do also with the character of their religion.

When the Israelites spoke of "the mountain of the house of the Lord" (Isa. 2:2), they could envision him "high and lifted up" (Isa. 6:1). They represented the strength and might of God with the figure of a mighty rock of salvation and strength (Psalm 62:6-7). One has but to see the massive mountains of stone in many parts of Palestine to understand the force of these and other similar figures of speech.

Such is the land to which God called Abraham and his family. Insignificant in size, containing an amazing variety of landscape, it nevertheless has remained a land of great importance because of the drama played out there as God dealt with the people of his choice. He acted mightily in history, using this little stage for a redemptive work which has significance for the whole family of man.

For Further Reading

AHARONI, YOHANAN. *The Land of the Bible.* Trans. A. F. RAINEY. Philadelphia: Westminster Press, 1967.

AVI-YONAH, MICHAEL. *The Holy Land.* Grand Rapids: Baker Book House, 1966.

BALY, DENIS. *Palestine and the Bible.* New York: Association Press, 1959.

————. *The Geography of the Bible.* New York: Harper & Brothers, 1957.

————. *Geographical Companion to the Bible.* New York: McGraw-Hill, 1963.

SMITH, GEORGE ADAM. *The Historical Geography of the Holy Land.* Revised edition. New York: Harper & Row, 1967.

McCown, C. C., "Palestine, Geography of," IDB, III, 626-639.

SCHOFIELD, J. N. "The Geography of Palestine," *Peake's Commentary on the Bible,* pp. 29-36.

WRIGHT, G. E. and F. V. FILSON. *The Westminster Historical Atlas to the Bible.* Philadelphia: Westminster Press, 1956.

Oxford Bible Atlas, (ed.) Herbert G. May. London: Oxford University Press, 1962.

Archaeology and the Bible

Three miles north of Jerusalem is a high, rounded hill topped with a mound of rocky earth. The Arabs for centuries have called it Tell el-Ful, or "the Hill of Beans," because its summit is a good place to grow beans, or chick-peas. This is the principal ingredient in a tasty Middle Eastern dish, popular for at least the past five thousand years.

Standing on top of the Hill of Beans, one can see to the northeast a large elongated mound, shaped like a giant grave. The local people call it Et-Tell, or "The Ruin," because it was a ruin when the Arabs came to Palestine in the seventh century. For at least thirteen centuries, it has been planted in wheat. Directly north of the Hill of Beans, and across a wide valley, is a small village of flattop huts strewn across the crest and south slope of another hill. It is called Er-Ramah, a name that has been handed down by inhabitants of the site for centuries. And to the west is another village called El-Jib, located on the highest point of another mound. Its pencil-straight minaret points up toward Allah, the Moslem deity.

Within a radius of 40 miles, there are literally hundreds of villages and mounds of ancient cities that rest quietly on hilltops near springs of water. They are impressive, even to the casual observer. A reader of the Bible perceives at once in Er-Ramah the name of Samuel's home town, Ramah (1 Sam. 7:15–17). And El-Jib is none other than Gibeon, the city of the Hivites who negotiated peace with Joshua (Josh. 9:3–15). Et-Tell is the biblical Ai.

And the Hill of Beans is probably ancient Gibeah, the village of Saul (1 Sam. 10:26), whose fortress-palace ruins lay unnoticed for centuries just inches below the peasant's plow.

Covered by the dust of centuries are the cities and villages of the Bible, at least some of its people surviving from generation to generation. Here, within a radius of 40 miles, the greater part of the drama of biblical revelation was experienced—long before it was written in a book. This revelation was experienced by people who lived here before it was written in a book. And the book, our Bible, was affected by all the influences that shape the experiences of a people; i.e., race, language, geography, religious institutions, internal and foreign politics, cultural traditions, scientific knowledge, literature, art, economy, class conflicts, etc. To understand and interpret the Bible, we should get to know the people who handed it down to us as a legacy of their experience with God.

It is true that we can get acquainted with the people of the Bible by meeting them in the pages of Scripture. But these pages are rather two-dimensional, and a common tendency is to supply the third dimension that makes biblical people live from our experience, not theirs. For instance, how many church building programs have been promoted with the text, "Where there is no vision, the people perish" (Prov. 29:18, KJV)! Actually the word vision in this verse means revelation from God, a common Near Eastern term used of Isaiah's prophecy (1:1) but descriptive of his inaugural call in 6:1 ff.[1]

It is not in error to admonish a congregation to exercise foresight in planning and building, but to find this practical meaning in the proverb is to impose our own use of a word upon Scripture and rob the Scripture of its inspired meaning.

The true dimension of reality, and relevance, in the Bible is its own life, not ours. When the people of the Bible live their

---

[1] J. Lindblom, *Prophecy in Ancient Israel* (Oxford: Basil Blackwell, 1962), pp. 122–37, has a comprehensive discussion of the phenomenon of prophetic visions in the Bible and the ancient Near East.

own lives, they speak to us. On the other hand, if we impose the experience of our life and ways of thinking on the Bible, its meaning becomes confused and its message lost. A major quest of serious Christians, then, should be to find the living people of God in Scripture, for it is they who communicate the living Word. To find them in truth, one must meet them in their own houses, eat the food they eat, talk with them in their sanctuaries, think with them in their literature, art, and symbols, suffer with them in their poverty, and strive with them for their ideals and faith.

Biblical archaeology ultimately is dedicated to the task of leading modern man into the ancient living world of the Bible. The material remains of cities like Jerusalem are excavated by careful scientific techniques. We can thus know and recover the exciting drama of life in Jerusalem as Isaiah, for example, experienced it. The book of his prophecy was his dialogue with his world. Within the holy wedlock of his prophecy and the world to which he spoke was born the legitimate word which the speaks to us. Archaeology therefore seeks to discover the interactions of history in any given period, the usage of words that give them meaning, and the equivalents of money, weights, and measures which bring life into focus in concrete terms. Archaeology seeks equally to discover the symbols in art and literature that communicate the soul of a people, benchmarks of factual information that the theologian must take into account in his doctrine, and a knowledge of the people of God in their international context that, over the years, cultivates perspective and understanding. In short, the legacy of archaeology to the Bible is life, the life of the people who gave us the book.

I. Discovery of the Biblical World

Two centuries ago the biblical world was practically unknown. Biblical scholars wasted much time debating issues that could have been settled quickly with some factual information. For instance, there was quite a controversy in Martin Luther's time over whether the world was created in 4004 or 6000 B.C. Actually the two sides followed chronologies in two texts of the Old Testament—the Masoretic Text which contains a genealogy that yields a 4004 date of creation, and the Septuagint which yields a 6000 date. Bishop Lightfoot of Cambridge University solved the problem in a classic example of supporting limited information with an extra portion of imagination when he set the moment of creation at 9:00 A.M. on October 23, 4004.

Meanwhile, most of the history of Egypt slept in unintelligible signs and symbols on literally acres of monuments down the length of the Nile. The story of Assyrian and Babylonian imperialism was known mainly from the selected accounts in the Bible. Ashurbanipal's library at Nineveh hid the Babylonian flood and creation accounts in curious wedge-shaped script deep in the heart of the ancient city mound.[2] The amazing city of Jericho covered its 8000 B.C. foundations under 70 feet of successive cities. (Kenyon, pp. 39–42). And the bones of a man who lived 600,000 years ago south of the Sea of Galilee lay until recently among the remains of 40 extinct animal species under the alluvial soil of a cotton field. (Emmanuel Anati traces the earliest evidence of man in Palestine in Part II).

Over the last 150 years, however, the story of the biblical world has been pieced together again. The first breakthrough occurred when Champollion, a brilliant young French linguist, deciphered Egyptian picture-writing on the Rosetta Stone in 1822. On the heels of this achievement, a persistent Englishman, Henry Rawlinson, found the key to cuneiform, the strange, wedge-shaped writing on monuments and clay tablets in the Euphrates Valley. Other equally significant milestones were reached. The royal library of Assyrian kings from Sen-

2 Cf. Pritchard, for translations of the Enuma Elish (creation account), pp. 60–72; and the Gilgamesh Epic (Flood story), pp. 72–99.

nacherib to Ashurbanipal, with its store of more than 24,000 inscribed clay tablets, was found at Nineveh in 1853. And Captain Charles Warren inaugurated field excavation in Palestine with his exploration of underground Jerusalem in 1867.

Field excavations have been carried out in every country of the Near East where and when volatile political conditions permitted. Yet a conservative estimate has been published that only 2 percent of Palestinian antiquities have been excavated in the last 100 years. Gifted linguists have ferreted out every strange piece of writing known in the whole Near East, and the words of the ancients have been read right back to the dawn of writing itself, *ca.* 3000 B.C. And the vast prehistory (before the invention of writing) of man has been doggedly traced back a half million years in Palestine, and nearly two million years in East Africa. What the next century holds in store is beyond speculation, but if past achievement is a guide, the next 2 percent of total information will be revolutionary enough to require at all times an open mind and flexible position on any historical problem in biblical study.

II. The Integrity of Bible History

The result of a century of discovery has been a new respect for the historicity of biblical events and persons. Throughout the Scriptures, the historical foundation of the revelation is claimed. Now we can weave the threads of that history into the fabric of extrabiblical history and establish firmly its basic integrity.

Biblical scholars, generally, no longer undertake to literalize all of the Bible as history, because it is a complex book of poetry, prophecy, hymns, proverbs, and traditions as well as factual history. And we find that factual history is written in the contemporary forms of biblical times. However, the recovery of numerous synchronisms with extrabiblical events and records enables the Bible student to approach his study with new and solid confidence that is foundational to a secure faith in the revelation.[3]

Assyrian and Babylonian annals supply many of the references that echo and supplement events related in the Bible. The Obelisk of Shalmaneser III, a squared pillar about seven feet tall found at Nimrud, Assyria, records the payment of tribute by various rulers in Syria-Palestine during the ninth century B.C. (cf. Pritchard, pp. 120:351; 290:351).

One panel shows Jehu, king of Israel, bowing before the great monarch in the only known pictorial representation of an Israelite king. Another monument of Shalmaneser III mentions Ahab as one of the kings who fought the Assyrians at the battle of Karkar in 853 B.C. Sargon II left a record of his capture of Samaria *ca.* 721 B.C., and even noted that 27,290 captives were led away to Assyria (cf. 2 Kings 17). Sennacherib, the arrogant conqueror who devastated Judah in Isaiah's time, recorded in bas-relief the capture of Lachish on a wall of his palace at Nineveh. His chronicler also left an account of the seige of Jerusalem in which he claimed that he shut up Hezekiah in the city "like a bird in a cage"! The travail of Judah as she faced destruction is recorded in 2 Kings 18:13—19:36 and Isaiah 36–37.

A number of inscribed clay tablets called "The Babylonian Chronicle" record the fall of Assyria and the first Babylonian captivity of Judah. The date of surrender of Jerusalem to Nebuchadnezzar in 597 B.C. corresponds to March 16 on our calendar![4] This record enables us to reckon the final destruction of Jerusalem in 587 B.C. Additional tablets found near the Ishtar Gate in Babylon record the issue of rations to King Jehoiachim of Judah, who remained under house arrest in Babylon from 597 until 562 B.C. And the Murashu Tablets from Nippur,

---

[3] Edwin R. Thiele, *The Mysterious Numbers of the Hebrew Kings* (Chicago: Univ. Press, 1951), reconstructs the complex chronology of Old Testament history and synchronizes it with extrabiblical history by using Assyrian records mainly.

[4] Cf. D. Winton Thomas (ed.), *Documents from Old Testament Times* (London: Thomas Nelson & Sons, Ltd., 1958), pp. 80–81.

southeast of Babylon, list Jewish clients of the Murashu banking house who rented land and obtained loans in the fifth century. They apparently pursued profitable business interests at the same time that zealously religious Jews were rebuilding Jerusalem under the leadership of Nehemiah.

Other discoveries that relate to biblical history more indirectly take us into the unusual world of the Patriarchs. Haran, in Genesis 12:4, was the point of emigration to the land of Canaan, and communication was maintained between Canaan and the Haran region until the descent into Egypt. The Mari Tablets, discovered on the Euphrates south of Haran and dating to *ca.* 1800 B.C. reflect the closeness of patriarchal associations with Haran.

Several towns bear the names of Abraham's relatives, possibly named after their families. For instance, there is the town of Til-Turakhi, a name equivalent to Terah in Genesis 11:24. Haran, the brother of Abraham and son of Terah, is the name of the city from which the patriarch emigrated to Canaan. It was a flourishing caravan and trading center in the eighteenth century B.C. Nahor, a brother of Abraham to whom Eliezer went for a wife for Isaac, is a city named in the Mari Texts. Serug and Peleg, ancestors of Abraham, are reflected in the village names of Sarugi, west of Haran, and Phaliga, on the Euphrates southwest of Haran (cf. Wright, p. 41).

The coincidence of these names is hardly accidental. Instead, the Mari Tablets provide an extrabiblical record of places that bear the names of Abraham's kinsmen. They reflect the basic historical ties of the patriarchal narratives with a specific region at the time we should expect.

Countless other examples of historical ties between biblical and extrabiblical history could be cited, reaching into the New Testament period. However, the selected references named above are representative, and should indicate without question that the biblical revelation was indeed apprehended within the arena of historical event. The union of revelation with history cannot be annulled!

III. Illustration of Biblical Words, Customs, Ideas

During the late nineteenth century, archaeology was used to support preconceived ideas about the Bible. It was made a servant in the house of theology. Some scholars were concerned to prove Bible events, and historical information from archaeology was eagerly grasped to support their contentions.

Sir Leonard Woolley's discovery of a silty layer of earth at Ur was cited as historical evidence of Noah's flood (Gen. 6—9).[5] The fact that no silt layer was found four miles away was ignored, as was the evidence at Kish, Shurrupak, Nineveh, and Nippur, where floods occurred at different times.

Evidence like this was used, irrespective of all related facts, to prove certain theological positions. The point here is not the issue of the biblical event of the flood, but the use of archaeological evidence. Archaeology does support the historical context of the biblical revelation, but it should be used with integrity and never apart from all evidence, internal and external, related to the biblical revelation.

In the nineteenth century some scholars with different theological concern used archaeological findings to illustrate the Bible, because they had worked out the historical problems, or thought they had. Discoveries served to illuminate the theological house these scholars had built. By 1940, however, the illumination penetrated to the foundations of their historical theories of the evolution of Israel's religion, and the presuppositions of nineteenth-century liberals were modified in the light of factual evidence.

Fortunately, archaeology was soon emancipated from its role of servant to theological presuppositions. The man who did the most to liberate archaeology was W. F.

---

5 Cf. Werner Keller, *The Bible as History* (London: Hodder & Stoughton, 1959), pp. 48–51.

Albright, whose presidential address to the Society of Biblical Literature in 1939 in effect called for a new role of archaeology as a kind of moderator among biblical disciplines.[6] The result has been a generation of exciting rediscovery of the Bible. As moderator among the disciplines of history, language, literature, and theology, significant categories of information have accumulated that provide guidelines for the interpreter and a basis for understanding the people who stand behind the book.

The role of illustrating the Bible, however, is still a significant one, when its limitations are recognized. Many words would remain without meaning if their ancient usage had not been rediscovered. For instance, we are told in 1 Samuel 13:19 ff. that the Philistines had a monopoly on iron-making and that the Hebrews took their iron agricultural tools to the Philistines for sharpening. The Hebrew word *pim* in verse 21 defied translation in the older versions because its use was not known. It is translated "file" in KJV, in view of the fact that tools were being sharpened.

But its actual meaning has been discovered in excavations that yielded small stone weights marked with the word *pim* in Hebrew. Several of these were discovered in the Jerusalem excavations in 1963.[7] It is evident from the *pim* weight that the charge for sharpening the plowshares, mattocks, etc., was a "pim," as the RSV translated the verse.

Some obscure and strange social customs are reflected in the intensely personal narratives of the patriarchs. For instance, there is uncommon anxiety for a male heir by Abraham (Gen. 15—17). When Sarah bore no son, she gave Hagar, her Egyptian handmaiden, to her husband for a secondary wife (Gen. 16:1 ff.). Hagar presented Abraham a son, and forthwith incurred the

jealousy of Sarah, who drove her away into the desert (Gen. 21:10 ff.).

The archives of five generations of a Hurrian family discovered at Nuzi throw some realistic light on the family problem of Abraham (Wright, p. 43).

Apparently, male heirs were necessary for the continuity of the social and religious system of patriarchal times. In case no male heir was born to perpetuate the family name, adoption was practiced. The Nuzi Tablets contain a regulation concerning adoption of an heir, along with the provision that a true son born later would take precedence over the adopted heir. This practice illuminates the dilemma of Abraham when he renewed the covenant in Genesis 15:1 ff., but the heir of his house was Eliezer of Damascus, apparently adopted.

Marriage contracts in the Nuzi Tablets obliged a childless wife to provide the husband with a handmaid who would bear children in her stead. There are no similar contracts stated in the Bible, but the gift of Hagar to Abraham is evidence of the custom. Furthermore, in Genesis 21:10-14, when Sarah demanded that Abraham cast out Hagar, the slave woman, because Isaac was the legal heir, the displeasure of Abraham was more than emotional. The Nuzi Tablets state the obligation of the husband to a secondary wife, which indicates that Abraham had a legal duty to provide for Hagar, and Sarah's jealousy forced him to act unjustly with Hagar and Ishmael.

The family life and social customs of Abraham are therefore accurately reflected, and the patriarch simply lives his life in Scripture as he lived it in history. In human frailty as well as strength, and bound by the commonly accepted customs of his day, Abraham still had faith to reach for a revelation that called him and his posterity to a higher purpose of God in history.

Perhaps the most profound idea in the Bible, i.e., that of the covenant, is not really understood by one who cannot see it in its Near Eastern meaning. The covenant

---

[6] "The Ancient Near East and the Religion of Israel," *Journal of Biblical Literature*, LIX, 85–112.
[7] R. B. Y. Scott, "The Scale-Weights from Ophel, 1963–64," *Palestine Exploration Quarterly*, 1965, pp. 128–139; also Figs. 5,7.

is more than an agreement, or even a commitment. It is a state of being, a profound relationship.

We read in Genesis 15:17–18, for instance, that the Lord made a covenant with Abraham and that "a smoking fire pot and a flaming torch passed between" the pieces of a sacrifice. A possible parallel from Asia Minor illustrates the meaning of this covenant ritual and reflects its seriousness. When a covenant was "cut" (the oldest term in the Old Testament for making a covenant), a sacrifice was prepared, cut in half, and the parties to the covenant passed between the pieces of the sacrifice, as presumably did a representation of the deity. It is likely that the flaming torch in Genesis 15:17 represented the presence of God, and that Abraham himself walked between the pieces of the sacrifice, a custom still known in the time of Jeremiah (cf. Jer. 34:18 ff.).

A covenant was therefore effected through sacrifice, the giving of life that two parties might be confirmed in a new relationship. Life is mingled with life and the two parties enter a spiritual and psychological state that has its physical analogy in blood relationship.

IV. Guidelines for Interpreting the Bible

Certain landmarks of historical information have been discovered which guide the interpreter of Scripture. He cannot ignore them. The interpreter is, of course, free to search out the hand of God in history witnessed to by the Bible. But he is not free to create history from his imagination in which his notion of the revelation fits better. History is thus a discipline for the interpreter, a discipline as relentless as the law. And for the interpreter there is no release by faith from the discipline of history.

Perhaps the most widely known recent discovery is the rapidly emerging picture of prehistoric man. Evidence at Jericho integrates a rather complete cultural reconstruction of Natufian man, for instance (cf. Anati, pp. 139–80). Slight in build, he stood about 5 feet, 3 inches, but very busy and creative—a producer of wheat and builder of houses. His cranial capacity of ca. 1500 cc. suggests that he had as much brains as the average modern person.

And he was a religious man—at least, he founded the city of Jericho as a sanctuary ca. 8000 B.C. We cannot know the response of his soul to God, nor the articulation of his worship, because he lived 5000 years before the invention of writing. But he worshiped in his own way and understanding and lived a peaceful life. In fact, Natufian man perhaps was less savage and bloodthirsty than modern man, involved in a major war of death and destruction in almost every generation.

The remains of Natufian art suggest already, 10,000 year ago, a comprehensive view of the world, a protophilosophy that may have inspired the revolutionary new developments of food-producing and city-building. Natufian man belongs to the age of modern man, not to aboriginal life. He is ours.

Standing at a crossroads in prehistory farther back is Mount Carmel man. (There are 12 skeletons from this particular period at Mount Carmel; cf. Anati, pp. 105–9). Some 50,000 years ago, from the terrace of his cave-home at Mount Carmel, he watched the sun rise each day over the forest of central Palestine. His broad, placid face betrays his surrender to the capriciousness of nature for a home, in whatever cave he could find, and food, wherever it happened to grow.

Like most people who serve capricious masters, he saw little future in life, and thus lived in no hurry. But when he stood on the terrace of his cave, there were 5 feet, 11 inches of man! Mount Carmel man had the physical attributes of modern man, including brains, and scanty remains that survived the erosion of time suggest that he worshiped an unknown god.

And there are others, a long procession of people marching out of the past which is being illuminated farther back in each generation of research. There they are, and no theologian need tell them to go away. A room must be added for prehistoric man at the time of Adam. The interpreter of Scripture should no longer talk about the creation of man in 4004 B.C., because the facts of history will not allow it.

Where is the guideline from archaeology, then? Archaeology discovered prehistoric man and made untenable the simplistic medieval view of the origin of man. But it also provides guidance for discovering the true significance of the biblical account of man's origin. The guidance comes from literary texts outside the Bible that illuminate the meaning of the biblical account.

In the first place, Adam, like original man in other Near Eastern texts, is a representative man, all of mankind poured into one individual. He is different from Natufian man in that he is individualized mankind who lives in the world of thought, who has capacity for communion with God, and who is morally responsible.

Secondly, his ancestry is found in literature and art, not in burial places that archaeologists will uncover. His genealogy is much more sophisticated than scholars suspected two hundred years ago, because it is traced in the unfolding revelation of the interpretation of man, not the physical evolution of his body.

And, thirdly, Adam feeds on symbols, not bread. Indeed, the fruit he ate is often painted as literal fruit, because symbols have roots in concrete literal things. But the fruit that Adam ate evokes meaning that cannot be contained in an apple. His eating forbidden fruit generated a potential for guilt in unborn generations of the human race, and the terrible truth about Adam's deed created an emergency in the heavens, even in the counsels of the Godhead. Adam is a man, but a representative man who encompasses in a compact and intelligible form every man, including prehistoric and modern man.

A different kind of skill is needed to excavate Adam and his world. For instance, how would one get a Carbon 14 date of the tree of life? It is a palm tree in ancient art, but it is the tree of life in its symbolic meaning on cylinder seals, or described in writing on clay tablets, or in the Bible. Or how would a laboratory at Hebrew University in Jerusalem find the pollen grains of the tree of knowledge of good and evil in an archaeologist's sample of earth? Or how would a geographer find the latitude and longitude of the Garden of Eden? It is a representative garden, the archetype of every sacred temple area in the lower Euphrates Valley compacted into one.

To excavate Adam, we begin by reading the dead languages of Sumeria, Babylonia, Assyria, as well as Hebrew. The accumulated learning of these great cultures is locked tightly in their literature. Much of it is communicated in symbols that are as simple as Adam, the representative man, or the tree of life; but the symbols are at the same time so profound that the literary excavator never quite reaches bedrock in probing their full meaning.

It is in this world of profound, historical symbols that have fossilized living experience and wisdom that we trace Adam's ancestors and come to know him. And when we find Adam, we find ourselves. On the other hand, when we find Natufian man, we find him, not ourselves.

Is this falsifying Adam? By no means. It is finding the essence of historical substance in him, and also ultimate meaning that is far more profound than the skeletal remains of any one man, surrounded by his flint tools and weapons. Mankind, the historical Adam, emerged from creation, the head of the earthly creation, but related physically to the earth. His physical kinship is with his earthly environment, something every biology pupil learns in high school, and something the ancient sages knew before the invention of writing. His spiritual kinship is with God, in whose image man was created a moral being, something we learn from the Bible and we accept by faith.

If we rob Adam of his symbolic meaning and simply literalize him, then we reduce him to one historical individual for the anthropologist to study. His skeleton can be measured, his brain capacity calculated, possibly his blood count obtained by centrifugating the dust of his flesh. If this exhausts the meaning for us of man's creation, then we have abandoned Adam too soon! We have lost man!

We have a guideline from archaeology, therefore, for the interpretation of man's beginnings in the Bible. There is much more that could be said, even about man's beginnings. Also there are significant guidelines for interpreting the history-writing of the Bible, for understanding the various forms of literature, even for interpreting the doctrines of inspiration and revelation in the Bible. These are recent developments that are just now finding expression in periodicals and books. But they are needed and wholesome developments in Bible study in a time when scientific discovery has outdistanced theological research, which is too often medieval in foundation and prespective.

By rediscovering the intellectual and spiritual world of the Bible in archaeological research, we have the possibility of getting to the Bible with new insights into its timeless truth. We are enabled to approach the biblical revelation assisted by the steady guidelines of Near Eastern history and culture. And by working within the guidelines or actual history, we are led into the living world of the Bible, to the people who gave us the Bible.

The legacy of archaeology to the Bible is, therefore, life, its own life.

For Further Reading

ADAMS, J. McKEE, and JOSEPH A. CALLAWAY. *Biblical Backgrounds*, rev. ed. Nashville: Broadman Press, 1965, 232 pages.

ALBRIGHT, W. F. *The Archaeology of Palestine.* London: Penguin Books, 1954, 271 pages.

ANATI, EMMANUEL. *Palestine Before the Hebrews.* New York: Alfred A. Knopf, Inc., 1962, 453 + xvii pages.

Biblical Archaeologist, The. Periodical published by the American Schools of Oriental Research, Cambridge, Massachusetts 02138.

KENYON, KATHLEEN M. *Archaeology in the Holy Land.* New York: Frederick A. Praeger, 1960, 326 pages.

PFEIFFER, CHARLES F. (ed.). *The Biblical World.* Grand Rapids: Baker Book House, 1966, 612 pages.

PRITCHARD, JAMES B. (ed.). *Ancient Near Eastern Texts, Relating to the Old Testament.* Princeton: Princeton University Press, 1955, 544 pages.

PRITCHARD, JAMES B. (ed.). *The Ancient Near East in Pictures, Relating to the Old Testament.* Princeton: Princeton University Press, 1954, 351 pages.

THOMAS, D. WINTON (ed.). *Archaeology and Old Testament Study.* Oxford: The Clarendon Press, 1967, 493 pages.

WRIGHT, G. ERNEST. *Biblical Archaeology.* Philadelphia: The Westminster Press, 1957), 288 pages.

The Canon and Text of the Old Testament

BURLAN A. SIZEMORE, JR.

I. The Canon

1. The Concept of a Canon

The word canon as it is used in the context of the study of the Scriptures refers to the rigidly limited collection of literature which is believed by the religious community to be given by inspiration of God and to be the basic guide for the regulation of the religious life and the religious institution. Most of the world's great religions possess such a collection, with greater or lesser emphasis on its origin as the divine word of God.

The English word canon may be traced through a Greek word to an ancient Semitic root which meant reed. In Greek the word came to denote anything straight, such as a rod or a carpenter's rule. The Greek word came to be used metaphorically to refer to any norm or standard. As applied to a normative collection of writings, the word canon was first used by the Christians of the fourth century. The concept of a sacred collection, however, is much older than this use of the word. Prior to this designation, the normative literature of the Jewish and Christian communities (essentially the Old Testament) was referred to as the "Scripture" or the "Sacred Scriptures." These references occur in such sources as Philo (first half of first century), Josephus (died shortly after A.D. 100), and the New Testament. Although described in different ways, the concept of a normative literature which is recognized as the Word of God goes back in the Hebrew tradition at least to the time of Josiah's reformation and the discovery of the book of the Law (part of Deuteronomy, 2 Kings 22–23) in 621 B.C. The process of the development and fixation of the canon was, however, to take many centuries.

2. The Books of the Canon and Their Arrangement

It is important to recognize two distinct arrangements of the Old Testament canon —the order of the Hebrew Bible and the order of the Christian Old Testament. When the canon of the Hebrew Scriptures was finally fixed, it contained 24 books arranged in three major divisions. The number and arrangement of books in the Hebrew Bible differ from that of the Christian Old Testament, although the content is the same, except that the Roman Catholic and certain Orthodox Catholic traditions include the Apocrypha, which was not a part of the Hebrew canon as fixed in Palestine.

In printed Hebrew Bibles the books are: (1) The Law—Genesis, Exodus, Leviticus, Numbers, Deuteronomy; (2) The Prophets: former prophets—Joshua, Judges, Samuel, Kings; latter prophets— Isaiah, Jeremiah, Ezekiel, The Book of the Twelve (the minor prophets); (3) The Writings: Psalms, Proverbs, Job, Song of Solomon, Ruth, Lamentations, Esther, Daniel, Ezra-Nehemiah, 1 and 2 Chronicles.

The difference from the prevailing order in Christian usage results from early Christian use of Greek translations of the Hebrew Old Testament. These Greek translations were arranged topically and chronologically (at least this was attempted —the judgments concerning dates were not accurate in every case), while the Hebrew order represents an older arrangement, which to some extent reflects the order in which the materials came to be recognized as Scripture.

3. The Formation of the Canon

The establishment of the Old Testament canon was a development of postexilic Judaism. The process through which the canon became a reality has been shrouded in mystery, however, and the traditional view formulated by ancient Judaism has prevailed through most of the history of the church and through later Judaism.

Josephus was one of the first to speak definitively of a collection of sacred writings, describing a collection of 22 books (probably the same material as the usual 24, but with Lamentations joined to Jeremiah, and Ruth to Judges), all of which he said originated between the time of Moses and the time of Artaxerxes I of Persia, who was contemporary with Ezra (*Contra Apionem* I. 8, A.D. 95). Josephus does not credit Ezra with any part in the formation of the canon other than the last part of it, but other writers in the ancient period gave expression to the very persistent view that Ezra was responsible for the final collection and preservation of the canon.

It is now generally recognized, however, that the process through which a certain collection of books came to be considered normative was a historical development which covered a very extended period. The Old Testament materials apparently were accorded canonicity in the order of the three divisions of the Old Testament in the Hebrew Bible, and in every case the material enjoyed a long popular acceptance before any general recognition was made of its special qualities as the authoritative word of God.

The Law or Torah. That the Torah (Pentateuch), or the law of Moses, was the first part of the Old Testament to achieve the status of Scripture is undeniable. It seems that a part of the Torah was accorded the status of sacred Scripture in the preexilic period. The book of the law found by Hilkiah the priest, which was used as a basis for the reform of Josiah (2 Kings 22—23), is at least a portion of the book of Deuteronomy. The honor accorded to this law book indicates at least the beginnings of a recognition of a collection of authoritative laws.

After the Exile, the ministry of Ezra

demonstrates an expansion of this law and perhaps indicates its almost complete collection. The Law read to the people (Nehemiah 8) by Ezra evokes from them a profound emotional response followed by acts of obedience which indicate a submission to the authority of the collection. The completeness of the collection cannot be known, but it is not unlikely that it included the great priestly collection of ancient material, including the incorporated J and E narratives. Deuteronomy, already respected, may have been joined to this collection by that time, or, if not, this certainly was done soon thereafter. The date of these events is uncertain, but was not later than 398 B.C.[1]

The Law, from this point, is the principal force in shaping the postexilic Jewish community. It may have been modified somewhat, and additions may have been made in subsequent years, but the changes certainly could not have been dramatic. This Law was distributed among Jews everywhere, and very rapidly received a canonical status which made any major modification of its content quite impossible. Certainly the Law was basically accepted by the time of the Samaritan schism, because it was retained in essentially the same form by the two communities. The date of the Samaritan schism is uncertain but must not be later than *ca.* 300 B.C., and perhaps was earlier.[2]

The early canonical status of the law is also attested by the Septuagint, a translation into the Greek language which was made near the middle of the third century B.C. Translation was not common in the ancient world, and it is not likely that a major work such as this would have been

1 The date of the return of Ezra has been the occasion of much dispute in modern times. If his return came in the seventh year of Artaxerxes I, then the traditional 457 is accurate. If the seventh year of Artaxerxes II is intended, then the year was 398. Some, by textual emendation would date Ezra's return in 428. Cf. John Bright, *A History of Israel* (Philadelphia: Westminster, 1959), pp. 375–86.
2 The schism has been dated from 432 B.C. to 122 B.C. Cf. Bright, pp. 393–95.

translated unless it were of overriding religious importance.

We are thus probably safe in saying that the Law was given canonical status, that is, it achieved a fixed and final form and was recognized as uniquely authoritative, sometime around 400 B.C., or not long thereafter.

The Prophets. The prophetic literature is divided into two sections, the Former Prophets, commonly known as the historical books in the English Bible, and the Latter Prophets, which includes the three major prophets and the 12 minor prophets. Although the prophetic literature had been accorded a great deal of respect in preexilic times, it, like the material of the Pentateuch, did not achieve the status of a strictly limited body of authoritative Scripture until after the Exile, probably substantially after this status had been achieved by the Pentateuch. Important to the development of concern about a prophetic canon was the vindication by events of the preexilic message of doom, plus the prophetic message of hope, which lent sustenance to the often faltering Jewish community of postexilic times.

It is likely that serious concern with the collection of an authoritative body of prophetic literature came after the institution of prophecy began to weaken and to fall into disrepute. The effort at collection probably developed in the fourth century B.C., although it is impossible to say just when the prophetic canon became firmly fixed. It seems clear that the process was completed at least by 200 B.C., because Jesus ben Sirach in about 190 B.C. refers to each of the individuals whose names are given to books of the prophetic canon, including a reference to the Twelve Prophets (the minor prophets) as though they were represented by one book, thus implying the complete collection. The fact that the book of Daniel, which received its final form in the second century B.C., did not find its way into the prophetic canon, but is included in the third section, suggests that the prophetic canon was closed before its appearance.

It is very likely that for many of the Jews the prophetic canon was closed and enjoyed a place of importance similar to that occupied by the Torah by the end of the third century B.C., although for much of Judaism the Mosaic law was to remain the basic regulation of life.

The Writings. There is a homogeneity to the literature in the Pentateuch and the Prophets which is lacking in the Writings or Hagiographa, the third section of the Old Testament canon. This section includes a tremendous variety of materials originating at vastly different periods in history. The first clear indication that this collection of literature was reaching canonical status came in a statement by the grandson of Jesus ben Sirach in the prologue to his translation of his grandfather's work into Greek in about 132 B.C. He mentions "the Law and the Prophets and the other books of our forefathers," the latter allusion presumably being essentially to those materials which eventually comprised the third section of the Hebrew canon.

The material which comprised the Writings probably never equalled the Law and the Prophets in significance in the Hebrew community, and, indeed, the earlier canonical materials probably served as one of the bases for judging the use of the later materials. Of the materials within the Writings, the Psalter has probably been the most important, and was the first to be honored as the Word of God. It is, in fact, sometimes used as a name for the entire collection (Luke 24:44).

Probably different factors entered into the process of elevation to canonicity for the various books. Many of the books were associated with the names of ancient worthies and this eased the way for their acceptance (e.g., the name of Solomon with Proverbs, Ecclesiastes, Song of Solomon; Daniel with a sixth-century prophet, etc.). Some of the books apparently enjoyed regular cultic usage, especially Psalms and Lamentations, and Esther was associated with the popular Feast of Purim. Ruth may have been associated with the book of Judges, since it is set in the same period; and Ezra-Nehemiah and the Chronicles represent a history work similar to the Former Prophets, and also may have been important because of its exaltation of the Law and worship.

Whatever the reasons for canonicity, there was substantial disagreement concerning whether some of these books merited a place in the canon of sacred Scripture (especially Esther, Song of Sol., and Eccl.), and some were finally determined to be Scripture only by action of a council. Decisions made concerning the content of the canon by the Council of Jamnia in approximately A.D. 90 proved to be definitive, although even these decisions did not remain unchallenged. The fact that Josephus and IV Ezra can speak of what appears to be a closed canon around A.D. 100 indicates that there was no substantial disagreement after this point. The work of the Council of Jamnia was probably stimulated by challenges to normative Judaism, which made it very important to decide upon a fixed canon of Scripture to serve as a basis for Jewish faith and religious practice.

The Apocrypha and Pseudepigrapha. The materials which finally comprised the fixed canon did not, of course, exhaust the materials which were considered important by the ancient community. Many books which to many persons carried the authority of Scripture were never included in the canon. The canon was the product of the Palestinian Jewish life, and in the Diaspora, especially in Alexandria, there were other works which seem to have been honored in a manner equal to the deference given to the materials which were included in the Palestinian canon. These works were translated into Greek and were circulated with the rest of the Greek Scriptures.

Those books included in the Greek Scriptures which were never accepted into the Palestinian canon are very important to Christianity, because the early church used the Greek Scriptures, and thus for most early Christians these books were used alongside those materials included in the Palestinian canon and presently used as the Old Testament by Protestant Christianity. These books, contained in the ancient Greek Scriptures but never in the Palestinian canon, are now commonly known as the Apocrypha. They appear as Scripture in the Roman Catholic Bible and that of certain Orthodox communions, and they were used extensively within Christendom until the time of the Protestant Reformation, at which time the Palestinian Hebrew canon became normative for a large segment of Christianity. These books, of varying value, include 1 and 2 Esdras, Tobit, Judith, additions to the book of Esther, Wisdom of Solomon, Ecclesiasticus, Baruch, Story of Susanna, Song of the Three Children, Story of Bel and the Dragon, Prayer of Manasseh, and 1 and 2 Maccabees.

There were other important Hebrew materials which did not find their way into either the Hebrew Scriptures or the Greek Bibles. These are commonly called Pseudepigrapha, a word meaning "false titles." This description is not entirely accurate, but it derives from the common practice of attributing new materials to ancient men, such as the "Testaments of the Twelve Patriarchs" and "The Book of Enoch." Some of the materials, however, are as old as materials which were included in the canon, so it seems that for the most part they were deliberately rejected. Many of these were held in high esteem by the early church community, and for the most part we know of them because of their preservation within the early church, often in the language of the church community which used them.

II. The Text

1. The Problem of the Study of the Text

In any instance in which a religious community is dependent upon written tradition for its basic identity, it is exceedingly important to that community that the text of its sacred literature be preserved without modification in its oldest and purest form. Since the Old Testament is basic to both

Jewish and Christian communities, very substantial attention has been given to the preservation of the text, and this has been done in a variety of historical situations.

For a thousand years the text of the Old Testament has been stable. Our Hebrew Bibles are based on manuscripts of the ninth and tenth centuries A.D. Such stability, however, belongs to the modern era, since the process through which this stability was achieved was a long and confusing one. The principal task of Old Testament textual criticism is the task of tracing, insofar as possible, the transmission of the Old Testament text through the years of its formation and seeking to discover the best and most ancient text forms, although this can never mean the recovery of an original text. While this may be theoretically possible, we must assume that we can never hope to have anything better than the result of many generations of copying. We must assume that all of the Old Testament literature went through a period of use in which it was not accorded canonical status, and when there would have been the degree of effort that came later to preserve accuracy in every detail. Beyond this we are forced to recognize that even after canonicity was established there were divergent textual traditions and it was many years before a single textual tradition prevailed.

2. The History of the Old Testament Text

The Hebrew text which is the basis for our present Hebrew Bible is called the Masoretic Text, so named for Jewish scholars known as the Masoretes, who conscientiously devoted themselves to the preservation of the textual tradition they had received. The basic text they preserved so carefully seems to have been accepted as normative by many Jews (particularly in Palestine) at the beginning of the second century A.D.

Some scholars think that a single manuscript was accepted as the authoritative text about A.D. 100 and was the basis for all the textual traditions which followed.

Most scholars now would argue that there may not have been a single manuscript which was accepted as normative, but for the most part they do agree that there must have been a severe narrowing and restriction of text forms about this time. It is very likely that the fixing of an authoritative form of the text coincided with the fixing of the Old Testament canon (see above). The completion of the task is usually associated with the work of Rabbi Akiba, who died in A.D. 132.

The establishment of an authoritative text form toward the end of the first century did not mean the end of varying traditions concerning the proper form of the biblical texts. There obviously developed more than one set of traditions concerning the proper form of the text, the principal versions of these having been preserved in Babylon and in Palestine. There were major concentrations of Jewish scribal activity in these areas, especially after the drastic disruption of Jewish life following the end of Bar Cochba's rebellion and the vigorous suppression of the Jews by the Romans in A.D. 135. The Palestinian form of the text was destined to become definitive.

The basic text standardized in the early Christian era was essentially a consonantal text. That is, there was no way of writing all the vowels necessary for pronunciation.[3]

During the Masoretic period there developed a standard system for writing Hebrew vowels. It seems apparent that during this period there were substantially different traditions concerning the proper manner in which the ancient Hebrew text should be pronounced, and as the divergences and the problems of memory increased with the years, it became increasingly important that the vowels be written into the text.

Techniques for writing the vowels developed among both Palestinian and Babylo-

---

[3] Much earlier than this, consonants had been used in the text to indicate some vowels, although this system was incomplete and irregular. These vowel sign letters were called *Matres Lectiones*.

nian schools of Masoretes, and the process seems to have received very substantial impetus with the appearance of a sect of Jews known as the Qaraites, who were extremely concerned with accurate transmission and interpretation of the Hebrew Scriptures. Though they did not belong to rabbinic communities which eventually evolved the system of vowel points which has prevailed, their emphasis provoked the rabbinic scholars to develop a complete system of vowel points and to standardize pronunciation.

The system of vocalization which eventually prevailed was that developed among Palestinian Masoretes at the community of Tiberias. Their system was the scheme of vowel points familiar to the modern student of Hebrew. There are many evidences that reconstruction of a system of vocalization may have been somewhat artificial, because some textual witnesses indicate an entirely different pronunciation for some words. The new system is called the Tiberian, and is to be distinguished from the earlier Palestinian and Babylonian systems.

The consummation of Masoretic activity in the eighth to tenth centuries A.D. came in Tiberias where there were two principal Masoretic families, ben Asher and ben Naphtali. These two families preserved slightly different recensions of the text with variation in vocalization. The ben Asher text came to be the text generally accepted, although ben Naphtali readings often found their way into later manuscripts.

3. The Proto-Masoretic Text

The task of determining the status of the text of the Old Testament in pre-Christian times is a formidable one. The ancient Sopherim (men of the Book), the predecessors of the Masoretes, began as early as the fourth century B.C. to take elaborate safeguards against the intrusion of errors into the text. Their work was carried on long before the emergence of the consonantal text which became the basis of the Maso-

retic Text, and the problem has been one of determining whether these scribes preserved a variety of competing text forms or whether one text was generally accepted as normative quite early. Until very recently there has been no real evidence available to shed light on this problem except the presence of the Septuagint text, which obviously existed in a much more ancient form than the received Hebrew text of the tenth century A.D. The antiquity of the Septuagint text did not, however, give any real indication that it preserved a better recension of the text than its Hebrew counterpart represented by later manuscripts.

The Septuagint has remained suspect to many scholars, first of all because it is exceedingly difficult to arrive at any real consensus concerning the character of the original Septuagint text. It is represented in many different varieties from different periods and places, and is even represented by translations into foreign languages for which it served as the base. The difficulty in determining an original Septuagint text is manifest when any meaningful attempt is made to compare the Septuagint with the Masoretic Text.

Another aspect of the problem of the use of the Septuagint for textual criticism is the continuing uncertainty concerning the quality of the translation. Do differences from the Masoretic Text really reflect a different text form, or are they simply indications that the translators were inept or inclined to the excessive use of paraphrase as they made their translation?

Another possible source for textual criticism has been the Samaritan Pentateuch, the Scripture of the Palestinian sect whose origin is traced to a schism with postexilic Judaism. It is clear that the Samaritan Pentateuch represents a different textual tradition, although it is also likely that some of its variations represent sectarian coloring, or readings introduced by the scribes of their own community in the transmission of their text.

The possibilities for a meaningful criticism of the Hebrew text were transformed with the appearance of the Qumran scrolls in 1947.[4]

It had long been supposed that genuinely ancient Hebrew manuscripts did not exist, and thus it was assumed that criticism was going to have to remain highly speculative. The initial discoveries, with the great Isaiah scrolls, were exciting enough, but these were followed very rapidly by the voluminous discoveries from Cave IV and other locations. Very soon most of the books of the Old Testament were represented, at least in fragmentary form, and scholarship was faced with the task of examining a very large body of material which was older than the fixed Masoretic Text. The scrolls probably date from the end of the third century B.C. to the first years of the Christian era.

Although even now the work of interpreting the scrolls is not complete, and many scholars still give their attention to them, several observations can be made concerning their significance. For the most part, the scrolls do not represent any major deviations from our textual traditions which demand serious reconsideration of the meaning of canonical material.

It is very important to observe that the scrolls do represent varying textual traditions, however, and it is significant to notice that the sectarians did not have any qualms about preserving differing textual traditions within their community. There are places where the text of Qumran scrolls clearly support the textual tradition represented by the Septuagint as over against the Masoretic Text. This is evident from a careful study of the historical books and especially the book of Jeremiah, the text of which differs substantially in the Septuagint as over against the Masoretic Text.[5]

The evidence is sufficient to confirm the significance of the Septuagint for textual criticism. The evidence of the scrolls also makes it clear that the Samaritan Pentateuch likewise represents ancient textual traditions. The scrolls also represent substantially the proto-Masoretic Text.

The scrolls make it clear that there were several established textual traditions in existence prior to the substantial fixing of the text in the early second century A.D. There were probably forms of the text transmitted primarily in Egypt, in Palestine, and in Babylon. They also demonstrate that the text standardized in the time of Rabbi Akiba was not a newly created text but represented a choice of texts available. We can thus be sure that our received text has been preserved without substantial change from very early time.

4. Versions of the Old Testament

Various ancient versions provide additional information for a study of the text of the Old Testament. The extension of the Bible into the languages of the world began early and has never ceased. Soon after the Babylonian exile, popular paraphrases of the Old Testament appeared in the Aramaic language. At first oral, they were eventually reduced to writing and have come down to us in a form stabilized during the early Christian era. These Aramaic translations, called Targums, have been preserved in several forms, the most important being the Targum Onkelos (the Pentateuch) and the Targum Jonathan (the Prophets).

We have had occasion to mention the Septuagint, and there were other significant Greek versions. One of the most important of these was that of Aquila, a Jewish proselyte from Pontus, who rendered a slavishly literal translation from the Hebrew in about A.D. 130. A second important translation, that of Theodotion, was also from the second century. Theodotion shows heavy dependence on the Septuagint. Still later in the same century there appeared a third Greek translation, Symmachus, a work

---

[4] Other ancient scrolls from *Wadi Murabba'at* dating from about A.D. 135 offer additional textual witness. *Wadi Murabba'at* scrolls support the received Masoretic Text.

[5] Much of the information available for the interpretation of this data has come from the publications of Frank Cross. Cf. *For Further Reading.*

in fluent Greek, sometimes to the point of sacrifice of the Hebrew sense.

Early Christianity was probably responsible for the first translations into Syriac, these works appearing in the second century or slightly earlier. The standard Syriac translation came to be called the Peshitta. The Syriac translation was probably carried to the East by early Christian missionaries.

The first Latin versions of the Old Testament appeared in North Africa in the late second century A.D. These first translations, called the Old Latin versions, were replaced by the Vulgate, translated by Jerome in response to a request by Pope Damascus *ca.* A.D. 382. The Vulgate became the Bible of the Roman Catholic Church.

Other ancient versions appeared in connection with the spread of early Christianity. These include the Gothic (fourth century), the Armenian (fifth century), the Georgian (fifth century), the Ethiopic (fourth century), and the Arabic versions (date of the first translation unknown, but fragments from the ninth century are extant).

For Further Reading

CROSS, FRANK M. *The Ancient Library of Qumran.* London: Gerald Duckworth & Co. Ltd., 1958, pp. 124–45.

EISSFELDT, OTTO. *The Old Testament.* Trans. PETER R. ACKROYD. New York: Harper & Row, 1965, pp. 560–721.

JEFFEREY, ARTHUR. "The Canon of the Old Testament," *The Interpreter's Bible,* Nashville: Abingdon, 1952, pp. 32–45.

KENYON, FREDERIC. *Our Bible and the Ancient Manuscripts.* New York: Harper & Row, 1958.

NOTH, MARTIN. *The Old Testament World.* Trans. VICTOR I. GRUHN. Philadelphia: Fortress Press, 1966, pp. 301–58.

PFEIFFER, ROBERT H. "Canon of the Old Testament," *The Interpreter's Dictionary of the Bible,* Nashville: Abingdon, 1962 I. pp. 498–520.

ROBERTS, B. J. *The Old Testament Text and Versions.* Cardiff, University of Wales Press, 1951.

THOMAS, D. WINTON. "The Textual Criticism of the Old Testament," *The Old Testament and Modern Study.* Oxford: Oxford University Press, 1951, pp. 238–63.

WURTHWEIN, ERNST. *The Text of the Old Testament.* Trans. PETER R. ACKROYD. Oxford: Basil Blackwell, 1957.

The History of Israel

CLYDE T. FRANCISCO

The Old Testament does not attempt to write a history of Israel. Rather it gives its witness to the work of God in establishing the nation. The Hebrews were the first ancient people to have a sense of history. Their contemporaries thought in cyclic terms, and conceived of history as repeating itself. The Old Testament sees God as directing events toward the goal of the redemption of his creation. Its writers were concerned about the milestones along the way. Details that would fascinate us were of no interest to them. Conversely, each event presented by biblical writers is used for a theological purpose.

The earlier books of the Old Testament (Genesis-Deuteronomy), which we treat as history, they called the Law (Pentateuch); they called Joshua to 2 Kings the Former Prophets. For the Hebrews, history should teach men the will of God and warn them concerning their future. They preached their history, and believed it foreshadowed the future of the people of God. It is indeed "salvation history."[1]

In this study we will attempt to do what the biblical writers never intended. We will try to get behind their testimony to the event, to distill the essence of the history from the interpretation. Since the scriptural writers present such frustratingly incomplete data, many scholars contend that such an endeavor cannot succeed. Archaeology, however, is rapidly filling in the gaps. The events of Israel's history were the foundations upon which they built their theology. Hebrew theology without event is like a spirit without a body. Although it is appropriate to say that the theology of the Old Testament is the interpreter's principal concern, the building cannot stand without a secure foundation.

The Hebrew historical witness is presented in three basic sources: (1) old pop-ular traditions, particularly in Genesis–Exodus; (2) the Deuteronomic interpretation of Israel's past, found in Deuteronomy–2 Kings; and (3) the priestly history, which forms the framework of Genesis–Numbers but is supplemented by 1 and 2 Chronicles, Ezra, and Nehemiah. The earlier traditions of Genesis go far back into antiquity, but were written down at least by 950–850 B.C. in the time of Solomon or Jehoshaphat. The Deuteronomic history, containing early materials, many of which are as old as the time of Moses, was put in its final form about the time of the fall of Jerusalem (587 B.C.) and presents the perspective of that time.

On the other hand, the priestly history, which likewise used ancient traditions, some much earlier than Moses, was written during the Babylonian exile (ca. 500 B.C.) and reveals the views of the priestly group of that period. The chronicler, furthermore, speaks from the life situation in 350 B.C. In the will of God these various witnesses have been preserved for use in achieving a meaningful perspective on Israel's history.

It is obvious that the sources speak to us with more clarity when they deal with events close to the time when they were written. The longer the materials were transmitted before being written down, the more fragmented they are and the more they have been subjected to revision in the transmission. Yet in all this involved process a solid core of data remains to furnish us with reliable evidence for God's mighty acts in history. The early traditions of Israel are clearer and more complete than any others in the ancient world.[2]

Another problem arises in distinguishing between the nature of the event preserved in the tradition and the interpretation given that event by different writers. Al-

---

[1] Alan Richardson, "Salvation," IDB, IV, 170–71.

[2] W. F. Albright, "The Biblical Period," *The Jews*, ed. Louis Finkelstein (New York: Harper, 1949), I, 3.

though both the Deuteronomic and the priestly writers treat many of the same events, they often give them different interpretations (cf. 2 Sam. 24:1 ff. and 1 Chron. 21:1 ff.; the earlier interpretation attributes to God what the later applies to Satan). These distinct perspectives must be taken seriously, but when seen as supplementing one another, they enrich our understanding of the original occurrence.

I. Promise and Fulfilment

The early traditions of Israel cluster around the theme of God's election-promises and faithfulness to his word. This is presented against the somber background of man's sin and unfaithfulness. Yet God keeps steadily moving toward the fulfilment of his purpose. What he has begun in his grace he will complete in his own time. He only waits upon man's response which, although slow in coming, must nevertheless precede his confirming acts.

The old stories that were common to the people of the ancient Near East concerning creation and the Flood were seen by the Hebrews in the light of the redemptive purpose of Israel's God; and the accounts of their ancestors told by father to son were unified around that compelling theme. Man was created to serve this holy God, and all of his troubles stemmed from his refusal to do so. The ancient stories of Abraham, Isaac, and Jacob were viewed as the initial phase of a clear pattern: God's initiative in the midst of man's tragic failure. What he freely promised to Abraham, he fulfilled for undeserving Israel, miraculously preserving, delivering, and establishing the Israelites as a nation.

1. The Patriarchal Age

The narratives concerning the ancestors of the Hebrews are unparalleled in the ancient world. In wealth of detail, literary quality, and theological perception they stand alone. They inform us that their forebears migrated from Mesopotamia to Canaan, and roamed Palestine supported by the promise of God that one day it would belong to their posterity. Very little is known of this formative stage of Israel's history except what we read in Genesis.

Archaeology has confirmed the Old Testament's picture of patriarchal times. Names similar to the ones recorded in Genesis were common in Mesopotamia during the time when the patriarchs are said to have lived. Also, it was only during this period that they could have freely roamed through Canaan as Genesis pictures it. The customs revealed by the stories are consistent with what we now know to have been the situation during these days. The accuracy with which the social and political conditions have been presented is significant evidence of the care with which the traditions have been preserved.

We can safely assume, therefore, that the forefathers of the Hebrews passed to them a conviction that their God had a special purpose for them in history, which included the eventual possession of Canaan as the Land of Promise. They never lived to see the fulfilment of their dreams, but died confident that a later generation would see the assurances of God confirmed. The only part of Palestine which they possessed was the burial cave of Machpelah, where their bodies were laid as tokens of their hope. They were not buried in a foreign land but in their own.

2. The Exodus from Egypt

It is generally regarded by scholarship today that the fourteenth and thirteenth centuries B.C. mark the beginning of the Hebrews as a nation, although the patriarchs lived several centuries before (ca. 1700 B.C.). It was in the experience of the Exodus (ca. 1250 B.C.) that a family became a nation—several tribes, one people.

The Flight from Egypt. Although there is no reason to question the fact of the Exodus, there remain many difficult problems to solve. These center around the number of people involved in the experience, the constituency of the tribes participating, and the route of the journey from Egypt.

In respect to numbers, Israel, when entering Canaan, must have been numerous enough to effect the destruction of large cities in Palestine. In regard to the constituency of the tribes, it is possible that not all the Hebrews went into Egypt with Jacob. Others probably left Egypt before the sojourn was over. It is also likely that non-Hebrew elements were absorbed into Israel's tribal life. Such men were Caleb (Num. 14:6) and Hobab (Num. 10:29). When they joined Israel it could be truly said that by their act of identification they became a part of that people and could truly claim Abraham as their father, even as Gentile Christians do today.

Debates concerning the route of the Exodus center around the place of the crossing of the sea. Apparently the term "Red Sea" (Hebrew, Sea of Reeds or Sea of Sea Weeds) can be applied to the entire expanse of water in the Red Sea area and cannot be confined to any particular spot. However, it is no more necessary for us to know the exact spot of crossing than for us to know where Jesus was buried after the crucifixion.

During the sojourn in Egypt, the faith of the Hebrews in the promises to the fathers was sorely tried, but the Exodus experience supplied a confirmation that forever witnessed to Israel's destiny among the nations. Without the promise to the fathers the Exodus might have been viewed as a mere coincidence; without the Exodus the hope of Abraham would have seemed an idle dream. In the Exodus the latent power of Israel's faith received a thrust that would never be denied. As Abraham looked forward to the possession of the land as the fruition of his faith, even so, later Israel would look back to the deliverance from Egypt to keep its faith alive. Israel's God had demonstrated that he was mightier than the gods of the nations. The God of Abraham, Isaac, and Jacob proved himself to be Lord of all. This the fathers had believed, but now it was confirmed in history.

The Sinai Experience. At Sinai Israel became the people of God. Until then they were the inheritors of a promise. Now they were united with their God in a common purpose. The name Yahweh might have been known to them before, preserved in the Kenite tradition, but now it assumed a new significance. It was a covenant name to be used exclusively by Israel. In ancient usage the sharing of a name was an intimate experience. In giving his name to Israel God was offering himself.

Until Sinai the Hebrews were loyal to the God who had promised them his blessing. They knew little about his real nature. It was at Sinai that God revealed to them the law (*torah*, "revelation"), giving them a glimpse of his character and his moral demands. Abraham might lie to Pharaoh without being conscience-stricken, but now the Israelite knew he was not to bear false witness; Jacob could steal his father's blessing with a clear mind, but now his people were told they must not steal.

They already knew that they were to be true to God alone, but now it was confirmed that they served a God whose likeness could never be made, for he was always beyond their knowledge, only to be known as he chose to reveal himself to them. Thus were injected into Israel's history the elements that made it unique from all other nations of the Near East. The purpose of God toward which Israel worked was yet to be completely revealed.

Not only did God reveal his true character and demands at Sinai, but it was there that Israel as a people committed themselves to God and his purpose for them. In the covenant at Sinai Israel pledged to live in the light of God's expectations, aware all the while that divine blessing awaited faithfulness to that agreement. This covenant was a conditional one, but Israel was committed to its keeping. From now on they were not only inheritors of a promise, but dedicated to a cause.

3. The Conquest of Canaan

It is one of the most amazing turns of history that Israel hesitated at the edge of

Canaan and refused to enter into the land. To be sure the scouts had reported giants and walled cities in the land. Yet, as Caleb replied, the God who had driven back the forces of Pharaoh could give them the victory. Yet they did rebel, to the complete surprise of Moses. Throughout the long and miserable years of the wilderness wanderings (38 years) he nursed his dream and the new generation of Israelites. Dying before he could achieve his dream he passed it on to Joshua. It was his to fulfil.

The Campaigns of Joshua. The conquest of the land is pictured as occurring in three stages. There was first of all a swift thrust through the central section at Jericho and Ai, thus dividing the land north and south (Josh. 6—9). Then the kings to the south were conquered (Josh. 10); and finally, the northern strongholds were taken (Josh. 11). Thus Israel was quickly and decisively established in the land.

Some passages in the book of Joshua seem to mean that Joshua completely conquered every city and acre in Canaan. Joshua 11:23 says, "So Joshua took the whole land." But 13:1 declares that "there remains yet very much land to be possessed."

It is difficult for today's Western reader to comprehend how two such divergent views could appear in the same historical material. The editors of the book of Joshua, who declared that he had taken all the land, are the ones who included the material saying the conquest was only partial. A solution is found when we understand the way the Hebrew mind worked and the customary modes of expression in Hebrew literature. Writing at a later time and aware of the original nature of the early conquest, the writers idealized the age of Joshua because they saw in his spirit the resources that would surely win the land. After his contribution in the initial conquest, the final conquest was only a matter of time. At his death it was as good as done.[3] The fact that they included the original, more historically oriented materials, is their way of saying that the more compre-

hensive claims are to be understood against that background. They were honest men who saw more in a moment of history than statistical records could show.

How much of the method in Joshua's conquest was the way of conducting war at the time, and how much was the specific command of God, it is impossible to discover. Yet we must realize that the command issued by God to take the land was not necessarily dictated to Joshua word by word. Joshua understood the command in the only way possible, in terms of the culture and times in which he lived.

The Period of the Judges. The book of Judges continues the history of Israel following the death of Joshua. This period was one of the most difficult in the history of Israel. They were in the land but had not yet completely possessed it. The challenge of the first conquest was gone, yet their enemies were still all around. They had room to live but not to grow. They could survive by doing nothing, but they could expand only by a new heroic effort.

Baalism versus Yahwism.—The principal temptation that confronted Israel was the constant attraction of the Baal worship of her Canaanite neighbors. Baal, the supreme Canaanite god, was known in each community by a personal title ascribed to him. It is in this latter sense that his worship was such a threat to the religion of Israel. The typical Israelite saw no reason why he could not claim Yahweh as his national God and still pay allegiance to Baal in his local community.

Our knowledge of the nature of Baal worship has been immensely augmented by the discoveries at Ugarit (Ras Shamra), an abandoned harbor in northern Syria, just southwest of Antioch. Several hundred clay tablets were found there during the years 1929–39. All of these are dated in the first third of the fourteenth century B.C. These tablets contain sacrificial ritual, mythological epics, and religious poems. In them is

---

[3] Consideration of a future event as already accomplished is a common Hebrew stylistic feature expressed by a prophetic perfect. Cf. Isa. 53: 1 ff.

revealed the true nature of the Canaanite religion and the secret of its attraction to the ancient Israelites.

In the first place, it appealed to the sensual nature. It was believed that intercourse with sacred prostitutes at the temple of Baal would guarantee the fertility of the soil, animals, and even one's wife. Baalism also promised a way by which man could get the gods to do his will. Baalism taught that if one went through the proper rituals, he would be guaranteed the favor of Baal upon the crops for the year.

When the Israelites came into the land, they were shepherds, not farmers. It is certain they asked the Canaanite natives about the secrets of successful farming. It is also just as certain they were told that the most important thing was to secure the favor of the local Baal. Thus the Israelites drifted toward serving Yahweh as the great high God of battle, and toward serving Baal as the god to be reckoned with for material comforts. The masses of the Israelites were drawn from the austere Yahweh worship to the materialism and sensualism of Baalism.

A discouraging cycle.—The primary feature of the book of Judges is the framework binding the originally separate narratives. It emphasizes the Deuteronomic philosophy of history that characterizes Hebrew history-writing from Deuteronomy through Kings: If Israel were faithful to Yahweh, she would prosper economically and politically; if she were unfaithful, she would just as surely come into catastrophe. The situation described in Judges 2:11–23 is the key to the organization of the entire book. An automatic formula is reapplied to every new crisis in Israel: (1) the Hebrews yield to temptation; (2) apostasy leads to oppression; (3) faced with adversity, the people repent and call upon God for help; and (4) he hears their cry and sends them a deliverer.

This disheartening summary of the period resembles the cyclic view of history held by Israel's neighbors. At first glance it appears that the writers have lost sight of any goal toward which Israel is moving under the hand of divine providence. Yet behind this summary is the overtone that although Israel was apparently in a hopeless cycle in its sinful condition, God was still enthroned, patiently guiding the course of history to lead them into his purpose.

The office of judge.—During this period the judges were sent in order to keep Israel alive until a better way could be provided. These judges were summoned from various walks of life to lead Israel against her foes. Some of their tenures in office apparently paralleled others, since the total number of years assigned to each judge surpassed the length of time generally assigned to the period (*ca.* 1200–1050 B.C.). None, as far as we know, ever led a completely united Israel.

The different judges were of quite varying personal characteristics and piety. All of them, however, shared one thing: they were chosen because of the evidence that God had given them personal qualities of leadership. Such qualifications are referred to as charismatic (possessing gifts of the spirit). This method of recognizing rulers contrasts sharply with the later custom in Judah of choosing a king simply because he was the heir in David's line.

II. The United Monarchy

At the close of the period of the judges (*ca.* 1050 B.C.) Israel was in dire straits. The Philistine domination of Canaan was almost complete. These maritime people who had settled Palestine had been more successful in conquering the land than had the Hebrews. Although the prophets of Israel claimed this was due to the Israelites' lack of faithfulness to God, many elders felt this was oversimplification; they felt a king was needed, but recognized that this was contrary to the traditions of Israel. Israel's ideal was a theocracy, a nation ruled over by God, not by man. God was their king and they were supposed to have no other (cf. Judg. 8:23; 9:1 ff.).

Now the elders of Israel were so desperate that they were willing to try to have a king. The Philistine system of kingship seemed to offer more stability than Israel had been able to achieve through the spasmodic charismatic deliverances during the age of the judges. Many of the elders loved Samuel but feared for the future. They exerted pressure upon the reluctant judge to give the blessings of God upon a king for Israel. Let God continue to be king, but let him establish a more stable human system than the charismatic deliverance of the judges.

Although Samuel's fears concerning the kingship were confirmed by its later course, the divine wisdom in permitting a king was proved even more judicious. As the editors of the book of Judges perceived, a king was needed to offset the centrifugal forces threatening Israel (cf. 21:25). The occasional judge could not give the stability that a vested monarchy would provide. It was also through the monarchy that Israel began to take her place among the nations. Until the establishment of the monarchy the Hebrews were content to acquire and live in their land. Soon afterwards they became conscious of the world outside the boundaries of Palestine. The coronation of a king automatically propelled Israel into the community of nations.

It was the monarchy, so caustically condemned on many occasions, that nevertheless furnished the prophets with the concepts that undergirded their dream of the future: the kingdom of God, the ideal king to come, Israel supreme among the nations.

1. The Reign of Saul

The tragic rule of the son of Kish began about 1020 B.C. In spite of his personal failures, he made a lasting impression upon the people of Israel, both as a military hero and as their first king. David inherited a kingdom already prepared for him by Saul. At first glance the regime of Saul appears to be a complete departure from the older order of the judges. The title "king" was foreign to Israelite culture. There was also a permanency to the anointing which the

judges did not possess. Saul expected his sons to rule after his death. His dominion, unlike that of Abimelech, included all the tribes.

Yet the rule of Saul departed as little as possible from the accustomed role of the judge. It retained the uniqueness of Israel's government within the context of the new title. Little change was made in the internal structure of the nation. The tribal organization was left intact. There was no complex governmental machinery. Saul had no harem; his court life, as archaeology reveals, was simple and rustic. It is obvious that Israel, certainly at first, even while yielding to the pressure to have a king as did the Philistine enemy, did not intend to imitate slavishly their neighbors but rather to adapt what they considered a superior system of government to the distinctive life of Israel. God's prophet, so clearly portrayed by Samuel, would always keep the crown resting uneasily upon the head of the king. No other nation of ancient times permitted such open castigation of a reigning monarch. It was the prophet who was commissioned to preserve the uniqueness of the Hebrews in the presence of compromise. Even when the people stoned their prophets, they replaced them with others whom they thought spoke for God. When the king supported the cultic prophets of later days who mouthed what he wanted to hear, he was yielding to the demand that the prophetic office be retained.

It was in the tension between king and prophet that the uniqueness of Israel's faith was preserved in the crises of her history. The king was necessary to achieve national unity, the prophet to declare the faith. In every crisis, for better or for worse, the two were side by side.

2. The Davidic Reign

David's rule extended from *ca.* 1000 to 961 B.C. Although he encountered initial difficulties because of the refusal of northern Israel to accept him as king, he eventually became the most influential ruler in all of Israel's history. This was not merely the idealized opinion of a later age but the thrust of the records which we possess.

The Davidic kingdom was established upon quite a different basis from that of Saul. Saul was declared king because of a concerted effort on the part of all the tribes. David became king of Judah first, then united the tribes. Thus the union was a precarious one, which David fully realized. It could be dissolved as quickly as it had been formed. In fact, in allowing himself to be proclaimed king in Judah before he was accepted by the other tribes, David recognized the rivalry of the northern and southern tribes in such a way that it always proved to be a major factor in the history that followed. Now that he was king of all Israel, however, he was anxious to effect a permanent national order.

First, however, he must meet the danger outside of Israel. The Philistines well knew that his rise to power was a threat to their supremacy in Palestine. Immediately they endeavored to meet the challenge he presented. Seeking to separate Judah from the northern tribes, they attacked near Jerusalem. The result was a catastrophic defeat in two engagements and left the Philistine plain open to an offensive by David (2 Sam. 5:17–25). This he proceeded to exploit, bringing the Philistines to their knees and breaking their power forever (2 Sam. 8:1). Later the Philistines appeared as professional soldiers in David's army!

With the Philistine threat removed David was now free to consolidate his reign over Israel. At this point his genius is conspicuous in his every move. First he must decide upon a capital. If he retained Hebron, the seat of government in Judah, it would alienate the northern tribes unnecessarily. A site in the North would antagonize his loyal followers in Judah. His choice of Jerusalem ranks as one of the most significant decisions in Hebrew history. Not only did he unite Israel around a central location unassociated with tribal rivalry, but he built upon a site that would withstand all attempts at assault for five centuries. David knew the strategic value of the location, for

already the city had withstood the attacks of both Israel and Philistia for over two hundred years.

The destiny of Israel, however, was not bound up in a political dynasty. Unless David could establish a synthesis of the religious and political aspects of Israel's life his reign would be just another moment in history. Thus he proceeded to bring the ark to Jerusalem and declare himself the preserver of the unique religious institutions of Israel. Jerusalem would henceforth be both the religious and political capital of Israel. Whereas Saul had alienated Samuel by his usurping of the priestly function, David established the priests in a secure position under the protection of the monarch, thus winning their loyalty to the crown.

There were still other tasks to perform. Scattered throughout Israel were Canaanite strongholds like Jerusalem which had still not been permanently subdued by the Hebrews. These David conquered one by one, subjecting them to Israelite dominion. Whereas in earlier days the Canaanites were assimilated by the Hebrews into their tribal life, now Israel kept her new subjects segregated and distinct (Noth, p. 193). This move presented new problems of adjustment in relation to Canaanite culture and religion.

There yet remained the conquest of enemies outside Israel's borders. These were more of a threat now that the Philistines were no longer powerful. First, David conquered the countries endangering his flank in Transjordan, Ammon, Moab, and Edom. His most formidable foe was Syria, but this nation also soon fell before the Israelite armies. David's power extended all the way to Hamath and the Orontes River, Damascus being his greatest prize. Such exploits caught the attention of Hiram, king of Tyre, who negotiated a treaty with David. Thus in a few years David had extended his rule from the tribe of Judah to Asia Minor and Mesopotamia.

To maintain this newly acquired territory required more centralized and complex machinery of government. No longer was

Israel composed of twelve tribes governing themselves in a loose federation, but rather a nation united under a powerful monarch, seeking to expand its dominion.

3. The Solomonic Era

With the accession of Solomon began the most glorious period in the history of Israel. The nations around him were either subject to Solomon or payed regular tribute to him. His fame went beyond the borders of the territory over which he ruled. This was largely due to his commercial activities, which marked the real genius of his administration. It was not the task of Solomon to enlarge the bounds of the kingdom, for he had inherited his domain from David, his father, who had by his closing days conquered all the land allotted to Israel. It was the responsibility of Solomon to exploit the rich resources now lying within his reach. This was done by remarkable efforts in industry and trade.

Solomon realized Israel's advantage as a land bridge between East and West, North and South. He also saw the possibilities by sea in his alliance with Hiram of Tyre. Under the guidance of Hiram, he constructed a navy that sailed the Red Sea and brought back the riches of the South, even from Somaliland. The voyage took over a year and brought back such treasures as gold, silver, rare woods, jewels, and ivory. His camel caravans traveled from Egypt through Arabia and into the Euphrates Valley.

One of Solomon's most important industries was his copper mines to the south of the Dead Sea near Ezion-Geber (cf. Thomas, pp. 437 ff.). Another remarkable project was his trade in horses (1 Kings 10:28-29). At first he brought them into his kingdom to strengthen the army, but soon he discovered that he could sell these strategic military assets to other nations at a greater profit. This eventually became one of his best sources of income.

All this commercial activity was a royal monopoly. The individual merchants worked for the government, most of the profit going

to the king's court. The small independent merchant did not have the financial means to underwrite such grandiose adventures in trade. The king was the only one who could be regarded as independently wealthy. The subjects, even the most powerful, could get only the scraps that fell from his table.

Such projects as the copper mines, the royal navy, the camel caravans, the palace and the Temple could not be accomplished without a price. Taxation was heavy and burdensome. The most grueling aspect, however, was the drafting of labor for the work. Although the Israelites were not made bondmen, yet while they were serving in labor camps, they were often mistreated (1 Kings 12:4).

III. The Divided Kingdom

The division of the kingdom occurred at the death of Solomon *ca.* 922 B.C. Various elements made this inevitable: an impetuous young man (Rehoboam), a clever labor leader (Jeroboam), excessive taxation, jealousy between the Rachel and Leah tribes (Joseph and Judah), differences in geographical location, the fear of dictatorship among a free people, and the apostasy of Solomon. To those who could see, the dissolution of the kingdom witnessed to the dreadful consequences of forgetting the divine destiny of Israel.

1. Struggle for Stability

Upon the death of Solomon *Rehoboam* became king in Judah (922-915 B.C.)[4] and *Jeroboam* in northern Israel (922-901 B.C.). Hostilities were continual between the two. Jeroboam, freshly influenced by the worship of the Egyptians and appealing to an Israelite inclination as old as Sinai (Ex. 32:4), put golden bulls at Dan and Bethel to rival worship at Jerusalem. He well knew that he could not keep his political independence long if his people con-

---

[4] Cf. Bright for Hebrew chronology. These dates are often contestable, since the Old Testament records provide few fixed points in reference to world history, and the reigns of fathers and sons frequently overlapped.

tinued to cross the national boundaries to worship at Zion. From what they have learned about the worship of the period, many scholars believe it was not his intention to lead Israel into worshiping the golden calves themselves, which were supposed to represent the God Yahweh. The Hebrews were worshiping the invisible Yahweh through the calves that symbolized his presence. The danger, of course, was that they would soon worship what they could see rather than the hidden God. Yet it was not until the time of Hosea that a prophet of northern Israel is recorded as opposing the golden calves. Elijah and Elisha were quite silent on the subject.

Abijah (915–913), the son of Rehoboam, succeeded where his father had failed; he defeated Jeroboam in battle. The grandson of Rehoboam, *Asa* (913–873), was one of the few kings commended by the Deuteronomic editors of the books of Kings, primarily because he instituted an extensive campaign against idolatry, even removing his idolatrous mother from her royal position. His reign is also distinguished by the defeat of Zerah, the Ethiopian king, which reveals the effective buildup of military power during his long reign.

Meanwhile there was a continual struggle for the throne in northern Israel. The son of Jeroboam, *Nadab,* ruled only two years before he was slain, and thus the first dynasty ended. *Baasha* (900–877) was a strong king militarily but was hampered by the rise to power of Benhadad I of Syria (*ca.* 880–842). His son *Elah* (877–876) suffered the same fate that his father had dealt to Nadab. His murderer Zimri ruled only seven days, burning his palace down upon his head to avoid capture by his rival *Omri* (876–869).

2. The Omrides

Although the biblical writers dispose of Omri with a quick word of condemnation for his idolatrous practices, from a secular point of view he was perhaps the most influential king that northern Israel ever had. Until this time the Northern Kingdom suffered from a lack of unity especially because there was no permanent capital city to symbolize the ideals of the nation. Quite wisely Omri bought the hill that would become Samaria, and established the government as no other king had been able to do. He made a permanent impression upon the rising empire of Assyria, whose kings would henceforth refer to Israel's king as "the son of Omri" and to Israel itself as "the land of Omri." Conscious of international affairs, he married his son Ahab to Jezebel, daughter of the king of Sidon. Although the move was roundly condemned by the biblical writer, it seemed to be a shrewd political maneuver.

Omri's son *Ahab* (869–850), although weaker than his father, was nevertheless a warrior of no mean ability. In fact, the famous son of Asa, *Jehoshaphat* (873–849), just before the battle of Ramoth-Gilead (1 Kings 22:1 ff.) appears to be vassal of Ahab, since he has no choice but to wear Ahab's armor into battle. Although not the warrior Ahab was, Jehoshaphat achieved unusual success in the domestic field. A religious and political reformer, he was a popular king. Under his encouragement the law was taught throughout Judah, and peaceful pursuits prospered at his hand.

With the coming of Jezebel to northern Israel, however, the opposite was occurring there. From the first there was open war between her and the prophets of Yahweh. It was her intention to replace the religion of Israel with her own. When she collided with Elijah, she met a man in touch with the power of God and the agent of his judgment.

During the reign of Ahab a new world empire was developing: Assyria, the first to use iron chariots in warfare. It soon became the scourge of the world. It was the Assyrian threat that made Ahab spare Benhadad when he was helplessly in his power. Ahab needed a strong Syria as a buffer between himself and Assyria. The prophets knew that God could offer better protection than Benhadad, but Ahab had no place for God.

The battle of Karkar (Qarqar) was

fought in 853 B.C., the first date in Old Testament history to be located with exactness. This was a great battle between a coalition of western countries (including Israel and Syria) and Shalmaneser III of Assyria (859–824). Although the engagement probably ended in a draw, the tide was soon to turn in Assyria's favor.

3. The Jehu Dynasty

Jehoram (849–842), the son of Jehoshaphat, married *Athaliah,* the daughter of Ahab and Jezebel. She was a true daughter of Jezebel. When her husband was killed in the purge conducted in northern Israel by *Jehu* (842–815), she attempted to kill all the royal seed in Judah, and had herself declared queen (842–837). She failed to discover the baby Joash, who was hidden in the Temple by the high priest Jehoiada, and, in her turn, was slain when *Joash* was crowned (837–800).

The purge of Jehu also featured the murder of *Jehoram* the son of Ahab (849–842), who had succeeded his unfortunate brother *Ahaziah* (850–849), who had died as the result of an accidental fall. Jehu's reign was noted for its destruction of Tyrian Baalism in the Northern Kingdom, although the worship of the local fertility baals still continued. In 842 B.C. Jehu also paid tribute to Shalmaneser III, recognizing for the first time the supremacy of Assyria in the West.

Shalmaneser III was followed by a weak king in Assyria, enabling Syria to rise again to power. Accordingly, *Jehoahaz* (815–801) the son of Jehu became a vassal of Hazael, who even approached Jerusalem but was bought off by Joash with palace and Temple treasures. However, the rise of Adad-nirari III to the throne of Assyria (811–783) soon brought Syria into subjection once more, enabling *Jehoash* (801–786) son of Jehoahaz to recover the territory previously lost to Syria. Meanwhile *Amaziah* (800–783) had succeeded his father Joash on the throne of Judah. Feeling his power after defeating the Edomites, he attacked Jehoash of Israel but was soundly defeated. In retaliation the king of Israel plundered Jerusalem, tearing down a part of the wall.

4. Prosperity and Collapse

With the death of Amaziah and the crowning of *Uzziah* (Azariah) as king of Judah (783–742), a period of prosperity was inaugurated unlike any since the days of Solomon. This was paralleled in Israel by the reign of *Jeroboam II* (786–746) whose tenure was marked by similar success. The reason for this was twofold. On the one hand Assyria was impotent during these years and Syria was depleted, leaving the Hebrews free to prosper, uninterrupted by war. On the other hand, Uzziah and Jeroboam left each other alone.

The great eighth-century prophets (Amos, Hosea, Isaiah, and Micah) saw beneath the superficial prosperity the seeds of a sick society. The affluency was not due to the favor of God, as many thought, but to a temporary lull in hostilities. It was the calm before the storm. The end came quickly for Israel. The son of Jeroboam, *Zechariah,* reigned only six months before he was slain by *Shallum,* who lasted only one month. *Menahem,* his murderer, managed to reign a few years more (745–738), but he was forced to pay tribute to the new king of Assyria, the relentless Tiglath-Pileser III (745–727). His son *Pekahiah* (738–737) was killed, as his father had killed a king before him, by *Pekah* (737–732). He was in turn murdered by *Hoshea* (732–722), who was but a puppet of Tiglath-Pileser. When he rebelled against the next king of Assyria, Shalmaneser V (727–722), Samaria, was besieged by this monarch and finally captured by Sargon II (722–705) in 722 B.C.

What were the causes that contributed to the disintegration of the Northern Kingdom and its eventual extinction? (1) Since 922 B.C. Israel and Judah had spent themselves in feuding with each other, with the Northern Kingdom more exposed to foreign attack. (2) The throne was unstable. In a period of almost 200 years there were

9 dynasties and 19 kings, 10 of whom died violent deaths. (3) The shocking immorality of the people and the lack of concern for social justice was fatal, bringing the judgment of God on a nation committed to self-gratification.

5. Judah and Assyria

Uzziah was followed by his son *Jotham* (742–734), during whose reign Micah began to prophesy. His son, the idolatrous *Ahaz* (735–715), came to the throne just in time to inherit the Syro-Ephraimitic War from his father. This was an attempt on the part of Pekah of the Northern Kingdom and Rezin of Syria to force Judah into an alliance against Tiglath-Pileser. In desperation Ahaz appealed to the Assyrian monarch for aid. Glad to oblige, he moved against the attackers and lifted the siege. Judah paid a costly price in tribute for the favor and was left without a buffer between herself and Assyria. It was during this crisis that Isaiah delivered his famous Immanuel oracle to Ahaz (Isa. 7:1 ff.).

When Sargon died in 705 B.C., it was the occasion for a new rebellion in Palestine, fostered by Egypt and including Hezekiah (715–686 B.C.). The Assyrian said that he shut up Hezekiah "like a bird in a cage." Second Kings 18:13–16 and Sennacherib's claim are in remarkable agreement. However, 2 Kings 18:17—19:37 tells of a disaster which befell the Assyrian army in which 185,000 men were lost.

Judah learned nothing from the fate that struck the Northern Kingdom. The good king Hezekiah was succeeded by one of Judah's worst, *Manasseh* (686–638). During his long reign the Hebrew nation drifted away from the high purposes of God, and foreign cults and practices were encouraged. Temple worship was deemphasized, and the building itself was allowed to deteriorate. Manasseh was branded by the author of the books of Kings as the worst king ever to sit on David's throne (cf. 2 Kings 21:9–15; 23:3 f.).

The picture was greatly changed after *Josiah* (640–609) came to the throne at the age of eight. Nothing is known of the years immediately following his coronation, but by 628 B.C. Judah (now all that remained of Israel) was beginning to recover territory lost to Assyria when Samaria fell a century before. Repairs upon the Temple were begun in preparation for the renewal of the ancient faith of Israel. About 622 B.C., an electrifying discovery was made. The book of the law was found in the Temple. This book, generally associated with our book of Deuteronomy, became the basis for sweeping reforms. Judah and the territory of Israel were purged of all alien practices, and the public worship of Yahweh was reinstituted in the Jerusalem Temple. Plainly this reformation was political as well as religious. It amounted to a complete break with Assyria.

6. Judah's Closing Days

In 612 B.C. Nineveh, the capital of Assyria, fell before Cyaxares, king of Media, and Nabopolassar, king of Babylon. The Assyrian army continued the fight as it retreated west toward its ally, Egypt. In 609 Pharaoh Neco set out to join the Assyrians in a desperate attempt to push back the onrushing tide from the East. Perceiving the Egyptian purpose and apparently hoping that he would fare better in face of a Babylonian victory, Josiah tried to stop Neco. Instead, Josiah was killed, and consternation struck Judah.

His son *Jehoahaz* (Shallum) was made king in Jerusalem. Fearing further trouble from Judah, Neco, who was in Syria at the time, deported Jehoahaz to Egypt after only three months on the throne. In his place Neco put his brother Eliakim, whose name became *Jehoiakim* (609–597), and made certain that he would remain an Egyptian vassal. Heavy tribute was exacted from Judah.

Jehoiakim proved to be a dismal failure. The old pagan cults of the Manasseh era crept in again with the accompanying immorality. The impetus of Josiah's reforms, however, kept the worship at the Temple in full swing, for it was also the center of

Israel's nationalistic hopes.

Events were hastening toward a climax. In 605 B.C. Nebuchadnezzar completely routed the Egyptians at Carchemish, and Jehoiakim was forced to shift his allegiance to Babylon. By 598 he had rebelled again, causing Babylon to send an army once more against Jerusalem. Jehoiakim's mysterious death at this time occasioned the crowning of his son *Jehoiachin* (Coniah), who ruled only three months and was taken captive to Babylon in 597. Along with him were taken the leading citizens of Judah, numbering at least ten thousand, as well as priceless vessels from the Temple. *Zedekiah* (Mattaniah) was placed upon the throne by Nebuchadnezzar. Eventually he too joined in rebellion against Babylon.

Once more Nebuchadnezzar made his way to Judah and soon was encamped before Jerusalem. When the city finally fell in 587 B.C., Nebuchadnezzar, infuriated by Judah's constant provocations, killed most of the people and took comparatively few prisoners. Among these, however, was Zedekiah, who was blinded and taken in chains to Babylon. Peasants were left to cultivate the land, while a few pro-Babylonian superiors remained at Mizpah under a Jewish viceroy. Before 597 B.C., approximately 150,000 people were living in Palestine. By 520 these had been reduced to no more than 50,000 (Bright, p. 347).

IV. The Exile and Restoration

The destruction of the monarchy did not mean the end of Israel, for the tribal confederacy had existed during the two centuries before the kingdom was established. Israel was a people before the accession of her kings and survived after they ceased to reign. The monarchy had been only an episode in her continuing history (Noth, p. 290). There still remained the prophetic dreams of world conquest, and there were those who still believed this was bound up in the political structure they had previously known. Yet the years that followed indicated increasingly that Israel's destiny must be understood in terms of the new life situation in which she found herself.

From the beginning the tensions concerning the monarchy centered around the danger of Israel's losing its distinctive character as the people of God. The history of the kingdom is largely a portrayal of its frustrated attempts to establish itself militarily and politically as a typical nation. Since this was no longer possible after the fall of Jerusalem, its future was found in a unique direction. Exile and restoration provided the crucible in which Israel's distinctive contribution was determined.

1. Hebrew Life During the Exile

There is no attempt in the Old Testament to describe in detail the conditions prevailing during the Exile, either in Palestine or in Babylon. Even though the population was depleted, Palestine was not as desolate as we might suppose. Jerusalem was in ruins, but agricultural life continued. Gradually a new land aristocracy developed to replace the nobles who had been deported. Over the years, Babylonian and Canaanite cults came to permeate the Yahweh worship of Judea (Ezek. 8:3,14; Isa. 57:3–8; 65:3–5; 66:3,17).

There were, however, some faithful worshipers of Yahweh remaining in the homeland, for Jeremiah mentions eighty pilgrims from Shechem, Shiloh, and Samaria who brought offerings to be presented on the site of the ruined Temple (Jer. 41:4 ff.).

Meanwhile in Babylon the Jewish leaders were trying to put the pieces of their shattered lives together. Although the captives in 587 B.C. were treated without mercy and put into slavery, those taken in 597 were allowed considerable freedom (Jer. 29:5–7; Ezek. 8:1). They were permitted to conduct their own affairs and to acquire property, although prohibited from returning home. Deprived of the opportunity to sacrifice at the Temple, they learned that Yahweh could be worshiped without such practices. Obedience replaced sacrifice. Fasting became more common and the sabbath more prominent. Although we cannot be sure when formal synagogue worship began,[5] some simple form of religious gathering must have occurred, with antecedents going back to the religious life of remote communities in Judah, especially after Josiah destroyed the local altars. These would later be called synagogues.

The syncretism that was developing in Palestine contrasted sharply with the determined attempts of the exiles to preserve their identity in a foreign land. The freedom of community life allowed them by the Babylonians permitted retention of their essential cultural and religious patterns. These were observed with devoted diligence. Such faithfulness under trying circumstances encouraged an exclusivism that magnified the differences not only between them and the Babylonians but also between them and those remaining in Judea. Not only had they suffered more than the people at home, but by heeding the words of Israel's great prophets they had been benefited by their misfortunes. Upon their return this feeling of superiority forced a cleavage between them and those who remained (Ezra 4:1 ff.). Whether this was completely justified or not we cannot say; yet, from the subsequent development of the Samaritan sect after this schism, we can conclude that the exiles were traveling a higher road (Robinson, pp. 157–60).

2. The Persian Era

The year 559 B.C. is a landmark in world history. In that year Cyrus succeeded his father as king of Anshan. Soon he was threatening Astyages, king of Media. In 550 B.C. Cyrus led a victorious army through the streets of Ecbatana, the capital city of Media, looting it and carrying off its riches to Anshan. Further conquests in the East kept Cyrus busy until 539 B.C., when he began to march against Babylon. Nabonidus, king of Babylon, was in no position to resist, had he desired to do so. His resources had been spent in restoring and building the temples of the gods. His people were discontented with their king. Thinking that he had displeased the chief god Marduk, they were in no mood to oppose Cyrus.

After the fall of Babylon, Cyrus was ruler of all of western Asia, his domain extending to the northern boundaries of Egypt. Since that nation was the only threat to his power in the South, he began at once to devise some means to keep it away from mischief. His territory included Palestine. If people of that area were loyal to him, his kingdom would be more secure from the ambition of the Egyptian Pharaohs. Thus it is not strange that he permitted the return of the Jews from Babylon to their fatherland—though the overruling providence of God is our real clue to what happened (Isa. 45:1–6). The response of some of the more prosperous Jews was not enthusiastic, for a large number chose to remain in Babylon. Many others made the return with Zerubbabel ca. 538 B.C. The tiring march consumed a considerable time, as did the troublesome affairs necessitated by settling in a new community. Accordingly, the foundation of the Temple was not laid until 536.

3. The Restoration

The Temple was not completed until 516 B.C., after the encouragement of Haggai and Zechariah in 520. The city was still not a safe place to live since it had no protecting wall. This was provided by Nehemiah in 444 B.C., almost one hundred years after the first return. Cyrus had been succeeded by his mentally disturbed son Cambyses. With the coming of Darius the Great (Hystaspes, 522–486) a new momentum came to the Persian rule.

The international policies of Persia were quite different from those of Assyria perpetuated by Babylon. The system of deportation was abandoned, captive peoples being allowed to return home. Considerable self-rule was permitted. The Persians desired only an assurance of regular tribute from an appointed governor.

Darius was succeeded by Xerxes

---

[5] H. H. Rowley, *Worship in Ancient Israel* (London: SPCK, 1967), pp. 213–245.

(486–465) who was probably the Ahasuerus of the book of Esther. Artaxerxes I (Longimanus, 465–424) followed him. In chronological order the other Persian kings were Xerxes II (423), Darius II (Nothius, 423–404), Artaxerxes II (Mnemon, 404–358), Artaxerxes III (Ochus, 358–338), Arses (338–336), and finally Darius III (Codomannus, 336–331), who surrendered the empire to Alexander the Great.

There is considerable difficulty in placing Ezra in this chronological scheme. The traditional place for him is in 458 B.C. during the seventh year of Artaxerxes I. Many scholars contend, however, that he returned during the seventh year of Artaxerxes II (398 B.C.). Still others suggest that "the seventh year" originally read "the thirty-seventh year" and date him during the reign of Artaxerxes I (428). There is no certainty concerning this matter, though the 398 date seems most unlikely since the solid biblical witness insists that Ezra and Nehemiah were on the scene together.

4. The Beginnings of Judaism

Without question, later Judaism developed its distinctive emphases during the Persian era. The development of eschatology characterized the period. Frustrated in the present age, they were more receptive to thoughts about the future. How much Israel was influenced by Zoroastrian thought is a matter of debate (Robinson, p. 165). Regardless of outside influences, the Hebrews were being led to refine and develop their own theology in the context of their convinced monotheism.

Not only were attitudes toward the future changing, but also views concerning present responsibilities. With the coming of Ezra, a new direction was given the Israelites' life: emphasis upon the law. Whereas in the past the law had served the Hebrews, now they became servants of the law.[6] The divine instrument for the expression of the faith often became an end in itself. National loyalty was being replaced

by loyalty to tradition, written and oral.

Other significant developments resulted from the Persian system of governing their provinces. Although they kept strict control of all political life, the Persians permitted complete freedom of religion. The Hebrews, deprived of political independence, found an outlet in fresh articulation and application of their historic faith. Political frustrations were compensated by religious zeal. The unique emphases that have marked Israel's life ever since found expression during this time: a rich vocabulary of prayer and praise (found in the Psalms of the second Temple), a practical application of the prophetic principles in everyday life (expressed in the Wisdom Literature), and especially a stubborn refusal to yield to any pressure, social or political, to apostatize. In it all God was guiding his people toward his purpose for them. They who had been looking for the Second David were being prepared for the Suffering Servant.

A Selected Bibliography

ALBRIGHT, W. F. *From the Stone Age to Christianity.* Baltimore: Johns Hopkins Press, 1946.

ANDERSON, G. W. *The History and Religion of Israel.* ("The New Clarendon Bible," Old Testament, Vol. I.) Oxford: University Press, 1966.

BRIGHT, JOHN. *A History of Israel.* Philadelphia: Westminster Press, 1960.

DANIEL-ROPS. *Israel and the Ancient World.* London: Eyre & Spottiswoode, 1949.

MANSON, T. W. *A Companion to the Bible.* Edinburgh: T & T Clark, 1943.

NOTH, MARTIN. *The History of Israel.* 2d ed. Rev. English trans. P. R. ACKROYD. New York: Harper & Row, 1960.

OESTERLY, W. O. E., and T. H. ROBINSON. *A History of Israel.* Oxford: Clarendon Press, 1932.

ROBINSON, H. WHEELER. *The History of Israel.* London: Duckworth, 1938.

SNAITH, NORMAN H. *The Jews from Cyrus to Herod.* Wallington: Religious Education Press, 1949.

THOMAS, D. W. *Archaeology and Old Testament Study.* Oxford: Clarendon, Press, 1967.

WELLHAUSEN, JULIUS. *Prolegomena to the History of Israel.* London: Adam & Charles Black, 1885.

---

[6] Gerhard von Rad, *Old Testament Theology* (London: Oliver & Boyd, 1962), I, 91.

The Theology of the Old Testament

E. C. RUST

The theological ideas of the Old Testament concern the nature and activity of God himself, as he discloses himself to the Hebrew people; the relationship of nature to God as its Creator and Sustainer; man's responsible relationship to God; and the interrelationship of man to his fellows and to his natural environment, under God.

I. The Methodology of Old Testament Theology

We have to remember that, in studying the thought of the Old Testament, we are dealing with traditions and documents which cover one thousand years of Hebrew history. Because we are dealing with a historical revelation and not with the thought patterns of one circumscribed period of time, Old Testament theology presents a peculiar problem. We must decide on some norm around which to build the theological thought. We must differentiate the permanent elements in Israel's thought from those which are transient. We must systematize, but the systematization must be consonant with a disclosure through the long processes of history. It must faithfully represent the dialogue of the living God with his people. As a result of such issues, the methodology and attitude adopted by Old Testament theologians have been varied.

First of all, we must carefully differentiate Old Testament theology from the history of Hebrew religion. The latter studies the religion of Israel as a historical phenomenon, dealing with its changing structures and its transient as well as its permanent elements. It will be concerned with what is distinctive in Israel's religion, but it will also take note of the relation of Hebrew religion to the religions of neighboring cultures. Furthermore, it will consider the development of Israel's religious experience and study Hebrew religion chronologically. Such a study is a valuable background for and adjunct to Old Testament theology, but the approach of the latter is different. Here we are concerned about those permanent elements which persist in the historical development of Israel's faith and do not drop out of sight. Again, Old Testament theology will seek for the theological meaning of Israel's religious ideas and attempt to build them into a systematized pattern.

In the second place, we have to ask ourselves how we are to assess what is of abiding significance in Israel's faith. Since most Old Testament theologians are within the Christian faith, the final court of appeal must be Christological. They are agreed that in some way the Old Testament faith points to the faith of the New Testament and provides the latter with its historical undergirding. What is of abiding significance is related to the theological testimony of the New Testament. Old Testament theologians as divergent in their views as Th. C. Vriezen and G. von Rad agree with Otto Procksch that the Old Testament and New Testament so belong together that the Old Testament without the New is like a torso without a head. Our final standard for the judgment of what is significant must therefore be the Christological, what points to and is fulfilled in the New Testament faith.

We are still left with the third issue—the pattern in which to arrange the theological ideas of the Old Testament faith. Here we face the problem of a historical development in which such ideas attain richer dimensions and also the fact that the disclosure of God is intimately involved in the historical movement of Israel's life. Evidently an existential pattern involving the concept of dialogue and relationship between God and his created order is more satisfactory here.

Modern Old Testament theologians have tended to move from a purely systematic approach to a more dynamic approach, emphasizing the divine activity and the relation of God to his created order. Within this framework they have sought to systematize in various ways. We shall here adopt a synoptic or systematic stance, centering in the dynamic relationship of the living God to his creatures, emphasizing those theological ideas which are gathered up in transfigured form in the New Testament faith. The key must be the continuing disclosure to Israel of the living God.

II. The Characteristic Patterns of Hebrew Thought

The Hebrew was essentially a realist. He accepted the world as it appeared to him at the level of the senses and was very aware of the awesome forces and majestic beauty of the natural order. This is very much evidenced in the nature Psalms (e.g., 65; 104; 148), but it is manifested also in the imagery of the prophets, who draw largely on nature in their poetic similes. The Hebrew also trusted in his moral intuitions and his religious visions. At every level of his experience, he believed he was in touch with reality.

His realism was, however, characterized by a distinctive sense of "wholeness." Quite evident in the view of nature and of the animal "kinds," this sense of wholeness is especially evident in the case of man. The individual, especially in the early days of Hebrew thought, is always thought of in his setting of a corporate whole. He is within the family, the clan, the tribe, the nation —humanity as a whole. There is a sense of corporate personality at the social level. What a man does is the responsibility not only of himself but also of his family. This explains the terrible punishment inflicted on all of Achan's family and property because of Achan's sin (Josh. 7:24). The personality of the individual and the consequences of what he does are extended over those who are related to him.

This "extension of personality" depends for its range upon the significance of the social relationships of the individual concerned. Thus the king incorporates the whole nation in himself, and the well-being of the nation depends upon the well-being of the king himself. At the family level, there was developed the proverb: "The fathers have eaten sour grapes, and the children's teeth are set on edge" (Ezek. 18:2). This is reflected in the acceptance of the maxim that the sins of the fathers shall be visited upon the children to the third and fourth generations (Ex. 20:5). At the level of any close knit group, the practice of blood revenge required that the crime of one member of the group be paid for by the blood of another member (2 Kings 9:26).

The idea of extension of personality helps us to understand how all the Psalms could be described as within the corporate or extended personality of David, the typical psalmist; all laws within that of Moses, the typical lawgiver; all wisdom within that of Solomon, the typical wise man. We need, finally, to note that the very word *Adam* is more a corporate than a given name. It stands for the typical man, and all humanity is to be described by the inclusive humanity of Adam.

Hebrew Psychology. The sense of wholeness also pervades the Hebrew understanding of man himself. Man is viewed as a psychosomatic whole. His body is an intimate part of his personal being. This is very evident in the Hebrew understanding of "soul." This word is very different in meaning from our commonly conceived idea of the soul, which is derived more from Greek thought. The initial meaning of soul is animating principle, that which makes the difference between the dead and the living. For the Hebrew, man is not an incarnated soul in our modern sense but an animated body. The Hebrew had no word for "body" or for "personality." Here we see Hebrew realism, with its emphasis on the concrete rather than the abstract. The body is the man, and man is characterized by the concrete fact that his body is animated. The physical and the psychical are closely intertwined. Let a man's blood be shed and his life will literally pour out. At this level of meaning "soul" can be translated as "life" (2 Sam. 1:9).

At a higher level, "soul" means man in his totality as a personal self, and it is thus equivalent to "I." There is still the concrete reference, for man's selfhood is bound up with his bodily condition (Gen. 27:25; Psalm 3:2). The psychosomatic attitude is still present. As a man is within, so he is without. Well-being of soul is equated with fatness (Isa. 55:2; cf. Jer. 31:25). The "soul" is man in his personal unity of animating principle and flesh.

There is, however, a more inward connotation of soul when the word is used to describe man's inward desires, both physical and spiritual. A man of strong physical desire is a "greedy soul" (cf. Isa. 56:11, Hebrew text), and a soul also thirsts after God (Psalm 42:2 ff.). The emotions of love (1 Sam. 20:17) and hate (Isa. 1:14) center in the soul.

This becomes apparent in the Hebrew understanding of "heart." The heart is the center of thought and intention and comes to stand especially for that inner aspect of man which we call character. The Hebrew can therefore speak of "laying a thing upon the heart" or of "setting his heart upon a thing," that is to say, letting a thought or word act upon him (Isa. 57:1; Jer. 12:11; Mal. 2:2). The heart thus represents the inner life or character of man. Man *is* a soul, but he *has* a heart. The heart can, however, stand for the whole personality. A man's heart may be comforted, or it may be poured out (Gen. 18:5; Lam. 2:19). The Hebrew believed that by his word one man could empty some of his "soul" into another and give him the strength to act.

The seat of feeling is likewise regarded as the bowels (Jer. 4:19; Isa. 16:11), while the kidneys can also perform psychic as well as physical functions (Job 16:13). In all this, the psychosomatic wholeness of man is emphasized. His outward condition and inner state of spirit or character are bound together and reflect one another. Hence we have the ready assumption that outward calamity always results from inward estrangement from God, a problem which perplexed the author of Job.

Hebrew Cosmology and the Hebrew View of Nature. Just as the Hebrew does not share our modern psychological understanding, so he is also prescientific in his understanding of nature. His world is a three-tiered universe. He pictures a flat earth, like a disc, with mountains at the edge on which the solid dome of heaven, the firmament, rests. Under the earth is the enlarged family grave, Sheol, where the shades of the departed go. Above the dome of heaven is God's palace. Genesis 1 and Psalm 104 alike illustrate this cosmology. The Hebrew envisages the whole as surrounded by the "deep." That a similar view of the world prevailed elsewhere in the ancient Near East is a reminder that, in his prescientific outlook, the Hebrew shared some views of his contemporaries.

As for nature itself, the Hebrew understands it with the same sense of wholeness with which he understands man. Nature as a totality and the various groups of natural phenomena within that totality are regarded as "wholes." Furthermore, such "wholes" are regarded as capable of a psychic response. The land, as a psychic whole, has a psychic bond with both God and his people. It can be "Beulah" land, married to God (Isa. 62:4). The domestic animals form a psychic whole and can give a psychic response to man. They have a covenant with man by which they have become his servants, whereas the wild creatures have not (Job 41:4).

The Hebrew has no sense of the mechanistic structures of cause and effect with which modern science has made us familiar. Rather he thinks of chains of psychic response. Hosea can think of God's evoking a chain of psychic responses in the heavens: the corn, the wine, and the oil; and Jezreel (2:21–22). Even the sun and the other heavenly bodies are pictured both physically and psychically. Psalm 19:4–6 makes this clear in the case of the sun, and in Psalm 148 the sun, moon, and stars are summoned to praise God. The stars possess such psychic life that they can fight against Sisera (Judg. 5:20), while the author of Job pictures the morning stars as shouting together when God created the world (Job 38:7). This is not mere poetry, but an aspect of Hebrew realism with its sense of psychic wholeness.

III. The Divine Disclosure

The Old Testament is the testimony to the divine disclosure in the history of the Hebrew people. The Hebrew, unlike the Greek, did not arrive at his understanding of God by the processes of human reason. God was not thought of as static Being, a rational pattern which gave meaning to the universe. He was envisaged as the living God, dynamic personal Being, who was known in what he did. He was alive and personal. Central in this understanding of God was his will, expressing his intention, his purpose. Furthermore, man's response to God was the way of the will, of trust in and commitment to the divine disclosure. God acted as person, giving himself to men, revealing himself to them, in the vicissitudes of their historical life. He was no abstract system of rational ideas.

This personal and living nature of God lights up the Old Testament testimony at every point. As such he is continually active in Hebrew history, transforming its course, dealing with Israel redemptively in judgment and in mercy. The insight of faith grasped his reality through the historical actualities and the natural environment of Hebrew existence. Hence men may swear by the life of God (Judg. 8:19). As living God he speaks from Sinai with the voice of thunder (Deut. 5:26) and comes to the aid of his people in the invasion of Palestine (Josh. 3:10).

The Name of God—Yahweh. Hence God gives himself to men in personal form. This is seen especially in the disclosure of his name. For a Hebrew to give his name to someone was, in a real sense, to impart knowledge of his innermost being. So, when God gives his name "Yahweh" to

Moses, this is a personal self-disclosure. This is the central name for God in the Old Testament.

According to the E tradition, the name Yahweh was first disclosed through Moses (Ex. 3:15). There are, however, indications that the name was not entirely new to some Hebrew groups. The J tradition carries it back to the primeval times and associates it with Abraham (Gen. 4:26; 9:26; 15:7). These two traditions need not be regarded as contradictory. We know that the Hebrew invasion of Palestine was piecemeal, and it may well be that to some tribal groups the name Yahweh was already known, for example, the Leah tribes (cf. Jacob, pp. 49 f.).

It is quite evident that the living God was known to the patriarchs as *'El,* the God of the fathers. Various individuals and groups of individuals knew him as the familiar friend and guide who accompanied them in their wanderings. Many scholars hold that among the Semitic groups there was an original, if primitive, monotheism. Certainly the P tradition declares that, prior to the Exodus, God was known to the Hebrew people as *'El Shaddai,* God Almighty, and as such, in this tradition, he discloses himself to Abraham (Ex. 6:3; Gen. 17:1; cf. 28:3). Melchizedek's encounter with Abraham introduces the name *'El 'Elyon,* God Most High. Clearly, the religion of the patriarchs was associated with God as *'El,* and this name was associated especially with power.

It may well be that the name Yahweh was also used in this remote and darkened past. Yet to Moses the name came as a new disclosure of God's innermost nature. The actual vowels in the original name have long since been lost, for later devotion prohibited the enunciation of the divine name. The consonants YHWH alone remain, and, in the sacred text, their occurrence was always accompanied in speech by the substitution of the name "the Lord," *Adonai.* Hence the vowels of the latter were fitted into the consonants to produce the name Jehovah. This is not, however, the original form. Early parallels and pieces of evidence would seem to indicate Yahweh as the original form.

Yet if Yahweh was known to the patriarchs, it was not as in the disclosure that came to Moses. The *'El* of power became the God of personal activity in the disclosure of the burning bush. God comes to Moses as the God of the fathers, but he now discloses himself in a new way. However known before, the name carries a new significance. God is understood as, "He who is," a living, continuing actuality. The consonants of the divine name became linked up, in the consciousness of Moses, with the verb to be. The important thing is that God *is,* the enduring and living background of Israel's life. The God of power has become more personal, the guarantee of his people's redemption from slavery. God is Yahweh, and Yahweh conveys in its consonantal structure the disclosure "I am."

The Divine Disclosure—the Divine Glory. The Hebrew was very aware of God's hiddenness and transcendence. God was personal, and, as such, he was also clothed in mystery. God was both revealed through his created orders and yet hidden by them. He was the God of mystery whom man could not find out by his searching (Isa. 40:28; Job 11:7). He was beyond the processes of nature and history, the Holy One who inhabited eternity (Isa. 57:15), yet he was also very immanent in them. There was no part of his world which was not open to him and where he was not present (cf. Psalm 139). God could work within nature and history and disclose himself personally in them.

When the Hebrew sought to understand this divine activity of disclosure, certain characteristic words were employed. We find fairly frequent use of the term divine glory. The glory of God is the way in which he manifests himself—his visible appearance, with the accompanying feeling of awe on the part of man. Nature theophanies, such as fire and storm phenomena, manifest God's glory as a burning or fiery appearance—the burning bush (Ex.

3:2 ff.), the pillar of fire (Ex. 13:21), the fire that burns Elijah's sacrifice (1 Kings 18:24 ff.). The storm cloud becomes the theophany for Ezekiel (1:26–28). Lightning is probably the physical basis for the serpent-like seraphim in the prophetic visions (Isa. 6:2 ff.; Ezek. 1:5 ff.).

Yet God hides himself as he shows himself. His glory is hidden by the cloud. The rising clouds of incense hide Yahweh's presence for Isaiah (6:1 ff.). Moses sees only God's hinder parts. To behold God's glory in all its fiery splendor is death (Ex. 33:17–23).

We may say that God's glory is his radiant splendor which he sends forth when he appears in the storm and the fiery lightning.

The Spirit and the Word. Much more significant for the Old Testament understanding of revelation are the Spirit and the Word. In Hebrew thought the idea of the Spirit is more that of an impersonal power than of a personal presence, especially in the preexilic period. The word has physical connotations. It can also mean wind. The spirit or wind from God's nostrils heaps up the waters of the Red Sea (Ex. 15:8). Ezekiel, in the vision of the valley of dry bones, plays on the double sense of the word as "wind" and "spirit" (Ezek. 37:1–14). In this physical sense the divine Spirit could, in the early days, be associated particularly with manifestly violent aspects of human behavior, e.g., Samson's strength and Saul's paroxysms of rage and madness (Judg. 14:6,19; 1 Sam. 16:14). All extraordinary gifts are also due to the Spirit—Bezaleel's skill and Joseph's ability to interpret dreams (Ex. 28:3; Gen. 41:25 ff.). The Spirit of God is an extension of his personal being in powerful activity, taking possession of men.

The Spirit came to be especially associated with the prophets. Saul prophesied when the Spirit of God came mightily upon him (1 Sam. 10:10). Thus the Spirit becomes the instrument of the divine revelation (cf. Mic. 3:8; Ezek. 2:2; 11:5).

Another term intimately bound up with

the divine disclosure is the "word" of Yahweh. At the human level, the word could mean act or thing as well as speech in Hebrew thought. In communicating himself to others, something of the man went into his word. Taking visible or audible form, it carried in itself something of the man's own being and intention. An extension of his personal being, it gave to the one who received it the intention of him who sent it forth. Thus the human word was a powerful instrument, able to work good or ill in those to whom it was directed.

In the same way, the divine word was an extension of God's own personal being into his world. It communicated, in potent form, the divine intention. When it was uttered by the prophet, it initiated the divine intention, in microcosm, in the situation to which it was directed. Already it had begun its objective work in the world, and it could not return to God void (Isa. 55:10 f.). Hence the prophet could preface his oracles with, "Thus saith the Lord." Once uttered, the word of Yahweh went its own way, containing in itself the very power of God and acting independently of the prophet's own person. Thus the word could be sent by Yahweh and light on Israel in catastrophic judgment (Isa. 9:8 ff.). The prophet did not have *a* word from Yahweh. He had *the* word of Yahweh, implying the full divine disclosure for his own particular situation. The prophet both is inspired by the Spirit of Yahweh and has the word of Yahweh. They represent God's immanence and revelatory activity in his world and in history.

The Divine Disclosure and the Prophetic Consciousness. The divine disclosure in history centers in the prophetic consciousness. It was the presence of the prophet which transformed the historical actuality into a revelatory event and created a disclosure situation for Israel. Moses' prophetic word at the Exodus transformed a natural happening, wind driving the waters back, into a disclosure of Yahweh's redeeming his people. The word of Yahweh through Isaiah created out of the historical invasion of the Assyrian forces a disclosure of the divine judgment and a call to repentance (10:5 ff.). Deutero-Isaiah could declare that Cyrus the Persian conqueror would fulfil the divine intention and restore the Babylonian exiles to their homeland (Isa. 44:28—45:7). From Moses onward, the outstanding figures in Israel's life are the prophets.

These men were characterized by an inspired insight into the divine will and intention. They felt as God felt and were constrained to speak and act under his direction. We may say, in modern language, that they were given an intuitive grasp of the divine purpose. They could see into the pattern of the divine mind and share in the thoughts of God. They saw themselves temporary extensions of the divine personal being into historical activity.

What distinguishes the prophets is not the psychology of their activity but the content of what they said and did. Generally they appear to be classified into two types—the ecstatic and the seer—both present in Israel. The ecstatic type which threw itself into a frenzy and manifested abnormal behavior may well have been known earlier by the word now translated prophet. Examples may be found in the "schools of the prophets" associated with the work of Samuel, Elijah, and Elisha, under the contagion of whose emotional influence Saul also began to prophesy (1 Sam. 10:10; cf. 18:10). The seer type was characterized by calm, intuitive insight and reflective judgment, e.g., Samuel and Moses. The characteristic Hebrew words rendered "seer" describe seeing and hearing. Such men were intuitively in touch with the divine mind and purpose. Yet Samuel could at times show charismatic phenomena like an ecstatic.

It would appear that, by the time our traditions took written form, the word prophet had become a generally descriptive term covering all varieties of prophetic activity (cf. 1 Sam. 9:9). Furthermore, most of the great prophetic figures show a fusion of the two types of psychology.

There are ecstatic elements in their dreams, visions, auditions, sense of compulsion, and abnormal behavior. Yet the ecstatic aspect is more at the periphery of their consciousness. At the center of the consciousness of the great prophetic figures we find an assured intuitive insight into the divine mind and purpose and the exercise of a reflective moral judgment upon the issues before them. All of them might at times be classed as ecstatics, yet equally all show the characteristics of seers.

The distinctive characteristic of the content of their message rather than the psychological pattern of their behavior is indicated in the struggle with the false prophets. There were prophetic personnel associated with the shrines where Yahweh was worshiped—Bethel, Gilgal, and the Temple at Jerusalem. Undoubtedly many of these men were devout and honest followers of Yahweh. Yet, a religious institution inevitably breeds professionalism. False prophets arose who went through the same outward psychological behavior but uttered dishonest oracles, e.g., in the story of Micaiah ben Imlah (1 Kings 22). Micah describes the lying prophets as windbags (2:11). Jeremiah's agony of spirit was made the harder to bear because of false spirits who preached "peace" when he was declaring judgment and exile for Judah (23:15 ff.; 29:21 ff.; cf. Mic. 3:5,11). Such men mimicked the prophetic mode of utterance. Outwardly they seemed the same. Their message must be tested in two ways. The extrinsic test was the confirmation of their oracles in the historical events themselves. Micaiah affords a good example (cf. Zech. 1:6). The intrinsic test lies in the ethical consistency of the prophet's message with his life. Jeremiah attacks the false prophets because of their promise of peace without moral demands (22:17).

Because the false prophets claimed to have the Spirit of Yahweh, the canonical prophets before the Exile emphasize that they have the word of Yahweh. Only with the exilic prophet Ezekiel does the emphasis on the Spirit return. But whether claiming Spirit or word, the prophets believed themselves to be Yahweh's messengers, temporary extensions of his personal presence into his world, agents of his activity. They saw God as surrounded by his heavenly council, his assembly of holy ones, in the deliberations of which they shared and from which they had been sent forth to declare the divinely ordained decrees (Jer. 23:18,22; cf. 1 Kings 22:19 ff.). As messengers they had been drawn up temporarily into God's own life. Their words were his words and their acts his acts.

Their acts were important. They spoke the word of Yahweh, but they also acted it. Isaiah mimes the slavery of the Egyptians by walking in the garb of a slave (ch. 20). Jeremiah takes an earthen bottle and smashes it to symbolize God's judgment (ch. 19). Ezekiel knocks a hole in the wall of his house and takes out his furniture, enacting the siege of Jerusalem, the breach in its walls, and the people going into exile (12:1 ff.). The prophet believed that thereby God was initiating in miniature his intention for his people. The act initiated the actualizing of God's purpose.

Not only was the prophet the guardian and mouthpiece of the divine oracle, he was also a specialist in intercessory prayer. We see this in the cases of Abraham (Gen. 20:7; Job 42:8); Moses (Ex. 32:11–14); Amos (7:2 ff.); and Jeremiah. In a very real sense, the prophets were promises of the incarnation. They were mediators, standing between Yahweh and his people, disclosing his will to the people and interceding before him as representatives of rebellious Israel.

The Law and the Priesthood. Around the Decalogue, given through Moses on Sinai's height, there grew a considerable body of rules and laws. The laws themselves came in various ways. They comprise, on the one hand, moral and ceremonial injunctions, exemplified in the early law book, the Covenant Code (Ex. 20:22—23:33). Side by side with these we find the judgments—civil and criminal laws—administered by the king and the local judges. These secular laws are found in Exodus 21:1—22:7. The first group is the kernel of the Law. It crystallizes the insights of the prophetic movement from Moses onward and also the priestly practices of the local shrines. But the king and the judges also were under divine appointment. The anointing of the king pointed to his sacral nature. So all laws finally were grounded down in the will of God.

So there grew in Israel a corpus of laws consisting of moral injunctions, ceremonial rules, civil laws, and criminal judgments. It embodied laws arising from social custom, rulings of kings and judges, cultic and ceremonial practices, moral injunctions based on prophetic oracles. Ultimately all were incorporated in our Pentateuch and constituted the Jewish Law. Deuteronomy manifests very clearly the teaching of the eighth-century prophets on divine judgment. When the prophetic consciousness waned after the Exile, the Law began to take its place. God who had spoken to the fathers through the prophets now spoke through the injunctions of his "law." The Law was applied to every aspect of man's life, and, by our Lord's time, the Pharisees and their teachers, the rabbis, were zealous in such detailed application.

In the earlier days, the priests were especially concerned with preserving and declaring the legal traditions. Hence, Aaron and his sons are to teach Israel the divine statutes (Lev. 10:11). The book of Deuteronomy declares that the priests are to teach Israel God's law (Deut. 33:10). Jeremiah and Hosea both associate the law with the priest (Jer. 18:18; Hos. 4:6).

Thus the priests, like the prophets, were types of mediation and promises of the incarnate Lord. They declared God's will to the people as embodied in his statutes. They represented the people before God in the sacrificial aspect of Israel's worship.

IV. The Covenant God of Israel's Faith

The Covenant Model. The central model for Israel's relation to Yahweh was derived in the divine disclosure from the Hebrew understanding of covenant. Found also among other Near Eastern peoples, this form of relationship implied mutual commitment and mutual obligation in the persons related. It applied to the relationships entered into by men and tribes, and the characteristic description is to "cut" a covenant. It created an artificial brotherhood between the parties concerned and thus extended blood kinship outside its natural limits. It expressed a common aim, the acceptance of a common will and purpose. To cut a covenant is indeed to make "peace" (Ezek. 37:26). A typical example of a covenant between individuals is that between David and Jonathan (1 Sam. 18:1 ff.). In a covenant, two "souls" are bound together intimately into one whole. Jonathan gives even his clothes and armor to David, for they are extensions of his soul. So David's soul is enveloped in Jonathan's.

When the parties to a covenant are of equal status, the obligations are mutual. When one party is superior, as in the case of a treaty after war, it lays the obligations on the other (e.g., 1 Kings 20:29–34). Such a covenant points the way to the theological usage of covenant. The covenant of Yahweh with Israel is not between two parties on an equal footing. Man cannot bargain with his Creator. So, at Sinai, it is Yahweh who declares, through Moses, his conditions, expressed in the Decalogue. All that the Hebrews can do, under the shadow of a great deliverance, is to accept. They cannot lay any conditions on their Deliverer. God initiates such covenant relationships, and he alone sets the conditions.

The relation of Israel to God shows that Yahweh's bond with his people was not naturalistic but moral. He was no naturalistic ancestor. He had chosen Israel, and Israel chose him. The relationship was moral. Hence the model of husband and wife can be used to describe the divine covenant (Hos. 2; Jer. 3:20), for marriage is a covenant relationship with ethical implications.

The Electing God. This emphasis on choice is important. God had chosen Israel, and he had chosen Israel under no compulsion save that of his own love. Hence it was a free choice. He had set his love on Israel (Deut. 10:15). Israel was not a great people (Deut. 7:7 f.), nor were they chosen because of their uprightness of heart (Deut. 9:4 f.). Israel had nothing by which she could lay claim to such a choice. Yahweh chose her freely out of all nations.

The vocabulary of this divine election is various. God "chooses" Israel (Isa. 43:10; 44:1). He "knows" Israel (Amos 3:2; Hos. 5:3), as one person knows another person, especially his wife. He "buys" Israel (Deut. 32:6; Ex. 15:15 f.; Psalm 74:2).

The election is carried back in quite early traditions to Abraham (Gen. 15:7; 28:13 f.; Josh. 24:2 f.). It is more often associated by the prophets with the exodus out of Egypt (Amos 2:10; 3:2; Hos. 11:1; Ezek. 20:5 ff.; Deut. 32:10). Because the two traditions belong to different historical groups among the Hebrews, the difference is a historical one. For the tribal groups in Egypt, the Exodus became the focal point. For other groups, the memory of Yahweh went back to Abraham and his calling of Abraham was more central. The point is that the God of Israel is an electing God. The covenant structure of Israel's life was within Yahweh's free choice of his people.

The Love of Yahweh—Electing Love and Loyal Love. Yahweh's self-disclosure to Israel centers in his love. Here two Hebrew words are involved. The first is generally translated love, but it carries with it the connotation of choice or election. It is used especially in the book of Deuteronomy, but we find it also in the prophets (Deut. 7:6 f.; 10:15; Hos. 11:8 f.; Ezek. 16:8). The word carries the sense of preferred. Its antonym is "hate" which implies, not active hatred, but "not preferred." Yet such preference or choice springs out of Yahweh's innermost nature. Love is the essence of his personal being, shrouded though it be in mystery. Yahweh is continually giving himself and seeking out his beloved, a preview of that New Testament declaration that God is love. Hence we

have the God-given models of father and son and of marriage which run throughout the Bible (Hos. 11:1; Ezek. 16).

The second word is variously translated loving-kindness, steadfast love, loyal love. The last two translations are most frequent renderings in the RSV. The word carries the idea of faithfulness or loyalty and is frequently coupled with words translated "faithfulness" (e.g., Deut. 7:9). It is also intimately bound up with the covenant model—it is covenant love. At the human level, the two parties of the covenant pledge to remain loyal or faithful to one another. They will show steadfast love, e.g., David and Jonathan.

At the divine level, God's love in the covenant has this same quality of steadfast faithfulness (Isa. 54:10; Dan. 9:4). Yahweh will abide by his covenant and remain faithful to his people (Hos. 2:18 f.). This is the basis of God's saving activity. Although Israel fails to keep the covenant, it remains his people, even in its rebellion. Hence, because he is faithful, he will seek them out. His steadfast love, grace, will not fail (Hos. 2; Jer. 2:2 f.; 3:1–4; 31:20). On Yahweh's side, the covenant is unconditional. Once more there is presaged the New Testament disclosure of divine grace.

Yahweh Is Righteous. Yet the Old Testament men were sure that Yahweh is a righteous God. The word righteous is based on a forensic model. Righteousness is a forensic quality. It makes someone a just judge. Generally the word describes conformance to a standard or norm. The "paths of righteousness" are paths conforming to the right way, and the "sacrifices of righteousness" are those that conform to the ritual regulations (Psalms 23:3; 4:5; 51:19). The word righteousness is often associated with judgment, the sentence of a judge. Hence it can be called justice. At the religious level, a righteous act is one which conforms to God's law or justice.

For the Hebrew, justice or righteousness is the standard which God has set up in his world. In his dealings with men, he abides true to his statutes (Deut. 32:4). His norm is set forth in the ethical demands of the prophets, including the Decalogue.

Now this norm springs from God's innermost character. In his judgments he abides true to himself. He acts in accordance with his own nature. He is true to himself, and he expects his creatures to be true to those demands which express his innermost being. He will not deviate, and he requires that they do not (Zeph. 3:5). On this his judgment of them is based. His righteousness is the dynamic quality of his character. It is seen in his acts.

Just here the prophetic problem was brought to a focus. God is love, and he demands that his people conform to that love. But Israel is a rebellious and wayward people. They will not obey. Indeed, they seem unable to obey. Therefore they are under his judgment. Yet he is also love. Somehow love must find a way whereby God can be true to himself as love and also as one who demands conformance to his norm. Here is the seed of the New Testament vision of the divine grace in Christ, for grace is love meeting its own demands in the person of our Lord.

The Holiness of God. The men of the Old Testament were aware that at this point they touched the divine mystery. Righteousness and love met in the otherness of God. His ways were not their ways, nor his thoughts their thoughts (Isa. 55:8). God was other than his creature. This mystery and otherness of God was expressed sometimes in dimensional terms. God inhabited eternity (Isa. 57:15). His palace was above the firmament (Psalm 104:2–3). The dimensional model is also matched by the term holiness. God is the Holy One throughout Isaiah. The word holy describes God's innermost nature. Other persons and objects are holy only because they are appropriated to, dedicated to, God's service and used by him—the sabbath, the firstborn, the priest, the shrine, even Israel and the heavens.

"Holiness" thus expresses the mysterious otherness and transcendence of God. It places God in an exclusive category and discloses the chasm between God and man. God is Spirit and man is flesh (Isa. 31:3). God clothes himself in mystery, veiling his glory in the cloud, as in Isaiah's inaugural vision. Before such a disclosure of moral transcendence, man falls down, stricken by the vision, and confesses his creaturely frailty and moral weakness (Isa. 6:5; Ezek. 1:28). Thus the holiness of God in the great prophets has moral content. It describes the uniqueness and otherness of the divine love and righteousness.

Because of this moral transcendence, God will have ways of dealing with a rebellious people in which his demands will yet be met and his love will triumph. They will yet be his people.

V. The People of the Living God

The Covenant Structure of Israel's Life. The covenant model of relationship to Yahweh characterizes the life of the Hebrew people. The covenant idea is centralized in the covenant relationship of Sinai, established through the prophetic consciousness of Moses. To this the preexilic prophets continually return as the norm for their understanding of Yahweh and his purpose (Amos 3:2; Hos. 2:15; 11:1; Jer. 31:30). This covenant was renewed in the formation of the tribal league at Shechem (Josh. 24). On the side of Yahweh, it was unconditional. He would steadfastly abide by it. On Israel's side, it was conditional upon Israel's obedience. If they contracted out of it and transgressed the covenant, their act was treachery and rebellion, but they were still God's people (Hos. 8:1; Isa. 1:2,4; Jer. 3:20).

Within this covenant structure of Sinai, other covenants were set. The moral conditions of Sinai were met, in the covenant tradition which goes back to Abraham, by Abraham's faith (Gen. 15:6,18). Once more it is bound up on Yahweh's side with an unconditional promise. Abraham's seed shall become a great nation and through them all the nations shall invoke blessing (Gen. 12:2 f.; 18:18; 22:17 f.). This divine promise, Israel could never forget.

Again, within this covenant there was the unconditional royal covenant with David and his descendants (2 Sam. 7:13–16; 23:1–39; Psalms 89:35 ff.; 132:17 f.). God had chosen the Davidic line, and, however much it failed him, he would establish his Davidic King upon the throne. The king was a sacral person. He represented both God and the people. His righteousness, his right relation to God, guaranteed the righteousness of his people. If he was unrighteous, the people were unrighteous (Psalm 72). Associated with this kingship motif, many scholars suggest that there was an annual new year festival of covenant-renewal, in which the king played a significant part. Many psalms support this.

The Nature of Sin. That Israel dealt treacherously with Yahweh and continually broke the covenant was the theme of the great prophets. Because the covenant was with the nation, the prophets were more concerned with corporate than with individual sin before the Exile. The most characteristic words by which they described Israel's waywardness are translated usually as sin and transgression. The first word occurs frequently and means fundamentally deviation from the ethical standard set by Yahweh's demands in the covenant (Deut. 19:15; Ex. 32:32,34; Lev. 4:3). It is thus less concerned with the inward aspect of sinfulness than with external behavior. Intercourse with God is conditional upon obedience, and this is manifested in man's acts. Israel has deviated from the right way. Such "sin" could be unintentional; wrong behavior does not necessarily spring from a wrong motive. "Sin" applies to acts and is used often in the plural.

The other significant word occurs frequently in verbal form. Often translated transgression and to transgress, it is better rendered rebellion and to rebel (Amos 4:4; Hos. 14:9; Isa. 1:2,28; 43:27; 44:22; 50:1; 53:5,8; Jer. 2:29). Here we have moved beyond legal stipulations to personal attitudes. Sin becomes rebellion against God, an arrogant opposition of the will, of the whole man, to Yahweh's gracious claims. It

relates to the inward spirit. So Israel has "the spirit of whoredom" (Hos. 4:12; 5:4).

The most profound analysis of sin is contained in the Garden of Eden story (Gen. 3). The man of the story stands as a representative figure for all humankind. The woman's suggestion to him: "You shall be like God" holds the key. Man is tempted to take his life and its powers into his own hands. Partly from pride in himself, partly out of fear that God will not manage things as well as he can, he succumbs to sinful arrogance. The sequel to the man's rebellion is equally significant. In symbolic fashion, a picture is painted of the dire results of man's rebellious motivation. He finds himself back in the wilderness out of which God called him, with its meaninglessness and frustration and separation from God. The man cannot even return to that fellowship with God which the life in the garden symbolizes. The barred gate and the angel with the flaming sword stand in his way.

Judgment and Repentance. Salvation and grace are displayed within Hebrew history against a background of judgment. History provides the arena within which Yahweh is actualizing his intention and bringing his covenant relationship to its consummation. Yet history was also the scene of Israel's rebellion. Treachery to the covenant must inevitably bring dire consequences. The great prophets were very aware of the element of judgment in history. We find it too in the Deuteronomic history writings (Deut., Josh., Judg., 1 and 2 Kings), which especially were influenced by prophetic insight. Behind the judgment is the divine wrath (Deut. 1:34; 9:18 f.). Assyria is the rod of God's anger (Isa. 10:5 f.). God gives his people into the hands of Babylon in his wrath (Isa. 47:6). In this divine attitude of rejection, God gives men over to the forces of nature and history (Psalms 21:9; 89:38; 90:11). Such wrath was especially directed against the covenant people, but it also operated against the foreign nations especially those used as instruments of the judgment on Israel (Isa. 10:5–19).

The divine judgment on Israel was effected through historical forces like Assyria and Babylon or through natural forces like famine, drought, locusts, pestilence (cf. Amos 4:6–11). In preexilic thought the major emphasis was corporate—nation (Amos 9:1–4) and family (Hos. 1:4; Ex. 34:7). Yet there was also the individual emphasis, although even here the family was also involved, e.g., Amaziah (Amos 7:17). With the Exile and after, the emphasis moved from the group to the individual. The popular proverb: "The fathers have eaten sour grapes and the children's teeth have been set on edge" was attacked by both Ezekiel (ch. 18) and Jeremiah (31:27,30). Every man shall die for his own iniquity. This individual emphasis is echoed in Deuteronomy 24:6. Yet even so, the innocent are involved with the guilty and the corporate aspect remains. A ruler's unrighteousness may bring disaster to his people. The element of wrath and judgment remains as a permanent aspect of the biblical witness.

Yet this judgment had an evangelizing aim. The judgment was concerned to bring Israel to repentance. This word repentance had an active connotation. It did not mean mere feeling but an active turning of will. Repentance meant a return to Yahweh in active obedience to his covenant demands (1 Kings 8:48–50). It was an act of will and involved a confession of sin, an act of penitent submission, and a turning away from idolatry (Hos. 14:2–3). On such a basis, man could appeal for the divine pardon (Psalm 51:1,17). God's last word is mercy, and so we find the prophets pleading with Israel (Amos 5:14; Hos. 10:12; Isa. 30:18).

Forgiveness and Salvation. The three Hebrew words for forgiveness are translated in various ways, but generally convey the sense of pardon with the accompanying removal of guilt (Ex. 34:9; 2 Chron. 30:18). Such divine forgiveness is grounded in the divine magnanimity (Isa. 55:7–9), yet the moral conditions must be met. Israel must ardently seek forgiveness. Once it has truly repented and its heart has been renewed, God's pardon is sure (Jer.

31:34). Always forgiveness means restoration to the covenant relationship with Yahweh.

The word salvation in the Old Testament seems to have little to do with sin and thus not to have a spiritual connotation. We need to remember, however, the intimate relationship of the outward and the inward in Hebrew thought. Man's psychosomatic nature meant that inward rightness with God had the external concomitants of health and prosperity—a belief that later raised real issues for men like the author of Job! So, too, with the nation. Rightness with God meant national prosperity and peace. Hence salvation from external enemies could also signify salvation at the spiritual level—a restoration to the covenant relationship. In this sense some passages speak of Yahweh saving Israel out of the hand of foreign nations (Ex. 14:30 f.; 1 Sam. 10:18).

All earthly saviors, such as kings and judges, are effective only because they derive their power from Yahweh. They triumph only in his salvation (Psalm 20:5,6). Such salvation, when it comes at God's hand, means peace, a characteristic covenant word implying health, wholeness, prosperity. Salvation, however, discloses its inner and spiritual aspect in the Psalms. Here the emphasis falls, not so much on material blessings, as on spiritual fellowship with God (Psalms 69:1,3; 31:1,2,5). The saved individual knows the joy of God's presence in his life.

Beside the word salvation, we have the two words which carry the idea of redemption. One word actually is better rendered "to ransom," although it is usually rendered "to redeem." Closely bound up with it is the noun ransom. The emphasis on the ransom paid is found in Isaiah 43:3. Israel has been redeemed and Yahweh has paid the ransom. Most often, however, the thought of a ransom price disappears (Deut. 9:26). Here, too, there is a movement from the nation as a whole to the individual; e.g., Psalms 34:22; 49:15.

Once more it is the outward that is emphasized. Only in Psalm 130:8 is redemption specifically related to iniquity and sin. Other passages emphasize deliverance from outward calamity, and yet such deliverance betokens forgiveness and restoration to the covenant relationship.

The other word for redemption is much more theologically significant. It carries the idea of the kinsman-vindicator, one who plays the kinsman's part and fulfils the kinsman's obligations. He redeems his kin from slavery (Lev. 25:48 f.). Boaz, in a similar role, redeems the land and saves Ruth's family from extinction (Ruth 4:1–11). Yahweh himself is the kinsman-vindicator of the hapless Job, even after the latter's death (Job 19:25). Second Isaiah uses the word frequently of Yahweh (e.g., Isa. 44:6,22,24; 52:3). Here we have a promise of the incarnation, an identification of God with man in which God plays the role of kinsman and meets the obligations himself.

The Eschatological Hope. Israel remained stubborn and unrepentant (Hos. 4:16; cf. Jer. 13:23). The Covenant Renewal Festival may well have been held every autumn, but the outward ritual betokened no inward repentance. Indeed, it may well have fostered the idea that all was well. They were God's people still, and he was committed to looking after them! The prophets emphasize this. Jeremiah warns against a false trust in the Temple as a sign of Yahweh's presence among his people (7; 26). Amos tells of those who looked for a glorious future despite their moral waywardness.

The *Day of Yahweh* was a central feature of the prophetic hope. It was that future time which would be full of Yahweh's kingship, the day of his triumph. This hope rests back upon the promise to Abraham. The failure of the annual Day of Covenant Renewal may also have fixed men's eyes on a future Day when the covenant would indeed be renewed and Yahweh's purpose fulfilled. In popular thought, it appears to have been pictured, before the Exile, as a time of glory for Israel. The preexilic prophets, however, from Amos on,

saw it as primarily a day of judgment and purging (Amos 5:18; Hos. 5:9; Mic. 2:4; Isa. 2:12,17; 7:18 ff.; 10:3; 13:9–11,13; Zeph. 1:7,8,14 f.; Jer. 25:33). They were, in one sense, prophets of doom. After the Exile, the emphasis changed. The later Ezekiel, Deutero-Isaiah, Joel, and the rest, see the Day of Yahweh as one of salvation and restoration for his people, although the theme of judgment still remains.

The distinction between preexilic and postexilic eschatology is more than one of emphasis. In the preexilic period, the Day of Yahweh would be initiated by historical forces like Assyria and Babylon. Unusual natural happenings may accompany such conquerors, but the historical scene provides the media for God's final act and the consummation takes place on this earth. From the Exile onward, however, human intermediaries give place to a direct divine intervention (e.g., Zech. 14), the transcendence of God is emphasized, abnormal convulsions of nature accompany the act, and the movement is toward an order other than this world as the final consummation. Postexilic eschatology is becoming apocalyptic, although Daniel is the sole true representative of this type of thought. In the Gospels both the historical emphasis of preexilic eschatology and the suprahistorical emphasis of postexilic eschatology are brought together in our Lord's person.

The Day of Yahweh manifests the beginnings of a pattern, various fragments of which were grasped and emphasized by individual prophets. None of them wove these diverse elements into an integrated pattern nor did they grasp the full meaning of what they said. Yet their hope and their promise pointed toward that Christological act in which God acted in his Son to deliver men and reestablish a people of God, the church.

One element in the pattern is the *remnant* which will survive the purging and judgment of Israel (Isa. 1:25 f.; 4:2–4; 10:20–22; Zeph. 2:3; Joel 2:32; Amos 9:8–10; Micah 4:4–7; Mal. 3:16–18; 4:2). Over this restored "people of God" Yahweh will set as king his Messiah, the Anointed One of the Davidic line (Jer. 23:5–6; Psalms 2:6–9; 110). Possessing a special measure of the Spirit of Yahweh, the Anointed One is a human king, whose righteousness will guarantee the righteousness of his people (Isa. 9:6–7; Isa. 11:1–5). He is not portrayed as a man of war. Rather it is Yahweh who will set him on his throne (Psalm 2:6). He rules by the strength of Yahweh (Micah 5:2–4).

The Messiah's rule will be worldwide (Mic. 5:4; Zech. 9:9 f.). Here the attitude toward other nations varies. Sometimes we have a harsh exclusive nationalism. Esther is the supreme example. It was a promise of future Judaism. At other times, we have a missionary spirit manifested in various degrees of intensity. Jonah affords a good example of this, but it is reflected in a lesser way in passages like Malachi 1:11 and Isaiah 19:18–25. Those of all nations will call on the name of Yahweh. Assyria and Egypt will share with Israel in the blessings of the coming time.

The missionary and evangelizing motif is brought to a focus in the figure of the Suffering Servant (Isa. 42:1–4; 49:1–6; 50:4–9; 52:13—53:12). Here, too, we have an eschatological motif. The identification of the Servant varies among scholars. Is he a corporate figure, representing Israel, or is he individual? If the latter, is he some prophetic figure come back to life, such as Moses, or is he messianic? The best solution would seem to lie in the recognition that an individual figure such as a king can yet also be corporate since, in a very real sense, the nation or the redeemed remnant is embodied in him. If so, the Servant, who appears in some poems as individual and others as Israel, may actually be a messianic figure, acting for and with the remnant. We have the loftiest messianic vision of the Old Testament— one who redeems through his suffering and brings the nations near through himself as a guilt offering to Yahweh. The vision of Isaiah 52:13—58:12 is full of evangelical significance. It is the gospel in promise

before it became actual in our Lord.

If through his suffering, the Servant constitutes the remnant, other prophets provide other aspects of the redemptive dimension of "the Day." Ezekiel sees God recreating men from within, giving them a new heart and a right spirit, making it possible for them to be his people (11:19; 18:31; 36:26). Jeremiah sees Yahweh making a new covenant with his people, which will be inward and individual (31:31–34). Ezekiel catches the vision of the valley of dry bones in which a dead Israel is resurrected by God's Spirit (37:1–14). So the promise of a new human spirit within, a new covenant, a creative inbreak of the Holy Spirit points forward to the "fulness of time." This new situation will be individual, however. The people of God will be resurrected upon the basis of God's dealing with the individual rather than with the nation as a whole.

VI. The Living God and Individual Man

The Image of God. The emphasis on the individual was, of course, never absent. But it is significant that the deeper understanding of man's nature came with the Exile, when Jeremiah and Ezekiel emphasized individual responsibility. To this period belongs the final version of Genesis 1:26 ff. with its description of man in the divine image. The two words image and likeness are attempts to safeguard against any idea of exact replica, the second word qualifying the first at this point. For the Hebrew, man was a psychosomatic whole, and as such he is in God's image. Not in the sense of a miniature deity but in the sense of being capable of fellowship with God. The earlier story of Genesis 2 conveys the same idea. Yahweh walks with man in the Garden. Man has a capacity for responsible relationship with God. Furthermore, he shows his divine image in living responsibly with his fellows. Man and woman are made together in the image of God, a type of all social relationships. Man is social and morally responsible. Finally, man's divine image is seen in his authority over his world. He has a capacity for science and technology, for shaping and controlling God's creation.

Along with this solitary reference to man in the divine image, we must place the increased understanding of the place of spirit. By the Exile, spirit was no longer only a description of the invasive and inspiring Spirit of Yahweh. Man also had a "spirit" as a permanent possession. It served the same function as the heart in Hebrew psychology. With it, will and intellect were associated—all man's higher and spiritual qualities had their seat in his spirit (Job 32:8; Isa. 26:9). So there is that in man which gives him kinship with God, who is Spirit.

Human Survival. Once the emphasis upon the individual became central, the issue of life beyond death also became central. As long as God was thought of as relating himself to the individual through the group, an individual could think of himself as surviving death in the life of his descendants. They were extensions of his own personal being through time. So he wanted as many children as possible and, for himself, a span of threescore years and ten (Job 5:25; 2 Sam. 14:7).

As for himself, hemmed in by birth and by death, the Israelite thought of this life on earth as his real existence. Beyond death, he still had a vague degree of existence in Sheol. This subterranean cavern was the whole which embraced all family graves. To it men went as "shades," as "weakened ones," as "souls" emptied out of their vitality and capacity for real living. Here all moral and social distinctions ceased (Job 3:17 ff.; cf. Ezek. 32:18–32). The dead know nothing (Eccl. 9:4 ff.). There can be no worship of God in Sheol (Psalm 6:5). God's covenant love does not operate there (Psalm 88:10–12). The grave is the vestibule of Sheol, the land of darkness, corruption, and the worm (Job 10:21 f.; 17:14 ff.). Real life ends in death, and Sheol is almost nonexistence.

But once the emphasis on the individual became central, two problems arose—un-deserved suffering and individual survival. No longer could a man blame his suffering upon the sins of his fathers (Ezek. 18); nor could he think of survival in his children. Job deals with both problems. The undeserved suffering of righteous Job is met by three answers. His orthodox friends say his suffering must be because *he* has sinned. He knows this is not true. In the end Job faces the awful majesty and mystery of God and finds comfort in his belief that God understands (42:1–6). This is the second answer. Suffering must be left with God, who must have a meaning in it. So there comes the third answer, hidden from Job, and contained in the prologue. He must suffer to prove that his faith is not dependent upon outward prosperity. Job shows in the drama that he loves God for God's own sake.

Bound up with the second answer is the first glimmer of personal survival. Job will die and go down to Sheol, but in the end God will remember him. Yahweh will call Job from the grave and, apart from his skin, he will see God and be vindicated (14:13–15; 19:25–27). This vague expression of hope gained content in the divine disclosure. Since man is a psychosomatic whole, this hope is not immortality of the Greek soul, but resurrection of the personal whole. We find this expressed, after the Exile, in Isaiah 25:6–8; 26:19; Daniel 12:2. In two Psalms, the key is given. Man survives death because he is in fellowship with God here and now (49:15; 73:23 ff.). So the way was prepared for the New Testament faith. The trumpet call of hope sounded for the pious Hebrew as this idea was given individual significance.

VII. God the Creator

The Hebrew's concern with Yahweh as Saviour of Israel carried with it implications about the origin of both man and his world. At the Exodus, Yahweh had created Israel a nation. He had shown himself to be Israel's Redeemer through the vicissitudes of its history. Deutero-Isaiah, picturing the return of Israel from the Babylonian Exile, sees Yahweh leveling up and transforming the desert that his people may safely return (Isa. 42:14 ff.; 55:10 ff.). This prophet combines the model of Creator with that of Redeemer in his description of Yahweh (Isa. 43:1,14 f.). The implicit logic of the divine disclosure would appear to be that he who can remake nature must have originated nature.

Prior to the Exile, the way had already been prepared for this faith by the shaping in Israel's tradition of the creation sagas of Genesis 1:1—2:4a and 2:4b–25. However much influenced by the creation stories of the surrounding peoples, the Hebrew sagas are filled with the revelatory content of the divine disclosure to Israel. The theistic emphasis replaces all naturalistic association. The whole framework of creation ideas has been historified and lifted up into Israel's historical experience of the living God. Yahweh's creation of Israel at the sea of reeds becomes the historical base. Here he acts in the midst of chaos to produce his people, just as initially he shaped the chaotic deep and formless void to produce his ordered world (Isa. 51:9 f.).

The creation story of Genesis 1 belongs to the P or Jerusalem tradition and received its present form roughly in the same period as Deutero-Isaiah conducted his ministry. Both the story and the prophet use a word translated "create." Unlike the words translated "made" and "formed" (RSV) this verb is used only with God as subject. It is never qualified by reference to any preexistent material out of which the entity is created. Implicit, but not explicit, is a faith in God as absolute Creator. Creation is initially "out of nothing." Genesis 1:1 paints a picture of God shaping the chaos: this theme of the struggle of Yahweh with the formless deep is an abiding element in Old Testament thought. But when pushed at this point, the Hebrew mind would have confessed that even the chaos existed by God's will.

Furthermore, God's creation of the world and of man is an act of will, his active presence in the developing cosmos. God speaks and the world becomes. Just as the uttered word is an extension of the speaker's personal being, so God's word is God extending himself in creative act, his immanence in his creative order—hence John 1 is grounded in Old Testament thought. Yahweh's Spirit likewise broods over the chaotic deep (Gen. 1:1). God's transcendence is thus matched by his immanence. He is involved with his creation.

This immanence of God accounts for the Hebrew concern with the vertical dimension of depth and height rather than the horizontal dimension of physical causation which preoccupies modern science. Where the contemporary scientist looks for causal or observable relations between the entities of the world, the Hebrew was concerned with the relation of such entities to Yahweh (cf. Hos. 2:21 f.). All things, including man and his "times," leaned back directly upon God. Even a miracle or "wonder" was not a break in God's fixed laws, a divine "break-in," but a special manifestation of God's gracious presence which at the same time was everywhere ordering Yahweh's world. A wonder could be normal or abnormal, the formation of the embryo (Psalm 139:14), a thunderstorm, or an extraordinary event (Gen. 18:14). The Hebrew did not recognize the sharp division between the natural and the supernatural which has raised so many questions in our own time.

For Further Reading

EICHRODT, W. *Theology of the Old Testament.* Vols. I and II. Philadelphia: Westminster Press, 1961, 1967.

JACOB, E. F. *Theology of the Old Testament.* Trans. A. W. HEATHCOTE and P. J. ALLCOCK. New York: Harper & Brothers, 1958.

KOHLER, L. *Old Testament Theology.* Trans. A. S. TODD. Philadelphia: Westminster Press, 1957.

ROBINSON, H. W. *Inspiration and Revelation in the Old Testament.* Oxford: Clarendon Press, 1946.

————. *Religious Ideas of the Old Testament.* London: Gerald Duckworth & Co., Ltd., 1956.

RUST, E. C. *Salvation History.* Richmond: John Knox Press, 1963.

Contemporary Approaches in Old Testament Study

JOHN I DURHAM

The study of the Old Testament today is both vigorous and extensive in approach. The contemporary scholar must recognize that he is indebted to the scholars who have labored before him, and that he is a part of a continuing process of research and research-testing. But he should also recognize, as have those before him, that his word will be no final word; biblical study above all convinces the student of the living quality of the word of the God who continues to speak.

It is the purpose of this article to describe in brief compass the basic avenues of approach in contemporary Old Testament study. Because of limitations of space, little can be said of the history of these approaches. For the same reason, details of biblical research in the use of these approaches must be omitted. In the pages which follow, the fundamental problems, methods, and resources of current Old Testament study are enumerated and briefly treated under three basic categories: (1) the text of the Old Testament as we have it; (2) how this text came to be; (3) aspects of the meaning of the text.

I. The Approaches to the Text of the Old Testament

The Old Testament is a book, and at once a library of books. It is of great importance to three major religions of the world. No original copies of it, however, are known to exist, and there are many and differing versions of its text. Further, it was composed over a long period in a language which, though once alive, long ago ceased to be a living language. It is therefore appropriate that study of such a book should begin first with the text itself and then proceed to a word by word understanding of what the text says.

1. Textual Criticism of the Old Testament

Textual criticism or lower criticism attempts the most accurate reconstruction of the text which is possible, with attention to its earliest known form and the history of its transmission from earliest times to the present. Its object is to approach as closely as possible the purest and most original form of the Old Testament text.

With exception of a little more than nine chapters,[1] this text is written in the Hebrew language. Across the gamut of the 39 books which constitute the Old Testament, the style and quality of the Hebrew original varies considerably, a fact which is hardly surprising if one remembers that the Old Testament is the creation of many inspired minds across a period of as much as twelve to fifteen hundred years.

The state of preservation of this Hebrew text also varies considerably from book to book and sometimes from section to section within a given book. The task of the textual specialist is both complicated and made possible by the fortunate heritage of a variety of traditions of the Hebrew text of the Old Testament, both as a whole and in its various parts. He must seek to arrive at the best approximation of the Old Testament as it was originally compiled, and he does this by a painstaking analysis of all the versions available to him: first of all, the Hebrew versions, and then other ancient versions which are translations of the original Hebrew into such languages as Greek or Aramaic or Syriac or Latin.

In the search for a pure text, the specialist is confronted with omissions, scribal errors, and other corruptions which crept into

---

[1] Ezra 4:8—6:18; 7:12–26; Dan. 2:4—7:28; Jer. 10:11, and occasional words are in the Aramaic language.

the biblical text during the process of transmission. Since the words of the Hebrew text were originally written without vowels and without punctuation, some manuscripts preserve the addition of the wrong vowel points and improper division of words and even sentences. In some cases, letters and words have been omitted; in other cases, added.

It is the task of the specialist in textual studies to take account of all such errors and omissions, and to reconstruct as accurately as possible, on the basis of a comparative analysis of all available textual evidence, the Hebrew text which must have been. In some instances, the textual critics have been unable to make a single reconstruction which is fully satisfying. In these cases, the reader may be presented with a choice.[2]

It is apparent in what has been said that study of the text of the Old Testament must be a continuing study. This is demanded not only by the presence of new evidence but also by the need for a periodic reexamination of old evidence. Textual research can be ended only when an original text is discovered and then established as such, and this has not yet happened in the history of the biblical text.

Nor is this approach in contemporary Old Testament study one which does not offer a continuing challenge. The growing collection of scrolls and scroll fragments from the area of the Dead Sea and the expansion of resource materials for textual analysis in the age of the computer offer the textual scholar a wider field than ever. The Privilegierte Württembergische Bibelanstalt continues to make needed revisions in the standard critical edition of the Hebrew Old Testament, carrying forward the work of R. Kittel and his able successor, the late Paul Kahle. The Hebrew University Bible Project has been under way for 12 years, and has now published its first sample of a new and much needed critical edition of the Hebrew Old Testament.[3] The fact that this publication presents no less than eight closely printed pages of notes on four chapters from the book of Isaiah is clear testimony of the lively state of current Old Testament textual study.

It should be noted, finally, that the text of the Old Testament is remarkably well preserved, considering the length of its history and the complicated circumstances under which it has been transmitted.

2. Old Testament Philology and Grammatical Understanding

A second approach to the text of the Old Testament, while dependent on lower criticism, moves beyond the limits of research upon what the text is to the realm of what the text says. This approach is concerned with three things: Hebrew vocabulary, Hebrew grammar, and Hebrew thought patterns.

The first step in the translator's approach to Old Testament study must be a working knowledge of Hebrew vocabulary, and this involves consultation of the Hebrew dictionaries. Armed with this fundamental knowledge, the translator may then expand his understanding of a given word or word-family through the use of a concordance and through the study of kindred words and word-groups in related languages. The concordance, listing as it does all the biblical occurrences of a given word, enables one to arrive at his own definition. In the case of most biblical words, it is no difficult task to examine every usage of an important word, a process which often sheds considerable light on meaning. Examination of Old Testament synonyms and equivalent words in languages cognate to biblical Hebrew often extends further the scope of understanding which is brought to the words of the text.

There is much interest in the vocabulary of the Old Testament today. The years 1951–53 saw the publication of a new lexi-

---

[2] Note, for example, the RSV text on Gen. 4:8; Deut. 28:22· 1 Sam. 3:13; Psalm 74:11.

[3] M. H. Goshen-Gottstein, The Book of Isaiah: Sample Edition with Introduction (Jerusalem: At the Magnes Press, 1965).

con of the Old Testament which is nearly 1500 pages in length,[4] and is even now being republished in a fully revised edition. Innumerable articles of varying length dealing with Hebrew words and phrases have been published in recent years, and such scholars as Thorlief Boman and James Barr have joined a lively debate on the broader problems of Hebrew semantics.

Just as the words which compose a text must be known as fully as possible in themselves, so also must their arrangement into phrases and sentences be studied and understood. Hebrew, like English, has lost the case endings which once made distinctive the grammatical function of the major words in a sentence, and so depends often upon word arrangement for specific nuance of meaning. It is therefore important for the translator to understand both the specific forms [5] in which words appear and also the relation of these words one to another within a sentence [6] if he is to translate accurately into another language what the biblical text is really saying.

Contemporary Old Testament study is increasingly taking account of the fact that the classical Hebrew grammarians, despite their laborious attention to detail and their incalculable contribution, often forced Hebrew grammar into Western grammatical forms. This has obscured many of the finer expressions of biblical Hebrew, and there is today a proper concern to remedy this deficiency through an intensive analysis of the forms of Hebrew narrative and poetry and through a comparative study of grammatical form in languages related to biblical Hebrew. Such scholars as G. R. Driver, D. W. Thomas, A. Sperber, C. H. Gordon, M. Dahood, and the late C. Brockelmann are representative of a growing number of Old Testament specialists interested in these problems.

A further concern of contemporary Old

Testament study is related to Hebrew thought. Even when the text has been established and its words appropriately defined, parsed, and related to their context, it is yet possible to produce such translations as, "My juice (sap) was changed into summer's drought" (Psalm 32:4) or, "My insides are bubbling, my liver is spilled out on the dirt" (Lam. 2:11). Here, obviously, there is a need to communicate Hebrew ideas in terms more congenial to modern expression: so the psalm passage might better be read, "My strength was spent as in summer's heat"; and the sentence from Lamentations, "My stomach is in knots, my heart is sinking."

A great deal of attention has thus been given in recent years to the special peculiarities of Hebrew thought, and much of this attention has been stimulated, in one way or another, by the monumental work of Johannes Pedersen,[7] which first appeared in English in 1926 (Vol. I–II) and 1940 (Vol. III–IV). The list of scholars who have approached the understanding of the Old Testament text in this manner would have to include not only such scholars as H. Wheeler Robinson, A. R. Johnson, C. Tresmontant, and G. E. Wright but the Old Testament theologians as well. Their work has in part been to the end that profound ideas might not become ludicrous in literal translation, but rather be understood and then converted to contemporary thought patterns.

II. The Approaches to the Literary History of the Old Testament

Yet another approach of Old Testament study today is concerned with what lies behind the text. Who composed the text originally, and when? In what forms and styles was it composed, and how has it come to the form in which we have received it? This research, called higher criticism, may be broadly described under three categories: study of the sources of Old Testament literature; study of the forms

---

[4] L. Koehler and W. Baumgartner, *Lexicon in Veteris Testamenti Libros and Supplementum* (Leiden: E. J. Brill, 1958).

[5] This is called morphology.

[6] This is called syntax.

[7] *Israel, Its Life and Culture*, Vols. I–IV (London: Oxford University Press, 1959).

of Old Testament literature; and study of the history of Old Testament literature.

1. Source Analysis of Old Testament Literature

The study of the sources of Old Testament literature was begun with the first five books of the Bible, often called the Pentateuch. The Old Testament itself does not designate an author for these books, but tradition has assigned them to Moses, both because of his identification with this material in such references as Deuteronomy 1:1; 2 Kings 14:6; Ezra 6:18; 2 Chronicles 25:4; Mark 12:26; and because early Jewish literature [8] expressly names Moses as their author. This tradition was taken up by the early church, though not without reservation in some quarters.[9] In the first thousand years of the Christian era, however, various verses and short passages were attributed to other authors, and the unity of the Pentateuchal writings was questioned repeatedly. Following the Middle Ages, both the number and the precision of these questions were increased and biblical scholars presented long lists of passages which appeared to be against both Mosaic authorship and Pentateuchal unity.[10]

The approach of contemporary Old Testament study to Pentateuchal criticism is indebted to the questions of these early scholars. But it is indebted also to the work of isolation and analysis of separate sources within the Pentateuch, begun in the eighteenth century and continued with trial, error, and great profit since. It is associated in particular with such scholars as Julius Wellhausen, H. Holzinger, S. R. Driver, A. C. Welch, W. O. E. Oersterley, T. H. Robinson, and more recently, R. H. Pfeiffer, A. Bentzen, C. A. Simpson, C. R. North, Otto Eissfeldt, S. Mowinckel, Martin Noth, G. von Rad, and Karl Elliger.

This approach, recognizing within the

Pentateuch anachronisms, repetition, conflicting accounts, a variety of large and small discrepancies, differing conceptions of God, and several markedly different writing styles, has led most contemporary scholars to the view that the Pentateuch known to us is neither a unity nor, when considered as a whole, a composition of Moses.

This is not to say that Moses made no contribution to the Pentateuch, or that the biblical tradition associating him with the "law" and the "book of the law" is unreliable. While some modern scholars would deny even the historicity of Moses, by far a majority would espouse the view that there are within the Pentateuch both concepts and events which are genuinely Mosaic.

Current Pentateuchal study recognizes, in broad terms, the presence within the Pentateuch of three strata of sources: oral sources, written sources, and redactional or editorial sources. It may be noted, indeed, that a similar source-structure is applied, in varying degrees, to the other Old Testament books.

The possibility that oral traditions underlie the written sources of the Old Testament was advanced with some conviction late in the nineteenth century. It is within the past forty years however that the case for oral sources has been presented most persuasively, particularly by such scholars as H. S. Nyberg, Ivan Engnell, and Eduard Nielsen.

The spoken word had for Old Testament man a much greater significance than it has for men today; it had a dynamic all its own. The spoken word arose in spontaneous creativity from the real situations of life and faith which men faced and to some extent also preserved this same spontaneous creativity. Indeed, it was by the spoken word that most men learned the stories of the faith and the assertions based upon them.

The familiar and thrilling stories of the fathers and their faith, the hymns and devotional poetry, the pungent wisdom of the sages, the personal statements of dependence on a present and active God, the

---

[8] So Philo, Josephus, and the Talmud.

[9] So Porphyry and Celsus, and various Gnostic writers.

[10] So Carlstadt, Masius, Hobbes, Spinoza, and Richard Simon.

speeches of politicians, the oracles and judgments of priests and even the sermons of prophets, spoken to be remembered and respoken *were* remembered and respoken.

Further, the presence of oral sources in the development of the Old Testament was not discontinued when a truly literary stage was begun. Throughout virtually the entire history of the composition of the Old Testament a continuing oral tradition underlay the truly literary development. This oral tradition was of course extensive before writing became more normative with the advent of true nationhood; from that point on it diminished in proportion to the extent to which it was written down. But it never ceased to have an influence until the text of the Old Testament was actually fixed, and for a very good reason: an inspired verbal creativity is at the base of the creative process in the development of much of the literature of the Old Testament. The great prophets referred to such verbalizations, brought to them by the *ruah* or spirit of Yahweh, as "the word of Yahweh." [11]

In their most basic form, these oral units were brief, consisting as they did of single stories, laws, sayings, poems, and the like. In time however, related oral accounts were drawn together, a process which both became a stimulus to the literary stage and was itself augmented by the literary process.

It is to this truly literary period that we are indebted for most of the Old Testament as we know it. When the oral sources first began to be assembled and set down in writing, the results were not entire biblical books as we know them, but rather what are now sections or booklets within our larger books. Alongside these written collections of sources originally oral, there were very probably blocks of material composed for the first time in writing, some inspired by the older oral material, and some without any preliterary stage. There is good reason to believe that some of this written material was very old indeed, antedating even some of the oral sources.

[11] Cf. 1 Kings 22; Mic. 1:1; Isa. 43:1 ff.; Jer. 23:16–22; Ezek. 3:4.

These written collections were then, in time, the sources which came to constitute our Old Testament books. The book of Psalms is very much a case in point for this process. Most of these poems were the creations of the worshiping community in Israel, and were a part of the living oral tradition of the cult. Gradually, collections of these hymns were made, according to purpose, by the influence of special groups of musicians, and on the basis of content. So there are hymns of praise, hymns from the collection of Asaph, special occasion collections, and so on. These collections came in turn to be rearranged according to still other criteria, as for example the somewhat arbitrary five-book division of the biblical Psalter. At this stage, of course, the whole collection was assembled to make up our present book of Psalms.

A similar process is observable in most of the other larger books of the Old Testament, though it is much less obvious in a superficial reading, and though of course the approach to the study of each book must take into consideration that book's special nature.

The third source stratum present in the Old Testament is the result of editorial work. Insofar as extent of material is concerned, this is by far the smallest of the three source layers. At the same time, it is the most determinative source as far as *our* Old Testament is concerned, for it is the source which largely governed the final compilation of the Old Testament which has come to us.

The material added to the Old Testament by the hands of those who compiled it consists in the main of introductory and explanatory notes, transitional sections, and in some instances expositional commentary. The real contribution of the editors lies in their selection and arrangement of available sources. In some instances, their task has been accomplished with such respect for the material and such skill that the hand of the editor is virtually invisible. In other books (and sometimes in the *same* books), the seams are all too obvious. So, for example, the two stories about the creation in the book of Genesis [12] are obviously from different sources—they represent different interests, and the editor has made no attempt to reconcile them. So also, the first verse of the book of Amos represents what a modern publisher would put on the title page of a book, or in the preface.

In some instances, the work of the editors was done with great objectivity; so for example their inclusion of the great "Court History of King David," [13] which relates in a very candid way the succession to the Davidic throne. In other cases, special interests were influential, as in the books of Chronicles, which present a glorified picture of the Davidic dynasty, excluding as much as possible the history of the Northern Kingdom.

2. Form Analysis of Old Testament Literature

Another fundamental approach to the literature of the Old Testament seeks to isolate and analyze the special ways in which this literature is framed. This approach, called form criticism, was suggested early in the present century by Hermann Gunkel. It has been employed with increasing enthusiasm by Old Testament scholars, because it sheds light not only on the literary forms themselves but also on the sources which utilize them and on theological motifs which are recurrent throughout the sources. Following Gunkel's lead have been such scholars as Hugo Gressmann, Leonhard Rost, Albrecht Alt, Martin Noth, Gerhard von Rad, T. H. Robinson, E. A. Leslie, and still more recently Claus Westermann, B. W. Anderson, and Walter Beyerlin.

The question here of course is how the text was composed; i.e., in what forms and styles, quite apart from whether the composition was oral or written. The substance of this approach in Old Testament study lies in the smaller sections and units of

material discernible within the sources which make up our present Old Testament books. Form critical study has revealed, for example, that consistent styles and patterns are employed in prophetic sermons, in priestly blessings and cursings, in expositions of law, in hymnic praising, or in the lament of the individual worshiper throughout the Old Testament. Still further illumination is to be found in the comparison of Old Testament literary forms with those of the literature of Israel's ancient Near Eastern neighbors—a literature which has been provided in great abundance by archaeological excavation.

Thus Gunkel, then Sigmund Mowinckel, and still more recently Artur Weiser, Westermann, and H. J. Kraus have sought a better understanding of the Psalms and the context in life from which they came by placing together psalms of similar content and form. Hymns of praise, for example, are found always to contain an imperative call to worship (105:1-4; 113:1-3) and a creedal basis for praise in worship (105:5 f.; 113:4 f.). Similar work, in the form analysis of Old Testament legal literature, has been done by Alt, G. E. Mendenhall, J. J. Stamm, and R. Smend; in the historical literature, by Alt, Noth, and John Bright; and in the prophetic literature, by H. Wildberger, E. Würthwein, Westermann, H. W. Wolff, and H. Reventlow.

The most valuable advantages of this helpful approach are (1) that it enables us to see the Old Testament in its most basic, kernel form and (2) that it often sheds great light on individual passages by helping us to see them against the larger literary pattern, both within and without the Old Testament, of which they are a part.

Many types of literature and styles of composition are of course present in the Old Testament, and such standard Introductions to the Old Testament as Eissfeldt's, Bentzen's, Weiser's, and Fohrer's set forth extensive lists. For the more general purpose at hand, however, we shall consider three categories: poetry, prose, and the formal declarations of state and cult.

---

[12] Gen. 1:1—2:4a vis-à-vis 2:4b-25.
[13] 2 Samuel 6—1 Kings 2.

Approximately a third of the Old Testament is poetry. This poetry is bound to carefully regulated forms which vary surprisingly little, even across the expanse of time involved in the composition and compilation of the Old Testament. These forms are shared forms, recurrent also in the poetry of the Canaanite, Babylonian, and Egyptian neighbors of the Hebrews. It is the content of Hebrew poetry and not its style which is unique, but the style is important because it both describes and helps interpret content. The Hebrew poet was not free, as poets are today, to improvise new and original forms; the form which his poetry took was in large measure dictated by his subject. It is for this reason that the isolation and analysis of Hebrew poetic form has provided so much help in understanding the Old Testament.

The most important internal characteristic of Hebrew poetry is fortunately one which is not lost in translation. It is rhythm of thought, or parallelism, whereby a second line reinforces by repetition of some kind the point of the first line. There are some complicated elaborations of this basic principle, but the theory involved remains virtually the same.[14]

Recognition of this device is basic to an understanding of the poetry of the Old Testament, but it is one of the most obvious of all poetic devices and is recurrent throughout Hebrew poetry. Meter, and such devices as assonance and onomatopoeia are much more complicated, and of course untranslatable. They are important to the Hebrew specialist, to whom they are rewarding in themselves and for whom they often provide helpful clues concerning textual problems.

Of even greater importance for Old Testament study generally, however, is the study of the external forms of Hebrew poetry. Isolation and analysis of the types of poetry shed great light on each separate type as a species, each separate poem within a given species, and of course upon poetry as a substantial substratum of the Old Testament text.

Some Old Testament poetry consists of songs of many types: work songs (Num. 21:17–18),[15] love songs (Song of Sol. 2:8–14), battle songs (Judg. 5:2–31), songs for funerals (2 Sam. 1:19–27), songs for festive occasions (Isa. 22:13), songs for gibe and mockery (Num. 21:27–30). It presents a great many "sayings": folk proverbs (Ezek. 18:2), riddles (Judg. 14:14), fables (Judg. 9:8–15), aphorisms (Prov. 11:22), terse lessons from the wise teachers of Israel (Prov. 1:7).

There is further the poetry of the cult, a collection scattered throughout the Old Testament and constituting the major portion of the poetry of the Old Testament. In this religious poetry are the priests' formulae of sacrificial ritual (Lev. 9:1–4) and of blessing (Num. 6:24–26) and cursing (Deut. 27:15–19), the oracles (Isa. 14:28–32) and parts of the sermons of the prophets (Amos 3:3–11), the great praising hymns of the responsive confessional psalms (Psalm 95:1–7), the poems of individual lamentation and faith-assertion (Psalm 13), and a variety of special occasion hymns and psalms (Psalm 45, celebrating a royal wedding).

Each of these poetic types has a form all its own, one which is readily recognizable and usually varied only slightly throughout its occurrences. The study of a given form in repeated usage sheds great light not only on the form as a pattern but also upon the individual poems which use that form.

Nor has such comparative study of literary style been restricted to the poetic literature of the Old Testament. While poetic forms are easiest to identify, use of this same procedure has revealed recurrent literary patterns in Old Testament prose as well. The most used prose literary type is the narrative, which is itself subdivided

---

14 See, for example, Psalm 24:1–3, where each successive verse contains the same idea twice. Or cf. Proverbs 14:28, Psalm 14:1–2, Isaiah 1:3 for variations of the principle.

15 Examples could of course be multiplied, but only one is given for each type due to limitation of space.

into such varied narrative forms as those which describe the beginnings of the peoples (Gen. 27) and institutions (Gen. 28:10–22); those which preserve fables (2 Kings 14:9) and popular stories (Judg. 15: 1–8); and those which recount history in a more official manner (2 Sam. 9—20).

Shorter prose types exist in the speeches of politicians (2 Sam. 15:1–6); the sermons of the priests and prophets (Deut. 4); such social and business documents as letters (1 Kings 21:8–10); contracts (1 Kings 5:2–9); genealogical (Gen. 5) and personnel (2 Sam. 8:15–18) lists; editorial comments (Jer. 1:1–3); but most of all in what might be termed the formal declarations of state and cult. In this category belong the extensive legal literature of the Old Testament, the regulations and instructions of the cult, the royal notices and edicts of the kings, the laws of the land, and the commandments of God. Here, too, however each type has its own distinctive form; and here, too, kind of content dictates form to be employed.

3. Traditio-Historical Analysis of Old Testament Literature

A third broad approach of contemporary Old Testament study combines the results of both source-research and form-analysis in an attempt to arrive at a literary history of the Old Testament. The concern here is to set the Old Testament into historical context and, using all available evidence, to reconstruct its sequential biography.

Basically, the question in this case is authorship, but the answer is a very complex one for the Old Testament. It must be concerned with the origin of both the content and the forms in which this content is expressed, the time and circumstances of the composition of the various parts of the Old Testament, and its compilation into the array of books which we know. Nor can this question be answered in a traditional manner, for the Old Testament is the product of many authors, not a few of whom have remained completely anonymous.

Much helpful work has been done by scholars toward the reconstruction of an Old Testament literary history, and this work can aptly be called contemporary, since most of it has been done in this century. These efforts may be associated first of all with Hermann Gunkel and Hugo Gressmann, both of whom emphasized the need to study Old Testament literary forms and motifs in relation to their ancient Near Eastern context. Building upon their research, and utilizing the extensive discoveries of modern biblical archaeology, such scholars as Johannes Hempel, Otto Eissfeldt, Martin Noth, Gerhard von Rad, Gustav Hölscher, Adolphe Lods, Artur Weiser, and still more recently, H. H. Rowley, A. Robert, A. Feuillet, P. Auvray, G. W. Anderson, S. Sandmel, L. Rost, and G. Fohrer have sought to recover the "situation in life" of the Old Testament writings.

These scholars trace the history of the literature of the Old Testament from a preliterary stage, where it existed in succinct oral traditions, through an intermediary and truly literary stage of written composition to a final stage of editorial composition. From the beginning of the process, and throughout its progress, the influence of the peoples and nations from whom the Israelites sprang and with whom they lived is recognized. But from the beginning the distinctive stamp of a people whose genius was the presence of their God is discoverable, recasting content and utilizing form and style for higher purposes and more profound statement.

From the beginning of transmission and composition in writing, the anonymous hand of the editor is seen as present, arranging, rearranging, providing setting and context, sometimes restating. The first task of these editors, it is thought, was to collect and to preserve in the best possible form what came into their hands. But they also felt keenly the need to make the literary heritage as meaningful and relevant to their time as they possibly could, and in this concern, they sometimes made the text more difficult for later generations.

It is also true of course that this growing

text sometimes became inadvertently complicated through mistakes in copying and transmission or even through loss of a part of a manuscript. In some cases, the material which the scribes were given to copy was ill-organized or even in fragmentary form. This is particularly the case, of course, with the prophetic books, whose frequent disarray often makes them very difficult to grasp.

It is precisely for such reasons that contemporary Old Testament study has so concerned itself with the history of Old Testament literature. And while the concern has meant much painstaking work, it continues to pay great dividends in understanding. Further, the overall result of this study has both underscored the providential nature of the composition and preservation of the Old Testament text and revealed the richness of the Old Testament in many new dimensions.

It must not be forgotten, finally, that the approaches of Old Testament study outlined above are all tools employed for a purpose. That purpose is a better understanding of the Old Testament which we have. To gain such an understanding, it is of course necessary to consider the Old Testament in its constituent parts—the larger literary sources, the books which contain them, and the smaller units which comprise the books.

But the Old Testament is itself a book. Further, the arrangement of the text in the form in which we have received it is also to a purpose. As illuminating as the study of individual sources and literary forms continues to be, we must at the same time keep in view the whole text as an end product. Just as those who composed the oral traditions and those who composed the written sources were inspired, so also were the compilers and editors who gave our Old Testament its present form.

III. The Approaches to the Meaning of the Old Testament

Armed with information about what the Old Testament text is, how it came to be,

and what it says, a final approach in Old Testament study is concerned with what the text means. This concern is manifest, furthermore, in two directions: (1) the meaning of the text for those who composed it and for their contemporaries, and (2) the meaning of the text for man today. Sometimes of help in this quest is a consideration of what the text has meant through history to those who have read and studied it. And always of interest, because the Old Testament is so large a part of our Bible, is a consideration of its meaning for man in every age.

1. The Meaning of Old Testament Worship

During the second half of the last century, and well into the first quarter of the present one, there was a great deal of interest among students of the Old Testament in the nature and history of Israel's religious institutions. The contemporary fascination with Old Testament theology, which may conveniently be dated from the appearance, in 1933, of the first volume of Walther Eichrodt's *Theologie des Alten Testaments*, eclipsed this interest. Recently, however, there has arisen a new interest in the religion of the Old Testament. While no single scholar has had so profound an influence on this revival as has Sigmund Mowinckel, many others have made very significant contributions to it. Among them are R. de Vaux, H. J. Kraus, H. Ringgren, Th. C. Vriezen, and H. H. Rowley, all of whom have published major works on this subject since 1960.

While it is true that these scholars are of necessity concerned with the history of Old Testament religion and its forms of worship, they are also much occupied by its meaning for the Israelite faith and for contemporary biblical understanding.

Thus the approach to the meaning of Old Testament worship seeks to isolate, from the periods to which they are indigenous, the forms of Old Testament worship. Once this is done, the meaning of these forms is considered a key to a fuller understanding of the people who employed them and of their conception of the God to whom they directed their worship.

Such a study must of course consider such subjects as the places, rituals, personnel, regulations, times, special ceremonies, equipment, music, and literature of Old Testament worship against its ancient Near Eastern background. Above all, however, it must consider the rationale for this worship.

Nor can this study be made only once and applied then to the entire Old Testament. Since so great an expanse of time and circumstance is involved, the study must be made in context and then assembled in historical survey of the continued evolution of a living religion. But as this is done, New Testament forms of worship and then our own today take on exciting new dimensions of meaning.

2. The Meaning of Old Testament Faith

A second approach to the meaning of the Old Testament is concerned with the meaning of its theology or faith. The objective of scholars here is to discover from the Old Testament text, which is Hebrew man's own affirmation of his faith, what that faith actually was.

No few scholars have made important contributions to this approach, but most important of all are W. Eichrodt and G. von Rad. Eichrodt in particular has had a formative influence on the contemporary exposition of Old Testament faith; but the impact of von Rad's major work, the two volumes of which were published in 1957 and 1960 respectively, is increasingly evident as well. Especially valuable also is the research on this subject of H. H. Rowley, E. Jacob, Th. C. Vriezen, R. C. Dentan, G. E. Wright, G. A. F. Knight, and Norman Porteous.

These scholars recognize that the study of Old Testament theology must first of all concentrate upon the theology of given periods in Old Testament history, each with its own historical circumstances and problems. That is to say, that one must consider the *theologies* of the Old Testament, each

against its own time, before one can consider the *theology* of the Old Testament. They hold that there is, however, a theology of the Old Testament, just as there is a larger biblical theology which it anticipates (and of which, of course, it is a constituent part).

By contrast with the study of Old Testament religion, which is concerned among other things with the methodology and rationale of worship, Old Testament theology is concerned with belief—faith as stated and lived by the people of Israel. Involved in this interest is Hebrew man's concept of God both as he experienced God's self-revelation and also as he made response to this revelation.

Old Testament theology thus deals with such matters as the nature of God in the Old Testament—what is the person of God, what are his attributes, his deeds, how does he make himself known, and what is his purpose and plan? In this process it considers such subjects as the names and titles for God in the Old Testament; the ways in which God reveals himself to men; God's active involvement in the world from creation onward; the basis of God's demands upon man; the understanding of God manifested on different levels of life and at different times; and God's relationship to the whole creation and to all men. In sum it may be said that Old Testament theology is concerned, as its name implies, with the statements of God and about God in the Old Testament.

3. The Meaning of Old Testament History

The study of the meaning of the history of Israel might be called the theologian's approach to Old Testament history, dependent upon the historian's approach but at the same time different from it. The historian seeks, primarily on the basis of what the Old Testament text itself says, and utilizing the invaluable secondary information of the ancient extrabiblical sources and of archaeological and geographical research, to reconstruct the history of Israel. Old Testament history is approached this way in contemporary study, and the excellent books and articles of such men as Albrecht Alt, W. F. Albright, Martin Noth, Johannes Hempel, Kurt Galling, John Bright and G. W. Anderson are the result. Thanks to such work, we are now able to say that we know a great deal of the history of the people of the Old Testament with a high degree of accuracy.

This history remains however a reconstructed history, and one quite different in basic emphasis from the presentation of history in the Old Testament itself. In recent years, scholars have given an increasing amount of attention to the history of Israel just as the Old Testament records it, primarily because of what such a study reveals about Israel's faith. C. R. North contributed one of the earliest studies in this vein, in 1946, and he has been followed by a host of scholars, important among which are R. C. Dentan, Millar Burrows, H. H. Rowley, G. E. Wright, G. von Rad, R. A. F. Mackenzie, and John Bright. There has also been much interest of late in special emphases and styles in the history-writing of the Old Testament, and many articles and monographs dealing with the form critical study of Israel's history have been produced.

The theologian's approach to Old Testament history-writing recognizes that the history presented in the text of the Old Testament has a higher purpose than reportage. It is a history of meaning, a history which has aptly been called salvation history. It is history theologically interpreted, which seeks primarily to set forth God's active and purposeful movement in the life of his people. It is creedal or confessional history, and thus is a very rewarding source in the search for the meaning of the Old Testament.

4. The Meaning of the Biblical Message

A fourth approach to the meaning of the Old Testament is concerned with a meaning which is wider than the Old Testament itself. Indeed, this approach involves the meaning of the Old Testament for the biblical message as a whole and for man in the past, at present and in time to come. This fascinating question has attracted considerable interest in contemporary biblical study, and has provoked no little activity among Old Testament scholars, in part because of its bearing on the important question of the authority of the Old Testament. It involves, in one way or another, nearly every approach to the study of the Old Testament.

Recent biblical scholarship has referred to this subject generally under the broad term "hermeneutics," which essentially involves interpretation. For the Old Testament, this interpretation can be said to involve three levels. First of all, what is the precise meaning of the text itself? What, literally, did the writer intend to say to his own time? This can be determined only on the basis of careful grammatical and historical research.

Second, what is the theological significance of the text in its setting? What is the basis in faith for what the text is saying? What motivated the statement? How is it an expression of the larger theology of which it is a part? It is the theology from which the text springs that unlocks the more universal relevance, the living message of the Word of God.

Third, what is the significance of the text for *biblical* theology, in relation to the New Testament as well as to the Old Testament? It is at this point in particular that the Christian must bring to focus the approaches of Old Testament study and apply them to *biblical* understanding. It is at this point also that the recent discussion of Old Testament hermeneutics has been most lively and provocative, since there is a variety of opinion about how the Testaments stand related. Thus such scholars as G. von Rad and H. W. Wolff suggest a typological connection between the Testaments, with the Old Testament representing the prefiguration, the beginning of which the New Testament is the end. W. Vischer has remained the most thorough exponent of the Christological view: "Everywhere the scripture is about Christ alone." R. E. Brown, J. Coppens, and N. Lohfink have advocated the "fuller sense" lying behind the literal meaning of Old Testament Scripture. Much influenced by von Rad, such scholars as W. Zimmerli, G. E. Wright, and to some extent John Bright espouse a relationship of promise-fulfilment. Along with these scholars, such men as Claus Westermann, B. W. Anderson, F. Bäumgartel, W. Eichrodt, Franz Hesse, W. Pannenberg, James Barr, and Daniel Lys have written important articles or books on the subject.

It is of course a fact that the relation between the Testaments is a very complex one, involving both continuity and discontinuity, and no one interpretative principle thus far suggested is adequate at every point. Essential to a proper understanding of the Old Testament is the honesty of the reader to let it speak its own unique word of God. Equally important for the Christian however is the significance of the message of the Old Testament in view of the presence in his own life of Christ as risen Lord. It is after all the coming of Christ which both fulfil the Old Testament and makes the New Testament truly new. When through the exercise of every approach to the Old Testament text the scholar has come to know it as it was, to know also what it is saying, and what this meant to those who heard or read it first, he must then make it his own by making the most profitable discovery of all: what is it saying to him, in *his* situation, and at *this* time? It is in this process that one begins to know both the unity of the Bible, that Old Testament and New Testament are really one, and also what the Bible is saying to man in every age.

Such, in broad and all too brief outline, are the major approaches of contemporary Old Testament study. These approaches require long preparation and the discipline of a devoted mind. They involve hard and painstaking work—work which is often concerned with the smallest details, even the very letters of the text. But it cannot be forgotten that these small details, these very letters, are a part of the living word of God. It cannot be forgotten that in this text, from the time of its composition, God has not ceased to speak.

Thus, Old Testament study, wielding its tools with loving care and honesty, continues in the pursuit of a purpose which is basically a religious one, a purpose motivated by the same force which compelled those who began the long process with the first composition. It is the perpetual attempt to hear God speaking more and more clearly.

For Further Reading

Ap-Thomas, D. R. *A Primer of Old Testament Text Criticism.* 2d rev. ed. Philadelphia: Fortress Press, 1966.

Auvray, Paul. "Hebrew and Aramaic" in Auvray, Poulain, and Blaise, *The Sacred Languages.* Trans. S. J. Testor. London: Burns & Oates, 1960, pp. 11–71.

Bright, John. *The Authority of the Old Testament.* Nashville: Abingdon Press, 1967.

Hahn, Herbert F. *The Old Testament in Modern Research,* with "A Survey of Recent Literature" by H. D. Hummel. Philadelphia: Fortress Press, 1966.

Jacob, Edmond. *Theology of the Old Testament.* Trans. A. W. Heathcote and P. J. Allcock. New York: Harper & Brothers Publishers, 1958.

Otwell, John H. *I Will Be Your God.* Nashville: Abingdon Press, 1967.

Kock, Klaus. *The Book of Books: The Growth of the Bible.* Trans. M. Kohl. London: SCM Press Ltd., 1968.

Ringgren, Helmer. *Israelite Religion.* Trans. D. E. Green. Philadelphia: Fortress Press, 1966.

Schofield, J. N. *Introducing Old Testament Theology.* Philadelphia: Westminster Press, 1964.

Westermann, Claus. *Handbook to the Old Testament.* Trans. and ed. R. H. Boyd. Minneapolis: Augsburg Publishing House, 1967.

Wright, Ernest and R. H. Fuller. *The Book of the Acts of God.* Anchor Book 222. Garden City: Doubleday & Company, Inc., 1960.

Genesis
Exodus

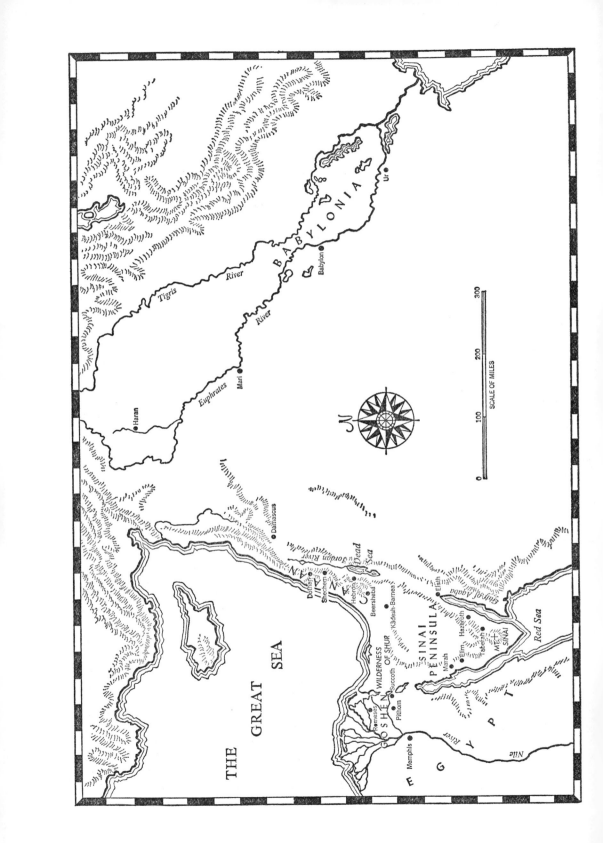

Genesis

G. HENTON DAVIES

Introduction

I. The Task

How does the commentator on the Scriptures approach his task and what attitude does he adopt? How does he deal with a famous book—in the present instance, the book of Genesis, commonly called "the First Book of Moses"?

The first responsibility is to ask: Is this present book of Genesis what the author said or wrote? Of course such a question belongs properly to the book of Genesis in Hebrew, the language in which all but a few words of the book was first written. Our English book of Genesis is a translation. For the moment, then, and in the interests of simplicity, let us keep in mind the original Hebrew book of Genesis. Therefore, the first question to be faced is, Is the text sound? This question must be asked, because we do not possess the author's actual manuscript. We possess only a copy of a copy, and we do not know how many copies have intervened. Errors then and faulty copyings could have crept in. So the Hebrew text has to be examined verse by verse.

The second question arises naturally out of the first. If we are reasonably satisfied that this is what the author said, or wrote, then we must ask: What did he say, and what did he mean when he said it? If we are sure of what he said, we must be equally sure that we know what he meant and that we are able accurately to interpret his meaning. The experienced reader will be aware that it is as easy to read into a book as to read out of it.

In ascertaining the meaning of the book the first of the ancillary questions will be to examine the forms employed by the author(s) to convey his meaning. How did he say it? What particular literary forms carry the context and convey his meaning? He sometimes wrote in poetry as well as in prose. A wide variety of literary forms are employed in the book of Genesis, and these will help us to understand the book.

Some may claim that the task of the commentator is complete when he has established what the original author said and what he meant when he said it. This would apply, I suppose, to a book in isolation. The book of Genesis, however, as we shall see, is both a very international book and one which points to generations beyond its last hero and story. Its international context then, and especially the people and events which it predicts or assumes, compel us to ask about the context of the book of Genesis. What is the relation of this First Book of Moses to the second, the third, the fourth, and the fifth books of Moses? How does Genesis appear the first of the five books of the Old Testament, the Pentateuch?

Further, if Genesis is related to Moses, it must also be related to the prophets and to the New Testament, too. What then is the relation of Genesis to the Pentateuch, to the entire Old Testament, to the New Testament, and indeed to the Bible as a whole? Inevitably the commentator, as he seeks to interpret, will meet passages of great difficulty and doubtful meaning. He will ask, What did the author mean? Thus he will look within the confines of the book and then beyond it in the Bible for the use and meaning of words, sayings, and thoughts occurring in similar passages. In the first place, Scripture unlocks the meaning of Scripture, for Scripture must be compared with Scripture within and beyond the particular passage in question. This principle of comparative interpretation, often overlooked, is quite essential to the understanding of any part of Scripture.

The commentator will receive further help if he is able to obtain answers to the questions: Who wrote the book, and when was it written? Nevertheless, and especially in regard to ancient books, the question of authorship is often of doubtful value. Questions about the authorship and date are very important, where they are practicable, but they are not always practicable in application to ancient books. Genesis in particular possesses such a universal and timeless quality that these questions are not as important as the questions of meaning and intention.

The state of the Hebrew book of Genesis, its scope alike in the original and in translation, the form of its expression, the person or kind of person who wrote it, and when and where he lived, all help us to answer the final questions. What was the purpose in writing? What led the writer to his task? Such a purpose is not stated in the book of Genesis as it is, for example, in the first paragraph of the book of Acts. The name Genesis, "beginning," serves mainly to identify the book, though it secondarily states its purpose. Thus the content and the scope of the book must serve to reveal the author's purpose.

When the attempt has been made to answer all these questions, the ultimate question still remains. Is what he said true? Did it happen like that? Is it historical? Is it still true even if it is not primarily historical in purpose and if all the details were not as

described? The larger part of such questions, however, is not really the task of the commentator. He is primarily concerned with what was said, and what was meant.

The tasks of the commentator, then, make their demand for humility, because the task is enormous and exacting. With all human helps, and with all his own abilities at full stretch, the task still lies beyond his power; and the commentator realizes that without the help of the Holy Spirit the book could never have been written, and could not now be explained.

II. What Is in the Book?

Reconnaissance is the first duty of soldiers—reconnaissance of the land to be gained and held. So the first duty of the commentator is to survey his territory. What is the lay of the land? What does the book of Genesis say? What is the total overall view?

A study of Genesis shows that first and foremost it is a book of personalities. The first book of the Bible is called Genesis—from its first Hebrew word, "In the beginning." Certainly the book describes the beginning of the world, of mankind, of sin and crime, of cities and the vocations of men, and of the geographical distribution of mankind. More particularly the book tells of the beginning of election and blessing, of covenant, of circumcision and a chosen race, and of the twelve tribes of Israel (Jacob).

All these topics, events, and themes are related, however, in a framework of personality. Genesis is a book of narratives or stories about persons. It is the first picture room in the portrait gallery of Holy Scripture.

The first chapter tells the story of the creation in six days. On the sixth, as the crowning work, man and woman appear, being described in their character as created in the image of God and in their destiny as exercising dominion over the created order. The results were at first so satisfactory that God approved and enjoyed all he had made, and then rested on the seventh day (2:1–3).

The second chapter is less a story of creation than a more detailed account of the making of man, of his intended career as a gardener, of the garden and its water supply, and of the making of a wifely companion for the man. The third chapter tells how this first couple committed their first sin and of the consequences of that sin for them and for the natural order. The fourth chapter is a story about the first two sons of the first couple, and how the elder slew the younger because of a quarrel about worship.

From now on life begins to spread rapidly, and we see the world peopled by a notable company of individuals living to very great age, and all their descendants. This portrayal of a consortium of very aged men, almost all contemporary with each other at some part of their life, is a vivid biblical picture of vitality at the beginnings of the human race.

Unfortunately, wrongdoing, that inevitable accompaniment of spreading life, also became manifest. A natural calamity brought about a great flood in which almost all mankind perished. The exceptions were Noah, his wife, and three sons and their wives—also examples of all known forms of life—who escaped in a great boat called an ark specially made for the purpose. The flood and the deliverance of these eight persons were interpreted as a personal intervention by God in a situation that called forth his judgment.

The new humanity sprung from the eight saved persons turned out no better than the first, and they were confused by division and weakened by dispersion through the world. Then a third beginning was resolved upon.

God called a man named Abram out of Ur and then out of Haran and promised him and his wife Sarai a numerous progeny, and a significant destiny in a new and promised land, the land of Canaan. The story of Abram—later called Abraham— lasts from chapters 11 through 25, and has as its most prominent theme, the alternat-

ing hope and despair of an everaging Abram and a barren Sarai—later called Sarah.

Isaac, their son, whose birth is anticipated from chapter 12, is born in 21, but plays a quite minor role until his death is recorded at 35:29. Thus in chapter 22 the story of the proposed sacrifice of Isaac is really a story of Abraham's obedience, and 23 is the story of the purchase of the burial place for Sarah, one of the principal characters of Genesis. In 24 a wife, Rebekah, is found for Isaac from among their own people in Haran. In 25 Abraham dies; but already Isaac's sons, Esau and Jacob, are apparently some fourteen years old, and the story now begins to revolve around them. Chapter 26 is the only chapter in which Isaac is the chief character. In 27:1 he is aged and helpless, the victim of his wife Rebekah and her ambitions for her younger son, Jacob, at the expense of the elder brother, Esau.

Jacob leaves home to go to his mother's and his grandfather's people in Haran. During the account of his journey to the north the story of the dream of Jacob's ladder is told. After his arrival Jacob enters the employment of Laban his uncle and eventually marries the two daughters: Leah, by whom he had six sons, and Rachel, by whom he had his two favorite sons, Joseph and, later in Canaan, Benjamin.

After some twenty years Jacob, now a wealthy man, returned to Canaan, being reconciled with Esau en route. He first established a foothold in the Shechem area, where two of the clans of Jacob, Simeon and Levi, brought disrepute upon the immigrants by treachery. Jacob then journeyed south and, at Bethel, received both a new name, Israel, and the renewal of the patriarchal promise. Further south near Bethlehem, Rachel died giving birth to Benjamin, and was buried there. Jacob reached the Hebron district just in time for Isaac's death and burial, in which Esau also shared.

Chapter 36 is largely concerned with the

descendants of Esau, and 37 sees the beginning of the comparatively long account of the life and adventures of Joseph. In 37 Joseph is discovered at the mercy of his jealous brothers and finds himself transported to Egypt. There he became the trusted steward of an Egyptian nobleman, Potiphar, whose wife nevertheless caused Joseph to be thrown into prison. Subsequently, by various pieces of good fortune he was delivered and made prime minister of the land of Egypt, second only to the king, Pharaoh, himself. Here, in due course, who should present themselves but his brothers, sent by their father Jacob to search for and beg food in Egypt? Joseph recognized them. The story has come full circle, and the brothers are now completely at his mercy.

In these chapters, as almost always in Genesis, the story moves from person to person: Joseph and his brothers with the Ishmaelites and the Midianites (37); Judah and his daughter-in-law Tamar (38); Joseph and Potiphar and his wife (39); Joseph and Pharoah's butler and baker (40); Pharaoh and Joseph (41); Joseph and his brothers again (42—45); Israel's (Jacob's) journey to Egypt (46); Joseph and his family and affairs in the land of Egypt (47); Jacob and his son Joseph and his grandsons, Ephraim and Manasseh (48). This great book comes to its close with the so-called blessing of Jacob, a review of the character and destiny of Israel's twelve sons, and with the death of Jacob and Joseph (49—50).

Adam and Eve, their children, and the long-lived patriarchs; Noah and his children; Abraham and Sarah and Hagar and Lot; Isaac and Rebeccah and Esau and Jacob; Jacob's wives, Leah and Rachel, and sons, especially Rachel's sons, Joseph and Benjamin—are the principal personalities of the book. There is in addition a line of secondary personalities too obvious and too numerous to mention, and beyond these again the names in the genealogies and in the lists of children, clan ancestors, princes, and leaders. Genesis is indeed a gallery of portraits, and all the principal portraits have their accompanying story.

This storybook of persons with their virtues, their follies, and their sins is however punctuated with several memorable and constant themes. Most notable among these are the themes of revelation and of blessing, which call for further consideration.

III. Revelation in the Book of Genesis

The book of Genesis is of course a part of the divine revelation recorded in the Scriptures. So the book is included in the doctrine laid down in 2 Timothy 3:16: "All scripture is inspired by God and profitable for teaching, for reproof, for correction, and for training in righteousness." It is, therefore, profitable to study the theme and terminology of revelation inspired by God in the book of Genesis.

The revelation to Jacob at Bethel is described as such, i.e., by the word "reveal" in 35:7, and the only other occurrence of the same Hebrew word for revelation in Genesis is in 41:25. A synonym "shown" appears at 41:28, and a third term (lit., made known) at 41:39. These last three references make plain the revelation behind Joseph's plans for the ordering of the Egyptian state during the famine crisis (cf. also 40:8; 41:16,32).

Though the technical terms for revelation are thus limited, the sentences descriptive of revelation are far more frequent. Every reader knows that the words, "And God said" punctuate the first chapter of Genesis. In the next two chapters appear the unique words, "And the Lord God said." In chapter 4 the words are, "And the Lord said." These are the principal formulae of spoken, as distinct from enacted, revelation in the Old Testament—so in Genesis. The first of the formulae, "And God said," and the third, "And the Lord said," occur, with exceptions presently to be noted, throughout the book. Thus they occur in chapters 1, 4, 6—9, 11—13, 15—18, 20—22, 25—26, 28, 31, 35, 46, and 48.

The formulae of revelation increase,

however, and become more varied as the following illustrations show: "commanded" (6:22; 7:5,9,16; 21:4); "remembered" (8:1); "the word of the Lord came" (15:1,4); "God spoke" (46:2); "the angel of the Lord . . . said" (16:7–11); "the Lord appeared to" (17:1; 18:1; 26:2,24; 35:9; 48:3); "God said" in a dream (20:3,6; 31:11); "as he had promised" (21:1); "God had spoken" (21:2; 35:13–15); "the angel of God called to" (21:17; 22:11,15); "spoke to me and swore to me" (24:7; 31:29; 50:24); "God who answered me" (35:3); "God will give . . . a favorable answer" (41:16); "God has revealed to" (41:25); God has shown you" (41:39).

Many of the foregoing formulae serve to introduce the very words of God. Thus the first occurrence of "and God said" introduces the first divine words, "Let there be light." These four words, represented by two Hebrew words, are not only the first specific act of creation but the first act of revelation since they inaugurate revelation by creating the possibility and mode of revelation. Revelation is light shown, and discovery is light seen. This first insight must surely have been one of the greatest insights ever made by man, but it was an insight made possible and achieved by a prior act of revelation by God himself. "In thy light we see light." The words "Let there be light" stand at the beginning of Genesis, for they inaugurate Scripture and revelation and indeed make them possible. These words are thus the text, the theme, the clue, and the hallmark of all Scripture.

The last time that one of the revelatory formula occurs in Genesis and is also linked with a new revelation is 46:2–4. (In 48:3 we have a recollection of a revelation made earlier in the life of Jacob.) In 46:2–4 we have the last example in Genesis of God's own words, and they are important because they authorize Jacob's new departure from Canaan and his descent into Egypt and because they confirm Jacob's destiny. They are the link with Exodus and the beginnings of the story of Israel's redemption.

God's first word in Genesis thus inaugurates revelation, but his last word brings into sight the history of redemption.

Between Genesis 1:2 and 46:2–4 the book affords many examples of the ipsissima verba of God. These words are generally brief oracles (e.g., 1:6,9 etc.; 2:18; 12:1–3; 18:26,28 etc.; 28:13–15; but longer examples are given, e.g., 3:14–19; 7:1–4; 9:1–7; 17:4–8, 9–15). The RSV fortunately prints these words of God in quotation marks, so that the reader may understand at once what these quoted passages are intended to be.

Although the divine oracles tend to decrease as the book proceeds, one fact emerges which is of great importance. All the principal stages of the book are inaugurated by these oracles. This has already been shown to be true of creation (1:1–2). God likewise states the terms of man's life in the garden (2:16 f.), also after his expulsion (3:23) from the garden (3:14–19). In the same way God announces the flood (6:13), the conditions of life for the second mankind (9:1–7), and later the confusion and dispersal of that race (11:6–7).

In the same way God's oracle inaugurates his redemptive purpose in Abram (12:1–3,7; 13:14–17; cf. 15:1,4,5,7; 17:1–2, 3–8; 22:15–18). A divine oracle likewise controls the birth of Isaac (18:10), and of Esau and Jacob (25:23). Revelations likewise confirm the place and part of Isaac (26:24) and of Jacob (28:13–15; 35:1,10–12). Primary revelations are thus made to Adam, to his children, and to Noah, Abram, Isaac, and Jacob. No such direct oracle is given to Joseph, but assurances of divine favor are not lacking (39:2,3,23).

Thus Genesis shows two movements. The one is the growth of sin, wickedness and corruption through the first two humanities sprung from Adam and Noah respectively, and to some extent in the lives of Abram, Sarah, Esau, and Jacob and the majority of his sons. The other movement is the line of revelatory points, where God is seen to intervene, inaugurate fresh directions in the selection of new individuals. These points are marked by divine oracles. From these points the overall pattern and progress of the redemptive purpose become clear as the book progresses. The revelation is made known in the divine oracles and realized and fulfilled in the narratives. This fulfilment is shown not only in the ongoing redemptive purpose described in the book, and particularly in the lives of Abram and Jacob, but also in the providential purposes illustrated in such episodes as the quest for a wife for Isaac (24), and the life of Joseph with which Genesis closes.

The spread of revelatory themes through Genesis is considerable. They tend to become fewer as the book proceeds and the revelation is made manifest less in direct divine oracles and more in the overall providential ordering of life. There are thus many references to God and to his deeds in the narrative about Joseph, but never once is God said to speak to Joseph as he spoke to his father and to Isaac and Abram before him. God speaks to Jacob in 46:2, but for directly quoted words of God before that we must go back to 35:11.

Many chapters in Genesis thus contain no examples of God's words and oracles. They are 5, 10, 14, 23, 27, 29, 36—45, 47—50. On the other hand, the revelatory theme is implied in these chapters or controls these chapters. For the rest, the chapters contain revelatory sentences, but often passages occur without such character. Thus, genealogies (as in 10:1–32; 11:10–30; 25:12–18), Terah's journey (11:31 f.), Sarah's grave (23), etc., are innocent of revelatory motifs, though germane to the redemptive purpose of the book.

The character of the God thus revealed in the book is very fascinating. He is of course represented as the great Originator of the universe and of all life and being. He is brought before us as the Lord of life and event as the successive events and crises unfold themselves in the progress of the story. God is besides actively involved,

for he not only speaks and commands, but also creates, fashions, breathes the breath of life into the first man, plants, sets, closes up, builds, walks, is sorry, shuts in, smells, promises, is with, etc.

All these successive pictures show the many-sided portrayal of the God of Genesis. The benevolent Creator and neighbor of chapters 1—2 is soon shown as the stern accuser and judge of chapters 3—4. The wronged God of chapter 5 soon becomes the planner of new expedients and possibilities for the correction of mankind and the administrator of the covenant for the second mankind (9:1–17). He is the inspector of the technological achievements of mankind at Babel, but the inspection soon leads to judgment, because technology is here joined with arrogance. Arrogance is inevitably the target of divine wrath, whether that arrogance is found in a serpent (3:1), a man (4:9), angels (6:2), engineers (11:4), citizens (19:5), a king (20:2), brothers (37:19 f.), a brother-in-law (38:7,9), or a firstborn (49:3). In Chapter 12 God resumes his role as initiator and selector to organize the beginnings and destiny of blessing for Israel and all mankind. He is seen as the protector of his own (12:17; 16:7), the giver of the land (12:1,7; 13:14–18; 15:7,18; 17:8). He is the shield and God Almighty of Abram (15:1; 17:1), the giver of life (18:10), and the merciful judge of all the earth (18:25). He is the trier and reward of Abraham (22:1–19), the God of heaven and earth (24:3), and the God and friend and companion of the fathers of Israel.

This many-sided portrayal of the God of Genesis thus shows the two main motifs resident in that God. On the one hand, he is shown in lofty, transcendent terms as Creator, Judge, Lord, and Arbiter of all destiny. There is a deliberate, organized divine intervention and control at the major crises and turning points of the drama of the book.

On the other hand, he is shown, if one may reverently use the description, as the great opportunist in the successive scenes.

He intervenes, addresses himself to the contemporary situation, decides what is necessary, and does what is required. He is the friend of men, conversant with their lives and experiences, concerned in their anxieties and griefs. He is the God of help, of succor, of relief, and of redemption. Genesis nowhere describes him as a God of love, but the incipient and embryonic lines of that character are plain to see. He is essentially the God of the process, ever working towards the fulfilment of his benevolent purposes. He is flouted, delayed, opposed, prevented, and resisted, but he never gives up. He is never defeated. He is infinite in his resourcefulness, supremely adaptable in his expedients, and indefatigable in his objects and methods. He is no abstraction but an ever-present God, the Lord of life, the contemporary of the successive generations, and the Friend and Redeemer, if Judge, of men.

Hence in spite of the record of sin and guilt in the book, of suffering and of mortality, the book casts no shadow of pessimism.

IV. Blessing in the Book of Genesis

A survey of the book of Genesis also shows the place and significance of blessing in its development. Blessings like personalities abound throughout the book.

In the first chapter blessing in the form of fruitfulness is appointed for beasts, birds, and fish (v. 22); and blessing in the form of fruitfulness and dominion is bestowed upon man. The seventh day, the day of God's joy and rest also acquires blessing. The terminology of blessing—except by way of reminiscence as in 5:2— though not the activity (cf. 4:15,25; 6:8), does not recur until 9:1, when the second humanity is blessed as it is launched on its destiny after the flood. Later, with the sons of Noah, a curse sets in in the line of Ham through Canaan, but blessing is channeled in the line of Shem (9:25–27).

Blessing reappears at 12:1–3, where blessing is now concentrated in the person of Abram, in his own fortunes, and expressly in his own descendants. Then more remotely, from Abram as the fount or standard of blessing for others, blessing is promised for the families of the earth. Here in these verses Abram and his succession are first bound up in that bundle of promise and blessing which is decisive for the understanding not merely of the Book of Genesis, but of the whole Bible, and perhaps for the whole race.

In 13:14–18 the promise of fruitfulness is reserved to Abram, when Lot has taken the first move away from his uncle and so away from the sphere of blessing. Lot's life now progressively moves beyond blessing into weakness, to no grandchildren for example except by incest, and so to death.

In that first significant encounter between Abram, the father of all Israel, and the king of Jerusalem, the ancient and modern capital of Israel, blessing is given to Abram and is recognized in Abram (14:19). In 15:1,4–6 the promise of a son is renewed and in the rest of that chapter fruitfulness and a land are again promised.

Even the children of Abram by Hagar, his concubine, share in the fruitfulness (16:10; 21:18) and in the blessing (17:20); but the central line of blessing is to remain in Abram, now called Abraham (17:4–8), and in Sarai, now called Sarah, and their descendants (17:16). The note of blessing reappears fleetingly in the divine soliloquy in 18:18.

After the testing of Abraham (22:1–14), the full terminology of blessing, reminiscent of 12:1–3, reappears in 22:17–18. The terminology of blessing is not found again for some time, but the effect of blessing is manifest in the successful purchase of Sarah's burial ground and in the discovery of a wife for Isaac (cf. 24:42,48, prosper the way).

Upon the death of Abraham, "God blessed Isaac his son" (25:11), and the fulness of the blessing-promises is now settled upon Isaac (26:2–6,12,22,23–25,29). The transfer of blessing from Esau to Jacob is the outcome of Rebekah's plot (27). In 28:1–5 Isaac is said to bless Jacob and to pray that the blessing of Abraham be now applied to him, and this appears to be confirmed in the vision of Jacob's ladder (28:13–15). Certainly Jacob is prosperous in his adventures in Haran, Abram's homeland.

When Jacob and his two wives and their families depart from Haran, Laban is said to bless his grandchildren and Jacob's wives. The omission of Jacob is consistent with the run of the narrative, but perhaps the blessing for Jacob is thus thought of as exclusively from elsewhere. The struggle at Penuel is stated in terms of blessing (32:26–29). In the renewed theophany at Bethel, the promise of fruitfulness and land are reaffirmed, but the terminology of blessing does not reappear (35:9–15). Neither did it appear at the renaming of Abram (17:5), but it did when Sarai was renamed (17:15 f.). God is not said to bless Jacob at Isaac's death, as he blessed Isaac at Abraham's death (cf. 25:11 and 35:28).

In 36:6 Esau and his dependants remove themselves from Canaan and from Jacob, that is, from the land and the person of blessing, a parallel to or fulfilment of Isaac's prediction about him in 27:39–40. Jacob's love and preference rested on Joseph (37:3 f.), as did the divine favor and blessing (39:3,5,21,23), and Joseph was prospered in his fortunes and offspring (41:51 f.). The terminology of blessing is otherwise largely absent from the story of Joseph. The blessing rests of course on Jacob and he is in the land of Canaan, but Joseph is in Egypt. There he serves as a remnant and life preserver whereby Jacob and his eleven sons survive the famine and live to begin a new day in Israel's destiny (45:5–8). As Jacob sets off for Egypt the promise of posterity is renewed. Jacob twice blesses (thanks and praises) Pharaoh (47:7,10).

At the last Jacob recalls his own blessing (48:3) in terms of life and land, and then solemnly transfers the blessing to Joseph and to his two sons, giving the priority to Ephraim, Joseph's younger son. At the very last Jacob lays a charge and a blessing upon each of his sons (49:28); but it is remarkable that the terminology of blessing is confined to Joseph, and the word is reiterated several times.

The book of Genesis is then a book of persons and a book of blessings. People and blessings belong together, especially in the main line of descent. But the blessings often mark inaugural stages, e.g., the first couple, the family of Noah after the flood, the beginning of the life of Abraham, and also of Isaac—of Jacob, too, as he flees to Haran or resumes his life in Canaan or prepares to leave for Egypt. Blessings belong to beginnings, the beginning of people and important events in their lives. Genesis is the book of beginnings of many things, but especially of the beginnings of blessing and of the blessing that belongs to beginnings.

This survey has shown that Genesis makes little use of the language of promise. The RSV concordance lists promise or promises on few occasions. See 18:19 where the Hebrew word for speak or said is translated "has promised," i.e., "had said" (21:1).

Similarly in 47:29, "and promise to deal loyally" represents the Hebrew "and thou shalt deal with me loyally." Also the oath formula, putting the hand under the thigh, is the strongest form of promise (cf. 24:2,9; 47:29). The Hebrew word "to swear an oath" is also used frequently for the recitation of promises between human beings (cf. Gen. 21:23 f.; 24:3,37; 25:33; 47:31; 50:5 f.). And of course the Hebrew word for speak could be translated as promise in many more passages than RSV has done.

The language of promise does not figure very prominently in Genesis, but of course the idea of promise does. The reinterpretation of the blessings to the patriarchs in Deuteronomy and in Psalms is largely in terms of a promise theology and replaces the terminology of blessing used of the patriarchs in Genesis. Deuteronomy and Psalms are thus important links where the blessing terminology is replaced by the promise terminology, and Paul can speak mainly of "the promise to Abraham and his descendants" (Rom. 4:13 f.; cf. 4:16,20; 9:8 f.; Gal. 3—4; Heb. 6). The terminology of blessing in reference to the patriarchs is not absent in the New Testament, but it is quite diminished (cf. Gal. 3:9; Heb. 7:6).

In Genesis then the so-called promises to the patriarchs are more than promises. They are also blessings. Promises are spoken guarantees, but blessings are more than promises because they also impart guarantees. What is promised is also given, and is thus built into the makeup and destiny of the recipients. Only in some such way as this can the fundamental dimension of blessing in Genesis be grasped.

It may then fairly be claimed that revelation and blessing are two fundamental themes of Genesis, and in particular that blessing, second only to divine oracles, is the principal mode and manifestation of revelation in the book. In his understanding of Genesis, the reader must come to terms with the formulae of revelation and blessing which so largely pervade the book.

V. The Witnesses and Their Evidence

A Jewish tradition recorded in the Talmud Commentary on an old Jewish Book entitled *Baba Bathra* preserves the Jewish view of the authorship of the Pentateuch. It reads: "And who wrote them? Moses wrote his own book and the section concerning Balaam (Num. 22:2—25:9) and Job. Joshua wrote his own book and eight verses of the law" (the eight verses, Deut. 34:5–12, which tell of the death of Moses).

According to the Jews Moses wrote the Pentateuch, that is, the book of Genesis and the four books that follow. This tradition is still preserved on the title page of Genesis in the English versions. Thus the RSV says: "The First Book of Moses Commonly Called Genesis." On the other hand, Hebrew Bibles print the word "Genesis" in Hebrew and nothing more. The LXX used the Greek word for beginning which occurs in Genesis 2:4a. The Latin and English Versions followed suit.

Christian belief has followed the Jewish tradition for centuries and assumed that Moses wrote Genesis. Of course all the events in Genesis had taken place before Moses was born. In fact, the Bible states that a gap of four hundred years and more exists between the end of Genesis and the beginning of Exodus (Ex. 12:40). If Moses was the author of Genesis, then he wrote or compiled Genesis long after the events it records had taken place. So he must have employed accounts, stories, family trees, and lists of persons derived from other people. At best then the authorship of Moses, as distinct from the editorship of Moses, is not a very important element so far as Genesis is concerned.

In view of the chronological gap between Genesis and Exodus, the earlier book may first be considered in isolation. Genesis is the book of beginnings, from the beginning of the heavens and the earth to the death of Jacob and Joseph.

The formula, "These are the generations (lit., begettings) of . . ." occurs ten times in Genesis. It occurs in 2:4 of the heavens and earth and is here used metaphorically; 5:1 of Adam ("the book of the generations of"); 6:9 of Noah; 10:1 of Noah's sons; 11:10 of Shem; 11:27 of Terah; 25:12 of Ishmael; 25:19 of Isaac; 36:1,9 of Esau; and, lastly, 37:2 of Jacob. The use and locale of this formula may be said to represent the skeleton of the book of Genesis, so that an overall unity in the architectural design of the book may be discerned.

Within this unity and between the spread of the formulae occur traditions of the persons mentioned in the formulae and of their lives, sayings, and religious experiences in diverse forms. So important were the events, like the creation and the flood, and distinguished were the persons whose portraits are given that more than one witness preserved views and recollections of these events and people. Two stories of the beginning of the world exist and two stories of the flood. The covenant with Abram is twice recounted (15 and 17), the promise of a son to Sarah is twice given (17:17; 18:10 ff.). Duplicate accounts of places (21:31; 26:33), persons (17:17; 18:12;

21:6), and family trees (10; 11:1) can be observed as the book is read.

Of course this diversity has its occasional embarrassment. Sometimes the stories show differences which represent interesting variants; sometimes the dates of the people do not fit the lives of the persons concerned (e.g., 17:17; 12:4). These differences, however, and these variants should not be of concern in view of the fact that in the main two witnesses, sometimes three, preserve their testimony to the events they describe, and preserve for us an underlying unity of historical structure and basic tradition.

The study of Genesis as part of the first five books—or six books or even four books of the Bible, has continued through many stages. Moses is nowhere said in Genesis to be the author of any part of Genesis, though he is said to be the author of sections of Exodus and Numbers, and of the bulk of Deuteronomy. The Jews began to diminish the idea of Mosaic authorship when they ascribed the last eight verses of Deuteronomy to Joshua. It was also pointed out that Genesis 12:6; 22:14; and 36:21 (cf. 14:16; 13:18) refer to conditions long after the days of Moses. These passages are now universally regarded as post-Mosaic additions.

Thus some ancient scholars concluded that Ezra was the real author of the Pentateuch, while a Roman priest, Richard Simon, claimed in 1678 that the Pentateuch was a collection and compilation of divine commandments and numerous human documents. In the eighteenth century a French physician, Jean Astruc, claimed that Genesis contained one major source which used the word God, and a second source, which used the divine name Yahweh, plus traces of ten other sources.

The clue derived from the use of the divine name led scholars to further discoveries. At first men thought there were three main sources which were initialed E, P, and J. Other scholars thought that the Pentateuch was made up of two collections of fragments written in the days of King

Solomon. Still others thought of a basic substratum which had been supplemented and expanded into the present Pentateuch.

A still more recent position was reached when the idea was put forward that the Pentateuch was made up of four documents named P, E, J, and D, though opinions differed concerning their date and sequence. After further investigation of the four documents, a new position was reached and the four documents were rearranged and dated in the following sequence: J about 850 B.C.; E about 750; D (Deuteronomy) about 621; and P about 500–450. More recently J has been divided into J^1, J^2, and J^3—or another source S (Seir = Edom) or L (lay) or K (Kenite) has been discovered within J—but these later developments have not commanded universal assent.

This four- or five-document theory became the orthodox view of the liberal scholars for a long time, and it was all but unanimously held among such scholars. In the last 50 years, however, there have been signs of increasing revolt. Scandinavian scholars have stressed rightly the role and importance of oral tradition; have rightly insisted on a new trust for, and acceptance of, the Hebrew text; and have urged that the logical categories of Western thought do not of necessity apply to the literary processes of the Hebrews or to their way of thinking. Thus some have found the original nucleus of the Pentateuch in Exodus 1—15, to which great additions before and after have been made.

Other scholars have seen original nuclei in such passages as Deuteronomy 26:5–9 or 6:20–24 or Joshua 24:2–13. These passages are akin to liturgical confessions made at sanctuaries on festal occasions, something like an Israelite's "Apostles' Creed." These credal statements are thus the depositories, the magnets, and the nuclei of expanding traditions and histories. From these the major themes of Israel's early history, it is thought, began to emerge. These were: the deliverance from Egypt, the wilderness wanderings, the settlement in Canaan. Later were added the traditions relating to Sinai and the complex of traditions about the patriarchs. So the five mother themes of the Pentateuch are reached. Lastly, the traditions of the primeval history, Genesis 1—11, were added as the great introduction to the whole work.

Beginning with the sentences of the cultic confessions, a great author and editor used the materials he had available, and so wrote a work which told the story of mankind from the creation to Canaan and to the rise of the Davidic monarchy. In particular, Gerhard von Rad has claimed that this basic and fundamental pattern is the work of the person known in the schools of Old Testament literary study as J, and in the following pages as the J witness, that is, the witness from the Southern Kingdom of Judah.

Thus, if the architectural ground plan of Genesis is seen in the tenfold use of the words, "These are the generations of . . . ," the thematic unity, the overall pattern, and the context of Genesis in the ongoing history of mankind are the work of the great J witness or writer.

All these later emphases and developments have been connected, some more loosely than others, with the prevailing four-document theory of the schools. But modifications of a very important kind have set in. Thus in the contemporary scene the four documents are no longer seen as successive points on a date line: e.g., J, 950 B.C.; E, 850; D (Deuteronomy), 621; P, about 400. They are seen to represent streams of traditions—largely parallel—all of which contain early and rich material as well as expansions from later times. Indeed, some have claimed that behind J and E lay a still earlier composition—the fundamental work—whose sequence, basic structure, and pattern were followed by J and E and indeed P.

These modifications have meant that the records are now thought to have arisen much nearer to the days of the events. Certainly the traditions behind the records in some cases go back to those days.

Of course no one could have witnessed the creation before man was created. There were witnesses of the flood, namely, Noah and his household. The narratives of the patriarchs are largely contemporary with the events they record. A new and healthy respect for the traditions of Genesis is thus abroad.

Alongside this never-ceasing investigation into the problem of the origins of the Pentateuch, the ancient, orthodox Jewish and Christian belief in the Mosaic authorship of the Pentateuch has persisted. A long line of competent scholars has succeeded not only in resisting the excesses and extremes of the critical position, and in helping to correct them, but also in maintaining to their own satisfaction the Mosaic authorship of the Pentateuch.

So the issue was neatly defined long ago in the terms: Is the Pentateuch Mosaic or is it a mosaic?

For more than a century the Mosaic authorship of the Pentateuch has been defended and expounded. Generally, conservative scholars have denied the validity of the criterion of the use of the divine names in Genesis for the separation of strands of narrative. Similarly, they have pointed out that a very subjective element is present in those judgments concerning the style and vocabulary detected in the strands which have been separated. They have also interpreted the apparent presence of double narratives (the so-called doublets) and the undoubted facts of repetition, not as evidence for the separate sources or strands, but as part of the literary art of the Hebrews: as expressing their delight in exact reiteration, their desire to emphasize and convince by eloquent repetition. These points of view undoubtedly have taken their place and have been of value in the long debate.

On the other hand, the exponents of the orthodox critical view of the J, E, D, P documentary theory maintain that as yet no really valid interpretation of the syntax and meaning of Exodus 6:2–3, other than the obvious meaning and claim of the words, has yet been put forward by conservative scholars.

Similarly, so-called liberal scholars have, in the main, pointed out that the differences in the use of the divine names and in the use of words and differing styles are not fortuitous. Blocks of material recur at regular intervals. There are sequences of different materials, and the sequences also show the concomitant criteria. The conservative scholars have not devised an explanation of the constancy of the sequent alternatives, represented by such a pattern as ooooo ..... ooooo ..... ooooo .... ++++ oooo ..... ooooo ....., etc. In this pattern oo regularly recurs, as do the periods and the crosses; and when they do recur, they recur always with the same characteristics.

The problem is not resolved, and the debate continues. Moses may have used the materials belonging to the ten "generation" passages ("These are the generations of . . .") as the sources, as he may have kept a diary during his lifetime. The issue is still mono- or multi-authorship, the authorship of Moses or the four-document theory represented by J, E, D, P.

It would not be too much to say that by and large the four-document theory is held by the majority of scholars and teachers, however powerful and indeed numerous the minority of those who accept the Mosaic authorship.

The four-document hypothesis does not remain unaltered. The documents are not sequels, but often contemporary, revealing different emphases and points of view. In this sense J, E, D, P, are not stages in an evolutionary development, but are the bearers of a manifold witness to the events they record. In Genesis J, E, and P present a triple tradition of witness to the doctrines of God, creation, revelation, judgment, sin, election, covenant, and blessing, which are the dominant themes of that book.

There is widespread recognition of the work of the Priestly witness in the Pentateuch, and his work may be distinguished because of his favorite terminology, his attention to chronology, and the systematic treatment of his material.

When the material contributed by the Priestly witness is isolated, quite a considerable amount of material is left. This comes mainly from the J writer, supplemented by sections and additions from an E writer. By and large, three witnesses have gathered material of all sorts from various places: family, shrine, and tribal life. Finally, with the ground plan of the J author before him, expanded by other parallel versions from the E witness, the P witness used his own special material and Deuteronomy to produce the work we now have as the Pentateuch.

At all stages in Scripture more than one witness seems to have been employed. Apostolic writings come to us not only from Paul, but also from Peter, James, and John. The testimony to Jesus Christ is given in the four Gospels. Further back, successive groups of prophets testify to the problems of their age and the divine revelation addressed to it. Similarly, the historical books are paralleled by 1 and 2 Chronicles. So, no surprise is occasioned when the Jewish idea of the monoauthorship of Moses eventually is seen to give way under the influences of the Protestant Reformation and the insights of Jewish and Roman scholars as to the idea of the triple tradition of Genesis. The accounts of the beginnings of the world and mankind and of the lives of Abraham, Isaac, and Jacob are given to us through the testimony of two or three witnesses. Each with his own emphasis and his own interpretation, together they add up to the impressive whole and unity of Genesis. So far as Genesis is concerned, it has been no loss to the value of the book to give up the authorship of Moses, born so long after the days Genesis describes, and instead to have very often the early and sometimes the contemporary traditions of the persons and events of Genesis gathered and preserved for us by three great witnesses, two of whom are masters of their craft: J, a storyteller and a historian of the first order, and P, a poet theologian of imagination and insight—all three being the instruments of the purpose of God.

The book of Genesis thus may be said to contain the work of three great witnesses, J, E, and P. Those sections which belong to P are very easily separated from the rest of the book. Not only the skeleton sentence, "These are the generations of," but many characteristic words and phrases help us to identify the contribution of the P witness.

So students of Scripture are generally agreed that the following portions of Genesis belong to the P witness: 1:1—2:4a; 5:1–32; 6:9–22; parts of 7 and 8; 9:1–17,28–29; 10:1–7 and most of vv. 22–32; 11:10–32; 12:4b–5. The rest of 1 —14 belongs to J except that 14 is probably a quite separate and ancient tradition of very great importance.

P continues his witness in 16:15—17:27; 19:29; 21:2–5; 23:1–19; 25:7–20; 27:46— 28:9; 29:24,28–29; 31:18b; 33:18a; 34:(most of) 4–29; 35:9–16; 35:22b–29; (most of) 36; 46:6–27; 47:5–11,27–28; 48:3–7; 49:28b–33; 50:12–13.

The separation of the material belonging to the J witness from that belonging to the E witness is not so easy. The longer passages belonging to the J witness after 15 are given by S. R. Driver as follows: 15; 16; 18; 19; 24; 25:21–34; 26; 27:1–45; 29:2–14.

The principal contributions made by the E witness are seen in the following passages: 15:1–2,5,20; 21:6–32; 22:1–14; part of 28; 29:15–30; parts of chapters 30, 31, 33, 35, and 37; almost all of 40—42; 45; 46:1–5; 48:8–22; 50:15–26.

Such is the generally agreed distribution of the material among the three great witnesses whose evidence has gone to make up our present book of Genesis and indeed of the Pentateuch.

VI. *The Religious Message of the Witnesses*

The analysis given in the preceding chapter has shown those sections and verses in the book of Genesis which are generally attributed to each of the witnesses. The analysis has shown that Genesis possesses a double tradition in the very early material of 1—11 and, even more fortunately a triple tradition in the history of the patriarchs. In turn the examination of the writings of each witness enables us to estimate his contribution to the religious teaching of the book.

In brief it may be said that J is the inspired genius of Genesis, E the commentator—and occasionally as in the Joseph history, a contributor—and P the genealogical architect. Some have argued that the plan of Genesis is anterior to J, and that he and others such as E found it already in existence either orally or in some basic document, a lost source of the Pentateuch. The view taken here is that J, the supreme literary artist of the Pentateuch, is also the author of that great design to which Genesis serves as the introduction.

The great plan of the J witness was to write a history of mankind from the creation to the settlement of Israel in Canaan and possibly as far as the Davidic monarchy itself. J's contribution in Genesis is thus seen as the beginning of that history, and must be seen in the light of that context.

For J Yahweh the God of Israel is the God of creation and the Lord of history. For him God has brought the world and history into being in order to bring the people of Israel on to history's stage. In this sense J, not the author of the Succession Document (2 Sam. 9—20, etc.), and not Herodotus, is the real father of history. J's witness thus leads him to Abram and through Abram to Israel. Election, blessing and promise are the methods of the divine ordering which the J witness describes.

Within this grand design must be set all those narratives which bear the marks of that simple, clear and living style of the J witness, the meaning of which the following commentary seeks to set forth. To leave the matter there, however, would be to leave unmentioned one further characteristic feature of this witness. In setting forth his God as the God of Creation, of history, and of Israel, the J witness delights also to show his God in the closest relations with the people he has created. S. R. Driver (pp. xx f.), lists no fewer than sixteen verbs by which J describes in Genesis the activities of the Lord. The result is that it has become fashionable to describe J's portrayal of God as highly anthropomorphic, i.e., he describes God in terms used of human resolutions, feelings, and activities. The description of the Lord in the Garden of Eden, in regard to the flood and the tower of Babel, and in the dialogues of the book sufficiently illustrate the point. This definition or description of the anthropomorphic must not be allowed to conceal its religious meaning, for J seeks to set forth the fellowship which exists between God and men. Just as he describes the consanguinity and oneness of man and woman, so he portrays the Lord and his subjects in terms of the closest relationship. The vivid anthropomorphisms are surely justified to present this picture of harmony and cooperation initially complete but later disrupted.

The material contributed by the E witness is much less extensive, and so his work is much less complete and unified. Nevertheless, by taking the whole of the Hexateuch into account, E's representation of the development of religion may be traced through three well-defined stages. In the first, the ancestors of Israel are depicted as idolaters (Josh. 24:2,14 f.; cf. Gen. 31:19; 35:2–4). The second stage is the fully monotheistic pattern of faith and worship depicted in the lives of the patriarchs. How the patriarchs reached this higher enlightenment is not stated. No doubt E once contained an account of Abram's breakthrough into this higher religion parallel to the account by the J witness. The third stage consists in the identification of the God of the patriarchs as Yahweh, whose name was first revealed to Moses (Ex. 3:14 f.).

Accordingly, E did not in Genesis use the name Yahweh, but speaks only of God, and his work first appears in 15:5. He is concerned to correct the more distasteful features of the J narrative. He presents Abraham as a prophet, and also shows that God reveals himself not in person but by more indirect modes—by visions, in dreams, and by angels. His major contributions are, first, the story of the proposed sacrifice of Isaac in which he combines a remarkable feeling of sympathy towards Abraham and his son with a demand for their inexorable obedience towards God; and secondly, the history of Joseph. In this history E shows how God rules and shapes, transforms and overrules the ordinary events of human relationships to bring about his own plans for the benefit of his people. Through incident and interpretation he conveys his inspired lessons, and shows himself more consciously a teacher of morality.

The third writer to offer his witness and interpretation of the events recorded in Genesis is a priestly writer, commonly designated P. The sections attributed to him, so easily identified, show that chapter 1 with its account of a creation in seven days is his first great contribution to the book of Genesis. He follows this with the record of the divine and heavenly sabbath as the prototype for the earthly sabbath to be instituted later. The P witness then links Adam to Noah by a genealogy, and expands his account to tell of the flood and the covenant with Noah. A table of nations follows and another list to link Shem to Abram. Following fuller accounts of the circumcision and the purchases at Machpelah, a sporadic series of notices is concerned with Jacob, Esau, and Joseph. But in effect P has little to contribute to the period between Abraham and Moses. He is content to let his fellow witnesses tell the story, provided he may indicate its essential features. Thus in 19:29 he summarizes the gist of 18 and 19.

By the use of the word God, by a distinctive style, detailed, chronological, and even juristic, P gives his witness. Especially remarkable is his elevated conception of God, who creates and reveals by his word:

"And God said" is the refrain of Genesis 1. He also supplies a framework for the book by using no less than ten times the formula: "These are the generations of . . ." (2:4a being the first, 37:2 the last).

This architectural and genealogical framework serves a double purpose. It serves as the framework for three world ages which he seeks to bring before us. These are in sequence.

The first world epoch is from the creation to the flood. During this period God is known as Elohim (God); the age is marked by vegetarian rules for men and beasts. The heavenly sabbath was also instituted at the creation, though it is not properly an institution for the period, because it was brought into being for God. The sabbath on earth, according to the biblical record, does not begin until the days of Moses. The second world epoch is from the flood to Abraham. God is known as God, and his dispensation towards the new mankind is marked by the sign of the rainbow. Meat drained of blood is now permitted to mankind. The third world epoch is from Abraham to Moses. God is now known as El Shaddai, and circumcision is the mark of the covenant between God and Abraham and his descendants. To complete the story, the fourth epoch begins with Moses, to whom God revealed himself as Yahweh; and the fully priestly systems of laws, including the sabbath, the tabernacle, and the sacrifices, were instituted.

The genealogical framework is the substructure which bears P's testimony to the cosmic history he sets forth. But, secondly, the framework reveals the steps by which the cosmic history led to Abraham and to Israel. This is the secret process enshrined in the story. All the descendants of Adam, except the house of Noah are destroyed. Then all the descendants of Noah except the line of Shem disappear from the story. Later Ishmael disappears, and Isaac only is left; then Esau goes, and Jacob the father of all Israel alone occupies the stage. At other points in the story, Moab and Ammon (19:30–38), the descendants of Nahor (22:20–24), and the descendants of Keturah, Abraham's concubine, appear but to disappear.

In his discourse P is all the time on his way to Abraham and to Israel. By destruction or omission of peoples he is narrowing down the story from mankind to Israel, for it is the people of Israel who are to be the bearers of the law, who are to settle in the designated land, and who, under the direction of these divine laws, are to exhibit to all mankind the pattern and example of an ideal hierocratic community, for which purpose they were chosen.

This brief account of the testimonies of the three witnesses of the triple tradition of Genesis will help to show the rich and varied treatment present in the book. Yet within this variety and diversity there is an impressive unity of testimony which may be briefly summarized.

First, God has created the ordered cosmos that in it the earth should be the stage, the garden, and the laboratory of man. There is, secondly, the clear testimony to the unity of mankind. Created by God, meant for blessing both present and future, made guilty by sin, divided into nations, and subject to the limits imposed by death, mankind is one. The teaching of Genesis is yet the unattained goal of our modern mankind. Thirdly, the three witnesses combine to propound in the election of Abraham the concept of agency. Adam to begin, Noah to conserve, but Abraham to concentrate and fulfil, they are the agents of the divine purpose. The descendants of Abraham—Israel and the spiritual heirs of Israel, the Christian church—are the agents of the divine salvation which is God's purpose for the world.

Many agencies are at work in the modern world. An aristocracy of doctors is concerned with the cure of cancer, an aristocracy of scientists with the inauguration of the space age, and many others with high purpose. But the first of all these agencies was the agency of Israel, an aristocracy of revelation and election, to witness to the revelation, to bear the purpose within its womb, and eventually to deliver to the world the promised Messiah.

Lastly, Genesis teaches that God is the first cause of all things. He is the Creator, the Lord, the Providence, and the Blessing of all the world. By this doctrine the book stands or falls.

This survey of the contributions and characteristics of three witnesses of Genesis must not be concluded without some reference to a literary appreciation of the book.

Genesis is a delightful as well as an inspired book. The importance of its divine character finds a counterpart in its human character and in its interpretation of the psychology of the attitudes and relationships of the people it describes. The descriptions are ever clear, the use of language ever economic, and the understanding of personality ever true.

The reader must be directed to a few examples of the narrative art of the book. Take for example Jacob's discovery of the real significance of his sleeping place at Bethel. The sequence of events, the dream, the assurances, and Jacob's realization of the sanctity of the place are memorable writing (28:10–17). Similarly, 29: 1–3 is a masterpiece of description, which needs to be read clause by clause so that the full weight of the dramatic action may be realized.

Particular attention should be paid to the conversations, which are a feature of the book of Genesis, as they are of the Gospels. Since Genesis is characteristically a book of personalities, it is also inevitably a book which abounds in conversations (e.g., 18; 19; 24; 43; 44). Notice how frequently the narratives are linked and the progress achieved by conversations.

Among the literary masterpieces of the J witness are the following: Consider first chapters 2 and 3. We have in 3:14–19 a perfect model of summation in order, progress, and climax when the persons and events of these verses are seen against the background of 3:1–13. Note further: serpent, woman, man (3:1–7); man, woman,

serpent (8–13); and, finally, serpent, woman, man (14–19).

Again, J preserves for us the story of Babel, where the achievement, arrogance, and judgment of man are so simply yet so ultimately described. Then again, the theophany to Abraham in 18 and Abraham's intercession for Sodom in the same chapter show the J witness at his best. Lastly, 24 must not be left out as it is one of the best stories of all Scripture, but it must be left to speak for itself.

The witness E must be commended for his account of the trial of Abraham's faith (22) and for his special masterpiece, the story of Joseph, with which the book closes.

Perhaps the first chapter of Genesis retains its place as also the best chapter in the book. The lofty quality, the transcendent tone, and the moving sublimity and majesty of the chapter show that the book —and thus the Bible—has the best of all possible beginnings.

VII. The Historical Value of Genesis

The historical evaluation of the book of Genesis is conveniently organized by separating the early primeval stories in 1—11 from the patriarchal histories in Gen. 12—50.

1. The Account of Creation. The first chapter of Genesis makes it clear that the heavens and the earth were prepared for man and woman, so that humans were not witnesses of the creation. "Where were you when I laid the foundation of the earth?" (Job 38:4). The divine question is a healthy and valid corrective. So the record of the creation must either be a revelation of the completely unknown, or an imaginative description based on observation, experience, and poetic insight; though of course these modes of apprehension are not incompatible. In Genesis 1 God created by fiat, and this spoken word is further defined in John 1 as the Word that was with God and eventually became flesh.

Creation then is prehistory, and is more a matter of belief than of history. That God created the universe, that man and woman were created in the image of God with a ruling destiny, and that sin played havoc are spiritual and moral facts which Genesis proclaims for our acceptance or rejection.

The question then arises whether God created the universe in that way and time described in Genesis 1. How can such a description be tested? The answer is that the account must be tested in the light of that "other Bible" which has been given to us, namely, the created order of the universe. "All scripture is inspired by God and profitable for teaching, for reproof, for correction and for training . . ." (2 Tim. 3:16). May it not be said—with special relevance to the creation—that the whole universe is inspired by God and profitable for all these purposes? God has thus graciously given us two sources of revelation, the universe and the Holy Scriptures, and in that order. Thus the historical value of Genesis 1 must be seen in the light of the coherence of that chapter with the order revealed in the universe.

To attempt to correlate Genesis 1 and the findings of science is for the present inadvisable. God has folded his secrets of the universe in the universe itself and has given man the means for increasing discovery. But to try to correlate Genesis 1 and the findings of science is premature, if not futile. The scientists as yet have no agreed explanation of the origin of the universe with which the biblical account may be compared. Further, the inauguration of the space age reveals a conception of space entirely unknown in Genesis 1. Thus, though the order of events in Genesis 1 may be substantially a scientific order, the space and duration of the creation account are only hints of the reality. Genesis 1 abides as a glorious proclamation, not of science, but of faith.

2. The Flood Stories. The book of Genesis transmits a double account of the devastation of a flood which inundated the whole earth and destroyed all but a few selected human beings and animals. The double account represents the Israelite transformation of a Canaanite account, that is, western version of flood stories originally circulating in the Babylonian or eastern area of the Fertile Crescent. No doubt historically speaking a flood existed which in its particular area did cover the territory concerned, and did destroy all but a few survivors. Particularly severe flooding due to the retreat of the ice ages or to particularly severe floodings in the great river valleys could be a sufficient explanation.

The book of Genesis, however, goes beyond this. Here it is not only a question of a very severe flood, but a total flood to inundate and cover the whole earth destroying all life except for chosen representatives of man and beast. In turn the flood is the means whereby the God of the universe deliberately brought all life, with the exceptions mentioned, to an end. The biblical flood brought the destruction of the first mankind [and the first animal kingdom, except for marine life] as the judgment of God upon mankind for its sin.

The student of Scripture is thus faced with a double problem. The extent of the flood is one that can only be decided by experts. To imagine the world covered by water to a depth of five miles, or that Noah could have gathered pairs of all the animals from all over the world in the time mentioned, or housed them all in the ark, calls for belief beyond reason. For many persons, the moral question is even more disturbing. Is God such a being that he would destroy the first mankind and so bring his first experiment with man to an untimely end? People will grapple with these questions in different ways, chiefly determined by their view of God and of the Scriptures.

God judges sin and condemns it. The soul that sins shall die, and the wages of sin is death. All these great sayings are true, but it is quite another thing to affirm that God wills and brings about the destruction of mankind. The question of the historical value of the flood story must be considered in the light of the moral and theological problems of the account. Genesis 1—11 presents us with the Hebrew version of the beginning and early course of the universe, and in that light these chapters must be evaluated.

3. *The Patriarchal Narratives.* At the beginning of the present century S. R. Driver was able to claim in his commentary that the patriarchal narratives, though not historical authorities, were nevertheless "*substantially* accurate" and exhibited a "*general* trustworthiness" (p. xliv). Driver rightly claimed that these narratives were modest in character and geographically well based.

The principal effect of archaeological discovery in the Mesopotamian area has been to show that patriarchal nomenclature, journeys, shrine building, and social and legal customs are typical of the inhabitants from whom Terah and his family moved. To the above may now be added a certain verification of detail, not as historically confirmed for the individuals concerned, but as typical for their day and age. The progression in the evaluation of the patriarchal stories is thus clear. They are more and more to be accepted. The days are gone when the patriarchs could be seen as gods, as the objects of ancestor worship, or as personified tribes. No doubt the narratives of Moab and Ammon (19), of Simeon and Levi (34), or of Judah (37), are basically tribal; but Abraham, Isaac, and Jacob are real individuals, and the individual stories about them are basically true and reliable. True, the narratives lack absolute verification, but the circumstantial evidence is very strong, and the coherence of the Scripture narrative highly credible. Full verification from other sources may never be forthcoming, but the setting and life of the patriarchal narratives are those of the patriarchal and not some subsequent age (cf. Driver, p. liii).

Really the most important question about the patriarchs is that of their religion, namely, was Abraham a worshiper of Yahweh? The older views that they were animists or that they were moon worshipers have ceased to be relevant. Indeed, the minimum basis for the contemporary religion in Canaan and of the patriarchal narratives in Genesis is a polytheistic view of religion. Further, recent writers have claimed that Abraham was a monotheist, as he is certainly represented in the Genesis narratives. This higher estimate of Abrahamic religion is altogether welcome. Certainly in any polytheistic context there is always a henotheistic possibility. That Abraham was a practical monotheist is altogether reasonable. But the real question remains. Was the God that Abraham worshiped known to him as Yahweh? The J witness affirms this, but the E and P witnesses both agree that the name Yahweh was first known to Moses (Ex. 3).

In this writer's view, the J witness appears to have the truth of it. The kind of personal God described by all the witnesses and the type of experience enjoyed by the patriarchal adherents at the receiving end of this religious relationship, are typical of Yahwism. When the deposit of Yahwism claimed by the Kenite hypothesis for the Kenite and Midianite slaves of the desert (Ex. 18), described as the descendants of Keturah, Abraham's concubine, is also considered, the evidence is all the more impressive. Grave difficulties still exist before the continuity of Yahwism in Genesis and Exodus may be safely postulated, but Abrahamic Yahwism cannot be ruled out. Even the old theory of a double origin of Yahwism, patriarchal and especially Abrahamic, and also Mosaic, may have to yield before the more satisfying view of the continuity of Yahwism as proclaimed by the J witness.

Conclusion

The book of Genesis will always remain of abiding interest for various reasons.

The early chapters, dealing with the beginnings of the world and of the race, will always interest men because they describe the means and methods whereby early middle eastern peoples thought everything had begun. The quest for origins and their explanations is perpetual. The early stories in Genesis illustrate that quest with the added significance that these stories are the vehicle also of a transcendent religious faith which ascribes all things ultimately to the activity of *the* God of the universe.

Similarly the literary value of the narratives of Genesis is very high. The narrative art in Genesis is one of the foundations of such art, and so will ever abide as a model and a standard. Indeed within Scripture it is only surpassed by the art of the parables of Jesus Christ.

But the book presses in upon us in yet more engaging concern. No doubt there are those who are versed in such matters who would take a few pages from the writings of Plato or Aristotle or some other ancient philosopher and, turning to the realm of philosophical thinking today, would suggest the parallels and point out the next steps forward in the investigation. Similarly, the major concern of Genesis is paralleled by a major concern in the modern world, namely, the question of the land of Palestine, the land of the Israelis and the Arabs. Whatever may be the terms employed to illustrate the theme, patriarchal journeys, altars, and grave and land purchases, they all point to that preoccupation with the land which, including the promise of progeny, is the earliest and most historical element of the many patriarchal elements. The life story of each patriarch in turn is set in the context of and against the background of the land of Canaan.

Finally, the relevance and indeed the mystery of Abraham for the New Testament remains. Abraham is mentioned 75 times, Isaac 19 times, and Jacob 23 times in the New Testament. Their persons bestraddle the New Testament as they do the book of Genesis, and both books are books of beginnings. Jesus Christ is numbered among the descendants of Abraham, who is one of the principal guests in the kingdom of God. A great arc embraces Abraham and Jesus Christ, as another arc binds the New Testament and the believer of any and every age.

Outline of the Book

I. The first account of creation (1:1—2:4a)
   1. The authenticating preface (1:1)
   2. The initial chaos (1:2)
   3. The first day of creation and the first work (1:3–5)
   4. The second day and second work (1:6–8)
   5. The third day and third and fourth works (1:9–13)
   6. The fourth day and fifth work (1:14–19)
   7. The fifth day and sixth work (1:20–23)
   8. The sixth day and seventh work (1:24–25)
   9. Sixth day completed (1:26–31)
   10. The seventh day (2:1–3)
   11. Authenticating conclusion (2:4a)

II. An account of paradise (2:4b—3:24)
   1. Man and the garden (2:4b–9)
   2. The four rivers (2:10–14)
   3. Test for man (2:15–17)
   4. Man's need and discovery of a companion (2:18–25)

III. The first sin and its consequences (3:1–24)
   1. The first sin (3:1–19)
   2. Expulsion from the garden (3:20–24)

IV. Stories about Adam's descendants (4:1–26)
   1. First acts of worship (4:1–7)
   2. First murder (4:8–16)
   3. Cain and the Kenites (4:17–24)
   4. The family of Seth (4:25–26)

V. Priestly family tree: Adam through Noah (5:1–32)

VI. Evil mankind and the records of the flood (6:1—8:22)
   1. Divine beings and the daughters of men (6:1–4)
   2. Divine judgment on the creation of men (6:5–10)
   3. The J and P witness to the flood record (6:11—8:22)

Selected Bibliography

DILLMAN, AUGUST. Genesis. Eng. Tr. W. B. Stevenson. 2 vols. Edinburgh: T. & T. Clark, 1897.

DRIVER, SAMUEL ROLLES. The Book of Genesis. "Westminster Commentaries." London: Methuen and Co., 1904.

EICHRODT, WALTER. Theology of the Old Testament. Two volumes. Translated by J. A. Baker. "The Old Testament Library." Philadelphia: The Westminster Press, 1967.

HERBERT, A. S. Genesis 12–50: Abraham and His Heirs. TBC. London: SCM Press Ltd., 1962.

HOLT, JOHN M. The Patriarchs of Israel. Nashville: Vanderbilt University Press, 1964.

HOOKE, SAMUEL HENRY. "Genesis". Peake's Commentary on the Bible. Edd. Matthew Black and H. H. Rowley. New York: Thomas Nelson and Sons. 1962. Pages 175–207.

RICHARDSON, ALAN. Genesis I–II. TBC. London: SCM Press Ltd., 1953.

RYLE, HERBERT EDWARD. Genesis. "Cambridge Bible." Cambridge: at the University Press, 1914.

SIMPSON, CUTHBERT AIKMAN. Genesis. IB 1. Nashville: Abingdon-Cokesbury Press, 1952. Pages 437–829.

SKINNER, JOHN. Genesis. ICC Sec. ed. Edinburgh: T. & T. Clark, 1963.

SPEISER, EPHRAIM AVIGDOR. Genesis. Anchor Bible 1. Garden City: Doubleday & Co., Inc., 1964.

THOMAS, D. WINTON, ed. Archaeology and Old Testament Study. Jubilee Volume of the Society for Old Testament Study, 1917–1967. Oxford: Clarendon Press, 1967.

VAWTER, BRUCE. A Path Through Genesis. London: Sheed & Ward, 1957.

VON RAD, GERHARD. Genesis. Trans. J. H. Marks. The Old Testament Library. Philadelphia: The Westminster Press, 1961.

Abbreviations

Abbreviations used in the Commentary on the Text include the following:

BDB—Brown, Driver, and Briggs, *Hebrew and English Lexicon*
ERV—English Revised Version (1885)
IDB—*Interpreter's Dictionary of the Bible*
JTS—*Journal of Theological Studies*
LXX—Septuagint (Greek Old Testament)
M.T.—Masoretic Text (Hebrew Old Testament)
NBD—*New Bible Dictionary*
WC—"Westminster Commentaries" (see Driver in Bibliography)

Commentary on the Text

I. The First Account of Creation (1:1— 2:4a)

The first eleven chapters of the Book of Genesis relate the very beginnings of the universe and all its contents, man included. The first chapter records the absolute beginning, and the works of creation in six days, followed by a seventh day on which God rested after all his works.

The biblical writer is almost certainly a priest and a learned man who writes succinctly, with a special diction and out of accumulated priestly knowledge. He does not waste a word, but by brevity and repetition sets forth a story of great dignity and power. His peculiar diction includes such words and phrases as create (1:1); kind (vv. 11–12,21,24–5); beasts of the earth (vv. 24–25, 30); swarm (vv. 20 f.); creeping (vv. 21,24–26,28–30); be fruitful and multiply (vv. 26,28); male and female (v. 27); and such conceptions as bless (vv. 22,28; 2:3); separate (vv. 4,6,14,18); and image (v. 26; cf. 5:1,3). The dominant note of the chapter is found in the tenfold "and he said," and the sixfold "it was so" (cf. v. 3). Also the divine approval is mentioned seven times (LXX, eight times).

His plan provides for eight works in six days. It has long been recognized that corresponding works are spread over the six days, divided into two pairs of three days each, in a relationship of preparation and accomplishment. By his creative word (Psalm 33:6), God brought the world into being as follows:

Day	Work	
1	first	light
2	second	firmament
3	third	dry land
	fourth	plants
4	fifth	heavenly light-giving bodies
5	sixth	birds and animals from the waters
6	seventh	beasts of the earth
	eighth	man

Compare the work of the first day with the work of the fourth day, and so on.

Thomas Aquinas, one of the great theologians of the Roman Church, wrote a summary of Christian theology, in which he draws attention to the three principal stages in the creation: first, the creation; then the work of separation; and lastly, embellishment. More particularly, separation and embellishment are the two methods employed (cf. *Summa* 1q 65 ante al).

The separating activity is seen in the following instances: the light from the darkness (v. 4); morning and evening (v. 5); the firmament separating the waters (vv. 6 f.); earth and seas (v. 10); plants and trees according to their kind (v. 11); day from the night; sea animals and birds (vv. 20–21,25); man and all other living creatures (v. 26); the seventh day from the first six (2:1–3). Creation was thus largely achieved by separation.

By embellishment, Aquinas of course meant the furnishing of the heavens and the earth with things, institutions, plants, birds, animals, and men.

Nevertheless the chief separation or distinction is between God and all the created order. God is one; he is unique; he is apart from and over all else that exists. Genesis 1 testifies to the singleness, invisible nature, glory, and power of the God of creation, presently to be known as the God of Israel too. There is no hint of any story or myth of the birth of gods, for Israel's God is the Lord of all. The chapter achieves sublimity.

The purpose of the chapter is thus to

show the relationship of the created universe to God. He is the origin and cause of the created order, and upon him it is dependent. In some measure the chapter also seeks to show the HOW of creation. In reality, it comes short of doing that. Rather, it may be said that it is the task of modern science to give the explanation. Genesis 1 shows that creation was not only the act of God but also a divinely planned movement —creation progressed to a goal and a consummation. The progressive stages reveal the beneficent intentions of the Creator as well as the beauty of the orders of being thus created. The immediate goal is man as the crown of the earthly creation and the sabbath rest as the goal of all creation. But the more ultimate goal is to set the scene for the story of mankind, and this leads us inevitably from Adam through Noah to Abraham and to Israel. In this sense the story of creation serves also the purposes of redemption.

1. The Authenticating Preface (1:1)

¹ **In the beginning God created the heavens and the earth.**

With this eloquent sentence, the priestly writer launches his account of the creation of the world and sets forth God as the only Creator. In its Hebrew form the sentence may be taken in several ways. The first and most widely accepted view is to read it as a sentence complete in itself. A second view regards the sentence as a temporal clause, indicating a point of time: "In the beginning when God created the heavens and the earth, then the earth was." A third view also treats the sentence as temporal, but postpones the main clause until verse 3, "And God said." The three clauses of verse 2 are then regarded as three parentheses: "In the beginning when God created the heavens, and the earth, the earth being . . . with darkness upon . . . and with the Spirit of God moving . . . God then said . . ." with the main clause "then God said" at verse 3. These old Jewish alternatives sought to avoid the view that God could have created the conditions said to exist in verse 2.

Nevertheless the sentence, testifying to the ultimate reality of God, summarily describes the absolute beginning of the universe, for the *heavens and the earth* is a Hebrew way of saying "everything." The verb create, which never occurs in the Old Testament of human creation or with the accusative of the material employed, is an unusually graphic Hebrew word to describe the spontaneous and supernatural activity of God in bringing into being something new and finite (cf. Ex. 34:10; Num. 16:30; Isa. 45:18; 48:7; Jer. 31:22; Psalm 51:10).

The Hebrew word for God here employed is the plural form *'Elohim*, of which the singular is *'Eloah*. The etymology of this word is uncertain, whether it be in terms of strength, goal, or leadership. Of more importance is the usage. The word may be construed as plural or singular (as here with singular of the verb), and the usage probably contains a frequency and oscillation between one and more, which is rich and wide-embracing (cf. BDB).

The Hebrew conception of God is therefore probably a singular-plural, which may be illustrated from the phrase "my face," and in Hebrew only occurs as "my faces." Man has but one face, though many faces are manifest through it. God is one but also more; he is also many who is not more than one.

Genesis 1:1, though itself a preface, was written of course long after the creation had been completed. Its purpose is not merely to introduce the story of creation but to set the scene, of which the writer himself and the people to whom he belonged were a part, not only for the history of mankind, but for the particular history of Israel.

2. The Initial Chaos (1:2)

² **The earth was without form and void, and darkness was upon the face of the deep; and the Spirit of God was moving over the face of the waters.**

Following this summary sentence, the story begins at the beginning with the state and fact of nothingness and of chaos. The earth was *tohu wabhohu without form and void,* which means not that the earth was preexistent as chaos, but that it was non-existent. The two Hebrew words together describe what is without form and empty. *Tohu* describes nothing (Isa. 40:17) and is synonymous with nothing. *Bohu* indicates empty and is always used with *tohu* which controls it—an empty nothingness! Even if the earth was somehow present, it was submerged. As formless, it was unidentifiable; and as submerged, invisible; for a chaos of waters—a deep—was present, covered by darkness (cf. Psalm 104:5 f.). This *t'hom* or "deep" is a common Semitic word for depths, and the Hebrew term is probably parallel to but not dependent on the Babylonian monster Tiamat, from whose body Marduk, the god of Babylon, made the heavens and earth, as described in the Babylonian myth of creation, *Enuma Elish.*

The depths, plunged in darkness, represent a primeval though not preexistent watery mass over which a tempest was raging. The Hebrew phrase represented by "spirit of God" is capable of interpretation at different levels. At its maximum it means *the Spirit of God* or the divine Spirit. In the present context the word God is a superlative, a maximum of meaning, not merely a divine spirit but a spirit of divine proportions. Similarly the word for spirit also means breath or wind, so the basic meaning is a howling wind, a hurricane. This wind is moving, stirring up (Dan. 7:2; cf. Deut. 32:11; Jer. 23:9) the waters of the deep, and thus adds to the wildness and terror. The entire phrase is part of the description of the initial chaos. It does not introduce the first part of the creative activity and is not meant to offset or compensate for the darkened watery mass. The initial act of creation begins in verse 3 with the utterance of God.

Nevertheless it must be remarked that the earth (whatever its condition), the deep (which was somewhere), and the wind which was moving, are not specifically said to be created. We must therefore assume that either they were preexistent and so prior to verse 1, or else that verse 1 serves also an introductory purpose—which seems certainly the case. In addition to being a statement of a theological principle in abstract, it marks also the beginning of creative activity, the result of which were the three elements of verse 2. God, so to speak, brings into being or creates the general locality of creation, albeit covered with a deep, darkness, and wind, the raw material from which the order and transformation of all things are to be gained.

In creation, then, nothingness gives way to chaos; and, in turn, chaos gives way to order, and this ordering begins in verse 3. The intention of these opening sentences is almost certainly to show that creation *ex nihilo* is implied.

3. The First Day of Creation and the First Work (1:3–5)

3 And God said, "Let there be light"; and there was light. 4 And God saw that the light was good; and God separated the light from the darkness. 5 God called the light Day, and the darkness he called Night. And there was evening and there was morning, one day.

God creates *light,* his first positive work, on the first day by his creative word. This is the first of the "ten sayings" by which, according to Jewish interpretation, the world was created. With planned and powerful and consummate ease God brings his divine will into action through his word. The priority or prevenience of the word thus shows the primacy of the word, as it also reflects the character and initiative of him who speaks it. The result of course is to bring into being something that resembles the creative principle of the word itself. Word and light have in common the ability to illuminate. They have too the quality of priority; and light, like its originating word, is good. Because God creates the whole world through the agency of his word, then the whole world will also reflect in itself the operation and the character of that originating word. This affinity between the creating principle and the created order justifies the claim that the earth is the Lord's and that what God saw was good, and indeed very good.

To Statius, the Roman poet, and his epic *Thebais* (ix, 661), we owe the famous line, *Primus in orbe Deos fecit timor* (First in the world fear fashioned gods). This is far removed from the revealed insight that God's word first created that which was most like itself—LIGHT. Light is the first, as it is the presupposition, of all the works of God and of men. Light is not merely switched on *in* the darkness but, as Paul says, is called *out of* the darkness (2 Cor. 4:6). God approves the light thus elicited and then separates, by act and by name, this new light from the old darkness. He gives the resultant body of light the name *Day*, and to the remains of darkness, the name *Night*. The naming is thus not only the ordering of the boundaries of light and darkness but also the title deeds to their ownership. He names his first possessions.

These verses associate light, darkness, day, night—and one day is reckoned from morning to morning. The original reference is therefore to daylight; i.e., physical light. The priestly writer would however be aware of other senses of the word light. He would surely know, for example, the line, "Oh send out thy light and thy truth" (Psalm 43:3), or the phrase "the light of thy countenance" (4:6), in which of course the idea of light as a spiritual principle is intended. The priestly writer probably used it in this sense, being of course quite aware that daylight came from the sun. The word light in this verse accordingly reflects differing levels of interpretation, originally daylight, and then by deeper and later insight, the spiritual principle of understanding by which all knowledge and all progress became possible.

4. The Second Day and the Second Work (1:6–8)

⁶ And God said, "Let there be a firmament in the midst of the waters, and let it separate the waters from the waters." ⁷ And God made the firmament and separated the waters which were under the firmament from the waters which were above the firmament. And it was so. ⁸ And God called the firmament Heaven. And there was evening and there was morning, a second day.

The importance of the work of the second day must not be underestimated. A whole day is now given to the making and siting of a firmament, whereby all that already existed is divided into two. The words *let it separate* translate a Hebrew participle "and let it be separating," whereby the permanence of the division is emphasized. Firmament is the English form of the Vulgate translation *firmamentum* of the Hebrew word *raqia'*. The Hebrew word means that which is beaten or stamped or spread out, and so a solid division is apparently thrust through the waters strong enough to support a weight of water above it (cf. Psalm 104:3; 148:4) and containing the water beneath it.

The *firmament* was then like some universal basin or even bell (von Rad). We must also infer that when the firmament was inserted it left some waters, and the light, and the heaven (v. 1), now to become the topmost heaven, the heaven of heavens above. In turn the firmament trapped beneath itself the waters that covered the earth, and the darkness together with the tempest of 1:2 (cf. Job 38:19; 26:10). God names this *firmament Heaven,* that is our sky as seen from below. Above the firmament would be waters (cf. Psalm 29:3,10), and above these, light. References to darkness under God's feet (cf. 18:9), or around him (92:2; cf. 18:9), are of course theophanic; i.e., they occur below the firmament.

The *firmament* is thus a permanent barrier between what is above and below it, and the idea of this separation persists. It appears again in the story of the Flood (Gen. 7:11; 8:2). It appears again in the prologue of Job (1:6–12); in Ezekiel (1:22–23, 25 f.; 10:1); and in Daniel (12:3). There is also the explicit reference to the open door into heaven (Rev. 4:1). Various biblical ideas, such as the heavenly council, and figures, such as the descent and ascent of the Son (John 16:28; Eph. 4:8–10) and of the Spirit (John 16:8), depend for their meaning on this picture of a divided universe.

The completion of the work is marked by the usual *And it was so.* The LXX has this formula at the end of verse 6, and usage in this chapter (vv. 9,11,15,24,30) suggests the LXX is right, but the formula of approval is missing. The LXX has it, and it would be reasonable to add it here, unless of course the priestly writer omitted it because this work is continued in the third day (von Rad), though hardly because he regretted the separation of what is above from what was to be below! Some writers, like von Rad, have seen in the use of the verb *made* (7,16,25,26) evidence of a record of creation other than that which employs the verb create.

5. The Third Day and Third and Fourth Works (1:9–13)

⁹ And God said, "Let the waters under the heavens be gathered together into one place, and let the dry land appear." And it was so. ¹⁰ God called the dry land Earth, and the waters that were gathered together he called Seas. And God saw that it was good. ¹¹ And God said, "Let the earth put forth vegetation, plants yielding seed, and fruit trees bearing fruit in which is their seed, each according to its kind, upon the earth." And it was so. ¹² The earth brought forth vegetation, plants yielding seed according to their own kinds, and trees bearing fruit in which is their seed, each according to its kind. And God saw that it was good. ¹³ And there was evening and there was morning, a third day.

The story now moves into the flooded dark cavern below the firmament. The first activity here below is the redistribution of the waters by an act of separation to permit the hitherto submerged earth to appear as *dry land* and to gain from God its name *Earth.* The *waters* now set within their boundaries (Job 38:8–11; Psalm 104:7–9; Jer. 5:22) are named *Seas.* Apart from the unlit darkness the chaos is now largely overcome, if only kept in check as surrounding the dry land (Job 26:10; Psalm 139:9) and

also placed beneath it (Psalm 24:2; 136:6; Ex. 20:4). The new arrangements command God's approval.

With the appearance of dry land above the waters the first act of adornment may take place. God's word is addressed *over* rather than *to* the earth, and the dry land becomes the soil for vegetation and for fruit trees. *Plants* is in apposition to vegetation, which is generic. So plants (grass, vegetation), comprise one form of growth and fruit trees the second. The distinction is then between plants which produce seed and trees which produce fruits which contain seeds. Others, following ERV, have thought of three types of growth—grass, herbs, i.e., larger plants tended by man (Gen. 3:18; Psalm 104:14), and fruit trees. Whether two or three types are meant, they all produce seed, i.e., have the ability to propagate themselves. *According to its kind* or "according to their own kinds," literally "his own kinds," brings out the manifold variety.

6. The Fourth Day and the Fifth Work (1:14–19)

¹⁴ And God said, "Let there be lights in the firmament of the heavens to separate the day from the night; and let them be for signs and for seasons and for days and years, ¹⁵ and let them be lights in the firmament of the heavens to give light upon the earth." And it was so. ¹⁶ And God made the two great lights, the greater light to rule the day, and the lesser light to rule the night; he made the stars also. ¹⁷ And God set them in the firmament of the heavens to give light upon the earth, ¹⁸ to rule over the day and over the night, and to separate the light from the darkness. And God saw that it was good. ¹⁹ And there was evening and there was morning, a fourth day.

More space is given to this fifth work, the creation of the heavenly lights, than to any other work. This is thus the supreme instance of adornment in the story and the counterpart of light in the first day. The luminaries are given a threefold purpose:

First, they are *to separate the light from the darkness,* and so to limit the darkness hitherto all pervading below the cupola of the firmament, and thus bring to an end the remaining area of chaos. Day and night now have their appointed duration.

Second, they are to serve as *signs*—that is, indications of the normal (like points of the compass) or of the extraordinary (like eclipses); and as *seasons* (better, religious festivals and weeks, months and seasons of the year); and *for days and years;* i.e., to number them and to decide their length.

Third, they are *to give light upon the earth.*

The plan is then stated to have been carried out in two stages. First, two great luminaries, the sun and the moon, are created, and then the lesser lights, the stars; then they are set in or on the lower surface of the firmament. The three purposes already stated in 14 f. are stated again in reverse order in 17 f., and with a stronger emphasis upon the control to be exercised by the major lights. The repetition of the threefold purpose, far from being confused or too much elaborated, is elegant, as may be seen when verses 14–19 are read aloud. The second half of 14 is no attempt to reduce the significance of 18a, but 18a summarizes this part of their function. Of no other works, apart from man, is the purpose so emphasized.

The passage thus clearly emphasizes and reiterates the purpose for which they are brought into existence. These lights are not gods or divine beings. They are institutions, working within limits and for purposes which are clearly laid down. Their creaturely and subordinate role is thus stressed, even if that role is even more clearly stated in terms of ruling. The Creator does not even name the sun and the moon but describes them as lights.

7. The Fifth Day and the Sixth Work (1:20–23)

20 And God said, "Let the waters bring forth swarms of living creatures, and let birds fly above the earth across the firmament of the heavens." 21 So God created the great sea monsters and every living creature that moves, with which the waters swarm, according to their kinds, and every winged bird according to its kind. And God saw that it was good.

22 And God blessed them, saying, "Be fruitful and multiply and fill the waters in the seas, and let birds multiply on the earth." 23 And there was evening and there was morning, a fifth day.

The various acts of separation had produced an ordered world with its sky, seas, and earth below the firmament into which the first animals may now be introduced. By his word and by his own distinctive act of creating, God gives life to the animals. Apart from the general summary in 1:1, the verb create now appears for the first time in the story. Added to this we read that God blessed the living creatures and the birds, giving them thereby the expectation and means of multiplying themselves, for fundamentally blessing is the gift of life. By his spoken word, then, by the act of creation, by the expressed approval, and by the endowment of blessing, the links between God and the first forms of life are expressed and stressed.

Let the waters bring forth is better translated, "Let the waters swarm with swarms of living creatures, that is, living beings." The Hebrew word *sherets* describes creatures that appear in swarms, whether in water, on land, or in the air. *Creatures* translates *nephesh,* a word expressing the principle of life, and then by transfer, the self, which contains the life principle. Since plants are not and do not contain a *nephesh,* they are not living creatures. So living creatures in the Hebrew sense first occur as this sixth work, the first appearance of life proper in the shape of massive animals; i.e., reptiles, fish, and fowl. *Across the firmament* translates the Hebrew words "upon the face of the firmament"; i.e., the under surface of the firmament which faces earth. Against this under surface the birds are seen to fly. *Be fruitful and multiply and fill* are some of the priestly author's typical expressions (1:28; 8:17; 9:1,7). At the end of verses 20 f. the LXX adds "and it was so." If this is the original reading, which the Hebrew has omitted, then its restoration to the Bible adds a touch of completeness in this context.

8. The Sixth Day and the Seventh Work (1:24–25)

24 And God said, "Let the earth bring forth living creatures according to their kinds: cattle and creeping things and beasts of the earth according to their kinds." And it was so. 25 And God made the beasts of the earth according to their kinds and the cattle according to their kinds, and everything that creeps upon the ground according to its kind. And God saw that it was good.

As the earth brought forth grass (v. 11), so it now brings forth, at God's command, three groups of animals, whose bodies are presumably made, on the analogy of the formation of man (ch. 2) from the dust of the earth. This origin from the earth material is more likely to be the link than any "material participation" (Delitzsch and von Rad) by the earth, which is a semi-idolatrous idea. This idea is in fact precluded by the precise statement *and God made,* which is not said of the plants (cf. v. 12). The three groups of animals are: wild animals, like carnivora and game; domestic animals, like cattle; and creeping things, like reptiles, snakes, and lizards. These are mentioned in the reverse order in verse 25—all living creatures—that is, they are not less in value than the animals of verse 20. The omission of the "blessing" formula and the "be fruitful and multiply" formula is therefore surprising.

The Hebrew form of the words *beasts of the earth* at the end of verse 24, represents an archaic way of expressing the nominative case in a genitive (that is, a relationship) construction. The clause must therefore be "from the oldest period of the language" (Dillman). *After their kinds,* more correctly "after its kind," appears to be distributive and to refer to all three classes of animals.

9. Sixth Day Completed (1:26–31)

26 Then God said, "Let us make man in our image, after our likeness; and let them have dominion over the fish of the sea, and over the birds of the air, and over the cattle, and over all the earth, and over every creeping thing that creeps upon the earth." 27 So God created man in his own image, in the image of God he created him; male and female he created them. 28 And God blessed them, and God said to them, "Be fruitful and multiply, and fill the earth and subdue it; and have dominion over the fish of the sea and over the birds of the air and over every living thing that moves upon the earth." 29 And God said, "Behold, I have given you every plant yielding seed which is upon the face of all the earth, and every tree with seed in its fruit; you shall have them for food. 30 And to every beast of the earth, and to every bird of the air, and to everything that creeps on the earth, everything that has the breath of life, I have given every green plant for food." And it was so. 31 And God saw everything that he had made, and behold, it was very good. And there was evening and there was morning, a sixth day.

The Eighth Work (vv. 26–28). By a special decision, by its fulfilment, and by a comprehensive blessing, God creates man. By his creation as the last act of the whole series, by the status and destiny which are prescribed for him, by some quiet exultant undertone which may be detected in the semipoetic form of the Hebrew sentences, and in the triple use of the word create, the coming into being of man is seen as the crown and climax of the creation story. Indeed Gunkel has suggested that these verses were based upon an old creation hymn. We must not overlook Delitzsch's remark that man is not only the noblest because the last of the creation but also "the most needy of all: for he is in need of all the creatures that precede him, without their being in need of him." [1] The verses convey a sense of completion, of consummation, and indeed of rapture.

Let us make man faithfully transcribes the plural of the Hebrew verb. This plural is not an illustration of self-address as if God were a plurality of persons. It is not an instance of the royal plural, the plural of majesty here used of and by God. It is not an expression of what was later known to be the Trinitarian character of God: it is not an expression inclusive of the heavenly host, the angels, the sons of God, the mem-

[1] Franz Delitzsch, *A New Commentary on Genesis,* 2 vols., tr. S. Taylor (Edinburgh: T & T Clark, 1894).

bers of the heavenly council (Isa. 6:8; Job 1: cf. *sodh,* 1 Kings 22:19 f.; Job 15:8; Psalm 89:8). All these views, though rejected by this writer, have been put forward by responsible scholars, and many persons find themselves in agreement.

For the Hebrew, God speaks out of a plurality or singularity of being, and so a plural is as coherent as a singular. In the present passage both forms occur: *Let us make man in* our *image, after our likeness.* So God created man in *his* own image. The Trinitarian explanation given above, though actually incorrect, is in fact much nearer the mark than any other. The same construction is seen in the singular collective noun Adam (man), which means mankind and which permits the plural pronoun *let them have dominion;* the singular pronoun "created him"; the plural "them"; and the plural subject in apposition "male and female." This extraordinary interchange of plural and singular both of God and man in the same context suggests not merely the similarity to be found in the image and the likeness but shows "that any Israelite who thought his ['Elohim] to be Many, also thought his ['Elohim] to be One." [2]

Several variations may be noted: "In our image, after our likeness" (v. 26), but in verse 27 "in his own image, in the image of God," almost as if to exclude the word "after [like] our likeness" (cf. 9:6), but in 5:3, "in his own likeness, after his image," where the prepositions in and after exchange their place in the description of Adam's image. In 5:1 "after the likeness of God" alone appears. Verse 26 thus uses two words to describe the character of God's created man. The first, "image," is obviously the more important and means an actual duplicate in the nature of a plastic work, i.e., conveying "the idea of material resemblance" (Driver). It is "something cut out" (BDB): images (1 Sam. 6:5); idols (2 Kings 11:18); painted pictures of men

(Ezek. 23:14). On the other hand, the second word *likeness* is more abstract and suggests appearance, similitude, pattern, copy, i.e., conveying "an idea of immaterial resemblance" (Driver). Driver's final conclusion that "both words refer here evidently to spiritual resemblance alone" represents too much of a division between the two words employed in the context, which in fact tend to shade into each other in meaning. This neglects the unity of man by separating the spiritual from the physical. Indeed the researches of scholars like Humbert and Koehler [3] have shown "that the original idea was of man's outward form as a copy of God's" (Eichrodt). Yet the effect of adding the word *likeness* to *image,* even if it did not define it more closely, was to qualify the purely physical interpretation. The priestly writer tries to spiritualize the idea by emphasizing the idea of correspondence. The use of the two words together effects a "shift of the *tselem* concept from physical similarity to spiritual correspondence" (Eichrodt). Man in his total being corresponds to the likeness and image of God.

We may safely assume that the use of the two nouns together is intended to emphasize the fact of likeness, correspondence, or "consimilarity" rather than the identity or nature of the similarity, shared by God and man.

The meaning of the phrase "image of God" however is a difficult and vexed question which has been approached in two main ways.

First, the image is defined in terms of man's essence, or of his state, or of his endowment, thus almost metaphysically.

The image of God in man is "the whole pre-eminence of man above the animal," as Delitzsch puts it. It belongs to man in general, transmitted by procreation, and found in man always and not merely in a state of

[2] A. R. Johnson, *The One and the Many in the Israelite Conception of God,* 2d ed. (Cardiff: Univ. of Wales, 1961), p. 28; cf. Dillman: "the fulness of the divine powers which he unites in himself."

[3] Paul Humbert, *Etudes sur la récit du Paradis et de la chute dans la Genése* (Neuchâtel: Secretariat de l'Université, 1940), pp. 153–75. Ludwig Koehler, *Old Testament Theology,* tr. A. S. Todd (Philadelphia: Westminster, 1957).

original innocence. It is in fact "the gift of self-conscious reason which is possessed by man, but by no other animal" (Driver), and is the presupposition of all his progress in all fields, including his ideals and his relationships.

Psalm 8:5, "Yet thou hast made him little less than God, and dost crown him with glory and honour," suggests however that the image is a dignity or a status or a rank in the divine economy. So the image could consist of "bodily resemblance, spiritual capacity, intelligence, will, freedom, differentiation or reciprocity of the sexes," as Jacob [4] puts it, or man's upright posture (Koehler). Thus Eichrodt rejects the concept of the image "as a quality bestowed on man, an item of equipment . . . whether . . . as the gift of psychic powers or of reason, or of the sense of the eternal, the good and the true, or of intelligence and immortality."

This interpretation of the image passage in terms of essence or state has thus commanded a wide variety of ideas by way of elucidation. The very multitude of ideas shows that there is no agreement among interpreters, and also that the text itself emphasizes the fact of correspondence without stating wherein the correspondence lay.

One particularly objectionable form of interpretation is that which sees in the plural form "let us make man in our image" a reference to the beings of the heavenly court, and then to argue from that that "the image of God does not refer directly to Yahweh but to the angels" (von Rad). This must be ruled out for at least three reasons:

(1) Any suggestion that the heavenly beings cooperated in or served as the prototypes of man must be expressly denied and is ruled out by the "God created" and "he created" (twice) clauses of verse 27.

(2) The priestly writer of Genesis 1 shows no knowledge of angels in the rest of

his work.

(3) Very emphatically verse 27 states "so God created man in his own image," and this precludes anything outside the being of God.

It is altogether safer to remark that verses 26 f. state the fact of the image without defining it further metaphysically or in terms of essence or of qualities. We rest then in a general emphasis on spiritual correspondence without further definition.

With this admitted, the second principal method of defining the image is more easily reached. Many of the church fathers, as well as the Socinians, believed that the image consisted not in a status or rank but rather in a function—and that the dominion over the creatures. This is an interpretation of the image in terms of expression and function rather than in terms of being or ontological similarity. Von Rad rightly emphasizes that the weight of the narrative in these verses is less on the image and more on the purpose, less on the gift and more on the task. Certainly dominion immediately follows image and likeness in verse 26, and occupies the rest of the verse. Again in verse 28 God's blessing has the usual results in the words "be fruitful and multiply." But now two further expressions are added: "subdue it" (the earth) and the reiterated "have dominion" clauses in 28*b* recapitulate the dominion of verse 26.

The common objection to the view that the image in man means the lordship of man is based on the fact that in that case the image would be merely "a consequence of the possession of the divine image, not that image itself" (Dillman). To that extent the objection is valid but does not thereby destroy this view. The image is not a thing in itself. It has to be seen, apprehended as it is in the dominion. Von Rad and Jacob refer to the custom of ancient monarchs setting up statues as a sign of their presence and authority in the remote areas of their kingdoms. The image thus represented the king. So man as the image of God is also the representative of

God in the world. He is in J. Hempel's happy phrase, quoted by Jacob, "the vizier" of God in the world. Image and dominion, or image with or through dominion reflects the teaching about man in verse 26. Certainly image and dominion were created together, were given to man together, and belong together in him.

The effect of this view therefore is to leave the character of the image without definition but to see the content and issue of the image in the endowment of dominion. So the image points to dominion, as dominion testifies to the presence of the image. So closely are they joined that one could suppose the loss of one would mean the loss of the other and vice versa. Similarly the impairment of the image would imply the reduction of the dominion, and again vice versa. But image and dominion belong together in man as he comes forth new from God's creative act.

One further point must be mentioned in reference to verse 26. In the list of living things mentioned in the verse, mention is suddenly made to "and over all the earth." The position of these words in the verse leads us to expect a reference not to the earth or its inhabitants but to a definite class of land animals. Thus the Syriac reads "the beasts of the earth," as verse 25, though the LXX and the Samaritan Pentateuch follow the Masoretic Text. Some scholars—Delitzsch, Dillman, Skinner, and others—have restored the word "beasts" to the verse.

Verse 27 should really be printed in a poetic form of three lines as follows:

So God created man in his own image,
In the divine image he created him,
Male and female, he created them.

The verse, with its undertone of triumph, shows quite clearly the distinction of sex. Any thought of an androgynous or hermaphrodite being is excluded by "them." The male and the female share equally in the image. God's blessing upon them equally confers upon them the ability to propagate and multiply. The word subdue in verse 28 means properly to tread

down and is used of conquest (Num. 32: 22; Josh. 18:1).

The Last Provision (vv. 29–30). God's tenth saying provides that seed-bearing herbs and fruit-bearing trees shall serve the need of man, and grass and herbs—literally, "all the green of herbs," i.e. leaves —the needs of animals. It is altogether a vegetarian food supply, and man is only better off by the use of fruit trees also. In this way the priestly writer pictures an ideal world in which man's overlordship does not include the right to kill animals for food. The right to kill for food was not given until after the flood (cf. 9:3).

The picture of the "paradisiac peace" of Genesis 1 is thus the priestly counterpart to the Garden of Eden in chapter 2 (cf. v. 30 with 2:9). The words *for food* replace the archaic and misleading "for meat." The slightly different form of some of the Hebrew words and some new Hebrew words does not justify the view that these verses are an addition to the chapter or that they were written by a different author.

The Final and Full Approval (v. 31). The expression of approval which marks the end of the sixth day is remarkable, not only for its position at the end, but also for its universality—*everything that he had made* —and for its superlative expression *very good!* The whole verse unmistakably conveys a double aspect. There is the completely perfect character of what has been created, without flaw, without pain, all in its adorned order; but there is also the pleasure and the delight of the divine viewer. Last of all, God looks at, surveys, and dwells upon the world in all its attractiveness as his own creation. "The heavens are telling the glory of God; and the firmament proclaims his handiwork" (Psalm 19:1).

He pronounces his generous approval. Intention has been matched by achievement.

10. The Seventh Day (2:1–3)

¹ Thus the heavens and the earth were finished, and all the host of them. ² And on the seventh day God finished his work which he

had done, and he rested on the seventh day from all his work which he had done. ³ So God blessed the seventh day and hallowed it, because on it God rested from all his work which he had done in creation.

The work of creation after the second and through the sixth day has been carried out below the firmament. God completes his work on the seventh day, but the story then continues above the firmament. This ending of the work probably means his ceasing from further work, and of course the work below the firmament is being described. Now, and surely in consequence, above the firmament God inaugurates on the seventh day a rest, and because his rest fell on the seventh day he both blesses that day, and sanctifies it; that is, he enriches it and appropriates it to himself.

With his work below the firmament completed, he inaugurates above the firmament the rest, which is a new act and state. This rest above the firmament is therefore heavenly, and presumably without end; i.e., eternal. The sabbath of Genesis 1 was thus the heavenly sabbath, a sabbath of God, by God and for him. It is thus surely clear that these verses do not intend in the first instance to mention a sabbath on earth, or any cultic seventh-day festival, even though the heavenly sabbath or rest of God was destined to point the way to and become the prototype of the institution on earth, as Exodus 20:8 shows (cf. Ex. 31:17). *All the host of them.* The word means army, the starry host, the angels. But it refers specifically to the contents of everything below the firmament which served to adorn the created order.

11. Authenticating Conclusion (2:4a)

⁴ These are the generations of the heavens and the earth when they were created.

This verse is regarded either as a subscription to what has gone before, which is confirmed by the special word *created,* or else as the heading to what follows. Certainly the verse marks a division between the two accounts of the beginnings. In the record so far the priestly witness has made

his contribution, but hereafter the witness takes up the story. The first seven words of the verse comprise a formula found some ten times in the priestly writings of Genesis. The word *generations* means begettings, family tree, genealogy, generations. It is used here in a general sense of "story of origin" (von Rad), serving as a boundary mark between the foregoing priestly material and the narrative that follows. The verse may even have been introduced here by an editor to serve such a purpose.

II. An Account of Paradise (2:4b—3:24)

The priestly material of the first chapter of Genesis has its sequel in the list of names in the family tree connecting Adam with Noah (ch. 5) and in the story of the flood (ch. 6).

In 2:4b—3:24 we pause to consider a further narrative about the first man and his wife and their fate. The higher or literary critics have been much preoccupied with these chapters, but many of their findings have been worked out almost to nothing at some points. First of all, it had seemed necessary to compare Genesis 2—3 with Genesis 1 to the advantage of the latter. In fact, however, Genesis 2 is not really a creation narrative at all. True there is the making of man (v. 7), but this story is not primarily interested in his making, but rather in the fact that this was a man whom God could put in a garden he had prepared. Similarly the growth of trees is merely a link to the presence of the two very important trees in the garden. Verse 19 tells of the making of the animals, and verse 22 tells of the making of the woman. Yet, these stories are not told as creation stories but as stories of the problem of finding a counterpart for the first man. At most, Genesis 2 is the story of the making of man and his wife. In other words chapter 2 introduces the creation parenthetically.

The real purpose of the story is to set the stage and assemble the actors so that the disastrous story of man's expulsion from God's garden could be told. Genesis 1 is a careful and amazing record of the stages of creation, as Israel's priests had divinely thought it out. Genesis 2—3 is a collection of stories about man's food, about finding a wife for him, about their marriage, their clothes, her subjection and child-bearing, the life of a serpent, and the drudgery of agriculture. Theologically, these chapters are also the primary source for the doctrine of the fall of man.

Equally there is no need to trace within these chapters two stories each concerned with one of the two trees, or even a basis of three separate narratives in these chapters. These attempts have failed to recommend themselves. We turn rather to a group of stories which show internal difficulties but which nevertheless have a plain message in the outcome. If these chapters are a partial parallel to chapter 1, that is only incidental, for they also succeed chapter 1 and go beyond it.

The stories of chapters 2—3 differ not only in purpose but in style and indeed in layout and presentation. In Genesis 1, God speaks, calls, acts, and creates. In these chapters he makes, breathes, places, takes, sets, brings, builds, closes up, walks. In fact, he only speaks twice, once to man (2:16) and once about him (2:18). These chapters are less sublime but more interesting, less centered in God and more human, but nevertheless fascinating and compelling. In Genesis 1 man is at the end of an ascent of creative days and acts; in Genesis 2—3 he is at the center of creation, which revolves around him and for him. That these two chapters are closely linked together may be seen from the following columns:

Chapter 2	Chapter 3
Man's origin out of dust (7)	is confirmed in 3:19, 23.
he is put into a garden (8)	he is expelled from it (23).
The tree of life is only incidental (9)	The tree of life is central (22)
Man has an easy lot (15)	He has hard labor in the field (17–19).
The tree is prohibited (16)	The prohibition is defied (6).
Their nakedness is noted (25)	The nakedness is part of the account in 3:11 and is corrected (21)
God is called Yahweh (Lord) God.	God is Yahweh (Lord) God.

This phrase Lord God only occurs once outside the Pentateuch and Lord is printed in capital letters in order to show that it is not the title Lord which is meant but the actual divine name Yahweh. Compare Psalm 8:1: "O Lord, our Lord," which in the Hebrew is, "O Yahweh, our Lord." Also see Genesis 15:2: "O Lord God," where the Hebrew says "O Lord Yahweh." Yahweh God could mean the divine Yahweh or Yahweh who is God, or, less likely, Yahweh who is of the class of 'Elohim.

1. Man and the Garden (2:4b–9)

In the day that the Lord God made the earth and the heavens, 5 when no plant of the field was yet in the earth and no herb of the field had yet sprung up—for the Lord God had not caused it to rain upon the earth, and there was no man to till the ground; 6 but a mist went up from the earth and watered the whole face of the ground— 7 then the Lord God formed man of dust from the ground, and breathed into his nostrils the breath of life; and man became a living being. 8 And the Lord God planted a garden in Eden, in the east; and there he put the man whom he had formed. 9 And out of the ground the Lord God made to grow every tree that is pleasant to the sight and good for food, the tree of life also in the midst of the garden, and the tree of the knowledge of good and evil.

Since the paragraph clearly begins with a subordinate sentence, the question is where the main sentence begins, for the passage is rather involved. Some have thought that the principal clause begins with verse 5, others with 6, and yet others, as RSV, with verse 7. To join 4b and 7 shows that the making of heaven and earth and of man all fall on the same day or at the same time. But verse 6 seems to indicate a long period, though this is ruled out if the events of verse 7 also took place on the same day, or at the same time, as those of 4b. Von Rad concludes that because man is the center of the story, then the principal clause must be 7, for it tells of man's making. The choice lies between 5, which describes the barren state of the steppe, and 7, which brings man on the stage. Verse 6 is part of the background.

By a succession of picturesque sentences, probably without a grammatical (except in 5b "for the Lord God," etc.) or chronological sequence, the primal conditions are sketched. Indeed some scholars have suggested that the story was originally without verses 5,9,10–15,19–20, but there is no agreement and many of these rather subjective views cancel one another out. Previous to shrubs and herbage, the earth was without rain "and man there was none to serve the ground"; but a mist or perhaps a flood was used to water the steppe. The statement about man suggests that his natural occupation would be to till the ground, but according to 3:23, this became his fate after his disobedience in the Garden. Genesis 2:15 only refers to circumstances within the Graden prior to the disobedience. Since the "mist" went up from the ground, perhaps only ground water from springs or wells is intended. Von Rad rightly contrasts the chaos-cosmos theme of Genesis 1 with the desert-sown theme of chapter 2, and again the absence of the fertilizing water in 2 with the hostile mass of waters in chapter 1.

Yahweh God formed, i.e., literally fashioned, molded (LXX *eplasen*, cf. plastic) man. The word also describes the work of a potter. Man is a combination of dust (which becomes his body) and divine breath (which is life) which is love breathed into him to make him a living being and is withdrawn to cause him to die (Psalm 104:29). The Lord God is directly responsible for the two constituents of man's being. He molds the first human body, and breathes in his own uncreated breath into the molded body. Not even Genesis 1 is as direct and immediate as this, for God's hands at work in modeling and his mouth at work in breathing and not merely his word (1:26) are here involved. Man came into being by an act of God, and is a being sustained by the breath of God. Without God, man does not begin, and only with God does man continue to be.

There is, however, another side to the story. Man is formed from the dust of the ground, but the Hebrew makes the connection even closer. Man and ground in Hebrew are *'adham* and *'adhamah* (sing. fem. noun; indeed the fem. form of man). The meaning of the word is not known, but man is certainly earthborn, made out of the substance known as the dust of the earth.

With 2:8 we come to the first important lead in the story. The Lord Yahweh transfers the already made man into a ready-made garden. After man's transfer, trees are made to grow everywhere in the world, but apparently only trees so that his life may be easy. Perhaps, however, verse 9 refers back to 5a, as it does certainly to 3:18, where he is condemned to live on the plants of the field by hard toil.

The Lord Yahweh had prepared a garden in Eden, a land away in the east; i.e., of Israel or Palestine. This land named Eden would remind an Israelite of his own Hebrew word *'edhen* which means delight. The two words however are not connected; hence, the LXX rendering, Paradise. This garden of delight is obviously a garden of trees and was prepared as an estate for the first man. The garden is a fenced in area as distinct from the open steppe and is notable for two trees—a central tree of life and the tree of the knowledge of good and evil. By comparing all the passages dealing with the two trees in these chapters, some scholars have thought that the tree in the midst of the garden was the tree of knowledge and that the tree of life is a later addition. However both trees are necessary to the present form of the story. Because the first human pair infringed the rule concerning one tree, they forfeited the benefits of the other also.

2. The Four Rivers (2:10–14)

10 A river flowed out of Eden to water the garden, and there it divided and became four rivers. 11 The name of the first is Pishon; it is the one which flows around the whole land of Havilah, where there is gold; 12 and the gold of that land is good; bdellium and onyx stone are there. 13 The name of the second river is Gihon; it is the one which flows around the whole land of Cush. 14 And the name of the third river is Tigris, which flows east of Assyria. And the fourth river is the Euphrates.

The priestly editor of Genesis found this notice in his collections of material, and although it has little relevance for the present context he retained it. These verses are a real geographical note attempting a brief description of the ecumenical (cf. Zech. 2:1) river system. A river rose in the land of Eden and passed through the garden, watering it in its flow. There, literally thence, i.e., the garden rather than Eden, it divided into four "heads"—rivers. The rivers of the four quarters of the world have their source at or from the garden. Since rivers are generally confluent and not divisive, as here, the emphasis must lie in the fact that this river watered the garden and that the rivers of the world took their rise in the garden. The rivers and thus the fertility of the world, depend upon the surplus of waters not required for the wetting or irrigation of the garden. Presumably at the end of the story they still do flow through and out of the garden, even though access to the garden is otherwise denied. The river, like the garden, is supernatural. The four rivers are only mentioned here in the Old Testament.

The first river is called Pishon. It encircled the land of Havilah, probably a district in eastern Arabia (cf. Gen. 10:7,29; 25:18; 1 Sam. 15:7), a land of gold, of bdellium (cf. Num. 11:7), a precious stone (LXX anthrax might be beryl or onyx), or a fra-

grant gum (medicinal in Sir. 24:25). The river may therefore be the Indus or the Ganges, or the ocean around Arabia.

The second river Gihon encircles Kush, i.e., Ethiopia (cf. Ezek. 29:10; Num. 12:1; Hab. 3:7), and the traditional view was that the Nile, or the Nubian Nile, was meant. Israel knew the Nile well by name, and if this river is the Nile or part of it, then obviously this is a pre-Israelite name for it, preserved in the Israelite tradition.

Gihon is also the name of the spring southeast of Jerusalem (1 Kings 1:33,38).

The third river Hiddekel is identified by Sumerian and Akkadian equivalents, and by Daniel 10:4, as the Tigris. This flowed east of Assyria, literally in front of Asshur, i.e., the city. This probably means on the eastern side of the city of Asshur, so that the story was written by someone in the west. This suggests that the story of Eden had already traveled to the west before 1300 b.c., when Asshur was replaced by the capital city Calah.

The fourth river has the Hebrew name Prath, seen in the second syllable of Euphrates, which it is. It is the great river of the Old Testament and needed no further identification.

The mention of Tigris and Euphrates suggests that Eden was thought to be located near the sources of these rivers, in the vicinity of Armenia.

This account of four vast rivers springing from one describes something unknown in the present world, but this view may represent what was thought in really olden days. The enumeration suggests that the first two mentioned are the most easterly. Dillman illustrates the attempts to reconcile the account of the four-headed river with what later came to be known of the end of the world. The exercise is superfluous, because not the geography but the supernatural character of the abundance of waters is important. Such an immense flow of water explains the fertility of the garden and may suggest that the garden must have been very large indeed.

3. Test for Man (2:15–17)

15 The LORD God took the man and put him in the garden of Eden to till it and keep it. **16** And the LORD God commanded the man, saying, "You may freely eat of every tree of the garden; **17** but of the tree of the knowledge of good and evil you shall not eat, for in the day that you eat of it you shall die."

Verse 15 is resumptive and mentions man's settlement and horticultural employment in the garden as natural and rewarding. It in no way contradicts 3:23, which speaks of man's agriculture outside the garden (and in other conditions), i.e., without ready access to what must surely have been an immense water supply, now canalized outside the garden into four rivers.

In verse 9 two trees are stated to be in the garden, one and possibly both at the center of it. Now the plot deepens, for a divine veto under penalty of certain death rests upon the eating of one tree only, the tree of the knowledge of good and evil. The Hebrew phrases emphasize the stringency of the veto and the certainty of death. A comparison of 2:9,16–17 and 3:3 has led some scholars to suppose there was only one tree in the story originally and that the tree of the knowledge of good and evil identified as in the center of the garden in 3:3. However a mural painting from the second millennium (found in Mari, a city on the right bank of the Euphrates), depicts the essentials of the Eden story. Two goddesses are shown each with a vase from which four streams flow. Two trees are also shown, one being guarded by three cherubim (cf. Parrot, in Thomas, p. 139).

Verses 16–17 clearly reveal the purpose of the story—to show how man was tested. Everything was in his favor; abundant fertility, many varieties of vegetarian food in perpetuity, complete freedom, natural and delightful activity, and only one snag—no eating from one tree. At this one point man comes under God's veto. His obedience and his decision are on trial; hence, at this point, his destiny too is at stake.

To ask what would have happened if he had eaten from the other tree first is to ignore the realism and absorption of the story. Man is confronted with one tree and this fills the center of the story and is the next necessary stage in the plot. Man's freedom to obey or to disobey is now put to the test.

Knowledge of good and evil. The phrase good and evil is not here used primarily with a moral sense. Rather the pair of terms as expressing opposites signifies totality—knowing everything is the meaning. See for example: turn neither to the left nor right, i.e., do not turn at all (Num. 20:17); or from the least of them to the greatest of them, i.e., everybody (Jer. 31:34).

4. Man's Need and Discovery of a Companion (2:18–25)

18 Then the LORD God said, "It is not good that the man should be alone; I will make him a helper fit for him." **19** So out of the ground the LORD God formed every beast of the field and every bird of the air, and brought them to the man to see what he would call them; and whatever the man called every living creature, that was its name. **20** The man gave names to all cattle, and to the birds of the air, and to every beast of the field; but for the man there was not found a helper fit for him. **21** So the LORD God caused a deep sleep to fall upon the man, and while he slept took one of his ribs and closed up its place with flesh; **22** and the rib which the LORD God had taken from the man he made into a woman and brought her to the man. **23** Then the man said,
"This at last is bone of my bones
    and flesh of my flesh;
she shall be called Woman,
    because she was taken out of Man."
24 Therefore a man leaves his father and his mother and cleaves to his wife, and they become one flesh. **25** And the man and his wife were both naked, and were not ashamed.

Verse 18 states the theme. *It is not good that the man,* the male, *should be alone.* Not good means not advantageous, not wise, not comfortable, not beneficial. *I will* —both LXX and Vulgate read "We will," as in 1:26. *Helper fit for him,* literally a helper according to what is in front of, i.e., corresponding to, equal and adequate to himself (BDB), i.e., a friend, companion conceived as his equal.

The Lord Yahweh now sets about his task. Having produced trees and man himself out of the ground, he now proceeds to produce the animals from the same medium. He made man outside the garden, and then placed him inside the garden. Similarly he makes the animals outside the garden and then brings them from outside the garden to the man in the garden, so that the man may name them and through the name express his description; and then, upon their rejection, returns them outside the garden. Beasts and birds all alike fail to gain man's approval. All this activity postpones the climax of the story and so creates suspense. The indefatigable Lord Yahweh then anesthetizes man by a swoon of a sleep (cf. 15:12; 1 Sam. 26:12). The purpose of the sleep may have been to conceal the divine activity, or to effect the operation without pain for man. The Hebrew word for this sleep suggests its supernatural origin.

God then abstracts a rib, healing the wound, and builds the rib into a woman. The choice of the word "build" is striking. The result is devastating. In ecstasy the man cries out in testimony to the divine success:

This is it, this time
Bone of my very bone
and flesh of my very flesh."
She (this one) shall be named Woman,
For from the man she was taken (v. 23).
(Heb., "was taken this.")

The man ('adham) then names his partner woman ('ishshah), taken from a man ('ish). Man's favorable appraisal is thus expressed through the name as well as in this poetical commendation. Particularly fascinating is the threefold "this" in reference to her! The whole story is a parable of the closeness and dependence of the sexes upon each other. First, verses 22 f. describe the relationship from woman's side

—she springs from man, is close to him, depends upon him, and is organically bound to him. Verse 24 shows that man too needs a woman, seeks after her, is dependent upon her, and renews an organic relation with her. This verse, far from being a later addition or an editorial comment, is the complementary of the previous verse, written by the same realist thinker, and not of course the words of the man (cf. Matt. 19:4 f.). Once man and woman were one, and so they tend to each other, for they belong to each other. A matriarchal form of society may be basic to the story.

The naked man and woman are together in the garden like small children. But children know they are bare only because they know what it is to be clothed. The first pair did not even know what it was to be bare nor did they realize they were nude.

Literary critics of the chapter have often made much of the fact that whereas in chapter 1 man and woman are created after the animals and as the final stage in the ladder of life, in chapter 2 man is before the animals who are before the woman. But the emphasis of the second story is not on their order, though it is different from that in chapter 1. The priestly editor himself could surely see that the stories were different. If he was aware of the difference, his purpose was not to point that out. The center of the story is man. In reference to man, the animals are not a stage of life above which the first pair emerge. The animals are, in chapter 2, a failed creation, insofar as man's finding a companion is concerned. As they are brought in turn to man they are judged, and found wanting. If one animal had succeeded, that animal would have remained with man as his companion in the garden. But they fail, they all fail to satisfy man. So they are led out and remain a part of the creation that failed to satisfy man. Their rightful place is thus outside the garden, where man was later to find them. The garden was empty after the man and his wife left it. They will not be there long by themselves!

III. The First Sin and Its Consequences (3:1–24)

Chapter 3 is the last of that great trilogy of chapters with which the book of Genesis and the history of mankind begin. It records the story of woman's weakness, man's weakness in sharing disobedience, and their consequent expulsion from the garden to the sweat and toil of life outside the garden. The narrative art of the first 13 verses and the conclusion of the chapter are only matched by the almost perfect literary and thematic balance of the poem in verses 14–19.

Beside the majesty and sublimity of the first chapter must be set the intimacy and warmth of chapters 2—3. These latter chapters reveal the fellowship between God and the children he has created, and show the close relations between the divine Lord and the first couple, relations disrupted by their folly, and a fellowship destroyed by their sin.

1. The First Sin (3:1–19)

(1) The Act (3:1–7)

¹ Now the serpent was more subtle than any other wild creature that the Lord God had made. He said to the woman, "Did God say, 'You shall not eat of any tree of the garden'?" ² And the woman said to the serpent, "We may eat of the fruit of the trees of the garden; ³ but God said, 'You shall not eat of the fruit of the tree which is in the midst of the garden, neither shall you touch it, lest you die.'" ⁴ But the serpent said to the woman, "You will not die. ⁵ For God knows that when you eat of it your eyes will be opened, and you will be like God, knowing good and evil." ⁶ So when the woman saw that the tree was good for food, and that it was a delight to the eyes, and that the tree was to be desired to make one wise, she took of its fruit and ate; and she also gave some to her husband, and he ate. ⁷ Then the eyes of both were opened, and they knew that they were naked; and they sewed fig leaves together and made themselves aprons.

The scene is set inside the garden, where man has been placed, where woman has joined him, and where, what must be called a gatecrasher, the serpent, appears.

We learn four things about this serpent: (a) Like the animals, the serpent had been made by Yahweh God; (b) he had a name "serpent." Presumably then he had gone through the same process as the other animals in 2:19. The serpent had been made, presented to man, named and rejected by him, and had gone back to life outside the garden. (c) But this serpent was the craftiest creature of all that God had made. He had not been content to live outside the garden; instead, he had contrived an entry into the garden. (d) The serpent's ability to speak shows that he has a symbolic role in the story, the role of the tempter. He addresses the woman, the more likely victim, for she had heard the veto only secondhand. (2:16 f.). The serpent is merely at this stage of the story the cleverest of God's creatures. He is not the agent of the devil, or a symbolic embodiment of lust or evil, as he has become for many commentators. As yet there is no sin or evil in the world. The first sin has not yet happened. The serpent approaches the woman, cunningly expressing his astonishment and actually falsifying or distorting the divine prohibition. To that extent he opposes God by pretending to be man's benefactor. The RSV fails to bring out the psychological subtlety of the serpent's first words: "So it is the case that God said . . . ?" "Has God really said . . . ?" "Did God actually say . . . ?" In this clandestine conversation neither serpent nor woman mentions Yahweh; each mentions only God. The omission is deliberate (cf. the usage in the rest of the ch.).

The woman corrects the serpent by stating that all trees are available except the tree in the midst of the garden. To eat that tree would be to incur the penalty of death. They are not even to touch it. The serpent openly challenges this and points out that to eat will confer upon the couple similarity to God (perhaps to gods, 'elohim), a likeness not of character but of power and of knowledge. *Your eyes will be opened* (v. 5) implies supernatural insight, *like God, knowing good and evil,* i.e., like God, knowing everything. The serpent thus achieves his aim by telling lies about God. God is aware, he says, that you will become like him, so he has needlessly threatened you with death. He thus suggests that God is envious and so is unreliable. His role in the service of wickedness and as the opponent of God increases and becomes more evident.

Faced with the serpent's denial, with his alluring prospect (v. 5), and with the evidence of her own eyes, the woman took, ate, and got her husband to do the same. Her own senses completed the tempter's work. *To make one wise* is understood by the LXX, Vulgate, Syriac, and many scholars to mean to look at, to contemplate; this meaning is doubtful because it occurs only here. A more intensive meaning is required; e.g., to look at intently, to ponder, to profit from the pondering, understand, make wise. In fact, their eyes are opened, and the first, because most immediate, discovery is their own nakedness. They become conscious of sex. But the sense of shame implies sin before God, and so they feel themselves to be wrong before each other. They sew foliage of fig trees together to make girdles or aprons with which to cover themselves.

Man's attempt to embrace the reality described by the serpent in verse 6 has failed, and he finds himself involved in an experience quite different from what was promised. Von Rad appositely quotes 1 John 2:16, "the lust of the flesh" (for food), and the lust of the eyes (pleasant to the eyes) and the pride of life (as gods). To this may be added the contrast in the behavior of the second Adam who "did not count equality with God a thing to be grasped" (Phil. 2:6).

(2) The Investigation (3:8–13)

⁸ And they heard the sound of the LORD God walking in the garden in the cool of the day, and the man and his wife hid themselves from the presence of the LORD God among the trees of the garden. ⁹ But the LORD God called to the man, and said to him, "Where are you?" ¹⁰ And he said, "I heard the sound of thee in the garden, and I was afraid, because I was naked;

and I hid myself." ¹¹ He said, "Who told you that you were naked? Have you eaten of the tree of which I commanded you not to eat?" ¹² The man said, "The woman whom thou gavest to be with me, she gave me fruit of the tree, and I ate." ¹³ Then the LORD God said to the woman, "What is this that you have done?" The woman said, "The serpent beguiled me, and I ate."

Yahweh God takes his usual evening (lit., in the breeze of the day) turn in the garden and reveals his presence by the rustle of his steps (not voice as KJV and ERV; cf. 2 Sam. 5:24; 1 Kings 19:12). Yahweh God's presence brings man into the second consequence of his action. He becomes afraid. Shame and fear are the basic consequences of wrongdoing, and that wrongdoing as now recollected in the divine presence becomes sin. So man and wife flee to hide themselves in the garden.

The serpent had begun with a supercilious question to the woman, but Yahweh God addresses his question to man. This is the first question addressed by God to man, and of course it is God's perpetual question as far as man is concerned. The divine questions are not asked to establish facts, but, rather, to hear the couple convict themselves out of their own mouths. The man at first parries the question, thereby giving God the necessary lead (v. 11).

The man betrays the woman but suggests by the words, *The woman whom thou gavest to be with me,* that God was also to blame. But his statement nevertheless ends *and I ate* (v. 12). The woman puts the blame on the serpent (v. 13), but the serpent is given no chance to speak.

Verse 11 does not contain the word sin or sinned; nevertheless it shows what sin is. Whereas vice is a deed directed against oneself; crime, a deed against a fellowman; sin is a deed known to be wrong and performed in rebellious defiance of a command of God accepted by man as such (cf. 2 Sam. 12:9,13). "Against thee, thee only, have I sinned, and done that which is evil in thy sight, so that thou art justified in thy sentence and blameless in thy judgment" (Psalm 51:4).

(3) *The Sentences (3:14–19)*

14 The LORD God said to the serpent,
"Because you have done this,
    cursed are you above all cattle,
    and above all wild animals;
upon your belly you shall go,
    and dust you shall eat
    all the days of your life.
15 I will put enmity between you and the wo-
    man,
    and between your seed and her seed;
he shall bruise your head,
    and you shall bruise his heel."
16 To the woman he said,
"I will greatly multiply your pain in child-
    bearing;
    in pain you shall bring forth children,
yet your desire shall be for your husband,
    and he shall rule over you."
17 And to Adam he said,
"Because you have listened to the voice of
    your wife,
    and have eaten of the tree
of which I commanded you,
    'You shall not eat of it,'
cursed is the ground because of you;
    in toil you shall eat of it all the days of
    your life;
18 thorns and thistles it shall bring forth to you;
    you;
    and you shall eat the plants of the field.
19 In the sweat of your face
    you shall eat bread
till you return to the ground,
    for out of it you were taken;
you are dust,
    and to dust you shall return."

The announcement of the penalties re-
verses the order of the questions. Successively serpent, woman, man are sentenced,
and their punishments represent the explanations of conditions under which they
now live; i.e., they are aetiological. The
verses have an irregular poetic structure
and are very ancient.

**The Sentence on the Serpent (vv.
14–15).** Yahweh God condemns the serpent
to be cursed among all animals, to wriggle
henceforth on its belly, to eat dust (cf. Isa.
65:25), and to suffer perpetual war with
mankind. *Above all cattle, and above all
wild animals* suggests that all animals were
cursed, but the serpent most of all. The Hebrew probably means out of or among; i.e.,
the serpent has the distinction of being the

only animal to be cursed. The rest were
only rejected. Cursing is basically disintegration.

The serpent's life collapses. The enmity
described between man and serpent gathers
to it overtones of the perpetual and inevitable struggle between man and evil (von
Rad). A certain demonic character appears
to attach itself to the serpent, which apparently has to abandon its upright posture
and crawl on the ground. Also implied is
the serpent's second expulsion from the garden, for its enmity is with man also shortly
to be expelled. *Enmity* is the first word in
the Heb. of verse 15, and this shows the
emphasis—"enmity I will put."

He (i.e., the seed of woman—mankind—
individual and collective), and *you* (the
serpent) as representative are both emphatic. The verb *bruise* (cf. Job 9:17) is
appropriate to describe the man's action,
but less appropriate to the serpent; the
meaning, however, is clear, even if the use
of the verb is uncertain. Ultimately of
course *he* was understood to refer to the
Messiah and so applied to Jesus Christ. The
struggle between Jesus Christ and evil is
nevertheless but one if the decisive event in
the continuous feud (cf. Skinner). Thus in
Christian interpretation the Christological
bruising of the serpent's head came to be
regarded as the first promise recorded in
the Bible, and was given the technical title
the *Protevangelium*, literally, the first gospel.

The Sentence on the Woman (v. 16).
This sentence is pronounced in four (Heb.,
five) lines whereas ten (Heb., eleven)
were devoted to the serpent's punishment,
and fourteen (Heb. uncertain) to the
man's punishment. Woman and man are
not cursed—as the serpent—but afflicted
and eventually expelled.

The woman's punishment is to involve
her in greatly increased pains (the word is
used in Hebrew in physical and spiritual
senses) in pregnancy and especially child-
birth (cf. Isa. 21:3; Jer. 6:24; Psalm 48:6),
a desire for intercourse with her husband,
either for enjoyment or for conception, and

her consequent subordination to him. Her role is represented here as an evil for the woman, and so for the man too. Relationship should be mutual, but here it is domination by the man as part of woman's punishment, and as such an evil.

The Sentence on the Man (*vv. 17–19*). First the divine Judge recapitulates the crime, and so by creating curse conditions in the soil achieves the conditions whereby man is to be punished. The punishment affects his strength and his food supply, due to the alienation between man and the ground brought about by the curse. Blessing brings fertility, but curse spells barrenness (Isa. 24:6). *And to Adam.* The Hebrew of these two chapters requires that these words should be read, "And to the man." Many scholars have traced a double tradition in these verses as follows:

(a) 17*c*,19*a*,19*b*

"Cursed is the ground because of you; in toil [lit., **pain**] you shall eat of it all the days of **your** life. In the sweat of your face you **shall eat** bread till you return to the **ground, for out of** it you were taken."

(b) 18,19*c*

Thorns and thistles [cf. Hos. 10:8] it shall bring forth to you; and you shall eat the plants of the field. You are dust, and to dust you shall return."

Von Rad further claims that (a) gives the reason for the hard life of the small peasant farmer, and credits (b) for the steppe life of the nomad. The double tradition appears to be most clear in the last two lines in each column. This means that the difficulty is in verse 19. Other scholars have preferred to omit verse 18, or part of it, as an explanatory gloss. *You shall eat bread* probably means "gain your livelihood" (cf. Amos 7:12), and so is not a parallel to **you shall eat the plants of the field.** The repetition is probably due to emphasis and not double tradition, because the double motif (a) "for" or "because" of the Hebrew **for out of it** and (b) **for dust you are** give two separate reasons for man's destiny: (a) his origin from the dust and (b) his makeup as dust.

These verses do not teach that work itself is a curse or a punishment, but rather the toil of work, its excessive cost, and the failure of commensurate reward—these are the penalties. The threatened punishment for eating from the tree was death (2:17), but when they did eat, they did not die.

Nevertheless the fact of the death sentence is confirmed. No implication of the immortality of the soul may be found here. The passage is concerned to teach death not as a punishment but as an inevitable terminus to human life. The judgment upon man brings about a cruelly hard life for him, with its inevitable end. The real punishment, however, is separation from God, a state which is depicted in symbolic fashion in expulsion from the garden.

2. Expulsion from the Garden (3:20–24)

20 The man called his wife's name Eve, because she was the mother of all living. 21 And the Lord God made for Adam and for his wife garments of skins, and clothed them.

22 Then the Lord God said, "Behold, the man has become like one of us, knowing good and evil; and now, lest he put forth his hand and take also of the tree of life, and eat, and live for ever"— 23 therefore the Lord God sent him forth from the garden of Eden, to till the ground from which he was taken. 24 He drove out the man; and at the east of the garden of Eden he placed the cherubim, and a flaming sword which turned every way, to guard the way to the tree of life.

Man's first meeting with woman was for him so sudden, astonishing, and rapturous that he could not have named her if he had tried; all he could say was "Part of me, part of me." Now face to face with their new destiny he names her as his partner in that new destiny. He calls her *chawwah,* Eve; i.e., life. This recognition of her life-embodying, life-conceiving, and life-delivering role is the answer, the compensation, and the eventual remedy for the toil and pain and death of the life previously described. This view is confirmed, for if God gives them "an outfit for misery," he has nevertheless done something which is different from punishment, and which is an expression of his care and his providential planning for what lies ahead.

According to 2:17, the punishment for the illicit eating was death. In actual fact that punishment took the form of retribution upon serpent, woman, and man. The possibility is now present, and is anticipated, that on the basis of his likeness to God in one respect, viz. knowledge, man may be clever enough to work out the advantages of eating from the other tree, the tree of life; namely, immortality. God therefore resorts to a precautionary measure—he puts them beyond the reach of this temptation, he expels them from the garden where this tree is, and prevents their reentry.

Because of his arrogant and disobedient behavior, man has forfeited his life in the garden, and so he is expelled. *Like one of us*—this is the singular plural description of God. After the expulsion the garden must have been empty, for the story of life goes on outside the garden. Inside the garden is life, and outside, presumably, the opposite. Verse 24 is not necessarily a double of verse 23, for the latter mentions the expulsion in order to describe the consequence; namely, agriculture, while verse 24 mentions the forcible expulsion to show what steps were taken to make it final and irreversible. Cherubim are half-human, half-animal, companions and intercessors with deity, and attendants or guardians of sacred places (cf. 1 Kings 6:23 ff.; 8:6 f.). The armament of the cherubim is a flaming sword turning this way and that. Its permanence rules out the view that it might be mythical lightning.

In Genesis 1 man is created to live on earth below the firmament in ideal surroundings. In Genesis 3, having forfeited such surroundings, he is now separated from those conditions and compelled to follow the hard lot of human life as known to man. He is excluded from the possibility of immortality. The RSV omits "and caused [LXX adds him] to dwell to the east," and

with LXX reads "and he placed" or "stationed," though RSV could be a paraphrase of the Hebrew text.

The story of Genesis 2–3 may be seen as based on an experiment in living. Instead of seeking prototypes or similar material from the Near Eastern cultural background it is easy to see that the story is based on the idea of a movement from the steppe to the sown, and the failure to establish oneself in the fertile areas. The story may thus be basically interpreted in terms of a sociological experiment that failed. Incursion from the desert into the fertile areas of the riverine valleys is thus the original motivation. Nevertheless such a natural event has been made the basis of this story about the first couple, and how they, through arrogance, forfeited the right to remain in a garden where God had placed them and intended them to live.

The story is also for many persons chiefly a record of man's original innocence and his first fall. The basic pattern is thus filled out with a number of themes; e.g., the organic link between man (*'adham*) and the ground (*'adhamah*); the organic corporateness of man and woman; a picture of sin as rebellion against the declared and known will of God; the separation of man from life, not to mention all the lesser aetiological motifs whereby human life and its conditions as now existing are explained by reference to events in this story. Man's troubles and sorrows were not created for him by God; rather, they are due to man's own behavior and folly. God is not responsible, but man is. Sorrow comes from sin, and confusion and man's bad relationships in any direction stem from his failure in his relationship to God.

It is remarkable that the rest of the Old Testament does not make use of or even refer to Genesis 2 f. Nevertheless the story has its counterpart in the New Testament.

The first couple in the best of all surroundings as provided by God nevertheless fell victim to temptation. Yet their counterpart Jesus Christ overcame temptation in a wilderness at the beginning of his earthly ministry (Mark 1:12–13 and parallels), and at the end of his life in a garden (Mark 14:32–42), and, dying helplessly on a cross, put aside temptation as to his destiny and his own faith (Mark 15:33 ff.).

IV. Stories About Adam's Descendants (4:1–26)

1. First Acts of Worship (4:1–7)

¹ Now Adam knew Eve his wife, and she conceived and bore Cain, saying, "I have gotten a man with the help of the Lord." ² And again, she bore his brother Abel. Now Abel was a keeper of sheep, and Cain a tiller of the ground. ³ In the course of time Cain brought to the Lord an offering of the fruit of the ground, ⁴ and Abel brought of the firstlings of his flock and of their fat portions. And the Lord had regard for Abel and his offering, ⁵ but for Cain and his offering he had no regard. So Cain was very angry, and his countenance fell. ⁶ The Lord said to Cain, "Why are you angry, and why has your countenance fallen? ⁷ If you do well, will you not be accepted? And if you do not do well, sin is couching at the door; its desire is for you, but you must master it."

The first couple are now identified by their names, Adam and Eve; and he *knew* her. The Hebrew know, which depicts intellectual knowledge and experience, is also used here euphemistically of sexual intercourse (4:17,25; 24:16). The firstborn son of the first couple is Cain. Eve says, *I have gotten a man with the help of* Yahweh. What the word translated *gotten* really means is doubtful. The etymology is popular, but erroneous. *Qanah* is the verb from which in its secondary form the word Cain is derived. Cain means spear or reed, not creature or "gotten thing." *With the help of* is an English interpretative addition of the Hebrew which has Yahweh as a second accusative, or says simply "with Yahweh," and, as it stands, is unintelligible. Many interpreters have tried to retain Yahweh as this second accusative in apposition to man, which itself is a strange designation for a baby, though its use here is a reference to its sex and not its size. The Jerusalem Targum translates, "I have obtained a man, the

angel of Yahweh." But Yahweh cannot be a suitable object to the verb. Others have altered the sign of the accusative '*eth* to '*oth*, and read "a man, the mark of Yahweh." This is no better.

Perhaps the story had once a larger context which carried a veto against childbearing. Eve overcomes the veto, offering a religious reason for her success. The English gloss is probably right, and the sentence is rather a pious acknowledgment. After all, for her and for the author, Cain was the very first child born into the world. This first birth is thus matched by the devout ascription. Eve's second baby was also a boy, hardly a twin as some have suggested. His name was Abel (Heb. is *hebhel*), which means a breath, vapor, vanity —and his life was but a brief breath. Cain was a farmer, tilling the ground; Abel, a shepherd, tending flocks. Flocks had at least been tamed and domesticated. In course of time each brother brings to Yahweh an offering from the product of his toil. Cain, a first-fruit, a simple present to Yahweh (cf. Ex. 23:16,19; 34:22,26; Num. 13:20); Abel, a firstling, not excluding the fat pieces (cf. Lev. 1:8; 3:3 f.; Num. 18:17). The bringing of the presents is simply noted, and no motive, such as thanksgiving or tribute or conciliation is intended. The passage simply records the first great division of men into the agricultural and the pastoral livelihood.

Yahweh accepted Abel and his offering, but looked with disfavor on what Cain had brought. The text gives no reason for the preference. The preference may have been due to: (a) a different disposition of spirit in the brothers; (b) the material of the offering, flesh and fat not fruit; (c) the method of the offering—the first-fruits by presentation only, the firstling, by sacrifice, that is, by death, and presentation. This means that only a blood ritual was acceptable.

Cain became angry (literally, "it became hot to him") and dejected (literally, "his faces fell"—note the Hebrew plural "his faces" for "his face" as another illustration of Israelite plural-singular thinking).

The implied warning and rebuke of verse 6 is followed by a diagnosis and cure in verse 7. Yahweh points out that if Cain behaves he will be acceptable. Hebrew, "If you do well will there not be a lifting": the lifting of course refers to the face. The phrase is nearly equivalent to face-saving, though not quite. Cain's face has fallen, but if he behaves it will be lifted, i.e., he will recover his honor (cf. Job 10:15; 11:15; 22:26). If Cain does not behave, then sin lies in wait "at the door" (cf. Prov. 9:14).

The figure of the couching animal or snake(!) in wait for its prey and man's victory over it describe the onset and foiling of sin. Man's defeat of sin is his mastery or rule over it. The psychology is sound, for the harboring of discontent is explosive. The relation of 4:7b with the same words in 3:16b is illuminating, especially for the latter passage.

The events of the fourth chapter continue the beginnings, because they are essentially the account of man's new life outside the garden. For the editor of the book of Genesis as he compiled it, and for us as we read it, the first couple are where they belong under the firmament, but they are also where they were not meant to be, outside the garden, to the east of it.

Now occur perhaps the first marriage, for perhaps no marriage was described or perhaps intended in the garden, and certainly the first sexual act, the first birth, the first trades, the first rituals of worship, the first murder, the first city, the first and seven-fold family tree, the first polygamy, the first arts and crafts, the first song and the first public worship. Chapter 4, then, is the first chapter after the beginning.

For strict analysis the chapter is not without its difficulties. Why was one sacrifice preferred to another (v. 5)? Where did Cain get his wife (v. 17)? How reconcile the reference to sacrifices offered to Yahweh with the note of the later beginnings of the worship of Yahweh (v. 26)?

The chapter is easily separated into three sections: the Story of Cain and Abel (1–16); Cain's family tree (17–24); part of Seth's family tree (25–26).

2. First Murder (4:8–16)

8 Cain said to Abel his brother, "Let us go out to the field." And when they were in the field, Cain rose up against his brother Abel, and killed him. 9 Then the Lord said to Cain, "Where is Abel your brother?" He said, "I do not know; am I my brother's keeper?" 10 And the LORD said, "What have you done? The voice of your brother's blood is crying to me from the ground. 11 And now you are cursed from the ground, which has opened its mouth to receive your brother's blood from your hand. 12 When you till the ground, it shall no longer yield to you its strength; you shall be a fugitive and a wanderer on the earth." 13 Cain said to the LORD, "My punishment is greater than I can bear. 14 Behold, thou hast driven me this day away from the ground; and from thy face I shall be hidden; and I shall be a fugitive and a wanderer on the earth, and whoever finds me will slay me." 15 Then the LORD said to him, "Not so! If any one slays Cain, vengeance shall be taken on him sevenfold." And the LORD put a mark on Cain, lest any who came upon him should kill him. 16 Then Cain went away from the presence of the LORD, and dwelt in the land of Nod, east of Eden.

The passage is notable for a number of features. "Let us go out to the field" is not found in the Hebrew, but is in the Samaritan Pentateuch and the LXX. Syriac and Vulgate versions suggest this RSV insertion. A contrast between living in the house and working out in the fields is implicit. The almost monosyllabic form of the verse portrays vividly the ghastly event, a compound of envy, hatred, and brutality. The Lord is instantly present at the scene of the crime, and his question now is not evangelical, as it was after the first sin (3:9), but ethical. *Where is Abel your brother?* Men are responsible for one another. Cain's reply is both an evasion and a lie, for Cain has buried Abel. (See Driver's note on the typical psychology of the passage.) Cain's first question is also the first question asked by man in the Bible, and by implication denies man's first concern for his fellows.

Cain's crime against his brother becomes a sin against God in verse 10. Cain has both slain his brother and usurped the divine rights in blood. The blood is the seat of life, which in turn is the possession and the gift of God. Murder robs man of life but challenges and takes away God's right to bestow and maintain life. On this view not even execution by the state may be justified, let alone individual homicide. Other Old Testament laws, especially in regard to idolatry, etc., provide otherwise. Murdered blood cries out from the grave to God, its owner (Job 16:18; Ezek. 24:7 f.). The Hebrew word for crying is outcry, especially as directed to and heard by God. It is the absence of righteousness (Isa. 5:7) and embraces the suppressed sufferings and injustices of the oppressed and slain (Ex. 3:7; 22:7).

Cain's punishment is parallel to his crime. His crime came between human blood and its source in God. His punishment breaks the harmony between himself as man (*'adham*) and the ground (*'adhamah*) from which he was taken. Instead of harmony with and dependence upon mother earth, a curse intervenes whereby earth will withhold its fertility and will be no home to him. Wherever he should find himself, he will not be at home and will move on only to be restless.

Cain describes his unbearable iniquity and punishment by the words, "Thou hast expelled me from upon the face of the ground." Unless by *ground* a particular territory is meant, e.g., Palestine or the garden in Eden, and Cain is exiled, the punishment is threefold: homelessness, absence from God, and these in perpetuity. Cain recognizes that his future condition will be an open invitation to anyone (who?) to slay him. The Lord then tattoos Cain with a protecting mark to preserve him from death. The idea of the mark was not merely to afford him divine protection but to ensure that he would live to bear his punishment of homelessness and godlessness. By his own words (4:14), Cain ensures the continuation of his fate. The amelioration of his lot prolongs the sufferings of his lot.

The land of Nod is Cain's new home. This word means wandering. Absence from God is the consequence of sin and is achieved for the living by expulsion from paradise, or by dispersion (cf. Gen. 11: 1–9), of which Cain's aimless wandering is the first example. *East of Eden* has two alternatives—a garden or homelessness; the first is out of the world, the second in the world.

3. Cain and the Kenites (4:17–24)

17 Cain knew his wife, and she conceived and bore Enoch; and he built a city, and called the name of the city after the name of his son, Enoch. 18 To Enoch was born Irad; and Irad was the father of Mehujael, and Mehujael the father of Methushael, and Methushael the father of Lamech. 19 And Lamech took two wives; the name of the one was Adah, and the name of the other Zillah. 20 Adah bore Jabal; he was the father of those who dwell in tents and have cattle. 21 His brother's name was Jubal; he was the father of all those who play the lyre and pipe. 22 Zillah bore Tubalcain; he was the forger of all instruments of bronze and iron. The sister of Tubalcain was Naamah.

23 Lamech said to his wives:

"Adah and Zillah, hear my voice;
  you wives of Lamech, hearken to what
  I say:
I have slain a man for wounding me,
  a young man for striking me.
24 If Cain is avenged sevenfold,
  truly Lamech seventy-sevenfold."

Cain is of course the representative or ancestor of the tribe of the Kenites. The story about Cain is a story about the second generation of man. If Abel is good, Cain is evil, and in his wandering expects death as inevitable. Evil is becoming universal. The expulsion from security with the soil to homelessness as a wanderer in the land of wandering shows separation from God as a result of sin. This primal picture also serves to show how the descendants of Cain, the Kenites, are related to Palestine and Israel.

The Kenites were worshipers of Yahweh (cf. Ex. 18; also the exploit of Jael, Judg. 4). They may have been for a time part of Israel (Ex. 17; cf. 18:27; Judg. 4:11) but were not heirs of the promise of the land (i.e., their Yahwism is pre-Abrahamic). They never lived in the land but were wandering smiths, gypsies on the fringe of the field. They may have worshiped Yahweh before Israel did, and may have borne a tattoo mark in evidence of their relation to Yahweh. They may also have been ruthless, cruel, and given to stealing and murder. Cain was to remain an example and a spectacle, and these features are perhaps figured in the reputation of the Kenites as wanderers.

The writer now gives us the family tree of Cain which is expanded with items of information as it proceeds. The material of this genealogy and its form are different from the preceding stories about Cain. Some interpreters have decided that there are two sources in the chapter, or that there were two genealogies, or that the original order of the verses has been lost. The editor simply preserves materials of different kinds and intentions.

The intention of the editor of the material is obvious. Although the character of Cain and his destiny are different from those of the Cain of 1–16, nevertheless only one Cain is intended—not two different men of the same name, as some have supposed. Cain, condemned to wander, nevertheless as an act of defiance attempts to settle. The wanderer tries to overcome his destiny by taking a wife and founding a settled home and a city. Then either because he could not help it—being insufficiently at peace with himself to name his city with his own name—or else to avoid drawing Yahweh's attention to himself as settling and building a settlement, he names the city Enoch, his son's name. Enoch is a name in the line of Seth also (5:18) and is a Midianite name in 25:4, and a Reubenite name in 46:9. Although apparently the only person in the world, apart from his parents, Cain seemingly has no difficulty in finding a wife and becoming the founder of urban life. On the editor's view of one family Cain's wife could only have been Adam's daughter and his own sister (cf. 5:4; Jub. 4:1,9).

Apart from the family tree no further news is given for four generations. Lamech's children by his two wives become

shepherds, musicians, and smiths. In Cain's family the life of the city and of the steppe have their beginnings.

The working of iron follows that of stone and bronze and is obviously much later in the cultural scale than is here represented. Verses 23 f. contain Lamech's ancient boasting song and illustrate the growth of polygamy and brutality among men. Perhaps verse 24 is echoed in Matthew 18:22. The song itself is a good illustration of a Hebrew poem consisting of six lines, where the second, fourth, and sixth lines virtually repeat the thought and form of the first, third, and fifth lines. This is what is meant by the parallelism of Hebrew poetry.[5]

4. The Family of Seth (4:25-26)

25 And Adam knew his wife again, and she bore a son and called his name Seth, for she said, "God has appointed for me another child instead of Abel, for Cain slew him." 26 To Seth also a son was born, and he called his name Enosh. At that time men began to call upon the name of the LORD.

As in Genesis 10 the families of the abandoned or other lives, e.g., Japheth and Ham, are given before the families of the line of promise, Shem. So here Cain's tree has been given, and the way is clear for the main line of the story to reappear. The line of Seth reappears in chapter 5 with Cainite names, Enosh and Lamech, but this would be natural in closely related families. Obviously the editor had two traditions of the Seth family tree.

In this story of the alternative family tree, the line of life and promise, the story invokes God again, as at 4:1, and leads in the third generation, that of Enosh, to the widespread cult of Yahweh. Perhaps the verse was originally a tradition about the first man ('enosh means man, especially in his frailty and mortality) and the first worship. In its present place the tradition emphasizes that worship is characteristic of the descendants in the family with which

---

[5] Cf. G. B. Gray, *The Forms of Hebrew Poetry* (London: Hodder & Stoughton, 1915). Also cf. Theodore H. Robinson, *The Poetry of The Old Testament* (London: Duckworth, 1947).

God proposes to further the history of mankind. Yahwism is closely related to the Cain and Seth families and was thus conceived as the original religion of men.

To call upon means in Hebrew to call out with the name; i.e., to say the name out loud in invocation. It thus means to pronounce the word "O Yahweh" (cf. 12:8; 13:4; 21:33; 26:25; Ex. 33:19; 34:5; Psalm 116:13).

V. *Priestly Family Tree: Adam Through Noah* (5:1-32)

¹ This is the book of the generations of Adam. When God created man, he made him in the likeness of God. ² Male and female he created them, and he blessed them and named them Man when they were created. ³ When Adam had lived a hundred and thirty years, he became the father of a son in his own likeness, after his image, and named him Seth. ⁴ The days of Adam after he became the father of Seth were eight hundred years; and he had other sons and daughters. ⁵ Thus all the days that Adam lived were nine hundred and thirty years; and he died.

⁶ When Seth had lived a hundred and five years, he became the father of Enosh. ⁷ Seth lived after the birth of Enosh eight hundred and seven years, and had other sons and daughters. ⁸ Thus all the days of Seth were nine hundred and twelve years; and he died.

⁹ When Enosh had lived ninety years, he became the father of Kenan. ¹⁰ Enosh lived after the birth of Kenan eight hundred and fifteen years, and had other sons and daughters. ¹¹ Thus all the days of Enosh were nine hundred and five years; and he died.

¹² When Kenan had lived seventy years, he became the father of Mahalalel. ¹³ Kenan lived after the birth of Mahalalel eight hundred and forty years, and had other sons and daughters. ¹⁴ Thus all the days of Kenan were nine hundred and ten years; and he died.

¹⁵ When Mahalalel had lived sixty-five years, he became the father of Jared. ¹⁶ Mahalalel lived after the birth of Jared eight hundred and thirty years, and had other sons and daughters. ¹⁷ Thus all the days of Mahalalel were eight hundred and ninety-five years; and he died.

¹⁸ When Jared had lived a hundred and sixty-two years he became the father of Enoch. ¹⁹ Jared lived after the birth of Enoch eight hundred years, and had other sons and daughters. ²⁰ Thus all the days of Jared were nine hundred and sixty-two years; and he died.

²¹ When Enoch had lived sixty-five years, he became the father of Methuselah. ²² Enoch walked with God after the birth of Methuselah three hundred years, and had other sons and daughters. ²³ Thus all the days of Enoch were three hundred and sixty-five years. ²⁴ Enoch walked with God; and he was not, for God took him.

²⁵ When Methuselah had lived a hundred and eighty-seven years, he became the father of Lamech. ²⁶ Methuselah lived after the birth of Lamech seven hundred and eighty-two years, and had other sons and daughters. ²⁷ Thus all the days of Methuselah were nine hundred and sixty-nine years; and he died.

²⁸ When Lamech had lived a hundred and eighty-two years, he became the father of a son, ²⁹ and called his name Noah, saying, "Out of the ground which the Lord has cursed this one shall bring us relief from our work and from the toil of our hands." ³⁰ Lamech lived after the birth of Noah five hundred and ninety-five years, and had other sons and daughters. ³¹ Thus all the days of Lamech were seven hundred and seventy-seven years; and he died.

³² After Noah was five hundred years old, Noah became the father of Shem, Ham, and Japheth.

Doubtless there once existed a book entitled *The Book of the Generations of Adam*.⁶ The priestly writer now connects his account of creation with the story of Noah and the flood by means of this ten-generation family tree. The priestly account is like a series of hourglasses and the family trees are the stems which connect each book.

This list (vv. 1-32) closely corresponds to the list of 4:17, with which it must be compared. Each item conveys stereotyped information (cf. the lists in Driver, pp. 80 f.).

This list of ten patriarchs also compares with the Babylonian list of nine or ten antidiluvian Babylonian kings. The seventh Babylonian king was supernaturally removed, and the tenth is the hero of the stories of the flood. The reigns of the Babylonian kings varies from 18,600 years to almost 65,000 years. These figures are

---

⁶ James B. Pritchard (ed.), *Ancient Near Eastern Texts Relating to the Old Testament*, 2d ed. (Princeton: Univ. Press, 1955).

much reduced in Genesis. According to these figures the pre-flood patriarchs of Genesis overlap, and so extend over a period of 1,656 years (cf. Sam., 1307, and LXX, 2262 years). Nine of the patriarchs were alive at the same time. Lamech, the ninth, was born before Adam died. Seth died just before Noah was born. Noah died when Abraham was sixty. Shem lived longer than Abraham and saw the birth of Esau and Jacob. This family tree thus presents us with a society of patriarchs and a company of related, yet isolated, very old men alive at nearly the same time.

The figures of the duration of life no doubt have some symbolic value, but as a whole the figures of duration of life of the pre-flood patriarchs are 700 to 1000 years; but from Noah to Abraham the life span is between 200 to 600 years, for the patriarchs 100 to 200 years, and thereafter the proverbial threescore years and ten. Thus the progressive diminution of the successive life spans is obvious, and it betokens the lessening of vitality and virility. This process is part of the priestly parallel to the spread of sin and death in the world. In the Samaritan Peutateuch and the Septuagint the figures are considerably reduced.

Generations, literally, begettings. Here the word is used in a literary sense as register or record of. In 2:4 the generations of heaven and earth end the story; here the generations of Adam begin the transition to Noah. Adam's Seth is born in his father's likeness.

The effect of this passage is thus not to reiterate that each successive generation is also created in the image of God, but that Seth, in his father's image, is thus one generation away from the divine image—hence the beginning of the lessening of dominion, the lessening of vitality already noticed. The name of the fourth man, Kenan, may be a variant of the name Cain. In verse 22 Enoch is said to walk *with* God (cf. Ecclesiasticus 44:16, Heb.), but Abraham *before* God. Perhaps the lessening longevity is matched by lessening fellowship with God.

In Genesis as a whole we begin in the garden, then go outside it: then Enoch and Noah walk with God but Abraham walks before God. Enoch was translated to God without passing through death, as was Elijah. Lamech lived 777 years and the figures are reminiscent of his song (4:23–24). Verse 29 pays an anticipatory tribute to Noah, the hero of the flood stories about to be related. The Sethite Lamech was much different in temperament from the Cainite Lamech.

VI. Evil Mankind and the Records of the Flood (6:1—8:22)

1. Divine Beings and the Daughters of Men (6:1–4)

[1] When men began to multiply on the face of the ground, and daughters were born to them, [2] the sons of God saw that the daughters of men were fair; and they took to wife such of them as they chose. [3] Then the Lord said, "My spirit shall not abide in man for ever, for he is flesh, but his days shall be a hundred and twenty years." [4] The Nephilim were on the earth in those days, and also afterward, when the sons of God came in to the daughters of men, and they bore children to them. These were the mighty men that were of old, the men of renown.

This brief and mysterious story illustrates two points concerning the traditions which make up the book of Genesis. It is in itself an independent story of unknown origin and uncertain purpose, but the author or editor of Genesis includes it in his story to illustrate his main purpose.

The story is dated to a time when men and women were plentiful; and persons of unusual stature, giants to ordinary mortals, had also appeared. These giants are present both before and after the incidents recorded, though such giants as were born of the marriages described are further defined as of primitive origin and men of great reputation. The story is not really presumed to explain the origin of the giants. These were on earth before the marriages, and even the mighty men of old. Perhaps originally verses 1–3 and verse 4 were not related.

Verses 1–3 describe marriages between *sons of God,* i.e., divine men, superhuman males, and the marriageable *daughters of men.* By sons of God are meant members of the heavenly court, angelic, divine, male beings (cf. Gen. 28:12; 1 Kings 22:19–22; Psalm 29:1; 89:7; Job 1:1–6; 2:1; 38:7) who marry human girls. The wickedness in the story then is that the heavenly beings marry at all, and when they do, they marry mortal women. They do not rape the women but marry them. But if they had been true to themselves they would not have sought sexual relations. How they did this, whether by assuming male bodies or by indwelling human males, is not stated.

In verse 3 Yahweh is displeased with what happens. He does not however punish the heavenly beings; he addresses himself to their progeny. Unfortunately the second verb of the verse and another key word are obscure. By *spirit* of course is meant man's life force as distinct from *flesh.* The RSV *shall not abide* replaces the KJV and ERV, "shall not strive with" (shall not shield, Speiser). Rule in, be humbled in, be powerful in are other meanings suggested, but the word is difficult.

From the descendants of Seth and/or Cain have come these giant men. Among them have now come the prodigies of these divine-human marriages. Yahweh feels compelled to put a limit on this expanding, strengthening life. He decides that man's life span shall be no more than 120 years; or, less likely, that life may remain on earth for 120 years more, i.e., before the Flood comes.

For may mean because or since, though some have taken it to mean "by reason of going astray he is flesh." The Nephilim or giants (cf. Josh. 15:14; Deut. 1:28; 2:10–11,21; 9:2; Amos 2:9) are only mentioned again in Numbers 13:33 (LXX, *gigantes*). The word may mean the fallen, the unnaturally begotten bastards. The limit of life is to apply to all men.

Perhaps the story originally told that the giants were the offspring of the divine-human marriages, but that is not clear in the present form of the story. Rather, the story appears to suggest man's life force is becoming explosive, that a sudden supercharging of this force took place in the marriages, and so limits had to be applied.

In the larger context of the narrative this story is used to illustrate the further spread of life and evil, affecting heavenly life as well as life on earth. The involvement of heavenly beings in the evils of earth is frightening and brings about a race of supermen who are also supersinners. Hence the limit on life to curb the spread of sin by shortened lifespan. The present position of this story, so difficult for us in ethos and outlook, shows however that it served as an introduction to the story of the flood and partly as a way of justification.

2. Divine Judgment on the Creation of Men (6:5–10)

5 The Lord saw that the wickedness of man was great in the earth, and that every imagination of the thoughts of his heart was only evil continually. 6 And the Lord was sorry that he had made man on the earth, and it grieved him to his heart. 7 So the Lord said, "I will blot out man whom I have created from the face of the ground, man and beast and creeping things and birds of the air, for I am sorry that I have made them." 8 But Noah found favor in the eyes of the Lord.
9 These are the generations of Noah. Noah was a righteous man, blameless in his generation; Noah walked with God. 10 And Noah had three sons, Shem, Ham, and Japheth.

The subject in the first three of these verses is Yahweh, and the progress of thought in Yahweh's mind is succinctly told. Yahweh reflects upon the extent of man's wickedness, grieves on it, and resolves upon action. The evil in the hearts of men is contrasted with the grief in Yahweh's heart, which is poignantly expressed (v. 6*b*). So the verses are a piece of theological reflection which sum up the progress of the history hitherto, and lead in to the narratives that follow. The verses are the bridge which links the stories of the beginning to the stories which tell of the end of the Adamic humanity. Here the author or the editor of Genesis reveals some of the framework of his drama. Not only are the hearts of man and of Yahweh contrasted, but the totality of man's wickedness is matched by the announcement of total destruction—except for Noah, the man of favor.

Man's great wickedness is flagrantly widespread in the earth, but also secretly. Every flight—fancy, form, fashion, imagination, impulse, purpose—of heart-mind-will is exclusively and continually evil. Were it not for the example of Noah, a picture of total depravity would be seen. The whole inner life of man is entirely bad.

The word for *imagination,* found again in this sense in 8:21, Deuteronomy 31:21, 1 Chronicles 28:9 and 29:18, and Isaiah 26:3 became a very important word in Jewish discussion on the psychology of man's inner life. The first and last verbs in verse 6 vividly describe the emotions of grief, vexation, and regret in Yahweh. The first verb means to take a deep breath, so to grieve and so to repent. The last verb means to feel pierced, and here to the very heart. References to Yahweh's change of mind do occur (Gen. 34:7; Ex. 32:14; 1 Sam. 15:11; Isa. 63:10; Jer. 18:7 f.; 26:3), though the belief that "God is not man that he should repent" (1 Sam. 15:29) is also clearly stated. Nevertheless now Adamic man is to be written off, and a new enterprise begun with Noachic mankind.

The Old Testament preserves two narratives of the flood as the sequels of the stories of the creation and the Fall. These are the biblical stories of the flood of which many examples have been found in the Ancient Near East and in other parts of the world. Best known are the flood stories from Babylonia with which the Old Testament stories are often and must indeed be compared.[7]

Two narratives may be traced in Genesis 6–9, but they are not successive as are the two stories of Genesis 1–2. They are rather interwoven, and so form the first really composite section in Genesis. As the following details show, the strands may be disentangled so as to reveal two almost complete and quite distinct stories.

First narrative (J)	Second narrative (P)
6:5–8	6:9–22;
7:1–5,7–10,12,	7:6,11,13–16a,
16b (last 6 words)	18–21,24.
17b,22–23	
8:2b–3a, 6–12,	8:1,3b–5,13a,
13b,20–22	14–19;
	9:1–17

These two strands are generally called the J and P narratives, corresponding to Genesis 2 f. and 1—2:4. The verses above show that: (a) 6:5–8 is parallel to 6:9–13; 7:1–5, to 6:17–20,22; and 7:7–9 to 7:13–16a; (b) in J one pair of unclean animals and seven pairs of clean animals are taken into the ark, whereas in the P story one pair only of all animals; (c) in J the flood lasts for forty days plus twenty one days (cf. 8:8,10,12), that is, 61 days, but in P the flood lasts 150 days. The waters increased and fell over a period of one year and 11 days; (d) J gives rain as the cause of the flood, but P the flood of waters from above and below the earth; (e) J uses the name Lord—Yahweh—whereas P uses the name God. Other expressions characteristic of each source also occur.

The two strands have been carefully threaded together, though the older J story is set in the context of the larger and later account of P. The two accounts are followed in turn.

3. The J and P Witness to the Flood Record (6:11—8:22)

11 Now the earth was corrupt in God's sight, and the earth was filled with violence. 12 And God saw the earth, and behold, it was corrupt; for all flesh had corrupted their way upon the earth. 13 And God said to Noah, "I have determined to make an end of all flesh; for the earth is filled with violence through them; behold, I will destroy them with the earth. 14 Make yourself an ark of gopher wood; make rooms in the

---

[7] For a brief account, see the article "Flood," NBD, especially pp. 428a, 429a.

ark, and cover it inside and out with pitch. [15] This is how you are to make it: the length of the ark three hundred cubits, its breadth fifty cubits, and its height thirty cubits. [16] Make a roof for the ark, and finish it to a cubit above; and set the door of the ark in its side; make it with lower, second, and third decks. [17] For behold, I will bring a flood of waters upon the earth, to destroy all flesh in which is the breath of life from under heaven; everything that is on the earth shall die. [18] But I will establish my covenant with you; and you shall come into the ark, you, your sons, your wife, and your sons' wives with you. [19] And of every living thing of all flesh, you shall bring two of every sort into the ark, to keep them alive with you; they shall be male and female. [20] Of the birds according to their kinds, and of the animals according to their kinds, of every creeping thing of the ground according to its kind, two of every sort shall come in to you, to keep them alive. [21] Also take with you every sort of food that is eaten, and store it up; and it shall serve as food for you and for them." [22] Noah did this; he did all that God commanded him.

[1] Then the LORD said to Noah, "Go into the ark, you and all your household, for I have seen that you are righteous before me in this generation. [2] Take with you seven pairs of all clean animals, the male and his mate; and a pair of the animals that are not clean, the male and his mate; [3] and seven pairs of the birds of the air also, male and female, to keep their kind alive upon the face of all the earth. [4] For in seven days I will send rain upon the earth forty days and forty nights; and every living thing that I have made I will blot out from the face of the ground." [5] And Noah did all that the LORD had commanded him.

[6] Noah was six hundred years old when the flood of waters came upon the earth. [7] And Noah and his sons and his wife and his sons' wives with him went into the ark, to escape the waters of the flood. [8] Of clean animals, and of animals that are not clean, and of birds, and of everything that creeps on the ground, [9] two and two, male and female, went into the ark with Noah, as God had commanded Noah. [10] And after seven days the waters of the flood came upon the earth.

[11] In the six hundredth year of Noah's life, in the second month, on the seventeenth day of the month, on that day all the fountains of the great deep burst forth, and the windows of the heavens were opened. [12] And rain fell upon the earth forty days and forty nights. [13] On the very same day Noah and his sons, Shem and Ham and Japheth, and Noah's wife and the three wives of his sons with them entered the ark, [14] they and every beast according to its kind, and all the cattle according to their kinds, and every creeping thing that creeps on the earth according to its kind, and every bird according to its kind, every bird of every sort. [15] They went into the ark with Noah, two and two of all flesh in which there was the breath of life. [16] And they that entered, male and female of all flesh, went in as God had commanded him; and the LORD shut him in.

[17] The flood continued forty days upon the earth; and the waters increased, and bore up the ark, and it rose high above the earth. [18] The waters prevailed and increased greatly upon the earth; and the ark floated on the face of the waters. [19] And the waters prevailed so mightily upon the earth that all the high mountains under the whole heaven were covered; [20] the waters prevailed above the mountains, covering them fifteen cubits deep. [21] And all flesh died that moved upon the earth, birds, cattle, beasts, all swarming creatures that swarm upon the earth, and every man; [22] everything on the dry land in whose nostrils was the breath of life died. [23] He blotted out every living thing that was upon the face of the ground, man and animals and creeping things and birds of the air; they were blotted out from the earth. Only Noah was left, and those that were with him in the ark. [24] And the waters prevailed upon the earth a hundred and fifty days.

[1] But God remembered Noah and all the beasts and all the cattle that were with him in the ark. And God made a wind blow over the earth, and the waters subsided; [2] the fountains of the deep and the windows of the heavens were closed, the rain from the heavens was restrained, [3] and the waters receded from the earth continually. At the end of a hundred and fifty days the waters had abated; [4] and in the seventh month, on the seventeenth day of the month, the ark came to rest upon the mountains of Ararat. [5] And the waters continued to abate until the tenth month; in the tenth month, on the first day of the month, the tops of the mountains were seen.

[6] At the end of forty days Noah opened the window of the ark which he had made, [7] and sent forth a raven; and it went to and fro until the waters were dried up from the earth. [8] Then he sent forth a dove from him, to see if the waters had subsided from the face of the ground; [9] but the dove found no place to set her foot, and she returned to him to the ark, for the waters were still on the face of the whole earth. So he put forth his hand and took her and brought her into the ark with him. [10] He waited another seven days, and again he sent forth the dove out of the ark; [11] and the dove came back to him in the evening, and lo,

in her mouth a freshly plucked olive leaf; so Noah knew that the waters had subsided from the earth. 12 Then he waited another seven days, and sent forth the dove; and she did not return to him any more.

13 In the six hundred and first year, in the first month, the first day of the month, the waters were dried from off the earth; and Noah removed the covering of the ark, and looked, and behold, the face of the ground was dry. 14 In the second month, on the twenty-seventh day of the month, the earth was dry. 15 Then God said to Noah, 16 "Go forth from the ark, you and your wife, and your sons and your sons' wives with you. 17 Bring forth with you every living thing that is with you of all flesh— birds and animals and every creeping thing that creeps on the earth—that they may breed abundantly on the earth, and be fruitful and multiply upon the earth." 18 So Noah went forth, and his sons and his wife and his sons' wives with him. 19 And every beast, every creeping thing, and every bird, everything that moves upon the earth, went forth by families out of the ark.

20 Then Noah built an altar to the Lord, and took of every clean animal and of every clean bird, and offered burnt offerings on the altar. 21 And when the Lord smelled the pleasing odor, the Lord said in his heart, "I will never again curse the ground because of man, for the imagination of man's heart is evil from his youth; neither will I ever again destroy every living creature as I have done. 22 While the earth remains, seedtime and harvest, cold and heat, summer and winter, day and night, shall not cease."

J's introduction to his flood narrative (6:5–8) was no doubt followed by an account of the making of the ark, but that account is no longer extant. Instead, the story tells how the family enters the ark. Noah's personal righteousness saves him and his entire family.

The missing section no doubt gave the reason for the building of the ark which is repeated now in 7:3 f., namely, to preserve some life in face of the flooding of the world and the destruction of all life. If the missing section gave no hint of the reason why the ark was to be built, then Noah is shown to have acted "in the dark." Noah obeyed God, doing exactly as he was bidden, and built a ship on dry ground by faith (cf. Heb. 11:7). So Noah is "right-

eous." This word not only describes a guiltless person but has a positive social meaning in the sense of a faithful member of the clan or the group. But Noah is righteous before God, that is, he is loyal in his relation to God also. To be righteous is to be right with God and with members of the society to which a man belongs. Thus through Noah and his family the continuity of human life in the world is assured. Beyond the disaster there is to be a future, and that future is part of the purpose of God and is in his gracious will.

The J witness speaks of 7 pairs of the clean animals and a pair of the unclean animals. The Hebrew for 7 pairs is actually "seven, seven," i.e., literally "by sevens." The words would mean 7 pairs, i.e., 14 animals; but they could mean 7 animals in each species, i.e., 3 pairs and 1 male over, as a spare or for a sacrifice after the flood.

J's distinction between clean and unclean animals can only be explained in the light of later texts in the Old Testament (cf. Lev. 11; Deut. 14), and from practices in old Canaanite religion. *Clean* means suitable for sacrifice and also human consumption. The P story does not recognize the distinction, which was only made later in Israel's history.

The male and his mate (7:2) are words quite different from the "male and female" in 6:19 and 7:3. The greater numbers of clean animals would produce a far greater supply of these animals, which in themselves would be of more use to men. After Noah and his family had entered the ark the Lord shut him in. Forty days' rain and twenty-one days of inundation blotted out all life from earth with the exception of the remnant family of Noah.

He blotted out. The pronoun "he" has no antecedent in the passage. It is better to read the same Hebrew verb in the passive sense and translate it, "Every living [subsisting] thing was blotted out." *Every living thing* (vv. 4,23) is not the usual word for living. Every subsisting thing is better. J continues his witness in 8:6–13.

The beautiful narrative of the birds in

8:6–13 needs only reading and not exposition, except to remark on the clear and picturesque details. The Babylonian account says that experiments were made with three different birds—the dove, swallow, and raven. From the behavior of the birds, the wild raven and the domestic dove, Noah understood the time of waiting and recognized the day of release.

Genesis 8:10,12 refers to 3 periods of 7 days each, a total of 21 days, between the dispatch of the raven and the nonreturn of the dove. So they left the ark, and Noah begins the new life with an altar and with a sacrifice of thanksgiving and perhaps of reconciliation as suggested by 8:22.

The word for altar in Hebrew means literally, the place where you slay. The word "burnt offerings" means sacrifice completely burnt on the altar, of which worshipers retain no part. The simplicity and primacy of the altar, the very first altar in the Bible, in that devastated world, reveal the dramatic art and religious feeling of the J writer.

In 8:22 the six terms, seedtime through winter, do not imply six two-month periods to make up a year, but two halves of the year in two series—*seedtime* (cold and winter) *and harvest* (heat and summer, cf. Psalm 74:17; Amos 3:15; Zech. 14:8). The last pair of terms, day and night, suggests a return to normal conditions after the dark night of the flood.

The P or priestly witness to the flood begins with his usual formula about the generations (6:9; cf. 2:4; 5:1). Noah is not only righteous as in J, but P also describes him as blameless; the Hebrew word is positive and means complete, sound, wholesome, having integrity, (cf. Job 1:1; Gen. 17:1; Psalm 18:23,25). "It was with God that Noah walked." The three tributes describe Noah's correct behavior, his acceptable integrity, and the humble conduct of his life as in God's presence. Even Abraham only walked before God (17:1). This man had three sons, but their significance only begins in the new era after the flood.

P describes the total corruption of the

earth and all flesh. The nauseous Hebrew word means destruction, ruin, and the decay and ruin due to corruption is overarched by violence—a rasping word of ruthless cruelty and unprincipled wrong. This dreadful picture compels the attention of God who resolves to end the evil by destruction.

The Hebrew is graphic: "The end of all flesh has come before me," almost as if the scene of the corruption before God's eyes is now succeeded by a new phase or condition. It means of course: I have decided that the end has come. The end is an eschatological (end of the world) word of great psychological power (cf. Amos 8:2; Hab. 2:3; Lam. 4:18; Ezek. 21:25,29).

All flesh. This phrase occurs 13 times in P's account of the flood, and really means all living beings, including animals.

Both J and P use the same word for the ark, which was made of gopher or cypress wood. This three-storied houseboat is 450 feet long, 75 feet broad and 45 feet high, that is reckoning the cubit at 18 inches, with a total displacement of about 43,300 tons.[8]

Pitched within and without, the ark with its cells (literally, nests) has a solitary window, unless the word means roof. The phrase *finish it to a cubit above* is difficult to understand. Perhaps it meant the window had that height, or that above the window there was a cubit of wood to the top of the ark. Others suggest a clerestory all around the ark. The ark also had a single door in one of its long sides. The Hebrew word for window in 6:16 is quite different from that in 8:6.

This vessel becomes the home of the remnant family of Noah and of the male and female animals and birds, one pair of every kind is chosen for preservation. The word for birds is the same as in Genesis 1. Sufficient food is also taken on board for animals and humans who are also fortified by the hint of a new covenant, an arrange-

---

[8] Alexander Heidel, *The Gilgamesh Epic and Old Testament Parallels*, 2d ed. (Chicago: Univ. Press, 1949), p. 236.

ment to be introduced and put into effect after the flood.

The method of destruction is by a flood of water by which is meant not rain or inundation in the normal sense, but the cosmic ocean which is above the firmament (1:7), and beneath the earth. The Hebrew word for flood is used only of Noah's flood and occurs 12 times in chapters 6–9. This cosmic ocean floods the earth through the opened windows of the firmament, and the springs in the ground, through which the waters well up (7:11).

This flood restores the watery chaos of 1:2 and thus reveals a terrifying catastrophe before which all life is helpless. It came upon the earth when Noah was 600 years old, on the seventeenth (LXX says twenty-seventh) day of the second month, seven days after they had entered the ark and begun to get used to life within the boat. The flood catastrophe lasts one year (either a lunar year of 354 days or a solar year of 365 days) and ten days.

So vast was the deluge of waters that the whole world was drowned, even the highest mountains were about 28 feet below the surface, and all life—men and beasts —was obliterated.[9]

When flood and destruction were complete, *God remembered Noah.* This does not mean that God had forgotten him, but it means the turning of the divine attention to the people who are to pioneer the new life in the world after the flood. Von Rad relates this moment of recollection to a turn toward salvation leading up to Jesus Christ. This is broadly true, but within this angle the more decisive turn in Abraham is the more significant. God really turns his attention to the founders of the second mankind, to the eight of the remnant family from whom the earth is to be peopled for a second time.

At once a divinely sent wind causes the waters to go down, because the sources of the inflowing water are cut off. After 150 days, on the seventeenth day of the sev-

9 Cf. J. Bright, *The Biblical Archaeologist*, Dec., 1942, V, 55–62.

enth month the ark grounded on Mount Ararat, a region in present-day Armenia. Nearly two and a half months were to pass before the tops of the mountains became visible. Two statements, 8:13a and 8:14, give different dates for the drying of the earth.

The departure from the ark is a combined operation of men and beasts under divine orders. The beasts are again under the new familiar blessing *be fruitful and multiply,* as in 1:22.

VII. The Second Humanity (9:1—11:32)

The renewal of the blessing is also extended to Noah and his sons who are to be fruitful, to multiply, and to fill the earth. Life is always and everywhere God's peculiar possession. This truth was probably first realized in Israel's priestly thinking (cf. Lev. 7:26 f.; Deut. 12:16; 24:15,23), but here that cultic truth is universalized and made a law of all life—human and animal. The second mankind is speeded on its way like the first. There are several differences to consider.

1. Covenant with Noah (9:1–17)

1 And God blessed Noah and his sons, and said to them, "Be fruitful and multiply, and fill the earth. 2 The fear of you and the dread of you shall be upon every beast of the earth, and upon every bird of the air, upon everything that creeps on the ground and all the fish of the sea; into your hand they are delivered. 3 Every moving thing that lives shall be food for you; and as I gave you the green plants, I give you everything. 4 Only you shall not eat flesh with its life, that is, its blood. 5 For your lifeblood I will surely require a reckoning; of every beast I will require it and of man; of every man's brother I will require the life of man. 6 Whoever sheds the blood of man, by man shall his blood be shed; for God made man in his own image. 7 And you, be fruitful and multiply, bring forth abundantly on the earth and multiply in it."

8 Then God said to Noah and to his sons with him, 9 "Behold, I establish my covenant with you and your descendants after you, 10 and with every living creature that is with you, the birds, the cattle, and every beast of the earth with you, as many as came out of the

ark. [11] I establish my covenant with you, that never again shall all flesh be cut off by the waters of a flood, and never again shall there be a flood to destroy the earth." [12] And God said, "This is the sign of the covenant which I make between me and you and every living creature that is with you, for all future generations: [13] I set my bow in the cloud, and it shall be a sign of the covenant between me and the earth. [14] When I bring clouds over the earth and the bow is seen in the clouds, [15] I will remember my covenant which is between me and you and every living creature of all flesh; and the waters shall never again become a flood to destroy all flesh. [16] When the bow is in the clouds, I will look upon it and remember the everlasting covenant between God and every living creature of all flesh that is upon the earth." [17] God said to Noah, "This is the sign of the covenant which I have established between me and all flesh that is upon the earth."

(a) The first man's beneficent lordship is here not mentioned. Instead, a tyranny emerges whereby the animals are to live in fear and dread of man, because they are to be at his disposal for food and use.

(b) Nevertheless men are not to eat meat which contains blood; i.e., they are not to eat blood. The Hebrew must be translated literally thus: "Only flesh with its soul, that is its blood, ye must not eat" (v. 4); and again, "And surely your blood, according to your souls"; i.e., the blood of each person will be required, and "the soul of man" (v. 5). The word soul or souls means here of course the principle of life, seated in the breath and/or the blood. A man who has ceased to breathe is dead, so there is life in breath. Similarly a man who has lost all his blood is a corpse, so there is life in blood. The Hebrew thus thought of a breath-soul and a blood-soul, in each of which of course life was present. On either count then the word for each describes that principle of conscious life distinct from the body, and so means the "person" or "self."

(c) Such a valuation of life inevitably means that even if men may destroy the life of animals, neither man nor beast may take the life of men (vv. 5 f.). Verse 6 is an ancient and precisely formed semilegal poetic fragment. It reads literally

Shedder of blood of man,
By man his blood will be shed

when a law of exact requital is stated in two alliterative lines where the terms exactly correspond. Murder must be countered by death, and man is made responsible to ensure the death of the murderer. This law is then grounded in the reminiscence that God (had) made man in God's image. The reference to the image as expressing man's dominion is absent at the end of verse 7 where it would be expected. Verse 7 then repeats verse 1. The second mankind, like the animals, is also under the blessing of God. They are meant to be fruitful and fill the earth, but the proliferation of life (so complicated now by the admixture of corruption, violence, and ruin) must be controlled within the limits presented.

Chapter 9 thus states the new divine arrangements for the second humanity, whereby God's blessing is adapted to the changing circumstances. God is still gracious and forbearing (Rom. 3:25), but there is a divine watchfulness and a policy for the new life.

God is now said to propose to Noah and his sons the institution of a covenant. *Establish* is the more sophisticated of the two main verbs to describe the making of a *covenant*. The earlier form is "cut" a covenant, and is typical of the earlier writings of the Old Testament. The word establish, literally to set up in its place, is the later word, and suggests the maintenance as well as the beginning of the covenant. P also uses "give a covenant" (17:2; Num. 25:12).

The covenant is to embrace Noah and his descendants; i.e., his sons and the new humanity to spring from them, and all life that survived the flood. The covenant inevitably selects and particularizes, for it is also the expression of the elective principle.

The covenant does not have the form of a mutual arrangement with mutual obligations. Rather God out of his own initiative gives a unilateral undertaking never to flood and destroy the earth again. This undertaking, without conditions, is vested in the rainbow which will serve as the sign of the undertaking and also as a reminder to God of his obligation. The covenant is thus absolute and everlasting. The word for *bow* elsewhere means a military bow. Here its string lies flat on the ground, and so the bow is unusable. The military sense is gone, and the bow is a sign of an undertaking only. The arrangement is more like a testament or dispensation than covenant in the usual sense. Everlasting covenant (cf. 17:7,13,19; Ex. 31:16; Lev. 24:8; Num. 18:19; 25:13, all P).

The second mankind is thus launched on its new life. Grace, salvation, and blessing are present. Then, as man's dealings with man and the beasts are controlled to safeguard human life, so God's dealings with men are also subject to the promise that life will never again be destroyed by divine punishment by flood.

Note: Traditions Concerning the Flood

Nearly one hundred stories of a great flood are said to exist in various parts of the world. The location of such stories poses interesting problems not only in the comparison of literature but also in protohistory. Of all these stories the Babylonian and biblical are the best known and the most closely related. The Babylonian story is inscribed on the eleventh tablet of the so-called Gilgamesh epic.

Gilgamesh, a young ruler of the first dynasty of the city of Uruk, suffers the loss of his bosom friend, Enkidu, by death and resolves to seek advice from his ancestor Utnapishtim on how to gain immortality. After many adventures he encounters Utnapishtim who tells him the story of the flood.

The parallels between the Babylonian story and Genesis are clear. The Babylonian gods decree a deluge, but one of them warns Utnapishtim of the impending catastrophe. Utnapishtim is the tenth Babylonian king before the flood, as Noah was the tenth patriarch before the flood. Both heroes are said to have built a huge ship, but the Babylonian vessel was much bigger than Noah's ark, for it was a cube with a displacement of 228,500 tons. The vessel housed a considerable number of people besides the animals. Noah's ark had but eight human occupants and the animals. Both stories give different versions of the duration of the flood, the grounding of the vessel, the dispatch of the birds, of the exit from the ark, and of the sacrifice after the flood.

Such a brief comparison shows that in some way the Babylonian and biblical stories are closely related, and the scholarly fashion was to claim that the biblical story was dependent upon the Babylonian. Nevertheless the many differences in ethos, religious feeling, and actual detail between the two stories, which are now increasingly recognized, render such a view very unlikely. The two stories have probably a common origin, or else the Babylonian story has traveled from its original home and been adapted to new conditions as it traveled. The stories are thus related, and parallel, but not interdependent.

Certainly in Genesis the flood stories now exhibit an exalted monotheism and are also clearly the vehicles of a moral judgment, and receive a unique ethical quality from these features. (For a full and carefully reasoned account, cf. Heidel, pp. 224–69.)

2. Farmer Noah (9:18–29)

18 The sons of Noah who went forth from the ark were Shem, Ham, and Japheth. Ham was the father of Canaan. 19 These three were the sons of Noah; and from these the whole earth was peopled.
20 Noah was the first tiller of the soil. He planted a vineyard; 21 and he drank of the wine, and became drunk, and lay uncovered in his tent. 22 And Ham, the father of Canaan, saw the nakedness of his father, and told his two brothers outside. 23 Then Shem and Japheth took a garment, laid it upon both their shoulders, and walked backward and covered the nakedness of their father; their faces were turned away, and they did not see their father's nakedness. 24 When Noah awoke from his wine and knew what his youngest son had done to him, 25 he said,

"Cursed be Canaan;
     a slave of slaves shall he be to his
          brothers."
26 He also said,
   "Blessed by the Lord my God be Shem;
          and let Canaan be his slave.
27 God enlarge Japheth,
     and let him dwell in the tents of Shem;
          and let Canaan be his slave."
28 After the flood Noah lived three hundred
and fifty years. 29 All the days of Noah were
nine hundred and fifty years; and he died.

The concluding story about Noah is not a
very happy one. Indeed some have even
claimed that this story is not about the
Noah of the flood at all, but about another
man also called Noah, who was the first
agriculturalist (not Cain, as in 4:2), and
who first specialized in the growth of vines.
The close connections however between
the Noah of the flood and this Noah require that they must be one and the same
person. A culture myth connecting agriculture and viticulture is thus used to further
the story of the second mankind.

The passage has several difficulties. The
people of the Old Testament were very
touchy about nakedness, and they possessed divine laws, listed in Leviticus 18,
which forbade the uncovering of the genital organs. This was a very serious matter,
and those scholars who suggest that other
vices as well as exposure are implied, are
not taking the story seriously enough. As it
stands the story says:

(a) Ham, Noah's second son, happened
to notice that his father was naked because
he was drunk (cf. Hab. 2:15; Lam. 4:21).
Ham is not said to uncover his father, but
to have noticed and told his brothers. He
could hardly be blamed, unless of course
his fault was that he entered his father's
tent, when he should not have done so.

(b) In fact, he is not blamed. Noah's
youngest son is blamed (v. 24), but Noah's
wrath is not vented on his youngest son,
Japheth, but on Canaan, Ham's fourth and
youngest son.

(c) Noah was naked in his tent and was
so seen. In verses 22 f., the phrase *nakedness of his* (their) *father* occurs three times.
By Leviticus 18:7 f., the "nakedness of your
father" can actually mean the nakedness of
his wife also. The text may therefore refer
to the nakedness of Noah and his wife in
an inner part of the tent, where Ham had no
business to enter.

(d) But why is Canaan and not Ham
blamed? The most common explanation is
to suppose that this is a story about (another) Noah who had three sons, Shem,
Japheth, and Canaan. If this assumption is
correct, then you must alter 9:18 to cut out
Ham and read Shem, Japheth, and Canaan;
and then you must cross out the words
"Ham, the father of" in verse 22. If you
accept this, then the story is all about
Shem, Japheth, and Canaan and may have
to be moved to follow Genesis 11:9. This
solution is very neat but Noah's three sons
usually are Shem, Ham, and Japheth
(5:32; 6:10; 7:13; 10:1; cf. 10:2,6,21).

This proposed reconstruction also assumes that once two cycles of stories existed. The one cycle concerned Shem,
Ham, and Japheth and the growth of the
second mankind from them. The second
cycle was much more limited and concerned Shem, Japheth, and Canaan, and
the interrelations of people in Palestine.
On this view Shem has to be limited to the
Israelites; Japheth to either the Hittites or
other people of Asia Minor—the Phoenicians, Cretans, or Philistines; and Canaan
of course, the Canaanites. Japheth is to
have an enlarging destiny and dwell in the
tents of Shem, but this corresponds to nothing in the later history of the Hittites or
Philistines, who unlike Japheth have no
future of blessing. This proposed reconstruction founders on the enlarging Japheth
and creates more difficulties than it solves.
The story also links one world context after
the flood to another world context—the
spread of the nations in Chapter 10. Localized traditions about the future inside Canaan would have been premature here and
so out of place.

An even more radical and unacceptable

form of the story would be to suppose that Canaan's offense was against his own father Ham.

On the other hand if we suppose the story is abbreviated, then by supplying some details another reconstruction is possible. Canaan must be fairly young, perhaps a child, with freedom to run in and out of all parts of his father and grandfather's tent. Canaan then must have seen the grandparental nudity and told his father, who checked and so committed the fault. Shem and Japheth covered their father by walking backwards and letting a garment fall off their own shoulders on to Noah (and ? wife). Noah awoke to find himself (themselves) covered, and on inquiry learned that the youngest son of the entire family had seen him (them) and told his father, Ham. Then Noah curses Canaan for the seeing, and for telling Ham, and so making Ham go wrong also. The words *his youngest son* naturally refer to Noah's youngest son, but they cannot refer to Japheth. They must refer to Noah's youngest son just as the words of the women of Bethlehem, "A son has been born to Naomi," really refer to Ruth's son and Naomi's grandson (Ruth 4:17).

The character of Noah poses some problems too. Remembering his excellent and devout character until now, we must suppose that he was the innocent victim of his own experiments with wine. Being the first person to till and cultivate vines, he began to eat grapes, drink their juice, store it, and one day in all innocence he became drunk. This first scientist is thus in this view quite free from blame.

On the other hand Noah tills the ground, and here again the ground ('adhamah— earth) theme reappears. Noah is the son of Lamech, and it was predicted of him in 5:29 that Noah would wrest relief (the Hebrew word is a play on Noah's name) from the cursed ground. This prediction is now fulfilled in Noah's discovery of the vine and its fruit the wine. But instead of being a relief, the curse of the ground still

pursues man, and Noah falls victim to or abuses the relief he is meant to bring to men. So the curse passes on from the 'adhamah through the vine, through Noah and on to Canaan. Noah is thus by no means guiltless, and thus serves to act as a link in the ongoing curse.

This particular story ends in a poem of three verses, in the form of a historical prospect of the ethnic groups descended from Noah. Canaan is to be the "slaviest" slave of his brothers. By Genesis 10:6 these are named as Cush, Egypt, and Put. In the future Canaan was often to be ruled by the descendants of Cush, i.e., Babel and Assyria (cf. 10:7–12), and by Egypt.

The middle verse is an ascription of praise not to Shem but to the God of Shem, but RSV has altered this. In Shem God has provided for mankind an ancestor—a family and a nation—from whom and from which salvation is to come (John 4:22).

The third verse of the poem invokes God's (not Yahweh's) blessing on Japheth, who is to enlarge and dwell in Shem's tents. The word *enlarge* is a pun on Japheth's name and the translation is uncertain. The meaning of the blessing must be the independent "expansion" of Japheth, some of whose people will reside among the Semites, or else a figure of security for the Japhethites insofar as the Semites are concerned, an anticipation of 12:3, or even of Isaiah 2:2–4 (Driver). Common to all three verses is the slave-estate of Canaan. Shem and Japheth are for blessing.

Noah lived for 950 years. This simply means that he had a long experience of the first mankind, survived the flood, and saw his own mankind well on its way.

3. Descendants of Noah: The Table of Nations (10:1–32)

[1] These are the generations of the sons of Noah, Shem, Ham, and Japheth; sons were born to them after the flood. [2] The sons of Japheth: Gomer, Magog, Madai, Javan, Tubal, Meshech, and Tiras. [3] The sons of Gomer: Ashkenaz, Riphath, and Togarmah. [4] The sons of Javan: Elishah, Tar-

shish, Kittim, and Dodanim. ⁵ From these the coastland peoples spread. These are the sons of Japheth in their lands, each with his own language, by their families, in their nations.

⁶ The sons of Ham: Cush, Egypt, Put, and Canaan. ⁷ The sons of Cush: Seba, Havilah, Sabtah, Raamah, and Sabteca. The sons of Raamah: Sheba and Dedan. ⁸ Cush became the father of Nimrod; he was the first on earth to be a mighty man. ⁹ He was a mighty hunter before the LORD; therefore it is said, "Like Nimrod a mighty hunter before the LORD." ¹⁰ The beginning of his kingdom was Babel, Erech, and Accad, all of them in the land of Shinar. ¹¹ From that land he went into Assyria, and built Nineveh, Rehoboth-Ir, Calah, and ¹² Resen between Nineveh and Calah; that is the great city. ¹³ Egypt became the father of Ludim, Anamim, Lehabim, Naphtuhim, ¹⁴ Pathrusim, Casluhim (whence came the Philistines), and Caphtorim.

¹⁵ Canaan became the father of Sidon his first-born, and Heth, ¹⁶ and the Jebusites, the Amorites, the Girgashites, ¹⁷ the Hivites, the Arkites, the Sinites, ¹⁸ the Arvadites, the Zemarites, and the Hamathites. Afterward the families of the Canaanites spread abroad. ¹⁹ And the territory of the Canaanites extended from Sidon, in the direction of Gerar, as far as Gaza, and in the direction of Sodom, Gomorrah, Admah, and Zeboiim, as far as Lasha. ²⁰ These are the sons of Ham, by their families, their languages, their lands, and their nations.

²¹ To Shem also, the father of all the children of Eber, the elder brother of Japheth, children were born. ²² The sons of Shem: Elam, Asshur, Arpachshad, Lud, and Aram. ²³ The sons of Aram: Uz, Hul, Gether, and Mash. ²⁴ Arpachshad became the father of Shelah; and Shelah became the father of Eber. ²⁵ To Eber were born two sons: the name of the one was Peleg, for in his days the earth was divided, and his brother's name was Joktan. ²⁶ Joktan became the father of Almodad, Sheleph, Hazarmaveth, Jerah, ²⁷ Hadoram, Uzal, Diklah, ²⁸ Obal, Abimael, Sheba, ²⁹ Ophir, Havilah, and Jobab; all these were the sons of Joktan. ³⁰ The territory in which they lived extended from Mesha in the direction of Sephar to the hill country of the east. ³¹ These are the sons of Shem, by their families, their languages, their lands, and their nations.

³² These are the families of the sons of Noah, according to their genealogies, in their nations; and from these the nations spread abroad on the earth after the flood.

The tenth chapter of Genesis is an admirable illustration of the ecumenical thinking, universal and comprehensive, in the book and of the strategy of its composition. Stories of one complete mankind lie behind us. Stories of the beginnings of a second mankind have been reached. Ahead, as the author or editor knew, lay fresh disasters for this second mankind combined with a new rescue operation—a rescue that involved another man, Abraham, and his descendants—the seed of Abraham and the children of Israel. Now is the moment then to survey the worldwide disposition of the second mankind, the descendants of Noah. This must surely be one of the earliest attempts to survey mankind as a whole.

Note the word for *nations* in verses 5,20,31–32. The table of nations thus serves two purposes. Retrospectively, it concludes the history of the second humanity, the mankind sprung from Noah. It is also the backcloth or introduction to the discovery of the real theme of Genesis, of the Old Testament, and indeed of the Bible itself: The call of Abram and the real beginnings of salvation-history. The table has a theological character and a theological purpose (Acts 17:26), for it seeks to answer such questions as, Who and where are the second or Noachic mankind?

The table is mainly priestly but has some J passages, and ethnic and linguistic divisions of mankind are subordinated to a geographical arrangement. The table begins of course with the sons of Noah, but different sections reveal evidence of widely varying dates. Von Rad and others have shown that several names in the text, and several portions of the text, reveal the position belonging to and following the days of the coming of the sea peoples at the end of the second millennium B.C. The omission of Israel is striking. This is not humility or theology. It merely reflects the pre-Israelite date of the main edition of the table. The geographical range is from Transcaucasia to Ethiopia and from Iran to the Aegean.

(1) Japheth

The descendants of this man are traced to various localities in Anatolia (Asia

Minor) and the fringes of the Aegean. The general reference then is to peoples of Indo-European stock here subsumed under Noah's third son.[10]

Gomer. That is, Gimirrai, mentioned by the Assyrians or Cimmerians of classical sources, and ancestors of the Cymru—the modern Welsh. An Ukrainian people who conquered Urartu, Armenia, at the beginning of the first millennium B.C.

Magog (cf. Ezek. 38:2). "Gog, of the land of Magog, the chief prince of Meshech and Tubal" links several names in the present context.

Madai. The Medes of the eighth and later centuries, an Aryan people who settled in northwest Iran, west of the Caspian Sea.

Javan (cf. Isa. 66:19; Ezek. 27:13; Zech. 9:13, i.e., Ionians; cf. Iōnes, *Iliad* xiii, 685). References in Isaiah, Ezekiel, Zechariah, and Daniel all refer to Greeks or Hellenists.

Tubal (cf. Isa. 66:19, Ezek. 27:13, 32:26; 38:2; 39:1). Eastern Anatolia.

Meshech (cf. Ezek. 27:13; 32:26; 38:2; 39:1). Probably an Indo-Aryan group who settled in Eastern Anatolia.

Tiras. Perhaps connected with the Tursha and the Etruscans, thirteenth century B.C.

(2) Gomer

Ashkenaz (cf. Jer. 51:27). Ancestor of various peoples settled between the Black and Caspian seas.

Togarmah (cf. Ezek. 27:14; 38:6). See *Tegarama* near Carchemish: a people of Asia Minor.

Elishah (cf. Alashia of the Amarna letters). A place, Enkomi, or part of Cyprus.

Tarshish (cf. 1 Kings 9:26; 10:22; Isa. 66:19). Maybe Tartessos in Spain but possibly some place in the eastern Mediterranean, or a general description for land where minerals were mined.

Kittim (cf. 1 Chron. 1:7). Greeks— Aegean islands and coastlands. See Kition (Larnaka) in Cyprus (cf. Jer. 2:10).

[10] Cf. E. A. Speiser, "Man, Ethnic Divisions of," in IDB, pp. 235–42.

Dodanim. Probably for Rodanim, inhabitants of Rhodes.

Cush. In the Old Testament, Cush generally refers to Ethiopia, as here. Cush in Genesis 2:4 is some other place. See the Kassite country (cf. 10:8).

(3) Ham

Egypt. Listed with Cush as the first people of the Hamitic nations.

Put. See Punt; i.e., Africa and, most probably, Libya (cf. LXX, Jer. 46:9, MT).

Canaan. Linguistically the term belongs to Hebrew and Phoenician (cf. 10:15; Isa. 19:18). The listing of Canaan in an Egyptian context suggests political and military relations. The Canaanites had come into Palestine in the third millenium.

(4) Cush

Seba. Probably land of Sheba and its people.

Havilah (cf. 2:11). By 10:7 a descendant of Ham; by 10:29 a descendant of Shem. Perhaps a south Arabian people.

Sabtah. Probably a south Arabian people.

Raamah. Unidentified but probably near and akin to Havilah and Sheba.

Sabteca. Probably a south Arabian people.

(5) Ra-amah

Sheba. Genesis 10:7,28; and 25:3 mention three Shebas, who may be one and the same. The problem is to explain the Shemite and Hamitic contexts of the name.

Dedan. Perhaps the famous trading depot of Jeremiah 25:23; 49:8, and Ezekiel 25:13.

These last seven names take us to the eastern shore of the Red Sea and beyond. The following notice concerns Cush and Nimrod. The words "before Yahweh" are obscure. Apparently by Yahweh's will Cush was the conqueror rather than founder of cities in the eastern areas of the Fertile Crescent. *Beginning:* better mainstay.

Nimrod—Nimrood. An ancient site on the east bank of the Tigris bears the name of the goddess Ninurta, or Nimurta. Ninurta was the patron deity of hunting, so that Nimrod may conceal the name of that god. The city is not mentioned in the Old Testament and Nimrod is only described as a hero, as he is in The Koran also. The frequency of the name in city names and in the literature of the eastern Fertile Crescent suggest widespread traditions about him.

Babel is Babylon. Its Semitic name may show that it was not among the oldest cities of that area. It was said to have been founded by Marduk and destroyed by Sargon.

Erech. A famous and often mentioned city of the third millenium—one of the earliest of the Sumerian city states. The Sumerians called it *Unu(g)*, the Assyrians, *Uruk,* modern *Warka,* about 40 miles northwest of Ur, and site of some of the earliest inscribed clay tablets.

Accad. Founded by Sargon of Accad in the late third millenium. Later the term was used of northern Babylonia, and Akkadian now describes the Assyrian and Babylonian languages. Verse 11 indicates a movement and a priority. The movement is from the southern centers of ancient Babylonia into the northern and northeastern areas of the Fertile Crescent. Likewise, Nineveh became the Assyrian capital about the turn of the eighth century B.C.

Rehoboth-Ir and *Resen* are unknown. Albright and Speiser interestingly suggest that Rehoboth-Ir, which means wide open city, is a description of the piazzas of Nineveh. *Calah* is Assyrian Kalhu and is the name of the city of Nimrud, founded by Asshur and rebuilt by Shalmanezer 1, ca. 1250 B.C., and three centuries later by Ashurnasirpal. The city is of immense archaeological significance.[11]

(6) Egypt

The eight names in verses 13–14 and in the Hebrew masculine plural, showing that people, not places, are mentioned.

[11] Cf. M. E. L. Mallowan, *Nimrud and Its Remains* (2 vols.; London: Collins, 1966).

Ludim. Genesis 10:13,22 speak of Ludim and Lud. The former from Ham were famous bowmen (cf. Isa. 66:19; Jer. 46:9). Lud is a descendant of Shem and may be Lydiaus. Some read as *Lubim* and equate with Lehabim (below).

Anamim. Unknown.

Lehabim. Unknown; cf. Ludim above.

Naphtuhim. Uncertain, possibly Nile Delta to offset the Pathrusim.

Pathrusim. Pathros is south land, i.e., upper Egypt. See Isaiah 11:11; Jeremiah 44:1.

Casluhim. Unknown (LXX, *Chaslōnim*). Whence came the Philistines. Ethnically they belong to Japheth in 10:5. Here the reference is geographical. See Amos 9:7. Israel's great rivals in the days of the judges and early monarchy.

Caphtorim. Caphtor is Crete (cf. Amos 9:7; Jer. 47:4). According to Deuteronomy 2:23 the Caphtorim were settled near Gaza.

(7) Canaan

Canaan the word is of unknown meaning. In Hurrian sources the term was applied to the main product of Canaan, a purple (red or blue?) dye and cloth. The term refers narrowly to Phoenicia (cf. 10:15–19) and its coastal strip; then more generally to Syria and Palestine. Canaanite also has the meaning of trader. For language and literature, history, culture, and religion see "Canaan" in a biblical dictionary (NBD or IDB, 1962).

Sidon. Reputedly the first of the Phoenician cities. The present context thus reflects the Egyptian hegemony in the second half of the second millenium, especially the eighteenth and nineteenth dynasties.

Heth. The inhabitants of Asia Minor. The term is mixed, for Hatti is the name given to their land by the original inhabitants of Asia Minor. The Hittites are Indo-Aryans who settled there in successive invasions from the third millenium onward. They obviously settled widely (cf. Ezek. 16:3; Gen. 10:15; 23; and Josh 1:4).

Jebusites. Probably Hurrians. Inhabitants

of Jerusalem in David's days and probably for centuries before.

Amorites (Amurru). Western Semites, akin to and settled among the Canaanites. Frequently mentioned in the Old Testament as a people in Canaan and as a general term for the people of Canaan (cf. Ezek. 16:3,45).

Girgashites. Possibly the *Qaraqisha* mentioned by the Hittites (Albright), otherwise unknown except as part of the mixed Canaanite population.

Hivites. Probably for Horites—Hurrians. Often confused in the Old Testament (M.T. and LXX). If Hurrians, they were probably a people so numerous and widely scattered as to be separately named. Otherwise a separate people settled mainly in the hills of Lebanon (Judg. 3:3; cf. Josh. 11:3).

Arkites. A people settled in Lebanon, whose city was widely known in the second half of the second millenium.

Sinites. A Canaanite people of the Lebanon area.

Arvadites. Arvad is an island city off northern Phoenicia, approximately fifty miles north of Byblos (cf. Ezek. 27:8,11; 1 Macc. 15:23).

Zemarites. The context shows that this people must be Canaanite, living between the Arvadites and the following.

Hamathites. Hamath a city frequently mentioned in the Old Testament; capital and trading center of a great Orontes kingdom. "The entering in of Hamath" is descriptive of Israel's northern boundary (Num. 34:8; Josh 13:5).

The territories in which the Canaanites dwelled stretched from Sidon in Phoenicia on the northwest coast of the region, almost due south to the Philistine plain, then eastward to Sodom and Gomorrah. The reference to these cities suggests the great age of the tradition, that is, before the destruction of these cities reported in the days of Abraham.

Admah. One of the cities of the plain, now submerged under the southern Dead Sea.

Zeboiim. Another city of the plain, and mentioned in chapter 14.

Lasha. Possibly the most easterly of the localities of the context.

These territories thus appear to be within the Egyptian hegemony.

(8) Shem

In verses 21–31 Shem's family is listed. Shem is always listed first as the eldest of Noah's sons (5:32; 6:10; 7:13; 9:18; cf. vv. 23,26; 10:1). In the table he and his descendants are listed last, and this may contain the suggestion that the story is to go on through the line of Shem. Certainly in 11:10 the family tree of Shem serves as the bridge to Terah and Abram.

Many of Shem's descendants used related languages and so Shemitic or Semitic has become an ethnic and philological term which covers a wide range of peoples, migrations, and languages.

Two observations are made about Shem (10:21). There is the umbrella observation that all Hebrews, i.e., the children of Heber, are Shem's descendants. Eber is the great grandson of Shem and the eponymous ancestor of the Hebrews (11:14 ff.). The word means "one who passes over," and is the same as Hebrew and probably Habiru (cf. Num. 24:24). Secondly Shem is described as the elder brother of Japheth. Why is Noah's third son not also mentioned? The omission can only be noted, for it may not certainly be explained.

Elam. The Elamites are grouped here geographically because their language is not Semitic. They are the persistent rivals of the powers of the eastern Fertile Crescent. They go back to the third millenium. The reference is somewhat mysterious in the Shem context, and so all the more reliable for that reason.

Asshur. First prominent in the second millennium, Asshurites come to new significance in the first half of the first millenium. The term Asshur describes both the land in the upper Mesopotamian plain, and the people—the Assyrians there resident—and frequently occurs in the Old Testament.

Arpachshad. No certain explanation of the name exists. The omission of Babylon from the list is astonishing. Perhaps *ch sh d* may refer to Kasdim, i.e., Chaldeans, as often has been suggested. Kirkuk also has been suggested.

Lud. Probably the Lydians of Anatolia (cf. 10:13) and if so not Semites at all (cf. Isa. 66:19).

Aram. The ancestor of the biggest group of Semites, the Arameans, whose center eventually became Aram, i.e., Syria. Their migration falls in the centuries 1500–1200, though their name is known long before this. They have a long and abundant history. Part of Terah's family settled in Haran in Aram-naharaim, the area of the later Mitannian kingdom. Both people and language appear prominently and fairly continuously in the Old Testament.

(9) Aram

The disorder of the sections is shown in that Aram is taken before Arpachshad through whom the story really goes on, as is seen in 11:10–12.

Of Uz, Hul, Gether, and Mash, nothing beyond the present context is known. There are persons and a place (Job 1:1) of the name of Uz.

The parallel account about Shem in 11:10 ff. is fuller, for it also gives the family tree of Arpachshad, Shelah, Eber, and Peleg. But 10:26 alone mentions another son of Eber, Joktan, who was the ancestor of southern Arabian families and tribes (cf. 1 Chron. 1:20–23 for the parallel list). Joktan must have been at one time a very considerable person, since so many southern Arabian tribes are attributed to him.

Hazarmaveth. Hadramaut in southern Arabia, east of modern Yemen, and this confirms the south Arabian locale of the foregoing and following in 10:26–28.

Jerah. The word means "mouth" in southern Arabian inscriptions and in Hebrew.

Obal. Ebal in 1 Chronicles 1:22.

Sheba. In the Yemen. Several persons have this name (cf. 10:7; 25:3). The name

of the most prominent southern Arabian states in the days of Solomon (1 Kings 10).

Ophir. East coast of Arabia. Entrepot between India, the Near East, and the West (cf. 1 Kings 9:28; 10:11; 22:48).

Havilah. South Arabian and not Kassite areas as in 2:11.

Jobab. Five persons bear this name in the Old Testament.

This account of the growth, spread, and location of the peoples of antiquity is a very remarkable piece of work. In the absence of easy communication, assembled knowledge, and printed works, the table is altogether a praiseworthy attempt to describe the peopling of the world.

4. Tower of Babel (11:1–9)

¹ Now the whole earth had one language and few words. ² And as men migrated from the east, they found a plain in the land of Shinar and settled there. ³ And they said to one another, "Come, let us make bricks, and burn them thoroughly." And they had brick for stone, and bitumen for mortar. ⁴ Then they said, "Come, let us build ourselves a city, and a tower with its top in the heavens, and let us make a name for ourselves, lest we be scattered abroad upon the face of the whole earth." ⁵ And the LORD came down to see the city and the tower, which the sons of men had built. ⁶ And the LORD said, "Behold, they are one people, and they have all one language; and this is only the beginning of what they will do; and nothing that they propose to do will now be impossible for them. ⁷ Come, let us go down, and there confuse their language, that they may not understand one another's speech." ⁸ So the LORD scattered them abroad from there over the face of all the earth, and they left off building the city. ⁹ Therefore its name was called Babel, because there the LORD confused the language of all the earth; and from there the LORD scattered them abroad over the face of all the earth.

This brief narrative possesses a double interest, namely, its place in the strategy of the overall narrative of Genesis and its own meaning as a unit of the tradition.

Broadly speaking this story corresponds in its place to the story of Noah's flood, for each story marks a decisive point in the overall discourse. In Noah's flood the first mankind is drowned and perishes, and a new beginning is centered in Noah and his family. In the Babel story the second mankind, that sprung from Noah himself, is dispersed and disqualified. The strategy of the story is controlled by 8:21 and 9:8–17, where the divine vow never again to destroy mankind is recorded. By his vow and his covenant God has bound himself no more to resort to curse or flood. His sovereign will must therefore find another way.

Noah himself had made a bad beginning (9:20–27), and the new mankind sprung from him and mainly located in Babylonia, continues the spirit and hubris of their ancestor. In its present context, and as distinct from the original meaning and intention of the story, the narrative leads up to a punishment by dispersal. This instance of punishment points back to the overall theme of general wickedness, as it also points forward through dispersal to the impotence and insignificance of Noah's mankind, and to a new beginning centered in the house of Terah and, especially, his son Abram.

The story thus marks a third point of major beginnings in Genesis, for it points to the story of the beginnings of Israel. Creation is the necessary beginning of the story, Noah is a transitional beginning, but Babel is the turning point out of which the central story of the Bible—that of redemption— begins.

In itself the story appears to possess several layers of meaning. Originally it appears to have been the record of a new type of scientific achievement, the designing and erecting of the biggest building yet attempted. Inevitably such an effort would have incurred opposition. So the original theme no doubt is the familiar "I wonder what they will try next." This daring architectural experiment is successful. An enormously high building is erected, but the achievement is matched by a spirit of arrogance. Arrogance bred revolt, faction, and dispersal. Dispersion inevitably brought about development in language and the end of the unity of the people involved. In these successive stages of the develop-

ment of the human spirit of arrogance, disruption, and failure are to be seen the successive stages of God's judgment. This judgment is of course not related to the technological achievement as such, but to the spirit it engendered. With such men God's purpose may not be furthered. He will block this generation by dispersal and seek an alternative agent for his purpose (cf. Deut. 8:17).

This original base of the story has been overlaid by themes of the unity of mankind and of the geographical centrality here of Babylon.

The unity of mankind is seen in 11:1 to be a linguistic unity, though verse 2 suggests an assembly of all mankind, or a major part of it, in the plain of Shinar, i.e., Babylon, where they plan a permanent home and defense system. City and tower are not marks of separate narratives but aspects of a complete living unit, implying community, residence, and security. This picture of geographical unity must however be qualified, because as the tables of nations in chapters 10—11 show, some dispersal has already occurred—and tribal and national units are already in existence. The numbers too of men are already too great, the lapse of time too long to permit of the unified picture of a one-language mankind in one place.

So the picture is an ideal one, of something that must have been, of something which to lose was loss indeed, and a something that belongs to men ideally, whose loss must have been caused by sin, and which it is the purpose of redemption to recreate and reestablish. So the uniting of tongues at Pentecost (the first great Christian Whitsuntide) is the firstfruits and promise of the new linguistic unity of the kingdom of God, a unity whose foretaste we already see in the language of science, in the needs of international radio and television, and in the conditions of modern communication.

This ideal of the unity of mankind carries with it to a certain extent the idea of a geographical center. Students of Babylonian mythology have made us familiar with the concept of centrality. This idea marks not only the center of the earth but the bond of heaven and earth and the bond of earth and the underworld, as the temple at Babylon was known.

The Babylonian milieu of the story is shown by the name, which means "gate of God," by the building materials and by the ideas in the passage (cf. D. J. Wiseman, "Babel," NBD, pp. 116 f.).

This idea of centrality persists too in the Bible. The ideas of the navel of the land and of Jerusalem as the center of the world (Psalm 74:12; Isa. 2:1–4; 45:22) are paralleled in the thought of other religions and literatures and, of course, in Christianity are fulfilled in Calvary as the center of mankind (John 12:32). The geographical center will be mentioned once or twice in Genesis and persists in Scripture, but nevertheless in Scripture it was destined to be replaced by the fact of a person at the center. In the Bible the highest range of values belongs to a central people and a central person rather than to a central place. The story of Abraham begins this story of the central person and is thus the counterpart, the saving counterpart to the lost unity and the lost center of the rejected mankind of Babel in 11:1–9.

Thus the meaning of this unit is deepened as it is considered in the larger context of the entire Scriptures. In themselves the religious values of the story are considerable. True the picture of God is somewhat anthropomorphic, for the Lord is said to come *down to see,* to *confuse their language,* and to scatter *them abroad.* His triple action is the action of judgment, but it is not only negative. The growth of languages and the displacement of people are viewed by the author as God's judgment on the arrogance of men at Babylon, but in the ongoing social process they may also be viewed as the stages necessary to the development of the divine drama of redemption.

5. Line from Shem to Terah (11:10–32)

¹⁰ These are the descendants of Shem. When Shem was a hundred years old, he became the father of Arpachshad two years after the flood; ¹¹ and Shem lived after the birth of Arpachshad five hundred years, and had other sons and daughters.

¹² When Arpachshad had lived thirty-five years, he became the father of Shelah; ¹³ and Arpachshad lived after the birth of Shelah four hundred and three years, and had other sons and daughters.

¹⁴ When Shelah had lived thirty years, he became the father of Eber; ¹⁵ and Shelah lived after the birth of Eber four hundred and three years, and had other sons and daughters.

¹⁶ When Eber had lived thirty-four years, he became the father of Peleg; ¹⁷ and Eber lived after the birth of Peleg four hundred and thirty years, and had other sons and daughters.

¹⁸ When Peleg had lived thirty years, he became the father of Reu; ¹⁹ and Peleg lived after the birth of Reu two hundred and nine years, and had other sons and daughters.

²⁰ When Réu had lived thirty-two years, he became the father of Serug; ²¹ and Réu lived after the birth of Serug two hundred and seven years, and had other sons and daughters.

²² When Serug had lived thirty years, he became the father of Nahor; ²³ and Serug lived after the birth of Nahor two hundred years, and had other sons and daughters.

²⁴ When Nahor had lived twenty-nine years, he became the father of Terah; ²⁵ and Nahor lived after the birth of Terah a hundred and nineteen years, and had other sons and daughters.

²⁶ When Terah had lived seventy years, he became the father of Abram, Nahor, and Haran.

²⁷ Now these are the descendants of Terah. Terah was the father of Abram, Nahor, and Haran; and Haran was the father of Lot. ²⁸ Haran died before his father Terah in the land of his birth, in Ur of the Chaldeans. ²⁹ And Abram and Nahor took wives; the name of Abram's wife was Sarai, and the name of Nahor's wife, Milcah, the daughter of Haran the father of Milcah and Iscah. ³⁰ Now Sarai was barren; she had no child.

³¹ Terah took Abram his son and Lot the son of Haran, his grandson, and Sarai his daughter-in-law, his son Abram's wife, and they went forth together from Ur of the Chaldeans to go into the land of Canaan; but when they came to Haran, they settled there. ³² The days of Terah were two hundred and five years; and Terah died in Haran.

The line begins with Noah's first mentioned son, Shem, and through his son Arpachshad. He was born two years after the flood, when Shem was a hundred years old. According to 10:22, he was Shem's third and middle son; 5:32 with 7:13 are difficult to reconcile with 11:10.

The line continues through Arpachshad's son, Shelah, and grandson, Eber. By 10:25 Eber had two sons, Peleg and Joktan. In the days of the former, mankind was dispersed or divided, and Peleg is a play on the word meaning division. Peleg becomes the father of Reu; Reu the father of Serug, the name of a district and city west of Haran, and Serug became the father of Nahor (Til-hahiri near Haran), father of Terah and grandfather of Abram.

Of all the men from Shem to Terah similar information is given: his age when he sired the next in order, the duration of his life after the birth, and the notice of other sons and daughters. Similar numbers even suggest some correspondence of the figures. Each link in the chain is thus equally treated, and the purpose is merely to identify the link and to achieve the family tree without gap or failure to Abram. Note too how begetting begins earlier in life, and life itself is of increasingly shorter duration.

The account of Shem and his descendants in chapter 10 is part of a world survey of families and nations, but in chapter 11 he stands at the head of a line that leads to Abram. The link of descent and not survey is the aim now, and the descent is to lead to and serve the saving story.

As we reach Terah, the bald statements are interrupted and the names of Terah's family are given. Obviously the story has arrived at a new starting point, and names and details must now be given (vv. 27–32). Whereas most of the chapter is P, verses 28–30 are J.

Terah is the father of Abram, married to the barren Sarai, and Nahor, married to Milcah, and Haran, whose wife is not mentioned but who had three children—Lot, the already named Milcah and Iscah—and who died before his father Terah. Nahor had thus married his niece, his brother Haran's daughter. The reference to Iscah is really pointless, but this very fact tends to authenticate the tradition.

Terah sets out with Abram, Sarai, and his grandson Lot, *from Ur of the Chaldeans to go into the land of Canaan,* but they settled at Haran (crossroads) en route. Although only these are mentioned, Nahor must either have accompanied or followed the first party, because later in the story they are presumably located at Haran. The LXX still reflects the difference between the person Haran and the place name Haran, a central Mesopotamian city on the left bank of the river Balikh which flows into the Euphrates.

The LXX reads "land" for Ur, but the Masoretic Text is better. Ur is almost certainly the ancient and extensive city of that name in Babylonia, Tell el-Mukayyar, though another locality in the neighborhood of Haran has much in its favor. The title Ur of the Chaldees is incorrect because Ur is never so listed, and the use of the word Chaldeans in reference to Ur must be anachronistic. Both Ur and Haran were centers of moon worship, but Terah's migration from Ur to Haran is not religiously motivated. Abram was born when Terah was seventy (v. 26), he went on to Canaan when he was seventy-five (12:4), that is sixty years before Terah's death at the age of two hundred and five.

VIII. The Call of Abram and the Promise (12:1—17:27)

1. Abram's Call (12:1–3)

[1] Now the LORD said to Abram, "Go from your country and your kindred and your father's house to the land that I will show you. [2] And I will make of you a great nation, and I will bless you, and make your name great, so that you will be a blessing. [3] I will bless those who bless you, and him who curses you I will curse; and by you all the families of the earth shall bless themselves."

These three verses are among the most important in Genesis and indeed in the whole Bible.

They are the consummation of what lies behind the narrative. Von Rad indeed includes them with 12:4–9 as the end of the biblical primeval history. Certainly their back cloth is the judgment of God seen in the dispersal of mankind from Babel. This dispersal involves abandonment too, for interest was then concentrated on the life-line from Shem to Terah and Abram. The selection of Abram is the beginning of the divine remedy against that dispersal and abandonment. Their retrospective significance is beyond doubt. The universal expanse of the table of nations, the idealistic unity of mankind at Babel vanish from sight. We follow the narrow pass from Shem to Abram and suddenly the universal expanse of mankind opens before us again.

This new vision of universalism begins with the selection of one man Abram, and so the remedy against the past and for the future dawns with one man and his family. A seed may begin a forest, and one man—elect, righteous, and dedicated—the beginning of a new mankind. Essentially promises, and promises for the future, these verses pose the far question: "Why was Jesus a Jew?" Each reader must decide for himself whether these verses answer that question. Their prospective significance for Israel, the Old Testament, the New Testament, and Christianity, is no less sure than their retrospective value. These verses point backward and forward.

The immediate question is whether these verses belong in their present context, or whether they are an addition from a later time to serve as a link in the narrative.

Unlike most of the units that go to make up the patriarchal narratives which contain incidents and adventures of various kinds, these verses have the character of a schedule, a program of promises for a man, his descendants, and indeed for mankind. They have accordingly been regarded as specially composed for the present context as a theological link between Genesis 1—11 and the patriarchal narratives. In themselves they are said to reflect the political conditions of the days of David, and these conditions have been summarized as a series of promises made to Israel's great ancestor Abram.

This explanation raises various difficulties. It ignores the poetic structure of the verses as shown in the Hebrew text. This poetic structure helps us to appreciate the antiquity of these verse lines in what is otherwise a prose context. Again other places in the patriarchal narrative, such as the stories of Jacob, the Exodus from Egypt, and even the settlement would have been more suitable for the interpolation—if interpolation they really are. They begin too with a peremptory command as sudden and as dramatic as anything in the patriarchal stories. "Be off with you," says Yahweh to Abram.

The verses, however, begin the real story of Abram. Their summary form shows how potential and pregnant they really are. Is it feasible that they really do belong there, and actually arose out of the story of Abram itself? Are these verses coherent with, or are they alien to, the context in which they occur? Not their literary form, not their theological character, not their similarity to the conditions in David's days, but rather their psychological coherence with their context must be the criterion of their authenticity.

An explanation along the following lines may be ventured:

(a) By 11:30 Sarai is barren. The longing and the need for children would be sufficient to set up the thought, the dream, the hope of children which is basic to the blessing: *I will make of you a great nation.* The juxtaposition of "barrenness" and "a great nation" is not merely a paradox; it exhibits the psychological principle of compensation. The term for nation, *goy,* has political and territorial overtones.

(b) Abram leaves home sixty years before his father's death. Only a divine compulsion (12:1) would account for such a rupture from a man's family. Under the influence of 12:1–3, Savonarola, the Italian reformer, was to make a similar decision. But Abram's departure leaves him a solitary adventurer and migrant into unknown territory. Again for the solitary and the insignificant, there is the dream of the destiny of a great name and a great family. Once again a psychological compensation is at work. Indeed a measure of overcompensation may possibly be seen in the Orientally described terms of the promise, in the presentation of Abram as the mediator of blessing to the whole world. This extraordinary statement will find further explanation and justification as the life story of this man is pursued.

(c) Abram leaves home and family, but the homeless finds comfort in the thought of a homeland somewhere. Abram has to seek a home. The obedience of Abram in leaving home, and his subsequent homelessness are real features of the story. The picture of the migrant Abram, with its attendant typology of a homeless Israel, the motif of the wandering Jew, must not be overdrawn, though it is attractive.

(d) Joshua 24:2 shows that Terah's family had "served other gods." The call of Abram suggests a henotheistic if not a monotheistic breakthrough. A new divine compulsion is perhaps the only adequate explanation of Abram's conduct in leaving his family.

The experiences of Abram are thus the psychological raw material for the promises contained in verses 1–3. In turn, these experiences become the vehicle of a divine revelation as they are more and more understood. The value of revelation may be placed upon these experiences, and the revelation is no less real and valid because it takes place through and within the categories of human experience. The call of Abram by God is worked out in the successive stages of his experience and spiritual needs.

The substance of the promises is *blessing*. The word itself is used five times, the root *great* is used twice, and further blessing is seen in the promise of a land, a name, personal welfare, and security. The final promise reads: "In you all the families of the earth shall be blessed" (marginal reading). The meaning could be that the standard of life and prosperity achieved by Abram will become the standard for his contemporaries, but the fuller meaning that Abram would become not the standard but

the agent of blessing for others is probably to be preferred. In Abram all the families of the earth will be blessed. This rendering in the passive given in the RSV margin is preferable to what is in the text: "will bless themselves." On either view the idea of personal centrality replaces geographical centrality prominent in the Babel story. *So that you will be a blessing* suggests Abram as the embodiment of blessing, and so blessed indeed.

On such grounds then the credibility of these verses must not be too quickly surrendered. The attempt is also abroad to argue for the monotheistic values of Abraham's religion, and certainly the three great monotheistic faiths of the world look back to him. Such new evaluations show that the spiritual stature of Abram has no doubt been underestimated in recent biblical scholarship, and perhaps the insights of Genesis and of the New Testament are more likely to be true (cf. Luke 16:22; Acts 3:25 f.; Rom. 4:13; Gal. 3:8,16). After all, Abraham is mentioned between seventy and eighty times in the New Testament.

Finally we note that the promises of 12:1–3 are repeated for him (13:14–16; 15; 17), for Isaac (26:24), for Jacob (28:3–4,13–15; 32:12; 35:9–12; 48:16). Promises, blessings, life, posterity, and so to incarnation—this is the salvation theme now inaugurated.

2. From Haran to the Negeb (12:4–9)

4 So Abram went, as the LORD had told him; and Lot went with him. Abram was seventy-five years old when he departed from Haran. 5 And Abram took Sarai his wife, and Lot his brother's son, and all their possessions which they had gathered, and the persons that they had gotten in Haran; and they set forth to go to the land of Canaan. When they had come to the land of Canaan, 6 Abram passed through the land to the place at Shechem, to the oak of Moreh. At that time the Canaanites were in the land. 7 Then the LORD appeared to Abram, and said, "To your descendants I will give this land." So he built there an altar to the LORD, who had appeared to him. 8 Thence he removed to the mountain on the east of Bethel, and pitched his tent, with Bethel on the west

and Ai on the east; and there he built an altar to the Lord and called on the name of the Lord. ⁹ And Abram journeyed on, still going toward the Negeb.

Abram, Sarai, their household, and Lot their nephew set out from Haran for the south. Their first mentioned call in Canaan is Shechem, and thus the biblical importance of that great city and shrine is inaugurated. The gateway through which the little family probably passed into the city is still to be seen. Shechem is a very old Canaanite city, and the oak of Moreh one, and perhaps the most famous, of its several shrines.

The journey is marked by two altars, one in the valley at or near Shechem. This altar at Shechem also marks the revelation by Yahweh and the realization by Abram that he is now in the land of promise (v. 7). This is where the descendants will live. The tree is the oak or terebrinth of Moreh. Moreh could be a personal name or could mean "of the teacher" (cf. Judg. 9:37). The second altar was on the highlands near Bethel. He invoked Yahweh's name over the second and so staked a claim for divine ownership. The journey takes them into the highlands between Hebron and Beersheba. Negeb means dryland and describes southern Palestine.

Names, journeys, and altar-building are three general marks of the patriarchal narratives, and they reflect conditions of the early second millenium.

The note about the Canaanites in verse 6 is editorial. It implies changed circumstances in days when the Canaanite predominance and majority had given way to Israelite possession.

3. Abram and Sarai in Egypt (12:10—13:1)

¹⁰ Now there was a famine in the land. So Abram went down to Egypt to sojourn there, for the famine was severe in the land. ¹¹ When he was about to enter Egypt, he said to Sarai his wife, "I know that you are a woman beautiful to behold; ¹² and when the Egyptians see you, they will say, 'This is his wife'; then they will kill me, but they will let you live. ¹³ Say

you are my sister, that it may go well with me because of you, and that my life may be spared on your account." ¹⁴ When Abram entered Egypt the Egyptians saw that the woman was very beautiful. ¹⁵ And when the princes of Pharaoh saw her, they praised her to Pharaoh. And the woman was taken into Pharaoh's house. ¹⁶ And for her sake he dealt well with Abram; and he had sheep, oxen, he-asses, menservants, maidservants, she-asses, and camels. ¹⁷ But the Lord afflicted Pharaoh and his house with great plagues because of Sarai, Abram's wife. ¹⁸ So Pharaoh called Abram, and said, "What is this you have done to me? Why did you not tell me that she was your wife? ¹⁹ Why did you say, 'She is my sister,' so that I took her for my wife? Now then, here is your wife, take her, and be gone." ²⁰ And Pharaoh gave men orders concerning him; and they set him on the way, with his wife and all that he had.
¹ So Abram went up from Egypt, he and his wife, and all that he had, and Lot with him, into the Negeb.

Why did Abram leave Haran? All we know is that he set out in obedience to a divine command to look for a land. That command was in itself the inauguration of a further stage in God's purpose for mankind. Yet all that is not at first fully known to Abram. Nevertheless for what purpose? A man must live, and he must make a living in order to live. This motif, though not mentioned, does come to the surface from time to time. Does Abram's erection of altars at various stages mark not only thanksgivings for journeying mercies, but also for good business deals as well in the early struggle to make a living?

Abram's journeys in chapters 12—13 are something of a problem: from Haran to the Negeb (vv. 4–9); to Egypt because of a famine (v. 10); back to the Negeb (13:1), and thence to Bethel (13:1–3). They are surely journeys connected with his living. Are they trade journeys? Verse 16 mentions his flocks and herds; verse 10, a famine. He visits the same places in the return. Was he calling on his old customers? Trade and making a living and the getting of possessions give coherence to the story.

Nevertheless the first story is unpleasant. The shrewdness and foresight of Abram, the exceptional beauty of Sarai, and her compliance are praiseworthy. But at the heart of the story is a lie (v. 13), even if Sarai was his half sister (20:12). There is also a suggestion that Abram did very well commercially out of Sarai's admission into Pharaoh's harem. Was some arrangement or commercial transaction involved? Abram's good fortune is somehow due to Sarai.

A coincidence seen as the work of God saved the day. Sarai's admission to the harem was followed by sickness, by plague. The superstitious Egyptians connected the two events. Did Sarai take in some infection? Was she a carrier? Were there some miscarriages among the women in the harem, and were they attributed to the advent of Sarai, herself barren? The outcome was fortunate. Abram got his wife back, and retained his flocks and herds. They leave Egypt, Abram and Sarai, and all that they had.

The unit is included, not because it was an example of a familiar motif applied also to Abram (cf. ch. 20, also of Abraham; 26:6–11, of Isaac), but because it marked the beginning of the material wealth of Abram. That the wealth had come out of a shoddy transaction was part of the story; that it had come at the expense of Egypt was eventually to be very funny; economics justifies the story even if it clearly and rightly condemns Abram's part. Nevertheless he got away with it.

The chapter thus shows both the religious conviction and the wicked behavior of Abram. Both the good and the bad must be accepted, for neither one cancels the other. Abram's weakness and faith and God's care and correction are present in the story.

The long journey to the south, the hard struggle to make a living, the crisis of the famine, the visit to Egypt and the upturn in fortune, not to mention the increase of flocks and herds, all took time, and perhaps a period of several years. By 12:10 Abram sojourned in Egypt. Probably the word *sojourn* does not have here its technical meaning of becoming a resident alien, though a stay of some years is quite feasi-ble. Abram has begun to amass his personal wealth. The blessing is at work.

4. Separation of Abram and Lot (13:2–18)

2 Now Abram was very rich in cattle, in silver, and in gold. 3 And he journeyed on from the Negeb as far as Bethel, to the place where his tent had been at the beginning, between Bethel and Ai, 4 to the place where he had made an altar at the first; and there Abram called on the name of the LORD. 5 And Lot, who went with Abram, also had flocks and herds and tents, 6 so that the land could not support both of them dwelling together; for their possessions were so great that they could not dwell together, 7 and there was strife between the herdsmen of Abram's cattle and the herdsmen of Lot's cattle. At that time the Canaanites and the Perizzites dwelt in the land. 8 Then Abram said to Lot, "Let there be no strife between you and me, and between your herdsmen and my herdsmen; for we are kinsmen. 9 Is not the whole land before you? Separate yourself from me. If you take the left hand, then I will go to the right; or if you take the right hand, then I will go to the left." 10 And Lot lifted up his eyes, and saw that the Jordan valley was well watered everywhere like the garden of the LORD, like the land of Egypt, in the direction of Zoar; this was before the LORD destroyed Sodom and Gomorrah. 11 So Lot chose for himself all the Jordan valley, and Lot journeyed east; thus they separated from each other. 12 Abram dwelt in the land of Canaan, while Lot dwelt among the cities of the valley and moved his tent as far as Sodom. 13 Now the men of Sodom were wicked, great sinners against the LORD.

14 The LORD said to Abram, after Lot had separated from him, "Lift up your eyes, and look from the place where you are, northward and southward and eastward and westward; 15 for all the land which you see I will give to you and to your descendants for ever. 16 I will make your descendants as the dust of the earth; so that if one can count the dust of the earth, your descendants also can be counted. 17 Arise, walk through the length and the breadth of the land, for I will give it to you." 18 So Abram moved his tent, and came and dwelt by the oaks of Mamre, which are at Hebron; and there he built an altar to the LORD.

Abram and Lot his nephew return to their trading activities in Canaan, and both become very wealthy. Abram has money, but their bank balance is mainly to be seen in their *flocks and herds and tents* for people and possessions. From 12:16 to 13:2, fine discussions have arisen whether Abram was nomadic and whether his life was controlled by the search for pastures. The search for pastures tends to fluctuate more between the deserts and Canaan, and the presence of camels and he- and she-asses show that more than pasture is involved. The reference to camels may be an anachronism, but could be a tribute to Abram's business acumen. Commerce, not pasture, caravans of goods, not grazing, these are the clues to the story. The quarrels between the herdsmen are inevitable, for overnight pastures amidst the small holdings of the Canaanite farmers would not be easy to find. The names of only two peoples are given here but no fewer than ten peoples in 15:19 f. The Hebrew for *very rich* is "very heavy with." The successful partnership inevitably brought about rivalry and strife, especially among the herdsmen who had to find the pastures and do the foraging.

The outcome of a peaceful and generous move by Abram was that Lot chose the Jordan for himself, and Abram remained in the highlands. The hills at Bethel and Ai afford a striking view of the countryside as you look southward. Not only are Jerusalem's hills visible some ten miles to the south, but away to the east is the sweep of the Jordan Valley to the southern end of the Dead Sea and the mountains beyond the River. The valley is compared with the Garden of Eden and with Egypt for its water and fertility.

Abram is apparently prepared to renounce the promise of the land. He gives the choice of location to Lot, and if Lot had chosen otherwise, then Abram could have been dispossessed. The writer may well have intended to astonish the reader as he reads of this.

The incident of the separation is immediately followed by a new divine revelation. Abram is bidden to survey all that he can see to the four points of the compass. All the land visible is now promised to him and his descendants, whose fabulous increase is also promised. Abram is bidden

also to walk the length and breadth of the land to know, to learn, and to recognize his inheritance. In fact, he moves off to Mamre some two miles north of Hebron and to his third altar. The site has shown Arab, Christian, Israelite, and Bronze Age, that is, pre-Israelite remains. The shrine may well have been pre-Abramic, and the existing shrine the reason for Abram's act of worship there. A square foot of ground and a few stones within a sacred area probably are all that is intended by Abram's altar. Again Mamre may well be a personal name (cf. 14:13).

Was Abram's generous offer to Lot a flouting of the divine intention? Was the new revelation in verses 14–17 not merely a renewal for his faith but a judgment on his casual treatment of the divine promise? It was at least the working out of the promise in greater detail. In 12:7 the northern central highlands had been already identified within the promise. Now in 13:14 the area of the promise is enlarged and further identified. We are approaching the usual dimension of "from Dan to Beersheba." Commentators have found evidence of interpolation in verses 14–17, but basically the verses are relevant.

Commentators seek to relieve the editor of Genesis of the necessity of providing a unified picture. The three stories about Abram so far show him as devout, as lying, and as generous. There is nothing incredible about these different traits present in one remarkable man. Acceptance of human nature as it is would prevent a lot of literary and religious theorizing.

5. Abram's Victory and Tithe (14:1–24)

Genesis 14 is one of the most puzzling chapters of the book. It relates the story of a victory in battle by four invading kings over five local kings after which Lot was captured. Abram rescued his kinsman, and later encountered the king of Sodom. In turn this event includes the story of a meeting between Abram and the king of Jerusalem.

Lot is thus the link between the stories.

The chapter has been viewed with great skepticism and is still regarded by some as a fairy story—a midrash, a piece of composition to teach religious truths and to magnify the importance of particular people. Nevertheless the story is finding new acceptance, even if some of the details remain unexplained. There is nothing necessarily unhistorical about the military expedition of verses 1–10. A new explanation of Abram's private army is available. The account of El Elyon as the god of Jerusalem is reliable, and the encounter between Abram and the city's king-priest, Melchizedek, typical of the encounter between Yahwism and a cult of Canaan.

The chapter has this very great importance. It is distinctive in its context, and quite dissimilar in words, ideas, and customs from the general run of traditions relating to the patriarchs. The chapter is independent, often antiquarian, often sound in its details if obscure in others, almost international, and may well have been composed by somebody outside Israel. The word "Hebrew" is always used of Israelites by foreigners or to foreigners. This suggests that the traditions of the chapter are non-Israelite, and if this is true, then the chapter is an independent witness to the life and work of Abram. Various factors in the chapter point to a date in the first half of the second millenium B.C. (Speiser).

(1) The War (14:1–12)

¹ In the days of Amraphel king of Shinar, Arioch king of Ellasar, Chedorlaomer king of Elam, and Tidal king of Goiim, ² these kings made war with Bera king of Sodom, Birsha king of Gomorrah, Shinab king of Admah, Shemeber king of Zeboiim, and the king of Bela (that is, Zoar). ³ And all these joined forces in the valley of Siddim (that is, the Salt Sea). ⁴ Twelve years they had served Chedorlaomer, but in the thirteenth year they rebelled. ⁵ In the fourteenth year Chedorlaomer and the kings who were with him came and subdued the Rephaim in Ashterothkarnaim, the Zuzim in Ham, the Emim in Shavehkiriathaim, ⁶ and the Horites in their Mount Seir as far as Elparan on the border of the wilderness; ⁷ then they turned back and came to Enmishpat (that is, Kadesh), and subdued all the country of the Amalekites, and also the Amorites who dwelt in Hazazontamar. ⁸ Then the king of Sodom, the king of Gomorrah, the king of Admah, the king of Zeboiim, and the king of Bela (that is, Zoar) went out, and they joined battle in the Valley of Siddim ⁹ with Chedorlaomer king of Elam, Tidal king of Goiim, Amraphel king of Shinar, and Arioch king of Ellasar, four kings against five. ¹⁰ Now the Valley of Siddim was full of bitumen pits; and as the kings of Sodom and Gomorrah fled, some fell into them, and the rest fled to the mountain. ¹¹ So the enemy took all the goods of Sodom and Gomorrah, and all their provisions, and went their way; ¹² they also took Lot, the son of Abram's brother, who dwelt in Sodom, and his goods, and departed.

The construction of the opening words is to some extent typical of regnal or military notices. The difficulty of a hiatus in Hebrew between verses 1 and 2 is overcome in the ERV by interpolating "these kings" at the beginning of verse 2. *All these* in verse 3 are the five defenders. Inevitably very little is certainly known of them.

Amraphel remains unknown, and the old identification with the great Hammurabi, not to mention several others of that name, is untenable. *Shinar* is Babylon. Amraphel must have been a smallish king, if one of the most notable, because he is first mentioned.

Arioch King of Ellasar. The locality is uncertain. The old identification with Larsa is probably untenable, because Arioch is a Hurrian name known in the cities of Nuzi and Mari. Perhaps Arioch is actually Arriwuk, a contemporary of Zimri-lim, king of Mari, himself a contemporary of Hammurabi of Babylon ca. 1728–1686.

Ched-or-laomer King of Elam. For Elam see 10:22, but its king, though leader of the expedition (vv. 4,5,9,17) is unknown.

Tidal King of Goiim. Tidal is probably the same as Tudhaliya, the name of five known Hittite rulers, of whom the first would be chronologically relevant. *Goiim* means nations and the reference is obscure.

Two of the four kings are unknown. That a king of faraway Elam should have been involved in a minor campaign in the Jordan Valley is difficult. The five kings of that valley are unknown, but they revolted after twelve years. Evidence exists of an early local civilization in Middle Bronze 1 (1950–1550 B.C.) and this is the background of those rebellious kings. The conquering coalition occupies Transjordania and from one end of Edom to the other to the Gulf of Akaba, turns northwest to Kadesh, sixty miles south of the Dead Sea, then northeast to the sea near to which are all the conquered cities (Deut. 29:23).

Valley of Siddim, otherwise unknown, must be the ancient name for most or part of the Jordan Valley, especially the part south of the Dead Sea. The early inhabitants of the cities are listed as Rephaim, a pre-Israelite giant stock (cf. 15:20; Deut. 2:11,20; 3:11,13 for geographical description). The Zuzim may be the same as Zamzummim (Deut. 2:20), giant inhabitants before Ammon; the Emim (Deut. 2: 10 f.) before Moab: the Horites are of course Hurrians, but the term is also used loosely of the early inhabitants of Edom and of Palestine too. The reference to the Amalekites, ancient enemies of Israel, is geographically correct, but the Amorites (10:16), seem rather far south, though the reference is not to be rejected for that reason. Hazazon-tamar by 2 Chronicles 20: 2 is Engedi on the west coast of the Dead Sea.

The description of the battle as four (outside) kings against five shows the proportions of the affair and consequently its memorable character. To doubt the historicity of so well described an event is unreasonable. The name of the fifth resisting king and the details of the battle are not mentioned. The flight of the defeated is impeded by the "wells upon wells of bitumen," for the supply of which the Dead Sea was known.

Sodom and Gomorrah were sacked, and Abram's nephew Lot was taken prisoner. So the link with Abram is either seen or, as some say, invented. It could better be argued that the person who binds the whole chapter together is the king of Sodom who appears in verses 2,8,17,21–23.

(2) The Rescue (14:13–16)

13 Then one who had escaped came, and told Abram the Hebrew, who was living by the oaks of Mamre the Amorite, brother of Eshcol and of Aner; these were allies of Abram. 14 When Abram heard that his kinsman had been taken captive, he led forth his trained men, born in his house, three hundred and eighteen of them, and went in pursuit as far as Dan. 15 And he divided his forces against them by night, he and his servants, and routed them and pursued them to Hobah, north of Damascus. 16 Then he brought back all the goods, and also brought back his kinsman Lot with his goods, and the women and the people.

News reaches Abram who is now in (commercial) partnership with Mamre, Eshcol, and Aner. The Hebrew implies that the head of the partnership, the senior partner or managing director is Abram. He is described as the Hebrew, and this suggests a reference by foreigners. The association of the four men shows how Abram has consolidated his own position and that again more years have passed. With the passing of the years and the increasing wealth of those concerned, we may infer too that Lot had increased his wealth (vv. 12,16), so that he had become a rich and well-known inhabitant of the area and thus worthy of capture.

Abram led forth his trained men. Both the verb and the accusative noun are uncertain, but fortunately this picture of Abram's private army is no longer as puzzling as once it was. Contemporary evidence shows the existence of commercial princes who used donkeys and asses for carrying their merchandise on long journeys, and who were compelled to equip themselves with armed bands for protection. Abram's private army is thus another feature that belongs to the picture of a wealthy merchant prince. The route of the pursuit and its distance are familiar, but that Dan is named Dan and not Laish (cf. Judg. 18:29) and that 318 men could conquer five kings and their armies, even by a surprise attack at night, are surprising. Oriental exaggeration has obviously blown up the victory, for the figure of 318 warriors sounds so reasonable. His retainers are born of his household, that is, not brought in as slaves. Hence their loyalty would be strong. Their numbers, their age, as able to fight, show that chapter 14 reflects a later stage in Abram's life, and reveals him as not only wealthy but a well-known and influential person in the area. The last word of verse 16 is ambiguous. It may refer to the captured soldiers of the five kings, to Lot's private soldiers, or to the citizens captured by the four kings.

(3) Abram and Melchizedek (14:17–24)

17 After his return from the defeat of Chedorlaomer and the kings who were with him, the king of Sodom went out to meet him at the Valley of Shaveh (that is, the King's Valley). 18 And Melchizedek king of Salem brought out bread and wine; he was priest of God Most High. 19 And he blessed him and said,
"Blessed be Abram by God Most High,
    maker of heaven and earth;
20 and blessed be God Most High,
    who has delivered your enemies into your hand!"
And Abram gave him a tenth of everything. 21 And the king of Sodom said to Abram, "Give me the persons, but take the goods for yourself." 22 But Abram said to the king of Sodom, "I have sworn to the LORD God Most High, maker of heaven and earth, 23 that I would not take a thread or a sandal-thong or anything that is yours, lest you should say, 'I have made Abram rich.' 24 I will take nothing but what the young men have eaten, and the share of the men who went with me; let Aner, Eshcol, and Mamre take their share."

On his return Abram is involved in a not too pleasant encounter with *the king of Sodom* about the question of the division of booty. The king seeks to reward Abram, or perhaps drive a bargain with him. But Abram, established in his independence, his wealth, and his increasing reputation, will not claim more than the expenses of the expedition, plus rewards for the victorious soldiers and his three partners, whose wealth and personnel were at risk in the venture. The story does not tell whether Abram's partners accompanied him. It ap-

pears more likely that Abram went alone, for it was the rescue of his kinsman that was at stake. Nevertheless Abram remembers his partners. The verse is conclusive that Abram and these three men were in business together.

In this setting are the climax and real significance of Genesis 14. The *king of Salem,* that is Jerusalem (cf. Psalm 76:2), who bears the name Melchizedek, "the king is just, righteous," comes forth to meet Abram with gifts of *bread and wine.* The element "zedek" (righteousness) is characteristic of the kings and priests of Jerusalem, of the Davidic ideology [12] and of the characteristics of the city (cf. Isa. 1:21–27). Kings of Jerusalem are known centuries before David, and the priest-king concept is familiar too.

Of outstanding significance is the reference in verse 18 to *God Most High.* This is *'El 'Elyon,* presumably the god of Jerusalem. The patriarchal narratives tell us of many such Els: *'El Shaddai* (17:1); *'El 'Olam 'El Pachadh* (Job 31:23), *'El Ro'i* (16:13); *'El,* god of Israel (33:20); *'El-Beth'el* (35:7). *'El* is a god, an important, sometimes supreme, sometimes a localized deity, but often associated with a person rather than a place. The number of *'Els* means that further differentiation is required. Hence *'El 'Elyon* (God Most High) of the present passage. It appears that he was a very important god in ancient Palestine; that elements of universalism were attached to him. He is pictured here as the creator of heaven and earth and in Deuteronomy 32:8–9 organized the disposition of early mankind, even assigning Yahweh to Jacob. *'El 'Elyon* is therefore a high god of universal proportions and originally quite distinct from Yahweh. It is almost certain that *'Elyon* and Yahweh were merged after David captured Jerusalem, for it is only after this time that *'Elyon* increasingly becomes used as an epithet of Yahweh. The usage of the name in the Psalms shows this.

12 Cf. Adonizedek, Josh. 10:1, A. R. Johnson, *Sacral Kingship in Ancient Israel* (2d ed.; Cardiff: University of Wales Press, 1967), pp. 35 ff., 47 ff.

Of course in verse 22 Abram is said to make this identification himself in the words "Yahweh, the *"Elyon."* The LXX does not have the word Lord Yahweh, and so there is some doubt, especially as the words are addressed to Sodom's king and not to Melchizedek.

Genesis 14 thus records the first encounter of two great religious traditions: (1) *'El 'Elyon,* God of Jerusalem, and its king Melchizedek; (2) Yahweh, the God of Abram. The indigenous and the invasive encounter each for the first time, and all their paths were peace.

The king offers gifts and pronounces a blessing. In return Abram tithes. The reference may be to a tithe of the booty, or of the possessions he had with him—hardly of all his personal wealth. Perhaps the royal gifts and the worshiper's tithe reflect the ritual of Jerusalem's sanctuary. Bread and wine could have sacral significance in the present instant, and perhaps they gave to Jesus Christ much later the notion of the elements for the ritual acts of the Last Supper, as distinct of course from the occasion and intention of the Last Supper.

In the last resort a decision must be made about the story. It may well be a free composition to associate Abram with Jerusalem and to set forth Abram's attitude toward Jerusalem and its king as an example for future generations and particularly for that generation contemporary with the composition of the narrative. The imagination and daring of the story in bringing together the father of all Isarel and that great city (the capital city, actually and ideally of all Israel) are valid motives for such composition.

On the other hand, is it necessary to postulate the fiction of such a bold and exemplary story, as many in fact do? Perhaps it is less miraculous and superfluous to take the story as it is and to see in it an exchange of courtesies and gifts without regarding these as the toleration of a heathen cult, and without making the gift of a tenth a religious tithe. The story appeals to many as too good to be true—

Abram, Jerusalem, and David's predecessor all in a few sentences! Nevertheless it may be it really was like that, and the amazing coincidence of place and personality is its vindication and the cause of its recollection and preservation.

6. Revelation to Abram (15:1-21)

¹ After these things the word of the LORD came to Abram in a vision, "Fear not, Abram, I am your shield; your reward shall be very great." ² But Abram said, "O Lord GOD, what wilt thou give me, for I continue childless, and the heir of my house is Eliezer of Damascus?" ³ And Abram said, "Behold, thou hast given me no offspring; and a slave born in my house will be my heir." ⁴ And behold, the word of the LORD came to him, "This man shall not be your heir; your own son shall be your heir." ⁵ And he brought him outside and said, "Look toward heaven, and number the stars, if you are able to number them." Then he said to him, "So shall your descendants be." ⁶ And he believed the LORD; and he reckoned it to him as righteousness.

⁷ And he said to him, "I am the LORD who brought you from Ur of the Chaldeans, to give you this land to possess." ⁸ But he said, "O Lord GOD, how am I to know that I shall possess it?" ⁹ He said to him, "Bring me a heifer three years old, a she-goat three years old, a ram three years old, a turtledove, and a young pigeon." ¹⁰ And he brought him all these, cut them in two, and laid each half over against the other; but he did not cut the birds in two. ¹¹ And when birds of prey came down upon the carcasses, Abram drove them away.

¹² As the sun was going down, a deep sleep fell on Abram; and lo, a dread and great darkness fell upon him. ¹³ Then the LORD said to Abram, "Know of a surety that your descendants will be sojourners in a land that is not theirs, and will be slaves there, and they will be oppressed for four hundred years; ¹⁴ but I will bring judgment on the nation which they serve, and afterward they shall come out with great possessions. ¹⁵ As for yourself, you shall go to your fathers in peace; you shall be buried in a good old age. ¹⁶ And they shall come back here in the fourth generation; for the iniquity of the Amorites is not yet complete."

¹⁷ When the sun had gone down and it was dark, behold, a smoking fire pot and a flaming torch passed between these pieces. ¹⁸ On that day the LORD made a covenant with Abram, saying, "To your descendants I give this land, from the river of Egypt to the great river, the river Euphrates, ¹⁹ the land of the Kenites, the

Kenizzites, the Kadmonites, [20] the Hittites, the Perizzites, the Rephaim, [21] the Amorites, the Canaanites, the Girgashites and the Jebusites."

Genesis 15 must be considered as one of a group of chapters, 12, 15, and 17, all with a similar theme. Doubtless the basic and original call of Abram came in 12:1–3, J source. Genesis 17 is almost certainly a tradition from the P source with clear indications of Jerusalem ideas.

How then is chapter 15 to be understood in relation to these chapters? The structure is easily analyzed. Verses 1–6 comprise one unit with some possible overlapping in 2–3. Then verses 7–21 are a second unit with some later elaborations in verses 13–16 and 18b–21. The theme of the first unit is Abram's descendants; the second, a covenant with Abram about the possession of the Promised Land. Neither unit is fully parallel with 12:1–3, where the land and descendants are spoken of. Two features of these units are, however, important.

The first is the prophetic cast of 15:1–6, seen in the phrases *the word of the Lord.* This has led to the likely view that this is the first passage in Genesis from the stock of E, i.e., Ephraimitic or northern Israel traditions. More difficult is to see in 15:1–6 the E parallel to the J version in 12:1–3; 15:1–6 does not appear to resemble a story at the beginning of a man's life. The claim that the words "seeing I go childless" refer to Abram's departure from Mesopotamia or Haran is not convincing. The RSV better translates the Hebrew *for I continue childless.* The idiom of the Hebrew describes not a journey about to begin but a continuing state of affairs.

The second feature is that Abram's doubt is met by a covenant, and the covenant includes not only reassurance to Abram but an increasingly accurate definition of the land in question.

Common to both units is Abram's concern expressed in the complaining question of 15:2 and the doubting question of 15:8. These considerations lead to the conclusion not that 15:1–6 is a parallel to 12:1–3, but that 15:1–6 and 7–21 belong to some period of Abram's life long after his departure from Haran. The passing of the years, ten such years are mentioned in 16:3 which is consistent with 12:4 (Abram, 75) and 16:16 (Abram, 86—ten years plus one for the conceiving and gestation of Ishmael), bring about a crisis of faith for Abram. He remains childless, having no personal heir for his business enterprise, and no hope of any permanent settlement in the land to which he has felt himself called.

Chapter 15 then probably represents a time of spiritual crisis for Abram some nine to eleven years after his migration to Canaan.

After these things. These words are merely a formula of transition, which loosely connects the present with what goes before, and so do not imply any special or chronological sequence (cf. 22:1,20; 39:7; 40:1; 48:1).

The core of 15:1–6 is Abram's doubt in the form of a recapitulation. This repeated retrospect (2-3) shows the welling-up of Abram's anxiety from within. This is the essential historical core. It wells up in defiance of his conviction of God's goodness here described in later religious and prophetic terms.

Shield is both a military term and, especially in the Psalms, a cultic term. The word *reward* is mainly economic, wages, or a reward for work well done. Here the word refers to progeny. To claim a cultic origin for 15:1 is to overstate the simple fact of later religious terms. Rather it describes in figurative fashion the divine protection and destiny which Abram feels himself to enjoy, which is prior in his experience, and is also the sounding board for his doubts. The adoption of a slave as personal heir reflects a custom well known in the texts from the city of Nuzi. So the claim that verses 2–3 is the historical core is confirmed by the reference to a very old custom which they contain.

Out of the conflict of complaint and conviction, Abram achieves renewed assurance that he is to have his own son and from him a numberless progeny. Abram believed, accepted the Lord's word, committed himself in trust to God. The word *reckoned* is basically a formula of imputation (Lev. 7: 18; 17:4; Num. 18:27), implying either divine approval as here, or rejection. Righteousness describes what is correct behavior to and within a clan by a member of that clan. The righteousness of God is divine behavior appropriate and necessary to the maintenance of his kingdom. The righteousness of an Israelite is his behavior appropriate to his membership of the covenant community.

Verse 6 contains but five pregnant Hebrew words, and so rounds off the unit with a theological conclusion. The words may be a later formulation of an attitude and demeanor constantly exhibited by Abram.[13]

In the second unit the recapitulation comes not from Abram, as in 15:2 f., but from the Lord. Verse 7 is a characteristic Yahwistic sentence, and to discuss whether it or Exodus 3:6 or 20:2 is the prototype is not very profitable. *I am the Lord who*, the divine self-introduction or self-predication, or in W. Vischer's fine phrase "the divine auto-kerygma," that is, the divine self-proclamation or preaching, is the description of the being, activities, and purpose of God, uttered by God himself.[14]

This is the supreme sentence of all Scripture. The four words are total and absolute. Very often they are accompanied by a further sentence beginning with who, and these additional sentences mention a particular characteristic attribute or activity. They accordingly exclude other attributes or activities and are therefore partial. The words "I am Yahweh" alone are absolute, but "I am the true vine" for example is something less. "I am Yahweh who brought you from Ur of the Chaldeans" similarly concentrates on that activity rele-

vant to the context. The "I am" sentences of Scripture contain a fund of living theology.

Abram's response to the divine retrospect takes the form of a request for proof. Here doubt witnesses to some struggle or conflict in Abram's life (as in verse 2). The juxtaposition of verses 8–9 is astonishing. The cry for proof is met by a ritual response—the selection of animals for slaughter, possibly for sacrifice—though that is not certain. The passage is basic for the understanding of Israelite thought. The promise, for which Abram demands proof, is shown to be real and dependable by means of a ritual of slaughter. The animals are cut in two, then the two halves are parted with their bleeding sides toward each other. The birds are not divided and their presence in the story is a mystery. Abraham falls asleep in a sleep as deep as a trance (cf. Job 4:13; 33:15), and in a vision *a smoking fire pot and a flaming torch passed between* the halves of the animals. The passage between the animals is a well-known covenant procedure, whereby the partners to the covenant, who pass between the pieces, invoke upon themselves in the event of their infidelity the fate of the animals (cf. Jer. 34:18–19). The sequence of thought is therefore a promise—Abram's challenge—the ritual of covenant-making. This is confirmed in verse 18, where the making of the covenant is noted.

The fire pot or oven and torch may be explained in one of two ways. They may be a symbol of the Lord's binding himself to the promise of the covenant by passing between the pieces. The thought that God thus threatened himself with the fate of the animals is very difficult indeed, even if it is impossible to think that God could be faithless. Or, if the fiery symbols do not represent God, then they have some psychological, almost nightmarish, explanation from out of the waking experience of Abram no longer preserved to us.

Verses 7–11,12,17 ff. must be a genuine story of an experience of Abram. This ex-

---

[13] Cf. W. Robertson Smith, *Lectures on the Religion of the Semites* (3d ed.; New York: Macmillan, 1927), pp. 655–71 for extended note by S. A. Cook. Also cf. G. von Rad, *The Problem of the Hexateuch and Other Essays*, pp. 125–30.

[14] Wilhelm Vischer, *The Witness of the Old Testament to Christ*, tr. A. B. Crabtree (London: Lutterworth, 1949).

perience arose out of his questionings and doubts about his future, some nine years or more after he had arrived in Canaan. This conflict was severe, so severe as to give rise to the images of a red hot oven and a flaming torch, but in turn to be resolved in a new faith embodied in a covenant. Abram's experiences and journeys and his knowledge of the land enabled him to gain a more precise definition of the boundaries of the territory promised to him. Verse 18 defines the extent of the land from the river of Egypt (not the Nile but the Brook of Egypt; cf. 1 Kings 8:65, the modern Wadi Arish) and the Euphrates, an extent only actually achieved in the days of Solomon's empire. As in 13–16, where a later hand has written in the tradition of the sojourn in Egypt and Israel's deliverance therefrom in terms of the history and judgment of Egyptians, Israelites, and Amorites, so in 18–21 there is evidence of some comprehensive cataloging born of a fuller but later knowledge. Nevertheless behind verses 18–21 is doubtless an original reference to Abram's ever-widening knowledge of the land of his adoption and its people.

The assurance of the promise is thus embodied in ritual. An idea, a promise, a thought is expressed in a series of actions. Here is a parallel to the prophetic symbols of the great prophets of Israel, and, it may even be suggested, the prototype of the mission of Jesus, embodied in baptism, and his cross, set forth in bread and wine.

Von Rad describes verses 13–16 as a "cabinet piece of Old Testament theology of history" and shares the view of many commentators that they are a late interpolation into the tradition (*Genesis*, p. 183).

The items of this passage may be listed as follows. The descendants of Abram over many centuries: their sojourn and oppression in alien territory (Egypt): their exodus with great wealth from bondage. These verses are therefore in their present context a prediction of Israel's fortunes over at least four centuries; and provided a cen-

tury and a generation are equated, this is a remarkably accurate prediction. Many commentators therefore prefer to see in these verses not a prediction but the retrospect of a later witness interpolated into Abram's life. To bring in another writer is really to add another witness whose accurate testimony renders unnecessary the idea of the miraculous prediction.

In the passage the people of Israel, the Egyptian oppressors, and the Amorites are all seen as participating in the history, but Egypt and the Amorites, if not Israel, are under judgment. That the iniquity of the Amorites is not yet full means that the time for their conquest has not yet arrived. The passage must be pre-Davidic and probably belongs to the days of the early settlement.

7. Sarai's Barrenness (16:1–16)

[1] Now Sarai, Abram's wife, bore him no children. She had an Egyptian maid whose name was Hagar; [2] and Sarai said to Abram, "Behold now, the LORD has prevented me from bearing children; go in to my maid; it may be that I shall obtain children by her." And Abram hearkened to the voice of Sarai. [3] So, after Abram had dwelt ten years in the land of Canaan, Sarai, Abram's wife, took Hagar the Egyptian, her maid, and gave her to Abram her husband as a wife. [4] And he went in to Hagar, and she conceived; and when she saw that she had conceived, she looked with contempt on her mistress. [5] And Sarai said to Abram, "May the wrong done to me be on you! I gave my maid to your embrace, and when she saw that she had conceived, she looked on me with contempt. May the LORD judge between you and me!" [6] But Abram said to Sarai, "Behold, your maid is in your power; do to her as you please." Then Sarai dealt harshly with her, and she fled from her.

[7] The angel of the LORD found her by a spring of water in the wilderness, the spring on the way to Shur. [8] And he said, "Hagar, maid of Sarai, where have you come from and where are you going?" She said, "I am fleeing from my mistress Sarai." [9] The angel of the LORD said to her, "Return to your mistress, and submit to her." [10] The angel of the LORD also said to her, "I will so greatly multiply your descendants that they cannot be numbered for multitude." [11] And the angel of the LORD said to her, "Behold, you are with child, and shall bear a son; you shall call his name Ishmael;

because the LORD has given heed to your affliction. 12 He shall be a wild ass of a man, his
hand against every man and every man's hand
against him; and he shall dwell over against all
his kinsmen." 13 So she called the name of the
LORD who spoke to her, "Thou art a God of
seeing"; for she said, "Have I really seen
God and remained alive after seeing him?"
14 Therefore the well was called Beerlahairoi;
it lies between Kadesh and Bered.

15 And Hagar bore Abram a son; and Abram
called the name of his son, whom Hagar bore,
Ishmael. 16 Abram was eighty-six years old
when Hagar bore Ishmael to Abram.

Life continues at Mamre (13:18). Presumably Abram's business continues to
flourish, but his problem remains. Still he
has no son and heir. If chapter 15 lifts the
veil to show the struggle in Abram's own
mind, chapter 16 shows the effect of the
situation on his wife Sarai. We must suppose that Abram was increasingly difficult
to live with or that he openly complained
of his sonlessness. Sarai must increasingly
have felt and acknowledged her disability.
To satisfy her husband and to quiet her
own mind, she has recourse to a legal custom well known in her day, whereby she
brought her own personal maid into the
sphere of her marriage. This entitled her
to acknowledge a child born to her husband
and her maid as her own, born on her own
knees (30:3,9). *I shall obtain children by
her* is literally, "I shall be built up from
her." The maid Hagar, an Egyptian, grows
arrogant in her pregnancy and is driven
out by Sarai, with Abram's consent.[15]

The story is thus a poignant one and calls
for no theological interpretation. No doubt
the affair had the effect of intensifying
Abram's doubts over his initial convictions
(12:1–3).

Two stories (16:7–14; 21:8–21) are
given about Hagar and her son, and many
have supposed that they are variants of one
story. Chapter 16 is however prior to the
birth of Ishmael and chapter 21 after his
birth and also after the birth of Sarai's son.
Verse 6 shows Abram's compliance, but
21:11 shows his displeasure, only overruled

15 Cf. Pritchard, p. 172; Code of Hammurabi, Nos.
145 ff.

by a divine command. This chapter contains no thirst-death motif as 21 does. Although both stories are concerned with the
destiny of Ishmael and divine assurances to
Hagar, the differences so far outweigh the
similarities that the stories are more truly
regarded as sequels than parallel.

Hagar, now reduced to her former status, flees toward Egypt. Shur must be some
place near or on the Egyptian border, possibly within Abram's trading area (20:1),
and certainly where Ishmael's descendants
dwelt (25:12–18); however, the well was
not at Shur but on the road to it. It lay
somewhere beyond Kadesh (16:14; cf.
21:14,21).

Hagar obviously falls into a position of
great difficulty. In her distress she is found
by a messenger of Yahweh who comforts
her and advises her. *Angel* in verse 7 may
well mean a divine visitant. If Yahweh's
angel is meant, then of course the phrase
does mean Yahweh in human form. For
the Hebrew mind, little difference exists
between Yahweh and his angel. The phrase,
however, may well have a simple explanation. To a person in distress, the sudden
appearance of a sympathetic man, wise in
counsel and ready to help, would qualify,
especially in retrospect, for the title "angel
of Yahweh." This messenger advises her
to return home and submit to her mistress.
This is the real advice, but then follows the
usual courtesies to a wife or pregnant
woman. "May you have an unnumbered
progeny." The stranger then suggests a
name for the unborn child (son), Ishmael.
"God hears" or "May God Hear," by which
he suggests that he has been divinely led
to Hagar and that she may safely regard
his advice. In verse 12 the character sketch
of Ishmael is a description from a later time,
born of actual experience of the Ishmaelite
tribes as proud, foolish, and isolationists.
This can hardly be original to the story,
whether the stranger was a real angel or a
chance passerby. In retrospect, Hagar believes she has seen a god whom she names
God of seeing. Verse 13 follows a well-
known emendation of a German scholar,

Wellhausen. The actual Hebrew reads, "Have I here indeed seen after the one who saw me?" This might mean that she only really realized who it was when the stranger withdrew from her (cf. Isa. 37:22, Heb.). Hagar thought she was speaking with a man, but then realized he must have been a god.

Hagar returns home, submits, and tells her story which was convincing enough to persuade Abram that he should call Hagar's son Ishmael. The concluding verses, 15–16, are probably from the priestly editor who thus links the story with 12:4 and 16:3.

The first story about Hagar is thus really about Sarai's frustration and belongs naturally to that context of frustration. Mentally the fulfilment of the promise of 12:1–3 and 15:4 remain suspended. The reader is left to infer the suspense, and he need not import into the story any theological motivation or any typological overinterpretation. The story is a plain story of a jealous barren woman, a frustrated if compliant husband, and a lively young woman.

8. Covenant and Circumcision (17:1–27)

The time is Abram's hundredth year, 13 or 14 years after Ishmael's birth, but the contents appear to parallel chapters 12 and 15. The question thus arises whether the time setting is correct and the story now takes a leap of thirteen years, or whether the sequence of Abram's life is halted for the time being, to permit the introduction of an account of Abram's call and covenant by that other great author and witness, the P editor as he is commonly called.

The latter is the view adopted here; and, as so often with this P witness, the contents and distinctive witness of his story are more important than his time settings. On the assumption then that chapter 17 is P's general corroboration of events already recorded of Abram's life rather than a sequel, the parallels may be noted, though these are not without their difficulties. Chapter 17 is the impressive account by the P witness of the theophany, the cove-

nant, the promises to Abram, and the all-important role of Abram in the purpose of God.

As in the J witness, God declares himself (v. 1; 15:1,7); promises a covenant, numerous posterity (vv. 2–7; 15:4–5,18), and a land (v. 8; 15:7–8,18); promises for Ishmael also are given (vv. 18–20; 16:10). These parallel traditions however include other and significant features. The divine self-introduction is in different terms; Abram and Sarai are to have new names; the covenant essentially resides in the physical mark of circumcision; the covenant is to be bilateral and everlasting; kings are numbered among Abram's descendants.

(1) The Theophany (17:1–8)

[1] When Abram was ninety-nine years old the LORD appeared to Abram, and said to him, "I am God Almighty; walk before me, and be blameless. [2] And I will make my covenant between me and you, and will multiply you exceedingly." [3] Then Abram fell on his face; and God said to him, [4] "Behold, my covenant is with you, and you shall be the father of a multitude of nations. [5] No longer shall your name be Abram, but your name shall be Abraham; for I have made you the father of a multitude of nations. [6] I will make you exceedingly fruitful; and I will make nations of you, and kings shall come forth from you. [7] And I will establish my covenant between me and you and your descendants after you throughout their generations for an everlasting covenant, to be God to you and to your descendants after you. [8] And I will give to you, and to your descendants after you, the land of your sojournings, all the land of Canaan, for an everlasting possession; and I will be their God."

I am God Almighty renders "I am El Shaddai." J had preserved "I am Yahweh." The P witness, however, believed that the divine name, Yahweh, was first revealed to Moses, and that consequently God could not have been known as Yahweh to Abram (Ex. 3:6; 6:2–4). This conflict of Scripture passages (15:7; 17:1) precludes a decision concerning the original wording of the revelation to Abram. Other Scriptures support each view. Genesis itself testifies that Yahwism is present in Abram's religion, and in his descendants by Sarai (Israel) and by

Keturah, his third wife (Midian, Kenites). Genesis also testifies, as will be seen, to a striking variety of El gods who are further distinguished in some way: e.g., *'El 'Elyon* (14:18–20, God Most High); *'El Shaddai* as here; *'El Ro'i* (16:13); *'El Pachadh* (31:42, the Fear [or kinsman] of Isaac); *'El Beth'el* (31:13). This Genesis picture of many *'Els*—gods—is confirmed by what is known of the polytheistic religion of Canaan as shown in the tablets from Ras Shamra. P's witness to *'El Shaddai* therefore preserves an early and reliable tradition. The question thus arises whether P's tradition was replaced by J's "I am Yahweh," or whether both traditions existed together. These are questions that cannot yet be answered.

'El Shaddai rendered "God Almighty," an old Jewish interpretation based on the idea of God the sufficient. Another possible view is that *Shaddai* is the same word as the Akkadian word for mountain. Neither view is certain.

Various characteristics of the narrative, such as this newly introduced divine name, the renaming of Abram, and the feature of the everlasting covenant,[16] show that P witnesses to a new era in the development of the world as he saw it. Creation, the first mankind, and the sabbath were the marks of the beginning; the flood, the second mankind, and the blood laws are the second great stage in P's account of the divine ordering of the world; the covenant with Abraham and his descendants, and circumcision are the third stage. Each stage falls within the previous one, as the next, the Mosaic, falls within the Abrahamic.

Verse 3 appears to be repetitive and certainly repeats verse 2. Abram is the same as *Abiram* "my" or "the father is exalted." "Abraham" is regarded by some as a meaningless lengthening of the name, but the alteration in name marks a new stage in the divine plan. Abram could

---

[16] Cf. 2 Sam. 23:5—David; Isa. 55:3; the new covenant in the prophets: Jer. 32:40; 50:5; Ezek. 16:60; 37:26.

mean exalted father, and Abraham father of a multitude. The covenant is to be extended to Abraham's descendants, and they are to include nations and kings. Such a precise promise shows that this verse must be dated to the days of the early monarchy. Israel not Edom is meant (36:31). The use of the word "everlasting" (vv. 7 f.) also probably reveals a late date. The terms describing the promise should be compared with similar statements in 1:28; 28:3–4; 35:11 f.; 48:3 f.; Ex. 1:7; 6:2–8, all deriving from the P witness.

I will make (lit., give) and *I will establish my covenant.* The J witness generally uses the word "cut a covenant" (e.g., 15: 18), but the P witness has a more formal and institutional word; establish, set up, institute, inaugurate. Verse 7 also illustrates a later covenant formula, "to be God to you," "to become your God," where the covenant is described in terms of God's relations with rather than his works for them (cf. v. 2). Verse 8 is a particularly majestic verse—divine action: giving to Abraham and his descendants Canaan as *the land of . . . sojournings* for an *everlasting possession;* and God as *their God.*

This analysis of the divine monologue explains, even if it fails to convey, the authority and majesty of this passage. Abram is silent in worship (v. 3), and his worship expresses the acceptance of the ethical role embracing his whole life now laid upon him.

(2) The Requirement (17:9–14)

9 And God said to Abraham, "As for you, you shall keep my covenant, you and your descendants after you throughout their generations. 10 This is my covenant, which you shall keep, between me and you and your descendants after you: Every male among you shall be circumcised. 11 You shall be circumcised in the flesh of your foreskins, and it shall be a sign of the covenant between me and you. 12 He that is eight days old among you shall be circumcised; every male throughout your generations, whether born in your house, or bought with your money from any foreigner who is not of your offspring, 13 both he that is born in your

house and he that is bought with your money, shall be circumcised. So shall my covenant be in your flesh an everlasting covenant. [14] Any uncircumcised male who is not circumcised in the flesh of his foreskin shall be cut off from his people; he has broken my covenant."

These verses contain the third divine speech of the chapter. Just as the promise of 15:7 f. is vested in the divinely prescribed ritual of 15:9–11,17–18, so the covenant of 17:4,7 is vested in the divinely prescribed mark of circumcision in the males among Abraham's descendants. Circumcision was a widely practiced custom and was not peculiar to Abraham's descendants. What is peculiar to them is that the mark of circumcision among them is not a sign of puberty, or of initiation, or of readiness for marriage, or even of dedication, but is the sign of their being covenanted to God. Other explanations of circumcision occur in Exodus 4:24 ff.; Joshua 5:2 ff., and indeed these passages seem to presuppose the beginnings of covenant circumcision in the patriarchal age. The use of stone as a knife suggests a period long anterior to the patriarchs (Ex. 4:25).

Other commentators have tended to see the covenant circumcision of chapter 17 as instituted, or at best revived, when the Israelites were exiled among the uncircumcised Babylonians in 586 and afterwards. Whether patriarchal, or belonging to the days of the early settlement, or of the Exile, this circumcision is a mark of relationship for the divine community pointing to the origin and character of their being and salvation. Into this estate every Israelite boy and every foreign boy who has been bought as a slave must enter. Hence the uncircumcised will automatically forfeit his membership of the people of God. *Cut off* means excommunication, not death.

This religious interpretation of covenant circumcision inevitably gave rise to the idea of a spiritual circumcision as described in such passages as Deuteronomy 10:16; 30:6; Jeremiah 4:4; 6:10; 9:26; Ezekiel 44:7,9; Leviticus 26:41. Compare also the Christian problems connected with circumcision in Acts 15:1–29; Romans 2:25—4:12; Galatians 5:2–12.

(3) *Two Promises* (17:15–21)

[15] And God said to Abraham, "As for Sarai your wife, you shall not call her name Sarai, but Sarah shall be her name. [16] I will bless her, and moreover I will give you a son by her; I will bless her, and she shall be a mother of nations; kings of peoples shall come from her." [17] Then Abraham fell on his face and laughed, and said to himself, "Shall a child be born to a man who is a hundred years old? Shall Sarah, who is ninety years old, bear a child?" [18] And Abraham said to God, "O that Ishmael might live in thy sight!" [19] God said, "No, but Sarah your wife shall bear you a son, and you shall call his name Isaac. I will establish my covenant with him as an everlasting covenant for his descendants after him. [20] As for Ishmael, I have heard you; behold, I will bless him and make him fruitful and multiply him exceedingly; he shall be the father of twelve princes, and I will make him a great nation. [21] But I will establish my covenant with Isaac, whom Sarah shall bear to you at this season next year."

Verse 15 introduces the fourth divine speech out of which a conversation and indeed a prayer develop. The mother of the promised son is to change her name. Sarai is simply an old feminine form of Sarah. The name means princess. The change in name of husband and wife signal the moment of a decisive change in their lives. The moment of their parenthood is at hand. The birth of a boy is precisely promised and his name is given.

Abraham's laughter, doubt, and questions lend a human touch not always evident in the stories of the P witness. Abraham's laughter may betoken ridicule or disbelief, or a compound of relief and unbelief. Abraham's concern for Ishmael is not refused. Ishmael shall have blessing, progeny, and destiny; but the covenantal favor will reside in Sarah's son who is to be called Isaac. This name means "he laughs" and is a play on Abraham's laugh as Ishmael (God has heard) is a play on Abraham's prayer. *Princes*, literally "exalted ones" i.e., in clan gatherings, suggest by their number an amphictyonic arrangement.

(4) Circumcision of Abraham's Family (17:22-27)

22 When he had finished talking with him, God went up from Abraham. 23 Then Abraham took Ishmael his son and all the slaves born in his house or bought with his money, every male among the men of Abraham's house, and he circumcised the flesh of their foreskins that very day, as God had said to him. 24 Abraham was ninety-nine years old when he was circumcised in the flesh of his foreskin. 25 And Ishmael his son was thirteen years old when he was circumcised in the flesh of his foreskin. 26 That very day Abraham and his son Ishmael were circumcised; 27 and all the men of his house, those born in the house and those bought with money from a foreigner, were circumcised with him.

Abraham came from Ur where circumcision was not practiced, and no doubt he was circumcised as was proper in Canaan. Ishmael's circumcision at thirteen years of age reflects Arabian custom.

That very day is the measure of Abraham's obedient submission.

IX. Abraham and Lot: Sodom and Gomorrah (18:1—19:38)

This comparatively large block of material comprising a number of units is the work of the J witness. It reveals a religious as well as a literary unity and marks a well defined point in the progress of the story in Genesis.

The units or pieces of the tradition are: Abraham's visitors, 18:1-16; God's confession to Abraham, 18:17-19; the reputation of Sodom and Abraham's intercession, 18:20-33; Yahweh's messengers in Sodom, 19:1-11; the warning to Lot, 19:12-23; the destruction, 19:24-29; the last story about Lot, 19:30-38.

Chapters 13, 18, and 19 tell the story of Lot. Even if the tradition about Sodom was once an independent unit, it has now been incorporated into the story of Lot, which in turn is part of the account about Abraham. The theme of the story is not easily under-

stood. Theophany links chapters 18—19; Sodom links 18:1-15 with what follows. The polarity of the chapters is the gift of life in the barren womb of Sarah, and the destruction of all life in the cities of the plain. The theme of destruction is so complete that Lot's daughters recognize that there are no men left to become their husbands. No necessity exists to create out of this story the idea of a universal destruction of all mankind comparable to the flood. Rather the clues are life (for Sarah) and death (for Lot's generation). Chapters 18—19 together present us with another example of the life-death theme which has appeared in Genesis at decisive points already. Creation has its counterpart in the expulsion from Eden and the institution of death. The choice of the house of Noah precedes the death of mankind by drowning. The election of Abram is preceded by the dispersal of mankind. The promise of life in Sarah's womb, which marks the resumption of the ongoing story of God's purpose, is matched by the degredation of Lot from wealth to poverty and by the destruction of his generation. Once again, in face of the prevailing disaster, the light of the divinely given life shines. The barren Sarah is to bear a son. Set in this recurring pattern of life, in face of or after disaster, is the clue to the religious unity of these two chapters, in themselves of such eloquence and narrative art.

1. Abraham's Visitors (18:1-19)

1 And the LORD appeared to him by the oaks of Mamre, as he sat at the door of his tent in the heat of the day. 2 He lifted up his eyes and looked, and behold, three men stood in front of him. When he saw them, he ran from the tent door to meet them, and bowed himself to the earth, 3 and said, "My lord, if I have found favor in your sight, do not pass by your servant. 4 Let a little water be brought, and wash your feet, and rest yourselves under the tree, 5 while I fetch a morsel of bread, that you may refresh yourselves, and after that you may pass on—since you have come to your servant." So they said, "Do as you have said." 6 And Abraham hastened into the tent to Sarah, and said, "Make ready quickly three measures of fine

meal, knead it, and make cakes." 7 And Abraham ran to the herd, and took a calf, tender and good, and gave it to the servant, who hastened to prepare it. 8 Then he took curds, and milk, and the calf which he had prepared, and set it before them; and he stood by them under the tree while they ate.

9 They said to him, "Where is Sarah your wife?" And he said, "She is in the tent." 10 The LORD said, "I will surely return to you in the spring, and Sarah your wife shall have a son." And Sarah was listening at the tent door behind him. 11 Now Abraham and Sarah were old, advanced in age; it had ceased to be with Sarah after the manner of women. 12 So Sarah laughed to herself, saying, "After I have grown old, and my husband is old, shall I have pleasure?" 13 The LORD said to Abraham, "Why did Sarah laugh, and say, 'Shall I indeed bear a child, now that I am old?' 14 Is anything too hard for the LORD? At the appointed time I will return to you, in the spring, and Sarah shall have a son." 15 But Sarah denied, saying, "I did not laugh"; for she was afraid. He said, "No, but you did laugh."

16 Then the men set out from there, and they looked toward Sodom; and Abraham went with them to set them on their way. 17 The LORD said, "Shall I hide from Abraham what I am about to do, 18 seeing that Abraham shall become a great and mighty nation, and all the nations of the earth shall bless themselves by him? 19 No, for I have chosen him, that he may charge his children and his household after him to keep the way of the LORD by doing righteousness and justice; so that the LORD may bring to Abraham what he has promised him."

Verse 1 sets the scene at Mamre in the heat of the day. This verse is almost like a stage direction which also supplies the meaning of the following story. This verse must be seen as if it existed in brackets; not part of the story, but a guide to its real meaning. The author or editor intends to say: "This story tells how God visited Abraham at Mamre at midday. It happened like this."

Abraham at his tent door, perhaps nodding, suddenly sees three men before him. We learn how the patriarch entertained three other men without at first knowing who they were. Abraham is the perfect host. His reverential obeisance (v. 2), his respectful address, *My lord,* or My lords—Sirs: his hospitality proffered in the form of a request for a favor (v. 3); his care for

their physical comfort (v. 4), the modest description of his hospitality—*a morsel of bread*—in contrast to the actual provision—a baking from Sarah—and calf-meat—a rare luxury—chosen by himself and prepared by his own servant. After some time the guests partake, but Abraham stands in hospitable concern. The story silently marks the passing of time, time to find out his wife's name, their barren marriage, their disappointed hopes. Courtesy alone would demand of guests that they should express good will to Abraham and wish the couple a son, and say that they would have a son. The good will and the wish become a prediction in spite of Sarah's unbelieving laughter, through which her curiosity and futile attempt to deceive are betrayed. In the precise timing "in the spring" (Heb. is lit., according to a living or the living time) or perhaps "according to the time of a living (pregnant) woman," or even "when its life time," and in the promise of intervention "I will return," the identity of the visitors begins to dawn on Abraham, and then on Sarah. Sarah's laughter is doubtless J's witness to Isaac's name, a parallel to 17:17. The words: *Is anything too hard,* too wonderful for Yahweh? seals the self-identification. The birth of Isaac is the will and the work of Yahweh (cf. Psalm 113:9; Luke 1:37).

The story brings us by revelation, by conversation, by insight, to Abraham's new and sudden conviction. He really is to have a son by Sarah. The moment of conception, of life, of pregnancy, of divine visitation, is at hand. Abraham sets his departing visitors on the way to Sodom. The moment of doom and destruction is also at hand.

Von Rad and others brilliantly describe these verses as God's soliloquy, but such a description can only refer to verse 17, for 18:23 shows that Abraham knows all about it. Possibly, the soliloquy was overheard or possibly, God confided in Abraham.

These verses are not a literary device to link the conversation pieces which precede and follow. They are the link necessary to the preceding life and the subsequent death theme, though some of the phraseology of verse 19 is reminiscent of the prophets. The theme itself finds its justification in the well-known words of Amos 3:7, according to which God always reveals his plans to his prophet servants.

2. Abraham's Intercession (18:20–33)

20 Then the LORD said, "Because the outcry against Sodom and Gomorrah is great and their sin is very grave, 21 I will go down to see whether they have done altogether according to the outcry which has come to me; and if not, I will know."

22 So the men turned from there, and went toward Sodom; but Abraham still stood before the LORD. 23 Then Abraham drew near, and said, "Wilt thou indeed destroy the righteous with the wicked? 24 Suppose there are fifty righteous within the city; wilt thou then destroy the place and not spare it for the fifty righteous who are in it? 25 Far be it from thee to do such a thing, to slay the righteous with the wicked, so that the righteous fare as the wicked! Far be that from thee! Shall not the Judge of all the earth do right?" 26 And the LORD said, "If I find at Sodom fifty righteous in the city, I will spare the whole place for their sake." 27 Abraham answered, "Behold, I have taken upon myself to speak to the Lord, I who am but dust and ashes. 28 Suppose five of the fifty righteous are lacking? Wilt thou destroy the whole city for lack of five?" And he said, "I will not destroy it if I find forty-five there." 29 Again he spoke to him, and said, "Suppose forty are found there." He answered, "For the sake of forty I will not do it." 30 Then he said, "Oh let not the Lord be angry, and I will speak. Suppose thirty are found there." He answered, "I will not do it, if I find thirty there." 31 He said, "Behold, I have taken upon myself to speak to the Lord. Suppose twenty are found there." He answered, "For the sake of twenty I will not destroy it." 32 Then he said, "Oh let not the Lord be angry, and I will speak again but this once. Suppose ten are found there." He answered, "For the sake of ten I will not destroy it." 33 And the LORD went his way, when he had finished speaking to Abraham; and Abraham returned to his place.

The outcry, that is, the outcry about Sodom's climbing to heaven and calling for retribution, is continuing and notorious. The Hebrew word is tsa'aqath. Compare its use in Isaiah 5:7, where it is contrasted with righteousness, which in Hebrew is ts'dha-

qah. The second part of verse 22 contains one of the so-called alterations in the sacred text deliberately made by the postexilic scribes in the interests of reverence. At present the text reads but Abraham still stood [paused] before the Lord, whereas before the deliberate alteration it read "but the Lord stood still (paused) before Abraham." This original form of the text accords well with verse 23, according to which Abraham is sensitive to the divine hesitation and advances towards God.

Abraham accompanied the three men to a vantage point on the hills east of Hebron, whence the southern end of the Dead Sea was visible (v. 16). Two of the three proceed to Sodom, but the third, now known to be Yahweh, remains with Abraham (v. 22).

Verses 23–33 tell of Abraham's concern for God and his intercession for Sodom, but verses 23–25 give the real theme of the passage. How can there be any suggestion of injustice or lack of fair play in God? Is it right that the just should suffer? The verses convey a wonderful picture of the suppliant Abraham in all his compassion and concern. He draws near in supplication to God (v. 23); his continuing questions are marked by abject obeisance (27,30–31), and the final plea for ten persons is supported by his promise that this is the last time of asking.

On the other hand the alacrity and immediate acquiescence in the divine response are striking, almost amounting to a divine "Of course; of course!" The real problem is in the last petition. Does the plea for the saving of ten persons mark the end of Abraham's compassion, that he dared not ask for fewer? Certainly at the end of verse 32, it is Abraham's turn to speak next, despite his words. A short pause may be imagined, after which the Lord withdrew and Abraham returned home to Mamre.

The question inevitably remains. What would the answer have been if Abraham had finally pleaded not for ten, but for five, or for three, or even for only one? The

Christian view can go even one further and claim divine forbearance on the ground of divine mercy alone.

The passage is often thought to represent the religious attitudes and activity of a much later Israel and indeed of a postexilic Judaism. But intercession after all is only concern on a heavenly axis. It is too much to deny that Abraham interceded for Sodom. After all, his nephew Lot was there. Nevertheless the developed form of the dialogue may well be the work of the J witness himself, using the basic core of an old tradition about Abraham at prayer (cf. 20:7,17) built up into an intercessory prayer. This prayer is concerned with the problem of whether a righteous minority can justify the cancellation of judgment on the wicked majority.

Yet a more precise and original interpretation may be possible. Did Abraham slowly work toward ten persons and stop at ten persons, because that was his real objective? If so, he must have had ten persons in mind. Ten such persons could be mentioned: Lot and his wife; his two younger engaged or married daughters and their fiancees or husbands (19:12,14), all four of whom perished in the subsequent destruction; his two other daughters, either his two elder daughters, or two daughters by another wife, who fled with their father and reappear in 19:15, 30–38.

The reference in 19:15 to the two daughters "who are here," literally, "who are found or findable," suggests that they are not the same as the betrothed or married daughters who would of course prefer to be with their men rather than with their father. The two *men* who went on ahead to Sodom (v. 22; 19:1–16) make up the required number of ten whom Abraham had in mind. The two men appear to Abraham (18:2), to Lot (19:1–3), and to the townsfolk of Sodom (19:4–16) as men, as human beings. Abraham looks at Sodom before and after the catastrophe and this betokens a vital interest in the fate of the city. Nevertheless four of the ten refused to escape and so the city was doomed, because the agreed number was not achieved.

The RSV uses "men" in verse 16, but speaks of angels (lit., messengers) in 19:1, and this corresponds to two different words in the Hebrew. The usage in these chapters helps us to understand the fluidity of meaning between men and angels, unless the term *angels* in 19:1 should be given up and the term messengers employed.

3. Yahweh's Messengers in Sodom (19:1–11)

[1] The two angels came to Sodom in the evening; and Lot was sitting in the gate of Sodom. When Lot saw them, he rose to meet them, and bowed himself with his face to the earth, [2] and said, "My lords, turn aside, I pray you, to your servant's house and spend the night, and wash your feet; then you may rise up early and go on your way." They said, "No; we will spend the night in the street." [3] But he urged them strongly; so they turned aside to him and entered his house; and he made them a feast, and baked unleavened bread, and they ate. [4] But before they lay down, the men of the city, the men of Sodom, both young and old, all the people to the last man, surrounded the house; [5] and they called to Lot, "Where are the men who came to you tonight? Bring them out to us, that we may know them." [6] Lot went out of the door to the men, shut the door after him, [7] and said, "I beg you, my brothers, do not act so wickedly. [8] Behold, I have two daughters who have not known man; let me bring them out to you, and do to them as you please; only do nothing to these men, for they have come under the shelter of my roof." [9] But they said, "Stand back!" And they said, "This fellow came to sojourn, and he would play the judge! Now we will deal worse with you than with them." Then they pressed hard against the man Lot, and drew near to break the door. [10] But the men put forth their hands and brought Lot into the house to them, and shut the door. [11] And they struck with blindness the men who were at the door of the house, both small and great, so that they wearied themselves groping for the door.

Lot is no less a host than his uncle. He is sitting in the small open space at the city gate, and when he sees the strangers he deferentially presses his hospitality upon them. Verse 2 is the refusal, polite but not intended to be final, and they soon give way to Lot's renewed pleas. Apparently Lot lives in a house, Abraham in a tent in the countryside. The townspeople have observed what has happened and they gather to Lot's house and demand the persons of the visitors (v. 5). By reasons of hospitality rather than morality, Lot refuses and offers his own unbetrothed daughters instead. Lot's house is then so viciously attacked that destruction is only prevented by the temporary blinding of the attackers.

Lot's visitors put forth a blinding flash, discomfiting the townspeople but revealing their own identity. The blinding flash represents a Hebrew word *sanwerim* akin to an Akkadian word for something very bright. The condition here is not ordinary blindness, but a temporary but complete blackout by excess light.

4. Warning to Lot (19:12-23)

12 Then the men said to Lot, "Have you any one else here? Sons-in-law, sons, daughters, or any one you have in the city, bring them out of the place; 13 for we are about to destroy this place, because the outcry against its people has become great before the LORD, and the LORD has sent us to destroy it." 14 So Lot went out and said to his sons-in-law, who were to marry his daughters, "Up, get out of this place; for the LORD is about to destroy the city." But he seemed to his sons-in-law to be jesting.

15 When morning dawned, the angels urged Lot, saying, "Arise, take your wife and your two daughters who are here, lest you be consumed in the punishment of the city." 16 But he lingered; so the men seized him and his wife and his two daughters by the hand, the LORD being merciful to him, and they brought him forth and set him outside the city. 17 And when they had brought them forth, they said, "Flee for your life; do not look back or stop anywhere in the valley; flee to the hills, lest you be consumed." 18 And Lot said to them, "Oh, no, my lords; 19 behold, your servant has found favor in your sight, and you have shown me great kindness in saving my life; but I cannot flee to the hills, lest the disaster overtake me, and I die. 20 Behold, yonder city is near enough to flee to, and it is a little one. Let me escape there—is it not a little one?—and my life will be saved!" 21 He said to him, "Behold, I grant you this favor also, that I will not overthrow the city of which you have spoken. 22 Make haste, escape there; for I can do nothing till you arrive there." Therefore the name of the city was called Zoar. 23 The sun had risen on the earth when Lot came to Zoar.

With the authority of their newly discovered identity, the visitors warn Lot and his family. Lot accepts the warning but his two intended sons-in-law are skeptical, and no doubt their fiancees were torn between two opinions. In the morning the argument was still not resolved, and so the angels compel the departure of Lot, his wife, and their two other daughters. Lot pleads to be allowed to enter the small city of Zoar which is thereby saved by the presence of Lot and his two daughters. The valley of verse 17 is the plain of Jordan, the *kikkar* (cf. 13:10); and Zoar was probably at the southeast corner of the Dead Sea.

5. Destruction (19:24-29)

24 Then the LORD rained on Sodom and Gomorrah brimstone and fire from the LORD out of heaven; 25 and he overthrew those cities, and all the valley, and all the inhabitants of the cities, and what grew on the ground. 26 But Lot's wife behind him looked back, and she became a pillar of salt. 27 And Abraham went early in the morning to the place where he had stood before the LORD; 28 and he looked down toward Sodom and Gomorrah and toward all the land of the valley, and beheld, and lo, the smoke of the land went up like the smoke of a furnace.

29 So it was that, when God destroyed the cities of the valley, God remembered Abraham, and sent Lot out of the midst of the overthrow, when he overthrew the cities in which Lot dwelt.

Sodom and Gomorrah and the surrounding territory are destroyed. *Brimstone and fire*—probably petroleum gas—and *overthrew* suggests an earthquake. Lot's wife too is turned into *a pillar of salt*, because she disobeyed the angelic command not to look behind. Abraham from afar beheld the aftermath of the overthrow of the cities, and the story ends with a retrospective reference, probably from the P witness to the leading events. There can be little doubt but that a great natural catastrophe in that area took place and was well known in the days of Abraham. The cities were probably located at the extreme southern end of the Dead Sea. Fantastic, free standing rock-salt pillars occur at the southwest corner of the Dead Sea, and one of these no doubt gave rise to this story about Lot's wife.

Chapters 18—19 then are a unity, and are basically historical with an interpretative overhang. Little need exists to point to a separate Sodom saga which has been fitted into a larger Lot legend (ch. 13, 18, 19), which in turn has been fitted into the still larger story of Abraham. The cross references and the recurrence of familiar motifs would presuppose not only a continuous fitting in but also an ingenious and intricate activity of cross reference through and through the stories. Such memorable coincidences were *part and parcel* of the original series of events and do not require the complicated literary processes proposed by recent commentators.

The theological overhang remains. The testimony of the Old Testament (cf. Deut. 29:23; Isa. 1:9; 13:9; Jer. 49:18; Ezek. 16:46 ff.; Amos 4:11; Psalm 11:6) is that God overthrew Sodom and Gomorrah. Sodom is the principal city in Genesis 18–19, because the story centers in Lot, but Gomorrah is not absent (18:20; 19:24–28). The cities of the plain (19:29) include no doubt "Admah and Zeboiim" (Deut. 29:23; Hos. 11:8) and possibly Zoar.

The reader and student of the Old Testament must recognize in such a sentence as "God overthrew Sodom and Gomorrah," the old Israelite way of describing natural calamity. It is part of their theocentric literary art and part of their theistic outlook to describe natural events in these terms. Each human being must eventually decide for himself whether this description corresponds to reality. Does God destroy cities and populations in this fashion? God is of course the ultimate cause, for this is his world. But that is not to say that he personally intervenes to bring about a calamity like an earthquake or the death of the Egyptian firstborn (Ex. 4:23).

6. *Last Story About Lot* (19:30–38)

30 Now Lot went up out of Zoar, and dwelt in the hills with his two daughters, for he was afraid to dwell in Zoar; so he dwelt in a cave with his two daughters. 31 And the first-born said to the younger, "Our father is old, and there is not a man on earth to come in to us after the manner of all the earth. 32 Come, let us make our father drink wine, and we will lie with him, that we may preserve offspring through our father." 33 So they made their father drink wine that night; and the first-born went in, and lay with her father; he did not know when she lay down or when she arose. 34 And on the next day, the first-born said to the younger, "Behold, I lay last night with my father; let us make him drink wine tonight also; then you go in and lie with him, that we may preserve offspring through our father." 35 So they made their father drink wine that night also; and the younger arose, and lay with him; and he did not know when she lay down or when she arose. 36 Thus both the daughters of Lot were with child by their father. 37 The first-born bore a son, and called his name Moab; he is the father of the Moabites to this day. 38 The younger also bore a son, and called his name Benammi; he is the father of the Ammonites to this day.

The story of Lot now comes to an inevitable and melancholy end, but not even his death is recorded. His two remaining unmarried daughters make their father drunk and conceive children by him. One of these children, boys, became the ancestor of the Moabites; the other, the ancestor of the children of Ammon. To the modern reader the story is a horrible record of incest, and something of this distaste is present in the story itself. The daughters had to intoxicate their father to achieve their ends.

If the story had its origin in Israel, then it partakes to some extent of a political taunt against Israel's neighbors—Moab and Ammon. If the story arose outside Israel, then it is told in honor of the two ancestresses of these peoples, who, rather than allow their father to die without descendants, and who rather than face childlessness, let life and children of pure blood take precedence over morality and honor.

The story, essentially, is a story about Lot, apparently in reduced circumstances, living in a cave, a widower and at the mercy of his two daughters. The Lot of this story must be seen in the context of the story of Abram.

Lot, Haran's son, accompanied Abram from Ur to Haran (11:31), and from Haran to Canaan (12:4). Lot shared in the prosperity of his uncle (13:5), but as the result of quarrels between their servants, Lot parted from Abram the man of blessing. Lot chose the fertile Jordan Valley, but nevertheless ended his life in poverty. Abram rescued Lot from capture and slavery (14:12,14,16), prayed for him and his family from the destruction of Sodom. It was because God remembered Abram that he delivered Lot (19:29), but Lot was delivered to live in a cave, the victim of his daughters.

Lot is thus selfish, fainthearted, and pathetic, but the real meaning of his life is that he parted from Abram the man of blessing. In Genesis, Lot is the man of the diminishing prosperity. The story of Lot in Scripture thus witnesses, if indirectly, to the primacy of Abram and Israel and to the fate of those who default from the sphere of blessing.

Such a view precludes any theory that the story is really about the only survivors of some catastrophe involving the whole earth. Such a theory takes the words *there is not a man on earth* too literally. The words mean no more than "there's no man available," and so make the crime more indefensible.

X. Abraham at Gerar (20:1–18)

¹ From there Abraham journeyed toward the territory of the Negeb, and dwelt between Kadesh and Shur; and he sojourned in Gerar. ² And Abraham said of Sarah his wife, "She is my sister." And Abimelech king of Gerar sent and took Sarah. ³ But God came to Abimelech in a dream by night, and said to him, "Behold, you are a dead man, because of the woman whom you have taken; for she is a man's wife." ⁴ Now Abimelech had not approached her; so he said, "Lord, wilt thou slay an innocent people? ⁵ Did he not himself say to me, 'She is my sister'? And she herself said, 'He is my brother.' In the integrity of my heart and the innocence of my hands I have done this." ⁶ Then God said to him in the dream, "Yes, I know that you have done this in the integrity

of your heart, and it was I who kept you from sinning against me; therefore I did not let you touch her. ⁷ Now then restore the man's wife; for he is a prophet, and he will pray for you, and you shall live. But if you do not restore her, know that you shall surely die, you, and all that are yours."

⁸ So Abimelech rose early in the morning, and called all his servants, and told them all these things; and the men were very much afraid. ⁹ Then Abimelech called Abraham, and said to him, "What have you done to us? And how have I sinned against you, that you have brought on me and my kingdom a great sin? You have done to me things that ought not to be done." ¹⁰ And Abimelech said to Abraham, "What were you thinking of, that you did this thing?" ¹¹ Abraham said, "I did it because I thought, There is no fear of God at all in this place, and they will kill me because of my wife. ¹² Besides she is indeed my sister, the daughter of my father but not the daughter of my mother; and she became my wife. ¹³ And when God caused me to wander from my father's house, I said to her, 'This is the kindness you must do me: at every place to which we come, say of me, He is my brother.' " ¹⁴ Then Abimelech took sheep and oxen, and male and female slaves, and gave them to Abraham, and restored Sarah his wife to him. ¹⁵ And Abimelech said, "Behold, my land is before you; dwell where it pleases you." ¹⁶ To Sarah he said, "Behold, I have given your brother a thousand pieces of silver; it is your vindication in the eyes of all who are with you; and before every one you are righted." ¹⁷ Then Abraham prayed to God; and God healed Abimelech, and also healed his wife and female slaves so that they bore children. ¹⁸ For the LORD had closed all the wombs of the house of Abimelech because of Sarah, Abraham's wife.

Genesis 20 sets the reader an intriguing problem, for the chapter tells a new story about the jeopardy of Abraham's wife, Sarah, the mother of all Israel, in the setting of a removal of Abraham from where he was (v. 1) to the southern areas of the land, *between Kadesh and Shur,* centered in *Gerar,* where the incident concerning Sarah took place. *From there* (v. 1) cannot mean the cave of 19:30, but must refer back to 14:13, that is, to Mamre.

The fact of Abraham's removal to the South fits in well with two features of the narrative. The succeeding chapters record events in the area well to the south of Mamre and Hebron. Verse 1 thus records

Abraham's removal from the areas in which the stories of Chapters 13—19 take place, to the area where the stories of Chapters 20—25 take place. Isaac too is centered in this more southerly area. Indeed the words in 20:1 *and he sojourned in Gerar* may well have the technical meaning of which they are capable, and which has been claimed for them; i.e., "and he became a resident alien there." Such a translation would imply a permanent removal, a new home and a new life in Gerar. The subsequent events tend to support this view.

Why then did Abraham go south and only return to Hebron for Sarah's burial? Chapters 13, 14, 18, and 19 show Abraham's interest in Lot and the area where he lived. In losing Lot, had Abraham lost a trading partner? Or had the earlier breach (ch. 13) between them been complete? If it had, then why had Abraham gone to Lot's rescue (ch. 14)? Perhaps Lot was no longer a partner of Abraham, but perhaps he was an agent for Abraham. Did Abraham go south because he had lost a trading area when the cities of the plain were destroyed? The cities of the Negeb, as listed in Joshua 15:21, belong of course to the tenth century but adjacent areas toward Egypt would then have become Abraham's new trading area. For some reason or other Abraham went south and 20:1 records this movement at the right time as the geographical references before and after 20:1 make clear. The framework is historical. The Negeb, literally the dry land, is the area from about 10 miles northeast of Beersheba as far south as Kadesh, i.e., Ain Kadish about 50 miles south of Beersheba. Shur is an area of desert in the northwest of the Sinai peninsula, and northeast of Egypt, (25:18; Ex. 15:22). Gerar is either modern Tell Jemmeh, some 8 miles south of Gaza, or probably Tell Abu Hureira, some 11 miles southeast of Gaza. Genesis 20:1 must therefore record two dwelling places of Abraham. He had his pastures between Kadesh and Egypt, but his citizenship was at Gerar.

On the other hand, within this framework is a story about an adventure suffered by Sarah, which is very similar to the story in 12:10–20. In that passage Sarah, young and beautiful was taken into Pharaoh's house with dire consequences. In chapter 20, Abimelech, king of Gerar, took Sarah into his house, presumably for the same reasons. Sarah must have been beautiful, attractive, and a great temptation, just as she was in chapter 12. But the facts now about Sarah are different. According to 18:11, Abraham and Sarah were old. She was past both the menopause and indeed delight in intercourse. So the adventure in the framework does not suit the time of life which Sarah had reached. The best explanation therefore seems to be that the story here parallels the earlier account and that it comes from another witness known as E. This is the first long extract from the E witness in the book of Genesis. Of course other interpreters recognize the existence of two separate incidents, and this could be the right explanation.

Admittedly the people are different— Pharaoh of Egypt, Abimelech of Gerar; the consequences are different—plagues and barrenness. Pharaoh discovers his fault, but Abimelech is divinely warned in a dream. The similarities are great, and it is fair to conclude that Sarah's adventure must have taken place before chapter 18, so that the story here is probably E's more ethical version of the chapter 12 story, and belongs earlier in Abraham's life, as verse 13 actually suggests. Genesis 26:6–11 contains yet a third story of a wife at risk, this time Isaac's wife, Rebekah, and again by Abimelech, king of the Philistines at Gerar. Perhaps one incident lies behind all three stories, and that incident took place at Gerar in connection with Sarah or Rebekah. Alternately the three stories may record three separate incidents, as some have maintained.

The E witness offers his own interpretation of the story. The first clause of verse 13 shows that this E witness too knew of Abram's migration from home. *Caused me to wander:* the verb in Hebrew is plural, not in deference to the possible polytheism of Abimelech, but as expressing the singular-plural polarity of the Hebrew God. He is elsewhere fond of using dreams as means of divine revelations (vv. 3,6). Abimelech is prevented from sin (v. 6) by sickness (v. 17). E is at pains to explain that Sarah really is Abraham's sister (v. 12), and that Abraham told the truth if not the whole truth. E also says that Abraham received a monetary compensation in addition to flocks, herds, and slaves. The comparison of the stories is thus instructive.[17]

Chapter 20, however, is much richer in religious ideas. The question of punishing the innocent is again to the fore (v. 4); the activity of intercession is prominent (vv. 7,17); the *fear of God* is a general term for piety and religion.

Especially interesting in the chapter is the first reference in the Old Testament to a prophet (v. 7), who is described as performing not those activities like proclaiming, preaching, more normally associated with the prophetic office, but the activities of prayer and intercession which recent study has shown to be such an essential part of Old Testament prophecy and has given acceptance to A. R. Johnson's dictum that the Old Testament prophet was "a specialist in prayer." The Hebrew words at the end of verse 16 are obscure in meaning, but the RSV gives the general sense. The wife of Abraham comes out of the incident innocent and with her honor in no way impaired.

The value of this chapter then in the life story of Abraham is that it records the removal of his family to the South and preserves the correct location of the story of the wife at risk; i.e., Gerar, and not Egypt. Certainly in contrast to the disasters of chapter 19, where Lot, bereft of blessing, does have two grandsons, and Abraham and Sarah are still without a child, chapter 21 brings the expected climax to

the Abraham source. The birth of a son, upon whose birth all the promises of chapters 12, 15, and 17 depend, is an unexpected postponement of the event expected after the end of 19.

If this interpretation is correct, and it is widely accepted, then the catastrophe of chapter 19 is at once followed by the birth of Isaac, and the unnatural conception of grandsons to Lot, who is outside the blessing, is offset by the divine ordering of the conception of Isaac who is the son of blessing. Chapters 20—22 are mainly the work of the E witness. Since he was probably a northerner, living in the days of Solomon, or soon after the monarchy was divided, his interest in these traditions, which belong to the Negeb and center in Beersheba, attests the reliability of the traditions.

XI. The Promise and the Test (21:1—22: 24)

1. The Birth of Isaac (21:1–7)

[1] The LORD visited Sarah as he had said, and the LORD did to Sarah as he had promised. [2] And Sarah conceived, and bore Abraham a son in his old age at the time of which God had spoken to him. [3] Abraham called the name of his son who was born to him, whom Sarah bore him, Isaac. [4] And Abraham circumcised his son Isaac when he was eight days old, as God had commanded him. [5] Abraham was a hundred years old when his son Isaac was born to him. [6] And Sarah said, "God has made laughter for me; every one who hears will laugh over me." [7] And she said, "Who would have said to Abraham that Sarah would suckle children? Yet I have borne him a son in his old age."

All three witnesses have a say in the records of Isaac's birth. Verses 1*a*,2*a*,6*b*–7 are J; 6*a* is E; and 1*b*,2*b*–5 are P. How important and valuable that all three witnesses testify in turn to the supernatural character of Isaac's birth—J in 1*a;* P in 1*b,* and E in 6*a.* Here analysis of the contributions of the witnesses is of incalculable help to the story.

At long last Abraham and Sarah have a son. For this event they have waited many, many years, and the reader has been wait-

17 Lev. 18:9,11; 20:17; Deut. 27:22 forbade marriage with half sisters, though it appears that Amnon could have married his half sister, Tamar (2 Sam. 13:13).

ing since chapter 12. The birth of a son to such aged parents is a mystery, to which verses 1–7 offer their own explanation. Was this birth a freak of nature, as occasionally happens, and which gives rise to good-natured amusement among neighbors and not a little sheepishness to the parents themselves? Was this belated birth the retrospective cause of the stories of the promises to Abraham?

In verse 1 the birth is said to be due to a divine visitation and a divine action. The interpretation can vary between a coincident intercourse on the one hand and a divinely created conception on the other. Driver, for example, cites Luke 1:68 among other references for the verb "visit." Genesis conceals the mode of the event but makes clear that God was responsible for the event itself and for its timing (cf. 18:10–14, the J witness; 21:1–2, the E witness). There is a divine reference about the birth of Isaac. Was there also, so to speak, a divine quantum or quality about his birth? The question may be put another way. Is there anything in the life and history of the descendants of Isaac, of the children of his son Jacob, who are the children of Israel, that points to a supernatural origin for the nation? Many nations have a longer identifiable presence through the millennia. The Jews have maintained their identifiable presence but without a land, without a home, and they have done that not only as foreigners in many lands but as the unwelcome, even the hated, the destroyed and yet not fully destroyed, almost universal, minority. Perhaps the evidence and proof of their supernatural origin is that they have survived when they ought not to have survived.

Isaac was born to Abraham and Sarah when she at least was long past the age of conception. As God called his father from outside of the Land of Promise to live in that land, so Isaac was born in some unknown place on the confines of that land if not actually outside its borders, later described by such terms as "from Dan to Beersheba." In a womb that could not conceive, Isaac was conceived and called to life within the promise. The record clearly testifies to divine intervention and to marvelous though unexpected quickening in Sarah's womb (18:14).

Genesis 21:1–7 is the bridge of the book of Genesis—a bridge which connects mankind on the one side with the sacred story of Israel and the gospel on the other side with the kingdom of God. Without the birth of Isaac the bridge could never have been completed. What was for Abraham and Sarah the far side of the bridge would never have been reached; what is for us the near side of the bridge would have remained useless. This record of the birth of Isaac is the keystone of the arch of the bridge and so was put in its place. Do verses 1–2 call in the first place for a decision of faith rather than an explanation of its meaning?

The baby is called *Isaac* and is *circumcised when he* [*is*] *eight days old;* thus he is appropriated to and set within the promise (17:9–14). The meaning of the name Isaac "may God smile" is one of the chief themes of the story. In 18:12 the reference is to Sarah's own amusement; in 17:17 to Abraham's incredulous laughter; in 21:6 to Sarah's thankful laughter and the merriment of the neighbors.

The verb in *would have said* is Aramaic and is limited to the poetical passages of the Old Testament (Psalm 106:2; Job 8:2). If 6b is read after 7 a well balanced poem of four lines becomes visible.

2. Abraham Loses His Option (21:8–21)

8 And the child grew, and was weaned; and Abraham made a great feast on the day that Isaac was weaned. 9 But Sarah saw the son of Hagar the Egyptian, whom she had borne to Abraham, playing with her son Isaac. 10 So she said to Abraham, "Cast out this slave woman with her son; for the son of this slave woman shall not be heir with my son Isaac." 11 And the thing was very displeasing to Abraham on account of his son. 12 But God said to Abraham, "Be not displeased because of the lad and because of your slave woman; whatever Sarah says to you, do as she tells you, for through Isaac shall your descendants be named. 13 And

I will make a nation of the son of the slave woman also, because he is your offspring." 14 So Abraham rose early in the morning, and took bread and a skin of water, and gave it to Hagar, putting it on her shoulder, along with the child, and sent her away. And she departed, and wandered in the wilderness of Beersheba.

15 When the water in the skin was gone, she cast the child under one of the bushes. 16 Then she went, and sat down over against him a good way off, about the distance of a bowshot; for she said, "Let me not look upon the death of the child." And as she sat over against him, the child lifted up his voice and wept. 17 And God heard the voice of the lad; and the angel of God called to Hagar from heaven, and said to her, "What troubles you, Hagar? Fear not; for God has heard the voice of the lad where he is. 18 Arise, lift up the lad, and hold him fast with your hand; for I will make him a great nation." 19 Then God opened her eyes, and she saw a well of water; and she went, and filled the skin with water, and gave the lad a drink. 20 And God was with the lad, and he grew up; he lived in the wilderness, and became an expert with the bow. 21 He lived in the wilderness of Paran; and his mother took a wife for him from the land of Egypt.

After two or three, or even more, years, Isaac was weaned and Abraham held—as the Hebrew word shows—a great drinking feast in celebration. In verse 9 the words *playing with her son Isaac* are not in the Hebrew but are supplied by the RSV and other texts from the Greek and Vulgate. "Playing" has often been given a sinister meaning; e.g., unchastity (39:14,17); idolatry (Ex. 32:6); attempted murder (2 Sam. 2:14; Prov. 26:19) have all been suggested. But the word only means that Ishmael was innocently amusing Isaac. At this time Ishmael would have been between fourteen and seventeen years old, and doubtless his equality with Isaac as one of the family, and perhaps his superiority suggested by his years aroused Sarah's fears.

Sarah demands Hagar's expulsion, and her words in verse 10 suggest that Hagar is not her own maid (16:3), but rather one of the female slaves who had become Abraham's concubine. Sarah's demand is resisted by Abraham, but he becomes convinced by a word from God that Sarah is

right; and Hagar and Ishmael are expelled to wander in the wilderness of Beersheba. Beersheba is nearly 30 miles southwest of Hebron. In 16:6 Abram is submissive to Sarai, but in 21:11 Abraham is far more independent. It takes a divine revelation to make him give way.

The position is very clear. Ishmael is Abraham's son, and is therefore a second string for the continuation of his father's life, business, and purpose. The divine instruction in verse 12 no doubt records Abraham's realization that he must be prepared to surrender the second string and rest all his hopes on his and Sarah's only son.

The submission of Abraham in faith explains the story, and the survival of Ishmael is promised (cf. Gal. 4:21—5:1). Early one morning, by divine command, probably in a dream, Abram loads Hagar with bread and water, and, according to some texts, puts Ishmael on her shoulder too. The present Hebrew text does not say this but is very awkward. The RSV is not clear. *Along with the child* could mean either that Abraham gave the food along with the child to Hagar, or that he put the food on her shoulder along with the child. The second sense could only mean that Ishmael was little more than Isaac's age, or that in putting the boy onto his mother's shoulder Abraham signified the end of his responsibility for him. In verse 15 she puts the child down under a bush, probably a broom tree. Such descriptions are difficult if Ishmael was between fourteen and seventeen years, however small he was in stature. Abraham was eighty-six when Ishmael was born (16:16), and he was one hundred when Isaac was born (21:5). Ishmael and Isaac played together (21:9), so Ishmael must have been fifteen, if not sixteen or seventeen years of age. At the end of verse 16 the Hebrew says "and she lifted up her voice and wept." The RSV follows the LXX: *The child lifted up his voice and wept.*

Verses 14–21 record a detailed if pathetic account of what happened, yet the inevitable does not happen. Given up by his father, abandoned by his mother, he is nevertheless saved. The anxious mother casting about in all directions suddenly finds some water. It is a providential discovery for her. God has answered the cries of her son and her own prayers, and mother and son are saved. The destiny of Ishmael (vv. 13,18) is reassured. Ishmael becomes the father of the camel nomads, Bedouin experts as bowmen, and eventually marries an Egyptian girl chosen for him by his mother (cf. 24:3 f.; 34:4) from among her countrywomen (16:1). The wilderness of Paran is et-Tih on the south side of the Negeb.

In 21:8–21 the E witness gives his version of the expulsion of Hagar and her son. For some reason he never gives the boy's name, though it is implied in the repeated *heard* of 21:17, for Ishmael means "God has heard." The story of the J witness is given in chapter 16. Many scholars believe that just as chapter 20 is the E version parallel to the J story in chapter 12 of Sarai's abduction, so 21 is E's parallel to the J story in chapter 16 of Ishmael's expulsion. To maintain this view 16:9, i.e., that Hagar returned home, must be regarded as an accommodation to prepare the way for 21:8–21.

That 21:8–21 is a parallel and not a real sequel to 16 is difficult to believe. In 16 only Hagar is expelled; in 21, Hagar and her son. The priestly witness thought of Ishmael as between fourteen and seventeen years of age, but 21:8–21 is the story of a small boy; but it also is the story of the E witness, who thought of the boy as much younger. Verses 8–21 should more reasonably be regarded as quite a different story from chapter 16. Sarah would undoubtedly have been upset when she saw Hagar's pregnancy. Equally she would have been angry when she saw Hagar's son and her own boy at play together as equals. Sarah's jealousy and opposition continued. Even if it could be shown that this is a parallel and not a sequel to chapter 16, then the story of the expulsion properly belongs to just

before chapter 22, where Abraham is facing the death of Isaac, having just before experienced the loss of Ishmael. After Ishmael had gone, Abraham had lost his option, and all he had left was Isaac.

3. Abraham and Abimelech (21:22–34)

22 At that time Abimelech and Phicol the commander of his army said to Abraham, "God is with you in all that you do; 23 now therefore swear to me here by God that you will not deal falsely with me or with my offspring or with my posterity, but as I have dealt loyally with you, you will deal with me and with the land where you have sojourned." 24 And Abraham said, "I will swear."
25 When Abraham complained to Abimelech about a well of water which Abimelech's servants had seized, 26 Abimelech said, "I do not know who has done this thing; you did not tell me, and I have not heard of it until today." 27 So Abraham took sheep and oxen and gave them to Abimelech, and the two men made a covenant. 28 Abraham set seven ewe lambs of the flock apart. 29 And Abimelech said to Abraham, "What is the meaning of these seven ewe lambs which you have set apart?" 30 He said, "These seven ewe lambs you will take from my hand, that you may be a witness for me that I dug this well." 31 Therefore that place was called Beersheba; because there both of them swore an oath. 32 So they made a covenant at Beersheba. Then Abimelech and Phicol the commander of his army rose up and returned to the land of the Philistines. 33 Abraham planted a tamarisk tree in Beersheba, and called there on the name of the LORD, the Everlasting God. 34 And Abraham sojourned many days in the land of the Philistines.

Two brief incidents concerning difficulties between Abraham and Abimelech are now related. The first in verses 22–24,27,31 concerns a general question in which *Abimelech*, the king of Gerar, and his army commander take the initiative. Following the incident concerning Sarah in chapter 20, the two men seek to put their relations with Abraham on a firm footing, and so protect offspring and posterity. The Hebrew words are *nini* and *nekhdi*, happily rendered by Speiser as "kith and kin." They recognize in the alien Abraham a rich and powerful person who could become a friend or foe. Abraham, anxious not to jeopardize the social and commercial position he has gained, is ready to cooperate and makes a present of sheep and oxen. The two men conclude a treaty of friendship (v. 27). Apparently Abimelech had actually journeyed to Beersheba for this purpose.

The other story is a dispute about the ownership of a well at Beersheba in which Abraham took the initiative, taking advantage of Abimelech's presence there. Abimelech's servants on a journey no doubt, had seized possession of one of Abraham's wells. Abimelech denied all knowledge of it and accepted *seven ewe lambs* from Abraham in token of the latter's ownership.

Beersheba means "well of the seven" or "well of the oath" (the Hebrew word for seven and oath is the same), and there is some play on the idea of seven. Perhaps to swear an oath was to "seven" oneself in some way, and indicate that an oath was seven times binding (cf. Skinner). Beersheba is certainly outside the domain of Gerar, being about twenty-five miles away, but Abraham must have been a very significant person in both areas.

Gerar is obviously an independent Canaanite city, ruled by a king whose name means "My father is king," either in reference to the king's royal father or to his god. *Phicol,* mentioned again in 26:26, is not a Semitic name but may be a form of *pylk,* meaning the Lycian.

Abimelech is described as the king of the Philistines, but the latter did not settle in this area until several centuries later, at the end of the second millenium. The name may therefore be the later name used to describe the earlier inhabitants of the area, but then earlier people may themselves have come from the same area of the Aegean as the Philistines. Philistines then in Genesis would broadly describe Aegean immigrants of any age.

The last two verses inform us that *Abraham planted a tamarisk tree* in honor of what must have been a local eminent deity, by name of *'El 'Olam,* which means the everlasting El or God. These verses do not suggest anything by way of animism, the worship of spirits—here in a tree; nor do they mention that Abraham erected an altar, which was generally his custom when Yahweh was concerned.

Beersheba, as the southernmost city of Judah, is about fifty miles southwest of Jerusalem and was an ancient sanctuary. Abraham, Isaac (26:23–25), and Jacob (46:1–5) are all associated with it. Samuel's sons were judges there (1 Sam. 8:2); and Amos denounces it as a pilgrimage sanctuary (5:5; 8:14).

Although living in Beersheba, Abraham used to spend considerable periods of time in Gerar. Here the commercial interests of Abraham's life come once again to the fore.

4. Proposed Sacrifice of Isaac (22:1–19)

1 After these things God tested Abraham, and said to him, "Abraham!" And he said, "Here am I." 2 He said, "Take your son, your only son Isaac, whom you love, and go to the land of Moriah, and offer him there as a burnt offering upon one of the mountains of which I shall tell you." 3 So Abraham rose early in the morning, saddled his ass, and took two of his young men with him, and his son Isaac; and he cut the wood for the burnt offering, and arose and went to the place of which God had told him. 4 On the third day Abraham lifted up his eyes and saw the place afar off. 5 Then Abraham said to his young men, "Stay here with the ass; I and the lad will go yonder and worship, and come again to you." 6 And Abraham took the wood of the burnt offering, and laid it on Isaac his son; and he took in his hand the fire and the knife. So they went both of them together. 7 And Isaac said to his father Abraham, "My father!" And he said, "Here am I, my son." He said, "Behold, the fire and the wood; but where is the lamb for a burnt offering?" 8 Abraham said, "God will provide himself the lamb for a burnt offering, my son." So they went both of them together.

9 When they came to the place of which God had told him, Abraham built an altar there, and laid the wood in order, and bound Isaac his son, and laid him on the altar, upon the wood. 10 Then Abraham put forth his hand, and took the knife to slay his son. 11 But the angel of the LORD called to him from heaven, and said, "Abraham, Abraham!" And he said, "Here am I." 12 He said, "Do not lay your hand on the lad or do anything to him; for now I know that you fear God, seeing you have not withheld your son, your only son, from me."

13 And Abraham lifted up his eyes and looked, and behold, behind him was a ram, caught in a thicket by his horns; and Abraham went and took the ram, and offered it up as a burnt offering instead of his son. 14 So Abraham called the name of that place The LORD will provide; as it is said to this day, "On the mount of the LORD it shall be provided."

15 And the angel of the LORD called to Abraham a second time from heaven, 16 and said, "By myself I have sworn, says the LORD, because you have done this, and have not withheld your son, your only son, 17 I will indeed bless you, and I will multiply your descendants as the stars of heaven and as the sand which is on the seashore. And your descendants shall possess the gate of their enemies, 18 and by your descendants shall all the nations of the earth bless themselves, because you have obeyed my voice." 19 So Abraham returned to his young men, and they arose and went together to Beersheba; and Abraham dwelt at Beersheba.

The first verse gives the theme of the story. *God,* and the word God is emphatically placed in the order of the Hebrew sentence, proposed to test the obedience of Abraham by commanding him to journey to *the land of Moriah* (identified in 2 Chron. 3:1 as Mount Moriah, the temple-hill of Jerusalem). The verb for testing is also emphatically placed at the beginning of the narrative. Thus *God tested* is a phrase that gives us the theological theme of the chapter and also helps to allay our fears, both about the character of God's requirements in the story and the outcome of the event itself.

For Moriah, the LXX has "lofty" and the Syriac reads "land of the Amorites." The suggestion that the original reading was Oak of Moreh (Shechem) is ruled out by the distance involved. There, Abraham is to offer his *only son Isaac* as a burnt offering, that is a sacrifice to be completely destroyed by fire on an altar. Abraham carries out the demands without complaint and without objection, and journeys for three days to within sight of the appointed place, which he recognizes from a distance. He leaves his servants behind, still hiding from Isaac his purpose, and father and son arrive at the place. The awful details of verses 9–10 are meticulously related, though nothing is said of the grief of Abraham or of the terror of Isaac. A last-minute intervention by God's angel, when Abraham had the knife in his hand, prevented the slaughter of Isaac. Instead, a ram caught in a thicket was slain and offered. The Hebrew for *behind him was a ram* is better read as "and behold a (literally, one) ram."

The story is marvelously related in simple, clear, polished, and logical style, and is one of the best of all the stories of Genesis. The emotional chastity of the chapter is almost incredible, but attention must be drawn to the repeated: *So they went both of them together,* and to the pathos hidden in the phrases: *My father,* and *My son.*

The story has been interpreted as a parable, just as the story of the prodigal son is a parable. The chief interpretation along these lines has been to see in it the divine repudiation of infant sacrifice, and in consequence the substitution of an animal in satisfaction for the divine claim to receive the firstborn of every womb (Ex. 22:29; 13:12–15). Infant, and indeed human, sacrifices were widely practiced customs and they did not die out in Israel until the eighth and seventh centuries (cf. 2 Kings 3:27; 16:3; 17:31; 21:6; 23:10; Mic. 6:7 f.; Jer. 7:31; 19:5; Ezek. 16:20 f.; 23:37; Isa. 57:5; Lev. 18:21; Deut. 18:10). Such an explanation, however, is not adequate to the full significance of the occasion, in which the whole future of Israel's sacred history is at stake, and not merely one sacrificial custom, barbarous as that was.

Another parabolic interpretation, suggested by von Rad (p. 240), would center not on the sacrifice but on the person of Isaac as typifying Israel: Israel, like Isaac, called into being by God; bound in a sacrificial servantship and apostleship; Israel given back by God, then renewed by God's life again. Unfortunately the parable does not really fit. Isaac is blameless, Israel was not. Israel's resurrection after the Exile is an act of forgiveness. Abraham, not Isaac, is the center of the story in Genesis.

The story may then be a parable of

obedience, Abraham's obedience, imitated by Isaac also. In obedience Abraham gives up all that had happened to him since his call. In like manner he now surrenders the future. He gives up everything to a command from God, incomprehensible in itself and contradicting everything that he had hitherto received from God, and had hoped to receive from God in days to come. Rising early one morning, no doubt the morning following the night in which the command was received by way of a dream, he immediately prepares for the journey. The journey into the third day measures his obedience. He himself carries the fire and the knife, the weapons of death. It is a picture of obedience unparalleled outside Gethsemane, and it is a part of the meaning of the story. *Fear God* in verse 12 is obedience.

If the story is a parable, then it must also be a parable of the way in which God tested his own friend, Abraham. The theme of the testing is given in verse 1, whereby the reader knows that the test will not be carried out to the bitter end, but Abraham does not know that the sacrifice will not, at the last, be exacted. God's test, as distinct from the devil or man's temptations, is part of the Old Testament. Thus the divine testing of Israel as a nation is part of the divine plan (cf. Deut. 8:2; 13:3; Judg. 2:22; Psalm 66:10; Jer. 9:7). Job too was tested, and Jeremiah's role was that of a tester. Testing was also part of cultic ceremonies (Ex. 15:25b; Psalms 7; 26).

The story in chapter 22 is not a ritual testing, and indeed it is too lifelike, too vested in actual persons, places, and circumstances, to be regarded as only a parable. This then is not a parable, even if it has a parabolic effect; it is rather the story of something that actually happened, something that Abraham intended to do, and would have done, had he not at the last moment been prevented.

Abraham believed he was called upon to sacrifice his son, and he set about doing it. The story thus records one of the deepest and most profound personal experiences in the Old Testament to be set besides the sorrow of Moses after the golden calf incident, the sorrows of David, the cross of Hosea, and the passion of Jeremiah. Without using one word to describe the feeling of the man, the writer yet lays bare the soul of Abraham in this experience of giving up his son, his beloved son whom he loves, his own Isaac, to the claim of God. The story is a true story of the greatest experience that Abraham or any other patriarch ever underwent.

The problem of the story is not in its events, but in its motivation. Why did Abraham feel that he had to make this sacrifice? The answer is that he felt that God required it of him, as Jepthah also was later to believe (Judg. 11:29–40). The problem of interpretation is this. Did Abraham's conviction or the writer's account of that conviction correspond to a real divine request? Did God make, would God in fact have made, such a demand upon Abraham or anybody else, except himself? There are those of course who would accept the command literally.

Our answer however is no. Indeed what Christian or humane conscience could regard such a command as coming from God? How then did this conviction arise in the mind of Abraham, since we believe that God did not put it there? The question can only be answered in part. Abraham's conviction that his son must be sacrificed is the climax of the psychology of his life.

Abraham's life is portrayed in a succession of experiences. It begins with his departure from his family, which is explained in terms of a divine commission and vocation; it is marked by the rupture from Lot, companion and partner of so much at the beginning; it is bedeviled by famine, by trading losses and by war; it is overshadowed by the unrelenting childlessness and the spiritual crisis of confidence and of faith that that state brought about; it is concentrated eventually, and especially after Ishmael's departure, into the thin thread of Isaac's life. Everything depends upon the life of Isaac in the days when child mortality must have been heavy.

The theme of Abraham's life after Isaac's birth must have been, "What if I should lose him?" Such a question is the raw material of the resultant conviction: "I am called upon to give him: God wants me to do it."

So Hannah reasoned even before Samuel was born, no doubt in hope of being given and of preserving Samuel (1 Sam. 3). So Abraham was driven by his good fortune, by his blessing, to the belief that his blessing must be surrendered. His son must be sacrificed. The discovery of the *ram* trapped *in a thicket* was the solvent of his own mistaken conviction and his release into the fulness of the God-given conviction about himself. He was not called upon to surrender his blessing.

Following the theophany (vv. 11 f.), the sacrifice (v. 13), and the customary designation of the place (v. 14), the immediate sequel is the divine reaffirmation of the promises to Abraham. The Lord swears by himself, there being no one higher than himself by whom the oath may be sworn. The oath is as absolute as God himself. The words "says the Lord" are in Hebrew, "The murmur of whisper of the Lord," a frequent expression in prophecy. Abraham is to be blessed, and the blessing will also be seen in the increase of his progeny, in their victories over their enemies, and in the blessedness of mankind. The Hebrew verb here is reflexive; i.e., bless themselves.

Isaac is not even mentioned, though the two servants are, and they all return to Beersheba. What did Isaac say, and what did Abraham say to Sarah?

5. Nahor's Descendants (22:20–24)

20 Now after these things it was told Abraham, "Behold, Milcah also has borne children to your brother Nahor: 21 Uz the first-born, Buz his brother, Kemuel the father of Aram, 22 Chesed, Hazo, Pildash, Jidlaph, and Bethuel." 23 Bethuel became the father of Rebekah. These eight Milcah bore to Nahor, Abraham's brother. 24 Moreover, his concubine, whose name was Reumah, bore Tebah, Gaham, Tahash, and Maacah.

No doubt news came from time to time of and from the distant family in Haran. Part of the news is now given by the J witness in the form of the family tree of Abraham's brother Nahor. This family tree consists of an Aramean alliance of twelve families, clans, or tribes who dwell in the northwest area of Arabia. The passage is inserted here in order to form an anticipatory link with the events of chapter 24.

Rebekah's father is Bethuel, though some verses suggest that her father was Nahor (24:24; 29:5). *Chesed* may be the ancestor of the Chasdim (Chaldeans), while the four tribes derived from the concubine show that they were not of such pure descent, that is they are related, or collateral, rather than full tribes. This is a feature characteristic of all such concubine tribes; e.g., Ishmael, Gad and Asher, Dan and Naphtali. Maacah lived in the region south of Hermon (Deut. 3:14; Josh. 13:11,13). The word used for concubine is not Hebrew but a foreign word borrowed from the Greeks or Hittites.

XII. Burial of Sarah (23:1–20)

1 Sarah lived a hundred and twenty-seven years; these were the years of the life of Sarah. 2 And Sarah died at Kiriatharba (that is, Hebron) in the land of Canaan; and Abraham went in to mourn for Sarah and to weep for her. 3 And Abraham rose up from before his dead, and said to the Hittites, 4 "I am a stranger and a sojourner among you; give me property among you for a burying place, that I may bury my dead out of my sight." 5 The Hittites answered Abraham, 6 "Hear us, my lord; you are a mighty prince among us. Bury your dead in the choicest of our sepulchres; none of us will withhold from you his sepulchre, or hinder you from burying your dead." 7 Abraham rose and bowed to the Hittites, the people of the land. 8 And he said to them, "If you are willing that I should bury my dead out of my sight, hear me, and entreat for me Ephron the son of Zohar, 9 that he may give me the cave of Machpelah, which he owns; it is at the end of his field. For the full price let him give it to me in your presence as a possession for a burying place." 10 Now Ephron was sitting among the Hittites; and Ephron the Hittite answered Abraham in the hearing of the Hittites, of all who went in at the gate of his city, 11 "No, my lord, hear me; I give you

the field, and I give you the cave that is in it; in the presence of the sons of my people I give it to you; bury your dead." 12 Then Abraham bowed down before the people of the land. 13 And he said to Ephron in the hearing of the people of the land, "But if you will, hear me; I will give the price of the field; accept it from me, that I may bury my dead there." 14 Ephron answered Abraham, 15 "My lord, listen to me; a piece of land worth four hundred shekels of silver, what is that between you and me? Bury your dead." 16 Abraham agreed with Ephron; and Abraham weighed out for Ephron the silver which he had named in the hearing of the Hittites, four hundred shekels of silver, according to the weights current among the merchants.

17 So the field of Ephron in Machpelah, which was to the east of Mamre, the field with the cave which was in it and all the trees that were in the field, throughout its whole area, was made over 18 to Abraham as a possession in the presence of the Hittites, before all who went in at the gate of his city. 19 After this, Abraham buried Sarah his wife in the cave of the field of Machpelah east of Mamre (that is, Hebron) in the land of Canaan. 20 The field and the cave that is in it were made over to Abraham as a possession for a burying place by the Hittites.

In this chapter the P witness makes his second great contribution to the story of the patriarchs. In chapter 17 he had told with much detail the story of the covenant and circumcision; now he gives the account of Sarah's death and the purchase of her grave. The national mark of Abraham's descendants, and the grave as the title deed to, or earnest of, their national home in that land are the two patriarchal themes to which the P witness testifies.

Sarah dies, one hundred and twenty-seven years old, *at Kiriath-arba*, literally city of four, i.e., four quarters or areas, the old name for Hebron. To read *Arba* as the name of a man (cf. Josh. 14:15) is probably an error. We last left Abraham and presumably Sarah at Beersheba (22:19). Abraham performs the customary wailing and mourning in the tent where she lay. *Mourn* represents the Hebrew word for wailing, for which professional women mourners were often employed (Jer. 9:17).

After the appropriate ceremonies are concluded, Abraham leaves the tent and proceeds, as verse 10 shows, to the gate of the city where the inhabitants of the city described as *Hittites* are gathered. It has been thought that the P witness is here describing the pre-Israelite inhabitants of the land by his own peculiar term, just as the J witness uses "Canaanite" and the E witness "Amorite" of the same people. Commentators are however careful to point out the very careful, quasi-legal character of the wording of this chapter (cf. vv. 17–20), so that P's use of the term children of Heth, i.e., *Hittites*, must be treated with great respect. No doubt at Hebron, as with the Jebusites at Jerusalem, the Hittites are a remaining pool of really Hittite stock who derived originally from Asia Minor and who had been assimilated to the life and language of Canaan.

The conversation that ensued is a skilful and delicate negotiation which passed through three principal stages.

In the first place, Abraham, a resident alien at Hebron, as he was at Gerar and doubtless at Beersheba too, presumably has no legal right to own ground. Abraham begins his plea with the frank admission that he has no legal claim. He is therefore begging a favor, but his admission is a point in his favor. The Hittites as a whole are said to answer: the inference is probably correct that to grant the right to purchase had to be a decision of the whole population. The Hittites had to confer and to decide to grant the favor. They immediately counter Abraham's admission by praising him as *a mighty prince*. The Hebrew words are "a prince of God." The words probably do not carry any sense of divine appointment. The word God is a genitive of quality, and is used in this phrase as in "trees of God" "mountain of God" (cf. Gen. 1:2) to indicate the extraordinary character of what is described. For them, Abraham is no mere resident alien. He is a mighty and famous man, indeed a great prince, and so, although they evade his request for purchase, they give him permission to bury in their territory. The choicest of their sepulchers is available to him.

Abraham has thus gained a great concession. Although only a resident alien he has succeeded in gaining a right to bury and thus probably to buy a piece of ground. A title to property would also inevitably improve his standing in the community. This purchase of the ground is probably the heart of the story and the secret to its meaning.

Second, Abraham accepts the right to bury and then goes on to make the particular proposition that he had in mind. He begs the good offices of the inhabitants in his interest to purchase *the cave of Machpelah* belonging to *Ephron,* one of their number, as a possession for its full value. Ephron's spontaneous response is remarkable for two points, apparently in generous mood he says he will give Abraham not only the cave but also the field where the cave is. Of course, in using the word *give* he meant "sell," and Abraham knew that; but perhaps the use of the word give rather than the word sell shows that Ephron begins his bargaining with a show of generosity. This deceives nobody, and Abraham knows that the concession he has already obtained will have to be dearly bought.

Third, Ephron throws in the field as well. Now it is well known that in the Hittite code of laws land tenure involved the owner in certain obligations of feudal service. If these people were Hittites, among whom Hittite laws still prevailed, then by ridding himself of the field, Ephron was also relieving himself of those further obligations. For this or some other reason Ephron clearly wants to sell his field as well.

The final stage of the negotiations is the price. Abraham accepts without demur that he must also buy Ephron's field, and virtually asks Ephron to name his price. Ephron mentions the trifling figure of four hundred shekels of silver which Abraham accepts again without any attempt to bargain. Mourners, especially when they seek favors, do not and cannot bargain. To assess the value of this silver is difficult, because the area of the field is not stated (cf. 1 Kings 16:24; Jer. 32:9 for comparisons).

That the price was exorbitant is certain, and Ephron no doubt made a most advantageous sale at the expense of the suppliant alien. Apparently Abraham pays down there and then the amount required.

The closing verses of the chapter define the location of the field; name its seller; list its contents—cave and trees; and stamp the sale publicly witnessed as a lasting possession for Abraham as a burial place. The verses reflect the contract of sale and title to the real estate.

The cave at Machpelah is now probably beneath the great mosque at Hebron which has a Christian and Jewish history as well. There, too, Abraham (25:9), Isaac (35:29), Rebekah and Leah (49:31), and Jacob (50:13) later were to be buried.

XIII. A Wife for Isaac (24:1-67)

The J witness, the prince of storytellers in the Old Testament, here tells of the last scene in Abraham's life, of the decision to seek a wife for Isaac, and how Abraham's steward fulfilled the commission laid upon him.

This very long narrative is divided into four parts, each largely made up of conversations connected by short narrative links. The parts however contain an inner movement. Abraham lays a last commission upon his house steward, a commission of great difficulty and perplexity. In turn the steward solves his problem by looking for a series of events which he himself cannot perform or even bring about. When these events do happen, then his problem is solved. The story is superb in its theme and narration.

Some commentators have seen evidence of a double narrative at some points in the story. Thus Laban is said to go to Abraham's servant twice (29b,30b), and 23b should be compared with 28; 50 with 53,55; 51 with 57,59; Rebekah's nurse, and 61a her own maidens. The duplicates are not really alternatives, and the unity of the piece seems assured.

In 36a Isaac appears to have inherited

his father's possessions, so it could be inferred from that verse that Abraham was already dead, and that therefore the evidence of the J witness recorded in 25:1–6 and 11b at one time preceded chapter 24. Others put 25:5 between 24:1-2. The witness of P in 25:7–11 is that Abraham lived for some thirty-five years after Isaac's marriage.

According to 25:11b Isaac was living at Beer-lahai-roi, and this would help to explain 24:62, which in the present Hebrew appears corrupt. Literally, the Hebrew reads, "Now Isaac came [had come] from coming to Beersheba." But the Samaritan Pentateuch and the LXX read "desert." "Now Isaac came into the desert of Beersheba." These probably refer to the same place differently described. There are also other suggestions, but the locality of the first meeting of Isaac and Rebekah is somewhat uncertain.

1. Abraham and His Steward (24:1–9)

[1] Now Abraham was old, well advanced in years; and the LORD had blessed Abraham in all things. [2] And Abraham said to his servant, the oldest of his house, who had charge of all that he had, "Put your hand under my thigh, [3] and I will make you swear by the LORD, the God of heaven and of the earth, that you will not take a wife for my son from the daughters of the Canaanites, among whom I dwell, [4] but will go to my country and to my kindred, and take a wife for my son Isaac." [5] The servant said to him, "Perhaps the woman may not be willing to follow me to this land; must I then take your son back to the land from which you came?" [6] Abraham said to him, "See to it that you do not take my son back there. [7] The LORD, the God of heaven, who took me from my father's house and from the land of my birth, and who spoke to me and swore to me, 'To your descendants I will give this land,' he will send his angel before you, and you shall take a wife for my son from there. [8] But if the woman is not willing to follow you, then you will be free from this oath of mine; only you must not take my son back there." [9] So the servant put his hand under the thigh of Abraham his master, and swore to him concerning this matter.

Sarah is dead, Isaac though marriagable is unmarried, and Abraham—successful in

all ways—addresses himself to his last responsibility. He must find a wife for his son, and thus hope thereby to ensure the succession and an heir to Isaac in the promise. Perhaps *take a wife* means "acquire" by paying the bride price. Abraham may be in his last days, for his words to his steward are his last recorded words, and the oath he extracts in verse 3 sounds so absolute that it was surely intended to apply after Abraham's death. Perhaps the J witness recorded Abraham's death after verse 9 or verse 61. Abraham's words in verses 1–9 thus appear to be part of his last will and testament, and the cooperation of the servant is ensured and vested in a particularly intimate act. The servant promises to carry out Abraham's requirements and signifies his willingness in an oath which is sworn at the same time as he places his hand under Abraham's thigh; i.e., on Abraham's genital organs. The oath thus taken is a matter of life and death, and the only other recorded example in the Old Testament is also at the request of a dying man (47:29).

The servant may be the Eliezer of 15:2 (cf. Ziba in 2 Sam. 9:1 ff.; 16:1 ff.). He swears on oath: (a) that he will not accept a Canaanite woman as a wife for Isaac; (b) that he will return to Abraham's family in Haran to seek the wife there; (c) that in no circumstances will he take Isaac back to Haran, because Isaac must remain in Canaan, for that land is promised to him and his descendants.

The servant is only to be relieved of this oath if the woman, apparently to be identified in some way by the angel of the Lord as a wife for Isaac, refuses to leave her people and come to Canaan.

Abraham is seeking to ensure the succession of his family, the succession of the family within the family, and that pure succession in the Promised Land. Abraham's last wishes therefore are his final act of obedience to the inaugural vision of his vocation. The beginning and the end of Abraham's life cohere in the promises of the Lord, the God of heaven and earth. God is thus pictured as living and ruling everywhere, and the idea suits the story. In verse 7, "and God of the earth" should probably be supplied from the LXX. Verse 7 then matches verse 3.

2. The Steward and Rebekah (24:10-27)

10 Then the servant took ten of his master's camels and departed, taking all sorts of choice gifts from his master; and he arose, and went to Mesopotamia, to the city of Nahor. 11 And he made the camels kneel down outside the city by the well of water at the time of evening, the time when women go out to draw water. 12 And he said, "O LORD, God of my master Abraham, grant me success today, I pray thee, and show steadfast love to my master Abraham. 13 Behold, I am standing by the spring of water, and the daughters of the men of the city are coming out to draw water. 14 Let the maiden to whom I shall say, 'Pray let down your jar that I may drink,' and who shall say, 'Drink, and I will water your camels'—let her be the one whom thou hast appointed for thy servant Isaac. By this I shall know that thou hast shown steadfast love to my master."

15 Before he had done speaking, behold, Rebekah, who was born to Bethuel the son of Milcah, the wife of Nahor, Abraham's brother, came out with her water jar upon her shoulder. 16 The maiden was very fair to look upon, a virgin, whom no man had known. She went down to the spring, and filled her jar, and came up. 17 Then the servant ran to meet her, and said, "Pray give me a little water to drink from your jar." 18 She said, "Drink, my lord"; and she quickly let down her jar upon her hand, and gave him a drink. 19 When she had finished giving him a drink, she said, "I will draw for your camels also, until they have done drinking." 20 So she quickly emptied her jar into the trough and ran again to the well to draw, and she drew for all his camels. 21 The man gazed at her in silence to learn whether the LORD had prospered his journey or not.

22 When the camels had done drinking, the man took a gold ring weighing a half shekel, and two bracelets for her arms weighing ten gold shekels, 23 and said, "Tell me whose daughter you are. Is there room in your father's house for us to lodge in?" 24 She said to him, "I am the daughter of Bethuel the son of Milcah, whom she bore to Nahor." 25 She added, "We have both straw and provender enough, and room to lodge in." 26 The man bowed his head and worshiped the LORD, 27 and said, "Blessed be the LORD, the God of my master Abraham, who has not forsaken his steadfast love and his faithfulness toward my master. As for me, the LORD has led me in the way to the house of my master's kinsmen."

The steward departs for Abraham's homeland with an impressive train of ten camels loaded with gifts—part of which without doubt were for the bride's price. The reference to camels is probably an indication of Abraham's wealth, for the evidence suggests that their more common use was still in the future. The LXX omits "and departed" in verse 10, but the RSV blends the several verbs describing the departure very satisfactorily.

Verse 10 records the journey to Nahor's city, probably Haran in Mesopotamia. Mesopotamia is in the Hebrew *'Aram Naharayim*, literally "Aram (Syria) of the two rivers." It could of course be a city called Nahor, namely, the Nahur mentioned in the Mari documents. During his long journey the servant has formulated a plan. He will attempt to discover the right woman by setting up a theoretical coincidence. He plans to ask a succession of women coming to the well outside the city for water to give him a drink. But he mentally lays down the proviso that if any of the women so addressed offers to water his camels also, he will accept that woman as the bride designated for Isaac. Presumably all the women coming to the well belonged to Abraham's family or the steward knew some sign, peculiarity of dress, etc. by which to recognize those who in fact did belong to Abraham.

As the steward waited, Rebekah a virgin, described as the daughter of Bethuel, Abraham's nephew (cf. 24:47), but who was more likely the daughter of Nahor, arrived on the scene. Laban is Rebekah's brother and he is the son of Nahor (29:5). The evidence of the P witness in 25:20 and 28:2,5 speaks of Bethuel as her father. Perhaps the Bethuel of 24:50, who is mentioned after Laban his brother, may be a different Bethuel, possibly a younger brother of Laban. Rebekah came to the well, descended the flight of steps, and came up with the pitcher full of water. At the steward's request she gave him a drink and then volunteered to satisfy the thirst of his camels also. This was no light promise, for it must have meant many descents and laden ascents of the steps until the beasts were satisfied. The steward watched in amazement as the coincidence was worked out to the last detail. Here then she was.

The steward accordingly adorned her with a *gold* (nose) *ring* and *two bracelets*, questioned her to find that she was a relative of Abraham, and recognized in that kinship the seal of God's guidance upon this chosen procedure. Commentators often describe these events in terms of an overruling providence. In fact nothing is overruled. What the steward proposes as a possible coincidence takes place, and the coincidence leads him to the home and family of his master. Not overruling so much as all things working together to ensure the end in view. Abraham had said, "He will send his angel before you" (24:7). Leading, confirming, and not overruling are the marks of the story. In verse 22 the Hebrew may once have had also the phrase "and put it on her nose," present in the Samaritan text here, and later in verse 47. The steadfast love and faithfulness of verse 27 express a loving loyalty and dependability used in other contexts of covenant love and fidelity.

3. In Rebekah's Home (24:28–61)

28 Then the maiden ran and told her mother's household about these things. 29 Rebekah had a brother whose name was Laban; and Laban ran out to the man, to the spring. 30 When he saw the ring, and the bracelets on his sister's arms, and when he heard the words of Rebekah his sister, "Thus the man spoke to me," he went to the man; and behold, he was standing by the camels at the spring. 31 He said, "Come in, O blessed of the LORD; why do you stand outside? For I have prepared the house and a place for the camels." 32 So the man came into the house; and Laban ungirded the camels, and gave him straw and provender for the camels, and water to wash his feet and the feet of the men who were with him. 33 Then food was set before him to eat; but he said, "I will not eat until I have told my errand." He said, "Speak on." 34 So he said, "I am Abraham's servant. 35 The LORD has greatly blessed my master, and he has become great; he has given him flocks and herds, silver and gold, menservants and maidservants, camels and asses. 36 And Sarah my master's wife bore a son to my master when she was old; and to him he has given all that he has. 37 My master made me swear, saying, 'You shall not take a wife for my son from the daughters of the Canaanites, in whose land I dwell; 38 but you shall go to my father's house and to my kindred, and take a wife for my son.' 39 I said to my master, 'Perhaps the woman will not follow me.' 40 But he said to me, "The LORD, before whom I walk, will send his angel with you and prosper your way; and you shall take a wife for my son from my kindred and from my father's house; 41 then you will be free from my oath, when you come to my kindred; and if they will not give her to you, you will be free from my oath.'

42 "I came today to the spring, and said, 'O LORD, the God of my master Abraham, if now thou wilt prosper the way which I go, 43 behold, I am standing by the spring of water; let the young woman who comes out to draw, to whom I shall say, "Pray give me a little water from your jar to drink," 44 and who will say to me, "Drink, and I will draw for your camels also," let her be the woman whom the LORD has appointed for my master's son.'

45 "Before I had done speaking in my heart, behold, Rebekah came out with her water jar on her shoulder; and she went down to the spring, and drew. I said to her, 'Pray let me drink.' 46 She quickly let down her jar from her shoulder, and said, 'Drink, and I will give your camels drink also.' So I drank, and she gave the camels drink also. 47 Then I asked her, 'Whose daughter are you?' She said, 'The daughter of Bethuel, Nahor's son, whom Milcah bore to him.' So I put the ring on her nose, and the bracelets on her arms. 48 Then I bowed my head and worshiped the LORD, and blessed the LORD, the God of my master Abraham, who had led me by the right way to take the daughter of my master's kinsman for his son. 49 Now then, if you will deal loyally and truly with my master, tell me; and if not, tell me; that I may turn to the right hand or to the left."

50 Then Laban and Bethuel answered, "The thing comes from the LORD; we cannot speak to you bad or good. 51 Behold, Rebekah is before you, take her and go, and let her be the wife of your master's son, as the LORD has spoken."

52 When Abraham's servant heard their words, he bowed himself to the earth before the LORD. 53 And the servant brought forth jewelry of silver and of gold, and raiment, and gave them to Rebekah; he also gave to her brother and to her mother costly ornaments. 54 And he and the men who were with him ate and drank, and they spent the night there. When they arose in the morning, he said, "Send me back to my master." 55 Her brother and her mother said, "Let the maiden remain

with us a while, at least ten days; after that she may go." 56 But he said to them, "Do not delay me, since the LORD has prospered my way; let me go that I may go to my master." 57 They said, "We will call the maiden, and ask her." 58 And they called Rebekah, and said to her, "Will you go with this man?" She said, "I will go." 59 So they sent away Rebekah their sister and her nurse, and Abraham's servant and his men. 60 And they blessed Rebekah, and said to her, "Our sister, be the mother of thousands of ten thousands; and may your descendants possess the gate of those who hate them!" 61 Then Rebekah and her maids arose, and rode upon the camels and followed the man; thus the servant took Rebekah, and went his way.

The maiden, excited by the golden gifts, rushed home and told her story. Her brother Laban rushed back to the well and greeting the man with an effusive welcome brought him home and provided for the needs of men and beasts. The steward, however, declined to eat until he revealed his identity and explained his mission. How electrifying must have been the words, *I am Abraham's servant,* and how eagerly the family must have heard news of Abraham and the commission he had laid upon the speaker. How fascinating they must have found his version of the events of the day and his compliment for Rebekah and her lovely behavior. How enthralled and surprised and perhaps a little alarmed must Rebekah herself have been. Verses 34–38 almost duplicate the previous narrative, but such repetition is characteristic of ancient literary storytelling and indeed of all literary art. In verse 41 the servant twice uses the Hebrew word for curse as his impression of what Abraham had meant by oath in verse 8. *Turn to the right hand* simply means "know where I stand."

Brother and father (v. 50) recognize the divine leading and agree that Rebekah shall be Isaac's wife. Then the steward brings forth yet more gifts for Rebekah, for her mother and her brother. Then comes the meal, no doubt a feast, and so to bed after a memorable and never-to-be-forgotten day.

Next morning the steward is anxious to begin the return journey. Her brother and mother propose a delay of some ten days,

but the steward is persistent, invoking the divine purpose. When consulted, Rebekah agrees, and with her nurse, named Deborah according to the E witness in 35:8, and her maids, Rebekah, Abraham's servant and his men set off that day. Her family take leave of her with blessings of marriage —numerous and victorious descendants. Thus was the permanent exile so speedily brought about. Rebekah was never to return home or to see her parents again.

4. Isaac and Rebekah Meet (24:62–67)

62 Now Isaac had come from Beerlahairoi, and was dwelling in the Negeb. 63 And Isaac went out to meditate in the field in the evening; and he lifted up his eyes and looked, and behold, there were camels, coming. 64 And Rebekah lifted up her eyes, and when she saw Isaac, she alighted from the camel, 65 and said to the servant, "Who is the man yonder, walking in the field to meet us?" The servant said, "It is my master." So she took her veil and covered herself. 66 And the servant told Isaac all the things he had done. 67 Then Isaac brought her into the tent, and took Rebekah, and she became his wife; and he loved her. So Isaac was comforted after his mother's death.

Verse 62 is very imprecise and the Hebrew is difficult to understand. Isaac may have come from the place known as Beerlahai-roi, or had been visiting there and was on his way back.

One evening he went out into the field to meditate. This could mean an evening gossip or walk or prayer, or the word may mean that he went to relieve his natural needs. In the fields the returning party came across Isaac. Rebekah alights and veils herself and is then brought into the tent. This admission is the essential feature of marriage. Rebekah became his wife and in his love for his wife Isaac was comforted for the loss of his mother. The new ancestress replaces Sarah, the former mother in the continuing line of descent.

XIV. Abraham's Last Days (25:1–18)

1. Abraham's Second Wife Keturah (25: 1–6)

1 Abraham took another wife, whose name was Keturah. 2 She bore him Zimran, Jokshan,

Medan, Midian, Ishbak, and Shuah. ³ Jokshan was the father of Sheba and Dedan. The sons of Dedan were Asshurim, Letushim, and Leummim. ⁴ The sons of Midian were Ephah, Epher, Hanoch, Abida, and Eldaah. All these were the children of Keturah. ⁵ Abraham gave all he had to Isaac. ⁶ But to the sons of his concubines Abraham gave gifts, and while he was still living he sent them away from his son Isaac, eastward to the east country.

After Sarah's death, Abraham married again and his second wife's name was **Keturah,** "the perfumed one." In 1 Chronicles 1:32 (cf. here v. 6), she is called a concubine. If she was a concubine, then she may have achieved that status during Sarah's lifetime. She bore Abraham six sons who became the ancestors of tribes and who lived in Northern Arabia. Trade in incense appears to have been part of the commerce of the area. From the six sons ten groups appear to have emerged. The Sabeans were rich caravan merchants on the Red Sea coast (1 Kings 10).

Zimran may be the same as Zabram west of Mecca. **Jokshan** and **Medan** are unknown. **Ishbak** is uncertain but **Shuah** may refer to an area south of Haran (cf. Job 2:11, Bildad the Shuhite, if the same area is meant). Nothing certain is known of the descendants of **Jokshan** and **Dedan.** Isaiah 60:6 refers to the camels of Ephah and Midian with their loads of gold and frankincense. In Genesis 37 Ishmaelites and Midianites appear together.

Of Keturah's six sons, Midian is both the best known and most important. The Midianites occupied the area from Moab to Edom and recur again in the stories of Joseph, Moses, and Gideon. The Midianites consisted of five families. Moses married into a Midianite family (Ex. 2:21; 3:1; Num. 10:29). Moses' marriage and the events of Exodus 18 have led to the so-called Kenite hypothesis, according to which Moses discovered not only his wife but his God, Yahweh, among the Midianites-Kenites.

The Kenites were a Midianite tribe (Num. 10:29; Judg. 1:16). The hypothesis in its extreme and original form is not soundly based, for it claims that originally Yahweh was the God of the Kenites only. According to this view, Moses discovered him after his flight from Egypt to Midian, and he returned to Egypt to introduce him as a totally new God to his people. This is very unlikely indeed, for the enslaved Israelites would hardly have embraced the religion of a totally new God.

In a modified form, the hypothesis shows the long connection between Yahweh and the Kenites. Thus Jethro's confession: "Now I know that Yahweh is greater than all gods" is not the rapturous confession of a new convert, but a joyful reaffirmation that his own God, Yahweh, is the greatest. Jethro presides at the sacrifice immediately following, which would be appropriate not for the new convert but for the long established and recognized priest. More likely then is the view that the Yahwism of Abraham was transmitted through Keturah to the Midianites and Kenites. Thus Moses, after his contact with his wife's family in Midian, brought about a revival of Yahwism among the main descendants of Abraham in Egypt. Yahwism had survived with various degrees of vitality in the different branches of Abraham's descendants, and Moses was able to revive the sterile Yahwism of his compatriots in Egypt with news of the vigorous Yahwism from the desert.

Verses 5–6 are Abraham's testamentary arrangements. Isaac is the heir and gets everything, but the sons of the concubines —Hagar and Keturah—receive gifts of slaves and cattle and are dispatched *away from his son Isaac,* so as not to be an obligation to him, to new living spaces beyond Jordan, the Syro-Arabian Desert.

2. Death and Burial of Abraham (25:7–11)

⁷ These are the days of the years of Abraham's life, a hundred and seventy-five years. ⁸ Abraham breathed his last and died in a good old age, an old man and full of years, and was gathered to his people. ⁹ Isaac and Ishmael his sons buried him in the cave of Machpelah, in the field of Ephron the son of Zohar the Hittite, east of Mamre, ¹⁰ the field which Abraham purchased from the Hittites. There Abraham

was buried, with Sarah his wife. ¹¹ After the death of Abraham God blessed Isaac his son. And Isaac dwelt at Beerlahairoi.

This chronological note bears the manifest hand of the P witness. Abraham lived for 175 years, and since he left Haran when he was seventy-five (12:4), he had lived in the land promised to him and to his heirs for a century. His burial is described as *gathered to his people*. The reference cannot be to the burial with Sarah but to the gathering of the departed in Sheol. Ishmael helps Isaac with the burial. If the P witness knew of Ishmael's expulsion, then he brings him back for his father's funeral.

Note the resumption of the theme of blessing. After Abraham's death, this is now centered on Isaac. Isaac's residence at Beerlahairoi appears to be the presupposition of the story in chapter 24.

The figures are confusing. Isaac married Rebekah when he was forty, (25:20) and he was sixty (25:26) when Esau and Jacob were born, and Abraham was one hundred sixty (21:5). So Abraham is said to have died before the twins are said to have been born. In fact Abraham died when the twins were between fourteen and fifteen years old.

3. Ishmael and His Descendants (25:12–18)

¹² These are the descendants of Ishmael, Abraham's son, whom Hagar the Egyptian, Sarah's maid, bore to Abraham. ¹³ These are the names of the sons of Ishmael, named in the order of their birth: Nebaioth, the first-born of Ishmael; and Kedar, Adbeel, Mibsam, ¹⁴ Mishma, Dumah, Massa, ¹⁵ Hadad, Tema, Jetur, Naphish, and Kedemah. ¹⁶ These are the sons of Ishmael and these are their names, by their villages and by their encampments, twelve princes according to their tribes. ¹⁷ (These are the years of the life of Ishmael, a hundred and thirty-seven years; he breathed his last and died, and was gathered to his kindred.) ¹⁸ They dwelt from Havilah to Shur, which is opposite Egypt in the direction of Assyria; he settled over against all his people.

The P witness now records the family tree of Ishmael, mentioning the names of the twelve princes of the tribes descended

from Ishmael (cf. 17:20). In these family trees from both the J and P witnesses, we see how the descendants of Abraham in their several branches are fanning out. Later on there will be considerable interplay among these various groups of descendants in the early stories of the Pentateuch. The Ishmaelite tribes and their princes exhibit a more organized basis.

The list contains some well-known names, *Nebaioth* and *Kedar* occur together in Isaiah 60:7. One of Esau's wives came from a Nebaioth tribe (Gen. 28:9) and Kedar is mentioned several times (Isa. 21:16; 42:11; Jer. 2:10; 49:28; and Psalm 120:5); localities in the deserts east of Edom appear to be intended.

Dumah and *Tema* are also the names of two well-known oases, the first some 140 miles north of *Tema* which is Teima, mentioned by Tiglath-pileser III of Assyria in his inscriptions. Teima (cf. Isa. 21:14; Job. 6:19) is most famous as the desert home of Nabonidus, the last native king of Babylon (555–539 B.C.), who maintained his home there even when Cyrus was threatening his capital and lines of communication. Nabonidus was also probably responsible for settling colonies of Jews in the principal oases of western Arabia. Tema is about 250 miles southeast of Aqaba.

Jetur and *Naphish* warred against Israel (1 Chron. 5:19); and Jetur is probably the Itureans (Luke 3:1), mountaineers of the Anti-Lebanon.

The word *encampments* is used probably to describe the circular form of the bedouin bivouac; *tribes*, the last word of verse 16, translates a word rarely used in Hebrew. The word may thus be the actual word used generally to describe the Ishmaelite tribes or clans.

Verse 18 is generally considered to be a fragment of the J witness, perhaps all that is left of his family tree of Ishmael. Since there were several Havilahs, the present one is further defined *Havilah to Shur. Assyria* here probably refers to the Ashurim of 25:3, hardly the great Assyria. Ishmael is said to have settled in front of all his brethren; i.e., they were farthest out from Palestine in the desert (cf. 16:12b). This is better than to suppose a reference to the various Ishmaelite tribes fighting one another. The general tenor of the verse is to describe a location rather than warlikeness as in 16:12b.

XV. The Family of Isaac (25:19—28:9)

Between the stories of Abraham the friend of God, and Jacob, a rather shady character who eventually was reformed, lie the traditions about Isaac, who, by contrast to these colorful personalities, was very pale. He is the hero of few events in chapter 26, and tends to be overshadowed by his brilliant wife or his quarrelsome sons, especially the adventurer Jacob.

Nevertheless 25:19 introduces us to the family of Isaac. Not until 35:29 is Isaac's death reported, but only after Jacob has received a new name and was thus rewarded for the new morality he had begun to show in chapters 32 f., and after Jacob's twelfth and last son, Benjamin, had been born. Isaac then is the second figure of promise and blessing, and the sparse records of his life are the arch which embraces 25:19—28:9. Thereafter the story centers in Jacob even though the material is largely concerned with Joseph.

1. Birth and Upbringing of Esau and Jacob (25:19–34)

19 These are the descendants of Isaac, Abraham's son: Abraham was the father of Isaac, 20 and Isaac was forty years old when he took to wife Rebekah, the daughter of Bethuel the Aramean of Paddanaram, the sister of Laban the Aramean. 21 And Isaac prayed to the LORD for his wife, because she was barren; and the LORD granted his prayer, and Rebekah his wife conceived. 22 The children struggled together within her; and she said, "If it is thus, why do I live?" So she went to inquire of the LORD. 23 And the LORD said to her,

"Two nations are in your womb,
    and two peoples, born of you, shall be divided;
the one shall be stronger than the other,
    the elder shall serve the younger."

24 When her days to be delivered were fulfilled, behold, there were twins in her womb. 25 The first came forth red, all his body like a hairy mantle; so they called his name Esau. 26 Afterward his brother came forth, and his hand had taken hold of Esau's heel; so his name was called Jacob. Isaac was sixty years old when she bore them.

27 When the boys grew up, Esau was a skilful hunter, a man of the field, while Jacob was a quiet man, dwelling in tents. 28 Isaac loved Esau, because he ate of his game; but Rebekah loved Jacob.

29 Once when Jacob was boiling pottage, Esau came in from the field, and he was famished. 30 And Esau said to Jacob, "Let me eat some of that red pottage, for I am famished!" (Therefore his name was called Edom.) 31 Jacob said, "First sell me your birthright." 32 Esau said, "I am about to die; of what use is a birthright to me?" 33 Jacob said, "Swear to me first." So he swore to him, and sold his birthright to Jacob. 34 Then Jacob gave Esau bread and pottage of lentils, and he ate and drank, and rose and went his way. Thus Esau despised his birthright.

Apart from 25:19–20 (cf. 21:1–3 and ch. 24) and 26b, which are brief notices from the P witness, the present account is the work of the J witness. P likes to give these statistical details, and he always uses the name Paddan-aram, literally field or plain of Aram (Syria), where J, as in 24:10, mentions Aram of the two rivers. Both terms describe the area around Haran, probably north of the junction of the rivers Euphrates and Chabur.

After twenty years without a baby (cf. Rachel, 29:31; Manoah's wife, Judg. 13:2; Hannah, 1 Sam. 1:2; Elizabeth, Luke 1:7), Rebekah's pregnancy was difficult. The Hebrew form of her question is, "If it's like this, why I?" i.e., is it worth it for me? So she resorted officially to the Lord, that is, to a shrine and received this oracle. She was told she was with twins, that they were quarrelsome and that the elder would serve the younger. The RSV rightly shows the poetic form of the four lines but omits the word "people" in the third line, after the one and after the other. This word for "people" in lines 2 and 3 is a poetic Hebrew word.

Shall be divided means not from Rebekah by birth, but from each other in their lives after birth. The oracle is thus about two nations and the future of Israel and Edom are being described (cf. Rom. 9:12). Speiser remarks that the two adjectives of the fourth line of the oracle reflect Akkadian terms and legal practice, whereby the elder son has twice the inheritance of the younger. Esau's sale of his birthright could then only mean that in this case he sold one-half of his inheritance to Jacob, and retained a half.

The source of the oracle is God and his medium is the priest, who uses his medical lore and the facts of the pregnancy for his judgment. The only other record of the birth of twins in the Old Testament is in 38:27–30. The Hebrew form of the words implies that nothing more than a priestly oracle is intended, though that is supported with the divinely given insight that the elder brother would be subordinate to the younger. This exactly reflects what is related of the subsequent stories of the descendants of the two brothers (Amos 1:11; Ezek. 35).

Like Sarah then, but less explicitly, Rebekah is able to conceive because the Lord yielded to her husband's prayer.

The J witness suggests a slight touch of ridicule in describing the firstborn twin as red and also hairy all over. "A fur coat by nature" (von Rad).

This first twin is called Esau, ancestor of Edom (36:1,8,19), and Edom is the same in Hebrew as the word for "red." A synonym for Esau is Seir (36:8), and this word in Hebrew also means "hairy." Perhaps Seir was once here in the story only to be replaced by Esau, which means press or squeeze. Jacob means "may God protect," but when the word for God was left out in the shortened form of the name, then the name Jacob was interpreted in terms of the word for "heel" (*'aqebh*), which the word Jacob resembles; namely, "He takes by the heel," or he supplants, so Jacob takes the heel (Hos. 12:3) and becomes the supplanter.

The vocations of the two boys are described. Esau is a skilful hunter, a food-gatherer, favored by his father. Jacob is a shepherd—also a food-gatherer, as distinct from food-grower. Jacob is described as quiet, for which the Hebrew is *tam* (blameless), but probably here means well ordered—fulfilling the regular and complete round of the shepherd life, as distinct from the irregular forays of the man who hunts when he is hungry and sleeps rough, whereas the shepherd sleeps regularly in his tent. Verse 28 must be read in the light of 27:1–45.

The disparity in living conditions leads to Esau's sale of his birthright. The Hebrew word for birthright expresses the right of the firstborn as showing special strength (49:3; Deut. 21:17); prospective headship of the family (29:29; 49:8); and a double share in the family estate (Deut. 21:15 ff.). Weary, *famished,* and half dead, literally "at the point of death," Esau desires food; he is said to speak in verse 30 of swallowing, eating ravenously, and so he agrees to sell his birthright but is compelled by his brother to do so under oath. The succession of verbs in verse 34 is striking. The story illustrates the cunning of Jacob and the carelessness of Esau. Jacob is avaricious and takes advantage of his brother. Esau is more spontaneous, impulsive, and heedless of the long term.

Clearly two brothers, two persons are described. Nevertheless beneath the two characters are the descriptions of two nations, and this is specially true of verse 23, where national destinies are prefigured. Some discord between the description of the individuals and the national histories is therefore inevitable, but points also to the reliability of the tradition whereby Esau was a hunter and Jacob seminomadic. In fact Edom was older and quite as urban as Israel became.

Within these personal-national themes, different levels of the interpretation exist. Daube [18] claimed that Jacob prepared a lentil soup in such a way as to make it look like a red soup, that is a blood soup, not

[18] David Daube, *Studies in Biblical Law* (Cambridge: Univ. Press, 1947), pp. 191–96.

only attractive but potent with life vigor. In fact it was only lentils, and so Jacob tricked Esau through the color of the soup. Because of this trick which would be found out as soon as the red soup was tasted, Jacob took the prior precaution of getting Esau to swear an oath. He thus prevented Esau's foreswearing his bargain when he discovered he had been tricked. In 27:36 Esau complains that Jacob had tricked him twice. Apart from this suggested deception over the soup, there is no real deception in the birthright story. It was a sale by which Jacob took advantage of, though hardly deceived, his brother. If there was a deception in the birthright story, it could well have been in a disguised soup.

Again the story reflects the outwitting of the fly-by-night hunter by the wily shepherd, and must have been a very acceptable story to shepherds.

The last clause of the chapter, that Esau despised his birthright, points to the larger theme of Genesis—the descent of blessing through the promised line. In the immediate context that theme of blessing and divine promise is not mentioned. But it is the overhanging arch of the narrative and so the Jacob-Esau, the shepherd-hunter, the two nations' oracle story must be understood in the light of the grand design. The story is destined to go on, not through Isaac's firstborn, Esau, but through his younger twin son Jacob.

2. Isaac at Gerar (26:1-11)

¹ Now there was a famine in the land, besides the former famine that was in the days of Abraham. And Isaac went to Gerar, to Abimelech king of the Philistines. ² And the LORD appeared to him, and said, "Do not go down to Egypt; dwell in the land of which I shall tell you. ³ Sojourn in this land, and I will be with you, and will bless you; for to you and to your descendants I will give all these lands, and I will fulfil the oath which I swore to Abraham your father. ⁴ I will multiply your descendants as the stars of heaven, and will give to your descendants all these lands; and by your descendants all the nations of the earth shall bless themselves: ⁵ because Abraham obeyed my voice and kept my charge, my command-

ments, my statutes, and my laws."
⁶ So Isaac dwelt in Gerar. ⁷ When the men of the place asked him about his wife, he said, "She is my sister"; for he feared to say, "My wife," thinking, "lest the men of the place should kill me for the sake of Rebekah"; because she was fair to look upon. ⁸ When he had been there a long time, Abimelech king of the Philistines looked out of a window and saw Isaac fondling Rebekah his wife. ⁹ So Abimelech called Isaac, and said, "Behold, she is your wife; how then could you say, 'She is my sister'?" Isaac said to him, "Because I thought, 'Lest I die because of her.' " ¹⁰ Abimelech said, "What is this you have done to us? One of the people might easily have lain with your wife, and you would have brought guilt upon us." ¹¹ So Abimelech warned all the people, saying, "Whoever touches this man or his wife shall be put to death."

Chapter 26 contains the few stories which have Isaac as their subject, but they are few. In all, only seven separate units have been discovered; namely, verses 1–6; 7–11; 12–14; 15–17a; 17b–22; 23–33; and 34–5. They are nevertheless quite independent, ancient, and authentic. Here are genuine stories about the middle patriarch Isaac, given to us by the J witness and rounded off in the last two verses by the P witness. The first four tell of Isaac's sojourn in Gerar. The fifth and sixth occur at Beersheba. Similar stories have already been recorded of Abraham in chapters 12, 20, and 21.

The stories reveal the outlook of the nomad, the travels of the small trader, the contrasts in morality, property rights in water, which are perhaps older and certainly more important than property rights in land and reflect the background of life which is passing from nomadic to agricultural and pastoral forms of society.

Faced with a famine, Isaac makes his way probably from Beerlahairoi to Gerar with the intention of going to Egypt. Egypt is the proverbial refuge from famine. At Gerar Isaac begins to perceive what is about to happen. He is about to go outside the Promised Land, something which Abraham had not even risked when he sought a wife for Isaac. The warnings and teachings of his father reassert themselves in the form and with the authority of a divine visitation. Isaac must abide in the Land of Promise, and then all the elements of the promise, prosperity (26:12 f.), possession of the land (26:22), growth of descendants as in the succeeding chapters will accrue to him (vv. 3–5).

As Abram entered the land and began to understand the promises (12:1–9), so Isaac remaining in the land is reminded of the scope of his father's testament. So Isaac remained in Gerar. He retraces some of the steps of his father. He becomes a resident alien in Gerar as his father had been. Abimelech who must be the same king as 20:2 is here expressly described as the Philistine king of Gerar.

Although these verses are parallel to the story of Abram and Sarai in 12:10–16, the differences outweigh the similarities. Whereas Abram and Sarai make a compact to tell the lie about his wife's identity, Isaac does not involve Rebekah, but lies directly to his Philistine neighbors. Instead of the Pharaoh and Egypt of the former story, Abimelech, the Philistines, and Gerar occur in the present context. In Genesis 12 Sarai was actually taken into the royal harem, but in chapter 26 Rebekah does not leave her husband's household. Harm accrues to the Pharaoh and his house but nothing calamitous occurs in Gerar. Isaac is seen besporting with his wife. Literally, Isaac (*Yitschaq*) fondles *m^etsacheq* his wife. Thus their real relationship is discovered, and Abimelech warns his people not to harm Isaac or his wife. To say that this Isaac episode is merely a variant of the earlier Abram story is too easy a solution. Both stories may recount separate experiences and the question must be left open.

In chapter 20 there is a similar story of Abraham and Sarah. That story resembles chapter 12 in that it happened, but it resembles chapter 26 in that it is placed in Gerar. The story in 20 thus appears to be an amalgam of the events of 12 with the locale of 26. Thus the two original stories may well have been those of chapters 12

and 26, supplied by the J witness, but the amalgam of 20, the work of the E witness. Chapter 26 may well be the oldest of all three stories.

3. Isaac's Increasing Wealth (26:12–22)

[12] And Isaac sowed in that land, and reaped in the same year a hundredfold. The LORD blessed him, [13] and the man became rich, and gained more and more until he became very wealthy. [14] He had possessions of flocks and herds, and a great household, so that the Philistines envied him. [15] (Now the Philistines had stopped and filled with earth all the wells which his father's servants had dug in the days of Abraham his father.) [16] And Abimelech said to Isaac, "Go away from us; for you are much mightier than we." [17] So Isaac departed from there, and encamped in the valley of Gerar and dwelt there. [18] And Isaac dug again the wells of water which had been dug in the days of Abraham his father; for the Philistines had stopped them after the death of Abraham; and he gave them the names which his father had given them. [19] But when Isaac's servants dug in the valley and found there a well of springing water, [20] the herdsmen of Gerar quarreled with Isaac's herdsmen, saying, "The water is ours." So he called the name of the well Esek, because they contended with him. [21] Then they dug another well, and they quarreled over that also; so he called its name Sitnah. [22] And they moved from there and dug another well, and over that they did not quarrel; so he called its name Rehoboth, saying, "For now the LORD has made room for us, and we shall be fruitful in the land."

Verses 12–17 have generally been thought to contain two separate units, but probably 12–14 and 16–17 contain one unit, and verse 15 really belongs to the well story of verses 18–22, as a sequel to the rivalry exposed in verses 12–17. The nomad trader Isaac is beginning to diversify. This is the first time the patriarchs are said to sow in the Promised Land (cf. 30:14; 37:7).

The crop is in accord with the blessings of the Promised Land. Isaac reaps *a hundredfold* and becomes increasingly wealthy. The Hebrew reads "a hundred of measures" or proportions. The LXX and Syriac assumed a different word and thought it meant, but wrongly, "a hundred of barley."

In these verses—in his planting, in his wealth, possessions, household, and retainers—Isaac's blessing is made manifest over a period of years.

The association of Isaac, land, and blessing is thus fully proved, for he is in the line of descent, and he is the inheritor of Abraham's promises. So much so that he incurs the jealousy of his neighbors and is compelled to leave the city and dwell in the nearby *valley of Gerar*. The word for valley probably means water course. *Nahal* means wady, often a torrent in winter, but a trickle or even dry in summer. On the whole, the story shows Isaac as mainly a nomad becoming a farmer. His movements are curtailed to a limited area. A hint of the merchant-trading of his father may be present in verse 14.

Verse 15 is not a later addition to the story. At worst it must be moved to be linked with verses 18–22, but the reason for its inclusion in the middle of the record of Isaac's prosperity is patent. Isaac's prosperity is his own. It owes nothing to his father, for in fact the wells dug by his father's servants had been stopped. Isaac shares the blessing of his father, but even so it comes to him in his own right. Each in his way is blessed and enjoys great success and wealth.

The tradition about Isaac and his wells is perhaps the most authentic and most significant of all the Isaac traditions. The tradition affords a clear illustration of how most of the traditions in Genesis must be considered. The tradition must be considered for its own intrinsic sake and value, but also it must be considered in the larger light of the theme of the book.

The tradition itself tells of three groups of wells. First, Isaac reopened his father's wells, which the local inhabitants had filled in, and brought them into use under the names which his father had given them. Isaac's rights are not contested. Second, by good fortune Isaac's servants found spring (Heb., living) water in a new well in the Gerar Valley, but the Gerar herdsmen contested the rights. So Isaac gave way over

two wells named *Esek* (Quarrel), verse 20, and *Sitnah* (Accusation), verse 21. Third, Isaac and his men move farther away, and no dispute occurs over the next well. Its name *Rehoboth* means breadth or space, and so it implies that the well was some distance away. Isaac's withdrawal is not an illustration of sociological stresses, but simply a testimony to his mild nature. Isaac thus establishes his rights in two ways—by renewing the use of his father's wells and by digging his own. The tradition is a valuable piece of social history, and its own intrinsic worth and its value for its context is found in the fact that "property in water is older and more important than property in land" (cf. Smith, *op. cit.*, p. 104).

This story is about the wells and is a property story—a story about real estate in water. Isaac is establishing his own right, not only to his father's real estate, but also to his own. The story is preserved because it is an ancient and true story about Isaac's real estate, and also because it illustrates how the promise of the land is working out in Isaac's life. Like his father, who possessed water and a burial place, Isaac too possesses water in the land promised to his family and to him. The meek have their reward.

4. The Renewed Promise (26:23–25)

23 From there he went up to Beersheba. 24 And the LORD appeared to him the same night and said, "I am the God of Abraham your father; fear not, for I am with you and will bless you and multiply your descendants for my servant Abraham's sake." 25 So he built an altar there and called upon the name of the LORD, and pitched his tent there. And there Isaac's servants dug a well.

These following verses also show how thoroughly grounded in real estate the chapter is. At Beersheba, Isaac receives a fresh confirmation of the promise of prosperity and progeny. In chapter 20 the Lord and Abraham had already been associated together at Beersheba, where Abraham had removed from Mamre. Accordingly many scholars have assumed recently that the two traditions were originally concerned with Abraham and Mamre; Isaac and Beersheba.

On this view Isaac is original to Beersheba, and the vision (v. 24), the altar and tent (v. 25) show the original dedication of Beersheba as Isaac's sanctuary. The alternative is to assume that Isaac in retracing his father's commercial journeys, records his conviction about his father's God and his father's claim to that area. Like wells and burial places, an altar also means a small piece, however little, of real estate. The cultic character of making altars must not blind us to its meaning as claiming a piece of land. This is in fact confirmed by the digging of another well in that locality too (v. 25).

In modern India today a man who scrapes a few stones together on another's land and calls those stones an altar, has thereby established an inalienable right to sanctify the land on which the stones stand. Verses 23–25 reestablish Abraham's rights in the person of Isaac, or else establish Isaac's own immediate rights. Thus the divine covenant is renewed, extended, and made relevant to the next generation.

5. Isaac's Treaty with Abimelech (26:26–33)

26 Then Abimelech went to him from Gerar with Ahuzzath his adviser and Phicol the commander of his army. 27 Isaac said to them, "Why have you come to me, seeing that you hate me and have sent me away from you?" 28 They said, "We see plainly that the Lord is with you; so we say, let there be an oath between you and us, and let us make a covenant with you, 29 that you will do us no harm, just as we have not touched you and have done to you nothing but good and have sent you away in peace. You are now the blessed of the Lord." 30 So he made them a feast, and they ate and drank. 31 In the morning they rose early and took oath with one another; and Isaac set them on their way, and they departed from him in peace. 32 That same day Isaac's servants came and told him about the well which they had dug, and said to him, "We have found water." 33 He called it Shibah; therefore the name of the city is Beersheba to this day.

The complicated arrangements in regard to the wells and the rivalries already described require recognition by a treaty arrangement. The king of Gerar and *Ahuzzath his adviser*, that is, his vizier or counselor (cf. 2 Sam. 15:37; 16:16; 1 Kings 4:5), *and Phicol*, the military leader, seek out Isaac with a view to an understanding. A similar incident is recorded of Abraham in 21:22–24, though some seventy years separates the events, and so the same people on the Gerar side could scarcely be intended.

Gerar may well have had two kings of the same name, but that each king should have had such a strangely named commander as Phicol, unless that name be a title, certainly suggests that the narratives in chapters 21 and 26 are duplicates. Their plea to Isaac for an understanding follows distinct steps. First they recite their hopes for the articles of the treaty. Then they make their submission by their recognition of Isaac's superiority and divine fortune. Isaac accepts and therefore confirms this acknowledgment by supplying a feast. As the superior, he is the host. In the morning they recite and make the oath, and the word used means "curse" which automatically follows covenant-breaking. Later that day Isaac hears of the new well mentioned in verse 25. Its name *Shibah* seems to reflect that morning's oath, Sheba, and the place where the well was dug, Beersheba —not to say another word meaning plenty, satiety, as some of the ancient versions read it.

6. Esau's Wives (26:34–35)

34 When Esau was forty years old, he took to wife Judith the daughter of Beeri the Hittite, and Basemath the daughter of Elon the Hittite; 35 and they made life bitter for Isaac and Rebekah.

The final two verses of the chapter are a brief notice from the P witness that Esau married two Hittite women, whose names are given. *Basemath* was the daughter of a Hittite, but both Greek and Syriac read Hivvite or Horite (cf. 36:2 f.). The two verses do not belong to the present context and must be understood as a well remembered tradition that Esau married against the advice of his parents, and outside the family. These wives were therefore a grief to Esau's parents because they were not from the family, as Isaac's wife was, and Jacob's wives were to be. The verse does not mean primarily that the foreign wives were troublesome women.

7. Scheming for the Blessing by Trickery (27:1–29)

The J witness now contributes a detailed and vivid picture of perhaps the most memorable event that ever took place in Isaac's household. The story is a real family story, the first one in such fulness in Genesis, for both parents and both sons all play a full part. The incident could be interpreted in terms of a deceived father, a scheming mother, a twice-tricked elder brother, or a compliant mother's darling. The four-part drama thus adds up to a story of family life, true in itself and memorable enough to be transmitted. The story is a unity from the J witness, who gives us a colorful and true-to-life account so typical of this writer. Some commentators have thought that verse 30 should be divided into separate parts, and that verses 11–13,16,21–23,33–34 were really parallel to 15,24–27a, and 35–38 respectively. Such analysis is somewhat subjective and does not really compel the reader to surrender the strong impression of unity of style which the narrative presents.

The story moves through a sequel of scenes. Verses 1–5, father and elder son; verses 6–17, mother and younger son; verses 18–29, father and younger son; verses 30–40, father and elder son again; verse 41, elder son alone; verses 42–45, mother and younger son again; verse 46, the parents alone; 28:1–5, father and younger son; 28:6–9, Esau again.

These last three units are however derived from the P witness, and thus 27:1–45 stands within the framework supplied by 26:34–35 and 27:46—28:9. In turn the

story (27:1–45) within that framework is the sequel of 25:34, or an illustration of 25:28.

The story is thus a family story which shows the family life coming to its breakup. The story is related quite objectively, and Rebekah is not blamed for her wickedness nor Jacob for his compliant deceit. The story is just related as it happened, but the consequences are no less clear. Isaac is wronged, and the estranged Esau departs to his household. The main punishment falls on Rebekah and her darling Jacob, for they are doomed to be separated for many years. In fact Rebekah and Jacob are not again said to meet, though that in fact they did may be inferred from 35:8,27–29.

Two reasons may be given for the preservation of the story: its own intrinsic value as a family tradition and as pointing to a permanent superiority of Jacob, the ancestor of Israel, over Esau, the ancestor of Edom. The subsequent rivalry and hostility between the two peoples may indeed be already reflected in the story itself, especially in the poetic fragments put in Isaac's mouth in 27:27–29,39–41. To point this out is not however to agree with von Rad for example that the narrative is only to be regarded as a literary recollection of tribal tradition. To claim that is to confuse the reason for the transmission with the origin of the tradition. The story is first and foremost a family story preserved for its own sake and transmitted because of its importance for the later history of Israel and Edom.

(1) Father and Elder Son (27:1–4)

¹ When Isaac was old and his eyes were dim so that he could not see, he called Esau his older son, and said to him, "My son"; and he answered, "Here I am." ² He said, "Behold, I am old; I do not know the day of my death. ³ Now then, take your weapons, your quiver and your bow, and go out to the field, and hunt game for me, ⁴ and prepare for me savory food, such as I love, and bring it to me that I may eat; that I may bless you before I die."

Isaac shows his love for Esau in a generous initiative. Isaac bids his son capture game to prepare it for a meal. The meal will be all the work of the son, and so in turn becomes the prerequisite of the father's testamentary blessing. Eating and blessing are closely connected, for eating strengthens the soul of the blesser and thus adds power to the blessing itself. Isaac is old, almost blind, and feels himself not far from death. He was sixty when his sons were born (25:26), and he died when he was one hundred and eighty (35:28). Either then Isaac was not so near death as he supposed and survived the incident by nearly eighty years (cf. Esau, forty in 26:34), or else the incident was just before Isaac's death, and then Esau and Jacob would have been quite old men. In fact Jacob would have been seventy-seven when Rebekah was afraid he would follow Esau's example and marry foreign women, and when he went tending sheep and love-making in Haran! (Cf. 27:46; 31:44.) The time sequence in the J witness and the P witness just happens to vary considerably. "That I may bless you" renders the Hebrew "that my soul, life, may bless you." It is almost a technical phrase recurring in verses 19,25,31 as a thematic refrain within the story.

(2) *Mother and Younger Son* (27:5–17)

5 Now Rebekah was listening when Isaac spoke to his son Esau. So when Esau went to the field to hunt for game and bring it, 6 Rebekah said to her son Jacob, "I heard your father speak to your brother Esau, 7 'Bring me game, and prepare for me savory food, that I may eat it, and bless you before the LORD before I die.' 8 Now therefore, my son, obey my word as I command you. 9 Go to the flock, and fetch me two good kids, that I may prepare from them savory food for your father, such as he loves; 10 and you shall bring it to your father to eat, so that he may bless you before he dies." 11 But Jacob said to Rebekah his mother, "Behold, my brother Esau is a hairy man, and I am a smooth man. 12 Perhaps my father will feel me, and I shall seem to be mocking him, and bring a curse upon myself and not a blessing." 13 His mother said to him, "Upon me be your curse, my son; only obey my word, and go, fetch them to me." 14 So he went and took them and brought them to his mother; and his mother prepared savory food,

such as his father loved. 15 Then Rebekah took the best garments of Esau her older son, which were with her in the house, and put them on Jacob her younger son; 16 and the skins of the kids she put upon his hands and upon the smooth part of his neck; 17 and she gave the savory food and the bread, which she had prepared, into the hand of her son Jacob.

This section reveals the doting mother as the evil genius of the piece. Eavesdropping, she learned Isaac's intention and, with Jacob's all too ready help, devised the stratagem to frustrate her husband's design. She supplied her darling with the necessary food, dressed him in Esau's clothes, and disguised his skin as Esau's skin. Rebekah adds to her account of Isaac's words, the extra phrase *before the Lord*, which heightens the solemnity of the occasion for her, and her own duplicity for us. Jacob's objection in verse 12 has a like effect. Rebekah has thought it all out and is prepared even to risk a curse. Doting and cynicism are strangely matched in her.

(3) *Father and Younger Son* (27:18–29)

18 So he went in to his father, and said, "My father"; and he said, "Here I am; who are you, my son?" 19 Jacob said to his father, "I am Esau your first-born. I have done as you told me; now sit up and eat of my game, that you may bless me." 20 But Isaac said to his son, "How is it that you have found it so quickly, my son?" He answered, "Because the LORD your God granted me success." 21 Then Isaac said to Jacob, "Come near, that I may feel you, my son, to know whether you are really my son Esau or not." 22 So Jacob went near to Isaac his father, who felt him and said, "The voice is Jacob's voice, but the hands are the hands of Esau." 23 And he did not recognize him, because his hands were hairy like his brother Esau's hands; so he blessed him. 24 He said, "Are you really my son Esau?" He answered, "I am." 25 Then he said, "Bring it to me, that I may eat of my son's game and bless you." So he brought it to him, and he ate; and he brought him wine, and he drank. 26 Then his father Isaac said to him, "Come near and kiss me, my son." 27 So he came near and kissed him; and he smelled the smell of his garments, and blessed him, and said,
"See the smell of my son
  is as the smell of a field which the LORD
  has blessed!

28 May God give you of the dew of heaven,
    and of the fatness of the earth,
    and plenty of grain and wine.
29 Let peoples serve you,
    and nations bow down to you.
Be lord over your brothers,
    and may your mother's sons bow down to
        you.
Cursed be every one who curses you,
    and blessed be every one who blesses
        you!"

The plot comes to its climax in the hesitations of Isaac and in the suspense of Jacob. In turn, Isaac's surprise at his son's speedy return, his desire to feel his son, his question (v. 24), and finally the kiss as enabling Isaac to smell his son, sustain his suspicions. Above all Isaac's words, "The voice is Jacob's voice, but the hands are the hands of Esau," are the classic form of the dilemma of doubting innocence. Jacob tells one lie after another on top of the deceit of his address. How Jacob must have trembled under the kiss, the smell, and the touch of blessing; and yet how elated that he survived these to hear the words of the testamentary blessing.

The blessing is not couched in the usual terms of the patriarchal blessings, but illustrates terminal blessings in exaggerated Oriental terms. The human smell is taken up into the smell of a very fertile field whose fruitfulness becomes the measure of Jacob's future success. In verses 28–29 the blessing is purely agricultural, with perhaps even a suggestion of the fertility of the Promised Land.

Fatness is literally fat, i.e., fertile areas of Palestine itself. The blessing is originally perhaps commercial, because wealth and not weapons would be its strength. The political overtones would inevitably intrude as the blessing was seen to reflect Israel's ascendancy over immediate peoples like the Canaanites, Moab and Ammon in the days of David, and over Edom then and in the succeeding centuries.

The couplet with which the blessing ends is reminiscent of 12:3 (cf. Num. 24:9).

8. Esau's Bitter Disappointment (27:30–40)

30 As soon as Isaac had finished blessing Jacob, when Jacob had scarcely gone out from the presence of Isaac his father, Esau his brother came in from his hunting. 31 He also prepared savory food, and brought it to his father. And he said to his father, "Let my father arise, and eat of his son's game, that you may bless me." 32 His father Isaac said to him, "Who are you?" He answered, "I am your son, your first-born, Esau." 33 Then Isaac trembled violently, and said, "Who was it then that hunted game and brought it to me, and I ate it all before you came, and I have blessed him? —yes, and he shall be blessed." 34 When Esau heard the words of his father, he cried out with an exceedingly great and bitter cry, and said to his father, "Bless me, even me also, O my father!" 35 But he said, "Your brother came with guile, and he has taken away your blessing." 36 Esau said, "Is he not rightly named Jacob? For he has supplanted me these two times. He took away my birthright; and behold, now he has taken away my blessing." Then he said, "Have you not reserved a blessing for me?" 37 Isaac answered Esau, "Behold, I have made him your lord, and all his brothers I have given to him for servants, and with grain and wine I have sustained him. What then can I do for you, my son?" 38 Esau said to his father, "Have you but one blessing, my father? Bless me, even me also, O my father." And Esau lifted up his voice and wept.

39 Then Isaac his father answered him:
"Behold, away from the fatness of the earth
    shall your dwelling be,
    and away from the dew of heaven on high.
40 By your sword you shall live,
    and you shall serve your brother;
but when you break loose
    you shall break his yoke from your neck."

Jacob had barely left when Esau comes in; then too Jacob's treachery is discovered and the very agitated Isaac (v. 33) passes through bewilderment to helplessness. Esau quickly grasps the situation and shouts out in bitter anguish and chagrin, because, like his father, he knows the blessing is irrecoverable and lost to him. The contrast of the superlative expressions of Isaac and of Esau bring the two parties and their two moods into high contrast. Isaac first identifies the miscreant *your brother,* and Esau in reply no doubt deliberately twists his brother's name to mean not "may God protect" but "he has supplanted" (cf. 25:26). Esau sums up his accusation against Jacob in a striking play of words: "He has taken my birthright and my blessing," in Hebrew *bᵉkhorathi* and *birkhathi*. Yet Esau foolishly sold his birthright, even though he was the innocent victim in the loss of the blessing.

In reply to Esau's plea for a blessing, Isaac shows that he has conferred, albeit unwittingly, status and welfare upon Jacob, and appears to have nothing left to give. Esau pleads again for only one blessing—a mini-blessing for himself alone. After the words "Oh my father!" the LXX adds, "but Isaac was silent." Perhaps the LXX retains here an original element of the story. The brief phrase is eloquent and makes Esau's renewed outburst all the more intelligible. In face of Esau's trapped helplessness, Isaac describes in predictive terms the habitat, the role, and eventual release of Esau from his destiny. The RSV rightly translates the ambiguous Hebrew preposition by the words *away from*, i.e., far from and outside the fertile places of the Promised Land, Esau is to live.

Isaac begins his utterance to Esau by a sentence upon him, which virtually confirms that Esau, because outside the land, is outside the blessing. No doubt, barren areas of Edom are described by implication. So his life first individually and then in his descendants will be a life of warfare and servitude. Later will come release. The conditions described in verse 40 no doubt reflect David's victories over Edom (cf. 2 Sam. 8:12–14) and later Edom's emancipation (cf. 1 Kings 11:11–22).

The solitary and unblessed elder son resolves to bide his time, and after his father's death to kill his brother. The motive is revenge only, for Jacob's death would not ensure the transfer of his blessing back to Esau. No doubt the oath born in silence was bruited forth in sullen hate and so reached his mother's ears, who summoning her beloved Jacob bids him depart to her old home in Haran to Laban her brother.

She contemplates but a short absence, but it was to be more than twenty years. Perhaps indeed they never met again. Her closing remark in verse 45 concerning the loss of both sons in one day means of course that if Esau killed Jacob, then his own life by blood revenge would be forfeit also. The story ends in family feud and flight and Isaac and Rebekah are left to go on as they began.

9. *Jacob's Flight* (27:41—28:5)

⁴¹ Now Esau hated Jacob because of the blessing with which his father had blessed him, and Esau said to himself, "The days of mourning for my father are approaching; then I will kill my brother Jacob." ⁴² But the words of Esau her older son were told to Rebekah; so she sent and called Jacob her younger son, and said to him, "Behold, your brother Esau comforts himself by planning to kill you. ⁴³ Now therefore, my son, obey my voice; arise, flee to Laban my brother in Haran, ⁴⁴ and stay with him a while, until your brother's fury turns away; ⁴⁵ until your brother's anger turns away, and he forgets what you have done to him; then I will send, and fetch you from there. Why should I be bereft of you both in one day?"

⁴⁶ Then Rebekah said to Isaac, "I am weary of my life because of the Hittite women. If Jacob marries one of the Hittite women such as these, one of the women of the land, what good will my life be to me?"

¹ Then Isaac called Jacob and blessed him, and charged him, "You shall not marry one of the Canaanite women. ² Arise, go to Paddanaram to the house of Bethuel your mother's father; and take as wife from there one of the daughters of Laban your mother's brother. ³ God Almighty bless you and make you fruitful and multiply you, that you may become a company of peoples. ⁴ May he give the blessing of Abraham to you and to your descendants with you, that you take possession of the land of your sojournings which God gave to Abraham!" ⁵ Thus Isaac sent Jacob away; and he went to Paddanaram to Laban, the son of Bethuel the Aramean, the brother of Rebekah, Jacob's and Esau's mother.

The first verse obviously resumes 26–34 f., and Rebekah's fear lest Jacob should imitate Esau's choice of wives leads Isaac to command Jacob to depart to the family's ancient home. The reference to

Paddan-aram shows that 27:46—28:9 is the testimony of the P witness. The two traditions ascribe Jacob's departure to the instruction of mother and father separately; but the traditions are not necessarily inconsistent. The P witness obviously did not think so. He thought that Rebekah achieved her real motive—the safety of Jacob (27:42–44)—through Isaac's fear, and her own, of Jacob's possible foreign wives. Two divergent traditions have thus been combined.

The P witness gives his own form of the blessing. It belongs to Jacob as he leaves home. The word "bless" should not be defamed to "greet" as some suggest. God Almighty, El Shaddai, one of P's terms for God (cf. 17:1; Ex. 6:3), will bless Jacob with a fruitful progeny. He will become a father of peoples (cf. 17:4), and they, with him, will possess Abraham's own blessing, here identified once more as possession of the Promised Land, described so often by P as "land of your sojournings" (17:8; 36:7). This incident is the only story about Isaac given by the P witness, but it confirms the J story at two points: that Isaac blessed Jacob and that Jacob, unlike his father, went to Haran.

10. Esau's Third Wife (28:6-9)

⁶ Now Esau saw that Isaac had blessed Jacob and sent him away to Paddanaram to take a wife from there, and that as he blessed him he charged him, "You shall not marry one of the Canaanite women," ⁷ and that Jacob had obeyed his father and his mother and gone to Paddanaram. ⁸ So when Esau saw that the Canaanite women did not please Isaac his father, ⁹ Esau went to Ishmael and took to wife, besides the wives he had, Mahalath the daughter of Ishmael Abraham's son, the sister of Nebaioth.

According to the P witness, Esau does seem to have tried to make amends. Recognizing that his father had blessed Jacob, and realizing that his own wives were vexatious to his parents, he paid a visit to Ishmael to seek a wife. *Ishmael* may be Abraham's actual son, though there are difficulties of date, but the word could

mean an Ishmaelite family or clan. From that clan he chooses his cousin, *Mahalath* (Gen. 25:13) for his third wife. Indirectly Esau is again shown to be outside the promise, for the line of promise had been through Sarah and Isaac, not Hagar and Ishmael. Like Jacob and Lamech, Esau practiced bigamy.

XVI. Jacob's First Sojourn Outside Canaan (28:10—31:55)

This section begins with an incident at Bethel during his journey but is otherwise concerned with Jacob's long stay outside Canaan. His stay with his mother's relatives lasted very much longer than was apparently anticipated (27:44). This was because he was compelled to work as a servant for fourteen years in order to gain his two wives, first, Leah and then Rachel. Jacob is persuaded to remain for a further period to work for what is apparently an insignificant wage.

Jacob the miscreant fugitive is thus punished for his misbehavior in several ways. His enforced exile is lengthened because of Laban's deceit. Jacob who had deceived his father is now in turn deceived by his mother's relative; he is denied the wife he really wants, and when he gets her she is for a long time barren. On the other hand during this enforced exile he is divinely protected and prospered (cf. 28:13). He does get his own way. He founds his family (29:31—30:24) and fortune (30:25-43), and wins the battle of wits with Laban.

1. Jacob and Bethel (28:10-22)

¹⁰ Jacob left Beersheba, and went toward Haran. ¹¹ And he came to a certain place, and stayed there that night, because the sun had set. Taking one of the stones of the place, he put it under his head and lay down in that place to sleep. ¹² And he dreamed that there was a ladder set up on the earth, and the top of it reached to heaven; and behold, the angels of God were ascending and descending on it! ¹³ And behold, the LORD stood above it and said, "I am the LORD, the God of Abraham your father and the God of Isaac; the land on which you lie I will give to you and to your

descendants; ¹⁴ and your descendants shall be like the dust of the earth, and you shall spread abroad to the west and to the east and to the north and to the south; and by you and your descendants shall all the families of the earth bless themselves. ¹⁵ Behold, I am with you and will keep you wherever you go, and will bring you back to this land; for I will not leave you until I have done that of which I have spoken to you." ¹⁶ Then Jacob awoke from his sleep and said, "Surely the Lord is in this place; and I did not know it." ¹⁷ And he was afraid, and said, "How awesome is this place! This is none other than the house of God, and this is the gate of heaven."

¹⁸ So Jacob rose early in the morning, and he took the stone which he had put under his head and set it up for a pillar and poured oil on the top of it. ¹⁹ He called the name of that place Bethel; but the name of the city was Luz at the first. ²⁰ Then Jacob made a vow, saying, "If God will be with me, and will keep me in this way that I go, and will give me bread to eat and clothing to wear, ²¹ so that I come again to my father's house in peace, then the Lord shall be my God, ²² and this stone, which I have set up for a pillar, shall be God's house; and of all that thou givest me I will give the tenth to thee."

This narrative is the direct sequel of the family events in 27:1–45. Jacob is on his way from Beersheba to Haran and on one of the nights of his journey has a dream described by some of the best known words of all Scripture, namely, the dream of Jacob's ladder.

The story is told by two of the earlier witnesses who gave us the book of Genesis. Among those who accept the idea of the witnesses, verses 10–12,17–18,20–22 are regarded as coming from E and verses 13–16,19, from J. The dream is a characteristic idea of the E witness.

Jacob *came to a certain place.* The Hebrew says, "He happened, lighted upon, the place." This means of course that he went to sleep at this place, not knowing it was the sacred place, a fact to be revealed to him only in his dream. Two accounts are given of what he saw in his dream.

According to E, the contact of his head with a local stone used as a pillow, brought about the dream of a ladder or stairway from earth to heaven, and angels, wingless

as often in the Old Testament, going up and coming down upon it. The word for ladder occurs only here and its verb "to heap up" suggests a ramp. Doubtless a recollection of the Babylonian ziggurat is joined here to the figure of human-heavenly intercourse. The direction of the ladder and of the movement of the angels is from the earth upwards. Presumably the direction is related from the point of view of the sleeper, though a description of divine messengers would be expected to say that they descended and then ascended in fulfilling their mission (cf. John 1:55). The suggestion that in ascending and descending the divine messengers are imitating worshipers does not accord with their character as messengers; i.e., having their starting point from above.

According to J, Jacob sees a vision of the Lord stationed above it (the ladder), or better, above him, or even beside him. The Lord identifies himself as the God of his grandfather and father, and reiterates the terms of the divine promises, the gift of the land, the numerous progeny, and that Jacob and his descendants are to be the fount or standard of blessing for others. The promises are further buttressed by two particular promises—the pledge of the divine presence—here to be understood as good fortune; and also the undertaking that Jacob will return to the land and thus remain within the divine intention and promise. Jacob awakes to a feeling of surprise. Only here in all Genesis does a theophany occasion surprise. Astonishment and fear are closely related. *Surely* is found only here and in Exodus 2:14 in the Pentateuch.

Jacob's description of the locality is striking. It is a terrible place (cf. Deut. 7:21; Dan. 9:4). *Awesome* best catches the mood of the awful sense of God's presence here described. The feeling of the place is numinous, and so Jacob describes it as *the house of God,* where God dwells, and *the gate of heaven,* i.e., from earth to heaven. The feeling gives way to the rudiments of a theology of place. Both the ziggurat shape of the ladder or ramp and the account of the place are reminiscent of the theology of the Babylonians. As was evident in the discussion of 11:1–9, the conception of the centrality of the sanctuary belongs to places like Shechem (Judg. 9:34–37), Jerusalem (Isa. 2:1–4; 45:22; Ezek. 38:12), and especially Golgotha and the cross of Christ (cf. John 12:32).

In the Bible of course centrality of place was to be accompanied by, and almost replaced by, a centrality of person, whether that person was Abram, or the Davidic king, or the Suffering Servant (Isa. 52:13–15), or Jesus Christ or the Lamb in the midst (Rev. 5:12; 7:17).

The Babylonian conception of the sanctuary is thus being transplanted to Canaan. Just as the patriarchs brought with them ideas of the beginning and flooding of the world, so here in Jacob's life is a sudden outcrop of some of the theological ideas which had not yet died out of the family, and were in fact to rise with new life in Canaan and Israel in the days of Solomon.

The remaining features of that memorable morning are the erection of a pillar, not necessarily a pillar many feet in height, but merely the small stone used for a pillow the previous night. Then comes the designation of the stone as *Bethel*—house of God—later interpreted as the renaming of the area previously called Luz (cf. 35:6; 48:3; Josh. 16:2; Judg. 1:23,26). The vow and the tithe (cf. Amos 4:4) follow. In the anointing (cf. 35:14), vow and tithe are doubtless to be seen as elements of the traditional worship associated with the Bethel sanctuary.

The question naturally arises how these elements are related to Jacob and how they emerge from out of his experience. Jacob is in flight from home and for a time a homeless migrant. Homesickness possibly, and certainly fear and concern in face of an unknown future could bring about a dream in which some of the traditional religious beliefs of his youth would emerge. The mind of the J witness is also probably to be seen in the siting of the revelation on Jacob's outward journey. Isaac had already

designated Jacob as the heir of blessing, but God now for the first time confirms this. Jacob is beginning his journeys and his own independent life. Yet his fear of the future, his loneliness, and the knowledge that he was not only leaving his home but the land of his birth, the Promised Land, are the circumstances which give rise to the dream and the revelation.

Just as the revelation was made spontaneously to Abram (12:3) without reference to his character or worthiness, so the revelation comes to Jacob at this point in his life, as he departs from home and people, without reference to his character, which at this point in the story is undeserving. Nevertheless his vow shows a glimmering of faith; and the terms of the bargain (vv. 20–21), and no one can deny that these terms are inconsistent with what we know of Jacob, exhibit the psychological beginnings of piety. The sequel of this story of Jacob's impending exit from the land is to be found in chapter 32, which tells of an experience before his impending reentry into the land. Exit from and reentry into the land—each is marked by an appropriate religious experience, which explains these incidents in Jacob's life in terms of the divine purpose in the patriarchal lives and his own place in that purpose.

Bethel must have been a very ancient sanctuary, probably pre-Israelite. The present story adds to its fame the prestige of association with, if not the actual founding by, one of the patriarchs. It remained significant in the settlement and was probably an ark sanctuary for a time (cf. Judg. 20:27). Jeroboam I made it a great pilgrimage shrine of the Northern Kingdom (1 Kings 12:26–29), and it remained an important shrine (Amos 5:4 f.; 2 Kings 17:28) until the days of Josiah who destroyed it (2 Kings 23:15). It appears also that there was a god called Bethel (Jer. 48:13).

2. Jacob Meets Rachel and Her Family (29:1–14)

¹ Then Jacob went on his journey, and came to the land of the people of the east. ² As he

looked, he saw a well in the field, and lo, three flocks of sheep lying beside it; for out of that well the flocks were watered. The stone on the well's mouth was large, 3 and when all the flocks were gathered there, the shepherds would roll the stone from the mouth of the well, and water the sheep, and put the stone back in its place upon the mouth of the well.

4 Jacob said to them, "My brothers, where do you come from?" They said, "We are from Haran." 5 He said to them, "Do you know Laban the son of Nahor?" They said, "We know him." 6 He said to them, "Is it well with him?" They said, "It is well; and see, Rachel his daughter is coming with the sheep!" 7 He said, "Behold, it is still high day, it is not time for the animals to be gathered together; water the sheep, and go, pasture them." 8 But they said, "We cannot until all the flocks are gathered together, and the stone is rolled from the mouth of the well; then we water the sheep."

9 While he was still speaking with them, Rachel came with her father's sheep; for she kept them. 10 Now when Jacob saw Rachel the daughter of Laban his mother's brother, and the sheep of Laban his mother's brother, Jacob went up and rolled the stone from the well's mouth, and watered the flock of Laban his mother's brother. 11 Then Jacob kissed Rachel, and wept aloud. 12 And Jacob told Rachel that he was her father's kinsman, and that he was Rebekah's son; and she ran and told her father.

13 When Laban heard the tidings of Jacob his sister's son, he ran to meet him, and embraced him and kissed him, and brought him to his house. Jacob told Laban all these things, 14 and Laban said to him, "Surely you are my bone and my flesh!" And he stayed with him a month.

The J witness presents another of his great stories (cf. Gen. 24; Ex. 2:15 ff.). Apart from the incident at Bethel, Jacob's long journey is told in one verse (v. 1). He is said to lift his feet and go—*went on his journey, and came.* The expression "lift his feet" only here in the Old Testament. *People of the east* normally designated the dwellers of the Syro-Arabian Desert, but as Numbers 23:7 shows, a northerly as well as an easterly area is intended. Jacob reaches a well besides which three flocks and their attendant shepherds are lying. In verse 3 RSV adds *the shepherds* to explain the meaning. In verse 3 and verse 8 the Samaritan Penteteuch and LXX read "the shepherds" instead of "the flocks." The

words from "for" in 2b to the end of verse 3 are parenthetical, describing the customary procedure. The verbs are thus best rendered, "used to roll the stone . . . used to water the sheep, and used to put the stone back."

Jacob has reached the right place for his conversation with the taciturn shepherds and soon elicits the fact that they know Laban, that he is alive and well, and that in fact a flock of sheep in the distance in charge of a girl is Laban's flock, tended by his daughter Rachel. Jacob probably understood from this description that Rachel was unmarried, because of her job. *Laban the son of Nahor* means of course the grandson of Nahor, for Laban is Bethuel's son (28:5).[19]

While waiting for Rachel, Jacob seeks to improve the occasion. He wrongly imagines that the flocks are gathered for the night, and so bids the shepherds be about their business because so much daylight is still left. The shepherds explain to this busybody that they cannot water and pasture the sheep, because it takes the combined strength of all the shepherds to roll the large stone *from the mouth of the well.* The climax of the incident is reached with Rachel's arrival. When Jacob sees Rachel at close quarters, gallantry so inspires his natural strength he rolls the stone away singlehanded. The commentators seem generally to overlook the middle phrase of verse 10, *the sheep of Laban his mother's brother.* In other words Rachel's charm is but half the explanation of Jacob's feat. Rachel's charm together with her father's obvious wealth spur Jacob on. The shouts of laughter at the retelling of such a story, revealing as it does Jacob's greedy nature, may well be imagined. The pathos of the actions and of the words in verses 11–12 are thus thrown in still higher relief. What Jacob said of course was "I am Jacob: I am your father's nephew: I am no other than the son of your aunt Rebekah." No

---

19 For this use of son as meaning grandson, cf. 2 Kings 9:14,20; Zech. 1:1; Ezra 5:1. Cf. J. R. Porter, "Son or Grandson (Ezra 10:6)?" JTS, xvii, 1966, p. 62.

wonder Rachel ran home and that Laban ran back and kept on hugging and kissing him. Laban is soon assured of Jacob's identity and so direct contact between the two parts of the family in Haran and in Palestine is restored, as far as is known, for the first time in over twenty years (but cf. the P witness in 26:34—more than forty years).

3. Jacob Marries Two Sisters (29:15-30)

15 Then Laban said to Jacob, "Because you are my kinsman, should you therefore serve me for nothing? Tell me, what shall your wages be?" 16 Now Laban had two daughters; the name of the older was Leah, and the name of the younger was Rachel. 17 Leah's eyes were weak, but Rachel was beautiful and lovely. 18 Jacob loved Rachel; and he said, "I will serve you seven years for your younger daughter Rachel." 19 Laban said, "It is better that I give her to you than that I should give her to any other man; stay with me." 20 So Jacob served seven years for Rachel, and they seemed to him but a few days because of the love he had for her.
21 Then Jacob said to Laban, "Give me my wife that I may go in to her, for my time is completed." 22 So Laban gathered together all the men of the place, and made a feast. 23 But in the evening he took his daughter Leah and brought her to Jacob; and he went in to her. 24 (Laban gave his maid Zilpah to his daughter Leah to be her maid.) 25 And in the morning, behold, it was Leah; and Jacob said to Laban, "What is this you have done to me? Did I not serve with you for Rachel? Why then have you deceived me?" 26 Laban said, "It is not so done in our country, to give the younger before the first-born. 27 Complete the week of this one, and we will give you the other also in return for serving me another seven years." 28 Jacob did so, and completed her week; then Laban gave him his daughter Rachel to wife. 29 (Laban gave his maid Bilhah to his daughter Rachel to be her maid.) 30 So Jacob went in to Rachel also, and he loved Rachel more than Leah, and served Laban for another seven years.

The story now continues with the account of Jacob's double wedding—two wives in eight days! Two such marriages defy the prohibition of Leviticus 18:18, and so surely represent very ancient tradition. Speiser is probably correct in seeing

the entire narrative of the chapter as a unity contributed by the J witness.

Rebekah was given more maids (24:61), but then Abraham's servant had gifts. Jacob probably could not afford the bride price and very generously offered instead to give seven years' labor for his Rachel. Jacob favored and loved Rachel. Her older sister Leah had weak eyes; they lacked the luster so necessary to Eastern ideas of beauty. Soft or tender would perhaps better give the meaning. Rachel was beautiful (v. 17; cf. 24:16). Jacob loved Rachel so much that the seven years passed as quickly as if they were but a few days.

Leah probably means "cow" and Rachel "ewe." Laban uses these circumstances to play a trick on Jacob. After seven years the bridal feast (Lit., drinking feast) is held, and Jacob's wife is given to him. Only the morning after does Jacob discover the trick and that he has in fact been given Leah. How Leah could have maintained the deceit of appearance and voice is not explained. Jacob must have been very drunk! Thus placed, Jacob agrees to *complete the week of this one,* that is, the marriage feast of seven days for Leah (Judg. 14:12), and then to receive Rachel on the eighth day against his promise to work for Laban another seven years in return.

Laban has been very cunning and successful. He has married off both his daughters within the family, and gained Jacob's labors for fourteen years. Laban's success appears complete, as his character as a selfish schemer certainly is clear. What coarse laughter must have been heard behind Jacob's back.

Von Rad rightly points out that Laban's defense that he could not give the elder before the younger must have cut the ground from beneath Jacob's feet, for Jacob the younger brother had supplanted Esau the elder brother. Yet, too, as von Rad also shows, without the Jacob-Leah marriage, Reuben, Levi, and Judah would not have been born, and that in turn means no Moses (tribe of Levi) and no David (Judah).

4. Jacob's Children (29:31—30:24)

Altogether Jacob had eight sons from his two wives and two sons each from the maids of his wives. All twelve sons except Benjamin and his daughter Dinah are born in Mesopotamia, and the list of births is marked by the maternal and quite personal explanations of the names given to the sons.

(1) Leah's First Four Sons (29:31–35)

31 When the LORD saw that Leah was hated, he opened her womb; but Rachel was barren. 32 And Leah conceived and bore a son, and she called his name Reuben; for she said, "Because the LORD has looked upon my affliction; surely now my husband will love me." 33 She conceived again and bore a son, and said, "Because the LORD has heard that I am hated, he has given me this son also"; and she called his name Simeon. 34 Again she conceived and bore a son, and said, "Now this time my husband will be joined to me, because I have borne him three sons"; therefore his name was called Levi. 35 And she conceived again and bore a son, and said, "This time I will praise the LORD"; therefore she called his name Judah; then she ceased bearing.

The account begins in ethical considerations, which arise because of the difficulties born of polygamy. Leah is less loved than Rachel, but the balance is divinely corrected. "Less loved" is more correct than *hated.* The meaning is relative (cf. Deut. 21:15). Leah has four sons but Rachel remains barren. Once again the long delay in the birth of the desired son occurs (cf. Isaac and Esau-Jacob). The womb is opened for conception (v. 31). Leah names her firstborn *Reuben,* and this word means literally, "Behold, a son," but Leah is said to think up a related Hebrew phrase "looked upon my affliction," i.e., that her husband prefers her sister. She names her second son *Simeon,* "the Lord has heard," and the explanation and the circumstance agree. She names her third son *Levi,* "adherent" (cf. Num. 18:2), and her fourth, *Judah,* "praise." Explanation and circumstance are in approximate agreement.

(2) Rachel's Substitute Children (30:1–8)

1 When Rachel saw that she bore Jacob no children, she envied her sister; and she said to Jacob, "Give me children, or I shall die!" 2 Jacob's anger was kindled against Rachel, and he said, "Am I in the place of God, who has withheld from you the fruit of the womb?" 3 Then she said, "Here is my maid Bilhah; go in to her, that she may bear upon my knees, and even I may have children through her." 4 So she gave him her maid Bilhah as a wife; and Jacob went in to her. 5 And Bilhah conceived and bore Jacob a son. 6 Then Rachel said, "God has judged me, and has also heard my voice and given me a son"; therefore she called his name Dan. 7 Rachel's maid Bilhah conceived again and bore Jacob a second son. 8 Then Rachel said, "With mighty wrestlings I have wrestled with my sister, and have prevailed"; so she called his name Naphtali.

Leah's fruitfulness gives rise to Rachel's jealousy. *She envied her sister.* The Hebrew word means "jealous" and expresses a more overt and active mood (cf. 26:14). Rachel has been described as envious and petulant, and this she may have been if despair is the only explanation. But her request to Jacob, *Give me children,* may not be petulance at all, but the precise reference to the custom about to be described, whereby a barren wife gives her personal maid to her husband, and children deriving from that union are counted as the wife's by a kind of adoption. Verses 1–8 are thus a parallel to 16:1–6. Jacob appears to misunderstand her and to deny that it is his fault that Rachel is barren (cf. 50:19; 2 Kings 5:7).

Rachel explains, *that she may bear upon my knees.* This expression is hardly figurative; it probably means that originally the travailing woman actually lay for the birth moment on the body of the adopting mother. The child was thus born between the knees of both women. Later the expression came to mean adoption (cf. 50:23; Job 3:12). *Even I may have children through her* represents the Hebrew "that I even I may be built up from her" (cf. 16:2).

Rachel names Bilhah's first baby *Dan,* which means "(God) has judged," i.e., vindicated, or given me my due (Psalm 26:1; 43:1). Rachel names Bilhah's second child *Naphtali*, combatant, because *with mighty wrestlings I have wrestled*, i.e., "enormous struggles I have had." The reference may be to the long drawn-out struggle with Leah over many years. Others have interpreted "mighty wrestlings," which represents the Hebrew "wrestlings of God," more literally, as "wrestlings with God in prayer" or more nebulously "numinous" wrestlings (Speiser), whatever they may be.

(3) Leah's Substitute Children (30:9–13)

⁹ When Leah saw that she had ceased bearing children, she took her maid Zilpah and gave her to Jacob as a wife. ¹⁰ Then Leah's maid Zilpah bore Jacob a son. ¹¹ And Leah said, "Good fortune!" so she called his name Gad. ¹² Leah's maid Zilpah bore Jacob a second son. ¹³ And Leah said, "Happy am I! For the women will call me happy"; so she called his name Asher.

Verse 9 resumes 29:31. So Leah now gives her personal maid to Jacob, and Zilpah bears *Gad* "good fortune" and *Asher* "fortunate." Gad, a god of good fortune, was widely known (cf. Isa. 65:11; Josh. 11:17; 15:37), and the coincidence has led to extravagant theories of this baby's divine ancestry or even identity with the god. The play on the word *happy* in verse 13 does not mean that a double etymology is actually given. Leah is happy, blessed because of the number of her children, and the women (literally, daughters, girls) compliment her.

(4) Leah's Last Two Sons and Dinah (30:14–21)

¹⁴ In the days of wheat harvest Reuben went and found mandrakes in the field, and brought them to his mother Leah. Then Rachel said to Leah, "Give me, I pray, some of your son's mandrakes." ¹⁵ But she said to her, "Is it a small matter that you have taken away my husband? Would you take away my son's mandrakes also?" Rachel said, "Then he may lie with you tonight for your son's mandrakes." ¹⁶ When Jacob came from the field in the evening, Leah went out to meet him, and said, "You must come in to me; for I have hired you

with my son's mandrakes." So he lay with her that night. ¹⁷ And God hearkened to Leah, and she conceived and bore Jacob a fifth son. ¹⁸ Leah said, "God has given me my hire because I gave my maid to my husband"; so she called his name Issachar. ¹⁹ And Leah conceived again, and she bore Jacob a sixth son. ²⁰ Then Leah said, "God has endowed me with a good dowry; now my husband will honor me, because I have borne him six sons"; so she called his name Zebulun. ²¹ Afterwards she bore a daughter, and called her name Dinah.

One day in May, the time of the wheat harvest, *Reuben,* now between seven and ten, or perhaps even older, accidentally discovers some *mandrakes in the field* and brings them back to his mother. Mandrakes are *Mandragora vernalis,* a small yellow ground fruit like potatoes and similar to plums or small apples in size. Both roots and fruit appear to have stimulating qualities for conception, and are much sought after for that purpose (Song of Sol. 7:13). The Hebrew word for mandrakes resembles the Hebrew word for desire, and the rendering "love apples" (ERV) is suitable.

Rachel asks Leah for some of them, but Leah's reply that Rachel has taken away her husband is the clue to a good deal in the story. Apparently Jacob had withheld conjugal rights from Leah (14 ff.; Ex. 21:10). No wonder then she had suddenly ceased to bear children (30:9), no wonder she gave her maid to Jacob, no wonder that a mighty struggle had taken place between the two wives. Rachel had presumably managed to keep Jacob and Leah apart.

The women strike a bargain. Leah has the service of Jacob for that night, conceives a child, but after nine months Rachel is still apparently without a child of her own. Leah is consistently represented as a woman of some wit. She says to Jacob, *I have hired you with my son's* "love-apples," and when a son is born she names him *Issachar,* meaning "there is a reward" or "man of hiring." The quiet, secular, rather funny, and indeed agricultural cast of these verses suggests real life rather than some imaginary story to account for the name Issachar.

Later, Leah has a sixth and last son, and for his name, **Zebulun,** two explanations are given. "He has given me a gift," i.e., a bridegroom's gift, or "My husband will dwell (lie, i.e., honor) with me." Another meaning—uphold, support, or even maintain—has also been suggested.

Leah also has a daughter, **Dinah,** literally, "judgment," but no meaning for the name is given. Dinah is the unfortunate victim of the story in chapter 34; 37:35 and 46:7 mention other unnamed daughters of Jacob.

(5) Rachel's First Son, Joseph (30:22–24)

²² Then God remembered Rachel, and God hearkened to her and opened her womb. ²³ She conceived and bore a son, and said, "God has taken away my reproach"; ²⁴ and she called his name Joseph, saying, "May the LORD add to me another son!"

As if to emphasize that her expedients, Bilhah first, mandrakes later, had failed, the E witness recalls that God remembered Rachel (cf. 1 Sam. 1:19), and consequently she bears a son. Two explanations of the name **Joseph** are given. The name is regarded as derived from a verb meaning to take away, i.e., her reproach, or from a verb to add, thereby indicating Rachel's prayer for yet more children.

Both witnesses, J and E, have contributed parts of the story of the birth of eleven of Jacob's sons (29:31—30:24). Basically the narrative is a J tradition with extra notes from the testimony of E, and it is a story about a family, especially the two rival wives. The notes about Bilhah and Zilpah introduce a well-known social custom, and this supports the view that the story is a genuine part of the tradition. Both witnesses testify to the personal and human aspects of the events, and even two etymologies are sometimes preserved, one from each witness.

The best explanation is that the narrative is a well remembered part of a well-known tradition. The story is memorable because of all its striking features. Jacob, the duped bridegroom, marries two sisters in eight days, giving fourteen years of his life for them. The wife he liked was barren, the disliked wife had six sons. Jacob cannot win. This is how it happened in that household all those centuries ago, and, largely without comment, the story has thus come down to us. What von Rad is pleased to style an etymological game is nothing other than the inventive wit of Leah, perpetually at a disadvantage in the one point that mattered to her; namely, her husband's preference for her sister, but with consolations in her sons which were increasingly vexatious to Rachel.

5. Turning Point in Jacob's Fortunes (30:25–43)

²⁵ When Rachel had borne Joseph, Jacob said to Laban, "Send me away, that I may go to my own home and country. ²⁶ Give me my wives and my children for whom I have served you, and let me go; for you know the service which I have given you." ²⁷ But Laban said to him, "If you will allow me to say so, I have learned by divination that the LORD has blessed me because of you; ²⁸ name your wages, and I will give it." ²⁹ Jacob said to him, "You yourself know how I have served you, and how your cattle have fared with me. ³⁰ For you had little before I came, and it has increased abundantly; and the LORD has blessed you wherever I turned. But now when shall I provide for my own household also?" ³¹ He said, "What shall I give you?" Jacob said, "You shall not give me anything; if you will do this for me, I will again feed your flock and keep it: ³² let me pass through all your flock today, removing from it every speckled and spotted sheep and every black lamb, and the spotted and speckled among the goats; and such shall be my wages. ³³ So my honesty will answer for me later, when you come to look into my wages with you. Every one that is not speckled and spotted among the goats and black among the lambs, if found with me, shall be counted stolen." ³⁴ Laban said, "Good! Let it be as you have said." ³⁵ But that day Laban removed the he-goats that were striped and spotted, and all the she-goats that were speckled and spotted, every one that had white on it, and every lamb that was black, and put them in charge of his sons; ³⁶ and he set a distance of three days' journey between himself and Jacob; and Jacob fed the rest of Laban's flock.

³⁷ Then Jacob took fresh rods of poplar and almond and plane, and peeled white streaks in

them, exposing the white of the rods. 38 He set the rods which he had peeled in front of the flocks in the runnels, that is, the watering troughs, where the flocks came to drink. And since they bred when they came to drink, 39 the flocks bred in front of the rods and so the flocks brought forth striped, speckled, and spotted. 40 And Jacob separated the lambs, and set the faces of the flocks toward the striped and all the black in the flock of Laban; and he put his own droves apart, and did not put them with Laban's flock. 41 Whenever the stronger of the flock were breeding Jacob laid the rods in the runnels before the eyes of the flock, that they might breed among the rods, 42 but for the feebler of the flock he did not lay them there; so the feebler were Laban's, and the stronger Jacob's. 43 Thus the man grew exceedingly rich, and had large flocks, maidservants and menservants, and camels and asses.

So far Jacob has been more or less at the mercy of his father-in-law, and torn between the rivalries of his wives. Even 14 years of his life have been signed over to Laban; but a signal has been given at last. Rachel, the favorite wife, barren for so long, has at last had a son. The interlude of serfdom is over for Jacob. Isaac has a grandson, and Jacob himself has a son—a son through whom the promise will be reactivated. Once again things may be expected to happen—freedom and prosperity, return to the destined land. The working of the promise has begun to move again with Joseph's birth.

Jacob resumes the initiative, which he appears to have lost for the last fourteen years, by requesting Laban's permission to return with his wives and children to his own place and land. Since Jacob is said to serve Laban for twenty years (31:38,41), the return must have been delayed for six more years, and the bargain about to be struck is regulative for Jacob's duties during those years.

The J witness contributes this story, and tells how two sharp businessmen drove what they thought was the best bargain they could. The bargaining is both progressive and repetitive. Verses 25–30 contain the negotiation; 31–34, the agreement; 35–41, its execution, 42, its outcome.

Jacob is said to ask that his wives and

children may accompany him. The release of a servant slave did not mean he took his wife and family with him, if the employer had given the wife (v. 43; cf. 21:4–6). Jacob has thus made two requests. Laban's reply is gracious and cooperative. *If you will allow me to say* represents the Hebrew, "If I have at all found favor in your eyes." This is Laban's way of admitting the justice of Jacob's claim that he has served Laban well. He also goes on to say "I have also divined," i.e., "the omens tell me" (cf. 44:5,15; 1 Kings 20:33). Laban brings the preliminary parley to an end by agreeing in general to Jacob's request, but he interprets that request as one for a bigger wage. Following the LXX, RSV omits the first Hebrew word of verse 28, "And he said." If retained, it could be rendered "and he concluded, name your wages." In verse 29 Jacob goes over his claim more fully. By referring again to the quality of his own personal service, the welfare and increase of Laban's cattle, Jacob strengthens his own case in the complicated quasi-legal argument between two men, neither of whose cases is quite clear. In verse 30, *increased abundantly* represents the Hebrew "broken forth to multiply," and *wherever I turned* renders the Hebrew "at my foot." Then from out of his strong position Jacob makes clear that he seeks none of Laban's money or livestock. Jacob's willingness to serve Laban without pay is unexpected, but is the crux of the story. Jacob will serve Laban for nothing provided he will agree to the following arrangement.

Some doubt exists concerning this arrangement. Since sheep are normally white, and goats dark or black, black sheep and spotted or speckled goats will be the minority. Jacob proposes to remove this minority of oddly colored animals from the flocks. Jacob then says, *Such shall be my wages,* meaning he will be content to take the oddly colored animals then existing and be content with them. But such a view is hard to reconcile with the later arrangements which Jacob works out to increase the oddly colored animals.

Jacob's proposal then probably means that the properly and oddly colored animals are to be separated; that he is to receive no payment for the time being; that he will shepherd only the properly colored, and that his honesty (lit., my righteousness) will be vouched for by the fact that Laban will find no oddly colored animals in the flocks later. This is, however, exactly what Jacob is working for, to ensure the birth and retention of the oddly colored animals. No fewer than five adjectives are used to describe the oddly colored animals. The distinction between striped and spotted animals first appears in 31:8, but must have some bearing on 30:37–42.

Difficulties arise on either view, and the narrative must be very condensed and must originally have illustrated Jacob's words in 31:6–7 when he complained that Laban kept on changing (lit., ten times) the terms of the bargain. The effect, however, is clear. Jacob was to keep the oddly colored animals born to the naturally colored animals. To achieve this he adopted several devices. He surrounded the white ewes with colored sticks, so they bore particolored young (vv. 37–39). He then kept the naturally and oddly colored flocks apart, but in such a way that the oddly colored were ever in sight of the naturally colored, and so influenced them (v. 40). He set up the peeled rods only when the stronger ewes were copulating (vv. 41–42).

Laban must have been greatly surprised by Jacob's apparent generosity, and no doubt was put on his guard thereby. He took steps to safeguard himself, for he not only separated the animals himself, but also removed his part of the flocks three days journey away so as to ensure that there would be no interbreeding.

Jacob carried out his plans. He *took fresh rods of poplar and almond and plane* and peeled them to show the white pith beneath. The green and white rods were thus oddly colored and so affected the animals in conception. Such practices apparently reflect widespread beliefs concerning the effects of environment on breeding habits and results.

Thus Jacob, by his own skill, knowledge, and experience, becomes very wealthy, though in 31:5–12 he ascribes his success to divine favor. Verse 43 *grew exceedingly rich* renders the same Hebrew verb noted above (30:30).

6. Jacob's Separation from Laban (31:1–55)

This chapter describes the concluding act of the threefold account of Jacob's dealings with Laban—his arrival, his stay, and now his departure. In verses 1–16 Jacob justifies his proposed flight; verses 17–21 record his flight; 22–25, Laban's pursuit; 26–43, their fierce altercation; 43–55, their treaty of understanding and separation.

(1) Jacob's Proposed Flight (31:1–16)

[1] Now Jacob heard that the sons of Laban were saying, "Jacob has taken all that was our father's; and from what was our father's he has gained all this wealth." [2] And Jacob saw that Laban did not regard him with favor as before. [3] Then the LORD said to Jacob, "Return to the land of your fathers and to your kindred, and I will be with you." [4] So Jacob sent and called Rachel and Leah into the field where his flock was, [5] and said to them, "I see that your father does not regard me with favor as he did before. But the God of my father has been with me. [6] You know that I have served your father with all my strength; [7] yet your father has cheated me and changed my wages ten times, but God did not permit him to harm me. [8] If he said, 'The spotted shall be your wages,' then all the flock bore spotted; and if he said, 'The striped shall be your wages,' then all the flock bore striped. [9] Thus God has taken away the cattle of your father, and given them to me. [10] In the mating season of the flock I lifted up my eyes, and saw in a dream that the he-goats which leaped upon the flock were striped, spotted, and mottled. [11] Then the angel of God said to me in the dream, 'Jacob,' and I said, 'Here I am!' [12] And he said, 'Lift up your eyes and see, all the goats that leap upon the flock are striped, spotted, and mottled; for I have seen all that Laban is doing to you. [13] I am the God of Bethel, where you anointed a pillar and made a vow to me. Now arise, go forth from this land, and return to the land of your birth.' " [14] Then Rachel and Leah answered

him, "Is there any portion or inheritance left to us in our father's house? [15] Are we not regarded by him as foreigners? For he has sold us, and he has been using up the money given for us. [16] All the property which God has taken away from our father belongs to us and to our children; now then, whatever God has said to you, do."

Some telltale words in verse 18 indicate a note from the P witness, but the narrative as a whole is the work of the E witness, though some comments from the J witness too are scattered through the chapter. Verses 1–3 appear to be the notes of the J witness who points a human reason, the criticism of Jacob's conduct by Laban's sons, and a divine reason, a precise instruction from the Lord for Jacob's departure. *Wealth* in verse 1 represents the Hebrew word for "glory" (cf. Psalm 49:17; Isa. 10:3; 66:12).

The E witness also gives both a human and a divine reason for Jacob's departure: Laban's changed attitude toward Jacob (v. 2); and a precise instruction from the God of Bethel (v. 13). The E witness then employs Jacob's clandestine conversation with his two wives as the means whereby he can bring home to his wives the unreasonable and unjust conduct of their father to him, and also justify his acceptance of the divine command that he with them should return to his homeland.

This parenthetical conversation is chiefly remarkable for the further light it throws on the happenings in the previous chapter. Jacob charges his father-in-law with cheating (v. 7), literally, mocking; "ten times" means, of course, time and time again (cf. Num. 14:22), and only by divine favor was Jacob able to overcome all his difficulties. Verses 8–9 describe the continuous action over the best part of six years. In verses 10–13 two brief revelations belonging originally to separate occasions are grouped together as if they were one revelation. The first revelation from *the angel of God* (the divine messenger) belongs to the beginnings of the struggle with Laban but the theophany of verse 13 belongs obviously

toward the end. *I am the God of Bethel.* These are obviously the opening words of a fresh revelation (cf. 28:10 ff.). The Hebrew is strictly, "I am the god, Bethel," or else the Hebrew should be expanded, as the LXX, to read: "I am the god who appeared to thee in Bethel." The Targums suggest a similar expansion. The E witness thus shows in this way that Jacob's devices for the increase of the oddly colored animals, no less than the decision to leave Laban, are divinely inspired.

Jacob's argument is stated against a legal background which he does not himself employ. In response to his statement, his wives state that legal background. They point out: (a) that no interest in the family estate remains to them; (b) that they are already regarded as not really belonging to their father's house, but are counted as strangers or foreigners (cf. Gen. 17:12); (c) that their father sold them, and no portion of the dowry (i.e., Jacob's labors) will ever benefit them; and (d) that what Jacob has gained is compensation for the above losses and are due to them and their children.[20]

The agreement of Leah and Rachel is remarkable, and also shows that they were well aware of what was legally at stake. It appears that their third claim shows that Laban had defrauded them, too, and thus had broken certain laws. They do not merely sympathize with Jacob or agree with his side of the story. They either point out the real meaning of Jacob's argument or they add this legal interpretation to strengthen Jacob's attitude, and justify their decision to go along with their husband.

The version of the E witness thus tends to put Jacob in a very favorable light. It is God who has really ruled the affair, by frustrating Laban, prospering Jacob, and summoning him back home. This "moral purification" (von Rad) of Jacob is almost complete, but not quite. Verse 12 suggests

[20] Cf. Millar Burrows, "The Complaint of Laban's Daughters," *Journal of the American Oriental Society* 57 (1937), pp. 259–76.

that Jacob's frustration of Laban was also divinely inspired. This verse is difficult for those like von Rad who wish to see a complete moral purification in the story, and so they reject it. But it claims to be retained as what is left of Jacob's crude belief that his devices for defeating Laban also came from God.

(2) Flight and Pursuit (31:17–24)

¹⁷ So Jacob arose, and set his sons and his wives on camels; ¹⁸ and he drove away all his cattle, all his livestock which he had gained, the cattle in his possession which he had acquired in Paddanaram, to go to the land of Canaan to his father Isaac. ¹⁹ Laban had gone to shear his sheep, and Rachel stole her father's household gods. ²⁰ And Jacob outwitted Laban the Aramean, in that he did not tell him that he intended to flee. ²¹ He fled with all that he had, and arose and crossed the Euphrates, and set his face toward the hill country of Gilead. ²² When it was told Laban on the third day that Jacob had fled, ²³ he took his kinsmen with him and pursued him for seven days and followed close after him into the hill country of Gilead. ²⁴ But God came to Laban the Aramean in a dream by night, and said to him, "Take heed that you say not a word to Jacob, either good or bad."

So Jacob flees with his family and possessions, and crossing the Euphrates reached Gilead. Rachel, without Jacob's knowledge, takes Laban's household gods with her. Jacob chose a good time—the time and feast of sheep-shearing (1 Sam. 25). Even so, Laban heard of Jacob's flight as soon as it was possible for him to do so (because they were separated by a journey of three days; cf. 30:36). The long journey required the use of camels (cf. 24:61), but how Jacob came by them is not known. *Outwitted* in verse 20 is for the Hebrew "stole the heart of," i.e., heart as the seat of the intelligence.

Laban is described as the Aramean only here and in verse 24. He is said to speak Aramaic in verse 47. The *Euphrates* represents the Hebrew for "the river." The hill country of Gilead is the area north and south of the river Jabbok, east of Jordan,

from just south of the Sea of Galilee to just north of the Dead Sea.

The distance of 350 miles from Haran to Gilead is probably far too far for a journey of only seven days. Laban's anxieties, in face of Jacob's successes and boldness, well up in a dream. Taking the form of a warning, regarded as of divine origin, not to do any harm to Jacob (i.e., for fear of Jacob's retaliation), he was to *say not a word to Jacob, either good or bad*, i.e., "nothing at all." Laban must have lived a long way from Haran to have made the journey in the time, or else the days allowed for the journey are too few. On the other hand Laban traveled light, and if he took seven days, Jacob must have taken far longer. The three days between the location of the flocks is also an unknown factor.

(3) Reproaches and Accusation (31:25–42)

²⁵ And Laban overtook Jacob. Now Jacob had pitched his tent in the hill country, and Laban with his kinsmen encamped in the hill country of Gilead. ²⁶ And Laban said to Jacob, "What have you done, that you have cheated me, and carried away my daughters like captives of the sword? ²⁷ Why did you flee secretly, and cheat me, and did not tell me, so that I might have sent you away with mirth and songs, with tambourine and lyre? ²⁸ And why did you not permit me to kiss my sons and my daughters farewell? Now you have done foolishly. ²⁹ It is in my power to do you harm; but the God of your father spoke to me last night, saying, 'Take heed that you speak to Jacob neither good nor bad.' ³⁰ And now you have gone away because you longed greatly for your father's house, but why did you steal my gods?" ³¹ Jacob answered Laban, "Because I was afraid, for I thought that you would take your daughters from me by force. ³² Any one with whom you find your gods shall not live. In the presence of our kinsmen point out what I have that is yours, and take it." Now Jacob did not know that Rachel had stolen them.

³³ So Laban went into Jacob's tent, and into Leah's tent, and into the tent of the two maidservants, but he did not find them. And he went out of Leah's tent, and entered Rachel's. ³⁴ Now Rachel had taken the household gods and put them in the camel's saddle, and sat

upon them. Laban felt all about the tent, but did not find them. ³⁵ And she said to her father, "Let not my lord be angry that I cannot rise before you, for the way of women is upon me." So he searched, but did not find the household gods.

³⁶ Then Jacob became angry, and upbraided Laban; Jacob said to Laban, "What is my offense? What is my sin, that you have hotly pursued me? ³⁷ Although you have felt through all my goods, what have you found of all your household goods? Set it here before my kinsmen and your kinsmen, that they may decide between us two. ³⁸ These twenty years I have been with you; your ewes and your she-goats have not miscarried, and I have not eaten the rams of your flocks. ³⁹ That which was torn by wild beasts I did not bring to you; I bore the loss of it myself; of my hand you required it, whether stolen by day or stolen by night. ⁴⁰ Thus I was; by day the heat consumed me, and the cold by night, and my sleep fled from my eyes. ⁴¹ These twenty years I have been in your house; I served you fourteen years for your two daughters, and six years for your flock, and you have changed my wages ten times. ⁴² If the God of my father, the God of Abraham and the Fear of Isaac, had not been on my side, surely now you would have sent me away emptyhanded. God saw my affliction and the labor of my hands, and rebuked you last night."

Laban finally overtook Jacob and his family. Both parties appear to be encamped on some unnamed hill. The location is uncertain, but the best location appears to be somewhere in the northeastern border of Gilead. Jacob is not said to cross the Jabbok until 32:23. The reference to Mizpah in verse 49 and Judges 10:17 is too indeterminate, because there could be many such watchtowers, which is what Mizpah means. The hill country in Gilead, north of the river Jabbok, known as the Jebel 'Ajlun, seems best to fit the story.

Laban's complaints are skilfully presented. He begins with the obvious, and in the role of a wronged father charges Jacob with cheating (i.e., stealing the heart, v. 26; cf. 20:5), and stealing his daughters in a secret flight. Had he known he would have sent Jacob on his way with a fanfare after having kissed them good-bye! This sentimental and ludicrous pose fits the part beautifully. Laban's attitude changes when

he tells Jacob that but for a divine warning he could have dealt seriously with him. The expression, *It is in my power* (v. 29), represents the Hebrew, "There is to the god of (or) to the power of my hand," i.e., it is entirely within my power. The climax comes when Laban recognizes Jacob's desire to return home, but not even that justifies the theft of his household gods. In reply, Jacob confesses his fears that Laban would have withheld his daughters from him, but recognizes the gravity of Laban's final accusation. He sentences the thief who stole the gods to death, and in so doing is unaware that he has sentenced his own beloved Rachel to death (cf. 38:24; Judg. 11:31).

The household gods (*t*ᵉ*raphim*) are small religious object(s), with the mask, or face or figure of a man (1 Sam. 19:13,16), used at home and in the sanctuary (Judg. 17:5; 18:14; Hos. 3:4), often for divination (Zech. 10:2; Ezek. 21:21). Although the word is plural, one object is probably meant, and Laban means to find it. He goes anxiously from tent to tent, without success. Rachel is in fact sitting on it on a saddle litter, a sort of howdah, and she begs to be excused from rising because she is in the middle of menstruation (Gen. 18:11; Lev. 15:19). So Laban fails to find them. Rachel's behavior suggests an utter ridicule of idolatry, but she at least is concerned to conceal it. In her uncleanness (Lev. 15:19 ff.) she sat on the holy thing.

This theft of the gods is the point of the passage. Rachel has stolen the gods, not because she is a godly girl or because she wanted to ensure for her husband the blessings of her family gods upon her new home, but because, according to the laws of Nuzi, the person who could show possession of the household gods could claim a legal right to the family estate in question.

By her theft Rachel had taken the law into her own hands, and was laying claim to a part of her father's estate of which they all believed he had robbed them. Thus in the light of archeological discovery, the central point of the story is discovered, and is seen to rest on a legal custom of those days.[21]

With such a firm historical feature in sight, it is difficult not to believe that the other great feature of the Laban-Jacob traditions—the mutual trickery—is historical too. The final act of the treachery is thus described: the father who has robbed his own daughter (29:25; 31:16) is now in turn tricked by her.

Laban's failure to find his god(s) enables Jacob to take full advantage of Laban's discomfiture. Jacob rhetorically demands what misconduct on his part could justify such a pursuit and such a search. Laban has found not even household goods, let alone household gods. In verses 38–42 Jacob, with great eloquence, recounts the hardships of a shepherd's life, in which he had triumphed. His care had prevented miscarriages (Ex. 23:26; Job 21:10); he even bore losses himself (Ex. 22:12); Laban has been an exacting employer; thefts by day or night were restored (Ex. 22:11); he has suffered exposure and loss of sleep. In verse 41 he summarizes his life with Laban, and attributes to his family God all his own success. Here the God of Abraham ('El Shaddai) and Isaac's God, the Fear (or Kinsman) of Isaac, are assimilated, as later they were at one time identified with Yahweh.

(4) Agreement (31:43–55)

[43] Then Laban answered and said to Jacob, "The daughters are my daughters, the children are my children, the flocks are my flocks, and all that you see is mine. But what can I do this day to these my daughters, or to their children whom they have borne? [44] Come now, let us make a covenant, you and I; and let it be a witness between you and me." [45] So Jacob took a stone, and set it up as a pillar. [46] And Jacob said to his kinsmen, "Gather stones," and they took stones, and made a heap; and they ate there by the heap. [47] Laban called it Jegarsahadutha: but Jacob called it Galeed. [48] Laban said, "This heap is a witness between you

and me today." Therefore he named it Galeed, [49] and the pillar Mizpah, for he said, "The LORD watch between you and me, when we are absent one from the other. [50] If you ill-treat my daughters, or if you take wives besides my daughters, although no man is with us, remember, God is witness between you and me."

[51] Then Laban said to Jacob, "See this heap and the pillar, which I have set between you and me. [52] This heap is a witness, and the pillar is a witness, that I will not pass over this heap to you, and you will not pass over this heap and this pillar to me, for harm. [53] The God of Abraham and the God of Nahor, the God of their father, judge between us." So Jacob swore by the Fear of his father Isaac, [54] and Jacob offered a sacrifice on the mountain and called his kinsmen to eat bread; and they ate bread and tarried all night on the mountain.

[55] Early in the morning Laban arose, and kissed his grandchildren and his daughters and blessed them; then he departed and returned home.

Laban reverts to legal arguments. Everything is his, but, as is said in England, possession is nine-tenths of the law—Jacob holds possession. So Laban proposes and Jacob accepts a treaty of friendship based on the status quo. In this paragraph the evidence of the hands of both the J and E witnesses is apparent. Two names, Galeed and Mizpah, are mentioned; a cairn, to witness that Jacob will not maltreat Laban's daughters, and a stone pillar (monolith) to witness a boundary beyond which neither will pass with evil intent. No doubt this pillar was erected at some prominent point where it could be widely observed. A covenant meal is mentioned twice (46, J and 54, E). This covenant meal signifies kinship, reconciliation, and as here, agreement. It resembles the later sacrifice known as the peace offering (cf. Ex. 18:12; 24:11; 32:6; 1 Sam. 9:13; Psalm 22:26).

These duplications suggest that two agreements are present, one recorded by the J witness in 46–50; the other by the E witness in 51–54. In 47, the words Jegar-sahadutha are Aramaic for "the heap of witness," and in 49, The Lord watch between you and me does not mean "the Lord be with you till we meet again," but let the Lord keep a lookout lest either of

---

[21] Cf. Cyrus H. Gordon, "The Story of Jacob and Laban in the Light of the Nuzi Tablets," Bulletin of the American Schools of Oriental Research 66, 1937, pp. 25–27. Cf. C. J. Mullo Weir, "Nuzi," in Archeology and Old Testament Study, pp. 73–86.

us should plan any evil toward the other.

The second agreement suggests a tribal as well as a personal agreement about a landmark now named *Mizpah,* in which Laban and Jacob represent the Syrians and Israel, whose borders adjoin in northeastern Gilead. Similarly *the God of Abraham* represents Jacob's side, and *the God of Nahor* Laban's side, for the custom was to vest such treaties in the gods of both parties. The Hebrew word for *judge* is plural, though the words *God of their father* identifies both gods as the one God of their common father Terah. The quoted phrase is not in the LXX and may be a gloss to identify as one God two gods originally distinct. Jacob further invokes his own personal God, his father's God, *the Fear of . . . Isaac.*

Radical scholars have been inclined to think that this second agreement, the story of which originally arose out of the need to explain the landmark, related to Israelite settlers in Gilead and a Laban Aramean tribe settled not at Haran but in the Gilead area. Thus in time the story created to explain a landmark, used in turn as a frontier agreement, eventually became associated with Jacob. The story of this agreement is the oldest part of the narrative and is now set in the context of family life. This roundabout reconstruction illustrates the dangers of presuppositions in biblical exegesis.

The more realistic presupposition assumes that the Laban-Jacob cycle is the account, largely reliable, of the rise of Jacob's family inside Laban's household, and that it goes back, to the middle of the second millenium B.C. At times the mind and language of the witnesses reappear, and at times portions, like this treaty, are adapted and set in a larger, tribal according to some, and indeed national framework (cf. 1 Kings 22:3 ff.; 2 Kings 8:12; 10:33; Amos 1:3), reflecting the period 860–770 B.C.

After all the celebrations were ended, Laban takes leave of his daughters and their families and returns home. Jacob thus comes to the end of a long but formative period in his life, and resumes his homeward way.

Laban is one of the less pleasing characters in the portrait gallery of Genesis. He is a hard and grasping man, marked by a specially strong self-interest, and is not at all selective in the means he adopts to achieve his ends. His greed, duplicity and downright cheating are plain for all to see. To a lesser extent these same characteristics were present in his sister Rebekah, and in his two daughters, as well as in Jacob.

Obviously, all these are members of one family group, faithfully portrayed in the tradition. The alternative is to suppose that the stories are fictitious and that the witnesses have specially invented these doubtful characteristics in this particular family group. Perhaps Jacob would not have behaved so badly had Laban not first broken faith with him and indeed consistently treated him badly. Jacob is generally the victim, and so perhaps the moralization of his character, found to be specially typical of the presentation by the E witness, may have some foundation in fact.

7. Return and Reconciliation (32:1—33:20)

On his return journey Jacob experiences several encounters. After the episode with Laban, the mysterious and brief visitation at Mahanaim, the preparations for the meeting with Esau, the mysterious struggle at Penuel south of Jabbok, and the dramatic encounter with Esau, he arrives and purchases land at Shechem.

(1) Mahanaim (32:1–2)

¹ Jacob went on his way and the angels of God met him; ² and when Jacob saw them he said, "This is God's army!" So he called the name of that place Mahanaim.

On his way Jacob was suddenly encountered by divine messengers. Some have found evidence of a hostile nuance in the word *met,* "fell upon." As he saw the messengers, Jacob deduced that he was at

God's camp, and so he named the locality *Mahanaim,* literally, two camps, i.e., hardly God's and his own, but more likely an anticipatory reference to verses 7 f. and 10 below. If there is a hostile aspect in the story, and this is not inevitable, then the angels may have been thought to resent human intrusion at a sacred enclave. The meaning of the story is the discovery of a sacred place to which the encounter with the angels is ancillary.

Mahanaim must be north of Jabbok (cf. v. 23), on the border of Gad (Josh. 13:26) and Bashan (Josh. 13:30), and not far from the Jordan (Gen. 32:10). It was presumably the capital of Ishbosheth, Saul's son (2 Sam. 2:8), and David's headquarters during Absalom's revolt (2 Sam 17:24,27), and the capital city for one of Solomon's taxation districts (1 Kings 4:14). The present story thus describes the discovery of the site and Jacob's association with it, and comes from the E witness.

(2) *Preparing to Meet Esau (32:3-21)*

³ And Jacob sent messengers before him to Esau his brother in the land of Seir, the country of Edom, ⁴ instructing them, "Thus you shall say to my lord Esau: Thus says your servant Jacob, 'I have sojourned with Laban, and stayed until now; ⁵ and I have oxen, asses, flocks, menservants, and maidservants; and I have sent to tell my lord, in order that I may find favor in your sight.' "

⁶ And the messengers returned to Jacob, saying, "We came to your brother Esau, and he is coming to meet you, and four hundred men with him." ⁷ Then Jacob was greatly afraid and distressed; and he divided the people that were with him, and the flocks and herds and camels, into two companies, ⁸ thinking, "If Esau comes to the one company and destroys it, then the company which is left will escape."

⁹ And Jacob said, "O God of my father Abraham and God of my father Isaac, O Lord who didst say to me, 'Return to your country and to your kindred, and I will do you good,' ¹⁰ I am not worthy of the least of all the steadfast love and all the faithfulness which thou hast shown to thy servant, for with only my staff I crossed this Jordan; and now I have become two companies. ¹¹ Deliver me, I pray thee, from the hand of my brother, from the hand of Esau, for I fear him, lest he come and slay us all, the mothers with the children.

¹² But thou didst say, 'I will do you good, and make your descendants as the sand of the sea, which cannot be numbered for multitude.' "

¹³ So he lodged there that night, and took from what he had with him a present for his brother Esau, ¹⁴ two hundred she-goats and twenty he-goats, two hundred ewes and twenty rams, ¹⁵ thirty milch camels and their colts, forty cows and ten bulls, twenty she-asses and ten he-asses. ¹⁶ These he delivered into the hand of his servants, every drove by itself, and said to his servants, "Pass on before me, and put a space between drove and drove." ¹⁷ He instructed the foremost, "When Esau my brother meets you, and asks you, 'To whom do you belong? Where are you going? And whose are these before you?' ¹⁸ then you shall say, 'They belong to your servant Jacob; they are a present sent to my lord Esau; and moreover he is behind us.' " ¹⁹ He likewise instructed the second and the third and all who followed the droves, "You shall say the same thing to Esau when you meet him, ²⁰ and you shall say, 'Moreover your servant Jacob is behind us.' " For he thought, "I may appease him with the present that goes before me, and afterwards I shall see his face; perhaps he will accept me." ²¹ So the present passed on before him; and he himself lodged that night in the camp.

The J witness now contributes a story which illustrates Jacob's character very clearly. He shows Jacob as fearful, yet pacific at heart; willing to make some amends at some cost to himself, yet resolved to retain as much as he possibly can of his fortune. He also shows withal the religious background to Jacob's life.

Jacob's servile and conciliatory message only elicits the news that Esau is on his way from Edom, where he has apparently moved, with four hundred men. Esau's intentions are not stated. In distress, Jacob divides his possessions into two parts (lit., two camps) in the hope that if Esau captures one part (camp) the other part (camp) will escape; he then resorts to prayer.

When in his youth the late Sir Winston Churchill was captured by the Boers, he said: "I prayed long and earnestly." Jacob too in a crisis prays, though he shows no mood of confession or penitence. The prayer, born of the passing crisis follows a well-defined pattern. Verse 10 is the invocation coupled with the Hebrew participial *who didst say to me* reference to God's grace in the past; verse 11 is the self-depreciatory recital of his own fortunes; verse 12 turns to the future, with a petition for deliverance and indeed is the grounding of that petition in the divine promises. The phrase *the mothers with the children* is in Hebrew, "Mother with (or upon or over) child" (cf. Hos. 10:14). The references to two camps in Jacob's precautions (vv. 7–8), and in his prayer (v. 10) probably explain verse 2. Jacob is seeking to impress Esau and also to safeguard himself. The prayer is almost a perfect pattern of its kind, and because it does not possess the poetic style, including parallelism, or the usual diction of the Psalms, it must be a very early if free composition of what Jacob said in his prayer.

The prayer serves as a vigil for the Penuel incident, as the reassurance for the confrontation with Esau and as the preparation for the return to the Promised Land.

Following the division of his possessions into two camps and his prayer, Jacob, still at Mahanaim, now prepares a present from the one-half of his possessions he has with him. The word for *present* means not a tax or tribute, but a gift designed to win favor. The gift itself comprised some 580 head of the five kinds of beasts he had; these were divided into (three) droves, led and followed by servants, separated by good distances. Precise instructions are given to the (three) servants who precede and (the three who) follow each drove. Their story will be consistent (v. 18). Jacob's staggered presents suggest a naïve mentality, hoping for a cumulative effect. Yet Esau in turn proved to be no less naïve. Jacob hopes for a reconciliation, costly in terms of goods but painless personally to him. "I may appease him" is literally "cover his face" and is the Levitical word for "covering sin" by sacrifice, i.e. hiding it from God. The laws render it "make atonement for."

In the Hebrew of verse 20 the words "his face" and "my face" occur twice. Literally translated, verse 20 reads: "I may cover his face with the present that goes before my face, and afterward I shall see his face, and perhaps he will lift up my face." Some have seen these "face" references as anticipatory of the Penuel (face of God) story following, but the fourfold reference to "face" in verse 21 is due to Hebrew idiom and hardly anticipates the divine face of verses 22–32. In verse 21 we are told that that night Jacob lodged in the camp at Mahanaim.

(3) Struggle at Penuel (32:22-32)

22 The same night he arose and took his two wives, his two maids, and his eleven children, and crossed the ford of the Jabbok. 23 He took them and sent them across the stream, and likewise everything that he had. 24 And Jacob was left alone; and a man wrestled with him until the breaking of the day. 25 When the man saw that he did not prevail against Jacob, he touched the hollow of his thigh; and Jacob's thigh was put out of joint as he wrestled with him. 26 Then he said, "Let me go, for the day is breaking." But Jacob said, "I will not let you go, unless you bless me." 27 And he said to him, "What is your name?" And he said, "Jacob." 28 then he said, "Your name shall no more be called Jacob, but Israel, for you have striven with God and with men, and have prevailed." 29 Then Jacob asked him, "Tell me, I pray, your name." But he said, "Why is it that you ask my name?" And there he blessed him. 30 So Jacob called the name of the place Peniel, saying, "For I have seen God face to face, and yet my life is preserved." 31 The sun rose upon him as he passed Penuel, limping because of his thigh. 32 Therefore to this day the Israelites do not eat the sinew of the hip which is upon the hollow of the thigh, because he touched the hollow of Jacob's thigh on the sinew of the hip.

Verse 22 does not naturally follow 21, and some words or even an episode may have fallen out. Likewise some confusion exists between verses 22–23. In verse 22 Jacob and everybody with him crossed the Jabbok, but in verse 23 Jacob has everybody else cross and remains behind alone. Some have claimed that verse 24 must be divided between E and J, but Driver gains a good result, harmonious with what follows, by omitting the last 7 words of verse

22 and the first 3 words of verse 23, though he thereby loses the name Jabbok.[22] Most probably then verse 22 describes the crossing while in process and 23–24a the result. Jacob was passing to and fro across the river, but in the end remained behind alone.

As the narrative stands, Mahanaim and Penuel could be the same place, unless Penuel was immediately on the north bank of the Jabbok, and Mahanaim some miles farther north. "Everything that he had": the Heb. does not have the word "Everything." It rests on the Samaritan Pentateuch, LXX, Syriac, and Latin versions.

Jabbok is the river Zerkha (Blue River), and divides Gilead into two halves. Rising west of Rabbah Ammon it makes a wide arc through the northwest and falls through a great gorge nearly 30 miles long into the Jordan about 25 miles north of the Dead Sea.

In his loneliness Jacob found himself in a wrestling match until dawn with a man whom he only later recognized from his strength and authority to be God disguised as a man. The Hebrew word for *wrestled,* only here and verse 25, is chosen because it resembles the word for Jabbok. The "unknown" unable to vanquish Jacob appears to foul him, for he touches, i.e., hits him on, the socket of his thigh bone, so that Jacob's thigh is dislocated; but with that touch the unknown assailant has also revealed his supernatural identity.

Jacob, with the stranger firmly in his grasp, seeks to extract a blessing from him, and the story now begins to ascend into a more spiritual dimension of meaning. The stranger confers a blessing in the form of a new name—Israel—for Jacob. *For you have striven with God and with men, and have prevailed* (cf. Hos. 12:4). This last clause, though it may only give the reason for the imparting of the blessing, is more

commonly thought to be a play on the name Israel. *Israel* means God strives, but this becomes "he who strives with God." Others have taken the word to mean "he who perseveres" or "prevails" with God.

Such meanings suggest that Jacob had really won the fight, because the stranger, whose fighting time is limited to darkness, begs to be released and admits that Jacob has prevailed. The words *with men* may refer to his earlier struggles with Esau and Laban. Indeed the stranger only secures his release through the touch described above. These are the elements of the lowest level of the story, but to these the loftier theme of the blessing and the new name has been added. The visitant is able to withhold his own name.

Finally Jacob names the place Peniel (the face of God), and so the story reaches its highest level. Jacob has wrestled with God, seen his face, and still lives (cf. Ex. 33:20; Judg. 6:22; 13:22). In the morning Jacob passes by Penuel (site unknown), limping on his thigh; and so in honor of this event Israelites do not eat the sinew of the hips, the sciatic nerve, from those animals lawful to them to eat. This fact is not mentioned elsewhere in the Old Testament, but the rule is enjoined in the Mishnah (*Chullin* 7). Perhaps a ritual dance involving the imitation of limping was once characteristic of the ceremonies at the Penuel shrine. (The only difference between the words Peniel and Penuel is a grammatical case in old Hebrew which need not concern us further. For Penuel cf. Judg. 8:8 f.; 1 Kings 12:25). One wonders whether Jacob had developed in the later part of his life those symptoms now known as an arthritic hip.

Note on Jacob's Struggle

Although 32:22–32 is a separate story with several levels of meaning, it gains in importance when seen in the light of the context of the biography of Jacob. The two parts of the great journey of his lifetime may be set forth as follows:

---

22 Driver's reconstruction (WC *Genesis,* p. 294) reads: "22 And he rose up that night and took his two wives, and his two handmaids, and his eleven children, 23 and sent them over the stream, and sent over all that he had."

His defrauding of
Esau
His departure

The episode at
Bethel
  (a) The ladder

  (b) The theoph-
any

Struggle with La-
ban

The struggle with
Laban
His departure
His reconcilation
with Laban
The episode on the
return
  (a) Divine camp
at Maha-
naim
  (b) Struggle at
Penuel
  (c) His new
name
Reconciliation with
Esau
The Shechem epi-
sodes
Return visit to
Bethel

The two parts of Jacob's journey are thus approximately parallel to each other. It seems reasonable to suggest that what Bethel and its discoveries did for Jacob on his forward journey out of the land, Mahanaim and Penuel did for Jacob as he was about to cross the Jordan on his return. If Bethel represents divine assurances to the fleeing Jacob, then Penuel represents the qualifying of Jacob for return to and residence within the divinely promised homeland. This qualifying is seen in the giving of the new name as the outcome of Jacob's struggle with God.

At the same time the parallel is not artificially constructed. If such a parallel had been the literary invention of the witnesses or of the editor, then surely the return visit of Jacob to Bethel (ch. 35) would have stood solitary as a monumental equivalent of the Bethel incident on the forward journey. In Jacob's biography however the second Bethel visit is at present a consequence and sequel of the first.

Jacob's return journey is much more crowded with incidents, incidents which broke up any artificial symmetry between the two parts of the journey, and which could not be left out because they were so essentially part of that tradition to which the witnesses testify.

The struggle at Penuel was a further illustration of Jacob's great physical strength (29:10); it was a struggle for life. The struggle also illustrates Jacob's courage, but most of all his willingness to struggle with God for his grace and blessing. In that sense Jacob mirrors the upper side of his people's character.

The story is not a dream, a vision, a theophany, or an allegory. It is a real physical encounter with some explicable features to which all these layers of meaning belong. But its chief importance lies in its meaning for Jacob's biography, for it undoubtedly marks the turning point in his life. This is the end product in the light of which all the other and lower levels of meaning must be seen.

Behind him lies a life of deception and of struggle. Rebekah, his own mother, and Laban, her brother, are the evil geniuses of his life. The attack of the assailant is the accusation of his own conscience, opposing, denouncing, and condemning the kind of life which Jacob had led up to this point. So at this turning point Jacob is subjected to this struggle, the supreme test of his life, and, when physically disabled, proffers his elemental prayer for blessing from the assailant. In turn, the assailant counters this prayer by requesting Jacob's name, and Jacob is compelled to surrender his identity. He is thus revealed to his divine assailant as Jacob, the shady trickster of the events so far narrated. But this Jacob is now locked in a struggle with God and seeks of his own free will to obtain God's blessing. Then it is that Jacob is given his new name. At the very least the new name, as for Abram—Abraham (17:5) and Sarai—Sarah (17:15), means a change in status and in relation with God, and so in character too. His new name is an honorable name.

The contest at Penuel is thus finally seen as a test for his fitness to take up his new life in the Promised Land. The heir of the promises, son of Isaac and grandson of Abraham, must qualify in his own life as the bearer of the promises and of the blessing in the land promised to his family. It is a fact that thereafter, after some diplomatic resourcefulness (ch. 33), deceit and fraud are absent from his behavior, and Jacob is seen in the rest of Genesis as "a just and God-fearing Israelite." The ultimate victor is God who preserves the secret of his own identity, and yet resumes his purposes in the transformed life of Jacob. (cf. Driver, p. 297, for a list of typical homiletical expositions of the passage.)

(4) Jacob and Esau Reconciled (33:1–20)

¹ And Jacob lifted up his eyes and looked, and behold, Esau was coming, and four hundred men with him. So he divided the children among Leah and Rachel and the two maids. ² And he put the maids with their children in front, then Leah with her children, and Rachel and Joseph last of all. ³ He himself went on before them, bowing himself to the ground seven times, until he came near to his brother.
⁴ But Esau ran to meet him, and embraced him, and fell on his neck and kissed him, and they wept. ⁵ And when Esau raised his eyes and saw the women and children, he said, "Who are these with you?" Jacob said, "The children whom God has graciously given your servant." ⁶ Then the maids drew near, they and their children, and bowed down; ⁷ Leah likewise and her children drew near and bowed down; and last Joseph and Rachel drew near, and they bowed down. ⁸ Esau said, "What do you mean by all this company which I met?" Jacob answered, "To find favor in the sight of my lord." ⁹ But Esau said, "I have enough, my brother; keep what you have for yourself." ¹⁰ Jacob said, "No, I pray you, if I have found favor in your sight, then accept my present from my hand; for truly to see your face is like seeing the face of God, with such favor have you received me. ¹¹ Accept, I pray you, my gift that is brought to you, because God has dealt graciously with me, and because I have enough." Thus he urged him, and he took it.
¹² Then Esau said, "Let us journey on our way, and I will go before you." ¹³ But Jacob said to him, "My lord knows that the children are frail, and that the flocks and herds giving suck are a care to me; and if they are overdriven for one day, all the flocks will die. ¹⁴ Let my lord pass on before his servant, and I will lead on slowly, according to the pace of the cattle which are before me and according to the pace of the children, until I come to my lord in Seir."
¹⁵ So Esau said, "Let me leave with you some of the men who are with me." But he said, "What need is there? Let me find favor in the sight of my lord." ¹⁶ So Esau returned that day on his way to Seir. ¹⁷ But Jacob journeyed to Succoth, and built himself a house, and made booths for his cattle; therefore the name of the place is called Succoth.
¹⁸ And Jacob came safely to the city of Shechem, which is in the land of Canaan, on his way from Paddanaram; and he camped before the city. ¹⁹ And from the sons of Hamor, Shechem's father, he bought for a hundred pieces of money the piece of land on which he had pitched his tent. ²⁰ There he erected an altar and called it El-Elohe-Israel.

The honor for the narrative about the meeting of the two brothers belongs to the J witness, though P has added verse 18, and the E witness the notice in verses 19–20.

On the near approach of Esau, Jacob divided his own camp into three parts. No doubt fortified by his physical strength, he changes his strategy and now himself leads the van and behind him were arranged his wives' maids and children, then Leah and hers, lastly Rachel and her precious Joseph, i.e., the least valued in front. Rachel at the rear might escape if flight should prove necessary.

Jacob obsequiously approaches Esau with a sevenfold obeisance, characteristic of Canaanite kings in their letters to their Egyptian overlord as described in the Tell El Amarna letters (fourteenth century B.C.). Esau is accompanied by 400 men, perhaps to impress Jacob but possibly with hostile intent, but he is won over to a most generous forgiveness by the diplomacy of Jacob. Esau embraces his brother and receives each company in turn. How well Jacob had schooled them all in their submissive role. To see the scene pass before the eyes is entrancing, so vivid and clear is the description. Esau refuses his brother's gift, but then shows still further generosity in agreeing to accept the gift pressed upon him (32:13,21). In verse 10 the *present* is described by the usual word, but in verse 11 a synonym is used. The synonym translated by RSV as *gift* is the Hebrew word for blessing (cf. 1 Sam. 25:27; 30:26;

2 Kings 5:15). Jacob pays Esau a high compliment in saying of him "as one seeth the face of God" (cf. 43:3,5). Perhaps a parallel to Penuel is intended. There a divine antagonist passes from hostility to friendliness; here Esau does the same.

Now Esau offers his company as a vanguard, but Jacob declines on the ground that his company with its nursing animals could not keep pace with Esau. Jacob promises to follow Esau to Edom. Esau then offers a posse of his men to accompany Jacob, but Jacob again refuses. He desires his independence. Esau departs on his long journey to Edom, and Jacob goes to Succoth (i.e., not Edom). Jacob appears to have deceived Esau about his destination.

Esau took a great journey to meet his brother, and it is evident that during the twenty years he has grown in stature. He is as impulsive as ever (v. 4), but he has matured and prospered. He behaves most generously toward Jacob, far better than Jacob deserved. Yet so marked is the change in Esau's character—once rude now princely—and so great the distances involved, that some have supposed two separate Esaus, or two sets of traditions about Esau: in one he is located in Gilead as in this story, and in the other in the deep south of Edom.

Difficult as these different portrayals are, no better explanation has yet been forthcoming than the account in the biography of Jacob.

Esau now disappears from the stories of the J and E witnesses, and he only reappears in the burial notice of Isaac, his father, supplied by P in 35:29.

After the brothers parted, Jacob journeyed to Succoth, the site of which is not known. The place is nearer the Jordan than Penuel, and it is mentioned in Joshua 13:27; Judges 8:5,6,8, as being east of Jordan in the territory of Gad. The halt at Succoth obviously lasted some time, and probably Jacob reconnoitered Shechem from there.

From Succoth he crossed the Jordan and made his way safely, literally, in peace, to Shechem, where outside the city he bought a piece of ground. Perhaps this ground is the area around the present Jacob's well, not mentioned in the Old Testament (cf. John 4:6,12). Reference to this ground is made in the notice of Joseph's burial (Josh. 24:32), as Abraham had purchased in the South a burial plot for Sarah, and so began the symbolic title to the land. Jacob now has a plot in the North and so begins symbolically Israel's possession of the North. Jacob, for a sum that cannot now be calculated, bought the ground from the principal clan at Shechem (cf. 34:2; Judg. 9:28). The Hebrew word q°sitah may be a weight or a coin (cf. Josh. 24:32; Job 42:11 only in O.T.).

Erected represents a Hebrew verb which is never otherwise used of the erection of an altar. Perhaps the word pillar was original here. Jacob names the altar or pillar "El, the God of Israel"; i.e., the altar bears the name of the God to whom it is dedicated. Israel of course means not Jacob here, but Israel, the people. Ancestor, land, home, and worship are thus united in this notice.

XVII. Dinah and Shechem (34:1-31)

¹ Now Dinah the daughter of Leah, whom she had borne to Jacob, went out to visit the women of the land; ² and when Shechem the son of Hamor the Hivite, the prince of the land, saw her, he seized her and lay with her and humbled her. ³ And his soul was drawn to Dinah the daughter of Jacob; he loved the maiden and spoke tenderly to her. ⁴ So Shechem spoke to his father Hamor, saying, "Get me this maiden for my wife." ⁵ Now Jacob heard that he had defiled his daughter Dinah; but his sons were with his cattle in the field, so Jacob held his peace until they came. ⁶ And Hamor the father of Shechem went out to Jacob to speak with him. ⁷ The sons of Jacob came in from the field when they heard of it; and the men were indignant and very angry, because he had wrought folly in Israel by lying with Jacob's daughter, for such a thing ought not to be done.

⁸ But Hamor spoke with them, saying, "The soul of my son Shechem longs for your daughter; I pray you, give her to him in marriage. ⁹ Make marriages with us; give your daughters to us, and take our daughters for yourselves.

10 You shall dwell with us; and the land shall be open to you; dwell and trade in it, and get property in it." 11 Shechem also said to her father and to her brothers, "Let me find favor in your eyes, and whatever you say to me I will give. 12 Ask of me ever so much as marriage present and gift, and I will give according as you say to me; only give me the maiden to be my wife."

13 The sons of Jacob answered Shechem and his father Hamor deceitfully, because he had defiled their sister Dinah. 14 They said to them, "We cannot do this thing, to give our sister to one who is uncircumcised, for that would be a disgrace to us. 15 Only on this condition will we consent to you: that you will become as we are and every male of you be circumcised. 16 Then we will give you our daughters to you, and we will take your daughters to ourselves, and we will dwell with you and become one people. 17 But if you will not listen to us and be circumcised, then we will take our daughter, and we will be gone."

18 Their words pleased Hamor and Hamor's son Shechem. 19 And the young man did not delay to do the thing, because he had delight in Jacob's daughter. Now he was the most honored of all his family. 20 So Hamor and his son Shechem came to the gate of their city and spoke to the men of their city, saying, 21 "These men are friendly with us; let them dwell in the land and trade in it, for behold, the land is large enough for them; let us take their daughters in marriage, and let us give them our daughters. 22 Only on this condition will the men agree to dwell with us, to become one people: that every male among us be circumcised as they are circumcised. 23 Will not their cattle, their property and all their beasts be ours? Only let us agree with them, and they will dwell with us." 24 And all who went out of the gate of his city hearkened to Hamor and his son Shechem; and every male was circumcised, all who went out of the gate of his city.

25 On the third day, when they were sore, two of the sons of Jacob, Simeon and Levi, Dinah's brothers, took their swords and came upon the city unawares, and killed all the males. 26 They slew Hamor and his son Shechem with the sword, and took Dinah out of Shechem's house, and went away. 27 And the sons of Jacob came upon the slain, and plundered the city, because their sister had been defiled; 28 they took their flocks and their herds, their asses, and whatever was in the city and in the field; 29 all their wealth, all their little ones and their wives, all that was in the houses, they captured and made their prey. 30 Then Jacob said to Simeon and Levi, "You have brought trouble on me by making me odious to the inhabitants of the land, the Ca-naanites and the Perizzites; my numbers are few, and if they gather themselves against me and attack me, I shall be destroyed, both I and my household." 31 But they said, "Should he treat our sister as a harlot?"

Dinah, daughter of Jacob and Leah and mentioned otherwise only at 30:21 and 46:15, is the victim heroine of this dramatic chapter. During a visit to the women of Shechem, she is seen, seized, and raped by Shechem, son of Hamor. The action is greatly condemned, but an agreement is reached where Shechem and Dinah are to wed, the two families to merge, but the men of Shechem are to submit to circumcision. When the men of the city are ill after the operation, two of Dinah's brothers, Simeon and Levi, kill them all, and all the brothers plunder the city. Jacob disapproves of the violence of his sons. The action and highly dramatic movement of the plot are vividly illustrated by the use of the verbs in verses 2,5,7,26–29.

The analysis of the narrative is difficult, and most scholars have seen in the narrative a combination of two sources. Some have even ventured to identify these as the J witness and the P witness; others have not been so confident. The problem resides not so much in the differences of vocabulary and diction as in the personal and communal elements of the story. The rape of Dinah is a personal story. But that two men, Simeon and Levi, could have killed the male population of a city is difficult, so that *Simeon and Levi* must here represent tribal elements. The analysis has thus pursued the personal and communal elements as two sources. But these elements are too much interwoven and the narrative too much integrated for such a solution.

Similarly, to make the story entirely personal is difficult because of the tribal activity of Simeon and Levi. On the other hand to make it tribal throughout ignores the entirely personal adventure of Dinah, which is really personal and not the story of how an Israelite clan called Dinah achieved a footing near Shechem.

We, therefore, have to think of one

story, essentially from the J witness, in which personal and collective elements are combined in sequence. The violation of Dinah leads to an attack by some Israelite tribes on the city of Shechem.[23] Indeed from now on in Genesis the narratives will often exhibit a pronounced collective feature; whereas, up to this point the stories have been largely concerned with individuals and a family.

The personal story of Dinah is thus embedded in the larger context of the penetration of some Israelite tribes into the Shechem area. This event took place before the exodus and before the settlement of those Israelite tribes which came out from Egypt under Moses. This Shechem penetration is thus pre-Mosaic and is probably pre-Amarna age too. In short, the account inaugurates the long association of Israelite tribes with Shechem.

The story tends to break off suddenly leaving Simeon and Levi masters of the scene. This same event is, however, probably referred to in 49:5-9, where the military and ruthless character of these two tribes is described. Their fate however was to lose their footing around Shechem and to be dispersed in Israel, i.e., through the land. Nevertheless Jacob had bought land there, and Israelites remained in the locality (cf. 37:12-14). Further, Joshua's conquest of the land, related in the book of Joshua, does not necessitate the conquest of Shechem (but cf. 48:22), and the conquest of Shechem is not related. Joshua 24 presupposes the conquest of Shechem and gives an account of the character of the covenant set up between those Israelites long settled around Shechem, and who had become Canaanized, and Joshua's Israelites who had come from the desert and from Egypt. This seems best to explain the fact that Shechem is not listed in the conquest traditions among the cities captured by the Israelites, or which remained independent.

Tribal history is thus setting in in chapter

34, and in the traditions of any given person or event an interaction between personal and collective is visible. Not separate sources but layers of meaning appear to be the best solution of this all-important narrative. Even the figure of Jacob himself exhibits the personal and communal aspects. In the body of the story he is the aging Jacob—weak, indecisive, and ignored. In verse 30 he is the voice of the people of Israel.

At 30:21 and 31:41, Dinah and most of her brothers were quite small children. So some years must have passed, for she and the brothers mentioned in this chapter are now grown up. She was six when the family left her grandfather's home, and it follows that a number of years must have been spent at Succoth and near Shechem. Jacob too is much older and is more a background figure. Dinah is shown to be conversant with the area and the people. She goes visiting the women of the countryside, which suggests familiarity with the area.

Shechem's father is named a Hivite, but here, as in Joshua 9:7, the LXX reads Horite for Hivite (cf. 10:17). Hurrians are known to have settled in central Palestine before the fourteenth century, but perhaps a precise racial connection is once again unnecessary, and Hivite or Horite is simply a general term for the Canaanite dweller of the land.

Hamor, which means ass and thus may have some further reference not precisely known to us, is known as *the prince*, a word characteristic of the P witness (17:20; 23:6; 25:16). *Shechem*, who is certainly an individual in this passage, noticed Dinah, carried her off and seduced her. Love rather than the more usual repugnance (cf. 2 Sam. 13:15) ensued, and Shechem desired to marry her. In verse 17 Dinah is still with the Shechemites; so, pending negotiation, she was detained. Shechem sought to comfort and woo her.

When Jacob hears of the event and of the marriage proposal made by Hamor for his son (cf. Judg. 14:2), he holds his

---

[23] For a parallel, cf. Charles M. Doughty, *Travels in Arabia Deserta* (London: Jonathan Cape, 1936), II, 114.

counsel until his sons, away shepherding and herding over a wide area, return home. Their reaction is threefold. They are *very angry;* they describe Shechem's action as *folly*—a strong word reserved mainly for sexual evil; it is a shuddering wickedness in which the whole community feels itself involved (cf. Deut. 22:21; Judg. 20:6,10). They condemn the folly as something contrary to Israelite practice, i.e., contrary to custom, mores, or, to use the proper word, contrary to the *mishpat*—the rule that obtained in Israel (20:9; 29:6; 2 Sam. 13:12). By his reference to *in Israel* the witness or editor reveals a later standpoint, that of his own age.

Faced with such a position, Hamor renews and enlarges his proposal. He proposes a general relationship between the incoming family of Jacob and his own people. So he proposes intermarriage, integration of the peoples concerned with trade and property rights. The picture is not so much a settled agricultural community over against a more wretched landless immigrant group of nomads. Jacob is already a small landowner (33:19), and possessed of sufficient wealth to make the proposed arrangement profitable also to the Shechemites. In the parley Shechem is also present and presses his own plea for marriage. *Marriage present* does not mean dowry in our sense, but the price paid to the parents for their daughter (cf. Ex. 22:16 f.; 1 Sam. 18:25).

Jacob's sons apparently agree to the proposals on condition that the men of Shechem submit to be circumcised. Their real aim, however, is to destroy the Shechem men when they are ill from the operation. In their deceit Jacob's sons use an expression *and become one people* which recapitulates the total meaning of the proposal. The reference to Dinah in verse 17 does not conclusively say where she is, whether with the Shechemites or at home (cf. vv. 2,26).

So eager is Shechem for the marriage that he is circumcised forthwith, and no doubt hoped that his example, in view

of his personal position as *the most honored,* would be emulated. Hamor and his son call a meeting of the men of the city at the gate and publicly put the proposal to them for the first time. Hamor's speech is most persuasive. He emphasizes that Jacob's family is friendly; that the land is spacious, literally, broad in both hands (sides); and even the rather objectionable condition of circumcision is set amidst inducements of increasing wealth which the Shechemites will come to own.

Obviously Jacob and his family have been in the neighborhood for some time, and have amassed considerable possessions. *Property* (v. 23) is too precise, but property and land may be intended, in view of the Hebrew of verse 10 "and take possession in it," i.e., the land. Hamor even repeats the phrase "become one people," a community united in blood and by possessions. In verse 24, *all who went out of the gate* (cf. 23:10,18), i.e., the fighting men, so all the defenders of the city are out of action at the same time (cf. 17:23; Josh. 5:3 ff.).

In 25–31 the communal meaning is dominant throughout. The plan is carried out and total access to the city achieved, after the brothers (tribes), Simeon and Levi, had unhindered, i.e., without the inhabitants' knowledge, entered the city. The beginning of verse 26 seems to duplicate the end of verse 25, but the order of the Hebrew words in 26 shows that this is not true. At the end of verse 25 is a statement about the general massacre. Then verse 26 continues, "and (even) Hamor and (even) Shechem, his son, they slew with the sword." They are singled out because of the prominent part they have played in the events hitherto, and because the notice of their murder shows the completeness of the slaughter. The rest of the brothers (tribes) see the success of the initial attack and plunder the city.

Jacob condemns the affair from a practical rather than moral angle (49:6). Jacob fears the consequences for his whole people, in that they are exposed to the hatred and possible revenge of the majority in the area. *Brought trouble on me* is a strong word, meaning make turbid or undone. *Making me odious* is weaker than the Hebrew which reads, "make me to stink with." The narrative ends with the highly indignant question of outraged brothers.

XVIII. Jacob's New Name (35:1–29)

A cluster of stories and notices brings to an end the account of Jacob's fortunes. Thereafter he is increasingly a background figure until his demise is reported in chapter 49.

The first of the group of stories is concerned with the abolition of idolatry, followed by the second visit to Bethel; death and burial of Rebekah's nurse, Deborah; Benjamin's birth at the expense of his mother's (Rachel) life; Reuben's incest; Jacob's sons and Isaac's death and burial.

The P witness contributed verses 9–13 and 22b–29, and the remainder is from the E witness.

1. Return to Bethel (35:1–15)

[1] God said to Jacob, "Arise, go up to Bethel, and dwell there; and make there an altar to the God who appeared to you when you fled from your brother Esau." [2] So Jacob said to his household and to all who were with him, "Put away the foreign gods that are among you, and purify yourselves, and change your garments; [3] then let us arise and go up to Bethel, that I may make there an altar to the God who answered me in the day of my distress and has been with me wherever I have gone." [4] So they gave to Jacob all the foreign gods that they had, and the rings that were in their ears; and Jacob hid them under the oak which was near Shechem.
[5] And as they journeyed, a terror from God fell upon the cities that were round about them, so that they did not pursue the sons of Jacob. [6] And Jacob came to Luz (that is, Bethel), which is in the land of Canaan, he and all the people who were with him, [7] and there he built an altar, and called the place Elbethel, because there God had revealed himself to him when he fled from his brother. [8] And Deborah, Rebekah's nurse, died, and she was buried under an oak below Bethel; so the name of it was called Allonbacuth.
[9] God appeared to Jacob again, when he came from Paddanaram, and blessed him. [10] And God said to him, "Your name is Jacob; no longer shall your name be called Jacob, but Israel shall be your name." So his name was called Israel. [11] And God said to him, "I am God Almighty: be fruitful and multiply; a nation and a company of nations shall come from you, and kings shall spring from you. [12] The land which I gave to Abraham and Isaac I will give to you, and I will give the land to your descendants after you." [13] Then God went up from him in the place where he had spoken with him. [14] And Jacob set up a pillar in the place where he had spoken with him, a pillar of stone; and he poured out a drink offering on it, and poured oil on it. [15] So Jacob called the name of the place where God had spoken with him, Bethel.

No indication is given as to the length of time that Jacob spent in the vicinity of Shechem, or how long a time elapsed before he resumed his journey to the south, but 35:5 indicates an immediate departure. A divine command compels him to ascend to Bethel, one thousand feet or so above Shechem. The story presents a number of interesting parallels to the narratives.

The word to *go up* inevitably suggests "to make a pilgrimage," because sanctuaries were so often on elevated ground (cf. 1 Sam. 1:3; Psalm 122:4). Thus it has been claimed that this story is either the prototype of annual pilgrimage from Shechem to Bethel, or a deduction from that pilgrimage now adapted as a part of Jacob's return journey.[24] Certainly pilgrimage ideas appear to have influenced the narrative; e.g., washing and change of garments (Ex. 19:10; Josh 7:13; 1 Sam. 16:5).

Again in the narratives of Israel's settlement the central ark shrine appears to have been moved from Shechem (Josh. 24:1,25) to Bethel (Judg. 20:26 f.) and so the prototypal journey of the ancestor was repeated actually and, later perhaps, in ritual ceremony as well.

A third feature is the abolition of idols. This is doubtless a direct reference to

24 Cf. Albrecht Alt, "Die Wallfahrt von Sichem nach Bethel," in *Kleine Schriften zur Geschichte des Volkes Israel* (Munich: C. H. Beck'sche Verlagsbuchhandlung, 1953) I, 79–88.

Rachel's teraphim (31:19). The action, however, is paralleled by the abolition of idols commanded by Joshua again in the days of the settlement at Shechem (Josh. 24:14,23). This association of the abandoning of idols with Shechem may well be one of the roots of that great antipathy to idols and idolatry seen in such books as Deuteronomy (cf. Josh. 24:25–27), and may well have significance for the origin and character of that book.

On the forward journey Jacob had vowed an oath to be fulfilled in return for God's gracious providence (28:20 ff.). He had seen almost all these acts fulfilled in the last 20 or 30 years of his life. He had not yet in fact reached his home (28:21), but he was well on the way. He is divinely reminded of his oath and obediently prepared to visit Bethel again. The erection of the altar is additional to 28:22, replacing the temple. *An altar to the God* does not properly represent the Hebrew which reads "an altar to 'El" (so v. 7 is lit., *'El of Beth'el*). In these references 'El is the great high God of Canaan, manifested in various forms—*'El Shaddai*, *'El Pachadh*, and here *'El Beth'el*. In 35:3 Jacob recalls the days of his distress under Laban (31:24,29,42) and the prosperity that did not forsake him. Earrings were obviously also amulets and associated with the idolatrous practices. For the oak at Shechem see 12:6. Jacob's action has the effect of defiling the oak. By the ritual actions Jacob and his family fit themselves to visit and enter the holy place. This general picture of intolerance of idolatry is of the very essence of Israel's Yahwism and its expression in an El of Bethel story shows further evidence of Yahwism in the Jacob stories.

A terror from God is that divine or numinous panic which falls on Israel's enemies during the course of Israel's Holy War on behalf of Yahweh (cf. Ex. 23:27; Josh. 10:10; Judg. 4:15; 7:22; 1 Sam. 14:15,20). Von Rad has rendered useful service in his analysis of the features of Israel's Holy War. In the present context it prevents any pursuit of Israel by the Shechemites. The reference here must be to the events of chapter 34 (cf. 48:22).

On arrival at Bethel, Jacob erected an altar and named the place, i.e., the sanctuary, "God of Bethel" (31:13). *There God had revealed himself.* This clause is interesting grammatically, for it could be translated, "There gods had revealed themselves," i.e., noun and verb are plural in form; or, "There divine beings (angels) had revealed themselves." The RSV rendering is best; i.e., the verb is plural because it is construed with a noun (God) plural in form but singular in meaning. The phrase thus illustrates this singular-plural polarity in Israel's idea of God.

The reference to *Deborah* (v. 8), Rebekah's nurse (24:59), is very puzzling, for she had accompanied Rebekah to Canaan 140 years ago (cf. 25:20). The verse shows that some kind of communication must have been maintained between Jacob and his family during the absence from home. Had Rebekah died and Deborah joined Jacob at Shechem? Some such explanation seems best. Otherwise we must suppose that apart from 32:3 (cf. 27:45) there was no communication with the family. Judges 4:5 mentions "a palm of Deborah between Ramah and Bethel." This could of course mean the heroine of that chapter, but it could of course refer to the Deborah of Genesis and so be the origin of the tradition of Judges 4:5. Verses 14–15 may be partly a sequel to verse 8, or better a parallel to 28:18. The poured out drink offering of wine (Ex. 29:40; 2 Kings 16:13) is a frequent feature of Israel's worship both to Yahweh and otherwise (cf. Jer. 7:18; Isa. 57:6). Verse 15 is obviously a parallel to 28:19 (J.), to 35:7 (E), and so is a repetition of 35:7, or a stray verse from the P witness.

These verses, together with 22b–29 are the sum and substance of what the P witness has to report concerning Jacob. The terminology of P is apparent in the verses; e.g., Paddan-aram, *'El Shaddai*, and the terms of verses 11–12. These verses thus witness independently to the tradition concerning Jacob. Jacob receives a new name (32:28), Israel,[25] and the promises given to Abram-Abraham concerning offspring and territory are renewed to Jacob (17:1,6,8) in similar terms. In particular the royal cast of P's account of the revelation is again manifest.

The context of verses 9–13 shows the location of the theophany to be Bethel, though these verses themselves give no hint of the place. According to 32:28 Jacob received his new name at Penuel, but the context here is Bethel. Obviously Bethel was very important in the traditions of all these witnesses—J, E and P—and Jacob's new name also a firm part of the tradition. The P witness could hardly have contributed verse 14, for he nowhere speaks of altars or worship in Genesis. His view is that all these were part of the revelation to Moses (Ex. 25—31), and they could not have anticipated that revelation.

In his account the P witness confines himself to the bare bones of the divine revelation, the briefest summary record of God's transactions with Jacob. On the other hand the witnesses J and E include illustrations of the day-to-day story of Jacob's life. In theological summary then, and in the homely happenings of life, the divine purpose is expressed and worked out. It is no less present because it may not be so obvious in life's daily tale.

2. Death of Rachel (35:16–21)

16 Then they journeyed from Bethel; and when they were still some distance from Ephrath, Rachel travailed, and she had hard labor. 17 And when she was in her hard labor, the midwife said to her, "Fear not; for now you will have another son." 18 And as her soul was departing (for she died), she called his name Benoni; but his father called his name Benjamin. 19 So Rachel died, and she was buried on the way to Ephrath (that is, Bethlehem), 20 and Jacob set up a pillar upon her grave; it is the pillar of Rachel's tomb, which is there to this day. 21 Israel journeyed on, and pitched his tent beyond the tower of Eder.

25 Cf. O. Eissfeldt, C. A. H. Fas. xxvi A, p. 4.

The birth of Benjamin (vv. 16–21) completes Jacob's family which is now listed (vv. 22–26). The account of Isaac's death and burial completes the record of his life. The beginning of verse 16 repeats as it also continues the beginning of verse 5. The verb used means basically to pull up the tent pegs, and the imperative of the verb is sometimes printed on the green light of traffic signs in modern Israel.

The site of *Ephrath* is unknown, though it is here identified with *Bethlehem.* Two traditions of the location of Rachel's grave exist. A monument to Rachel is still to be seen about one mile north of Bethlehem and four miles south of Jerusalem. (Cf. Y. Aharoni "Beth-haccherem," in *Archaeology and Old Testament Study,* pp. 171-84). But Rachel is the mother of Joseph and Benjamin and traditions about her would be expected in those tribal areas. Thus 1 Samuel 10:2 describes Rachel's tomb as being on "the (N) border of Benjamin," i.e., not far from Bethel which is some ten miles north of Jerusalem. Jeremiah 31:15 speaks of Rachel weeping at Ramah, which is five miles north of Jerusalem. Ephrath must be some unknown locality north of Jerusalem, or it may be Ophrah in Benjamin (Josh. 18:23) to be distinguished from Ophrah of the Abiezrites (Manasseh), mentioned in Judges 6:24. Of course the actual identification of Ephrath with Bethlehem is against this second view. So too are the words *still some distance* by which RSV inadequately translates "by the length of the land." A literal interpretation would point to the Bethlehem locality, but 2 Kings 5:19 suggests a short distance.

Near Ephrath Jacob's twelfth son, Rachel's second boy, was born and here too Rachel died, and her grave is marked by a tombstone (pillar). Before she died she was told she had a second son (cf. 30:24), whom she named "Son of my sorrow," but her husband later changed the name to *Benjamin*—Son of the right hand; i.e., the right hand is the auspicious hand. After Rachel's burial, Israel, Jacob under his new name, resumed his journey. *The tower of Eder* is the tower of the flock. Many such towers would exist in the pastures and on the hillsides for protection of the flocks. The tower here appears to be a particularly well-known one, and it has been located at Bethlehem and at Jerusalem (Mic. 4:8).

The first part of verse 22 is a notice of the wicked behavior of Reuben, Jacob's eldest son. He lay with Bilhah, Rachel's maid, and his father's second concubine. A double significance seems to attach to this crime. It is the crime of incest, but since Reuben, the eldest son, is the guilty party, his action is open to the further interpretation that he thereby announced his intention of taking his father's place (cf. 2 Sam. 16:20–23; 1 Kings 2:13–25). This would point to Jacob's increasing age and feebleness. Genesis 49:4 (and Deut. 33:6) refers to this crime and the "pre-eminence" is withheld from him; i.e., he loses the rights of the firstborn (1 Chron. 5:1). The punishment thus did fit the crime. No doubt 35:22 once contained the sentence of deposition, or of the curse which is the basis of 49:4. The present ending of 22a, *and Israel heard,* is clearly incomplete.

3. Jacob's Sons (35:22–26)

22 While Israel dwelt in that land Reuben went and lay with Bilhah his father's concubine; and Israel heard of it.

Now the sons of Jacob were twelve. 23 The sons of Leah: Reuben (Jacob's first-born), Simeon, Levi, Judah, Issachar, and Zebulun. 24 The sons of Rachel: Joseph and Benjamin. 25 The sons of Bilhah, Rachel's maid: Dan and Naphtali. 26 The sons of Zilpah, Leah's maid: Gad and Asher. These were the sons of Jacob who were born to him in Paddanaram.

As Jacob almost reaches home again, the P witness reminds us of the twelve sons that Jacob is about to introduce to his father. Jacob went out from home alone, and has now returned with all these children, just as later he went down into Egypt seventy souls, and his people returned from there as a great company (Ex. 1:1–7).

Dinah is not mentioned in the present list.

Although all the information is already known to us, the passage as a whole calls for several comments.

This list, which is arranged according to the four mothers, must be compared with the similar lists in 49:1–28; Numbers 26:5–51; Deuteronomy 27:12–13; 33:6–25, which are arranged differently.

Leah has six sons, Rachel two sons, and the maid of each wife has two sons each. Leah precedes Rachel, but the latter's maid precedes Leah's maid.

All these twelve sons are said to be born to Jacob in Paddan-aram, in Mesopotamia, but the J witness has only just reported that Benjamin was born in Canaan (35:18–19).

The Leah sons may have represented one confederation—a southern confederation of tribes—and the Rachel tribes a second but northern confederation. Both confederations, if they existed, then united to form the people Israel. The four concubine tribes, Dan and Naphtali, Gad and Asher, may represent four of the lesser Israelite tribes, and some of these, but not all, are reproached for inactivity in face of Israel's need (Judg. 5:17–18), while others of the main tribes are not even mentioned in Deborah's song (Judg. 5).

Interest centers on Benjamin; a tribe of Benjaminites is mentioned in the texts from the city of Mari (eighteenth century B.C., North Syria). The Benjaminites of Mari and the Israelite Benjaminites may have been related in some way, for links other than the name exist. (Cf. A. Parrot, "Mari," in Thomas, pp. 140 f.). The effect of this identification would be that a Benjaminite tribe existed before Jacob's days.

4. Death of Isaac (35:27–29)

27 And Jacob came to his father Isaac at Mamre, or Kiriatharba (that is, Hebron), where Abraham and Isaac had sojourned. 28 Now the days of Isaac were a hundred and eighty years. 29 And Isaac breathed his last; and he died and was gathered to his people, old and full of days; and his sons Esau and Jacob buried him.

Isaac, who according to 27:2,41, was not far from death, survived according to the chronology of the P witness for another eighty years, and thus lived to see the return of Jacob and all his children. When Jacob first left home he was about forty (cf. 26:34), and he was 120 years when his father died at the age of 180 years, for Isaac had begotten them when he was sixty (25:26).

His sons Esau and Jacob bury him, as Ishmael and Isaac had buried their father Abraham (25:8 f.). According to 49:30–31, Isaac and Rebekah were buried with Abraham and Sarah in the cave of Machpelah.

XIX. Descendants of Esau (36:1–43)

Just as the P witness reported the death and burial of Abraham (25:7–11), and then listed the descendants of Ishmael (25:12–17), so having reported the death and burial of Isaac, he now transmits the equivalent lists and notices concerning Esau. So farewell is taken of Esau and his fortunes, and the story henceforth centers on Jacob's, i.e., Israel's, descendants (37:2). The notices concerning Esau naturally fall here, but 36:6–8 could well have come after 28:9 as the necessary presupposition of 32:3. But chapter 36 usefully collects the facts concerning Esau.

The lists are extant summary tables of self-perpetuating facts which the P witness has preserved for posterity, and they are also given with variations in 1 Chronicles 1:35–54. The lists are probably of Israelite origin rather than Edomite, and show that contacts between early Edom and early Israel were maintained.

The land of Edom is called Mount Seir, which Yahweh had given to Esau (Deut. 2:5; Josh. 24:4). The northern boundary of Edom is the river Zered (Wadi Hesa) which flows from the east into the southeast end of the Dead Sea. Its western boundary for about one hundred miles was the Arabah, the southern extension of that sea. The southern and eastern boundaries are lost in deserts.

Israel and Edom are brothers. They both occupied territories in which they became the dominant powers, founding kingdoms. The history of the two people remained closely related.

The present chapter begins with a title (v. 1) and comprises six lists and one brief notice: verses 2–5, Esau's wives and sons; 6–8, Esau's migration; 9–14, Esau's descendants; 15–19, clan leaders of Edom; 20–30, Horite clans and leaders; 31–39, eight kings of Edom; 40–43, second list of clan leaders of Edom.

1. Esau's Family (36:1–5)

¹ These are the descendants of Esau (that is, Edom). ² Esau took his wives from the Canaanites: Adah the daughter of Elon the Hittite, Oholibamah the daughter of Anah the son of Zibeon the Hivite, ³ and Basemath, Ishmael's daughter, the sister of Nebaioth. ⁴ And Adah bore to Esau, Eliphaz; Basemath bore Reuel; ⁵ and Oholibamah bore Jeush, Jalam, and Korah. These are the sons of Esau who were born to him in the land of Canaan.

Esau is Edom (vv. 8,19; cf. 25:30). In verses 9 and 43 Esau is described as the father of Edom. So the connection between Esau and Edom is made in two ways. If 36:1 is not a title to the whole chapter, then it is the beginning of the first list in 2–5—Esau's wives and sons (cf. 1 Chron. 1:35–37).

This list must be contrasted with the lists in 26:34 and 28:9.

26:34 and 28:9	36:2–5 and 36:9–14
Judith, daughter of Beeri the Hittite;	Adah, daughter of Elon the Hittite;
Basemath, daughter of Elon the Hittite;	Oholibamah, daughter of Anah, the Horite;
Mahalath, daughter of Ishmael and sister of Nebaioth.	Basemath, daughter of Ishmael and sister of Nebaioth.

Obviously the two columns represent two different traditions into which an error has at some time crept. To suppose that

Esau really had five wives, or that the same wife had more than one name does not really solve the difficulty. That two traditions are present is shown by the presence of sons in the lists in chapter 36. The marriages and the births are said to have taken place in the land of Canaan before Esau's migration.

Some confusion also exists concerning Oholibamah, the daughter of Anah, the son of Zibeon the Hivite. In reading *son of Zibeon,* RSV follows Sam., LXX, and Syriac against the Hebrew which reads, "daughter of Zibeon." In verse 24 Anah is described as the son of Zibeon (cf. Driver). Zibeon is declared a Hivite but this is generally considered to be an error for Horite (cf. v. 20 where Zibeon is the son of a Horite). The Horites are the original inhabitants of the land of Edom, and they are sometimes described as cave dwellers in Edom. The Hivites appear to be widespread over the area; e.g., Shechem (34:2); Gibeon (Josh. 9:7; 11:19); Lebanon (Judg. 3:3); and Hermon (Josh. 11:3), and throughout the land (cf. 2 Sam. 24:7; 1 Chron. 2). Hivites are not known outside the Old Testament and since V and R are in Hebrew very similar letters, then perhaps by Hivites is intended the word Horites, and Horites are either Hurrians or a non-Hurrian people called Hivites in Edom.

Esau is said in 26:34 to marry two Hittite women, and in 28:9 an Ishmaelite woman. In 36:2 he marries a Horite (Hivite) woman, and from 36:12 and 22 it is clear that Esau's son Eliphaz married a Horite woman by the name of Timna. The first of these marriages undoubtedly took place in Canaan (v. 5), and so does not reflect the mixture of Esau and Horite groups in Edom, as the marriage of Eliphaz probably does. Since Esau's migration to the area of Edom is unexplained, it is possible that the explanation may be found in the influence of a Horite wife and her family upon Esau. This is the only clue to Esau's choice of the land of Edom. Five sons were born to Esau in Canaan.

Adah is also the name of Lamech's first wife (4:19), but most of the names only occur here and in 1 Chronicles. *Oholibamah* means tent of the high place (cf. Ex. 31:6), and for Basemath, see 1 Kings 4:15. The Samaritan Pentateuch reads Mahalath for Basemath here and in verses 4,9,13,17, following 28:9.

2. Esau's Migration (36:6–8)

⁶ Then Esau took his wives, his sons, his daughters, and all the members of his household, his cattle, all his beasts, and all his property which he had acquired in the land of Canaan; and he went into a land away from his brother Jacob. ⁷ For their possessions were too great for them to dwell together; the land of their sojournings could not support them because of their cattle. ⁸ So Esau dwelt in the hill country of Seir; Esau is Edom.

Esau migrates with all his household, including daughters not previously mentioned, and possessions from Canaan to *a land away.* At this point Syriac adds "of Seir," and probably this name has at some time been accidentally omitted. Verse 7 presupposes that the migration must have taken place after Jacob's return home (cf. 32:3). *Away from* could also be translated "on account of." The hill country of Seir is the high plateau east of the Arabah (cf. 14:6; 27:39).

3. Sons of Esau and Princes of Edom (36:9–19)

⁹ These are the descendants of Esau the father of the Edomites in the hill country of Seir. ¹⁰ These are the names of Esau's sons: Eliphaz the son of Adah the wife of Esau, Reuel the son of Basemath the wife of Esau. ¹¹ The sons of Eliphaz were Teman, Omar, Zepho, Gatam, and Kenaz. ¹² (Timna was a concubine of Eliphaz, Esau's son; she bore Amalek to Eliphaz.) These are the sons of Adah, Esau's wife. ¹³ These are the sons of Reuel: Nahath, Zerah, Shammah, and Mizzah. These are the sons of Basemath, Esau's wife. ¹⁴ These are the sons of Oholibamah the daughter of Anah the son of Zibeon, Esau's wife: she bore to Esau Jeush, Jalam, and Korah.

¹⁵ These are the chiefs of the sons of Esau. The sons of Eliphaz the first-born of Esau: the chiefs Teman, Omar, Zepho, Kenaz, ¹⁶ Korah, Gatam, and Amalek; these are the chiefs of

Eliphaz in the land of Edom; they are the sons of Adah. ¹⁷ These are the sons of Reuel, Esau's son: the chiefs Nathan, Zerah, Shammah, and Mizzah; these are the chiefs of Reuel in the land of Edom; they are the sons of Basemath, Esau's wife. ¹⁸ These are the sons of Oholibamah, Esau's wife: the chiefs Jeush, Jalam, and Korah; these are the chiefs born of Oholibamah the daughter of Anah, Esau's wife. ¹⁹ These are the sons of Esau (that is, Edom), and these are their chiefs.

Note the double title, one in verse 9 and the second in verse 10.

This list classifies Esau's descendants by his three wives, and the names here are communal rather than personal. If we exclude the concubine's son, Amalek, in verse 12, the number of clans is 12 (so Ishmael, 25:12–16). The sons of Oholibamah rank with the grandsons of the other two wives (cf. v. 18).

The list may be tabulated in this way.

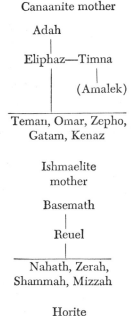

Hittite or
Canaanite mother

Adah
|
Eliphaz—Timna
| |
            (Amalek)
_____
Teman, Omar, Zepho,
Gatam, Kenaz

Ishmaelite
mother

Basemath
|
Reuel
|
_____
Nahath, Zerah,
Shammah, Mizzah

Horite
Mother

Oholibamah
|
_____
Jeush, Jalam, Korah

Eliphaz is the name of Job's senior friend (Job 2:11). Teman is often mentioned in the Old Testament as a district in northern Edom (Amos 1:12; Jer. 49:7; Ezek. 25:13). *Kenaz* is the ancestor of the Kenizzites, a group in southern Palestine later absorbed into Judah (15:19; Num. 32:12; Josh. 14; Judg. 1:13; 3:9). *Amalek* is a concubine, i.e., inferior tribe, and probably a part of the people known to the Old Testament as the Amalekites.

Basemath's son bears the name *Reuel,* and this is one of the names of Moses' father-in-law who was a Midianite (Ex. 2:18). Nearly all the remaining names can be paralleled from the Old Testament.

The word chief in Hebrew really means a thousand or family, indicating a leader of a thousand (cf. Ex. 15:15; Zech. 12:5 f.), a usage probably limited to Edom. This list in verses 15–19 is identical with the list of 9–14 except that *Korah* (v. 16) is wrongly introduced from verse 18; that is, from *Oholibamah* to *Adah. Amalek* shares an equal status in this list. The chiefs are virtually personifications of the tribal groups, but the sense would be best brought out by translating, "The chief of Teman," "the chief of Omar," etc.

Verse 19 appears to have the form of double ending—*sons* and *chiefs.* Consideration of these three lists reveals a pattern common to all of them.

4. Sons of Seir, the Horite (36:20–30)

²⁰ These are the sons of Seir the Horite, the inhabitants of the land: Lotan, Shobal, Zibeon, Anah, ²¹ Dishon, Ezer, and Dishan; these are the chiefs of the Horites, the sons of Seir in the land of Edom. ²² The sons of Lotan were Hori and Heman; and Lotan's sister was Timna. ²³ These are the sons of Shobal: Alvan, Manahath, Ebal, Shepho, and Onam. ²⁴ These are the sons of Zibeon: Aiah and Anah; he is the Anah who found the hot springs in the wilderness, as he pastured the asses of Zibeon his father. ²⁵ These are the children of Anah: Dishon and Oholibamah the daughter of Anah. ²⁶ These are the sons of Dishon: Hemdan, Eshban, Ithran, and Cheran. ²⁷ These are the sons of Ezer: Bilhan, Zaavan, and Akan. ²⁸ These are the sons of Dishan: Uz and Aran. ²⁹ These are the chiefs of the Horites: the chiefs Lotan,

Shobal, Zibeon, Anah, 30 Dishon, Ezer, and Dishan; these are the chiefs of the Horites, according to their clans in the land of Seir.

The list in these verses is concerned with the autochthonous inhabitants of Seir as distinct from the immigrants of Esau and his descendants. Deuteronomy 2:12 records that the sons of Esau dispossessed and replaced the Horites of Seir. The information is early, unique, and as yet cannot be confirmed or checked. Some of the names appear to have a Hurrian flavor and this helps to establish the connection with the Hurrians, a people who migrated into Mesopotamia and into Syria and Palestine in the second millennium B.C.

The list also shows that there were seven main branches of the Horites—*Lotan, Shobal, Zibeon, Anah, Dishon, Ezer, and Dishan* (vv. 20–21), repeated exactly in verses 29–30. But of these Anah reappears under Zibeon, and Dishon under Anah; i.e., Anah and Dishon figure as sons and grandsons of Seir, who is here treated as a person.

Some German scholars (Ewald and Dillman) identify Seir's eldest son Lotan with Lot, father of Moab and Ammon (19:30). The names of these men pass before us, and each name conceals a lifetime hidden and undiscoverable. Then suddenly a memorable event persisted in transmission and it is reported that Anah as he pastured his father's asses, suddenly discovered *hot springs in the wilderness.* Perhaps good fortune favored him or perhaps he really was more adventurous and made his discovery where others were afraid to venture. The Hebrew word translated "hot springs" only occurs here, and the translation is not certain. The seventh name is *Dishan* and this is very similar to the fifth name *Dishon.* LXX reads Rishon for Dishan (and in vv. 21,30). *Uz* is probably a branch of the Aramean Uz (cf. 10:23; 22:21). Verse 29 adds the information that Seir's seven sons (vv. 20–21) were also the clan leaders of the Horites.

The philologists point out that a large number of the names in verses 20–30 end in "an" or "on," suggesting that this nunation (use of *n*) was characteristic.

5. Kings and Chieftains in Edom (36:31–43)

31 These are the kings who reigned in the land of Edom, before any king reigned over the Israelites. 32 Bela the son of Beor reigned in Edom, the name of his city being Dinhabah. 33 Bela died, and Jobab the son of Zerah of Bozrah reigned in his stead. 34 Jobab died, and Husham of the land of the Temanites reigned in his stead. 35 Husham died, and Hadad the son of Bedad, who defeated Midian in the country of Moab, reigned in his stead, the name of his city being Avith. 36 Hadad died, and Samlah of Masrekah reigned in his stead. 37 Samlah died, and Shaul of Rehoboth on the Euphrates reigned in his stead. 38 Shaul died, and Baalhanan the son of Achbor reigned in his stead. 39 Baalhanan the son of Achbor died, and Hadar reigned in his stead, the name of his city being Pau; his wife's name was Mehetabel, the daughter of Matred, daughter of Mezahab.
40 These are the names of the chiefs of Esau, according to their families and their dwelling places, by their names: the chiefs Timna, Alvah, Jetheth, 41 Oholibamah, Elah, Pinon, 42 Kenaz, Teman, Mibzar, 43 Magdiel, and Iram; these are the chiefs of Edom (that is, Esau, the father of Edom), according to their dwelling places in the land of their possession.

The list of eight Edomite kings is important in itself as a piece of ancient history, but it is also important because of the comparisons which the list evokes with Israel's history.

Esau is the firstborn, and obviously achieved a state organization before Israel. Along with Moab and Ammon the Edomites are part of that Aramean migration which peopled these areas from about the twelfth century onward. The Edomites appear to have had eight kings before Saul ruled Israel. Numbers 20:14 and Judges 11:17 record kings of Edom, so that these kings cover the two centuries before Saul, back perhaps to the days of Moses. The writer responsible for the comparative note in verse 31, must of course have written after monarchy had become established in Israel.

None of the eight kings is said to be the son of his father. Perhaps then the Edomite monarchy was elective. Each king is mentioned along with his city, just as Saul remains closely connected with Gibeah. **Bela the son of Beor** may be the same person as Balaam son of Beor (Num. 22–24). **Bozrah** is known in the Old Testament as one of the principal Edomite cities (cf. Amos 1:12; Isa. 63:1): now Buseireh, 35 miles north of the Dead Sea.

Hadad is the name of an Aramean deity, and figures prominently in the names of the Aramean–Syrian kings; e.g., Benhadad and Hadadezer (cf. 1 Kings 11:14 ff.).

Shaul is the same name as the Israelite Saul. The river may be the Euphrates; if so Saul would be a foreigner to Edom. **Baal-hanan** means Baal is gracious, which indicates Baal worship but not necessarily in Edom. Baal-hanan was also the name of the man who slew Goliath (2 Sam. 21:19—El-hanan). So it has been conjectured that David's birth name was El (Baal) hanan, and David was his dynastic name. In turn, Shaul and Baal-hanan could also be the two first kings of Israel. The eighth king is **Hadar**—neither his death nor his successor is mentioned.

The last list enumerates eleven chiefs of Esau, and the names of almost half of them figure in verses 10–39. The explanation that this list incompletely duplicates previous names is no more certain than the view that the eleven here mentioned are the heads of subdistricts of Edom, possibly after Edom had lost its independence (cf. 2 Sam. 8:14). This cannot be proved, but if it is feasible then this list may be the latest in time, and that a rough chronological order may be discerned when the lists are numbered in this sequence: 20–30, Horite chiefs; 15–19 as parallel to 9–14, and 40–43.

Chiefs Timna, Alvah, . . . means of course chief of Timna, chief of Alvah, etc. **Elah** is probably Elath, the seaport on the Gulf of Aqaba. **Pinon** is probably the Punon of Numbers 33:42 f. The reference to Esau and Edom may link this sixth list with the second in 9–14.

XX. Joseph's Youth and Betrayal (37:1–36)

These chapters comprise the last principal section of the book of Genesis, and, apart from chapter 38, tell the story of Joseph, Jacob's firstborn by his favorite wife, Rachel.

The title is seen in verse 2 "These are the generations of Jacob" which is a note from the P witness, and may once have actually headed a family tree. Since Isaac is dead, and Esau is departed from the land, Jacob, back at home, is the head of the family. The note recognizes his primacy, even though Jacob is a background figure, except for chapters 48—49, until his death in 49:33. Jacob prominently reappears only after the climax of the Joseph story.

The story thus centers in Joseph. Except for chapter 38, where Judah is the hero, Joseph is the central figure in 37—50.

This section presents a long sustained narrative concerning Joseph. More chapters are concerned with stories about Abram-Abraham than are concerned with Joseph, but 37, 39—47, and 50 are concerned with the life of Joseph. This narrative is the longest unit in Genesis and indeed in the Pentateuch.

The story is a unity which moves to a climax to which all the successive scenes or parts contribute their topics. This theme is not "a rags to riches" theme (cf. Holt), but "a riches to rags to riches theme," which has been best described by Driver, who makes use of Aristotle's account of good drama to expound the Joseph story. For Aristotle the reversal of fortune—an action is turned into the opposite of what was intended—and the recognition, the realization of this reversal by the persons concerned, are the essence of drama.

From a background of envy, and from a scene in which the youth Joseph is entirely at the mercy of his elder brothers, the story moves to the scene in which those brothers are entirely at the mercy of Joseph, at first unknown to them, but then later made known to them. In the interval before his self-disclosure, Joseph uses his incognito not for revenge but for a trial of their character and real concerns. From the discovery of their sincerity, their concern for their father, and their own genuine remorse, Joseph realizes that they are worthy to be forgiven and his self-disclosure and his forgiveness belong to the same moment. The theme is without formal theophany and without explicit revelation (apart from 46:1–4); it is "personal and secular" (Speiser), but withal an uncovering of the ways of God in the affairs of men. God is seen to move in a mysterious way through dreams to perform his wonders, and though the bud had a bitter taste for Joseph, the flower was wonderfully comforting.

Skinner sees the Joseph narrative as a dramatic unity but as exhibiting such a perfect technique of description that it "must have passed through many successive hands" (p. 440) to reach its present perfection. He feels that this process has been assisted by the use of three kinds of material: (a) elements of tribal history, especially in the relations of Joseph and Benjamin, Ephraim and Manasseh, and in the role of Reuben; (b) elements of individual biography, some memory of an Israelite in charge of affairs in the great land of Egypt; and, (c) elements from the folklore of the Egyptians.

This view of a long continuing process of composition from such varieties of materials is hardly consistent with the picture of a unitary work. Von Rad supplies the correction: "It is from the beginning to the end an organically constructed narrative." Any account of its composition must be subordinate to its character.

Thus its character controls any explanation of the work of the witnesses. No doubt the J witness in the south and especially the E witness in the north possessed versions of this story of Joseph, but in the story itself the hand of one writer must surely be

seen. He wrote up essentially the E version with extracts from J and some notes from P, to present us with this organic whole. Were it not for the absence of features customarily used by E, the work might have been thought to have been written by him. Almost the only cue as to the presence of sources is the varying use of Jacob and Israel as the name of the patriarch. Israel is the name for Jacob customarily employed by the J witness.

Since these chapters are essentially the narrative about Joseph, it is important to realize that his character has been idealized as no other patriarch. As Skinner rightly says (p. 440): "Joseph is not (like Jacob) the embodiment of one particular virtue, but is conceived as an ideal character in all the relations in which he is placed: he is the ideal son, the ideal brother, the ideal servant, the ideal administrator." He was not always the ideal brother because of his talebearing tendency, but with age came wisdom, and Skinner's estimate is largely true.

1. The Young Dreamer (37:1–11)

[1] Jacob dwelt in the land of his father's sojournings, in the land of Canaan. [2] This is the history of the family of Jacob.

Joseph, being seventeen years old, was shepherding the flock with his brothers; he was a lad with the sons of Bilhah and Zilpah, his father's wives; and Joseph brought an ill report of them to their father. [3] Now Israel loved Joseph more than any other of his children, because he was the son of his old age; and he made him a long robe with sleeves. [4] But when his brothers saw that their father loved him more than all his brothers, they hated him, and could not speak peaceably to him.

[5] Now Joseph had a dream, and when he told it to his brothers they only hated him the more. [6] He said to them, "Hear this dream which I have dreamed: [7] behold, we were binding sheaves in the field, and lo, my sheaf arose and stood upright; and behold, your sheaves gathered round it, and bowed down to my sheaf." [8] His brothers said to him, "Are you indeed to reign over us? Or are you indeed to have dominion over us?" So they hated him yet more for his dreams and for his words. [9] Then he dreamed another dream, and told it to his

brothers, and said, "Behold, I have dreamed another dream; and behold, the sun, the moon, and eleven stars were bowing down to me." [10] But when he told it to his father and to his brothers, his father rebuked him, and said to him, "What is this dream that you have dreamed? Shall I and your mother and your brothers indeed come to bow ourselves to the ground before you?" [11] And his brothers were jealous of him, but his father kept the saying in mind.

Verse 1 deserves a special comment, for it is itself a comment on the fortunes of Jacob. Jacob is found supreme in the very situation from which he had to flee. At last, with his father dead, with Esau removed, and after many years of exile, Jacob is back home—home in the land of the sojourning (17:8; 28:4). In this summary note there is a measure of fulfilment and perhaps a touch of satisfaction. For a moment the major theme of the patriarchal story of Genesis is manifest. Jacob the heir of promise, the supplanter of blessing, is resident in the Promised Land. The verse records that he dwelt where Isaac sojourned, but perhaps it was Isaac who dwelt, for Jacob only sojourned. But now for ten years Jacob is back home.

This is the history of the family of Jacob represents the Hebrew, "These are the generations of Jacob." Speiser's view that the reference is retrospective—"This concludes the genealogy of Jacob"—is very doubtful indeed. Perhaps 35:22*b*–26 once followed 37:2*a*.

Benjamin is presumably too young to be mentioned. So Joseph as the only other son of his mother would only be one among the six sons of Leah. He is therefore set to work *shepherding* along *with the sons of Bilhah and Zilpah,* Jacob's concubines. Joseph is something of a sneak and a prig—a spoiled boy. He was a talebearer; he was Jacob's favorite for several reasons; he had also a special dress. That Joseph was a child of Jacob's old age is not strictly in accord with 30:23. He is therefore the object of the envy of his brothers—all ten of them. In verse 2 the *ill report* seems to be about Dan and Naphtali, Gad and Asher, but Joseph

was probably in their care, and told tales about all his ten brothers. Verse 3 could be the very beginning of J's story about Joseph. *A long robe with sleeves* correctly replaces the old and familiar "coat of many colors." This costume is a tunic extending to the ankles and with sleeves. The ordinary tunic had no sleeves and reached the knees. This sleeve and ankle garment is the dress of a princess in 2 Samuel 13:18 f. In verse 4 the first *him* is emphatic in Hebrew by reason of its inverted position, "him their father loved." (For, "could not speak him peaceably" cf. Deut. 18:21 f.).

Joseph experiences and relates two dreams to his brothers. The second he also mentions to his father. These two fancy-free dreams of his future greatness suggest a persistent feature in Joseph's mind, and for the hearers the certainty of fulfilment (cf. 41:32). The dreams are not concealed oracular revelations, but are psychological revelations of the real thoughts of Joseph's heart. Even his father is aghast, though he retained the word, i.e., pondered the situation (cf. Luke 2:19,51). Jacob's attitude thus serves as a kind of "carryover." The mystery implicit in the dreams has a future, even though that future will not be manifest until 42:6 (cf. 50:18). Thus the dreams carry a psychological meaning relating to Joseph's imagination, and also a prophetic element which anticipates the future.

Joseph dreams an agricultural dream in which the brothers are *sheaves,* and they *bowed down* to him. The reference to reign and dominion is not a particular reference to the political kingship in northern Israel later, but is simply a figure of dominance. Similarly any understanding of the second dream in terms of the zodiac is also quite unnecessary. The second dream is even more fantastic for *the sun, the moon, and eleven stars*—i.e., Jacob, Rachel (or Leah), and eleven brothers—*were bowing down* to him. The dreams are related, not merely as a further illustration of the hatred (J) and the envy (E) of the brothers, but as the final touch of arrogance on Joseph's part which leads to the ensuing action. The mental state described in verses 2–5 reaches boiling point in verses 5–11. In verse 10 *mother* can only refer to Rachel, who is thought of as still alive, though her death was in fact reported in 35:19.

2. The Plot Against Joseph (37:12–36)

12 Now his brothers went to pasture their father's flock near Shechem. 13 And Israel said to Joseph, "Are not your brothers pasturing the flock at Shechem? Come, I will send you to them." And he said to him, "Here I am." 14 So he said to him, "Go now, see if it is well with your brothers, and with the flock; and bring me word again." So he sent him from the valley of Hebron, and he came to Shechem. 15 And a man found him wandering in the fields; and the man asked him, "What are you seeking?" 16 "I am seeking my brothers," he said, "tell me, I pray you, where they are pasturing the flock." 17 And the man said, "They have gone away, for I heard them say, 'Let us go to Dothan.' " So Joseph went after his brothers, and found them at Dothan. 18 They saw him afar off, and before he came near to them they conspired against him to kill him. 19 They said to one another, "Here comes this dreamer. 20 Come now, let us kill him and throw him into one of the pits; then we shall say that a wild beast has devoured him, and we shall see what will become of his dreams." 21 But when Reuben heard it, he delivered him out of their hands, saying, "Let us not take his life." 22 And Reuben said to them, "Shed no blood; cast him into this pit here in the wilderness, but lay no hand upon him"—that he might rescue him out of their hand, to restore him to his father. 23 So when Joseph came to his brothers, they stripped him of his robe, the long robe with sleeves that he wore; 24 and they took him and cast him into a pit. The pit was empty, there was no water in it.

25 Then they sat down to eat; and looking up they saw a caravan of Ishmaelites coming from Gilead, with their camels bearing gum, balm, and myrrh, on their way to carry it down to Egypt. 26 Then Judah said to his brothers, "What profit is it if we slay our brother and conceal his blood? 27 Come, let us sell him to the Ishmaelites, and let not our hand be upon him, for he is our brother, our own flesh." And his brothers heeded him. 28 Then Midianite traders passed by; and they drew Joseph up and lifted him out of the pit, and sold him to the Ishmaelites for twenty shekels of silver; and they took Joseph to Egypt. 29 When Reuben returned to the pit and saw

that Joseph was not in the pit, he rent his clothes 30 and returned to his brothers, and said, "The lad is gone; and I, where shall I go?" 31 Then they took Joseph's robe, and killed a goat, and dipped the robe in the blood; 32 and they sent the long robe with sleeves and brought it to their father, and said, "This we have found; see now whether it is your son's robe or not." 33 And he recognized it, and said, "It is my son's robe; a wild beast has devoured him; Joseph is without doubt torn to pieces." 34 Then Jacob rent his garments, and put sackcloth upon his loins, and mourned for his son many days. 35 All his sons and all his daughters rose up to comfort him; but he refused to be comforted, and said, "No, I shall go down to Sheol to my son, mourning." Thus his father wept for him. 36 Meanwhile the Midianites had sold him in Egypt to Potiphar, an officer of Pharaoh, the captain of the guard.

Jacob's brothers return to the Shechem area on a shepherding expedition. That they should return to the vicinity of Shechem is astonishing in the light of the events of chapter 34, but their return to that area, planned before they left home, helps to explain Jacob's concern. A considerable lapse of time must also be supposed for the events of verses 2–11. Considerable ill feeling existed between the brothers, but no harm had ever come to Joseph, and so Jacob deems it safe to send Joseph to seek news of his brothers. The brothers must already have been weeks if not months away from home. To tend flocks all that distance would have taken time, and perhaps their return was overdue.

Joseph leaves the broad and pretty vale in which *Hebron* lies (23:2,20) and proceeds northward to the very pleasant areas near *Shechem*. He turned off the main path, visiting groups of shepherds as he sought his brethren. A passerby spotted his difficulty, and it happened to be a person who knew the brothers and who also knew that they had gone on to *Dothan*, some 15 miles north of Shechem. Dothan itself an ancient city of Canaan, represented now by a striking mound, Tell Dothan (2 Kings 6:13–15), stands on the edge of a broad and fertile plain. An entrant into the plain would be visible from a considerable distance.

Joseph's brothers plot to kill him, but

Reuben and Judah devise expedients to foil them. Joseph is carried into Egypt, and Jacob is eventually told that wild beasts have destroyed his son.

The story appears to be in reasonable sequence. Two brothers try in succession to save Joseph; two caravans of merchants pass by. Yet these facts have led many exegetes to regard the narrative as a conflate of two traditions.

According to one, Joseph's brothers agreed to sell him to a caravan of passing Ishmaelites, but according to the other, Joseph was rescued from the pit by Midianites (v. 28), but recourse to two sources is not always necessary. As soon as the brothers recognize Joseph in the distance they denounce him as **this dreamer.** The Hebrew has "this master of dreams." The expression is strong and contemptuous. Joseph was put into an empty waterless **pit here in the wilderness,** that is off the plain, out of earshot, and possibly out of sight. Escape from the pit or cistern would not be possible because it had the rough shape of a bottle. The narrow neck would prevent the entry of too much sunshine, and likewise make escape difficult (cf. Jer. 38:6; Lam. 3:53; Deut. 6:11; 1 Sam. 13:6; cf. the law, Ex. 21:33 f.). This was done at the suggestion of Reuben, the eldest brother, as an alternative to the proposal of the brothers to kill Joseph. His words are only three in the Hebrew, "No smiting [killing] life." His peremptory command surprises his brothers, and Reuben quickly follows up his advantage and gains a reprieve for Joseph. Reuben plays the lead as befits the elder brother, and he is also credited with the intention of saving Joseph later.

During the meal that followed they noticed a trading **caravan** (cf. Job 6:18 f.; Isa. 21:13) **of Ishmaelites** who were traveling on the road **from Gilead** through Jezreel, through Dothan and on to the coastal plain on their way **to Egypt.** The Ishmaelites are trading in **gum** (tragacanth), **balm, and myrrh.** Balm, (mastic) was a well-known product of Gilead (cf. Jer. 8:22; 46:11), and the gums were used for medical purposes, as well as for incense and embalming. The myrrh stands for *lot,* fragrant gum from the cistus rose.

Judah now proposes a different plan. Some hours had elapsed since Joseph had been hidden in the well, and no doubt Judah and the others had had time to cool off and to reconsider their murderous resolution. For profit, and because of kinship, the brothers resolve to sell Joseph to the Ishmaelites, instead of killing him and hiding his blood that it should not call for vengeance (Ezek. 24:7; Isa. 26:21). In the meantime, perhaps before negotiating with the Ishmaelites had even begun, or less likely, during those negotiations, another passing caravan, this time of Midianites, overheard Joseph's cries, lifted him out of the pit, and took him along (cf. 40:15). Soon they encountered the Ishmaelites, and were glad to sell Joseph to them for *twenty shekels of silver* (cf. Lev. 27:5). In turn the Ishmaelites took Joseph to Egypt. The only real variant in the entire account occurs in verse 36, which reports that the *Midianites* themselves *sold him [Joseph] in Egypt.*

The brothers did not know what had happened. *Reuben returned to the pit,* either to release Joseph, or to hand him over to the Ishmaelites, or even just to feed him, and found that he had gone.

The story is thus perfectly coherent until verse 36, and the brothers were both prevented from committing crime, or reaping any reward from their cruelty. They cover their tracks and invent a plausible story that Joseph had been killed by wild beasts, that they had found his bloodstained robe which they now took to their father, who drew the desired conclusion (v. 20) and was cast into deep mourning and despair. Of course by Exodus 22:13 the brothers would be absolved from all responsibility. Despite the consolations of his sons and daughters, here mentioned for the first time, unless daughters-in-law were meant, he laments that he has nothing left to live for and will mourn for the rest of his life until he goes **down to Sheol.** This means he will wear the mourning garments for the rest of his life.

Sheol was pictured as a vast assembly hall for the dead, situated beneath the earth in the lowest of the three stories which comprised the universe. Here all the dead were gathered, except such favored persons as Enoch and Elijah, who were translated. In Sheol all the dead were recognizable, having the same likeness as on earth. It was a ghostly place of shades and silence (cf. 35:8; Job 10:21–22; Psalms 6:5; 88:10–12; Isa. 14:9–10; Ezek. 32:21 ff.).

According to verse 36, the Midianites sold Joseph to an Egyptian official. This directly contradicts 39:1 which says that that same Egyptian bought Joseph from the Ishmaelites. In this double record of the sale of Joseph in Egypt is the only certain trace of a double narrative. On this doublet rests mainly the case for tracing a double narrative back through the chapter, though the chapter itself does not necessarily require such a solution. The choice before the exegete is thus a unified tradition or else the abandoning of either 37:27 or 39:1. The best explanation is probably that both the J and E witnesses did have their own accounts of how Joseph was raised from the pit and then dispatched to Egypt. Traces of these accounts still appear as at 37:27. It is however quite another thing to see different accounts at any point where there are differences which upon examination are only apparent.

The Egyptian official is *Potiphar,* a name which means gift of the sun or he whom the sun god has given. A more correct form of the name is given in 41:45 (Potiphera), though this is not to suggest that the two men are the same person. The present Potiphar is Pharaoh's officer, literally, eunuch: more generally, court official (40:2), officer (1 Kings 22:9), officials (2 Kings 8:6), eunuchs (Esther 1:12). He was the particular eunuch who was also *captain of the guard,* more accurately "head of the butchers." Other renderings are "head of the cooks" (1 Sam. 9:23), head of the guard, executioners or guards (2 Kings 25:8; Jer. 39:9).

Joseph is thus in Egypt and with this event another crisis point in the account is reached. The patriarchal narratives of Genesis, from chapter 12 onward, are ever concerned with the fate of the son of the family of promise. The theme of the son has its own particular development within the general theme of progeny, a numberless seed, a multiplying nation.

For Abraham the son is so long in coming, that the "future" son casts his shadow on the story. After his birth, and when still a boy, he has to be offered and is only redeemed at the last moment. Isaac spends his life within the Promised Land. His wife even is brought in. When her twins are born, the son of destiny is born second, but regains the birthright. Then for a long time he is absent from the Land of Promise. Eventually he returns and is found where he belongs, in Canaan (37:1). With him is the favorite son Joseph, but once again the problem reasserts itself. Joseph is unpopular, hated, and as a result gets sold into Egypt. The favorite son is once again out of the land. He is in Egypt and in fact nobody knows what has become of him. How will Joseph be recovered for the promise and for the family and for the land? These are the problems of the narrator as he proceeds with his narrative. They are, however, only problems as they are seen to delay, frustrate, or otherwise hamper the divine purpose which is the presupposition and foundation of all these records.

But within the theme of the absent son there lies at this juncture the theme which specially belongs to Jacob, namely, deception. He who deceived his own father, tricked his brother, was tricked by and tricked his father-in-law, is now in the matter of the absent son tricked by his own sons. Jacob is deceived and remains deceived for a number of years. Only in the rediscovery of the absent son will the deception be destroyed.

The unfolding narrative about Joseph is at this point interrupted. At this moment a new and apparently unrelated subject is introduced, and the main theme remains in suspense.

XXI. Judah and Tamar (38:1–30)

The J witness is now called upon to relate how the tribe of Judah, in whom the J witness is specially interested, because the J witness is mainly the Judean source, came to settle in the person of its ancestor, in the areas where the tribe eventually lived; also how the tribe came to possess a strong admixture of Canaanite blood, and how three of the principal clans of Judah came into being (cf. Num. 26:19–22). Our attention is thus directed to the location and growth of the tribe of Judah and its amalgamation with Canaanite elements. Chapter 38 which tells of Judah's settlement in the south is thus a counterpart to chapter 34 and related passages which tell of the parallel northern settlement of parts of Israel.

This tribal reference of the story is closely associated with and indeed worked out through a secondary purpose of the story; namely, the duty of marriage that rests upon the brothers and relatives of a deceased brother's wife. The fourth chapter of Ruth is an illustration of the same obligation and Ruth 4:12 refers to the Judah-Tamar incident of Genesis 38. For the actual law, see Deuteronomy 25:5–10.

Von Rad (p. 351) claims that "every attentive reader can see" that the present story (ch. 38) "has no connection at all" with the Joseph story. Let us then be even more attentive. To illustrate: often when the fortunes of some of the characters in a tale of Anthony Trollope or a saga of John Galsworthy are being related and we come to an interesting juncture, the author breaks off to pursue the life and adventures of some other characters. Disappointment gives way to patience with the realization that the interlude is necessary so that the author may catch up and maintain the balance of his overall story.

Certainly the interpolation of the Judah-Tamar incident into the Joseph story at this point is surprising. The Judah incident had to go in somewhere. The editor had to keep his story in balance so that no section of the full account of the future Israel should fall behind. There was comfort in the thought: if Joseph is gone out of the land, Judah remains within, and Judah is the womb of the Davidic house.

Three reasons may be discerned for this present setting of the Judah incident. First, the tradition originally reported that when Joseph had been sold into Egypt, Judah moved away from the family to a different part of the south country. Joseph's presumed death and Judah's removal belonged together in the inherited tradition.

Second, change and developments in Judah's family had to be reported in readiness for the report of the list who went down into Egypt with Jacob (46:8–26, espec. v. 12). Nevertheless it is sometimes claimed that the chronology of the Joseph narrative (37:2; 41:46; and 45:11 equal 15 years) is incompatible with Judah's descent into Egypt with grandchildren.

Third, Judah's tribe, glorious as its future was to be, had to be shown to have its origin in the patriarchal period.

The line is Judah, Perez, Hezron, and then Jerahmeel—a fruitful clan (1 Chron. 2:9,25–33,34–41): Ram, the ancestor of the royal Davidic line (1 Chron. 2:9, 10–17); Caleb, who settled at Hebron (Josh. 15:13 ff.; 1 Chron. 2:9,18–20,24,42–50).

The removal of Judah is thus seen as the beginning of a long series of events which culminate in the Hebrew monarchy. The line was preserved at the beginning by the audacious courage of a Canaanite woman, Tamar, as it was preserved at the end by the same courage of a Moabite woman, Ruth.

1. Judah's Family (38:1–11)

¹ It happened at that time that Judah went down from his brothers, and turned in to a certain Adullamite, whose name was Hirah. ² There Judah saw the daughter of a certain

Canaanite whose name was Shua; he married her and went in to her, 3 and she conceived and bore a son, and he called his name Er. 4 Again she conceived and bore a son, and she called his name Onan. 5 Yet again she bore a son, and she called his name Shelah. She was in Chezib when she bore him. 6 And Judah took a wife for Er his first-born, and her name was Tamar. 7 But Er, Judah's first-born, was wicked in the sight of the LORD; and the LORD slew him. 8 Then Judah said to Onan, "Go in to your brother's wife, and perform the duty of a brother-in-law to her, and raise up offspring for your brother." 9 But Onan knew that the offspring would not be his; so when he went in to his brother's wife he spilled the semen on the ground, lest he should give offspring to his brother. 10 And what he did was displeasing in the sight of the LORD, and he slew him also. 11 Then Judah said to Tamar his daughter-in-law, "Remain a widow in your father's house, till Shelah my son grows up"—for he feared that he would die, like his brothers. So Tamar went and dwelt in her father's house.

Birth of Judah's Sons (vv. 1–5). About the time of Joseph's disappearance, Judah separated himself from his brothers and went down from the high countryside around Hebron westward to the Shephelah to Adullam (Josh. 15:33–35). There he joined forces with a certain man named *Hirah* with whom he remained friendly for a long time. They doubtless had their shepherding or business enterprise in common. While there Judah married a woman whose name is not given, unless her description *daughter of a certain Canaanite whose name was Shua* was really her name, "Bathshua," and by her he had three sons— *Er, Onan,* and *Shelah*—the third while a resident in *Chezib* (cf. Achzib, Josh. 15:44; Mic. 1:14). For the sons of Shelah, see Numbers 26:20.

Tamar's Misfortune (vv. 6–11). Judah, as head of the family, chooses a wife for his firstborn, Er (cf. 24:3; 34:4; 21:21), named *Tamar,* which means date palm and which was a family name in David's household (2 Sam. 13:1; 14:27). Er died childless, and his death in youth was attributed to Yahweh, because of Er's wicked life. Judah's second son, Onan, in spite of his father's command, evaded the duty of a

brother-in-law and used to avoid begetting out of selfish interest in regard to primogeniture. His early death was put down to this misdemeanor.

The tenses of the Hebrew verbs in verse 9 are frequentative, and should be translated: "So whenever he used to go in . . . he used to spill the semen." The result of his failure to impregnate his sister-in-law was that he deprived his dead brother of someone to carry his name and inherit his share of the property. Judah suspected that something about Tamar might be malevolent, and so he bade Tamar wait until his third son was grown up. Tamar retired to her own father's house (cf. Lev. 22:13; Ruth 1:8).

2. Tamar's Successful Stratagem (38:12–23)

12 In course of time the wife of Judah, Shua's daughter, died; and when Judah was comforted, he went up to Timnah to his sheepshearers, he and his friend Hirah the Adullamite. 13 And when Tamar was told, "Your father-in-law is going up to Timnah to shear his sheep," 14 she put off her widow's garments, and put on a veil, wrapping herself up, and sat at the entrance to Enaim, which is on the road to Timnah; for she saw that Shelah was grown up, and she had not been given to him in marriage. 15 When Judah saw her, he thought her to be a harlot, for she had covered her face. 16 He went over to her at the road side, and said, "Come, let me come in to you," for he did not know that she was his daughter-in-law. She said, "What will you give me, that you may come in to me?" 17 He answered, "I will send you a kid from the flock." And she said, "Will you give me a pledge, till you send it?" 18 He said, "What pledge shall I give you?" She replied, "Your signet and your cord, and your staff that is in your hand." So he gave them to her, and went in to her, and she conceived by him. 19 Then she arose and went away, and taking off her veil she put on the garments of her widowhood.

20 When Judah sent the kid by his friend the Adullamite, to receive the pledge from the woman's hand, he could not find her. 21 And he asked the men of the place, "Where is the harlot who was at Enaim by the wayside?" And they said, "No harlot has been here." 22 So he returned to Judah, and said, "I have not found her; and also the men of the place said, 'No harlot has been here.'" 23 And Judah re-

plied, "Let her keep the things as her own, lest we be laughed at; you see, I sent this kid, and you could not find her."

With the passage of time Tamar became increasingly resentful of her lot as a twice "widowed," childless wife, and realized that Judah had deceived her because his third son, now grown up, had not been given to her. She suddenly saw an opportunity whereby she could inveigle her own father-in-law to fulfil the duty of the levirate marriage; i.e., give her a child of her own.

She heard that Judah was paying a visit near her home for some sheep-shearing (31: 19; 1 Sam. 24:2 ff.). This visit was made with his friend Hirah some time after he had completed the mourning ceremonies for his own wife who had died. Widows were apparently unveiled, unless the veil was used to conceal the identity of harlots. Tamar put off her widow's garments and stationed herself at the entrance to Enaim (cf. Jer. 3:2; Ezek. 16:25). Enaim (cf. Josh. 15:34) was presumably on the road from Judah's home to her own home at Timnah some ten miles west of Bethlehem, and not the Danite Timnah of Samson and the Philistines (Josh. 15:10; 19:43; Judg. 14:1). Judah, a widower, mistook Tamar for a harlot, and for the price of a kid (cf. Judg. 15:1), pledged by the deposit of Judah's *signet* and *cord* and his ornamented *staff*, lay with her. Thus Tamar conceived and withal retained proof of the identity of the father.

After the incident she resumed for a time the life of her widowhood. Seal, cord, and staff obviously indicated a man of some standing. The seal, no doubt a cylinder seal, was hung round the neck by the cord. Tamar was very astute to ask for such objects as a pledge, and Judah very amorous to yield them. The Hebrew word for *pledge* in verses 17 f. is transliterated as it reappears in Greek, 'erabhon—a loan word from Akkadian and used in 2 Corinthians 5:5 and Ephesians 1:14 as "guarantee."

Judah's subsequent behavior is informative. He is naturally anxious to recover his very personal possessions; but to hide his shame he sent his friend Hirah with the promised kid. Unable to find Tamar, who had returned to her father's house, he inquired for the harlot, and of course his inquiry was fruitless. No regular harlot was known at the entry to Enaim. When all this was reported to Judah he, to avoid being mocked (38:23), cut his losses, pointing out at least that he had honored his obligation by sending the kid.

The Hebrew word for **harlot** in verse 15 is the common word for such a person, but it must be contrasted with the word in verses 21 f., which means literally "a female sacred person," "a cult prostitute." (Cf. Deut. 23:17; Hos. 4:14; Prov. 7:1-27). Hirah, or even Judah himself, may have deliberately used this word to relieve the occasion of some of its nastiness, or Tamar may have made out by her dress that she was such a votary, prostituting herself in a service to the deity. It is however questionable whether Tamar could have asked for payment if she had adopted such a role.

3. Tamar's Vindication (38:24-26)

24 About three months later Judah was told, "Tamar your daughter-in-law has played the harlot; and moreover she is with child by harlotry." And Judah said, "Bring her out, and let her be burned." 25 As she was being brought out, she sent word to her father-in-law, "By the man to whom these belong, I am with child." And she said, "Mark, I pray you, whose these are, the signet and the cord and the staff." 26 Then Judah acknowledged them and said, "She is more righteous than I, inasmuch as I did not give her to my son Shelah." And he did not lie with her again.

Some three months later, Tamar's secret was known, and it came to Judah's knowledge. Judah ordered that she be brought out (Deut. 22:21,24) and burned. Quite literally on the way to the stake she produces Judah's seal and staff and thus establishes the identity of the father of her child. Judah is forced to acknowledge his complicity amidst the widest publicity. As Tamar is brought out, she makes her accusation to the crowd that would inevitably accompany her. Judah, no doubt from a distance, both justified Tamar and never repeated his action, for that would have been tantamount to incest. Judah accepted her as his daughter-in-law.

Tamar is treated as an engaged girl rather than a widow, for Judah has jurisdiction over her, and so she was counted as part of his family though resident with her father. In inveigling her father-in-law Tamar had resisted her severance from Judah's family. The usual punishment was death by stoning (Deut. 22:23 f.; Lev. 20:16; John 8:5). Burning was reserved for priests' daughters who sinned in this way, possibly because they were daughters of holy men (Lev. 21:9). The conclusion of the episode thus shows how much Tamar risked for her wifely rights, and how well Judah himself behaved in face of his proven guilt.

4. Birth of Perez and Zerah (38:27–30)

27 When the time of her delivery came, there were twins in her womb. 28 And when she was in labor, one put out a hand; and the midwife took and bound on his hand a scarlet thread, saying, "This came out first." 29 But as he drew back his hand, behold, his brother came out; and she said, "What a breach you have made for yourself!" Therefore his name was called Perez. 30 Afterward his brother came out with the scarlet thread upon his hand; and his name was called Zerah.

Tamar eventually gives birth to twins, and the story of the birth is similar to that of the birth of Esau and Jacob (25:24–26). The second boy, later named Zerah, was the first to be seen, actually putting out a hand. The midwife immediately tied a scarlet thread around that hand. But then the other child, later called Perez, achieved a violent and sudden birth, actually calling forth an ejaculation or admonition from the midwife, *What a breach you have made for yourself.* So they named this violent child *Perez* (breach) in recollection of the manner of his birth. The Perez clan eventually became not only the stronger and more numerous of the two but also the more distinguished because of Jerahmeel's, Caleb's,

and especially David's descent within it. *Zerah* is also the name of an Edomite clan (cf. 36:13). With Judah thus settled, and with the beginnings of his illustrious line thus established, the narrative now returns to its main theme.

XXII. Joseph in Egypt: Rise to Power (39: 1—41:57)

1. Joseph and Potiphar (39:1–23)

1 Now Joseph was taken down to Egypt, and Potiphar, an officer of Pharaoh, the captain of the guard, an Egyptian, bought him from the Ishmaelites who had brought him down there. 2 The LORD was with Joseph, and he became a successful man; and he was in the house of his master the Egyptian, 3 and his master saw that the LORD was with him, and that the LORD caused all that he did to prosper in his hands. 4 So Joseph found favor in his sight and attended him, and he made him overseer of his house and put him in charge of all that he had. 5 From the time that he made him overseer in his house and over all that he had the LORD blessed the Egyptian's house for Joseph's sake; the blessing of the LORD was upon all that he had, in house and field. 6 So he left all that he had in Joseph's charge; and having him he had no concern for anything but the food which he ate.

Now Joseph was handsome and good-looking. 7 And after a time his master's wife cast her eyes upon Joseph, and said, "Lie with me." 8 But he refused and said to his master's wife, "Lo, having me my master has no concern about anything in the house, and he has put everything that he has in my hand; 9 he is not greater in this house than I am; nor has he kept back anything from me except yourself, because you are his wife; how then can I do this great wickedness, and sin against God?" 10 And although she spoke to Joseph day after day, he would not listen to her, to lie with her or to be with her. 11 But one day, when he went into the house to do his work and none of the men of the house was there in the house, 12 she caught him by his garment, saying, "Lie with me." But he left his garment in her hand, and fled and got out of the house. 13 And when she saw that he had left his garment in her hand, and had fled out of the house, 14 she called to the men of her household and said to them, "See, he has brought among us a Hebrew to insult us; he came in to me to lie with me, and I cried out with a loud voice; 15 and when he heard that I lifted up my voice and cried, he left his garment with me, and fled and got out of the house." 16 Then she laid up his garment by her until his master came home, 17 and she told him the same story, saying, "The Hebrew servant, whom you have brought among us, came in to me to insult me; 18 but as soon as I lifted up my voice and cried, he left his garment with me, and fled out of the house."

19 When his master heard the words which his wife spoke to him, "This is the way your servant treated me," his anger was kindled. 20 And Joseph's master took him and put him into the prison, the place where the king's prisoners were confined, and he was there in prison. 21 But the LORD was with Joseph and showed him steadfast love, and gave him favor in the sight of the keeper of the prison. 22 And the keeper of the prison committed to Joseph's care all the prisoners who were in the prison; and whatever was done there, he was the doer of it; 23 the keeper of the prison paid no heed to anything that was in Joseph's care, because the LORD was with him; and whatever he did, the LORD made it prosper.

The J witness continues his account of the fortunes of Joseph and preserves his tradition that Joseph was brought down to Egypt and sold there by the Ishmaelites. The refrain of the narrative now appears in verse 2. Yahweh was *with Joseph,* and he was successful (cf. 21:20). This favor controls his fortunes in Potiphar's house, and again later in prison (vv. 21,23). Joseph's good fortune has a double consequence. Not only was the Lord with Joseph, but it was manifest to Potiphar that the Lord was with him, and that the Lord was the cause of his prosperity (v. 3). Potiphar took advantage of this and made him the overseer of his household, and as a result Joseph's good fortune spread to Potiphar's household, possessions, and enterprises. Potiphar's only concern was with his own food, whether for private reasons or, as in 43:32, for ritual reasons.

"With Joseph" and its variant "the Lord blessed" are the standard Israelite ways of expressing the origin of prosperity. The presence of the ark in Obed-edom's household had the same effect (2 Sam. 6:11 f.). But the most famous example is of course David (1 Sam. 16:18). The preposition with is thus important not only in its use in this general idiom of prosperity, and especially in the particular application to David and his house (cf. 2 Sam. 7:9 and variants throughout the chapter; cf. Psalm 89), but also because it reached its fulness when the idea of "God being with" was promoted to become a name for the Messiah. "Immanuel" means "with us (is) God." This brief survey shows the increasing importance of the "God with" concept in the Old Testament and of course in the New Testament (Matt. 28:20; John 17:12), though in the New the "with" conception ranks second to the "God in" conception, for God was in Christ (John 17:21,23; cf. 2 Cor. 5:19).

Joseph is beautiful like his mother Rachel (29:17), the beauty of mother and son being described in identical terms. Accordingly he falls victim to the amorous intentions of his master's wife. Joseph repels her advances on two grounds. He cannot take advantage of the position of trust given to him by his master, and, in any event, to agree to her suggestion would be to sin against God. This is the climax of Joseph's objection and the insuperable barrier to her desire, though it was daily urged upon him.

But one day (v. 11) is represented by an idiomatic Hebrew phrase, the meaning of which is lost to us; literally, "as this day" or possibly "on the day in question." In revenge she makes a false accusation about Joseph to the other servants and later to her husband himself. She supports her charge by producing Joseph's inner-house-garment, which she had seized and which he had left in her hand as he fled almost naked from her. Joseph fled not into the street but probably into the courtyard around the house. She strengthens the accusation by declaring that all the women in the house are at risk; i.e. *to insult us* (cf. 26:8), and by describing Joseph as *a Hebrew* (v. 14). She later repeats the story and shows the garment to her husband on his return home.

The use of the name *Hebrew* is important. It occurs five times in the Joseph story, then again several times in Exodus 1–10 and in 1 Samuel. The discovery of the term among the Babylonians, Assyrians, Hittites, and probably the Egyptians, shows that it was probably not an ethnic term at first. It is probably a term to describe a lower social class with nevertheless a well defined place and legal status in society (cf. Ex. 21:1 f.; 1 Sam. 14:21). Alongside this meaning, the national sense was also evident, as "land of the Hebrews" in 40:15 shows (cf. Deut. 15:12; Jonah 1:9; Gen. 10:21,25). In the Joseph narratives the term "Hebrew" is used three times by non-Israelites (39:14,17; 41:12); once by Joseph in regard to foreigners (40:15) and once in a contract between Hebrews and Egyptians. The contemptuous use in the present passage is obvious.

Potiphar's wife's complaint raises his anger which is directed of course against Joseph. The story gives no hint that he was suspicious of and angry with his wife, as some exegetes have suggested. He jails Joseph in the prison, literally, "house of roundness" or "house of enclosure," a phrase which only occurs in verses 21–23 and 40:3,5. Perhaps a tower of some kind is intended, unless the Hebrew word used is transliterated from Egyptian.

Even in his new adversity, Joseph is however marked out and is prospered in his fortune. Just as his former master had been led to recognize the mark of divine favor, so now the keeper of the prison recognizes Joseph's fortunate life, and gives him charge of the other prisoners. Thus in succession Joseph has care of a private household, a prison, and eventually a country; and his supervision is complete and unchecked by other officials or the chief person in each situation. The chapter ends with the reiteration of the reason for Joseph's success.

Note

An Egyptian story exists, entitled "The Tale of the Two Brothers," composed for Seti II of the nineteenth dynasty in the twelfth century. Two brothers live in one house with the elder brother's wife. Her advances are repulsed by the younger brother. The wife accuses her brother-in-law falsely, and eventually she is slain for her wickedness. The story has features parallel to this Joseph story, but to claim any other connection and even dependence is to go beyond the evidence. The differences between the stories are even greater than the similarities.

The crime of adultery was a very one-sided concept in the Old Testament. By adultery a woman could violate only her own marriage, but a man could only violate another marriage by his adultery. In other words, a wife could belong only to one man, whereas a husband could have intercourse with other women of his household, such as female slaves (16:2) or prisoners of war (Deut. 21:10 ff.). An engaged person was treated like a wife (Deut. 22:23 f.; cf. Gen. 38:24). Within these limits adultery was a terrible crime; it was apodictically, "Thou shalt not," forbidden; and punishment was the death penalty. One of the Ten Commandments was devoted to the sanctity and preservation of marriage (Ex. 20:14,17). Marriage was thus under protection of a divine law. Some evidence of a lower level of interpretation exists, where adultery is also considered as the infringement of property rights (Ex. 22:16 f.; Deut. 22:28 f.).

2. Joseph in Prison (40:1–23)

Although Joseph is now a prisoner, he has behaved so well, and has been so prospered by the divine care and blessing that he has been given charge of all the other prisoners. After some time two distinguished prisoners, royal officials, are thrown into prison, and are put in Joseph's charge. They each have a mysterious dream which Joseph interprets to them. He thus gives proof that he has a supernatural wisdom. Joseph's success in interpreting these dreams is the turning point of his life and career.

The study of Genesis has taught all the great commentators to see the work of the

E witness continuously in this chapter. The E witness pays great attention to dreams as a means for the revelation of God's will (cf. 20:3; 21:12; 28:12; 31:11,24; 37:5 ff.). Chapters 40—41 are mainly from this E witness; 40:1 continues the story from 37:29-30,36, but is of course directly in sequel here to 39:23. Whereas seven references to Yahweh occur in Chapter 39, they now cease, and Yahweh is not mentioned by name again in Genesis.

(1) Two Distinguished Prisoners (40:1-8)

¹ Some time after this, the butler of the king of Egypt and his baker offended their lord the king of Egypt. ² And Pharaoh was angry with his two officers, the chief butler and the chief baker, ³ and he put them in custody in the house of the captain of the guard, in the prison where Joseph was confined. ⁴ The captain of the guard charged Joseph with them, and he waited on them; and they continued for some time in custody. ⁵ And one night they both dreamed—the butler and the baker of the king of Egypt, who were confined in the prison— each his own dream, and each dream with its own meaning. ⁶ When Joseph came to them in the morning and saw them, they were troubled. ⁷ So he asked Pharaoh's officers who were with him in custody in his master's house, "Why are your faces downcast today?" ⁸ They said to him, "We have had dreams, and there is no one to interpret them." And Joseph said to them, "Do not interpretations belong to God? Tell them to me, I pray you."

The first four words of verse 1 represent a customary transition formula (cf. 15:1) without any indication of the length of time involved.

The head butler and head baker, eunuchs and personal servants of the king, unluckily offended Pharaoh and were thrown into prison. In Nehemiah 1 the same Hebrew word for butler is translated "cupbearer." Although Joseph was in charge of all the other prisoners, he is now made a servant to these two men, presumably because of their importance. Royal favor or displeasure is capricious, and Pharaoh's servants could have as easily and quickly be restored to favor. Von Rad's view that as a slave to prisoners, Joseph had now reached his lowest level is hardly correct. The overseer of the prisoners is a personal attendant on two very distinguished persons. His new task further distinguishes Joseph. For some time represents Hebrew "days" and is again used of an indefinite period (cf. 4:3).

(2) Their Dreams and Their Fate (40:9-23)

⁹ So the chief butler told his dream to Joseph, and said to him, "In my dream there was a vine before me, ¹⁰ and on the vine there were three branches; as soon as it budded, its blossoms shot forth, and the clusters ripened into grapes. ¹¹ Pharaoh's cup was in my hand; and I took the grapes and pressed them into Pharaoh's cup, and placed the cup in Pharaoh's hand." ¹² Then Joseph said to him, "This is its interpretation: the three branches are three days; ¹³ within three days Pharaoh will lift up your head and restore you to your office; and you shall place Pharaoh's cup in his hand as formerly, when you were his butler. ¹⁴ But remember me, when it is well with you, and do me the kindness, I pray you, to make mention of me to Pharaoh, and so get me out of his house. ¹⁵ For I was indeed stolen out of the land of the Hebrews; and here also I have done nothing that they should put me into the dungeon."

¹⁶ When the chief baker saw that the interpretation was favorable, he said to Joseph, "I also had a dream: there were three cake baskets on my head, ¹⁷ and in the uppermost basket there were all sorts of baked food for Pharaoh, but the birds were eating it out of the basket on my head." ¹⁸ And Joseph answered, "This is its interpretation: the three baskets are three days; ¹⁹ within three days Pharaoh will lift up your head—from you!—and hang you on a tree; and the birds will eat the flesh from you."

²⁰ On the third day, which was Pharaoh's birthday, he made a feast for all his servants, and lifted up the head of the chief butler and the head of the chief baker among his servants. ²¹ He restored the chief butler to his butlership, and he placed the cup in Pharaoh's hand; ²² but he hanged the chief baker, as Joseph had interpreted to them. ²³ Yet the chief butler did not remember Joseph, but forgot him.

By a coincidence each eunuch had a dream the same night and each felt that his dream had a special meaning for him personally. The coincidence is not really remarkable. If during the day or days previously, the two men had discussed their fates with animation, or even quarreled about them, and it had appeared that the baker had offended Pharaoh more seriously than the butler, then both the mental disturbance and the greater guilt complex of the baker could recur in a dream.

The morning after, they were obviously troubled, but Joseph's concern elicited the events of the night. Joseph unconsciously illustrates his superior wisdom by reminding the two men that the inner meaning of dreams is also part of revelation (cf. 41:16,38-39; Dan. 1:17; 2:19,30; 4:6; 5:12).[26]

In these verses a parallel between Joseph and Daniel begins to emerge. Both are members of the chosen race, resident in a foreign country, but in prison. Both are able but modest, both are divinely favored but meek, both are pious but attractive, both are specially gifted in the interpretation of dreams and are counted wise men. This quality of personal wisdom links the figures of Joseph and Daniel very closely, and is part of the background to the role of Jesus Christ in the Sermon on the Mount as among other things the Master Teacher. The Beatitudes (Matt. 5:1–12), for example, and the closing parables of 7:24–29 are couched in wisdom terminology.

In the butler's dreams a vine shoots forth its buds, its blossoms, and its fruits in immediate succession, and he saw himself press the grapes and place the cup of juice in Pharaoh's hands. The only part of the dream that causes difficulty is why *three branches* (v. 10), or the *three cake baskets* in the baker's dream should mean three days. Perhaps this is where occult understanding has its place, for the narrative continually emphasizes that the interpretation of dreams is the gift of God (v. 8; 41: 16,25). *Lift up your head* (cf. 2 Kings 25: 27, Jehoiachin), i.e., "restore you to honor." But the same phrase is used of the baker (v. 20), so perhaps it means release from prison. In verse 13 the word for *office* literally means base, pedestal, and so figura-

tively, standing, office (cf. Dan. 11:20–21, 38). In verse 14 Joseph's plea is even more compelling and piteous in the Hebrew, literally, "Only that you will remember me with you."

In verse 15 Joseph complains that he was stolen out of the land of the Hebrews (cf. 37:28). Therefore he was illegally detained as a slave in prison. *Dungeon,* literally pit (cf. 37:20).

Encouraged by the favorable prediction made to his colleague the head baker now relates his dream, only to receive warning of his impending death. His head will be lifted too, but in quite a different sense. The awful pun in *lift* suggests decapitation and hanging—death and humiliation (Deut. 21:22 f., Josh. 10:26; 2 Sam. 4:12; 21:9 f.).

Joseph's predictions were fulfilled after three days, and the butler returns to his post. Pharaoh's birthday was celebrated in later times by festival and amnesty as the inscriptions of Rosetta and Canopus show. The reader now shares with Joseph a hope that he will not be forgotten, and though the chief butler was at first forgetful, the hope is but deferred.

3. *Prison and Palace (41:1–57)*

Chapter 41 continues, as it depends upon, chapter 40 and is a further section from the E witness, who is responsible for most of the material from now until the end of Genesis. Reference to God as distinct from the name Yahweh, to dreams, and to the identical characters illustrate the continuity.

Two years after the events of chapter 40, and 12 to 13 years after Joseph had left Canaan, Pharaoh had 2 dreams about cows and 7 ears of grain which obviously had the same theme and meaning, but none of his magicians could explain the meaning. In these circumstances Joseph is summoned and explains the dreams. He predicts a great famine, makes suggestions for dealing with the emergency, and finds himself appointed under Pharaoh as absolute ruler over Egypt to deal with the crisis.

26 A. L. Oppenheim, *The Interpretation of Dreams in the Ancient Near East* (Philadelphia: American Philosophical Society, 1956).

(1) Pharaoh's Dreams (41:1-8)

¹ After two whole years, Pharaoh dreamed that he was standing by the Nile, ² and behold, there came up out of the Nile seven cows sleek and fat, and they fed in the reed grass. ³ And behold, seven other cows, gaunt and thin, came up out of the Nile after them, and stood by the other cows on the bank of the Nile. ⁴ And the gaunt and thin cows ate up the seven sleek and fat cows. And Pharaoh awoke. ⁵ And he fell asleep and dreamed a second time; and behold, seven ears of grain, plump and good, were growing on one stalk. ⁶ And behold, after them sprouted seven ears, thin and blighted by the east wind. ⁷ And the thin ears swallowed up the seven plump and full ears. And Pharaoh awoke, and behold, it was a dream. ⁸ So in the morning his spirit was troubled; and he sent and called for all the magicians of Egypt and all its wise men; and Pharaoh told them his dream, but there was none who could interpret it to Pharaoh.

Joseph remained two further years in prison. Then one night the Egyptian Pharaoh dreamed that he stood beside the Nile. The Hebrew word for Nile is probably borrowed from the Egyptian 'iotr, 'io'r, so that the Egyptian word is taken over into the Hebrew text of the Bible. This word in the Old Testament, with very few exceptions, always refers to the Nile. Herodotus once described Egypt as the gift of the Nile, and certainly the fertility of Egypt depends upon this great river and especially upon its annual floods. These are due to the melting of snows in the Abyssinian Mountains where the river takes its rise. The 14 cows have no symbolic value as representing the cow-headed goddess, Hather, but are simply water cows found in Egypt through the centuries. In his dream Pharaoh saw that 7 cows were fat, and 7 were thin. *Sleek* is exactly the same description in Hebrew of Joseph himself (39:6), and of Rachel (29:17). The 7 thin ate the 7 fat cows, a fantastic dream feature. The 7 fat cows graze on the reed grass, the 7 thin cows simply stand around. Since they depict famine no grass was available for them. The Hebrew word for reed grass is also borrowed from an Egyptian word meaning "to be green."

Pharoah awoke only to fall asleep again and dream this time of 7 fat ears of corn growing on a single stalk followed lower down by 7 thin and blighted ears, and these devoured the 7 fat ears. The east wind in the Old Testament is always the sirocco which blows from the east and southeast deserts with parching heat, and was laden with grains of sand. It blows from February to June so violently as to destroy vegetation and even planted seed corn. This reference is one of the few references in Genesis to weather.

Pharaoh awoke to discover he had been dreaming, and when he arose in the morning he recollected his dreams and related them to his dream experts. They failed to interpret the meaning of what Pharaoh had dreamed about. Whether magicians and wise men represent two classes of Egyptian experts, or whether the intention is merely to say that all the "brains" of Egypt were defeated is not certain. The word for magician only occurs here and is used also in Exodus 7–10, of Egyptian experts, and in Daniel, of Babylonian experts. It is not an Egyptian word, but is probably derived from the Hebrew word meaning graving tool, stylus, and so means engravers, writers, scribes, in the further sense of astrologers or magicians.

The meaning of verse 8 is quite clear. The interpretation of the royal dream is beyond human capacity, and can only be achieved through divine help. Magic is helpless but a Joseph, as here, a Moses (Ex. 7–9), or a Daniel (Dan. 2,5), are divinely gifted to reveal the meaning. In this sense too Joseph speaks in 41:16. The contrast between human knowledge and divine revelation is illustrated in the contrast between Isaiah 29:13 and 28:29 (cf. 47:12 f.).

(2) Joseph Enters the Palace (41:9-24)

⁹ Then the chief butler said to Pharaoh, "I remember my faults today. ¹⁰ When Pharaoh was angry with his servants, and put me and the chief baker in custody in the house of the captain of the guard, ¹¹ we dreamed on the

same night, he and I, each having a dream with its own meaning. 12 A young Hebrew was there with us, a servant of the captain of the guard; and when we told him, he interpreted our dreams to us, giving an interpretation to each man according to his dream. 13 And as he interpreted to us, so it came to pass; I was restored to my office, and the baker was hanged."

14 Then Pharaoh sent and called Joseph, and they brought him hastily out of the dungeon; and when he had shaved himself and changed his clothes, he came in before Pharaoh. 15 And Pharaoh said to Joseph, "I have had a dream, and there is no one who can interpret it; and I have heard it said of you that when you hear a dream you can interpret it." 16 Joseph answered Pharaoh, "It is not in me; God will give Pharaoh a favorable answer." 17 Then Pharaoh said to Joseph, "Behold, in my dream I was standing on the banks of the Nile; 18 and seven cows, fat and sleek, came up out of the Nile and fed in the reed grass; 19 and seven other cows came up after them, poor and very gaunt and thin, such as I had never seen in all the land of Egypt. 20 And the thin and gaunt cows ate up the first seven fat cows, 21 but when they had eaten them no one would have known that they had eaten them, for they were still as gaunt as at the beginning. Then I awoke. 22 I also saw in my dream seven ears growing on one stalk, full and good; 23 and seven ears, withered, thin, and blighted by the east wind, sprouted after them, 24 and the thin ears swallowed up the seven good ears. And I told it to the magicians, but there was no one who could explain it to me."

In the general bewilderment *the chief butler* recalls his own dreams in prison, and also the faults against Pharaoh which put him there. He then remembers Joseph—the young Hebrew—who gave the meanings, and whose interpretations of the dreams were exactly fulfilled.

I remember should be translated "I will (must) mention my faults," i.e., against Pharaoh, and not against Joseph. The butler's intervention is carefully and penitently phrased so as not to revive the anger of the now vexed Pharaoh, and so to justify the butler in introducing a possible solution for the royal perplexities. *I was restored* renders the Hebrew which is literally, "me he (or one, i.e., Pharaoh) restored; him he (one) hanged."

Following this information Pharaoh sent

immediately for Joseph, who was admitted to the royal presence after having washed, shaved off his hair and his beard, and changed his garments (cf. 35:2). Pharaoh himself recounts his difficulty and praises Joseph for what he has heard about him. As in 40:8, Joseph is able to draw the distinction between human insights and divine knowledge. Joseph thus politely declines the compliment and refuses to be numbered among magicians or any other experts in dreams; but he is confident enough to promise Pharaoh a favorable answer in reply to his request.

The Pharaoh then recounts his two dreams to Joseph, and once again they are given in full. The words are not always the same, and the thin cows and the thin ears of corn are described by a third epithet, *poor* and *withered* respectively, to heighten the impression of their poor quality. In fact Pharaoh had never seen such poor beasts in his realm, and when the thin beasts had eaten the fat beasts, the thin beasts were no fatter. The extra word "withered," used of the ears of corn, is found only here in the Old Testament and means hard dried. It is omitted here by the LXX, Syriac, and Vulgate. How he referred the matter to the magicians is much abbreviated (cf. v. 24 with v. 8).

(3) Joseph's Double Solution (41:25-36)

25 Then Joseph said to Pharaoh, "The dream of Pharaoh is one; God has revealed to Pharaoh what he is about to do. 26 The seven good cows are seven years, and the seven good ears are seven years; the dream is one. 27 The seven lean and gaunt cows that came up after them are seven years, and the seven empty ears blighted by the east wind are also seven years of famine. 28 It is as I told Pharaoh, God has shown to Pharaoh what he is about to do. 29 There will come seven years of great plenty throughout all the land of Egypt, 30 but after them there will arise seven years of famine, and all the plenty will be forgotten in the land of Egypt; the famine will consume the land, 31 and the plenty will be unknown in the land by reason of that famine which will follow, for it will be very grievous. 32 And the doubling of Pharaoh's dream means that the thing is fixed by God, and God will shortly bring it to pass.

33 Now therefore let Pharaoh select a man discreet and wise, and set him over the land of Egypt. 34 Let Pharaoh proceed to appoint overseers over the land, and take the fifth part of the produce of the land of Egypt during the seven plenteous years. 35 And let them gather all the food of these good years that are coming, and lay up grain under the authority of Pharaoh for food in the cities, and let them keep it. 36 That food shall be a reserve for the land against the seven years of famine which are to befall the land of Egypt, so that the land may not perish through the famine."

In the first place, Joseph offers his interpretation of the two dreams. He claims that both have the same meaning, and winds up his interpretation in verse 32 by pointing out that the doubling of the dream means that what he has just predicted in his interpretation will certainly and quickly take place. The doubled dream is thus a divine warning of great urgency.

In the interpretation itself, Joseph first concentrates on the number seven, just as he had fastened on the number three in the dreams of the butler and the baker. This time however the seven stands for seven years in both dreams, and not for days as before. Having clarified this clue, Joseph proceeds to define the seven thin cows, and the seven bad ears of grain as *seven years of famine.* Then he makes the general application. The land of Egypt will have seven years of plentiful food, followed by seven years of famine, and these years will be so bad that all the plenty will not only be consumed in the lean years, but will be forgotten.

In verse 27 RSV follows the Hebrew in reading *empty ears,* contrasting well with the "full ears" of verses 7 and 22. The Samaritan Pentateuch, LXX, and Syriac read "poor," as in the other verses. The Hebrew words for "empty" and "poor" are almost identical and could have been confused.

In verses 33–36, Joseph, having predicted the catastrophe, goes on to the second part of his solution. He proposes certain steps be taken forthwith to deal with the situation that not only threatens but is inevitable, even predestined. Pharaoh must appoint a director-general over the entire land who will be assisted by area superintendents, and together they will organize the collection of one-fifth of the food raised during each of the good years. Although "all the food of these good years" will be gathered, apparently only one-fifth in each year will be reserved as a food supply for the famine years. Thus, one-fifth for seven of the good years will be sufficient for a normal food supply for all seven lean years. This arrangement was eventually to prove so salutory that with the consent of the people, it became a law for Egypt in perpetuity (47:24–26). The reserve of food will be stored under the authority (lit., hand; cf. 2 Kings 13:5) of Pharaoh in granaries in the cities.

(4) Joseph's New Position (41:37–45)

37 This proposal seemed good to Pharaoh and to all his servants. 38 And Pharaoh said to his servants, "Can we find such a man as this, in whom is the Spirit of God?" 39 So Pharaoh said to Joseph, "Since God has shown you all this, there is none so discreet and wise as you are; 40 you shall be over my house, and all my people shall order themselves as you command; only as regards the throne will I be greater than you." 41 And Pharaoh said to Joseph, "Behold, I have set you over all the land of Egypt." 42 Then Pharaoh took his signet ring from his hand and put it on Joseph's hand, and arrayed him in garments of fine linen, and put a gold chain about his neck; 43 and he made him to ride in his second chariot; and they cried before him, "Bow the knee!" Thus he set him over all the land of Egypt. 44 Moreover Pharaoh said to Joseph, "I am Pharaoh, and without your consent no man shall lift up hand or foot in all the land of Egypt." 45 And Pharaoh called Joseph's name Zaphenathpaneah; and he gave him in marriage Asenath, the daughter of Potiphera priest of On. So Joseph went out over the land of Egypt.

Joseph speaks with clarity and conviction. He passes quickly from predictions to practical proposals. The logical sequence of his thought and its eloquent expression are very impressive, and all unknown to Joseph, Pharaoh is being convinced that Joseph is not only a person who can interpret dreams but is the heaven-sent person who can undertake the organization of the plan he has himself proposed. Joseph is like David, "prudent in speech" (1 Sam. 16:18, lit., "understanding words") and stands before Pharaoh in appearance, eloquence, and practical mindedness so attractive and compelling that Pharaoh is bound to attribute all these gifts to the work of the Spirit of God; i.e., Joseph is divinely endowed (cf. Ex. 31:3; Num. 27:18; Dan. 5:11,14; for other tributes to eloquence cf. Prov. 16:23 f.; 18:21; esp. Mark 1:22; Luke 20:39; John 7:46). This is the first time in Genesis that the Spirit is regarded as the author of these inward gifts of understanding and illumination.

Thus Joseph becomes viceroy of Egypt. Such a personage is the official representative of Pharaoh himself, and so the second most influential figure in the kingdom. Compare for verse 40 the person "who is over the house" in Judah (1 Kings 4:6; 16:9; 2 Kings 10:5; 15:5; 18:18; Isa. 22:15, 20 ff.). *And all my people shall order themselves* represents a Hebrew clause "and upon thy mouth shall all my people kiss." The phrase reflects a custom once perhaps literally performed, but with the democratization of custom and office it has probably become a figure of authority. This figurative interpretation is given by RSV. A literal translation would have been better, even if the precise meaning is not at present available to us. The sequence of thought and action is interesting. On the basis of Joseph's words and his obvious wisdom, Pharaoh announces his intention and defines Joseph's position (v. 40). Then follows the actual statute of Joseph's appointment, *Behold, I have set*—appointed—*you.* Following the statute comes the actual installation. This is performed through a series of ceremonies.

First Pharaoh puts his own *signet ring* on Joseph's finger. The ring is thus the official badge of his office and expresses his authority, for with the ring Joseph would seal and thus authorize all the royal commands (cf. Esther 3:10; 8:2; 1 Macc. 6: 15). Next, Pharaoh *arrayed him,* or had him arrayed, in fine linen garments. The word for *linen* used here is the Egyptian and not the Hebrew word. No doubt, not merely clothes of good quality, but a particular uniform appropriate to the office is intended. Third, Pharaoh adorns him with a *gold* necklet or *chain* or collar, possibly a reward rather than merely a mark of office. Like the actual insignia mentioned the phrase describes probably some Egyptian custom. Egyptian influence is thus paramount through the paragraph. The same applies to Joseph's public appearances. Joseph is permitted to ride in the second chariot, i.e., not of quality but of rank (cf. 1 Sam. 23:17; Esther 10:3; 2 Chron. 28:7). Horses and chariots first appear in the pictorial representations on Egyptian monuments of the eighteenth dynasty following the expulsion of the Hyksos invaders. Heralds or runners were to call out *'abhrekh.* The meaning of this word is still uncertain. The word closely resembles the Hebrew word for "kneel," e.g., "make to kneel down," hence the call, *Bow the knee.* Preferably the word is the Hebrew form of an Egyptian expression for which several explanations have been offered. Thus the word may be an ejaculation or instruction, "Attend," "Bow the knee," or it may be the title of some Egyptian office. The concluding words of verse 43 bring to an end the arrangements for Joseph's installation.

Following the glory attending the ceremonies, Pharaoh deems it wise to define their respective positions. Pharaoh proclaims his own royalty, then the authority of Joseph which is regulative of all behavior in Egypt: *lift up hand or foot,* i.e., "do anything whatsoever."

As Abram and Jacob received new names according to their new place in the purposes of God, so Joseph receives a new name to mark out his new position in the Egyptian government. This new name is *Zaphenathpaneah.* Egyptologists are increasingly agreed that the name means "the god speaks and he lives." Names of this form appear in inscriptions from the twentieth dynasty onward. Perhaps the reference to the god is to Pharaoh himself. This would obviate any clash between an Egyptian god and the God of the Hebrews, and could accurately reflect the context in which Joseph owes his life and new position to Pharaoh himself.

Another mark of the royal favor is Joseph's marriage with *Asenath, the daughter of Potiphera priest of On,* one of the most important persons in the religious life of ancient Egypt. The name *Asenath* means devotee of goddess, Neth. Potiphera must have been quite a common name, though none of the Egyptian names in the present context was frequent before the twenty-second dynasty. *On* is Heliopolis, about seven miles northeast of Cairo, a center of the worship of the sun god (cf. Jer. 43:3). The priesthood at On was distinguished for its learning, and according to Plutarch, was of royal rank.

Joseph's marriage, like his new name, could have become an opportunity for false worship, for it also certainly represented social advancement. The sequel of the story shows that they did not. Certainly in later Israel, and especially in the days of Ezra and Nehemiah, both the new name and marriage would have been condemned.

(5) Fulfilment (41:46-57)

⁴⁶ Joseph was thirty years old when he entered the service of Pharaoh king of Egypt. And Joseph went out from the presence of Pharaoh, and went through all the land of Egypt. ⁴⁷ During the seven plenteous years the earth brought forth abundantly, ⁴⁸ and he gathered up all the food of the seven years when there was plenty in the land of Egypt, and stored up food in the cities; he stored up in every city the food from the fields around it. ⁴⁹ And Joseph stored up grain in great abundance, like the sand of the sea, until he ceased to measure it, for it could not be measured. ⁵⁰ Before the year of famine came, Joseph had two sons, whom Asenath, the daughter of Potiphera priest of On, bore to him. ⁵¹ Joseph called the name of the first-born Manasseh, "For," he said, "God has made me forget all my hardship and all my father's house." ⁵² The name of the second he called Ephraim, "For God has made me fruitful in the land of my affliction."

⁵³ The seven years of plenty that prevailed in the land of Egypt came to an end; ⁵⁴ and the seven years of famine began to come, as Joseph had said. There was famine in all lands; but in all the land of Egypt there was bread. ⁵⁵ When all the land of Egypt was famished, the people cried to Pharaoh for bread; and Pharaoh said to all the Egyptians, "Go to Joseph; what he says to you, do." ⁵⁶ So when the famine had spread over all the land, Joseph opened all the storehouses, and sold to the Egyptians, for the famine was severe in the land of Egypt. ⁵⁷ Moreover, all the earth came to Egypt to Joseph to buy grain, because the famine was severe over all the earth.

A chronological note (v. 46), probably contributed by the P witness, places Joseph at thirty years of age at this critical point in his life. Comparison with 37:2 shows that Joseph's slavery and imprisonment must have lasted some 12 or 13 years. *Entered the service* represents the Hebrew, "stood before" (Deut. 1:38; 1 Sam. 16:21). Joseph made a tour of the land of Egypt.

Joseph's dream is exactly fulfilled. Egypt enjoyed abundant food for seven years, and each year Joseph stored up of the abundance in the granaries of the cities throughout the land. The story means of course that normal needs were met and what was superfluous was stored, unless the proportion of verse 34, i.e., one-fifth, was really observed.

Joseph, now second in command in the land, married to an aristocratic wife as befitted his new rank, is now blessed with two sons, *Manasseh* and *Ephraim.* The first name means "making to forget," but this does not mean that he forgot, or blotted out either the memory of his slavery or of his upbringing. It either means, as von Rad says, "to have something no longer" or better "was compensated for" or "received the comforting equivalent of," i.e., a national rank for hardship, his own family for his father's family. The second name, Ephraim, means to be fruitful, appropriate for a second son, and also descriptive of the land of Ephraim, i.e., northern Israel, where the tribes of Ephraim and Manasseh eventually settled. The sons are born during the period of plenty, so even Joseph's family fortunes are in accord with his predictions.

The circumstances of Joseph's marriage

should be contrasted with the marriages of the earlier favorite sons. Isaac was not allowed to leave the land when his wife was sought. Jacob flees from the land and finds his wife from the Haran branch of the family. Joseph is forcibly taken from Canaan to Egypt where he marries an Egyptian lady.

Isaac and Jacob thus married within the patriarchal family, but Judah married a Canaanite woman (38:2), and also had sons from his Canaanite daughter-in-law. Thus in the royal Judah-Davidic house there is a strong Canaanite element. Joseph's two sons by his Egyptian wife became the two principal tribes of northern Israel. Altogether Israel is eventually of very cosmopoliton origin, and the mixture of nationality in the tribes, in the royal house, as in the capital city, Jerusalem itself, are most marked (cf. Ezek. 16:3). Obviously if late Jewish influences were really responsible for the stories of the exclusive marriages of Isaac and Jacob, as it is sometimes claimed, such influences no longer applied in the story of Judah and Joseph. However, the better explanation is once again to be found in the strength and reliability of the traditions of the witnesses.

Again, as Joseph had predicted, the seven years of plenty were followed by seven years of famine, and the famine occurred *in all lands.* This is the Old Testament way of saying, "The famine was pretty universal" (cf. 1 Kings 10:24; 18:10). Emergencies and shortages would inevitably occur in spite of precautions and plans. There is therefore no necessary inconsistency between verses 54 and 55. The thriftless and the nervous would inevitably complain, but Joseph had provided. The RSV correctly supplies *storehouses* in verse 56.

Verse 57 is also the link, historical in itself, which provides the framework for the first visit of Joseph's brethren to Egypt.

Note

The Egyptian caste of the Joseph story is beyond doubt. Apart from the details of 41:37–46, references to famine, store-

houses, distribution of grain are typical (cf. the older commentaries by Driver and Skinner for illustrations from the Egyptian monuments themselves). What remains beyond discovery is the identity of the Pharaoh in Joseph's days.

Pharaoh is of course a title for the ruler of Egypt, and not the name of any given person. It is similar to the title of President for the head of the United States of America. By the title "President" any one of a number of persons could be intended. Similarly the chronological data of the Old Testament are insufficient in themselves, especially when compared with the genealogies to lead to a decisive result.

In general it may be said that there are two periods in Egyptian history when the career of such a person as Joseph was possible. The first of the periods is the Hyksos period of domination over Egypt. The Hyksos occupation of Egypt ended in about 1550 B.C., having lasted some two centuries or so, though for 511 years according to the ancient historian Manetho (cf. Josephus, *Contra Ap.* 1.14). In turn this would be supported by the chronological data of the Old Testament. According to this scheme, and beginning from 1 Kings 6:1 and Exodus 12:40, the date of the Exodus would be 1440 B.C. and Jacob's descent 1870 B.C. or 1655 (LXX). On this reckoning then the Pharaoh of the Joseph period will be one of the Hyksos kings.

The other possibility is of course what is called the Amarna age, *ca.* 1417–1362 B.C. Thus Rib-adda, the king of the city of Byblos in Phoenicia, often refers to a powerful Egyptian official by name of Yanhamu. He was an Egyptian viceroy in Syria, held the office of "royal fanbearer," and was charged with the supply of grain for the Syrian people in time of famine. His name is Semitic, and his position is comparable to that of Joseph. Thus Joseph's period has been set in the latter part of the Amarna age, and Joseph's Pharaoh identified with Akhenaton. This possibility, and it cannot at present be more highly rated, is confirmed by the evidence from Old Testament genealogies as distinct from the chronological data.[27]

The choice thus lies probably between the late Hurrian (late 17th century) or late Armarna (15th century) periods.

XXIII. The Brothers in Egypt (42:1—45: 28)

Chapter 42 begins the second part of the Joseph narrative which extends from *ca.* 42 to 45 in which nearly all the original characters of the first part of the Joseph narrative reappear. Two journeys to Egypt before the final descent of Jacob and all the family, four interviews with Joseph, a series of expedients to delay the denouement and to increase the suspense, finally brings the story to its climax in the reconciliation of Joseph and his brethren.

Jacob's ten sons visited Egypt to buy corn, were recognized by Joseph, imprisoned by him as spies, and released after three days. Simeon was detained as surety for the return of the nine brothers, who were enjoined to bring with them Benjamin, Jacob's twelfth and last son. The brothers secretly accept their treatment as due punishment for their treatment of Joseph years before. Their fear is increased by the discovery that the money they had spent in Egypt for corn was actually in their sacks. Jacob further complicates their position by refusing permission for Benjamin to go back to Egypt with them.

The E witness contributes the whole of the chapter with the possible exception of verses 27–28, which may be from J, who is said to begin his part of the narrative at 41:38 and continues to the end of chapter 44. The E witness reappears in chapter 45.

1. The First Visit (42:1–38)

(1) Famine in Canaan (42:1–5)

[1] When Jacob learned that there was grain in Egypt, he said to his sons, "Why do you

look at one another?" [2] And he said, "Behold, I have heard that there is grain in Egypt; go down and buy grain for us there, that we may live, and not die." [3] So ten of Joseph's brothers went down to buy grain in Egypt. [4] But Jacob did not send Benjamin, Joseph's brother, with his brothers, for he feared that harm might befall him. [5] Thus the sons of Israel came to buy among the others who came, for the famine was in the land of Canaan.

What von Rad describes as "a marked caesura" between chapters 41—42, Skinner describes as "another effective change of scene." The account returns from Egypt to Palestine to describe the effect of the famine upon Jacob's family. While the brothers vacillate, Jacob is decisive and executive. At his bidding the ten sons go to Egypt (cf. 12:10). Jacob retains his twelfth son, Rachel's second son (35:18) at home, for this boy, Benjamin, has taken Joseph's place in his father's affections (44:29–31).

(2) First Interview with Joseph (42:6–17)

[6] Now Joseph was governor over the land; he it was who sold to all the people of the land. And Joseph's brothers came, and bowed themselves before him with their faces to the ground. [7] Joseph saw his brothers, and knew them, but he treated them like strangers and spoke roughly to them. "Where do you come from?" he said. They said, "From the land of Canaan, to buy food." [8] Thus Joseph knew his brothers, but they did not know him. [9] And Joseph remembered the dreams which he had dreamed of them; and he said to them, "You are spies, you have come to see the weakness of the land." [10] They said to him, "No, my lord, but to buy food have your servants come. [11] We are all sons of one man, we are honest men, your servants are not spies." [12] He said to them, "No, it is the weakness of the land that you have come to see." [13] And they said, "We, your servants, are twelve brothers, the sons of one man in the land of Canaan; and behold, the youngest is this day with our father, and one is no more." [14] But Joseph said to them, "It is as I said to you, you are spies. [15] By this you shall be tested: by the life of Pharaoh, you shall not go from this place unless your youngest brother comes here. [16] Send one of you, and let him bring your brother, while you remain in prison, that your words may be tested, whether there is truth in you; or else, by the life of Pharaoh, surely you are spies." [17] And he put them all together in prison for three days.

---

[27] The most comprehensive and valuable discussion of the problem is still that of H. H. Rowley, *From Joseph to Joshua*, Schweich Lectures, 1948 (London: Oxford, 1950). For the genealogies cf. Gen. 46; Ex. 6; Num. 26; and "Genealogy" in *HDB*; cf. E. L. Curtis, "Genealogy," *ibid*, II, 121–37.

Governor renders a late Hebrew word meaning to have the mastery over. Perhaps the word is a technical term which remained extant in the tradition. Pharaoh owns all the land and its food, which Joseph as his representative sells to the people. The ten brothers are shown into his presence, and make obeisance with their faces to the ground. Thus without their knowing the dream prediction of 37:7 ff. is largely fulfilled. Joseph recognized them, but they did not recognize the apparently Egyptian regal figure before them. The play on the Hebrew words in verses 7–8 is forceful: *knew them* and *treated them like strangers* is in Hebrew *wayyakkirem wayyitnakker*. Verse 7 is not a duplication from J, but a reiteration for the sake of emphasis.

The narrative is really "obvious." Joseph plays the part of an overbearing potentate: he reiterates charges familiar and relevant to men in such circumstances. Joseph charges them with being spies who have come to spy out the defenseless character of the land, because the northeastern frontier of Egypt is vulnerable. This fact makes the accusation plausible, though in itself it is ridiculous but very terrible to the brothers. The reiterated accusation gains a slightly fuller rebuttal and Joseph inwardly realizes the truth of their statements. Facts, however irrelevant, are a wonderful form of defense. He takes the obvious step and resolves to test their story. They are to send one of their number home to bring back the brother of whom they have spoken. Joseph puts them in prison for three days for surety, and perhaps to help them make up their minds. The strength and strangeness of the oath *by the life of Pharaoh* adds strength to Joseph's purpose and terror to the minds of his hearers. In form the oath is parallel to, "As the Lord lives," or, "as your soul lives" (cf. 1 Sam. 14:39; 17:55). Joseph's behavior is quite reasonable in the circumstances (cf. v. 16).

(3) *Second Interview with Joseph (42: 18–25)*

¹⁸ On the third day Joseph said to them, "Do this and you will live, for I fear God: ¹⁹ if you are honest men, let one of your brothers remain confined in your prison, and let the rest go and carry grain for the famine of your households, ²⁰ and bring your youngest brother to me; so your words will be verified, and you shall not die." And they did so. ²¹ Then they said to one another, "In truth we are guilty concerning our brother, in that we saw the distress of his soul, when he besought us and we would not listen; therefore is this distress come upon us." ²² And Reuben answered them, "Did I not tell you not to sin against the lad? But you would not listen. So now there comes a reckoning for his blood." ²³ They did not know that Joseph understood them, for there was an interpreter between them. ²⁴ Then he turned away from them and wept; and he returned to them and spoke to them. And he took Simeon from them and bound him before their eyes. ²⁵ And Joseph gave orders to fill their bags with grain, and to replace every man's money in his sack, and to give them provisions for the journey. This was done for them.

During the following three days Joseph recasts his intentions regarding his brothers. He summons them to his presence and with an affirmation of his own honesty in the words, *I fear God*, i.e., "I am a godfearing man whose word may be relied upon," proposes a milder form of his test. He will retain but one brother; the others may return home alive and succour their family with food. In return they must bring back their youngest brother. In both interviews the names of Jacob, Joseph, or Benjamin are not used.

This second proposal is followed by a little scene which all but overwhelmed Joseph. Apparently he had spoken with his brothers in some language other than theirs through an interpreter. Did they speak Hebrew and did Joseph speak Egyptian to heighten the illusion concerning himself? On the one hand they agreed to Joseph's proposal, and having thus heard the worst, fall to recriminations among themselves. They come to the conclusion that their present distress is the punishment due for their treatment of Joseph. Reuben joins in with a forceful reminder of his warning to them (37:22) but speaks on the assumption of Joseph's death. No doubt Reuben's intervention was news to Joseph. This confession of their guilt and this discovery of Reuben's earlier intervention cause Joseph to break down. He retires from them to weep.

On his return he puts his plan into action and chooses Simeon, the eldest after Reuben, for detention. Does the choice go back to Joseph's memory of some unmentioned harsh treatment from Simeon, or is it simply another hint of Simeon's character (ch. 34; 49:5–7). Just as once they appeared before Jacob without Joseph, so now they must again appear before their father without another of his sons.

(4) Return to Canaan (42:26–38)

26 Then they loaded their asses with their grain, and departed. 27 And as one of them opened his sack to give his ass provender at the lodging place, he saw his money in the mouth of his sack; 28 and he said to his brothers, "My money has been put back; here it is in the mouth of my sack!" At this their hearts failed them, and they turned trembling to one another, saying, "What is this that God has done to us?"

29 When they came to Jacob their father in the land of Canaan, they told him all that had befallen them, saying, 30 "The man, the lord of the land, spoke roughly to us, and took us to be spies of the land. 31 But we said to him, 'We are honest men, we are not spies; 32 we are twelve brothers, sons of our father; one is no more, and the youngest is this day with our father in the land of Canaan.' 33 Then the man, the lord of the land, said to us, 'By this I shall know that you are honest men: leave one of your brothers with me, and take grain for the famine of your households, and go your way. 34 Bring your youngest brother to me; then I shall know that you are not spies but honest men, and I will deliver to you your brother, and you shall trade in the land.' "

35 As they emptied their sacks, behold, every man's bundle of money was in his sack; and when they and their father saw their bundles of money, they were dismayed. 36 And Jacob their father said to them, "You have bereaved me of my children: Joseph is no more, and Simeon is no more, and now you would take Benjamin; all this has come upon me." 37 Then Reuben said to his father, "Slay my two sons if I do not bring him back to you; put him in my hands, and I will bring him back to you." 38 But he said, "My son shall not go down with you, for his brother is dead, and he only is left. If harm should befall him on the journey that you are to make, you would bring down my gray hairs with sorrow to Sheol."

Joseph's last action before the departure of his brothers, and no doubt an impulse in sympathy with the feelings described in verse 24, was to place the money the brothers had paid him for the corn in each man's sack, and then on top of that to provide as well for the needs of their journey home. En route at one of the nightly stopping places, one of the brothers discovered the money. They looked upon this as another bad omen, but apparently refrained, possibly because of fear, from opening all the other sacks to see if they also contained the money. Otherwise it must be supposed that they all opened their sacks and all discovered their money. If this is correct, and since verse 35 says they actually found the rest of the money only after their return home, then verses 27–28 must be the J parallel to 35. That these verses are from J is further suggested by the word for sack used as the last word in verse 27. It is a different word from that used earlier in the verse, and it is used in verse 28 and 13 times in verses 43 f. and nowhere else in the Old Testament. Since chapters 43—44 are J, it would appear that 42:27 f. are also J. Again the double tradition adds verisimilitude to what is related.

On reaching home they tell Jacob of their experiences, recounting Joseph's accusations and their own defense, and how they finally agreed to leave Simeon behind as a bound hostage, pending the return of the remaining nine brothers with Benjamin as proof of the veracity of their defense.

In their father's presence they plucked up enough courage to open their sacks. From their discovery en route that one sack contained the money, they suspected that all sacks were the same. If they did not open all the sacks en route it was because they were too frightened. Also if they had been followed from Egypt, eight of the brothers could claim ignorance of the money in the sacks. When the sacks were opened, they and Jacob were all the more dismayed.

The discovery shows Jacob that his sons were telling the truth. Jacob recounts his sorrows. "Me you have bereaved" he says, in the emphatic order of the Hebrew. Joseph, then Simeon, *and now you would take Benjamin; all this has come upon me.* This last phrase needs to be turned around to bring out the emphasis of the Hebrew words, "Upon me are all these things." Thus Jacob throughout the verse is said to emphasize his misery. In spite of Reuben's guarantee to slay his own two sons if he does not bring Benjamin safely back, Jacob will have none of the arrangement, and once again a seeming deadlock is pointed out. (For note on Sheol, cf. on 37:35.)

2. Second Visit to Egypt (43:1—45:28)

(1) The Dispute About Benjamin (43:1-10)

¹ Now the famine was severe in the land. ² And when they had eaten the grain which they had brought from Egypt, their father said to them, "Go again, buy us a little food." ³ But Judah said to him, "The man solemnly warned us, saying, 'You shall not see my face, unless your brother is with you.' ⁴ If you will send our brother with us, we will go down and buy you food; ⁵ but if you will not send him, we will not go down, for the man said to us, 'You shall not see my face, unless your brother is with you.' " ⁶ Israel said, "Why did you treat me so ill as to tell the man that you had another brother?" ⁷ They replied, "The man questioned us carefully about ourselves and our kindred, saying, 'Is your father still alive? Have you another brother?' What we told him was in answer to these questions; could we in any way know that he would say, 'Bring your brother down'?" ⁸ And Judah said to Israel his father, "Send the lad with me, and we will arise and go, that we may live and not die, both we and you and also our little ones. ⁹ I will be surety for him; of my hand you shall require him. If I do not bring him back to you and set him before you, then let me bear the blame for ever; ¹⁰ for if we had not delayed, we would now have returned twice."

The J witness reappears at 42:38 or better with 43:1, and his version now continues through the next two chapters. The change of witness does not involve any break in the sequence. After Jacob's adamant refusal (42:38), the question of another visit to Egypt, even the problem that Simeon is still held in Egypt as a hostage, remain in abeyance. Faced with the obduracy of the aged, all that can be done is to wait until circumstances compel the issue to be raised again. The anxiety over the food supply, over Simeon, added to the sense of Jacob's grievance and the brothers' guilt over Joseph, imply an atmosphere of tension and great difficulty.

Jacob, in this chapter called Israel, as is usual in the J witness, resumes the initiative and in face of the waiting attitude of the brothers advises another shopping expedition to Egypt to buy corn. This time Judah takes up the cudgels on behalf of the brothers. It is really not sufficient to say that whereas according to the E witness, Reuben, but according to the J witness Judah, is the spokesman. Granted that there is a change of speaker, this may indicate a psychological development in the argument. In other words, if the whole of J and E were extant the argument in both witnesses might have been carried on by Reuben and Judah in succession. Thus in 37:22 Reuben begins the effort to save Joseph, but in 37:26 f. Judah succeeds. Likewise in 42:37 Reuben begins the attempt to break down Jacob's obduracy, but in 43:3,8 Judah actually succeeds.

The order of intervention by Reuben and then by Judah, and the degree of success they enjoyed, probably reflect the original tradition of both witnesses and thus bear testimony to the weight of influence that Judah was able to bring to bear on the debate. In 42:37 Reuben proposes a bargain, but in 43:3-5 Judah delivers an ultimatum compounded of Joseph's condition and their own demands. *See my face* means to have an audience (cf. 44:23,26; 2 Sam. 3:13; 14:24,28). Israel accuses his sons of telling "the man" too much, but they point out that they were compelled to answer his questions. In fact in 42:13 they do volunteer the information concerning the family. It is actually in J that they concede the information (cf. 44:19). Then finally Judah, with a mixture of appeal and guarantee and even reproach about the delay, wins Israel over.

The RSV in verse 7 with *questioned us carefully,* and *could we in any way know* makes a good effort to bring out the strong emphasis of the Hebrew verbs. "He cross-examined us" and "how could we possibly know" also indicate something of the petulance of the brothers' defense. Judah's words *then let me bear the blame for ever* renders the Hebrew, "I shall have sinned against thee for ever," and means "will be your debtor for the rest of your life"; i.e., the father will be able to do what he wills to his offending son (cf. 1 Kings 1:21). Judah thus commits his life into his father's keeping and this no doubt was the final gesture to convince his father.

(2) Preparation for the Second Journey (43:11–15)

11 Then their father Israel said to them, "If it must be so, then do this: take some of the choice fruits of the land in your bags, and carry down to the man a present, a little balm and a little honey, gum, myrrh, pistachio nuts, and almonds. 12 Take double the money with you; carry back with you the money that was returned in the mouth of your sacks; perhaps it was an oversight. 13 Take also your brother, and arise, go again to the man; 14 may God Almighty grant you mercy before the man, that he may send back your other brother and Benjamin. If I am bereaved of my children, I am bereaved." 15 So the men took the present, and they took double the money with them, and Benjamin; and they arose and went down to Egypt, and stood before Joseph.

Israel agrees to his sons' demands, but then prepares to make the best of a bad job. First, they must take some choice fruits of the land with them. *Choice fruits* renders the Hebrew "the praise (or less likely the pruning) of the land"; it may mean, less likely, "admirable products." Perhaps the Hebrew means "by praise of the land"; i.e., what we mean by first prize in the flower show. The sense is clear; the best of fruits must be taken. Second, they are to take *a present* of manufactured products (37:25)

and nuts. The Hebrew word for *pistachio nuts* is only mentioned here in the Old Testament. The *honey* is probably real wild bee honey (Ezek. 27:17), and not merely dibs, i.e., a sweet brown syrup gotten by boiling grape juice. Third, they are to take *double the money,* and the meaning probably is the money that they in ignorance brought back, and what they will owe for their new purchases. Fourth, they may take Benjamin, and thus at last Israel gives way. They are to go again *to the man.* These words are used six times in the first 13 verses of this chapter, and thus the mystery and objectivity of the distant Joseph is conveyed in the narrative. As soon as the narrative has returned to Egypt, and the reader is once more in his presence, *the man* resumes his name and is referred to as Joseph. Israel commits his family—all eleven sons are now involved—to the care of *'El Shaddai, God Almighty.* This title of God occurs nowhere else in the J or E witnesses, but no doubt Israel is here invoking the great God of Abraham as the ultimate protection for his family's fortunes. The reference is surely not accidental nor redactional but a mark of the deepest piety in the deepest perplexity. This is confirmed by the last words of verse 14 which express final resignation (cf. 42:26; 2 Kings 7:4; Esther 4:16).

The packing, the loading of the beasts, the departure, the journey, the entry to Joseph's office are all described in one verse. The duration of time is left to be inferred.

3. Joseph Entertains His Brothers (43: 16–34)

16 When Joseph saw Benjamin with them, he said to the steward of his house, "Bring the men into the house, and slaughter an animal and make ready, for the men are to dine with me at noon." 17 The man did as Joseph bade him, and brought the men to Joseph's house. 18 And the men were afraid because they were brought to Joseph's house, and they said, "It is because of the money, which was replaced in our sacks the first time, that we are brought in, so that he may seek occasion against us and fall upon us, to make slaves of us and seize our

asses." 19 So they went up to the steward of Joseph's house, and spoke with him at the door of the house, 20 and said, "Oh, my lord, we came down the first time to buy food; 21 and when we came to the lodging place we opened our sacks, and there was every man's money in the mouth of his sack, our money in full weight; so we have brought it again with us, 22 and we have brought other money down in our hand to buy food. We do not know who put our money in our sacks." 23 He replied, "Rest assured, do not be afraid; your God and the God of your father must have put treasure in your sacks for you; I received your money." Then he brought Simeon out to them. 24 And when the man had brought the men into Joseph's house, and given them water, and they had washed their feet, and when he had given their asses provender, 25 they made ready the present for Joseph's coming at noon, for they heard that they should eat bread there.

26 When Joseph came home, they brought into the house to him the present which they had with them, and bowed down to him to the ground. 27 And he inquired about their welfare, and said, "Is your father well, the old man of whom you spoke? Is he still alive?" 28 They said, "Your servant our father is well, he is still alive." And they bowed their heads and made obeisance. 29 And he lifted up his eyes, and saw his brother Benjamin, his mother's son, and said, "Is this your youngest brother, of whom you spoke to me? God be gracious to you, my son!" 30 Then Joseph made haste, for his heart yearned for his brother, and he sought a place to weep. And he entered his chamber and wept there. 31 Then he washed his face and came out; and controlling himself he said, "Let food be served." 32 They served him by himself, and them by themselves, and the Egyptians who ate with him by themselves, because the Egyptians might not eat bread with the Hebrews, for that is an abomination to the Egyptians. 33 And they sat before him, the first-born according to his birthright and the youngest according to his youth; and the men looked at one another in amazement. 34 Portions were taken to them from Joseph's table, but Benjamin's portion was five times as much as any of theirs. So they drank and were merry with him.

The J witness now takes ten verses to describe the events and words of a morning spent by the brothers in surmise and in suspense for Joseph's will to be made known. The brothers see Joseph, and Joseph sees them and Benjamin, but not a word is exchanged, though the brothers realize that instructions about them have

been given by "the man" himself. Joseph's house steward (cf. 44:1,4; 39:4 and 41:40), who by now was almost certainly a party to the plot, is to bring them to Joseph's home where they are to *dine . . . at noon.* A beast is to be slain and this itself is a mark of wealth and occasion.

But their admission to Joseph's home only frightens the brothers all the more. They can only imagine worse treatment than on the previous visit and find an explanation in the mysterious money inexplicably found in their sacks. They suspect a conspiracy which will lead to slavery and the forfeit of all their possessions. *Seek occasion* is literally "roll themselves over us" only here. They seek to forestall any accusation by trying to justify themselves to the house steward. They make a long speech, all of three verses, to explain their situation and their innocence about the money. The money returned was in full weight; i.e., it was the exact amount measured by weight. The man's reply is twofold. "That money was a divine windfall for I actually received your money." The mystery of the returned money thus gets deeper, but at least they can feel themselves not to be guilty. Then Simeon is restored to them. Then by washing, feeding their animals, preparing their present, they make ready for the promised meal.

This vivid scene is divided into three parts. Joseph first receives his brethren, and the account of his suavity is extraordinary especially in view of what he has in mind; then follows his withdrawal ostensibly to prepare for the meal, but really to conceal his tears, and lastly the extraordinary arrangements for the meal.

The brothers reenter Joseph's house with their present handy (cf. 24:10; Num. 22:7), and again prostrate themselves before Joseph (37:3–9; 42:6). Joseph politely inquires after their health; quickly establishes that which he most desires to know that his father was alive and well, and publicly identifies Benjamin whom he had already secretly recognized (v. 16). Joseph further marks out his own full brother, who is considered to be quite young, though the disparity in their ages was small, with a prayer-greeting. The tender movement of Joseph's mind (literally, bowels; cf. 1 Kings 3:26; Hos. 11:8) toward Benjamin was however too much for him, and he had to leave hurriedly but with as much dignity as possible to hide his distress. He returns, composed to order the serving of the meal.

The meal is arranged according to Egyptian custom. Egyptian eating arrangements were well known to Herodotus (cf. 1.2.41) as controlled by ritual ideas. Joseph eats apart; the brothers as visitors and non-Egyptians apart, but apparently facing Joseph (v. 33), and the Egyptians also apart. The room takes on a vivid and colorful scene in the mind's eye, as we think of the colors, the flowers, the food, the attendants and perhaps the dancing girls as well. Further, two surprising things occurred. The brothers noticed that they were placed in order of their ages. This must surely have betrayed Joseph's secret, unless more likely the ordering had been previously arranged with the brothers as a mark of courtesy to them. Then also everybody saw that Benjamin had received from top table a portion (cf. 1 Sam. 1:5; 9:23; 2 Sam. 11:8) five times greater than anybody else had received. Aided by such civilities, such correctness not to mention much wine, the visitors were completely relaxed and carefree. They were at least very merry (cf. Hag. 1:6; Song of Solomon, 5:1).

There is no adequate explanation why Benjamin's portion should have been five times (lit., hands) as large. Since the physical task of consuming so much would have been difficult, the number five, especially if it came in five dishes or in five parts on one dish, must have had some meaning as a mark of honor. It is sometimes claimed that the number five is particularly significant in Egypt, (cf. 41:34; 45:22; 47:2,24; Isa. 19:18).

4. Joseph's Last Test (44:1-34)

The J witness continues his story and his account is generally parallel to the story in chapter 43. The secret instruction to his steward (cf. 43:16-17 with 44:1-5), is followed by the interview between the steward and the brothers (cf. 43:19-24 with 44:6-13), and finally the encounter between Joseph himself and his brothers (cf. 43:26-34 with 44:14-34). Thus the essential ingredients of the plot are brought out. These are: (a) the correctness of Joseph's behavior; (b) this correctness throws into high relief his plan for testing the character and conduct of his brothers, a plan which he shares with his steward; and (c) the private purpose known only to Joseph which he nurtures secretly in his own heart, the collapse of which is discovered in the sequel to this present chapter.

(1) Last Secret Plan (44:1-5)

¹ Then he commanded the steward of his house, "Fill the men's sacks with food, as much as they can carry, and put each man's money in the mouth of his sack, ² and put my cup, the silver cup, in the mouth of the sack of the youngest, with his money for the grain." And he did as Joseph told him. ³ As soon as the morning was light, the men were sent away with their asses. ⁴ When they had gone but a short distance from the city, Joseph said to his steward, "Up, follow after the men; and when you overtake them, say to them, 'Why have you returned evil for good? Why have you stolen my silver cup? ⁵ Is it not from this that my lord drinks, and by this that he divines? You have done wrong in so doing.'"

Joseph privately instructs his steward to provide the men with corn, to return the purchase money, and to put his personal *cup* in Benjamin's sack. He is to give the men a few hours' start and then overtake them and accuse them of theft.

Many scholars have thought, unnecessarily, that the further deposit of the money in the sacks is a detail added by some editor later, because no further reference to this money is made. Interest thus centers on the cup. This is the new feature, and the means of the new and, as it turns out, the last test.

This paragraph reveals several interesting points. Each man has a sack, and his own sum of money. The size of the sacks is limited by the strength of the beasts of burden, but one sack per brother seems a small amount to justify a long journey to Egypt. There must have been other sacks; e.g., for Jacob. Perhaps each man's sack indicates that the brothers, except perhaps Benjamin, had each his own household. This would agree with the story about Judah in chapter 38, with the reference to Reuben's children (42:37). References are probably limited to each man's sack for the purposes of the story.

Then the cup is Joseph's personal and divining cup. The Hebrew word is not the usual word for cup. Perhaps goblet would be better. The word used here is also used of the golden cups of the candlestick of the tabernacle (Ex. 25: 31–34; 37:17–20), and of bowls in Jeremiah 35:5. Thus quite accidentally information is given about an Egyptian custom. Cups were used for divining, either by interpreting the shape, number, and size of the drops that dropped from the cup, or from the action of the contents of the cup when various metals or objects were put into the cup. No doubt Joseph who understood dreams also dabbled in cup divination (cf. v. 15).

Then again the brothers depart at first light. This is another of the rare references which the book of Genesis makes to weather conditions. Temporal references to early morning (19:15; 22:3; 28:18; 44:3), and to evening (15:5,17; 19:1; 24:63; 28:11; 32:13,22) are also indirect references to the prevailing heat and to the most suitable traveling conditions. Famine conditions imply periods of drought. No one would imagine that all the stories narrated in Genesis took place beneath a blazing and pitiless heat (cf., however, 18:1), which rendered early morning and late evening journeys preferable. The weather is too constant except for the rainy seasons and the exceptional conditions described in the flood stories, to merit frequent reference.

The fictitious accusation was theft, theft of a personal and possibly semisacred possession. A person convicted of theft would be fined according to his offense, but if the theft involved a sacred object then life was forfeit (Josh. 7:25).

At the end of verse 4 RSV supplies with the LXX, Latin, and Syriac against the Hebrew, *Why have you stolen my silver cup?* which introduces verse 5 more logically.

(2) *The Steward's Accusation* (43:6–13)

6 When he overtook them, he spoke to them these words. **7** They said to him, "Why does my lord speak such words as these? Far be it from your servants that they should do such a thing! **8** Behold, the money which we found in the mouth of our sacks, we brought back to you from the land of Canaan; how then should we steal silver or gold from your lord's house? **9** With whomever of your servants it be found, let him die, and we also will be my lord's slaves." **10** He said, "Let it be as you say: he with whom it is found shall be my slave, and the rest of you shall be blameless." **11** Then every man quickly lowered his sack to the ground, and every man opened his sack. **12** And he searched, beginning with the eldest and ending with the youngest; and the cup was found in Benjamin's sack. **13** Then they rent their clothes, and every man loaded his ass, and they returned to the city.

When the brothers are free of Joseph's household on the return journey they are suddenly overtaken and accused by Joseph's steward. They are flabbergasted. They recount their honest conduct, and are so confident of the issue, and rightly, for they are in fact innocent, that they agree that if any one of them has the cup, he shall be put to death and the rest will become slaves. The reference to death may be hyperbole or the recognized punishment for the crime. The steward limits the punishment to the enslaving of the guilty party, if such there be among them. The other brothers will be blameless. On this prior understanding they open their sacks and the steward finds the cup in the last he searched, in Benjamin's (cf. 1 Sam. 15:6 ff.). In grief and in despair, they return to the city where Joseph lives.

The plot centers on Benjamin. The steward's categorical and binding sentence— the guilty one only shall become a slave (v. 10)—is exactly echoed later in Joseph's sentence (v. 17). Obviously, beforehand, Joseph and the steward had agreed that the punishment was to fit the crime. Benjamin, and Benjamin only, was to appear to be punished. He was to be detained in Joseph's household in Egypt as a slave.

What was Joseph's purpose in this "insolent, almost wanton game" (von Rad) that he and his man were playing? Joseph maintains his correctness and justice in limiting the punishment to Benjamin. The brothers can have no complaint on that score. His plan is obviously to test the brothers at the most sensitive point of their relationships with the father. Joseph wishes to discover whether his brothers will now abandon Benjamin, as they did away with him, and as they were prepared to leave Simeon; and whether they would now return to Jacob and advise the old father to accept his losses and thus give up Benjamin, as he had been forced to give up Joseph and Simeon earlier in the story. The sequel shows that the brothers were not prepared to do this, and that Judah, or any one of them, was prepared to surrender himself so that Benjamin might return to Jacob.

The question is whether this is all that Joseph had in mind. In the earlier test the aim had been to have Benjamin brought down to Egypt. The inference seems to be that in planning to detain Benjamin he now had the further hope of having Jacob brought down to Egypt. Certainly after his disclosure in chapter 45, his first concern is his father (v. 3), and his first plan is to summon Jacob to Egypt (vv. 9–14). If this were his private purpose, then perhaps he had first resolved to delay the disclosure of his identity until he had accomplished the reunion of the entire family in Egypt, when he could reveal his stratagems in all its steps. But Joseph was overtaken in the execution of his plan by his own emotions, which were too much for him.

(3) Defense Before Joseph (44:14–34)

14 When Judah and his brothers came to Joseph's house, he was still there; and they fell before him to the ground. 15 Joseph said to them, "What deed is this that you have done? Do you not know that such a man as I can indeed divine?" 16 And Judah said, "What shall we say to my lord? What shall we speak? Or how can we clear ourselves? God has found out the guilt of your servants; behold, we are my lord's slaves, both we and he also in whose hand the cup has been found." 17 But he said, "Far be it from me that I should do so! Only the man in whose hand the cup was found shall be my slave; but as for you, go up in peace to your father."

18 Then Judah went up to him and said, "O my lord, let your servant, I pray you, speak a word in my lord's ears, and let not your anger burn against your servant; for you are like Pharaoh himself. 19 My lord asked his servants, saying, 'Have you a father, or a brother?' 20 And we said to my lord, 'We have a father, an old man, and a young brother, the child of his old age; and his brother is dead, and he alone is left of his mother's children; and his father loves him.' 21 Then you said to your servants, 'Bring him down to me, that I may set my eyes upon him.' 22 We said to my lord, 'The lad cannot leave his father, for if he should leave his father, his father would die.' 23 Then you said to your servants, 'Unless your youngest brother comes down with you, you shall see my face no more.' 24 When we went back to your servant my father we told him the words of my lord. 25 And when our father said, 'Go again, buy us a little food,' 26 we said, 'We cannot go down. If our youngest brother goes with us, then we will go down; for we cannot see the man's face unless our youngest brother is with us.' 27 Then your servant my father said to us, 'You know that my wife bore me two sons; 28 one left me, and I said, Surely he has been torn to pieces; and I have never seen him since. 29 If you take this one also from me, and harm befalls him, you will bring down my gray hairs in sorrow to Sheol.' 30 Now therefore, when I come to your servant my father, and the lad is not with us, then, as his life is bound up in the lad's life, 31 when he sees that the lad is not with us, he will die; and your servants will bring down the gray hairs of your servant our father with sorrow to Sheol. 32 For your servant became surety for the lad to my father, saying, 'If I do not bring him back to you, then I shall bear the blame in the sight of my father all my life.' 33 Now therefore, let your servant, I pray you, remain instead of the lad as a slave to my lord; and let the lad go back with his brothers. 34 For how can I go back to my father if the lad is not with me? I fear to see the evil that would come upon my father."

In view of Judah's decisive role in the earlier negotiations (37:26; 43:3–7), and in view of his oath to be the hostage for Benjamin (43:9), it is not surprising that it is Judah who leads the procession back to Joseph's house. Joseph, no doubt by arrangement, had not yet left home for his office. There they found him and there for the fourth time, and most abjectly of all, they fell to the ground before him. It appears that they lay before Joseph on the floor, as distinct from obeisance. Joseph's charge is loaded. He justifies the pursuit and the search by referring to his occult knowledge. The actual detection of the criminal was only the outward form of his insight into crime.

Faced with the fact of Benjamin's guilt, and with the knowledge of the man's occult powers, Judah, as spokesman for his brethren, confesses their helplessness and their guilt. The discovery of the cup is beyond explanation, like the money, unless Benjamin had been guilty. Although all ten brothers—Joseph and Benjamin of course being excluded—are innocent as far as any wickedness in Egypt is concerned; yet so terrible is the dilemma of their innocence, and so beyond rescue their condition, that they surrender to the nemesis of their present position, and find an explanation in their guilt: not merely their guilt as the brothers of and partly responsible for Benjamin, but their guilt, their secret, hidden guilt, of which nobody in Egypt can be aware, that guilt from the plain of Dothan years ago, when they dealt cruelly with Joseph. At last their crime has come home to them, and Judah expresses their communal guilt.

The man before them cannot possibly know, though in fact he better than any man knows, what the brethren have in mind. The brothers are confessing to Joseph, but they are confessing beyond Joseph. Without details they are confessing the events at Dothan to God, but Joseph also knows. Judah spoke for and with the ten, as once Peter preached with and for the eleven (Acts 2:14).

Yet Joseph controls himself. He refuses Judah's offer to enslave them all—for such an action would indeed have left Jacob bereft. Correctly as ever, he limits punishment to the criminal. They can be at peace (cf. 1 Sam. 1:17; 20:42), for Benjamin and Benjamin only shall forfeit his freedom. Joseph offers them the one thing they cannot in any circumstance accept—their freedom at the price of Benjamin's detention. From their decision Joseph will know whether their spirit as manifest in Dothan lives on, or whether they have changed.

Judah then virtually buttonholes Joseph, and speaks as a man himself condemned to death. Again the decisive moment and speech belong to Judah, who now speaks for himself alone. The speech really speaks for itself as it moves eloquently and submissively through the petition to be heard without wrath, through flattery (v. 18) to recital and recapitulation (vv. 19–29), to plea (vv. 30 ff.), and to proposal (vv. 33–34). The recapitulation is intended to introduce and indeed to justify the final proposal. It omits any reference to matters like the returned money and concentrates on the personalities involved.

Judah brings before Joseph first Jacob, then Benjamin, and then the "dead" Joseph, and then Benjamin again, Jacob's favorite (vv. 19–20). Then Judah with great skill and omitting all the unpleasantness refers to Joseph's great favor in desiring to *set . . . eyes* on Benjamin (v. 21). To set eyes upon a person is a phrase used in Jeremiah 39:12 and 40:4 (cf. Psalm 33:18; 34:15) of showing favor to a person. Judah is said to use the same phrase here, and thus to put Joseph in the place of a patron of (the now guilty) Benjamin. From this vantage point Judah recounts the difficulties of bringing Benjamin back, and goes more deeply into the tender history of Jacob, and leads on to the catastrophe that will follow upon Benjamin's nonreturn.

Judah now falls back on his own part in the drama. He himself has gone surety for Benjamin's return, and now asks that he may take Benjamin's place, bear Benjamin's guilt, so that Benjamin may be restored to his father. If Benjamin does not go back, he Judah can likewise not go back, for to go back without Benjamin would be to kill Jacob.

The recital thus moves not from event to event but from person to person within the family story. It begins with Jacob and Benjamin (v. 19), and it ends with Benjamin and Jacob (v. 34). During Judah's speech Jacob is mentioned some eighteen times, and he is also quoted in verses 27–29, while Benjamin is mentioned twenty times. This movement from person to person, and this dwelling upon personalities is the secret to the understanding and appreciation of the narrative.

Further, Judah quotes Jacob's own words in verses 27–29, and in these words Judah lets Jacob touch the tenderest chords. Jacob speaks of his favorite wife, Rachel (Joseph's own dead mother), of the loss of Joseph, *I have never seen him since,* of the possible dangers to Benjamin, and of his own death. The members of the family in their relationships thus create the tenderness and the beauty, the pathos and the compassion with which the speech is inspired.

The speech thus illustrates in its substance the words which may be taken as its text, *His life is bound up in the lad's life.* The phrase is a remarkable one. Closer than the bonding of bricks in a wall in all its circuit (Neh. 4:6), more personal than putting on ornaments (Isa. 49:18), Jacob's life was bound up with that of Benjamin, as Jonathan was with David (1 Sam. 18:1). Similarly, in another eloquent speech in the Old Testament, when Abigail, that gifted lady, addresses David (1 Sam. 25:24–31), she describes him with different Hebrew words, and in a figure of safety, rather than of love, as "bound in the bundle of the living in the care of the Lord" (1 Sam. 25:29).

Judah, in going to the very heart of Jacob's family life and love, has inevitably and all unconsciously touched Joseph to the quick. Judah has described that wholeness of family life which Joseph has but to speak the word to reenter. Judah has pictured

the dissolution of Jacob's family unit to the man who alone can prevent that dissolution, and indeed restore and recreate that unity beyond Judah's wildest dreams.

Thus Judah passed the test. Judah's deep sense of being in Jacob and within his father's family has triumphed over the Dothan spirit. The relation between Jacob and Benjamin is more precious to Judah than his own life. Whatever further purpose or desire Joseph had in mind, whether through the test and through Benjamin's detention to contrive Jacob's journey to Egypt (cf. 45:9–14), his experience with Judah is too much for him. The climax of the story is reached. Joseph the absent though present figure of the entire story must decide the fate of the family and must explain his plot. Thus Judah spoke, for Jacob's sake, and saw Joseph make an end to the scheme for testing his brothers.

5. Recognition and Reunion (45:1–28)

Following this long extract from the J witness, the editor turns to E, who now gives the account of Joseph's disclosure, his reconciliation with his brethren, his message to Jacob, Pharaoh's participation in the arrangements for the return home of the brothers, and the actual return and announcement to Jacob. Those commentators who insist that both witnesses would testify to the reconciliation, admit that their actual separation is very difficult and leads to different results in the work of several scholars. Driver probably rightly claims that apart from certain clauses, the story is from E. E's account was probably preferred because he offered an explanation of the story of Joseph's life in Egypt in terms of an overruling providence.

(1) Disclosure (45:1–15)

[1] Then Joseph could not control himself before all those who stood by him; and he cried, "Make every one go out from me." So no one stayed with him when Joseph made himself known to his brothers. [2] And he wept aloud, so that the Egyptians heard it, and the household of Pharaoh heard it. [3] And Joseph said to his brothers, "I am Joseph; is my father still

alive?" But his brothers could not answer him, for they were dismayed at his presence.

4 So Joseph said to his brothers, "Come near to me, I pray you." And they came near. And he said, "I am your brother, Joseph, whom you sold into Egypt. 5 And now do not be distressed, or angry with yourselves, because you sold me here; for God sent me before you to preserve life. 6 For the famine has been in the land these two years; and there are yet five years in which there will be neither plowing nor harvest. 7 And God sent me before you to preserve for you a remnant on earth, and to keep alive for you many survivors. 8 So it was not you who sent me here, but God; and he has made me a father to Pharaoh, and lord of all his house and ruler over all the land of Egypt. 9 Make haste and go up to my father and say to him, 'Thus says your son Joseph, God has made me lord of all Egypt; come down to me, do not tarry; 10 you shall dwell in the land of Goshen, and you shall be near me, you and your children and your children's children, and your flocks, your herds, and all that you have; 11 and there I will provide for you, for there are yet five years of famine to come; lest you and your household, and all that you have, come to poverty.' 12 And now your eyes see, and the eyes of my brother Benjamin see, that it is my mouth that speaks to you. 13 You must tell my father of all my splendor in Egypt, and of all that you have seen. Make haste and bring my father down here." 14 Then he fell upon his brother Benjamin's neck and wept; and Benjamin wept upon his neck. 15 And he kissed all his brothers and wept upon them; and after that his brothers talked with him.

Judah's appeal, the manifest readiness of the brothers to prefer Benjamin's freedom to their own welfare, and Judah's constant play upon the person of their father, overwhelm Joseph. He is unable to control himself before the bystanders, commands the withdrawal of all except his brothers, and when he is alone with them reveals his identity. At first he could not speak for weeping, but then managed to sob out the two great realities of his life at that moment. First he says: *I am Joseph;* and then he asks: *Is my father still alive?* Of course he knew very well that his father was alive, but such is the relief of grief that it asks silly questions, questions to which it knows the answer, and expects to hear: "Don't be silly, of course he is!" But the brothers are

paralyzed into silence (v. 3; cf. Isa. 21:3; Jer. 51:32), as Jacob was also to be when he heard the news (v. 26). How bewildered, shaking with undefinable emotions, how incredible this news must have been to the brothers and later to the father.

Joseph has had his attendants around and near him. Their withdrawal left wide the gap across which Joseph addressed his unbelieving brothers. He has to try again. First he summons them closer to him, no doubt immediately before him, so that they could recognize his features beneath the Egyptian disguise. Now his self-identifying sentence is again twofold. *I am your brother, Joseph,* and not again a reference to his father but a further reference to ten of them and himself, *whom you sold into Egypt.* In such circumstances the repetition was necessary, and was psychologically inevitable. Those commentators who claim that the repeated "I am Joseph" indicates the two witnesses, and that 1, 4 and 5a are J, and 2, 3, and 5b are E, fail to recognize the progressive impact of the disclosure which demands repetition, and in turn virtually guarantees the unity of the passage. Joseph's loud weeping is heard outside the room, and indeed outside his house, and news of it spread to the palace (v. 2).

But at once Joseph reassures his brethren. He is now magnanimous in his treatment of them, and sets their former sale of him within God's purpose for him and them. To look at a piece of embroidery from underneath, "from the wrong side," is to see threads and colors and patches, but the design is distorted and unrecognized. But to see that same piece of embroidery from above, from the right side, is to see the design in its color and meaning. Thus Joseph views the progress from Dothan to that day in terms of God's overruling providence, (cf. 50:20; Psalm 105:17 ff.).

Joseph says, "for God sent me before you to preserve life." Thus Joseph overlays *you* by *God,* and replaces *sold* by *sent,* and adds the remaining words to describe the divine purpose. The references to "sold" are probably reminiscences of the language of the J witness.

It simply must not be overlooked that the words "to preserve life" represent one of the few examples of one of the most interesting words in the Hebrew Bible. A technical explanation is necessary. One of the Hebrew devices to indicate a locality is to add the letter *m* to a verb. Thus if the Hebrew letter *m* is written before the Hebrew verb to slay *zbhch*, the combination of *m*, plus to slay gives the meaning "place where you slay," i.e., altar *mzbhch*. Thus *lun* is to lodge, but *malon* is lodging place, inn. In the present context the same formation is found, based on the Hebrew verb to live, i.e., *chyh*. So the Hebrew word *michyah* means place to live, preservation of life, existence. The present Hebrew words may be rendered in their order as follows: "For for a 'place of life' (*michyah*) God sent me before you." Joseph was thus destined to be the "place" where the brothers would find life. So Joseph is the focus, the nucleus, the cell, the preserving and saving point of life. With this word the witness summarizes the role and function of Joseph in Egypt.

The word is so fascinating that its other occurrences may be listed. In 2 Chronicles 14:13 (Heb., v. 12) the word is translated "(until now) remained alive"; in Judges 6:4 as "sustenance"; and in Judges 17:10 as "your living," i.e., keep or maintenance; in Ezra 9:8-9 as "reviving or revival"; and in Leviticus 13:10,24 it is used of the quick of the raw flesh in leprosy. The root of the word is to live, be alive, and the noun thus means the quick, the living, the preservation, the means of life, sustenance.

Against such a usage the word in the present context must be understood both in its immediate reference as a means of preserving life in the circumstances of the continuing famine, and also in the larger context as the savior of the descendants of Abraham, Isaac, and Jacob for the purposes of the Abrahamic election and blessing. God is the source, a human life is the means, and the welfare of a community is the goal of the providential ordering in the story.

No wonder at all that in Acts 7:9–16, Stephen sets the Joseph story and the sojourn in Egypt as a connecting link in the story of salvation in the Old Testament. No wonder that Hebrews 11:22 also lists Joseph in the heroes of faith and describes his role as predicting Israel's exodus to the Promised Land and his own burial there. No wonder too that Christian theology has seen in Joseph a figure of Christ, sent by the Father into captivity, to be the means of life and salvation for his brethren in the bondage of their own guilt.

Verse 7 is also a rich verse because of its use of the language of remnant. Two of the principal Hebrew terms for remnant occur behind the words *a remnant* in the land and to *keep alive for you* (a large escaped remnant) *many survivors*. In his commentary von Rad draws far too rigid a distinction between the remnant conceived as what is left of a catastrophe— e.g., Noah from the flood, the family of Abram from the dispersal from Babylon, Lot from Sodom, where the remnant survives as a family and community of hope into the future—and what he conceives to be the more negative idea of the remnant in Isaiah (6:13; 7:3; 10:20 f.; 14:32) as simply survival, escape, or what is left. Von Rad is able to maintain this distinction by denying such passages as Isaiah 4:2–6 to Isaiah, but this is by no means evident.

The remnant is composed of survivors in the Old Testament, but these survivors are also (a) chosen by God; (b) righteous in character; (c) destined to preserve and to give life; and (d) compassed about by the divine presence. Joseph exhibits all these characteristics. Remnant is elect not for conservation but for life and growth and hope. In 45:7 the words "keep alive" further remind us of the concept of life, basic and essential to the Old Testament idea of the remnant. Joseph and his family are the elected heirs of the Abrahamic promise and blessing.

In 45:8 Joseph makes the transition from

the past to the future through his present greatness. God is responsible for the past; he is responsible for the present; he may be trusted for the future. As viceroy, Joseph fulfils three roles: father (cf. Isa. 22:21; Rest of Esther 13:6; 16:11; 1 Macc. 11:32) to Pharaoh; lord of his house (41:40), i.e., lord chamberlain; and administrator of his kingdom (42:6).

In verses 9–14 Joseph makes arrangements for Jacob and all the family to return to Egypt and live out the remaining years of the famine there. The area he has in mind is the land of Goshen. This name is peculiar to the J witness, and so the clause has probably come from him. The area designated is probably the Wadi Tumilat, a depression running east to west between the delta of the Nile and the Bitter Lakes, i.e., between Port Said and Suez. Kesem is listed as the twentieth name or administrative district of lower Egypt. It lies east of the Nile and is one of the best pastoral areas in Egypt.

But suddenly the monologue collapses, and Joseph's preliminary arrangements melt into embrace and conversation and news. The reconciliation between Joseph and his brothers is complete.

(2) Pharaoh's Invitation (45:16–28)

16 When the report was heard in Pharaoh's house, "Joseph's brothers have come," it pleased Pharaoh and his servants well. 17 And Pharaoh said to Joseph, "Say to your brothers, 'Do this: load your beasts and go back to the land of Canaan; 18 and take your father and your households, and come to me, and I will give you the best of the land of Egypt, and you shall eat the fat of the land.' 19 Command them also, 'Do this: take wagons from the land of Egypt for your little ones and for your wives, and bring your father, and come. 20 Give no thought to your goods, for the best of all the land of Egypt is yours.' "
21 The sons of Israel did so; and Joseph gave them wagons, according to the command of Pharaoh, and gave them provisions for the journey. 22 To each and all of them he gave festal garments; but to Benjamin he gave three hundred shekels of silver and five festal garments. 23 To his father he sent as follows: ten asses loaded with the good things of Egypt, and ten she-asses loaded with grain, bread, and

provision for his father on the journey. 24 Then he sent his brothers away, and as they departed, he said to them, "Do not quarrel on the way." 25 So they went up out of Egypt, and came to the land of Canaan to their father Jacob. 26 And they told him, "Joseph is still alive, and he is ruler over all the land of Egypt." And his heart fainted, for he did not believe them. 27 But when they told him all the words of Joseph, which he had said to them, and when he saw the wagons which Joseph had sent to carry him, the spirit of their father Jacob revived; 28 and Israel said, "It is enough; Joseph my son is still alive; I will go and see him before I die."

When Pharaoh hears of the arrival of Joseph's brothers, he also is prompted to urge Joseph to invite his family to settle in Egypt. Thus Joseph's continued presence in Egypt and his policy to defeat the famine would be assured. Pharaoh offers the best things, i.e., the best of the produce; *wagons* for the return journey and bids them make speed, giving no thought—literally, "let not your eye pity" (cf. Deut. 7:16; 13:8)—to household furniture, for that would delay their return. The wagons are two-wheeled bullock wagons for the transport of baggage (Num. 7:3).

To return the compliment of Jacob's own present (43:11), to illustrate the affluence of his own standard of living, as well as in obedience to Pharaoh, and to reinforce his welcome, Joseph is lavish in his own gifts to his brothers, to Benjamin and to Jacob. *Festal garments* would be special and more costly raiment reserved for religious and other celebrations, and such gifts were common form (Judg. 14:12,19; 2 Kings 5:5,22 f.). Again Benjamin has five such garments and *three hundred shekels of silver*, pieces of metal cut off a bar and weighed. Jacob's present is on a lavish scale, *ten asses* being required for its carriage, and ten more milk asses with food for the return journey. The rather priggish element in Joseph's character emerges in his parting injunction: "Do not quarrel en route."

The brothers announce to Jacob the news about Joseph, and no doubt confessed their own miserable part in the story. At first incredulous and numbed, eventually his spirit revived, literally, came to life. Of all the news about Joseph, his position, his glory, his wealth, one thing suffices— Joseph is after all alive and well. Joseph, his Joseph and Rachel's, has come back from the dead. Jacob has but to travel to see him.

Jacob's return to the narrative means that it now centers on him rather than Joseph. The introduction of material in chapter 46 reminiscent of the earlier patriarchal narratives confirms this. Some passages in the closing chapters of Genesis, notably 47:13-26, are concerned only with Joseph, but the remainder are devoted to the closing years of Jacob's life.

The narrative concerning Joseph is thus an independent instalment in the traditions concerning Jacob. It is an amalgam of the testimonies of J and E, but it is not easy to assess the resultant work. It is not a collection of stories, but rather a story of organic unity with conflict and central purpose. It is often said not to be a saga, because it is not tied to any locality; and it is far too personal to be the personification of tribal legends and histories. The religious as distinct from theological interests are not sufficiently compelling to justify the term legend, for a legend is properly a sacred or religious story.

The real question is whether the Joseph story is a historical biography. There can be little doubt that the figures of Jacob, Joseph, Judah, and Benjamin are historical persons. The theme from riches to rags and once more to riches is not at all unlikely. The portrayal of Egyptian conditions is reasonably accurate, even if those conditions reflect an Egypt much later than that of Joseph's period.

Above all the delineation of the characters, their moods and makeup, their behavior and reactions, are lifelike—too lifelike to permit the view that the narrative is a mere psychological and fictional portrayal. The unity, the progress, the characters, and the portrayal compel once again the view that this is a record of the largely actual.

The succession of scenes must be a selection, for so much of these twenty years of Joseph's life are not recorded, and the gaps are significant. The memorable features of Joseph's life, and his relationships in these hidden years, insist on being preserved and transmitted because of their interest and vitality.

Perhaps embryonic features in theology (45:4-8), in Joseph's role as an interpreter of dreams (40—41), and in the wisdom aspects of the character of Joseph have been developed and rephrased. Even so, in the pathos of the circumstances, the encounters, and the conversations, real life is present. The criteria of the commentators for the interpretation of ancient books, and apparently of Scripture more than other ancient books, undergo great variation from generation to generation, and in that variation reveal their subjectivity. The great difficulty likewise, and indeed the failure to reach a widely acceptable judgment about the Joseph narrative, tends to confirm the fact that the least subjective view is to say that largely speaking this is how it was. The Joseph narrative is a unity, though it is an intermittent unity; but it is intermittent because it is memorable, and because it is so memorable it is convincing in the truth it teaches.

XXIV. Jacob in Egypt (46:1—49:33)

In the lives of Abraham and Jacob, journeys have a large part. Chapter 46 tells the story of Jacob's last journey. Jacob goes down into Egypt. The statement like the journey itself is astonishing, and that the father of Israel with all his family should have gone down to Egypt becomes even more astonishing as the centuries and the millennia go by.

This narrative obviously has been split by the insertion of the list of names in verses 8-27. The work of the P witness, it is inserted by him at the end of a section from the E witness (vv. 1-5) and before the continuation in verse 28 which comes from the J witness, and which continues to

47:6. Only by this separation of the witnesses can the narrative be truly evaluated.

1. Jacob's Journey to Egypt (46:1–7)

¹ So Israel took his journey with all that he had, and came to Beersheba, and offered sacrifices to the God of his father Isaac. ² And God spoke to Israel in visions of the night, and said, "Jacob, Jacob." And he said, "Here am I." ³ Then he said, "I am God, the God of your father; do not be afraid to go down to Egypt; for I will there make of you a great nation. ⁴ I will go down with you to Egypt, and I will also bring you up again; and Joseph's hand shall close your eyes." ⁵ Then Jacob set out from Beersheba; and the sons of Israel carried Jacob their father, their little ones, and their wives, in the wagons which Pharaoh had sent to carry him. ⁶ They also took their cattle and their goods, which they had gained in the land of Canaan, and came into Egypt, Jacob and all his offspring with him, ⁷ his sons, and his sons' sons with him, his daughters, and his sons' daughters; all his offspring he brought with him into Egypt.

Jacob, here named Israel, which suggests some words from the J witness, took his departure from Hebron (35:27; 37:14), where he was resident. However great was his desire to see Joseph, he cannot even have contemplated such a journey, or indeed have set out, without great misgivings. His previous stay away from Canaan had been very much longer than he had anticipated. His own father had not been allowed to leave the land even to look for a wife (ch. 24), and Egypt had been expressly ruled out (26:2). By the time that Jacob had reached Beersheba, his own father's ancestral shrine (cf. 21:31; 26:25), the doubts had become a preoccupation in Jacob's mind. The sacrifices he offered there included a feast, and following the offering Jacob experienced again a theophany of reassurance, such as he had experienced previously in similar situations (28:10–17; 35:9–15).

Jacob's spiritual anxieties concerning his exit from the Land of Promise are the seed bed and the occasion of the divine reassurance vouchsafed to him in the theophany. So often in the patriarchal stories, the theophany is followed by the activity at the altar. Here the order is reversed. The Joseph narrative nowhere reports that Joseph was the recipient of theophanies, unless the dreams have some such intention. This theophany is the last revelation in the book of Genesis, but Jacob-Israel is the recipient. He sought guidance on exit.

The first patriarchal entry into the land was marked by a theophany (12:1–3,7–9), and now the last patriarchal exit is also so marked. The theophany at the departure is thus motivated not only by Jacob's spiritual needs at that moment but also by the necessity to have the overall purpose of Genesis—the growth of Israel—reaffirmed, although that is to take place in Egypt. That Beersheba is the last patriarchal sanctuary on the way to Egypt is purely accidental.

The theophany is introduced and authenticated as usual by the divine self-predication—*I am God*. Its personal purpose is the removal of Jacob's anxiety—*Do not be afraid to go down to Egypt*—and its providential intention, the promise of increasing progeny—*a great nation* (cf. 12:2; 17:6). Its support is the accompanying presence of God in Egypt, whence his descendants will surely return, and where Joseph will attend him in death (v. 4). Thus Jacob, and all his family, with his Israelite and Canaanite children and grandchildren, with his profit of Canaan, all loaded in the wagons of Pharaoh, journeyed to Egypt.

Verses 6–7 are P's brief summary of Jacob's descent into Egypt. Jacob's daughters are mentioned, although one only is known by name—Dinah (but cf. 37:35). In the following list only one daughter (v. 15) and one granddaughter (v. 17; cf. Num. 26:46) are mentioned.

2. List of the Migrants (46:8–27)

⁸ Now these are the names of the descendants of Israel, who came into Egypt, Jacob and his sons. Reuben, Jacob's first-born, ⁹ and the sons of Reuben: Hanoch, Pallu, Hezron, and Carmi. ¹⁰ The sons of Simeon: Jemuel, Jamin, Ohad, Jachin, Zohar, and Shaul, the son of a Canaanitish woman. ¹¹ The sons of Levi: Gershon, Kohath, and Merari. ¹² The sons of Judah: Er, Onan, Shelah, Perez, and Zerah

(but Er and Onan died in the land of Canaan); and the sons of Perez were Hezron and Hamul. 13 The sons of Issachar: Tola, Puvah, Iob, and Shimron. 14 The sons of Zebulun: Sered, Elon, and Jahleel 15 (these are the sons of Leah, whom she bore to Jacob in Paddanaram, together with his daughter Dinah; altogether his sons and his daughters numbered thirty-three). 16 The sons of Gad: Ziphion, Haggi, Shuni, Ezbon, Eri, Arodi, and Areli. 17 The sons of Asher: Imnah, Ishvah, Ishvi, Beriah, with Serah their sister. And the sons of Beriah: Heber and Malchiel 18 (these are the sons of Zilpah, whom Laban gave to Leah his daughter; and these she bore to Jacob—sixteen persons). 19 The sons of Rachel, Jacob's wife: Joseph and Benjamin. 20 And to Joseph in the land of Egypt were born Manasseh and Ephraim, whom Asenath, the daughter of Potiphera the priest of On, bore to him. 21 And the sons of Benjamin: Bela, Becher, Ashbel, Gera, Naaman, Ehi, Rosh, Muppim, Huppim, and Ard 22 (these are the sons of Rachel, who were born to Jacob—fourteen persons in all). 23 The sons of Dan: Hushim. 24 The sons of Naphtali: Jahzeel, Guni, Jezer, and Shillem 25 (these are the sons of Bilhah, whom Laban gave to Rachel his daughter, and these she bore to Jacob—seven persons in all). 26 All the persons belonging to Jacob who came into Egypt, who were his own offspring, not including Jacob's sons' wives, were sixty-six persons in all; 27 and the sons of Joseph, who were born to him in Egypt, were two; all the persons of the house of Jacob, that came into Egypt, were seventy.

The list seems to give the names of Jacob's family at the moment of his departure for Egypt. It is summarized in Exodus 1:1–5, and it must be compared with the normative census list of those who came up out of the land of Egypt in Numbers 26:5–62. The two lists (Gen. 46; Num. 26) describe the families of Israel at different times, and so differences between them are inevitable.

Leah's sons and their families comprise thirty-three persons:

Reuben and his four sons (Ex. 6:14; Num. 26:5 f.).

Simeon and his six sons (Ex. 6:15; Num. 26:12 f.). Numbers 26 omits Ohad. Shaul clans had Canaanite blood.

Levi and his three sons (Ex. 6:16; Num. 26:57). The three are the ancestors of the three branches of the Levites: Gershonites,

Kohathites, and Merarites—officials of the cult (Num. 3:17–20).

Judah and his five sons and two grandsons (Num. 26:19–21). See Genesis 38 for the story of Judah's Canaanite marriage, etc.

The Judah citation involves well-known difficulties: (a) Er and Onan died in Canaan and so cannot be counted in the 70 persons who went down into Egypt, or in the 33 descendants of Leah who went down to Egypt. The net figures are thus 68 and 31 (cf. below). (b) According to 37:2 and 41:46 Joseph was 13 years in Egypt before he became viceroy, and according to 41:47; 45:6, 9 more years had elapsed before Jacob and his family came to him, a total of 22 years. Since Judah's marriage in chapter 38 is subsequent to the sale of Joseph, it follows that his 3 children were born, the first 2 grew up and died, and the third grew up, and after his refusal to cohabit with the widow of his brother, Judah marries and has a son and by him grandsons. Now all these events in the life of one family would have taken far longer than twenty-two years. So it follows that the list therefore cannot be harmonized with itself or with its context.

Issachar and his four sons (Num. 26:23 f. and 1 Chron. 7:1 read Jashub for Iob (46:13), and the LXX reads Jashub in Genesis also).

Zebulun and his three sons (Num. 26:26).

The sons of Zilpah, Leah's handmaid (vv. 16–18):

Gad and his seven sons (Num. 26:15–17 with Ozni for Ezbon).

Asher and his four sons and one daughter and two grandsons (Num. 26:44–46, without Ishvah), a total of 16 persons in all.

The sons of Rachel (vv. 19–22):

Joseph and his two sons, born of an Egyptian wife (41:50; Num. 26:28–37).

Benjamin and his ten sons (Num. 26:38–40, with only five sons listed; 1 Chron. 7:6 is different again, with only three sons). The portrayal of Benjamin as a lad in chapters 44—45 hardly accords with the account of Benjamin here as the father of ten sons.

The sons of Bilhah, Rachel's handmaid (vv. 23–25): Dan and his one son (Num. 26:42); Naphtali and his four sons (Num. 26:48)—a total of seven persons.

So the figures are: Leah, 33; Zilpah, 16; Rachel, 14; Bilhah, 7; a total of 70 persons in all (cf. Deut. 10:22). The figure can be maintained by the addition of Dinah and Jacob, for 46:26 quotes a figure of 66 which is reached by excluding Er and Onan (dead), Joseph and his two sons (already in Egypt), and adding Dinah.

The 66 can be made up to the traditional 70 by retaining Joseph and his two sons, and by including Jacob. Exodus 1:5 has 70 persons excluding Jacob. The LXX has five additional descendants for Joseph, and thus makes the number 75 (cf. Acts 7:14). The number 70 remained significant (cf. Ex. 24:1,9; Num. 11:16). It is also the number of the Jewish Sanhedrin, and of the seventy sent out by Jesus Christ (Luke 10:1).

3. Jacob in Goshen (46:28–34)

28 He sent Judah before him to Joseph, to appear before him in Goshen; and they came into the land of Goshen. 29 Then Joseph made ready his chariot and went up to meet Israel his father in Goshen; and he presented himself to him, and fell on his neck, and wept on his neck a good while. 30 Israel said to Joseph, "Now let me die, since I have seen your face and know that you are still alive." 31 Joseph said to his brothers and to his father's household, "I will go up and tell Pharaoh, and will say to him, 'My brothers and my father's household, who were in the land of Canaan, have come to me; 32 and the men are shepherds, for they have been keepers of cattle; and they have brought their flocks, and their herds, and all that they have.' 33 When Pharaoh calls you, and says, 'What is your occupation?' 34 you shall say, 'Your servants have been keepers of cattle from our youth even until now, both we and our fathers,' in order that you may dwell in the land of Goshen; for every shepherd is an abomination to the Egyptians."

Verse 28 obviously continues 46:5, where Jacob is the subject. As the caravan approaches Egypt, Jacob sends Judah ahead to prepare for their arrival. The RSV adopts to appear from some of the versions. The Hebrew reads "to show the way before him." On either reading, Joseph is the subject. Either as RSV, he is to make a rendezvous in Goshen and this is what happens in verse 29, or else provide directions in person, or through a guide, for that part of the journey that falls within Egyptian territory. Joseph goes up in his chariot to the slightly more elevated terrain of the Goshen district. There father and son meet, and Jacob's joy is full (cf. 45:28). Verse 30 with its hint of Jacob's death points to the deathbed scene in 47:29 ff., though seventeen years will elapse according to the P witness (47:28) before Jacob's death.

Joseph now begins to prepare for the approaching audience before Pharaoh. He instructs his family to confess their calling as shepherds and cowmen. Shepherds as a class must have had a low social status in Egypt, and were objectionable to Egyptians as not always conforming to Egyptian standards of cleanliness. By admitting this status the family would ensure their settlement at a distance from Pharaoh. The district of Goshen would suit all parties. Joseph's experience and consequent advice correctly anticipates the situation and leads to the desired result. Joseph is said to have to go up. This may not necessarily mean from Goshen, but the words may describe the usual way of calling on Pharaoh. Perhaps Pharaoh's palace was elevated, or his audience chamber, and certainly his throne would be elevated.

4. Audiences Before Pharaoh (47:1–12)

1 So Joseph went in and told Pharaoh, "My father and my brothers, with their flocks and herds and all that they possess, have come from the land of Canaan; they are now in the land of Goshen." 2 And from among his brothers he took five men and presented them to Pharaoh. 3 Pharaoh said to his brothers, "What is your occupation?" And they said to Pharaoh, "Your servants are shepherds, as our fathers were." 4 They said to Pharaoh, "We have come to sojourn in the land; for there is no pasture for your servants' flocks, for the famine is severe in the land of Canaan; and now, we pray you, let your servants dwell in the land of

Goshen." ⁵ Then Pharaoh said to Joseph, "Your father and your brothers have come to you. ⁶ The land of Egypt is before you; settle your father and your brothers in the best of the land; let them dwell in the land of Goshen; and if you know any able men among them, put them in charge of my cattle."

⁷ Then Joseph brought in Jacob his father, and set him before Pharaoh, and Jacob blessed Pharaoh. ⁸ And Pharaoh said to Jacob, "How many are the days of the years of your life?" ⁹ And Jacob said to Pharaoh, "The days of the years of my sojourning are a hundred and thirty years; few and evil have been the days of the years of my life, and they have not attained to the days of the years of the life of my fathers in the days of their sojourning." ¹⁰ And Jacob blessed Pharaoh, and went out from the presence of Pharaoh. ¹¹ Then Joseph settled his father and his brothers, and gave them a possession in the land of Egypt, in the best of the land, in the land of Rameses, as Pharaoh had commanded. ¹² And Joseph provided his father, his brothers, and all his father's household with food, according to the number of their dependents.

Joseph announces to Pharaoh the arrival of the family, presents five of his brothers, mentioning casually that they are for the time being in the district of Goshen, and so it is decided that the family is to settle in Goshen. Pharaoh then receives Jacob in audience, and later the family is settled in the land of Rameses. In verses 3–4 the brothers answer as directed in 46:34, and then proffer their petition to be allowed to settle in Goshen. Pharaoh then recapitulates with royal caution the facts of arrival and his promises and then agrees to their settlement in Goshen. He further seeks to suggest employment for some of them among his own herds.

The LXX reads in a different and fuller order, namely: 5a, "And Pharaoh said to Joseph, let them dwell in the land of Goshen, and if thou knowest any able men among them, then make them rulers over my cattle"; 5b, "And Jacob and his sons came into Egypt, unto Joseph. And Pharaoh, king of Egypt heard of it. And Pharaoh spake unto Joseph, saying 'Thy father and thy brethren. . . .'" But the Hebrew, as followed by RSV, may quite reasonably be retained. The purpose of the Greek

rearrangement is only to provide a direct answer to the petition of verse 4.

The expression *able men* implies moral and physical excellence, not to mention military abilities (Ex. 18:21,25; 1 Kings 1:42,52; Josh 1:14; 1 Sam. 9:1).

Verses 7–11 are probably from the P witness. *Jacob* comes before Pharaoh, *and Jacob blessed Pharaoh*, i.e., greets him (1 Sam. 13:10; 2 Kings 4:29). Pharaoh puts the question which is appropriate to an old man, and Jacob says he is 130 years and explains that he had not lived as long as his father or grandfather. (Isaac reached 180 years (35:28) and Abraham was but five years less (25:7).

The P witness is fond of the word *sojournings* to describe the lives of the patriarchs. They only sojourn in the Land of Promise. They do not properly and fully possess it until their descendants under Joshua occupy and settle in the land. Of course they own burial places, parcels of land, and wells in the areas around Beersheba, Hebron, and Shechem. But such possessions are only tokens, earnests of future possession. In fact his years have not only been fewer but evil (or, more evil) than his fathers. Whether this statement refers to the spread of evil, bringing about in turn a diminishing vitality shown by the progressively decreasing life span is uncertain. Perhaps Jacob is reflecting on his many travels outside the Promised Land, and that Egypt is the third land in which he has lived. Abram had spent 100 years, and Isaac all his years, in the Promised Land.

After the audience they all return to Goshen, described in P's terms as the best of the land, *the land of Rameses*. Probably the land of Rameses is larger in extent than Goshen. This title is also used by the LXX in 46:28, and it describes part of the eastern area of the Delta, where Rameses II, the great builder of the nineteenth dynasty, erected many cities in the thirteenth century. This Pharaoh was probably the Pharaoh of Israel's oppression and therefore lived a considerable time after the days of

Joseph, whatever date is given to Joseph. The use of the name thus anticipates history. *Their dependents* represents the Hebrew, "The little ones," literally, those who take quick, tripping steps, but the expression can include women (cf. 50:21).

5. Joseph's Food Policy (47:13–26)

13 Now there was no food in all the land; for the famine was very severe, so that the land of Egypt and the land of Canaan languished by reason of the famine. 14 And Joseph gathered up all the money that was found in the land of Egypt and in the land of Canaan, for the grain which they bought; and Joseph brought the money into Pharaoh's house. 15 And when the money was all spent in the land of Egypt and in the land of Canaan, all the Egyptians came to Joseph, and said, "Give us food; why should we die before your eyes? For our money is gone." 16 And Joseph answered, "Give your cattle, and I will give you food in exchange for your cattle, if your money is gone." 17 So they brought their cattle to Joseph; and Joseph gave them food in exchange for the horses, the flocks, the herds, and the asses: and he supplied them with food in exchange for all their cattle that year. 18 And when that year was ended, they came to him the following year, and said to him, "We will not hide from my lord that our money is all spent; and the herds of cattle are my lord's; there is nothing left in the sight of my lord but our bodies and our lands. 19 Why should we die before your eyes, both we and our land? Buy us and our land for food, and we with our land will be slaves to Pharaoh; and give us seed, that we may live, and not die, and that the land may not be desolate."
20 So Joseph bought all the land of Egypt for Pharaoh; for all the Egyptians sold their fields, because the famine was severe upon them. The land became Pharaoh's; 21 and as for the people, he made slaves of them from one end of Egypt to the other. 22 Only the land of the priests he did not buy; for the priests had a fixed allowance from Pharaoh, and lived on the allowance which Pharaoh gave them; therefore they did not sell their land. 23 Then Joseph said to the people, "Behold, I have this day bought you and your land for Pharaoh. Now here is seed for you, and you shall sow the land. 24 And at the harvests you shall give a fifth to Pharaoh, and four fifths shall be your own, as seed for the field and as food for yourselves and your households, and as food for your little ones." 25 And they said, "You have saved our lives; may it please my lord, we will be slaves to Pharaoh." 26 So Joseph made it a statute

concerning the land of Egypt, and it stands to this day, that Pharaoh should have the fifth; the land of the priests alone did not become Pharaoh's.

The J witness now contributes a full statement of Joseph's agrarian policy, which is an elaboration of what is briefly stated in 41:55 f. The policy is gradually worked out during the years of famine and could not have been reasonably inserted until the famine years were running their course. The result of course is that the present section is unrelated to its context, namely, the adventures of Jacob and his family. Nevertheless, it is part of the story of Joseph which could not very well have been stated earlier.

The purpose of the narrative is not by any means to set a pattern according to which Israelite politics would direct the life of any state under Israel's control. Rather, the purpose of the story is to show that Joseph's policy was equal to all the successive crises of the emergency. Thus Joseph and his policy dominate the story.

Verse 13 is resumptive, setting the scene for the following narratives. All was well until the people in Egypt had parted with all their money for the purchase of food. Their extremity must have been not before the third or even fourth year of the famine (cf. 45:6, for two years had gone even before Jacob had heard that Joseph was alive). With the passage of time, money would more quickly run out as the pressure of shortage increased.

The money was brought into the royal treasuries. Joseph therefore has to devise a new measure, and suggests the exchange of cattle for food. A literal exchange would be quite impossible, for how could Joseph manage the vast herds of cattle that would be assembled? Presumably the people brought such cattle as they possessed to prove ownership and thus to prove how much food they could claim. Then though Pharaoh owned the cattle, the people had the use of them. Of course Canaan could be mentioned in the negotiations only when money transactions were involved. Thereafter in the cattle transactions (from v. 15) Canaan is no longer mentioned. *And he supplied them with food in exchange* represents the Hebrew, "to lead to a watering place," so to pasture, to lead gently (Isa. 40:11; Ex. 15:13), here to refresh, support, so provide, maintain.

Verses 18–22 represent the third and most drastic stage of Joseph's policy. When the people have parted with their money and, presumably pledged their cattle, they themselves propose to Joseph that Pharaoh should take over their persons and their possessions. The population is virtually enslaved, private property is abolished and is instead nationalized. This is said to take place in the following year (Heb., second year), the second year that is, not of the famine, but the second year in succession following the exchange of cattle; that is, the fifth or sixth or even the last of the seven years of the emergency. The fact that seed corn is now mentioned suggests a return to more normal conditions, and that the acquiring of seed corn was in readiness for normal crops.

The loss of personal independence is indeed a drastic remedy and one, however inevitable in Egypt, which was extremely distasteful in Israel. The Israelites were free and held tenaciously to the family holdings, and incursions on personal freedom and the family patrimony were resisted (1 Sam. 7:10–18).

Verses 20–21 are again resumptive, setting the total position against which the particular exception now to be mentioned is to be understood. *He made slaves of them* rightly follows Samaritan Pentateuch and the LXX against the Hebrew which reads, "He removed them to the cities." The nationalization of Egyptian land did not extend to the temple estates. The private, priestly allowances in kind from Pharaoh precluded the necessity of loss of cattle or lands. (The rights are referred to in Diodorus 1.72 and Herodotus II 168.)

The allowance of seed to the people for sowing is subject at the following harvest time to a tax of one-fifth of the produce.

Thus from the following harvests the people will retain four-fifths for food and for further sowing. This became the permanent law of the land, so that the suggestion of the people is embraced by Joseph, and is incorporated into a permanent system, and has lasted to the days of the writer. A tax of one-fifth is not judged to be excessive in view of the very great fertility of normal seasons in Egypt, and in comparison with interest rates of up to 40 percent and even higher elsewhere in the ancient Near East (cf. 1 Macc. 10:30). Such a change from private estates to state property seems to have taken place following the Hyksos period in the days of the new kingdom, represented by the eighteenth dynasty. In the Old Testament tradition the change is attributed to the Israelite hero Joseph.

6. Joseph's Oath (47:27–31)

[27] Thus Israel dwelt in the land of Egypt, in the land of Goshen; and they gained possessions in it, and were fruitful and multiplied exceedingly. [28] And Jacob lived in the land of Egypt seventeen years; so the days of Jacob, the years of his life, were a hundred and forty-seven years.

[29] And when the time drew near that Israel must die, he called his son Joseph and said to him, "If now I have found favor in your sight, put your hand under my thigh, and promise to deal loyally and truly with me. Do not bury me in Egypt, [30] but let me lie with my fathers; carry me out of Egypt and bury me in their burying place." He answered, "I will do as you have said." [31] And he said, "Swear to me"; and he swore to him. Then Israel bowed himself upon the head of his bed.

Jacob is the third and last of that great triumvirate of men whose names—Abraham, Isaac, and Jacob—have become almost a popular saying, and beside whom even Joseph is a poor fourth. The last arrangements and death of Jacob are of great interest to all three witnesses, for all have preserved their account of these last events of Jacob's life. Altogether there are four main incidents: (a) Jacob's instructions to Joseph concerning his burial (47:28–31); (b) Jacob's blessing of Ephraim and Manasseh, Joseph's two Egyptian sons

(48:1–22); (c) the so-called blessing of Jacob—the collection of oracles concerning the sons or tribes of Israel (49:1–28); (d) Jacob's instructions concerning his burial in the cave at Machpelah (49:29–33).

Fortunately the division of the sources is not too difficult, and considerable agreement exists. The material is thus generally divided: (1) To the J witness: 47:29–31; 49:1–28a; 50:1–11; 14. (2) To the E witness: 48:1–2; 48:8–22; 50:15–26. (3) To the P witness: 47:28; 48:3–7; 49:28b–33; 50:12–13.

The evidence for the allocation is reasonably clear. In 47:27–28, the hero appears first as Jacob (P), and then as Israel (J); 47:28 is continued in 48:3–7 (P). In 47:29 Joseph is summoned and attends at Jacob's bed (J); in 48:1 he learns of his father's illness and takes his sons to pay a last visit (E); the claim that the blessing appears to be twice given, namely in 48:15–16 and 48:20, may not be well founded.

Verse 27 begins as a resumptive verse from J, but the verse changes to the P witness with the characteristic reference to *fruitful and multiplied,* and the chronological note so beloved of the P witness.

According to the J witness (vv. 29–31), Jacob summons Joseph to his bedside to make his son promise that he would arrange for his father to be buried in the ancestral burial place at Machpelah (49:29; 50:12 f.). Jacob's reference in 50:5 to the grave which he has himself dug need not be any contradiction to the general description of the ancestral grave.

Within the ancestral complex Jacob has also provided for himself. (For the form of the oath, the hand of the swearer on the genitals of him to whom the oath is made, see 24:2.) Israel bowed himself toward the head of the bed; presumably these words describe as much of an act of prostration as an aged and dying man could perform (cf. David, 1 Kings 1:47). The LXX reads "on the top of his staff" but RSV rightly follows the Hebrew. Jacob seeks to show his gratitude by his action.

7. Jacob Adopts and Blesses Joseph's Two Sons (48:1–22)

[1] After this Joseph was told, "Behold, your father is ill"; so he took with him his two sons, Manasseh and Ephraim. [2] And it was told to Jacob, "Your son Joseph has come to you"; then Israel summoned his strength, and sat up in bed. [3] And Jacob said to Joseph, "God Almighty appeared to me at Luz in the land of Canaan and blessed me, [4] and said to me, 'Behold, I will make you fruitful, and multiply you, and I will make of you a company of peoples, and will give this land to your descendants after you for an everlasting possession.' [5] And now your two sons, who were born to you in the land of Egypt before I came to you in Egypt, are mine; Ephraim and Manasseh shall be mine, as Reuben and Simeon are. [6] And the offspring born to you after them shall be yours; they shall be called by the name of their brothers in their inheritance. [7] For when I came from Paddan, Rachel to my sorrow died in the land of Canaan on the way, when there was still some distance to go to Ephrath; and I buried her there on the way to Ephrath (that is, Bethlehem)."

[8] When Israel saw Joseph's sons, he said, "Who are these?" [9] Joseph said to his father, "They are my sons, whom God has given me here." And he said, "Bring them to me, I pray you, that I may bless them." [10] Now the eyes of Israel were dim with age, so that he could not see. So Joseph brought them near him; and he kissed them and embraced them. [11] And Israel said to Joseph, "I had not thought to see your face; and lo, God has let me see your children also." [12] Then Joseph removed them from his knees, and he bowed himself with his face to the earth. [13] And Joseph took them both, Ephraim in his right hand toward Israel's left hand, and Manasseh in his left hand toward Israel's right hand, and brought them near him. [14] And Israel stretched out his right hand and laid it upon the head of Ephraim, who was the younger, and his left hand upon the head of Manasseh, crossing his hands, for Manasseh was the first-born. [15] And he blessed Joseph, and said,

"The God before whom my fathers Abraham
    and Isaac walked,
the God who has led me all my life long to
    this day,
[16] the angel who has redeemed me from all
    evil, bless the lads;
and in them let my name be perpetuated,
    and the name of my fathers Abraham and
        Isaac;
and let them grow into a multitude in the
    midst of the earth."

[17] When Joseph saw that his father laid his

right hand upon the head of Ephraim, it displeased him; and he took his father's hand, to remove it from Ephraim's head to Manasseh's head. [18] And Joseph said to his father, "Not so, my father; for this one is the first-born; put your right hand upon his head." [19] But his father refused, and said, "I know, my son, I know; he also shall become a people, and he also shall be great; nevertheless his younger brother shall be greater than he, and his descendants shall become a multitude of nations." [20] So he blessed them that day, saying,

"By you Israel will pronounce blessings, saying,
'God make you as Ephraim and as Manasseh' ";

and thus he put Ephraim before Manasseh. [21] Then Israel said to Joseph, "Behold, I am about to die, but God will be with you, and will bring you again to the land of your fathers. [22] Moreover I have given to you rather than to your brothers one mountain slope which I took from the hand of the Amorites with my sword and with my bow."

In chapter 35 the birth of Benjamin (vv. 16–19) and the list of Jacob's twelve sons (vv. 22–26) is immediately followed by the notice of the death of Isaac (v. 29). So now in the present context of Jacob's death and his blessing of Joseph's two sons, the oracles on the twelve tribes are also given. As farewell of Jacob is about to be taken, and he is seen in the context of his fathers before him, so provision is made for the future, and the continuity of blessing is spoken and enacted.

The narrative about Joseph's two sons, Manasseh and Ephraim, points to two facts in the later Israel, which were also prefigured in the words and deeds of their dying grandfather. The first fact is that the tribes of Manasseh and Ephraim count as the two half tribes of Joseph (Josh, 17:14; 18:5; Judg. 1:22 f.), and were the leaders in the settlement of the Rachel tribes in the mountains of Samaria west of Jordan. The second is that Ephraim gained the ascendancy over Manasseh; thus in Numbers 26:28, Manasseh is mentioned before Ephraim, and the notice about Manasseh in 26:29–34 precedes that about Ephraim in verses 35–37. But in the list in Numbers 1, which is generally regarded as a list later

than Numbers 26, the order is reversed; Ephraim, verses 32–33 and Manasseh, verses 34–35.

The E witness reports that when Joseph heard of his father's illness he went to visit him, his two sons, Manasseh and Ephraim, with him. The P witness, verses 3–7, then reports that Jacob adopts the two boys. In these verses the marks of the P witness are clear. 'El Shaddai, Paddan, and the familiar terminology are used. The verses make the continuity clear in the retrospective (3–4) and the prospective references (5–6). Jacob vests and grounds what he is about to do in his own spiritual experience at Luz (Bethel), and in the promises there made to him (35:11–12, P). Then on the basis of the promise of the land and progeny, Jacob adopts Joseph's two sons: *And now your two sons . . . are mine.* It has been suggested that this adoption scene was once linked with 49:28, and that it took place in the presence of all the other sons (Dillman). Reuben and Simeon are mentioned as Jacob's eldest sons to match Joseph's two firstborn. Jacob names them in the order Ephraim and Manasseh, and admits them to a new status as his own sons; i.e., full founding fathers of two distinct tribes among the ancestors of the tribes of the children of Israel.

The virtual withdrawal of Levi and his tribe from the list by reason of their sacralization, left eleven tribes. As Joseph began to count for two tribes so the number twelve was restored. On the other hand, the offspring born to the two sons will rank to Joseph, as the offspring of the other eleven sons of Jacob will rank to those eleven sons. That is, all those born late in the house of Joseph will be counted to either Ephraim or Manasseh.

The relevance of the pathetic reference to the death and burial of Rachel is difficult to ascertain. The sight of Rachel's grandchildren perhaps prompted the sad recollection of his favorite wife. The last three words of verse 7 define the locality of Ephrath and must be considered in the light of the discussion at 35:19 concerning that identity.

In verses 8–22 the E witness records Jacob's blessing upon Joseph's two sons, and the verses are the proper sequel of 48:1–2. Jacob has little sight because of age (v. 10), but enough to notice the two boys. The story creates the impression that this is the first time that Jacob has met them (cf. v. 11). Such an impression reveals the difficulty in the narrative. Did Jacob meet Joseph's sons soon after his arrival in Egypt, and was that also the time of his death according to E, rather than seventeen years later (47:28) when Jacob adopted the boys shortly before he died (P)? In this latter event the lads would not be lads to be placed between the knees of adults (v. 12), but men more than twenty years of age, for they were born before the seven years of famine (41:50).

According to E, Jacob blesses the two boys, but the action is really threefold: (a) Jacob embraces them (v. 10). (b) Verse 12 implies that the two boys were between Jacob's knees, whence their father removed them. This position in turn suggests some form of adoption parallel to the account in the P witness at verse 5 above. *From his knees* preserves the ambiguity of the Hebrew, "from with his knees." Probably not "on" but "between" is meant. Thus some commentators, Procksch[28] and others, have suggested that *bless them* in verse 9 should be translated "that I may take them upon my knee." But "bless" is probably an overall formula for the three actions described. Jacob's action at this point earns Joseph's prostrate appreciation and gratitude. (c) The third action is the extension of Jacob's arms in blessing (v. 14).

The story confronts the reader with two difficulties more apparent than real. The first difficulty is that according to verse 15 Jacob is said to bless Joseph, but in the actual blessing (vv. 15–16), the two lads are blessed. Then again, later in the story, Joseph's attempt to alter the position of his father's arms comes too late. Jacob crossed his hands, pronounced the blessing formula

and then only did Joseph intervene.

The clue to these difficulties and probably to the entire meaning of the account lies in the physical position which Joseph adopted during the ceremony. In verse 12 Joseph has prostrated himself in an act of tribute and thankfulness and courtesy to his father. He rises and places Ephraim on his right side, opposite his father's left arm, and Manasseh on his left side, opposite Jacob's right arm. Jacob would then extend his arms so that his right hand would rest on the head of Manasseh, the elder of Joseph's sons. This was obviously the treatment appropriate for the elder son.

Having thus stationed his sons Joseph, it is suggested, then resumes his prostrate position in front of his father and between his two boys, kneeling or standing on each side of him. Joseph thus places himself in a position to be blessed (v. 15). He is one of the group of three to be blessed, and the three are treated and become one entity as the recipients of the blessing. Then Jacob is mysteriously led to cross his arms, so that his right arm is laid on Ephraim's head, and his left on Manasseh's head. He thus depicts a reversal of seniority in the two boys. This crossing of Jacob's arms takes place above Joseph's prostrate body. Joseph does not protest because he does not know what has happened. Jacob goes on to alter the blessing, but still Joseph is unaware of the crossed arms above his head. When all is over, and Joseph raises or turns his head, either he notices the crossed arms, or even brushed against them, and realizing what his father had done remonstrates with Jacob.

On this view Joseph is included in the blessing, and the order of blessing is thus Joseph (v. 15), Ephraim (by the crossed arm), and Manasseh. Indeed Jacob's act in suddenly crossing his arms over the prostrate Joseph may not have been due to any sudden or mysterious impulse. By crossing his arms the action took place over and above Joseph, and not parallel to him. Thus Jacob included Joseph within the sphere of the blessing, and it is the coincidence of this memorable and unique act of Jacob's

28 Otto Procksch, *Die Genesis übersetz und erklärt*, Kommentar zum A. T. (Leipzig: A. Deichertsche Verlagsbuch, 1913).

with the later rise of Ephraim to supremacy among the house of Joseph which caused the story to be recollected. Jacob has adopted Joseph's two sons (48:5, P; 48:12, E) as his sons, and so he blesses them all three together in one act and with the same words.

This action is as essential to the blessing as the words. In the action what is spoken in the words is actually transferred to the recipients. All three feel the blessing as they hear it. The blessing is bestowed as well as spoken.

Jacob the grandfather is but the agent of the blessing and he imparts it with his action and pronounces it with his words. He is the descendant of Abraham and Isaac, he is the guided and redeemed man who transmits the blessing. He prays that the blessing may be a perpetuation of Abraham, Isaac, and himself in them, and that the lads will become a multitude in the world. Jacob is thus the link embracing the past and speeding that past onward, in and through the destinies of his two grandsons, now adopted and blessed as his own sons.

God is the author and giver of the blessing. Jacob dwells upon the God whom he is invoking in a three-line ascription of praise in which a sixfold predication of God is uttered. The use of the third person is even more impressive. He is the God . . . who; he is the God . . . who; he is the angel . . . who. No doubt the ascription was spoken slowly and with great deliberation, and this buildup of the fulness of the divine personality has its sequel in the fulness and effect of the blessing outcoming from the God so described. Perhaps the three lines about the Blesser match numerically, if no more, the three persons blessed.

The first and second lines speak of the God, but the third of the angel, by whom of course God is meant, God on earth, even if in some representative capacity. The first line is a relative sentence, but the second and third lines are in Hebrew participial in form, though they are translated in English

by who, who as if they were relative sentences. Further illustrations of these participial clauses or phrases of praise may be found in such passages as Psalm 103:1–5; the hymns in Amos 4:13; 5:8 f.; and is the form that lies behind many of Paul's parenthetical ascriptions of praise (cf. Rom. 4:17,24; 5:5; 8:11,34; 2 Cor. 2:14; 4:6,14; Gal. 2:20). Such instances may appear in the introductory sentences and epithets of the collects of some Christian churches.

Such brief clauses of praise are of course embryonic creedal clauses, born directly of religious experience, and include some of the golden sentences of Scripture. The wealth of the present sentences is also illustrated by the fourth and sixth predications employed. The fourth reads: *who has led me,* literally, "who has shepherded me." Shepherding is more than leading (cf. Psalms 23:1; 28:9). Likewise the sixth predication *who has redeemed me,* literally, "who has been my redeemer, my *go'el,*" where the Hebrew word means next of kin. The duties of this official person "next of kin" under the law were to redeem a relative sold into slavery, to pay his debts (Lev. 25:25 f.). The angel-God is thus Jacob's divine next of kin, and the idea is much employed in Isaiah (41:14; 43:1; 44:22; 48:20). The final verb of the passage *let them grow into a multitude* expresses an abundant fertility.

Too late then Joseph seeks to alter the position of his father's hands, explaining that Manasseh, not Ephraim, was the elder son. But Jacob refused, and justifies his refusal by a prediction of the future greatness of both sons, and the leadership and supremacy of the younger. A *multitude of nations* is literally "a fulness of nations," i.e., a figure of populousness (cf. Deut. 33:17).

The second blessing that day (v. 20) is thus not a parallel and duplicate of the blessing in verses 15–16, but a confirmatory repetition which indicates the certainty of what has been pronounced. Jacob *blessed them,* but the terms of the blessing are in the singular; i.e., both references to *you* are literally to "thee." The singular preserves the form of blessing. (For a parallel oscillation, cf. Num. 6:22 f.) The prosperity of these tribes will be proverbial in Israel, where Israel means the future people of that name.

In his final words, Jacob resumes the motif so characteristic of Joseph's life— *God will be with you* (cf. 39:2,3,23). Then he makes known one particular provision of his will whereby he bequeathes to Joseph a shoulder (*sheᵉkhem;* cf. Shechem) of land, a mountain slope which he had captured from the Amorite inhabitants of the Shechem area. The word for "shoulder" is the same word as the name, Shechem, and that city was the center of the Joseph area. The reference is not to chapter 34, where Simeon and Levi are denounced for their evil attack on Shechem, nor is it to 33:19, where Jacob brought a piece of ground. Rather, it is to some other event not recorded in our traditions whereby Jacob conquered Shechem or an area of territory in the vicinity of Shechem belonging to that city, such as the adjacent Mount Gerizim.

8. Jacob's Testament and Last Command (49:1–33)

¹ Then Jacob called his sons, and said, "Gather yourselves together, that I may tell you what shall befall you in days to come.
² Assemble and hear, O sons of Jacob,
　and hearken to Israel your father.

³ Reuben, you are my first-born,
　my might, and the first fruits of my strength,
　pre-eminent in pride and pre-eminent in power.
⁴ Unstable as water, you shall not have pre-eminence
　because you went up to your father's bed;
　then you defiled it—you went up to my couch!

⁵ Simeon and Levi are brothers;
　weapons of violence are their swords.
⁶ O my soul, come not into their council;
　O my spirit, be not joined to their company;
　for in their anger they slay men,
　and in their wantoness they hamstring oxen.

⁷ Cursed be their anger, for it is fierce;
　and their wrath, for it is cruel!
I will divide them in Jacob
　and scatter them in Israel.

⁸ Judah, your brothers shall praise you;
　your hand shall be on the neck of your enemies;
　your father's sons shall bow down before you.
⁹ Judah is a lion's whelp;
　from the prey, my son, you have gone up.
He stooped down, he couched as a lion,
　and as a lioness; who dares rouse him up?
¹⁰ The scepter shall not depart from Judah,
　nor the ruler's staff from between his feet,
until he comes to whom it belongs;
　and to him shall be the obedience of the peoples.
¹¹ Binding his foal to the vine
　and his ass's colt to the choice vine,
　he washes his garments in wine
　and his vesture in the blood of grapes;
¹² his eyes shall be red with wine,
　and his teeth white with milk.

¹³ Zebulun shall dwell at the shore of the sea;
　he shall become a haven for ships,
　and his border shall be at Sidon.

¹⁴ Issachar is a strong ass,
　crouching between the sheepfolds;
¹⁵ he saw that a resting place was good,
　and that the land was pleasant;
so he bowed his shoulder to bear,
　and became a slave at forced labor.

¹⁶ Dan shall judge his people
　as one of the tribes of Israel.
¹⁷ Dan shall be a serpent in the way,
　a viper by the path,
　that bites the horse's heels
　so that his rider falls backward.
¹⁸ I wait for thy salvation, O LORD.

¹⁹ Raiders shall raid Gad,
　but he shall raid at their heels.

²⁰ Asher's food shall be rich,
　and he shall yield royal dainties.

²¹ Naphtali is a hind let loose,
　that bears comely fawns.

²² Joseph is a fruitful bough,
　a fruitful bough by a spring;
　his branches run over the wall.
²³ The archers fiercely attacked him,
　shot at him, and harassed him sorely;
²⁴ yet his bow remained unmoved,
　his arms were made agile

by the hands of the Mighty One of Jacob
  (by the name of the Shepherd, the Rock
    of Israel),
25 by the God of your father who will help you,
  by God Almighty who will bless you
  with blessings of heaven above,
blessings of the deep that couches beneath,
  blessings of the breasts and of the womb.
26 The blessings of your father
    are mighty beyond the blessings of the
      eternal mountains,
    the bounties of the everlasting hills;
may they be on the head of Joseph,
    and on the brow of him who was separate
      from his brothers.

27 Benjamin is a ravenous wolf,
  in the morning devouring the prey,
  and at even dividing the spoil."

28 All these are the twelve tribes of Israel; and this is what their father said to them as he blessed them, blessing each with the blessing suitable to him. 29 Then he charged them, and said to them, "I am to be gathered to my people; bury me with my fathers in the cave that is in the field of Ephron the Hittite, 30 in the cave that is in the field at Machpelah, to the east of Mamre, in the land of Canaan, which Abraham bought with the field from Ephron the Hittite to possess as a burying place. 31 There they buried Abraham and Sarah his wife; there they buried Isaac and Rebekah his wife; and there I buried Leah— 32 the field and the cave that is in it were purchased from the Hittites." 33 When Jacob finished charging his sons, he drew up his feet into the bed, and breathed his last, and was gathered to his people.

Jacob assembled his twelve sons around him and addresses them all in turn. In verse 1 his words are described as predictions of destinies. The poem is called Jacob's blessing, from the description of what he did in 49:28, but in fact some of the so-called blessings are in fact denunciations (vv. 4,14). Simeon and Levi are actually cursed, not blessed (v. 7). Only Judah (vv. 8–12) and Joseph (vv. 22–26) command total approval.

Jacob speaks first to all six sons of Leah in the order of their birth, except that Zebulun precedes Issachar (cf. Deut. 33:18, but not in Gen. 30:17 ff.; 35:23; 46:13 f.). The four concubine tribes are addressed, not according to the order of

their birth—Dan, Naphtali (Bilhah), Gad, and Asher (Zilpah)—but in a geographical order, from south to north; namely, Dan, Gad, Asher, Naphtali. The Rachel tribes, Joseph and Benjamin, conclude the series.

The poem presents the reader with three great difficulties. The first is that this composition of high literary merit, and one of the most artistic pieces of poetry in the Old Testament, should be attributed to a weak, an aged, in fact, a dying man.

Second, the poem exhibits a reasonably accurate picture of the historical and geographical conditions of the tribes in the period of the Judges; although perhaps Levi ought to be excepted from that judgment. Thus the poem has nothing to say of the great events of the Mosaic era, and is silent concerning the division of the monarchy. Only the oracle on Judah presupposes the Hebrew monarchy and, specifically, the Davidic monarchy. Thus the poem appears to reflect a particular period in Israel's history.

Third, the poem breathes an upsurgent nationalism, unlike the spirit of Jacob, and more characteristic again of the end of the Judges period and the beginning of the monarchy. Thus the poem is concerned not only with individuals as such but also with tribal entities represented by Jacob's sons. The character of each of the twelve ancestors foreshadows that of the tribe. So 49:28a expressly asserts that the poem is concerned with the twelve tribes of Israel.

The loss of primogeniture is known in the ancient cities of Alalak, Ugarit, and Nuzi. Abraham deposed Ishmael (21:-10 ff.); Jacob deposed Reuben in favor of Joseph (48:14,22), and later Manasseh in favor of Ephraim (48:13 f.).

Reuben is destined to be deposed because of moral instability. Simeon and Levi are cursed for their violence, Judah is greatly praised, Zebulun has fair prospects, but Issachar can expect those of slavery. The four concubine tribes are favored in various ways. Joseph is famed for prosperity, and Benjamin is notorious for plunder.

The personal characteristics work out in the fortunes of the tribes sprung from them.

Inevitably Jacob's poem must be compared with the victory Song of Deborah in Judges 5, and the uniformly benign blessing of Moses in Deuteronomy 33. Although a great deal of interest is shown in the secular relationships of the tribes, nevertheless the idea that the tribes are fulfilling the destinies laid out for them by their father Jacob is of course an indirect expression of the divine purpose manifest in the patriarchal accounts. This divine purpose, implicit throughout, surfaces itself especially in the monarchical expectations of Judah, and again in the blessings granted to Joseph.

The main result of the critical interpretation has been to deny that Jacob could have been the author of this poem as it now stands, and to affirm that it belongs to that period at the end of the Judges, and at the beginning of the monarchy, which it reflects with substantial accuracy. The affirmation has become even more precise in the view that the author was a Judean of the time of David, to whom the high praise of Judah is specially due.

But the claims that Jacob was the original and only author, or, alternatively, that the blessing was not composed until the days of David, are both extreme views. The events described are not limited to the end of the Judges period, for not less than three hundred years separate the exploits of Simeon and Levi (vv. 5–7) and the rise of monarchy in Judah (v. 10). There is no hint of the sacralization of Levi (Ex. 32:25–29), and some of the features of the poem are personal to the tribal ancestor concerned. Similarly, archaeological evidence reveals that such testamentary dispositions were known in the Ancient Near East. (Cf C. J. Mullo Weir, "Nuzi," in Thomas, p. 76). Knowledge of human nature justifies the inference that such testaments would be everywhere common where possessions were held by the dying.

An intermediate view is accordingly more likely to be true. Basically Jacob on his deathbed takes leave of his sons and gives warnings, advice, curses, and favorable signs. Expansions indicating tribal fortunes are undoubtedly present, but these are additions to an early tradition at first contemporary with Joseph. The poem also possesses a number of archaic expressions which do not occur later in the Old Testament.

Verse 1 is a technical introduction, depicting a total and final scene. Once again Jacob confronts all his sons, and from his experience of their natures, their past conduct, and the resultant inferences, ventures into prediction. The last phrase literally, "in the end of the days," occurs fourteen times in the Old Testament and indicates the last period of the particular future envisaged by the speaker who uses the phrase (cf. Num. 24:14; Deut. 31:29; Hos. 3:5; Isa. 2:2; Jer. 48:47; Ezek. 38:16). This precise eschatological definition is probably out of place here, and the phrase is a general equivalent for "in the future."

Verse 2 is a poetical introduction, in synonymous parallelism, emphasizing the need for attention with an implicit stress on obedience also (4:23; Deut. 32:1; Isa. 1:10).

Reuben is the firstborn, yet weak and very guilty. In all the traditions and genealogies, Reuben is always the firstborn (29:32; 35:23; 46:8; Ex. 6:14; Num. 1:20; 26:5; 1 Chron. 5:3). In that capacity he speaks first (37:22; 42:22,37) or takes the lead (37:29 f.; cf. Num. 16:12; Deut. 11:6). Yet Reuben's interventions are rarely effective, and he appears as a weak protagonist. As a tribe he later settled east of the Jordan (Josh. 13:15–23), and did not join in Deborah's battle (Judg. 5:15), and there was a danger that he might become extinct (Deut. 33:6). The allusions by Jacob give no hint of these later developments, and the oracle is about Reuben personally. The estimate of his early importance is therefore uncertain. He dishonored his father's bed, an act which probably means he tried to wrest supremacy from Jacob (cf. 35:22). Reuben was thus the kind of man who had no future.

Verses 5–7 lump Simeon and Levi together as violent, too violent for the consultative assembly of the tribes, cruel in their behavior to men and beasts, destined for dispersal among the future Israel. The primary reference is to their conduct at Shechem (34:25–31). The word *swords* is of uncertain origin and meaning. It could mean something like "their stock in trade." *Council* denotes a circle of intimate friends and is used of earthly (Job 19:19; Jer. 23:18,22) and heavenly circles (Amos 3:7). Such antisocial behavior would lead to a situation in which "every man for himself" would obtain, and their isolation and dispersal become inevitable. Jacob might have inferred as much, and given them a very particular warning, though whether Jacob himself could have said *I will divide them in Jacob* is improbable.

Nevertheless the sentence is an early formulation, because Levi is still a secular tribe, and later never received an area of settlement in Canaan, and because Levi could never have become the object of a curse after the days of Moses. Simeon was weak at the end of the Mosaic era (cf. Num. 1:23; 26:14). The tribe allied itself with Judah in the settlement (Judg. 1:3,17; cf. Josh. 19:1–9) and then seems to lose its identity (Josh. 15:26–32,42). In Deuteronomy 33 and Judges 5 Simeon is not mentioned.

Verses 8–12 preserve the sayings concerning Judah. It has fallen to the lot of Judah to take the decisive part, and often the lead, in the negotiations about Joseph (ch. 37) and with Joseph in Egypt (chs. 43—44, 46). Jacob's words to Judah confirm those gifts of Judah, and his sentences are almost all laudatory. Judah is the first tribe; the lion tribe; the messianic tribe; the blessed tribe. Jacob begins with a play on his name: "Praise your name is, and praise you will have from your brothers because of your military successes." Judah is like *a lion's whelp*, successful in the hunt

(cf. Num. 23:24; 24:9; Deut. 33:20,22), and who has returned to the lair. So Judah has possessed his territory (ch. 38; cf. Judg. 1:1–7) and gone to live there.

Scepter (v. 10) is permissible but suggests royalty. The words for scepter and staff (not lawgiver, as RSV margin) can apply to rulers less than royalty, chiefs, etc. (Judg. 5:14; Num. 21:18). They indicate Judah's political preeminence and in this context probably point to the Davidic house. The *ruler's staff* probably stood on the ground, as he stood, but was placed between his knees when he sat.

The third line of verse 10 is still one of the unsolved mysteries of the Old Testament. Everywhere else in the Old Testament Shiloh is the city of Shiloh in the tribe of Ephraim. As it stands, the verse must be translated in a variety of ways.

(a) Until Shiloh comes. If this is correct, the identity and timing of the advent are unknown. Shiloh is unknown as a name of the Messiah before the Talmud, and this interpretation first appears in the sixteenth century.

(b) Until he comes to Shiloh. Judah's advent to Shiloh is only conceivable after the settlement, when Shiloh was the central sanctuary (Josh. 18:1; 1 Sam. 1–4). Note a slightly different reading of the Hebrew (as LXX, Syr., Targ.).

(c) *Until he comes to whom it belongs.* This probably is the best rendering in the present state of knowledge, where *it* means of course the scepter or kingdom in a messianic sense.

(d) Until that which belongs to him comes. Both (c) and (d) mean that Judah will not lose the kingship until he, i.e., the Messiah, comes, to whom the kingship rightly belongs.

(e) Until the one requested comes. A greater alteration of the text makes possible (f) and (g).

(f) Until his ruler comes; i.e., David, or David's ruler—i.e., Messiah.

(g) Until the peaceful one comes. Again a messianic motif; but (f) and (g) are unlikely on textual grounds. The view that the verse is an intrusion, breaking the connection between verses 9–11, is also unsound.

In general the clause obviously describes conditions which inaugurate a yet more splendid future. This thought is continued in the acknowledgement of the universal obedience of the nations (d). This splendid future may be found in (a) the advance of Judah, the leading tribe, to become the tribe of the house and kingdom of David. In turn this means the first two clauses of verse 10 do not have a royal significance but relate to the premonarchic role of the tribe. If 10c thus marks the Davidic ruler, then 10d is harmonious with it, as such references as Psalms 72:8–11 and 89:19–27 show. Likewise the splendid future may be found in (b), the messianic destiny of the tribe of Judah through the house of David. In turn this means that 10a and b refer already to the Davidic house.

The "messianic" cast of the Davidic-Jerusalem-sonship and sovereignty-ideology is so pronounced that inevitably the aspirations for the coming of the Messiah should find their origin here (cf. Isa. 11). Similarly, since the main stream of messianic expectation is so closely bound up with the house of David, it may be difficult to disassociate these ideas in the interpretation of 10c. Thus the verse may be described not as an either-or, i.e., historical or ideal, but as a both-and, i.e., as an actual Davidic ideal—messianic expectation. The Davidic ideology is implicitly messianic, and it is difficult to distinguish and draw the line between them. (Cf. Driver, Special Note Excursus II, pp. 410–15.)

Verses 11 f. describe the sheer abundance of his (v. 10) material blessings. No man in his senses would bind his animals to vines, for the animals would eat them; but such is the abundance that such conduct is of no consequence. Abundance is messianic and surrounds the Messiah (Isa. 11:1–9; Ezek. 34:23–31; Amos 9:11–15).

The synonymous parallelism in verse 12 is perfect. His eyes are darkened by much wine, but his teeth are dripping white with milk.

Verse 13 praises **Zebulun** in virtue of his favorable habitat, fronting the sea. Judges 12:12 mentions "Aijalon in the land of Zebulun," and thereby locates Zebulun in the western slopes of Samaria. So later they must have moved northwards to "suck the affluence of the seas" (Deut. 33:19, but contrast the landlocked position in Josh. 19:10–16). Israelite tribes on the coast is itself a phenomenon, for Hebrew has no word for harbor, and the Israelites were really landlubbers. Zebulun's territory stretched northward against Sidon, i.e., Phoenicia.

Verse 14 depicts the foolish decision of **Issachar,** who like Zebulun, took a valiant part in Deborah's great victory (Judg. 5:15). Dwelling south of Naphtali, on the east of Zebulun, north of Manasseh and west of Jordan (Josh. 19:17–23), strong and able to make its own way. Issachar yet decided to live in pleasant places at the price of its freedom.

The word for **resting place** has rich associations with Palestine as Israel's rest (Deut. 12:9), and with the thought of Yahweh's resting place (Psalms 95:11; 132:8,14; Isa. 66:1, cf. Zech. 9:1 of Yahweh's word). **Forced labor** means a body of men conscripted for forced labor (1 Kings 5:13). In Joshua 16:10 it is used of the lot of some of the conquered Canaanites. The independent Israelites in the hills poured scorn on such as Issachar who chose the fertile lowlands in Jezreel at the price of Canaanite domination. Similarly, Biridya, prince of Megiddo, organized forced labor in Esdraelon (cf. Pritchard, *A.N.E.T.,* p. 485).

Verses 16–21 pay tribute to the four concubine tribes, in which the two Zilpah tribes are inserted between the two Bilhah tribes.

At first Dan lived between Ephraim, Benjamin, Judah, and the Philistines (Josh. 19:40 ff.), but later, under pressure, moved north, conquered Laish, and settled there in a new area called Dan (Judg. 1:34;

18:7,27 ff.). The interpretation of the verse depends on the meaning of the words *his people.* If these two words mean Israel, then Dan will give a judge to Israel, will wage the struggle for Israel, just like any other tribe. If the two words mean Dan, then the verse honors Dan as a small tribe (Judg. 18:2,11,19 describe Dan as a clan) which conducts its own life and maintains its own independence in face of odds.

The use of *Dan* again in verse 17 reasserts Dan's vitality, and is not to be regarded as a separate saying. Rather, this suggests Dan's worrying, guerilla tactics. The figure chosen is that of the *serpent,* the horned viper, of which the modern equivalent would be the terrier snapping at the heels of men and horses. The thought of Dan's littleness and bravery against odds probably suggested the kind of prayer appropriate to Dan in face of Philistine harassment. This prayer in verse 18 thus points to Dan's first position in the southwest before the removal to the north. Salvation means mainly in that context deliverance.

Verse 19 praises *Gad,* dogged by Bedouin raids, because of its position in Gilead, south of Jabbok, bordering desert peoples, especially Ammonites (Josh. 13:25; Judg. 11:15). The alliteration in the Hebrew is striking—*Gadh gᵉdhudh yᵉghudhennu. Their heels* rightly translates by making the first Hebrew letter of verse 20 the last letter of verse 19 with LXX, Syriac, and Vulgate versions.

Asher dwelt on the fertile coast between Carmel and Tyre. Asher is so well off that he is famous for his own standard of living and for the delicacies supplied as exports (1 Kings 5:9; Ezek. 27:17; Acts 12:20). In particular the area was known for its oil (Deut. 33:24), wheat, and wine.

Verse 21 is a tribute to *Naphtali,* but interpretation is difficult. The Hebrew permits two readings of the first line. Thus: Naphtali is *a hind let loose,* or, according to an alternate reading, is "a spreading terabinth," but the second line "giving fair speeches" suits neither translation of the first line. So the second line is emended to read *that bears comely fawns* or "producing goodly shoots." These figures, whatever they mean, must be compared with Naphtali's territory on the west of the sea of Galilee and northward beyond Huleh to Lebanon (cf. Deut. 33:23; Judg. 5:18). Nothing more than the idea of the spread of Naphtali through a fairly large tract of country may be inferred from the passage.

Verses 22–26 praise the double tribe of *Joseph,* Jacob's favorite son. The house of Joseph was the most numerical and powerful of the tribes and gains great praises. Deuteronomy 33:13–17 appears to be based to some extent on the present passage. Four themes are present. The vigor of Joseph; his defense against the attack of the archers; the fourfold invocation of God; and the variegated blessings on Joseph's head. Joseph is likened to *a fruitful bow,* such as a vine tree. The Hebrew word is *porath* which resembles Ephratha, a name for Ephraim (41:52; Hos. 14:8). The tree is planted by a fountain, and is so well watered that it grows vigorously, surmounting the adjacent wall (cf. Psalm 1:3; Jer. 17:8).

The second theme is Joseph's successful defense against archery. The verse does not speak of a particular engagement or battle, but rather of a type of military activity. Joseph was staunch amidst the prevalent archer attacks, presumably from Canaanite and the more distant Arab neighbors, just as it might be said today that a certain regiment was good at jungle warfare or guerilla activity. The first half of verse 24 is difficult, the meaning unclear.

The third theme is the support which Joseph sustained from the God of his father, here described in four ways. He is the *Mighty One of Jacob* (cf. 17:1; 21:33; 31:13,42; Isa. 1:24; 49:26; Psalm 132:2,5). Mightiness was ever an attribute of the God of the patriarchs, and it is particularly apt in reference to Jacob, who himself was so strong. The title is thus a very ancient one, but was used in later Israel with special application to the ark, etc. The second title employs a well-known figure of God as *the Shepherd,* but the reference to the *Rock of*

Israel is mysterious (the word "rock" in Psalm 18:32; 1 Sam. 2:2; Deut. 32:4 etc. 95:1 represents a different Hebrew word), unless there is a reference to the stone of Bethel in 28:18 f., 22; and 35:14, i.e., to the God of Bethel or even to "the stone of help" (Ebenezer) in 1 Samuel 3:20; 7:12. The third title is a straightforward reference to the **God of your father.** The fourth title **God Almighty** is only gained by preferring Samaritan Pentateuch, 7 and LXX, Syriac to the Hebrew "and with the Almighty" (*Shaddai*).

The rest of verses 25–26 is obviously a formula of comprehensive blessing arranged in a series of couplets. The **blessings of heaven** are rain and dew and sunshine; **of the deep,** the springs, fountains, wells, and streams that come up from the great watery deep below the earth; blessings of healthy and numerous offspring, no doubt of men and beasts.

The meaning of verse 26 is not clear. The phrase **blessings of your father** may refer to the blessings heaped upon Jacob by his father, Isaac, or it may mean simply the blessings now being bestowed by Jacob. The second line of the text is corrupt and the RSV solution is uncertain though as good as any, depicting as it does the superiority of Jacob's blessings to anything in nature. The last two lines are as contemporary with Jacob as anything in the poems. **Separate** may be construed as "prince" (cf. Deut. 33:16).

Verse 27 praises **Benjamin,** Jacob's last son, and one of the most military of Israel's tribes, famous for its archers and slingers (Judg. 20:16). It is sufficient to recall the names of Ehud, Saul, and Jonathan. The tribe incurred the censure of the other tribes (Judg. 19–20). The present reference is of course entirely laudatory. The earlier Benjaminites of the Mari tablets who lived before the time of Jacob evince the same military and rapacious characteristics (Parrot, "Mari," in Thomas, p. 141). The Old Testament Benjaminites are ever on the prowl for booty.

A final review of Jacob's testament sug-gests on the basis of the foregoing that a minimum original nucleus composed by the patriarch himself might have consisted of the sentence of deposition of Reuben, most of the sayings about Simeon and Levi, some of the sayings about Judah, and those about Joseph linking father and son.

The first part of verse 28 is of course the postscript to the poem.

In 28*b*–33 the P witness reports another and different part of Jacob's testament, the arrangements for his burial, and adds a notice of Jacob's death. This passage follows 48:3–7, parallel to 47:29–31 (J), and is continued by P's final witness in Genesis, 50:12–13.

Jacob instructs his sons that he is to be buried in the family burial place in the cave of Machpelah at Hebron (23:8,16–18). Note the parallel between the verbs in 28:1 and here. The burials of Rebekah and Leah are recorded only here in Genesis (for Rachel, cf. 48:7). The persistence of the Machpelah tradition in Genesis is impressive. **My people** in verse 29 is singular but in verse 33 is plural, **his people,** (cf. 25:8). Jacob was sitting on the edge of the bed and then drew his feet up into the bed for the last time. Thus with this laconic note, Jacob, the father of all Israel, dies.

The final chapter (50) tells of Jacob's embalming, his notable funeral procession, and burial; the full reconciliation of Joseph and his brothers, and his provision for them; and, last, Joseph's own death and embalming.

XXV. Jacob's Burial and Joseph's Last Days (50:1–26)

1. Embalming and Burial of Jacob (50:1–14)

¹ Then Joseph fell on his father's face, and wept over him, and kissed him. ² And Joseph commanded his servants the physicians to embalm his father. So the physicians embalmed Israel; ³ forty days were required for it, for so many are required for embalming. And the Egyptians wept for him seventy days.

⁴ And when the days of weeping for him were past, Joseph spoke to the household of Pharaoh, saying, "If now I have found favor in

your eyes, speak, I pray you, in the ears of Pharaoh, saying, ⁵ My father made me swear, saying, 'I am about to die: in my tomb which I hewed out for myself in the land of Canaan, there shall you bury me.' Now therefore let me go up, I pray you, and bury my father; then I will return." ⁶ And Pharaoh answered, "Go up, and bury your father, as he made you swear." ⁷ So Joseph went up to bury his father; and with him went up all the servants of Pharaoh, the elders of his household, and all the elders of the land of Egypt, ⁸ as well as all the household of Joseph, his brothers, and his father's household; only their children, their flocks, and their herds were left in the land of Goshen. ⁹ And there went up with him both chariots and horsemen; it was a very great company. ¹⁰ When they came to the threshing floor of Atad, which is beyond the Jordan, they lamented there with a very great and sorrowful lamentation; and he made a mourning for his father seven days. ¹¹ When the inhabitants of the land, the Canaanites, saw the mourning on the threshing floor of Atad, they said, "This is a grievous mourning to the Egyptians." Therefore the place was named Abelmizraim; it is beyond the Jordan. ¹² Thus his sons did for him as he had commanded them; ¹³ for his sons carried him to the land of Canaan, and buried him in the cave of the field at Machpelah, to the east of Mamre, which Abraham bought with the field from Ephron the Hittite, to possess as a burying place. ¹⁴ After he had buried his father, Joseph returned to Egypt with his brothers and all who had gone up with him to bury his father.

Joseph's mourning is singled out as that of the favorite son. Jacob's body is embalmed by the Egyptians, experts in such matters, but it is so treated not for the reasons implicit in the Egyptian mythology but merely to preserve Jacob's body for it to be carried to Canaan and there buried.

The embalming was a costly and lengthy process and it took forty days. Including, though hardly additional to, these forty days were seventy days of mourning. Aaron and Moses were mourned for thirty days (Num. 20:29; Deut. 34:8). Egyptian mourning for a king was seventy days (Diodorus 1:72), and the mourning for Jacob was nearly as long, out of respect for Joseph.

Through intermediaries in Pharaoh's household, Joseph requests royal permission to go to Canaan to bury his father, as

he had promised his father. There is no necessary contradiction between 50:5 and 47:30. Individual graves in the family area had to be dug. He gives the undertaking that he will return to Egypt. Why Joseph used intermediaries is not known, for the mourning for Jacob was past. Perhaps Jacob was still in Joseph's dwelling, and therefore Joseph was to some extent isolated by taboo at least from Pharaoh's presence. Pharaoh readily agrees and a number of Egyptians accompany the cortege. The Egyptians went possibly for security reasons as well as respect, for a military escort (v. 9) is implied. Jacob's sons had to leave behind their children and flocks as surety of return. The funeral procession was obviously a very famous and memorable affair, long spoken of.

Verses 10–12 describe a locality beyond Jordan, i.e., east of Jordan, but not far from the river, for the locality was in sight of Canaanites on the west bank. This reference to an east Jordan locality has prompted the question as to whether or not Jacob was thought to have been buried there, not far from Jordan's east bank, for it is hardly likely that a funeral procession from Egypt to Hebron would have gone round via east Jordan. The only possible justification for such a detour was to enable Esau to participate in the mourning, but the narrative gives no hint of this.

The locality was *the threshing floor of Atad*, (literally, of the bramble) which may have been the same place as the field (or mourning) of the Egyptians. The customary period for mourning is seven days (1 Sam. 31:13). The final stage of the route and the burial itself is made by the family only. When all was over, Joseph, who had played a leading part, and all the members of the cortege, returned to Egypt, and Jacob remained buried in his native land.

2. Joseph Reassures His Brothers (50:15–21)

¹⁵ When Joseph's brothers saw that their father was dead, they said, "It may be that Joseph will hate us and pay us back for all the evil which we did to him." ¹⁶ So they sent a

message to Joseph, saying, "Your father gave this command before he died, 17 'Say to Joseph, Forgive, I pray you, the transgression of your brothers and their sin, because they did evil to you.' And now, we pray you, forgive the transgression of the servants of the God of your father." Joseph wept when they spoke to him. 18 His brothers also came and fell down before him, and said, "Behold, we are your servants." 19 But Joseph said to them, "Fear not, for am I in the place of God? 20 As for you, you meant evil against me; but God meant it for good, to bring it about that many people should be kept alive, as they are today. 21 So do not fear; I will provide for you and your little ones." Thus he reassured them and comforted them.

The E witness concludes the book of Genesis with some stories that reveal the magnanimity of Joseph to his guilty brothers, and his piety toward the traditions of his fathers. The story ends in reconciliation (vv.15–21).

Sinful and guilty men tend to project their consciousness of guilt. Liars rarely trust others. Joseph's guilty brothers fear that with the death of Jacob Joseph will now take his revenge for their past cruelty to him. First they send a message or deputation, which Joseph hears and receives with weeping. Joseph wept perhaps because he was grieved that they should attribute such motives to him, but more likely out of compassion for their fears. They then venture to come themselves. (There is no other reference to the command of Jacob here invoked by the brothers, v. 16.) Once again the brothers prostrate themselves before Joseph. Thus the predictions of the dreams (37:7,9) are fulfilled for the last time. Joseph again interprets the past in terms of God's overruling providence (45:5 ff.). Joseph denies that he can exercise God's function, and thus exact retribution. In fact God has already acted. The conduct of the brothers has already been embraced by God and transformed into part of his saving action for them. The proof is that they and so many others are still alive.

Thus as the brothers based their appeal to Joseph by reference to the God of Jacob (v. 17), so now Joseph finally resolves the

mystery in terms of the will of that God (v. 20). In token of his acceptance of that belief, he promises, no doubt not for the first time, to provide for them, and in full reconciliation he reassures and comforts them.

It is not necessary to suppose that the conversation falls within the time of the famine. The statements are too general for that.

3. Joseph's Old Age and Death (50:22–26)

22 So Joseph dwelt in Egypt, he and his father's house; and Joseph lived a hundred and ten years. 23 And Joseph saw Ephraim's children of the third generation; the children also of Machir the son of Manasseh were born upon Joseph's knees. 24 And Joseph said to his brothers, "I am about to die; but God will visit you, and bring you up out of this land to the land which he swore to Abraham, to Isaac, and to Jacob." 25 Then Joseph took an oath of the sons of Israel, saying, "God will visit you, and you shall carry up my bones from here." 26 So Joseph died, being a hundred and ten years old; and they embalmed him, and he was put in a coffin in Egypt.

Like Joshua his descendant (Josh. 24:29), Joseph reached the age of 110 years, an age for a lifetime considered in Egyptian circles to be ideal and blessed. What is more, Joseph actually saw his great-great-grandchildren from both his sons, even though he was the first of all Jacob's sons to die (v. 25).

Particular reference is made to Manasseh's son, Machir, and their children. Machir is one of the powerful clans of Manasseh and is mentioned in the Song of Deborah (Judg. 5:14). The numerous references to Machir and his descendants in the wilderness (Num. 26:29; 27:1; 32:39–40) and settlement (Deut. 3:15; Josh. 13:31; 17:1) traditions, coupled with the reference to the Exodus in verses 24–5, suggest that the gap between the days of Joseph and those following the Exodus could not have been as long as implied. The tendency of these verses then is to date Joseph, not in the sixteenth century, but rather in the fourteenth. Whether the birth on Joseph's knees means something more than a family custom, such as adoption, is uncertain.

Like his father Jacob (48:21), Joseph predicts the Exodus and instructs his brothers that his bones are not to be left in Egypt (Ex. 13:19; Josh. 24:32). Joseph died and was embalmed and placed in a chest, for which the word used in Hebrew is the same word as for the Israelite ark of the covenant; but of course no connection whatsoever exists between them.

The last Hebrew word in the book of Genesis means "in Egypt," but the last paragraph of the book has once again the Promised Land in view, not a land of sojourning but a land for political freedom and spiritual liberty.

Thus this last paragraph holds out the hope of a future in the Promised Land, but the last word of the book reminds them of their present stay in Egypt. As time went on no doubt the hope of a future grew more distant, but the realities of their present lot grew more permanent and cruel. This last paragraph of Genesis delineates the problem, the solution of which the book of Exodus is to portray.

Exodus

ROY L. HONEYCUTT, JR.

Introduction

Exodus is to the Old Testament as the Gospels are to the New Testament. Both proclaim the redemptive activity of God conceived in his compassion for the plight of man-in-bondage. Each anchors the revelation of God firmly to history, and each focuses in the activity of a covenant mediator who fulfils his calling by the selfless giving of his own person: Moses in Exodus, Jesus in the Gospels. Both portray the sealing of a covenant with those who have chosen to follow the redeemer God, and in both there is the revelation of the divine will for inward character and outward conduct among those who have so chosen to follow the Lord of the covenant. Exodus and the Gospels are in full accord in proclaiming the absolute lordship of God (Christ) over history, nature, and man.

Exodus is a book touched by the diversity of many hands in the process of compilation, but it reaches out to equally diverse readers: the professional scholar who spends hours analyzing sources; the sincere believer, professionally untrained but rewardingly devoted to the study of God's Word; the minister, translating its eternal message into terminology relevant to an age of confusion. To each of these, Exodus may speak in a different way, with strangely different accents. But to each of these the voice heard, the message discerned, and the impressions left should be uniquely alike, if not the same. For Exodus addresses each person—scholar, layman, minister—regardless of station or role, as God's challenging word of grace and judg-

ment, as a comforting word insisting that life need not be lived in bondage, as a reassuring word that the redeemer God is eternally Lord of history, nature, and man.

Thus, this is a book, a word breaking forth from God, that calls us from the anguish of our bondage and the humdrum purposelessness of life in Egypt to set our feet on a new way; a way forged through pestilence and plague, through sea and wilderness; a way bounded on both sides by his covenant revelation; a way overshadowed by his presence as he leads us through our wilderness, insisting all the while that no man need live and die in the futility of "Egypt," estranged and lost to the purposes of the covenant Lord.

I. Name

English translations refer to the second book of the Old Testament under the title "Exodus." The name came through the Latin Vulgate which refers to the book as *Liber Exodus.* However, the Vulgate itself was dependent upon the title which appears in the Septuagint, a Greek translation of the Old Testament made in the third century B.C. The Septuagint referred to the book by the simple title *Exodos* (exit, departure). The occurrence of the word *exodos* in the Septuagint in 19:1, may well be responsible for the title ultimately given to the book.[1]

[1] Cf. Ex. 19:1: "On the third new moon after the people of Israel had gone forth [*tes exodou*] out of the land of Egypt."

In keeping with the Old Testament practice of taking the opening word or words of a book as the title, the Hebrew text refers to Exodus as *w⁰elleh sh⁰moth*, "these are the names of" (i.e., of the sons of Israel who went into Egypt), or more briefly as *sh⁰moth*.

The name Exodus is quite appropriate. The event was foundational for many Old Testament writers as they theologically interpreted both Israel's beginnings and present existence. However, one should use Exodus as the title with this understanding: solely in terms of the deliverance from Egypt, the exodus motif occupies only 15 of 40 chapters. Exodus deals with much more than the actual exodus. It includes the additional emphases of the wilderness and Sinai themes, both of which are of singular importance.

II. Authorship

Technically the book of Exodus is anonymous, for no single person is specified as author of the entire book. Nonetheless, there is a lengthy tradition which identifies Moses as the author of Exodus; indeed, of the entire Pentateuch. Consequently English translations have consistently included in titles to Exodus such expressions as "The Second Book of Moses, Called Exodus" (KJV), or "The Second Book of Moses Commonly Called Exodus" (ASV, RSV). Such references appear in the titles later added to the book, however, and have never been present in the Hebrew text. Consequently, the reference to Mosaic authorship in the titles is valid only as an illustration of the long history among translators for the ascription of Mosaic authorship to the book of Exodus.

Within the book, however, there are occasions when writing is associated with Moses: "And the Lord said to Moses, 'Write this as a memorial in a book and recite it in the ears of Joshua, that I will utterly blot out the remembrance of Amalek from under heaven'" (17:14). "And Moses wrote all the words of the Lord.

. . . Then he took the book of the covenant, and read it in the hearing of the people" (24:4–7). "And the Lord said to Moses, 'Write these words; in accordance with these words I have made a covenant with you and with Israel'" (34:27).

Despite these references within the book, full Mosaic authorship depends essentially upon external evidence. For example, appeal is often made to later ascriptions of Mosaic authorship for the Pentateuch or parts thereof. One might compare in this regard 2 Chronicles 25:4, "But he did not put their children to death, according to what is written in the law, in the book of Moses, where the Lord commanded . . ."; or, Ezra 6:18, "And they set the priests in their divisions and the Levites in their courses, for the service of God at Jerusalem, as it is written in the book of Moses."[2]

Thus, there was a late tradition within the Old Testament which spoke of the "book of Moses" (cf. Dan. 9:11, 13). Later, the Talmud declared that any departure from the teaching that Moses wrote the Pentateuch was to be punished by exclusion from Paradise.

As important as these references may be for some, the greatest authority for many exponents of the Mosaic authorship of the Pentateuch is the New Testament. That the Pentateuch was synonymous with the "Law of Moses" in the thought of first-century persons appears clear. From the following and other references many conclude that Moses wrote the Law: "Jesus said to them, 'For your hardness of heart he [i.e., Moses] wrote you this commandment'" (Mark 10:5); "If you believed Moses, you would believe me, for he wrote of me" (John 5:46). (Cf. also Matt. 19:8; Mark 12:26; Luke 24:27, 44; John 7:19, 23; Acts 13:39; 15:5; 28:23; 1 Cor.

---

[2] These references are probably to the book of Deuteronomy with which Moses was more specifically identified (cf. 1 Kings 2:3; 2 Kings 23:25; 21:8; Mal. 4:4), and the belief in Mosaic authorship of the entire Pentateuch probably represents an extension of that conviction.

9:9; 2 Cor. 3:15; Heb. 9:19; 10:28.)

A majority of Old Testament scholars assumes that the authorship of Exodus is much more complex than the ascription of authorship to a single person would imply. Rather than having been written by a single person, it is much more likely that many persons from several different areas, both geographical and functional, were responsible for Exodus in its present form. Some of the material may well have originated in the time of Moses. Perhaps some was committed to writing by him. Other parts likely arose through the worshiping community. Although an individual probably produced these various parts, this person may have been anonymous even to his contemporaries.

Quite often contemporary emphasis in Pentateuchal studies is placed upon sources rather than authors. The Southern Kingdom, Judah, for example, possessed its own record of the exodus events (as of the entire Pentateuch, and other areas). The Northern Kingdom, Israel, would also have possessed its account(s), for it also was descended from the people involved in the exodus. Thus, one faces a situation in many ways similar to the Gospels of the New Testament and their parallel accounts. There is, however, at least one major difference. While the Gospels were not woven into a single account, the motifs of the exodus, wilderness, Sinai, and conquest were woven into a single narrative. Then to these were added the themes of the patriarchs and the creation narratives. Apparently the southern source was taken as normative and served as the framework so that when the Northern Kingdom fell its religious literature was assimilated into the Southern Kingdom's narrative. Later the process was repeated, and when the Southern Kingdom fell the priests wove the combined southern-northern accounts into their understanding of God's dealings with his people since creation.

Although few today would support all of the proposals associated with the work of Wellhausen, among the abiding contributions of nineteenth-century literary criticism have been the isolation of sources and their designation by the symbols J, E, D, and P. The characteristics of each of the sources are too involved to receive full consideration here, but it should be observed that among their several characteristics the use of the divine name is significant. The southern source preferred to use the name Lord (Jehovah, or Yahweh), while the northern source preferred the name God (in Hebrew *'elohim*). Consequently, during and following the nineteenth century the southern source came to be known as J for Jehovah, or Yahweh, and the northern source as E for *'elohim*. Material associated with Deuteronomy and the literary activity related to it was labeled D, and the priestly materials were identified by the symbol P. Although material contained therein may be earlier, the sources themselves date in final form approximately as follows: J, tenth century; E, ninth century; D, seventh century; P, sixth century in the main. This terminology will be used in the present treatment of Exodus when it proves helpful to distinguish various sources one from the other.

How is one to resolve the complex problem of the authorship of Exodus? Quite frankly, forging one's final opinion will be time-consuming if all evidence is considered, as certainly it should be before arriving at a decision. Since minute consideration of the problem is beyond the scope of the present work one should turn to books of introduction for more detailed treatment.[3]

In conclusion, it is the present writer's

---

[3] For support of Mosaic authorship of the Pentateuch, cf. E. J. Young, *Introduction to the Old Testament*, and Gleason L. Archer, Jr., *A Survey of Old Testament Introduction*. A helpful summary of the view that the Pentateuch is based on several sources or strata of material may be found in Cuthbert A. Simpson, "The Growth of the Hexateuch," in *The Interpreter's Bible*, Vol I; H. H. Rowley, *The Growth of the Old Testament*; Gerhard von Rad, "The Problem of the Hexateuch," in *The Problem of the Hexateuch and Other Essays*; Georg Fohrer, *Introduction to the Old Testament*, trans. David E. Green (Nashville: Abingdon, 1968), an excellent survey.

judgment that while Exodus may contain some material of which one may legitimately speak of Mosaic authorship, the book as we now possess it is much more complex. There is no intrinsic reason to deny to Moses a basic contribution to Exodus. He was a historical person, living at a time when writing was prolific (as even a casual reading of Ancient Near Eastern literature will reveal), and had participated in a momentous experience worthy of fixation in written form. Despite this, however, it is doubtful that extensive authentically Mosaic material can ever be extricated so that one can say with finality "it is here" or "it is there." Hence, if one is to speak of Moses as author of the Law, and of Exodus more specifically, this may best be done in the very general sense that the Law is ascribed to him as the first and greatest of the Israelite lawgivers. Just as one may speak of Solomon as the father of Israel's wisdom literature, although others also wrote wise sayings; or, as one may speak of David as the psalmist of Israel, although others also wrote psalms; so one may speak of Moses as the lawgiver of Israel, despite the fact that others also contributed to the formation of the fivefold complex known as the Pentateuch.

Thus, while one may legitimately ascribe materials both oral and written to Moses, the book of Exodus remains in the main anonymous. Let it be clearly understood, however, that this does not adversely affect the authority of the book. Biblical authority is dependent not upon the human mediator but upon divine origin or inspiration.

III. Composition

If one assumes the Mosaic authorship of Exodus, the problem of composition is greatly simplified. With this as a basic premise one is confronted with the picture of an individual's writing, as it were, his memoirs, framed in the context of Israel's beginnings. On the other hand, one may well assume that God led in the composition of the book over a much longer period.

So the book may have passed unit by unit through an oral stage. Then, shaped by usage in worship centers throughout the era of conquest and settlement, parts were written down in the North and yet other parts transcribed in the South, until finally through a series of redactions it reached the essential form in which it now appears. If the latter is correct, as probably it is, then the problem of composition is much more complex and deserves elaboration in order to clarify just how the book reached its present stage.

Nineteenth-century literary criticism, as well as the era immediately following, gave primary if not sole attention to literary criticism, seeking to isolate sources one from the other on the assumption that such sources were composed as documents ascribed to four basic origins, these were then woven into a single literary form constituting the Pentateuch in the essential form that it has been known for over two millennia. These documents were dated late in the history of Israel and it was felt, by Wellhausen and his disciples especially, that it would have been impossible for Moses to have written any of their contents. It is safe to say that this particular approach is supported by exceedingly few Old Testament scholars of the mid-twentieth century, despite the fact that many positive results of the literary-critical era have been preserved and are quite legitimate.

Beginning with the work of Herman Gunkel an attempt was made to get behind the written sources to the life situation of the biblical material. Although Gunkel's primary work dealt with Genesis, his conclusions are applicable to other areas as well. With the advent of this procedure, attention shifted to the preliterary histoy of the text. Admittedly, much of this work was inevitably characterized by conjecture. After all, one can deal definitively only with written sources, and preliterary material can only be dealt with on the basis of conclusions of greater probability. However, Gunkel's emphasis was wholesome in that it left the way open for the assumption that although the written form in which the biblical material may have come to us is relatively late, such written sources may well depend upon earlier preliterary forms of the biblical material.

One of the more articulate voices emphasizing the place of the worship center in the creation, transmission, and transformation of the biblical material has been that of Gerhard von Rad. It is his contention that the settlement tradition, the promise and fulfilment of a land for the people of God, constitutes the backbone of the Pentateuch. To the settlement tradition there were added the Sinai and the wilderness motifs. This was later elongated by the addition of the patriarchal narratives and the creation stories, plus the materials extending through Genesis 11.

Uniquely characteristic of von Rad's position is the assumption that the various themes of the settlement and Sinai were attached to separate religious shrines such as Shechem and Gilgal. His view allows for the growth of the biblical material over a long period of time and insists that the narratives, although they may have been oral during this time, were shaped by usage in the various worship centers. While this position is far removed from the older view of Mosaic authorship, it has much to commend it and should be examined seriously by those seeking the best understanding of the Exodus material, indeed of the entire Pentateuch.

More specifically, however, what were the precise stages through which the book of Exodus passed in the process of its compilation? While the general outlines of composition are essentially the same as those of the Pentateuch sketched above, it is likely that Exodus was composed in much the following manner.

The various elements within the book of Exodus tended to gravitate toward either accounts of significant places, cultic centers, or outstanding personalities. This is much as one would expect. Although this transpired under the providential guidance of the Lord, the mechanics whereby the literature grew consisted of what one might term a magnetic nucleus which attracted brief elements now contained in the book of Exodus. Thus, segments relating to the exodus motif gathered around the celebration of the Passover.

The Sinai motif may well have developed, as von Rad has suggested, at the worship center located at Shechem. The emphasis upon the settlement which appears briefly in Exodus may have gravitated toward the worship center at Gilgal. And the accounts of Moses' life flowed together because each separate element dealt with the all-important personality of Moses. In other words, the material did not flow together without a catalyst. Recognizing the element of divine leadership, there nonetheless was a mechanical agent present which precipitated the various elements. At times material flowed together because it dealt with a place, Sinai, Kadesh, or Trans-Jordan. Again, the material united around a great personality—especially Moses, but Aaron as well. Worship centers and specific celebrations within worship such as Passover, the Feast of Weeks, and the Feast of Tabernacles attracted yet other elements.

Assuming a legitimate historical nucleus for the book of Exodus, this material may well have gathered around at least three motifs: exodus, 1:1—15:21; wilderness, 15:22—18:27; and Sinai, 19—40. Within each of these motifs, however, there is a complicated development of literature with which we cannot deal fully at this time.

The *exodus motif* (1—15), which Pedersen associates with the Passover celebration, drew together numerous originally diverse elements. The Passover narrative, with its culmination in the slaying of the firstborn and the deliverance at the sea, may have once stood separately from the plague narratives but later assimilated with the accounts of the plagues. The birth narrative of Moses may have gravitated toward this motif because of his involvement with the exodus, although this may well have happened at a later time than the union of the Passover-plague theme. Thus, behind Exodus 1—15 there is a complex process of preliterary and literary development involving at least four areas: (1) the Passover narrative itself, including deliverance at the sea; (2) the plagues; (3) the birth narrative; and (4) the additional songs of Moses and Miriam found in chapter 15 (although this could be treated as the opening of the wilderness theme).

Before these diverse elements were brought together into a unified complex, whether oral or written, they in all probability existed in oral form and were told and retold around the campfires of Israel, within the family circle as children were taught the theological significance of their father's history, and at the centers of worship. This not only preserved the material but through exalting the Lord's deeds in worship caused them to live again as contemporary events.

The *wilderness theme* occupies a relatively brief part of the book of Exodus (15—18). This should be read, however, as part of the broader theme of settlement, which extends through the book of Numbers. The artificial division of the Pentateuch into five books should not be allowed to obscure the unity of the settlement theme. In fact, there is a real sense in which the wilderness theme is fulfilled in the conquest narratives of Joshua. Thus, the wilderness and conquest motifs are but part of the broader settlement tradition which saw the giving of the land as the fulfilment of the Lord's promise to his people.

The *Sinai* motif extends from Exodus 19:1—Numbers 10:10, but the essence of it insofar as Exodus is concerned appears in chapters 19—20, 24, and 34. The literary and sacral history of the Sinai theme is an often debated topic among contemporary Old Testament scholars. Von Rad, for example, has insisted that the Sinai theme was not originally connected with either the exodus or settlement traditions. He says it had a separate existence as a cultic

narrative at the Shechem sanctuary, only later being brought together with the exodus motif by the author from the Southern Kingdom who gave to the entire Pentateuch its overall theological structure. Thus, in the case of the Sinai motif, one is again confronted with a literary complex which was probably transmitted in oral form for many generations, during the process continuing to grow as briefer elements were attracted to the magnetic core constituting the essence of the theme.

To these three primary motifs within Exodus there were added narrative episodes such as those related to the apostasy involving the golden calf (cf. 32 ff.). Also, various bodies of law found their way into the book of Exodus between the period of its inception and its finalization late in the monarchial or even post monarchial period. With regard to the incorporation of the corpus of law into Exodus, G. W. Anderson's helpful and accurate parallel between the Pentateuch and the New Testament is illuminating when applied to Exodus. Within the New Testament one may discern behind the diversity of the literature the apostolic kerygma, the preaching of God's saving event in Christ. This may be recovered from allusions in the Epistles, and from the apostolic preaching in the book of Acts. It also reappears in the Gospels, very considerably expanded by the addition of miracle narratives, parables, and the like. The Pentateuch also has its kerygma, its proclamation of God's saving event. Von Rad isolates one such *confessio* in Deuteronomy 26:5 ff. and insists that the Pentateuch itself is but an expansion of this confession. "Just as, for example, St. Matthew's Gospel expands the *kerygma* by the addition of miracle stories and blocks of teaching, so, in the Pentateuch, the outline of the saving acts is expanded by codes of law, the stories of the Patriarchs, and the primeval history." [4]

The same analogy is applicable to the

---

[4] G. W. Anderson, *A Critical Introduction to the Old Testament* (London: Gerald Duckworth), pp. 55–56.

A Proposed Reconstruction of the Growth
and Composition of Exodus

Moses' birth narra-
tive and biography
Plague narratives   } Exodus Theme
Passover
Crossing the sea

Marah
Manna and quails
Water from the rock   } Wilderness Theme
Battle with Amale-
kites

Theophany (19)
Decalogue (20)   } Sinai Theme
Sealing covenant (24)
Renewal of covenant (34)

Moses, Aaron,
Pharaoh
Jethro and Moses   } Narrative Episodes
Aaron and calf
episode

Book of covenant (20–23)
Instructions for sanc-   } Legal Corpus
tuary and worship
(25—31; 35—40)

J (Southern, 10th century)
E (Northern, 9th century)
P (Priestly, 6th century)

Ca. 721 B.C.
Ca. 586 B.C.
EXODUS

book of Exodus. It, too, contains its ke-rygma, the proclamation of God's saving event epitomized in the deliverance from Egypt and the wilderness. Into this procla-mation, however, there have been inter-woven codes of law much as the miracle narratives and parables were added to the New Testament proclamation. Hence to the kerygmatic proclamation of Exodus, there have been inserted legal sections (cf. 21–23; 25–31; 34; 35–40) and narra-tive episodes so as to constitute the book in much the form that we know it.

As Anderson concludes, "As the Sermon on the Mount and the parables need the context of the saving acts of God, if they are to be understood, so we cannot appre-ciate what the laws meant for Israel unless we remember their setting, a setting which many of them doubtless had in worship long before they were given their present context in the Pentateuch."

In conclusion, the composition of the book of Exodus most likely followed a pat-tern in which brief sections, most likely oral in form, gathered together around the memory of a great person, a significant place, or a worship center. Often these sections were diverse in nature and their unifying feature lay primarily in their com-mon association with a place or a person. From these briefer sections larger elements such as the exodus, wilderness, and Sinai themes were formed; each with a complex preliterary and literary history. Finally, the three basic themes, interspersed with nar-rative episodes and legal material achieved much the same form as the present book.

Behind many of these traditions there is an involved preliterary and literary struc-ture. For example, the plague narratives are highly complex, and originally there may have been a much more basic and simple preliterary or literary form.

IV. The Historical Context

The broader historical context of Exodus is bounded in general terms by the eighteenth century B.C. as one terminus and the thirteenth century B.C. as the other. In addition to specific events within Egypt there are at least two movements which are of importance. These are the Hyksos of *ca.* 1800–1550 B.C., and the Habiru who are of especial importance for Exodus during the period of the Amarna literature, *ca.* fourteenth century.

The Hyksos are important for the book of Exodus because of the frequent tendency to identify their period of domination in Egypt as the period during which the descent of Isaac's son(s) may have occurred. Most if not all of them were of West Semitic stock, Syria-Palestine, and were called "Hyksos," i.e., "rulers of foreign lands" (sometimes referred to as shepherd kings; a questionable designation based upon Manetho, an Egyptian priest and historian of the third century B.C.). Their conquest of Egypt occurred in the anarchy which followed the twelfth dynasty (*ca.* 1991–1792) and was likely made possible by their use of the horse and chariot which they introduced to Egypt. The first Hyksos dynasty was established at Avaris in about 1730, supplanting the fourteenth dynasty. Discontent with foreign control led to the eventual expulsion of the Hyksos from Egypt by Ahmose in about 1570–1545.

The Joseph story suggests that the court of Pharaoh was not far from Goshen (cf. Gen. 46:28 ff.), a condition which coincides with the Hyksos occupation. This and other evidence suggest that this was the period when the rise to power of a person such as Joseph could be easily explained. As Wright and Filson indicate, "several lines of evidence suggest that it was during this time, probably not far from 1700 B.C., that Joseph came to power in Egypt." [5]

[5] *The Westminster Historical Atlas to the Bible,* ed. George Ernest Wright and Floyd Vivian Filson (Philadelphia: Westminster, 1946), p. 28. This and *The Interpreter's Dictionary of the Bible* represent excellent sources for a study of the historical background of Exodus; cf. also, George Ernest Wright, *Biblical Archaeology* (Philadelphia: Westminster, 1957).

During the fourteenth century B.C. a people known as the '*apiru* or "Habiru" are mentioned in correspondence between Egypt and Palestine. They had occupied the hill country of Palestine and generally contributed to the insecurity of the various political subdivisions owing allegiance to Egypt. They are important for the book of Exodus since some have identified their activity with the supposed presence of Israel following an exodus dated in the fifteenth century B.C. Others support a later date for the exodus but nonetheless associate the Habiru with the settlement of Canaan, interpreting the Habiru as a pre-Israelite phase of the Hebrew settlement of the land later joined by Israelites proper after their exodus from Egypt.

The Habiru were not a precise ethnic group but represented a social class living on the fringes of society. They most likely secured a livelihood through marauding raids (cognizance is taken of the fact that in isolated instances evidence indicates a particular ethnic group). They are mentioned over a very wide area during the second millennium but are of specific importance for Exodus with regard to their activity in Canaan.

The name is similar to Hebrew and while some Old Testament scholars have denied a direct relationship, there is an increasing recognition of the fact that in the Habiru one is confronted with some aspect of what we now term "Hebrews." Whatever the precise relationship between "Habiru" and "Hebrew," it is of importance to consider the activity of this group as testified by the Amarna literature, correspondence between governors in Palestine and the Egyptian government dating to the fourteenth century B.C. and discovered by Egyptian peasants in A.D. 1887. This literature clearly testifies to destructive raids on Canaan dating to the fourteenth century B.C.

Two dynasties in Egypt are of unique significance for the book of Exodus. These are the eighteenth (*ca.* 1570–1310) and the nineteenth (*ca.* 1310–1200), for it was during one of these two dynasties that the exodus from Egypt took place.

The eighteenth dynasty was the period when Egypt ruled the East, a period of international conquest paralleled by a golden age within Egypt when the flowering of the pharaonic empire may be considered to have taken place. This was the era of great personalities whose names and feats have remained to captivate the modern student of Egyptian history: Thutmose I, II, and III; Queen Hatshepsut; Amenhotep IV-Akhnaton, the religious reformer; and Tutankhamen, to mention but a few. During the period of the eighteenth dynasty the capital was located at Thebes, in upper Egypt, a fact which has bearing upon establishing the most likely date for the exodus.

Under the leadership of Ahmose, the previous dynasty had succeeded in completing the expulsion of the Hyksos. Because of the occupation of Egypt by the Hyksos during the fifteenth and sixteenth dynasties, considerable hostility would likely have existed in succeeding dynasties against foreign elements with Egypt. Both the extensive building operations of the eighteenth dynasty and the enmity for foreigners would parallel well both the building operations and the emergence of a "king" (Pharaoh) who "did not know Joseph" (cf. Ex. 1:8 ff.).

The nineteenth dynasty was the age of the Ramessids: Ramses I (1319–1318), Sethi I (1318–1299), Ramses II (1299–1232), and Merneptah, Amenmose, Siptah, and Sethi II (1232–1200). During this era the capital was moved from upper to lower Egypt in the reign of Sethi I, an action of particular importance for the dating of the exodus. This was also a period of intensive building operations in lower Egypt. Exodus 1:11 refers to the fact that the Hebrews built, or participated in building, "for Pharaoh store cities, Pithom and Raamses." This reference suits well the period of the nineteenth dynasty, for Pharaohs of the eighteenth dynasty did very little building in the area of the delta;

neither was their capital in the vicinity of Goshen as it was in the nineteenth dynasty. Thus, it is exceedingly probable that the exodus occurred in the nineteenth dynasty and that Ramses II was the Pharaoh of the oppression.

V. The Role of Exodus in Biblical Thought

Although the exodus event was determinative for much of biblical thought, quite strangely the word exodus as a technical term never appears in the Old Testament and is found only once in the New Testament (Heb. 11:22; cf. *Nelson's Complete Concordance of the Revised Standard Version*, p. 570). Despite the failure of a technical term to emerge, the event itself occupied a central role in biblical thought.

Throughout the Old Testament Yahweh was championed as the one who led his people out of Egypt, and the exodus was interpreted as his redemptive action (Josh. 24:16–18). Prophets recalled the deliverance, making that action one of the bases upon which they appealed to their generation. (Cf. Amos 2:10; 3:1; 9:7; Micah 6:4; 7:15; Hosea 2:15; 11:1; 12:9, 13; 13:4; Isa. 11:16; Jer. 2:6; 7:22,25; 11:4,7; 16:14; 23:7; 32:21; 34:13.)

The psalmists never tired of extolling the action of the LORD, and the centrality of the Exodus motif in Israel's worship is clearly reflected in the frequent use of this theme. It is the emphasis of nearly twenty psalms, either in whole or in part (cf. 18; 44; 60; 68; 74; 75; 78; 80; 81; 83; 89; 95; 100; 105; 106; 114; 135; 136), as well as other isolated references (cf. Psalms 66:6; 107:3).

The idealization of the wilderness period may well have been one of the contributing factors in the development of the concept of a new exodus. It was in the work of Isaiah of the Exile that the concept of a new exodus received its fullest treatment. He expected the eschatological reign of the Lord to follow the pattern of the exodus from Egypt. He proclaims that God's redemptive act is about to be recapitulated. The exodus is to be repeated in new form: "A voice cries: In the wilderness prepare the way of the Lord, make straight in the desert a highway for our God" (Isa. 40:3). Overtones of the new exodus appear in several contexts, but the theme is the specific subject of ten passages in chapters 40–55.

The significance of the exodus motif was not exhausted within the Old Testament, however, and it is not surprising that it continued to serve as a wellspring for Israel's eschatological hope. Within the so-called intertestamental literature Sirach of the second century appealed for final redemption and expressed this longing in terminology associated with the exodus; "Show signs anew, and work further wonders, make thy right arm glorious" (Sirach 36:6).

Especially in the New Testament, however, does the exodus theme find fuller expression, and the themes of exodus, wilderness, and conquest are as important for the New Testament as for the Old. The vocabulary used to express the saving work of Christ is drawn from the exodus event: "redeem" and "redemption," "deliver," "ransom," "purchase," "bondage," "freedom." [6]

One can hardly read of the attempt upon the life of Jewish children by Herod without recalling the earlier attempt upon those in Egypt (cf. Matt. 2:16; Ex. 1:16). Nor can one read of the emergence of Jesus out of Egypt, of John the Baptist as, "the voice of one crying in the wilderness: Prepare the way of the Lord," the forty days in the wilderness, or the similarity between the giving of the Commandments at Sinai and the Sermon on the Mount, without recalling the obvious parallels between the exodus motif and the life of Jesus.

Paul on occasion utilized passages from the context of Exodus, and "there are in all about forty references, or allusions, to the history of the exodus."[7]

[6] G. E. Wright, God Who Acts (London: SCM, 1952), p. 63.
[7] Harold Sahlin, "The New Exodus of Salvation According to St. Paul," in Root of the Vine: Essays in Biblical Theology, by Anton Fridrichsen and other members of Uppsala University (London: Docre, 1952), p. 83.

Thus, one finds the role of the exodus for biblical thought moving through three stages: (1) the event itself and its role as it was recited and as it recreated the redemptive event within worship circles in Israel; (2) the interpretation of Israel's eschatological hope in terms of a new exodus; an exodus not merely a duplicate of the old but an entirely new and eschatological experience; and (3) the manner in which the New Testament in numerous places portrays a propensity toward interpreting God's eschatological deed in Christ along the lines of the fulfilment of the new exodus motif.

VI. Unifying Theme

The exodus is superbly characterized by a triumphant shout of victory much akin to that of the New Testament resurrection: The Lord has triumphed, to him belongs the victory! This is well expressed in what may be the oldest written couplet in the book of Exodus: "Sing to the Lord, for he has triumphed gloriously; the horse and his rider he has thrown into the sea" (15:21). The entire Song of Moses is a grand exultation of the Lord's victory and power; Yahweh is triumphant Lord, Lord of all. He is "glorious in power" and "in the greatness of his majesty he overthrew his adversaries" (vv. 6–7). With climactic joy and victory the triumph song concludes, "The Lord will reign for ever and ever" (15:18).

Thus, the manifold themes within the book of Exodus have as their focus of unity the revelation of the Lord's power—his lordship over the totality of the created order: history, nature, and man. The descent of a people into Egypt, their providential sustenance, and their eventual redemption under the leadership of Moses reflect the Lord's sovereign power.

The confrontation with Pharaoh repeatedly portrays the triumphant power of Yahweh; triumphant over not only Pharaoh but the gods of Egypt and their representatives as well. When one considers the role of the sea in Israelite thought, as well as ancient Near Eastern mythology, to say nothing of the considerable fear of the sea by the Israelite, Yahweh's triumph over the sea is far more than the proclamation that the Lord allowed Israel to escape the Egyptians. Second Isaiah saw in this the demonstration of the Lord's cosmic power in triumph over the primeval forces of chaos: "Was it not thou that didst cut Rahab in pieces, that didst pierce the dragon? Was it not thou that didst dry up the sea, the waters of the great deep; that didst make the depths of the sea a way for the redeemed to pass over?" (Isa. 51:9).[8] Thus the plagues narratives, the crossing of the sea, plus the acts in the wilderness (often a symbol of hostility, much like the sea) are all grounded in the demonstration of Yahweh's lordship. He is triumphant over hostile powers in a land of other gods, he triumphs over the power of chaos in the sea, and even the demonic forces of the wilderness yield to his lordship.

The covenant is also a revelation of Yahweh's lordship, indirectly bearing witness to the reality of his sovereign power. Covenants were of two types in the ancient Near East—parity and suzerainty. Within the parity covenant the parties to the covenant stood as equals, each assuming mutual obligations within the covenant structure. The opposite was true of the suzerainty covenant, however, for it was formulated between lord and vassal, a superior and inferior. It is to this latter category that the Old Testament covenant form has been all but unanimously assigned. Thus, the covenant presupposes the sovereign power of the Lord. Yahweh is Lord of the covenant and within that structure is revealed as Lord of man.

Thus, there is a legitimate reflection of Yahweh's lordship throughout the book of Exodus. Within the present study the unifying theme of the book is assumed to be "The Lordship of Yahweh."

Yahweh is *Lord of history*, as reflected in

his providential guidance of a people and the raising up of a leader in the person of Moses (1:1—7:7). Yahweh is *Lord of creation* (or nature) and the powers within the world hostile to his sovereignty yield to his power (7:8–18:27). He is *Lord of man*, for his lordship is fundamental to the understanding of the covenant made with Israel (19:1—24:14). Within the context of the covenant relationship he is also *Lord of worship*, and against the background of this premise worship is structured according to his counsel (25:1—40:38; this might well be extended through Num. 10:10, but because of the limited purpose of this work Leviticus and Numbers cannot be treated).

VII. The Contributions of Exodus

Among the several contributions of Exodus to biblical thought which should be briefly considered are the concepts of God, history, and covenant.

First God is best known by his name and his action. Both are clearly underscored in the book of Exodus.

The personal name of the covenant God is given (3:14–15). While the detailed examination of this must wait for the commentary on that section, it should be noted even at this stage that the name conveys the concept of God as presently active in the life of his people. The phrase "I AM WHO I AM" or I Will Be What I Will Be" gives emphasis to the reality of God's being as presence as opposed to the abstract idea of being. God will be with his people. One cannot always specify how this presence will manifest itself, and he certainly cannot control it, for God will be whatever he chooses to be. But one can be sure of God's continuing presence.

How is one to pronounce the name for the covenant God? Within Judaism there developed the practice as early as the pre-Christian era of refusing to pronounce the personal name of the covenant God. The name revealed in 3:14 f. was thought to have been too holy to pronounce. Therefore, every time the Hebrew consonants YHWH appear in the Hebrew text Jews

---

[8] Both Isaiah's reference to "Rahab" the dragon (cf. 30:7; 27:1; Ezek. 29:3) and to the "sea" most likely refer to the Hebrew version of the primeval combat between God and chaos-monsters. Yet, here he associates this with the exodus motif.

pronounced the name Lord (*'adhonay*). During the Middle Ages biblical scholars adopted a compromise, coining a word never before heard: Jehovah. To do this they took the consonants of the Hebrew text and added to them the vowels of the Hebrew word for Lord. In German the yodh (Y) is written as J and the waw (W) as V. Hence in German the consonants for the name of the covenant God are JHVH (and practically all leading Old Testament scholars then were German). To the consonants JHVH were added the vowels of the Hebrew word for Lord, thereby producing the name Jehovah.

The RSV attempts to solve the problem by using capitals when translating the name of the covenant God, giving LORD. The primary difficulty of this is that it makes no effort to translate what is essentially a personal name and is confusing, since the RSV—and other translations as well—makes three uses of the same series of consonants and vowels. These can be distinguished only by the use of capitals. Hence, LORD is used of the personal covenant God, a name never used outside the context of the covenant and a name that needs to be specified with clarity because of the connotations implied within contexts where the word appears. *Lord* is used when the name described God. Finally, *lord* is used of an earthly ruler.

Contemporary Old Testament scholars are not unanimously agreed concerning the vowels that should appear with YHWH, but the majority prefers *Yahweh*. This is the name for the covenant God which appears in *The Jerusalem Bible* and is as close to the original name as we can perhaps arrive at present. It is the writer's personal judgment that Jehovah should not be used since it is a hybrid composed of the consonants of one word and the vowels of another, and never existed as a real word until the compromise was reached in the Middle Ages. Concerning the use of LORD, this fails to convey the overtones of the personal name and also is most confusing since translators use a word spelled the same way to convey three different meanings.

If God is known by his *name*, he is also known by his *actions*. In one sense the book of Exodus is a book of the action of God. If one would know what God is like, look at what God does. With providential guidance he leads a people into Egypt and through this same providence raises up a leader who acts under his guidance to free the people of God. He is a God who hears his people, remembers the covenant made with their fathers, who sees them and knows their condition (2:24 f.). He knows their suffering and he comes down to deliver them (2:7 f.). Individuals are the primary tool or agent of his service, although his lordship in power is such that he can also use the forces of the natural world. His redemptive nature is clearly revealed in his redemption of Israel, and his providential care is expressed in a multiplicity of deeds in both the exodus and the wilderness themes. The personal nature of God is clearly expressed in the covenant which he makes and the assurance of fellowship made possible through that covenant. The ethical and moral concern of Yahweh as well as his concern for the welfare of man is present in the giving of the law, for the law was not given as a penal burden to be borne but as a blessing to lighten the darkness of Israel's way.

Second, the book of Exodus provides a clear example of the Old Testament concept of history. Fundamental to the Old Testament understanding of history was its theocentric nature. It was God-centered, God-directed. Israel saw history under God's management. It was God who set the process in motion, and who limits it in accord with his will. Thus all history has its source in God and takes place for God (cf. von Rad, pp. 170 f.).

Especially in Exodus is this concept of history fundamental. The sovereign God is Lord of history; it is subservient to his purposes. Whether in the migration of tribes into Egypt, the raising up of a deliverer, the unique appearance of a series of catastrophes within Egypt culminating in the event at the sea, or the formation of a people held together by covenant bonds and common worship, Exodus portrays the way in which history is the vehicle of revelation.

Third, Exodus is the quarry from which the covenant concept is hewn. There are other covenants mentioned in the Old Testament, but there is a sense in which the covenant of Exodus 19–20; 23; 34 is the covenant par excellence. The prophets, for example, knew of the patriarchs and dealt with them at times, but no preexilic prophet ever discussed the covenant with Abraham. The covenant in prophetic thought was most often the covenant with Moses on Sinai, or the covenant with David.

Within the life of Israel the covenant served as the "touchstone" against which the life of the people was continually measured. The prophets, for example, were not innovators bringing a new religion to Israel (as they were once portrayed). Rather, they came to call Israel back to the demands of covenant life inaugurated generations previously.

Even in the most difficult of circumstances, when Israel appeared to have failed the Lord completely, the covenant concept continued to serve as an ideal. Jeremiah saw beyond the brokenness of his own generation to a new covenant that the Lord would write on the heart (31:31 ff.), a pledge fulfilled in the assertion of our Lord, "this is my blood of the [new] covenant" (Matt. 26:28). This statement is incomprehensible apart from Exodus 24, the sealing with blood of the covenant at Sinai, and Jeremiah 31, the promise that the covenant would continue to constitute the relationship of the Lord and his people, albeit a "new" covenant.

Indirectly the centrality of the covenant to biblical thought is constantly revealed in that we still refer to the Bible as the Old Testament (Old Covenant) and the New Testament (New Covenant). It would be difficult to overstate the importance of Exo-dus for an understanding of the entire concept of covenant.

Outline

2. New challenges for old loyalties (6:10–13)
3. New people from old tribes (6:14–27)
4. New responsibilities for old servants (6:28—7:13)
   (1) The renewed commission of Moses and Pharaoh's response (6:28—7:7)
   (2) The revelation of the sign to Pharaoh (7:8–13)

Part Two: Yahweh, Lord of Creation (7:14—18:27)

I. The plagues as revelations of power and lordship (7:14—11:10; 12:29–42)
  1. The pollution of the Nile: the first plague (7:14–24)
  2. The plague of frogs: the second plague (7:25—8:15)
  3. The plague of gnats: the third plague (8:16–19)
  4. The plague of flies: the fourth plague 8:20–32
  5. The pestilence upon the cattle: the fifth plague (9:1–7)
  6. The plague of boils upon man and beast: the sixth plague (9:8–12)
  7. The plague of hail: the seventh plague (9:13–35)
  8. The plague of locusts: the eighth plague (10:1–20)
  9. The plague of darkness: the ninth plague (10:21–29)
  10. The plague of death: the tenth plague (11:1–10; 12:29–42)
II. Cultic practices of Passover, unleavened bread, and dedication of firstborn (12:1–28,43—13:16)
  1. The Passover (12:1–13,21–28,43–50)
   (1) Instructions for the Passover (12:1–13)
   (2) Institution of the Passover (12:21–28)
   (3) Participants in the Passover festival (12:43–50)
  2. The feast of Unleavened Bread (12:14–20; 13:3–10)
   (1) The Lord's instructions to

    Moses and Aaron (12:14–20)
   (2) Moses' instructions to the people (13:3–10)
  3. Dedication of the firstborn (13:1–2,11–16)
   (1) The Lord's instruction to Moses (13:1–2)
   (2) Instruction given to the people (13:11–16)
III. Victory and freedom through Yahweh's lordship (13:17—15:21)
  1. Victory through strategy (13:17—14:4)
  2. Victory through Yahweh's support of Israel (14:5–20)
   (1) Egyptian might in pursuit of Israel (14:5–9)
   (2) Promise of the Lord's salvation (14:10–18)
   (3) The angel of God providing for Israel (14:19–20)
  3. Deliverance at the sea (14:21–25)
  4. Destruction in the sea (14:26–29)
  5. Dedication in response to the Lord's victory (14:30–31)
  6. Victory in retrospect (15:1–21)
   (1) The Song of Moses (15:1–19)
   (2) The Song of Miriam (15:20–21)
IV. Providential care through the wilderness (15:22—18:27)
  1. Thirst: bitter waters of Marah (15:22–27)
  2. Hunger: provision of quail and manna (16:1–36)
   (1) Murmuring against the Lord's leaders (16:1–3)
   (2) Moses' mediatorial office (16:4–8; 9–12)
   (3) Manna and quail for a hungry people (16:13–21)
   (4) Manna for the sabbath (16:22–30)
   (5) Israel's memory of the miracle of the manna (16:31–36)
  3. Despair: the frustration of national enemies and domestic problems (17:1—18:27)
   (1) Water from the rock (17:1–7)
   (2) External enemies: the battle

tabernacle (39:32—40:33)

(1) Presentation to Moses (39:32–43)

(2) The Lord's instructions concerning the erection of the tabernacle (40:1–15)

(3) Erecting the tabernacle and placing the equipment (40:16–33)

6. The glory of God fills the tabernacle (40:34–38)

Selected Bibliography

BRIGHT, JOHN. *A History of Israel.* Philadelphia: The Westminster Press, 1959.

CERNÝ, JAROSLAV. *Ancient Egyptian Religion.* London: Hutchinson House, 1952.

DAVIES, G. HENTON. "Exodus," *Torch Bible Commentaries.* London: SCM Press Ltd, 1967.

DRIVER, S. R. "The Book of Exodus," *The Cambridge Bible for Schools and Colleges.* Cambridge: At The University Press, 1953.

EISSFELDT, O. "Palestine in the Time of the Nineteenth Dynasty: The Exodus and Wanderings," *The Cambridge Ancient History,* Vol. II. Cambridge: At The University Press, 1965.

FINEGAN, JACK. *Let My People Go: A Journey Through Exodus.* New York and Evanston: Harper & Row Publishers, 1963.

McNEILE, A. H. "The Book of Exodus," *Westminister Commentaries.* London: Methuen & Co., 1908.

MUILENBURG, JAMES. *The Way of Israel.* New York: Harper & Brothers Publishers, 1961.

NOTH, MARTIN. "Exodus," *The Old Testament Library.* London: SCM Press, Ltd., 1962.

RYLAARSDAM, J. COERT. "The Book of Exodus," *The Interpreter's Bible,* Vol. I. Nashville: Abingdon-Cokesbury Press, 1952.

STEINDORFF, GEORGE, and KEITH C. SEELE. *When Egypt Ruled the East.* Chicago: The University of Chicago Press, 1947.

VON RAD, GERHARD. *The Problem of the Hexateuch and Other Essays.* Translated by E. W. Trueman Dicken. Edinburgh & London: Oliver & Boyd, 1966.

———. *Old Testament Theology,* Vol. I. Edinburgh & London: Oliver and Boyd, 1962.

WILSON, JOHN A. *The Burden of Egypt: An Interpretation of Ancient Egyptian Culture.* Chicago: The University of Chicago Press, 1951.

Commentary on the Text

Part One
Yahweh: Lord of History
1:1—7:13

Israel's history-writing expressed an essentially religious conviction: Yahweh is Lord of history.

Because Yahweh is Lord of history, through his providence Israel passed from bondage into freedom and eventual nationhood. Especially was God's providence reflected in those sections of Exodus dealing with the preservation of patriarchal descendants (1:1 ff.), the providential care of Moses (2:1 ff.), the emergence of a leader in the person of Moses to represent both the people and God before Pharaoh (3:1—4:17), the commitment of Moses to the task of deliverance (4:18—6:1), and

the second account of Moses' call (6:2—7:13).

I. These Came to Egypt (1:1–22)

Exodus opens with an account of the descendants of Israel (Jacob) who came to Egypt, thus maintaining continuity with Genesis 47:1 ff. Such continuity illustrates a much broader unity within the Pentateuch than is commonly recognized. One might well read the contents of the entire first six books as one lengthy account of the way in which God fulfilled his promise to provide a land for the descendants of Abraham. More specifically, Exodus 1:1 ff. is the story of a people who refused to die—or, better, of a God who refused to let his people die.

1. Patriarchal Backgrounds and Ancestry of Moses (1:1-7)

[1] These are the names of the sons of Israel who came to Egypt with Jacob, each with his household: [2] Reuben, Simeon, Levi, and Judah, [3] Issachar, Zebulun, and Benjamin, [4] Dan and Naphtali, Gad and Asher. [5] All the offspring of Jacob were seventy persons; Joseph was already in Egypt. [6] Then Joseph died, and all his brothers, and all that generation. [7] But the descendants of Israel were fruitful and increased greatly; they multiplied and grew exceedingly strong; so that the land was filled with them.

Viewed in retrospect, all of Jacob's descendants were portrayed as having gone into Egypt, but the migration itself was probably much more complex than the movement of a single family of seventy persons. Many today feel that while some descendants of Jacob as a tribal group were in Egypt (the Joseph tribe especially, but also Levi), others remained either totally or in part within Canaan. In any case, Exodus is clear—descendants of Israel (Jacob) were in Egypt and constituted Moses' genealogical background.

Descendants of Israel were fruitful and increased greatly. Part of the original promise to the patriarchs had been that of numerous posterity (cf. Gen. 15:5 ff.; 26:4; 28:14). The promise is here being fulfilled. The reference to the number of Israel as so great *that the land was filled with them* should be understood in a relative sense, for the remainder of Exodus consistently speaks of Israel as limited to Goshen, a northeastern section of the Nile delta.

2. Three Efforts to Destroy Israel's (Jacob's) Descendants (1:8-22)

[8] Now there arose a new king over Egypt, who did not know Joseph. [9] And he said to his people, "Behold, the people of Israel are too many and too mighty for us. [10] Come, let us deal shrewdly with them, lest they multiply, and, if war befall us, they join our enemies and fight against us and escape from the land." [11] Therefore they set taskmasters over them to afflict them with heavy burdens; and they built for Pharaoh store cities, Pithom and Raamses. [12] But the more they were oppressed, the more they multiplied and the more they spread abroad. And the Egyptians were in dread of the people of Israel. [13] So they made the people of Israel serve with rigor, [14] and made their lives bitter with hard service, in mortar and brick, and in all kinds of work in the field; in all their work they made them serve with rigor.

[15] Then the king of Egypt said to the Hebrew midwives, one of whom was named Shiphrah and the other Puah, [16] "When you serve as midwife to the Hebrew women, and see them upon the birthstool, if it is a son, you shall kill him; but if it is a daughter, she shall live." [17] But the midwives feared God, and did not do as the king of Egypt commanded them, but let the male children live. [18] So the king of Egypt called the midwives, and said to them, "Why have you done this, and let the male children live?" [19] The midwives said to Pharaoh, "Because the Hebrew women are not like the Egyptian women; for they are vigorous and are delivered before the midwife comes to them." [20] So God dealt well with the midwives; and the people multiplied and grew very strong. [21] And because the midwives feared God he gave them families. [22] Then Pharaoh commanded all his people, "Every son that is born to the Hebrews you shall cast into the Nile, but you shall let every daughter live."

Within the broader section of 1:8-22 there are probably two major parallel accounts drawn from several sources which tell of the persecution. The first is drawn from J (8-12) and P (13-14) and describes the enforced labor. The second is drawn from E and records the essential elements of the attempt on the lives of the male children (15-21), although verse 22 may be distinct from verses 15-21.

Effort to Break Their Spirit (8-14). The restrictions sought to make the Hebrews subservient and docile. This was an effort to conquer a people through the destruction of their spirit or will to oppose.

A new king over Egypt, who did not know Joseph. The specific date for the exodus is a highly debatable issue with conclusions largely divided between the advocates of a fifteenth-century date and those of a later date in the thirteenth century. The strongest arguments for the early date of the exodus are the chronological statements of the Old Testament, some datings of the fall of Jericho to the fifteenth century, and the activity of the *Habiru* in Canaan during the fifteenth century (which is identified or at least associated with the invading Hebrews by adherents of an early date). First Kings 6:1 dates the building of the Temple by Solomon as 480 years "after the people of Israel came out of the land of Egypt." Assuming that Solomon's fourth year was about 959 B.C., the exodus would have occurred 480 years previously, about 1439 B.C.

Concerning the 480-year period of time, however, it has often been noted that Israel believed twelve generations to have existed between the exodus and Solomon (cf. 1 Chron. 6:1 ff.; 6:50 ff.). Also Israel reckoned a generation in round numbers of 40 years, as did the early Greeks. Twelve generations of 40 years gives 480 years. But if a generation were nearer 20 or 25 years, then a date much nearer the thirteenth century for the exodus would harmonize the witness of 1 Kings 6:1.

There are, in fact, strong reasons for establishing the thirteenth-century date for the exodus. The most significant evidence may be classified as archaeological and historical.

The archaeological evidence rests primarily upon three areas of investigation.

First, Nelson Glueck demonstrated that the trans-Jordan kingdoms were not founded before the thirteenth century. For 600 years before 1300 B.C. inhabitants of Transjordan lived as nomads and did not settle in towns. Also, the kingdoms of Edom and Moab (cf. Num. 20—21) were not established before the thirteenth century. Yet this was the period when Israel met opposition in Transjordan by settled peoples, if Israel came out of Egypt in the fifteenth century.

Second, Canaanite cities such as Lachish and Debir, which figured so prominently in the conquest, experienced cataclysmic destruction in the thirteenth century.

Third, the Jericho evidence for a fifteenth-century date for the exodus has been brought under serious question by more recent excavations. So Jericho evidence now tends to confirm a thirteenth-century date for the exodus.

Historical evidence for the thirteenth-century date rests in the location of the Egyptian capital at the time of the exodus. When Israel went out of Egypt the Egyptian capital was located near Goshen (cf. the proximity of the royal family to Moses' geographical birthplace 2:1 ff.; the proximity of Goshen and the capital during the conversations between Moses and Pharaoh). It was during the nineteenth dynasty that the capital was moved from Thebes to the delta area, under the direction of Seti I (1308–1290 B.C.). During the fifteenth century the capital was far to the south.

Thus, the king who "did not know Joseph" was probably Seti I, the pharaoh of the oppression. His son, Rameses II (1290–1224), was the pharaoh of the exodus. The king of the oppression died (2:23).

The people of Israel are too many and too mighty for us. The ascription of such number and strength to the descendants of Israel (Jacob) stands in contrast to the relative ease with which the Egyptians maintained rigid control over them, plus the fact that two midwives could serve all the Hebrews. A malcontent and disloyal group of foreigners dwelling so near the military routes to the northeast was, however, a genuine threat to Egypt.

Let us deal shrewdly with them. Forced labor was common among rulers of antiquity, and was characteristic of later Israel (1 Kings 5:13; 14; 9:15; 12:18).

They built for Pharaoh store cities, Pithom and Raamses. The *store cities* served as storage points for war material and provisions, and may also have been a trade center (cf. 1 Kings 9:19; 2 Chron. 8:4; 16:4; 17:12; 32:28–29). *Pithom* means House of Atum (Tem), the sun god, and is to be located at either Tel el-Machkhutah or Tell el-Ratabah in Goshen in northeast Egypt. *Raamses* was also located in northeast Egypt in Goshen, and was the capital of the nineteenth dynasty (1319–1200 B.C.). It was the great capital of Raamses II and was called by him "House of Raamses."

Attempted Betrayal At the Hand of

Those Within (15–21). The change of title from "Pharaoh" to the "king of Egypt" when referring to the Egyptian Pharaoh is in keeping with a probable change of source material beginning at verse 15. The terms Pharaoh and king of Egypt are synonymous.

Hebrew midwives . . . Shiphrah and Puah. The term Hebrew is an older and broader term than Israelite (cf. Gen. 14:13). During 1500–1200 B.C. waves of Hebrews (Habiru) came into Syria-Palestine, and the Israelite Hebrews were most likely one aspect of this migration in the ancient Near East. More precisely, Hebrew refers in general to preconquest Israelites; Israelite should be limited to the time of the established nation; and Jew should be used no earlier than the period of the Exile.

Birthstool is based on the Hebrew *'abhnayim,* which means stones. The reference in all probability was to the stones, or stone (following a variant reading of the text), upon which the Hebrew women sat or knelt during labor, a common custom in the ancient world.

Annihilation from Without (*v.* 22). Illustrations of this pattern of oppression are embarrassingly numerous and contemporary. First, break the spirit of a people; second, betray them from within their own ranks; finally, if these have failed, destroy them by the application of force from without.

Yahweh, the God of Israel, is truly Lord of history. The coming of scattered tribal groups into Egypt was more than a quirk of circumstance or twist of fate. Within the broader purposes of God it constituted one part of his purpose to mold a people who would become a means of blessing for all mankind (cf. Gen. 12:1 ff.). Interpreted from the perspective of faith, both the migration and the preservation of a people ultimately called "Israel" were results of divine activity within history. God brought the factors of time and circumstance so to coincide as to meet the crucial demands of his sovereign purpose.

II. The Providence of God During Moses' Formative Years (2:1–25)

1. Moses' Birth Narrative (2:1–10)

¹ Now a man from the house of Levi went and took to wife a daughter of Levi. ² The woman conceived and bore a son; and when she saw that he was a goodly child, she hid him three months. ³ And when she could hide him no longer she took for him a basket made of bulrushes, and daubed it with bitumen and pitch; and she put the child in it and placed it among the reeds at the river's brink. ⁴ And his sister stood at a distance, to know what would be done to him. ⁵ Now the daughter of Pharaoh came down to bathe at the river, and her maidens walked beside the river; she saw the basket among the reeds and sent her maid to fetch it. ⁶ When she opened it she saw the child; and lo, the babe was crying. She took pity on him and said, "This is one of the Hebrews' children." ⁷ Then his sister said to Pharaoh's daughter, "Shall I go and call you a nurse from the Hebrew women to nurse the child for you?" ⁸ And Pharaoh's daughter said to her, "Go." So the girl went and called the child's mother. ⁹ And Pharaoh's daughter said to her, "Take this child away, and nurse him for me, and I will give you your wages." So the woman took the child and nursed him. ¹⁰ And the child grew, and she brought him to Pharaoh's daughter, and he became her son; and she named him Moses, for she said, "Because I drew him out of the water."

The unseen forces of God's providence overshadowed the life of Moses from the very beginning. Martin Noth suggests that the common element to the numerous accounts of great personalities who suffer tribulation early in life is found in the basic thought that from the beginning of their lives they have experienced the special working of divine providence which has proved effective in the face of all attacks directed against them.

A man from the house of Levi identifies Moses with a tribal group that became a priestly class early in the history of Israel (cf. 6:16 ff.).

Although people at the time were unaware, the most significant event of that year was the birth of a boy, Moses, to Jochabed. Over a thousand years later biblical writers were still extolling his life (cf. Heb. 11:23).

Bulrushes (*gome'*) were marsh rushes, better known as papyrus. They were widely used for writing material but were also used for baskets and vessels of various kinds, especially boats.

His sister. Since Moses is portrayed as the firstborn child, how can he have a sister old enough to watch over the small "ark," or boat? An attempted solution has been to suggest that both Miriam and Aaron (who was also older than Moses) were children of Amram by another marriage (cf. 15:20; Num. 12:1).

Nursing the infant established ethnic solidarity with the Hebrews, with whom it was more important for Moses to be linked than with the Egyptians. The fact that Miriam went immediately to Jochabed tends to confirm the belief that the entire experience was a deliberate plan to place Moses in the care of the princess. Thus, Jochabed is portrayed as a woman of superior wisdom, to say nothing of her matchless courage.

Egypt was especially noted for her wise men and their teachings on wisdom. So Moses would have shared in the very finest training. Thus, unknown to either mother or son, the providence of God which had delivered Moses also opened doors of opportunity and preparation for his destined ministry.

There is a pattern, the warp and woof of purpose and meaning, that runs throughout history. It is the pattern traced by the providence of God as an effectual force within history.

2. *The Egyptian Murder* (2:11–15a)

11 One day, when Moses had grown up, he went out to his people and looked on their burdens; and he saw an Egyptian beating a Hebrew, one of his people. 12 He looked this way and that, and seeing no one he killed the Egyptian and hid him in the sand. 13 When he went out the next day, behold, two Hebrews were struggling together; and he said to the man that did the wrong, "Why do you strike your fellow?" 14 He answered, "Who made you a prince and a judge over us? Do you mean to kill me as you killed the Egyptian?" Then Moses was afraid, and thought, "Surely the thing is known." 15 When Pharaoh heard of it, he sought to kill Moses.

The statement *Moses was afraid* gives a historic ring to the account of Moses' life, for he is not portrayed as the bold, heroic figure who could slay the Egyptian oppressor with never another thought. To the contrary, his very human quality is clearly portrayed in the fear which swept over him.

To debate whether or not the murder was within the will of God is to miss the point of the entire narrative. The account of the murder permitted the narrator to accomplish these things: indicate Moses' identification with the Hebrews, despite his Egyptian training; reveal the fiber of Moses' character, his sense of justice, his courage, his willingness to act decisively; indicate the rebuff suffered when attempting to mediate the argument between the Hebrews (this is a continuing motif of Moses' life); portray the human quality of Moses through exposing his fear; and, to offer an explanation of Moses' migration from Egypt to Midian.

3. *Moses' Exile in Midian* (2:15b–22)

But Moses fled from Pharaoh, and stayed in the land of Midian; and he sat down by a well. 16 Now the priest of Midian had seven daughters; and they came and drew water, and filled the troughs to water their father's flock. 17 The shepherds came and drove them away; but Moses stood up and helped them, and watered their flock. 18 When they came to their father Reuel, he said, "How is it that you have come so soon today?" 19 They said, "An Egyptian delivered us out of the hand of the shepherds, and even drew water for us and watered the flock." 20 He said to his daughters, "And where is he? Why have you left the man? Call him, that he may eat bread." 21 And Moses was content to dwell with the man, and he gave Moses his daughter Zipporah. 22 She bore a son, and he called his name Gershom; for he said, "I have been a sojourner in a foreign land."

During this period God revealed himself to Moses in a fuller way as Yahweh. Also, through his association with the Midianites, Moses doubtless learned much that would later equip him as leader of Hebrew tribes. Physical details such as geographical terrain, trails, oases, scattered sources of water, and other items necessary for a semi-nomadic leader were accumulated, perhaps with no view of their possible future use.

Few would likely have believed that during his exile from Egypt Moses was being prepared for a heroic task. Perhaps not even Moses himself. Yet, in retrospect it is not difficult to see the providence of God at work in this period of desert preparation—not difficult, that is, if one accepts the reality of Divine Providence.

The Midianites were distant relatives of the Hebrews, for Midian is described as the son of Abraham by Keturah (Gen. 25:2). It is entirely conceivable that elements of the Midianites maintained contact with the Judah tribe and that Moses' new insight into the nature of God as Yahweh was mediated to him through the Midianites during the time of his exile. Jethro, Moses' father-in-law, was a priest (v. 16), who later officiated at (or at least offered) a sacrifice to God (18:12). He also offered advice concerning the Hebrews, and Moses accepted it (18:13 ff.). There are, however, other explanations of Moses' understanding of the nature of God as Yahweh.

There are distinct points of correspondence between the lives of Moses and Jacob. Both fled for their lives to relatives in another country (although Moses was much more distantly related), both met their future wives at a well where both performed a physical feat of some importance in assisting the young woman in watering her flock. Both were taken home to the father, and both eventually married the girl met at the well.

The *priest of Midian* is obviously **Reuel,** although his name was evidently somewhat confused, even to the biblical narrators. He was at times called Reuel (v. 18), or Hobab (Num. 10:29; Judg. 4:11), but most often Jethro (3:1; 18:1). Reuel was probably the father of Hobab (Num. 10:29).

An Egyptian delivered us. Moses had so absorbed his cultural background that he would be identified by others as an Egyptian.

And he *was content to dwell with the man.* "Content" has no idea of concession about it, for *ya'al* means to show willingness, be pleased, or to accept an invitation. In later times Moses' marriage to Zipporah would have been forbidden (cf. Num. 25:6–9), and Rylaarsdam suggests that Zipporah is quite likely the "Cushite woman" involved in the controversy between Moses and Aaron and Midian (cf. Num. 12:1).

4. God's Pledge Through the Covenant (2:23-25)

23 In the course of those many days the king of Egypt died. And the people of Israel groaned under their bondage, and cried out for help, and their cry under bondage came up to God. 24 And God heard their groaning, and God remembered his covenant with Abraham, with Isaac, and with Jacob. 25 And God saw the people of Israel, and God knew their condition.

Whether mediated through Abraham, Moses, or David, and whether conditional or unconditional, the touchstone of Israel's religious experience was the covenant.

From the vantage point of a faith presupposition, the providence of God is a reality; and the covenant is fulfilled through the providential ordering of history. Beyond the series of secondary causes producing a given event or series of events there may be discerned an overarching purpose, a pattern or design, etched by God upon the course of history.

Four verbs express with simple yet majestic force God's personal involvement with the burdens of those within the covenant. God *heard,* God *remembered,* God *saw,* God *knew.* Whether the cry was directed immediately to God or whether their cry was simply one of anguish and pain wrung from them by the grief of their condition, God heard.

God *remembered his covenant* with Abraham, Isaac, and Jacob (Gen. 12:1–3; 17:1–14; 26:2–5; 28:13 ff.). Central to the action of God throughout the Old Testament is his faithfulness to the covenant relationship. The central point of emphasis which should be stressed about various personalities, therefore, is not that they pleased or displeased God but that God was faithful despite their unfaithfulness (cf. David).

God *saw the people of Israel.* There are numerous instances when the word *ra'ah* has the deeper sense of knowing. For example, the word may mean see, so as to learn to know (cf. Deut. 33:9) and is synonymous with experiencing something (cf. Jer. 5:12; 14:13; Psalm 89:48).

God *knew.* The word *yadha'* means to know experientially. The word always retains the personal, experiential emphasis with regard to the way in which God knows the condition of his people. We only know that as we look at life in retrospect there begin to emerge snatches of meaning here and there which we eventually begin to place together and conclude that they surely must form some part of a larger, coherent whole. When one strips away the numerous layers of causal factors in the experiences of Moses, he may discern a pattern of design and meaning that is more than chance coincidence.

At a point between the extreme of rejecting all divine presence in history and the belief that nations and individuals are puppets held on strings, there is a responsible view of the providence of God which allows for the freedom of man and the contingencies of events and circumstances without eliminating the reality of God's personal involvement in history. Such a view of God's providence is soundly based in the biblical revelation.

III. The Self-Revelation of Yahweh 3:1–22

The phrase "I have come down" characterizes the nature of the God who met Moses; a God who does not sit placidly in the heavens, lost in self-contemplation, oblivious to history as the center stage for his revelation. More positively, the phrase stresses the reality of a personal God

within the framework of history, thereby asserting that events are more than the conclusion of a series of causal circumstances held together either by chance coincidence or the solely physical power of human personality.

1. Moses' Call (3:1–6)

[1] Now Moses was keeping the flock of his father-in-law, Jethro, the priest of Midian; and he led his flock to the west side of the wilderness, and came to Horeb, the mountain of God. [2] And the angel of the LORD appeared to him in a flame of fire out of the midst of a bush; and he looked, and lo, the bush was burning, yet it was not consumed. [3] And Moses said, "I will turn aside and see this great sight, why the bush is not burnt." [4] When the LORD saw that he turned aside to see, God called to him out of the bush, "Moses, Moses!" And he said, "Here am I." [5] Then he said, "Do not come near; put off your shoes from your feet, for the place on which you are standing is holy ground." [6] And he said, "I am the God of your father, the God of Abraham, the God of Isaac, and the God of Jacob." And Moses hid his face, for he was afraid to look at God.

When Moses went back to Egypt, one primary mark of validation was his call experience in which he had come to know God by the personal name Yahweh.

Horeb, the mountain of God. Horeb and Sinai are synonymous. Probably, but not absolutely, they refer to the mountain of God, where Moses had his call experience and from which Israel probably received the Commandments. Horeb was characteristically used by the E and D sources, while Sinai was used by the J and P. Sinai appears twice as frequently in the Old Testament as Horeb (35 usages versus 17 for Horeb). Although some favor a location for Sinai to the east of the Gulf of Aqaba in the land of Midian, the great majority of Old Testament scholars locate Sinai at the traditional site in the southeastern area of the Sinai peninsula. Most often it is equated with *Jebel Müsa.* Some place the *mountain of God* at Kadesh, especially because of the strong connections of the tribes with Kadesh.

The angel of the Lord is normally interpreted as a theophany, that is, an appearance of God (Gen. 16:7 ff.; Ex. 19:1 ff.; Judg. 13:15 ff.). References to the angel of the Lord are consistently found in early passages of Scripture and the concept was not a long-range medium of revelation.

It is most difficult to harmonize all elements about the angel of the Lord with the bodily presence of a "being." For example, following the meeting with Manoah it is said that "the angel of the Lord ascended in the flame of the altar" (Judg. 13:20). Ancient patterns of thought readily accommodated to the belief in literal, semidivine beings, and such actions as those in the case of Manoah. For many students of the Bible the literal interpretation of the angel of the Lord, and other angelic beings, is both satisfying and in keeping with their understanding of the nature of the biblical revelation.

The question for many twentieth-century exegetes, however, is quite simple, but profoundly important: was the angel of the Lord an actual being whose presence can be so like that of a man that he can be entertained as a guest (Judg. 13:15 ff.), appear at times as a burning flame (Ex. 3:2), or ascend upward in a flame (Judg. 13:20)? Or, was the angel of the Lord a profound but nonliteral way of speaking of God's presence by the use of thought patterns of the ancient world? May it not be that the concept of a literal being in physical form was part of the passing background of the ancient world, while the truth contained with regard to the reality of God's presence was a permanent, immovable, affirmation?

Moses' experience with God depicted in the account of the angel of the Lord's appearance in a flame of fire was a most genuine experience with the Lord. Such a revelation, however, may well have been mediated through a visionary experience. The visionary experience would likely have assumed its descriptive character from the cultural ideas common to the era in which Moses lived. For Moses, the bush burned with the flaming presence of the angel of the Lord. But it may well have

been an inner experience, and one standing next to Moses may have seen nothing extraordinary. Belief in the angel of the Lord as a person who could be seen with the physical eye is hardly prerequisite to the deeper truth that the Lord confronted Moses at the burning bush.

A flame of fire out of the midst of a bush. The association of God's presence with fire probably had its beginnings in the storm theophany, especially the lightning (cf. Gen. 15:17; Ex. 13:21; 19:18). The flame of fire also symbolizes the burning presence of God in both Testaments.

Three possibilities immediately appear with regard to the bush that burned without being consumed. First, the bush may in some way contrary to all known laws of nature and science have burned with fire without being consumed. Second, the sun may have reflected upon the bush in such manner that it appeared to burn. Or, it bore a fruit or had leaves of such color that the bush seemed to burn as the sunlight reflected on them. Essentially such explanations are attempts to rationalize the experience in terms comprehensible to the scientific era. Third, there is the possibility that the narrator, speaking against the cultural and prescientific background of roughly 1200 b.c., believed that the angel of the Lord literally appeared and that the burning was the flame traditionally associated with the angel of the Lord.

It is also possible that the experience of Moses was a vision, an inner experience, in which the details were drawn from the thought patterns common to his generation; thought patterns that embraced a literal angel of the Lord and a literal flame of fire.

The latter appears to be the best alternative for the present writer. According to this view the biblical material conveys to us the profound truth of God's presence but does so in language that was part of the passing understanding of the era. It appears to be sounder exegesis to follow either (1) the literal view or (3) the view that reinterprets the ancient view of literal, semidivine beings in order to see the ultimate truth of God's presence. The nonliteral view is in keeping with the total nature of the biblical revelation: that is, to convey ultimate truth in thought categories compatible with the writer's cultural context. This in no way lessens the miracle of the direct and personal divine encounter with Moses.

Moses' experience took place at *the mountain of God,* a site that probably had sacred associations for many generations and for many people. The command to take off his shoes reflects a common attitude in the presence of that which is holy (cf. Josh. 5:15) and remains a custom upon entering a mosque or other holy place in the East today.

The Lord identified himself to Moses as *the God of your Father, the God of Abraham, the God of Isaac, and the God of Jacob.* Whatever else the phrase may mean it is certainly a movement toward continuity, an effort to bind the previous revelation of God to the revelation mediated through Moses. All that may have been dissimilar and all that was believed in common merged together into a single faith in the covenant understanding of Yahweh as the God of Israel.

2. Confirmation of Moses' Call (3:7–12)

⁷ Then the Lord said, "I have seen the affliction of my people who are in Egypt, and have heard their cry because of their taskmasters; I know their sufferings, ⁸ and I have come down to deliver them out of the hand of the Egyptians, and to bring them up out of that land to a good and broad land, a land flowing with milk and honey, to the place of the Canaanites, the Hittites, the Amorites, the Perizzites, the Hivites, and the Jebusites. ⁹ And now, behold, the cry of the people of Israel has come to me, and I have seen the oppression with which the Egyptians oppress them. ¹⁰ Come, I will send you to Pharaoh that you may bring forth my people, the sons of Israel, out of Egypt." ¹¹ But Moses said to God, "Who am I that I should go to Pharaoh, and bring the sons of Israel out of Egypt?" ¹² He said, "But I will be with you; and this shall be the sign for you, that I have sent you: when you have brought forth the people out of Egypt, you shall serve God upon this mountain."

The Great Condescension (vv. 7–10). The response of verses 7–8 is probably parallel to 2:23–25. The verbs are identical except that 2:23 f. refers to God as having remembered the covenant, while 3:7 f. speaks of God's declaring that he has come down. This point of difference is complementary rather than contradictory, however, and it is quite significant that remembering the covenant (P) leads Yahweh to come down and involve himself in events (J).

The fruition of God's response is the exodus of the Hebrews from Egypt and their entry into a "land flowing with milk and honey," the traditional way of describing the fertility of the Promised Land. Verses 7–8 represent the response of Yahweh to the plight of the people according to the southern source (J), while verses 9–10 represent the response of Yahweh according to the northern source (E). The two are thus parallel descriptions of Yahweh's response to the initial phase of Moses' call experience.

Come, I will send you . . . that you may bring forth my people. A comparison of verses 7–8 and 9–12 is quite revealing with regard to the fulfilment of the Lord's promise. Earlier (v. 8) Yahweh declared that he would come down and bring the people out of Egypt (J). Now (v. 10) he speaks of sending Moses (E). Although having a separate circle of usage, the two means of deliverance complement each other. The Lord does redeem his people, but he does so through his people. It is by humanity that God redeems humanity.

Commitment Without Confirmation (vv. 11–12). Courage to face the task was inherent in the promise of the Lord's presence. There is a direct relationship between the statement *I will be with you* (*'ehyeh*) and the name Yahweh, later revealed to Moses: "I AM WHO I AM," or "I WILL BE WHAT I WILL BE" (*'ehyeh*). The two verbs are identical in every way.

The sign is more than Israel's mere presence at the mount, more even than her worship there. The sign centers in the presence of God in Israel at the mount.

Thus, the future would validate Moses' present call. Like every man, in the nightmare of his crises there can be heard Moses' plaintive wail, *Who am I that I should go . . . ?* (v. 11). "Why didst thou ever send me?" (5:22). With inner desperation every man cries for some sure word of confirmation for his life. In return there is often only the ominous refrain: after the long course of your task has been completed; when the plagues are over, the shadow of the death angel gone, and the sea of chaos crossed; when the murmurings of the people are over, and the thirst has been quenched and the hunger filled; when you stand upon your mountain, wherever it may be, and your people worship in exultation in the presence of God who sees—then you will know that he has truly sent you. But you cannot know until then, not with ultimate certainty.

3. The Commission of Moses (3:13-22)

13 Then Moses said to God, "If I come to the people of Israel and say to them, 'The God of your fathers has sent me to you,' and they ask me, 'What is his name?' what shall I say to them?" 14 God said to Moses, "I AM WHO I AM." And he said, "Say this to the people of Israel, 'I AM has sent me to you.'" 15 God also said to Moses, "Say this to the people of Israel, 'The LORD, the God of your fathers, the God of Abraham, the God of Isaac, and the God of Jacob, has sent me to you': this is my name for ever, and thus I am to be remembered throughout all generations. 16 Go and gather the elders of Israel together, and say to them, 'The LORD, the God of your fathers, the God of Abraham, of Isaac, and of Jacob, has appeared to me, saying, "I have observed you and what has been done to you in Egypt; 17 and I promise that I will bring you up out of the affliction of Egypt, to the land of the Canaanites, the Hittites, the Amorites, the Perizzites, the Hivites, and the Jebusites, a land flowing with milk and honey." ' 18 And they will hearken to your voice; and you and the elders of Israel shall go to the king of Egypt and say to him, 'The LORD, the God of the Hebrews, has met with us; and now, we pray you, let us go a three days' journey into the wilderness, that we may sacrifice to the LORD our God.' 19 I know that the king of Egypt will not let you go unless compelled by a mighty hand. 20 So I will stretch

out my hand and smite Egypt with all the wonders which I will do in it; after that he will let you go. 21 And I will give this people favor in the sight of the Egyptians; and when you go, you shall not go empty, 22 but each woman shall ask of her neighbor, and of her who sojourns in her house, jewelry of silver and of gold, and clothing, and you shall put them on your sons and on your daughters; thus you shall despoil the Egyptians."

The Revelation of Yahweh's Name (vv. 13-15). In ancient Israel the name was the summation of one's character, the self-disclosure of the person (cf. Jacob-Israel, Gen. 32:27-28). The refusal to share one's name on the other hand, reflected the unwillingness to give one's self completely. For, to know one's full name implied the possession of some power or control over the person (cf. Gen. 33:20; Judg. 13:17 ff.). Hence, it is extremely significant that God revealed his personal name to Moses. It is as though God made a full declaration of his inmost being.

The God of your fathers has sent me to you. It is the God of Abraham, Isaac, and Jacob, who is also the God of Moses, and who now reveals himself in a new manner. More specifically the term "God of your fathers" connoted a distinct phase of religious life characteristic of patriarchial times. In 1929 Albrecht Alt suggested that "God of your father(s)" reflected a unique understanding of God, distinct from the local *'elim* (gods) of Canaan.[1] The "God of your fathers" was unique in that this God was not identified with a shrine, but was associated with persons—Abraham, Isaac, Jacob; he was not a local deity but the God of the clan. He was the God of history in that he entered into covenant with those in the clan.[2]

Thus, the phrase *God of your fathers* connoted the essence of patriarchial religion, and in the present context the writer underscored the distinction between pa-

---

1 "The God of the Fathers," in *Essays on Old Testament History and Religion,* trans. R. A. Wilson (Oxford: Basil Blackwell, 1966), pp. 1–77.

2 Cf. Frank Moore Cross, Jr., "Yahweh and the God of the Patriarchs," *The Harvard Theological Review,* LV, 4, 1962, pp. 225 ff.

triarchial religion and the revelation mediated through Moses, while at the same time indicating an essential continuity between the religion of the patriarchs and the worship of Yahweh during the era Moses.

As Alt suggests: "The specific function of this story in the plan of the whole Elohist narrative is, on the one hand, to make the reader conscious of the complete contrast in the sight of God between the time of the patriarchs and that of Moses, and on the other hand to compose the difference again in a higher unity by presenting the same God as bearer of the old and new divine names. The story thus becomes the link by which the Elohist sagas of the patriarchs and of Moses can be kept distinct and yet brought into a very close relationship with one another" (p. 11).

God said to Moses, "I am who I am." Several emphases make this passage of unique importance: (1) it is the only place in the Old Testament where any attempt is made to explain the meaning of the name Yahweh, although even here it is so exceedingly brief as hardly to be an explanation; (2) the revelation of the personal name of God, Yahweh, was intended to counteract disbelief in Moses' ministry as agent of God's deliverance; (3) the name Yahweh marks the transition from the loosely related tribal existence of the Hebrews and *the God of your fathers* to the collection of tribes eventually gathered around a central sanctuary, destined to become Israel, and Yahweh.

First, *I am who I am* is a verbal phrase based in all probability upon the verb *hayah,* to be. When others spoke of Yahweh in the third person, the probable verbal form was *yahweh*—"he causes to be" —or (assuming an older form of the simple stem) "he is," or "he will be." As it appears in the present Hebrew text, the phrase could well be translated "I am who (what) I am," or "I will be who (what) I will be," or, "I will be what (ever) I will be." [3]

Philip Hyatt has recently argued against the creative connotation in the divine name YHWH.[4]

The name Yahweh, and the use of the phrase "I will be what I will be" when Yahweh speaks of himself, is a declaration of the presence of God. The use of the verb *hayah* (to be) does not imply the philosophical concept of absolute existence or being in a metaphysical sense. In this regard verse 12 is instructive: "I will be with you" (*'ehyeh*). The form is identical with the verbs in verse 14 *'ehyeh 'asher 'ehyeh.* Thus the name Yahweh, "He will be," or "I am, I will be," connotes God's presence.

If verse 14 is a declaration of God's revelation of his inmost being as "presence," it is also a declaration of the "hiddenness" of God. God is not only "I am" or "I will be" but "I am what I am" or "I will be what I will be." The phrase is much like others in the Old Testament in which the speaker is deliberately vague, thereby leaving with the reader a pregnant statement designed to convey more than is actually stated in the particular text (cf. Deut. 1:46; 29:16; 1 Sam. 23:13; 2 Sam. 15:20; 2 Kings 18:1; the passages are normally a bit clearer in the Hebrew text). Compare 1 Samuel 23:13—*wayyithhall'khu ba'asher yithhallakhu,* "and they walked in whatever (way) they walked"—and Exodus 3:14 (*'ehyeh 'asher 'ehyeh*), "I will be whatever I will be"; or 2 Samuel 15:20 (*wa'ani holekh 'al 'asher 'ani holekh*): "And I walk wherever I walk" ("I go whither I may," KJV; "I go I know not where," RSV). Thus, the phrase "I will be what (ever) I will be" is indicative of a hiddenness of God, grounded in his incomparable nature. His definition of himself

---

[3] Another meaning of the name YHWH takes it from a causative stem and translates the phrase in verse 14, *'ehyeh 'asher 'ehyeh,* as "I cause to be what

comes into existence." Behind such a translation is the assumed phrase *Yahweh 'asher yihweh.* W. F. Albright has contended for such a meaning in *From the Stone Age to Christianity* (Baltimore: The Johns Hopkins Press, 1946), pp. 198 ff.

[4] "Was Yahweh Originally a Creator Deity?" J.B.L., LXXXVI (1967), pp. 369 ff.; cf. D. N. Freedman, "The Name of the God of Moses," J.B.L., LXXXIX (1960), pp. 151–56.

can be given only in terms of himself, and this is given in such a way as to leave more unstated about him than is apprehended at any given time.

Such an understanding of the phrase "I will be what (ever) I will be" underscores the continuing revelation of Yahweh. His presence is assured, but his self-revelation has such fluidity about it as to permit a continual unfolding of the divine nature without exhausting the total content of God's nature. Rather than being able to define God with such precision as to capture the totality of his essence, the phrase reveals the nature of God while allowing the possibility of further insight and revelation. Although continually present as a God who does not change, he is at the same time present in every generation with new connotations and implications.

The Fulfilment of the Covenant (vv. 16–22). The promise to bring Israel out of Egypt was understood, not only in the more immediate terms of deliverance from Egyptian bondage, but as the fulfilment of the covenant made to Abraham, and later reaffirmed in the course of events. There were times when the people of Israel did not hearken, when in fact they rebelled (cf. 5:20 f.), yet God's promise to Moses was fulfilled. The people did respond, bringing about eventual freedom from the tyranny of Egypt.

Three days' journey was probably a common expression for a considerable distance (cf. Gen. 30:36, where it is a distance sufficiently great to separate effectively the flocks of Jacob and Laban). The request that they be permitted to go to the arid region lying between Egypt and Palestine for the purpose of offering sacrifice was natural. National and ethnic groups worshiped gods unique to their own people or nation. The nature of the sacrifice is not specifically identified, but in all probability it was associated with some aspect of the spring celebration and the flock, perhaps the time of sheep-shearing. The request was perhaps a ruse in order to get out of Egypt, or it may have been a legitimate

request made to test the reaction of Pharaoh (with the further possibility of seeking release should his reply have been favorable to the first request).

I know that the king of Egypt will not let you go. Set in the context of the call experience, this narrative is a picture in miniature of the entire conflict between Moses and Pharaoh. It is designed both to warn Moses of the difficulty and at the same time to assure him of ultimate victory.

I will give this people favor. The ancient world looked with pride upon the ability to "outwit" another, especially an enemy, and the case at hand was probably recounted throughout Israel as they ridiculed Egypt for the manner in which the Israelites had gained advantage over them. Read in the context of its original environment it is a pointed story which exalts Israel at the expense of Egypt.

IV. Moses' Surrender and Commitment (4:1—6:1)

The giving of the signs was a means of strengthening Moses' faith (4:1–31), a faith soon tested by his encounter with Pharaoh, Pharaoh's repudiation of Moses' message, the retaliation taken against the Israelites, and the renunciation of Moses' leadership by his own people (5:1–21). The closing picture of Moses prior to the second account of his call (6:2 ff.) is that of a discouraged figure assured by Yahweh that faith will triumph (5:22–23).

1. Faith Tried (4:1–31)

(1) Faith Tried in Preparation (4:1–17)

¹ Then Moses answered, "But behold, they will not believe me or listen to my voice, for they will say, 'The LORD did not appear to you.'" ² The LORD said to him, "What is that in your hand?" He said, "A rod." ³ And he said, "Cast it on the ground." So he cast it on the ground, and it became a serpent; and Moses fled from it. ⁴ But the LORD said to Moses, "Put out your hand, and take it by the tail"—so he put out his hand and caught it, and it became a rod in his hand—⁵ "that they may believe that the LORD, the God of their fathers, the God of Abraham, the God of Isaac,

and the God of Jacob, has appeared to you."
6 Again, the LORD said to him, "Put your hand into your bosom." And he put his hand into his bosom; and when he took it out, behold, his hand was leprous, as white as snow. 7 Then God said, "Put your hand back into your bosom." So he put his hand back into his bosom; and when he took it out, behold, it was restored like the rest of his flesh. 8 "If they will not believe you," God said, "or heed the first sign, they may believe the latter sign. 9 If they will not believe even these two signs or heed your voice, you shall take some water from the Nile and pour it upon the dry ground; and the water which you shall take from the Nile will become blood upon the dry ground."
10 But Moses said to the LORD, "Oh, my Lord, I am not eloquent, either heretofore or since thou hast spoken to thy servant; but I am slow of speech and of tongue." 11 Then the LORD said to him, "Who has made man's mouth? Who makes him dumb, or deaf, or seeing, or blind? Is it not I, the LORD? 12 Now therefore go, and I will be with your mouth and teach you what you shall speak." 13 But he said, "Oh, my Lord, send, I pray, some other person." 14 Then the anger of the LORD was kindled against Moses and he said, "Is there not Aaron, your brother, the Levite? I know that he can speak well; and behold, he is coming out to meet you, and when he sees you he will be glad in his heart. 15 And you shall speak to him and put the words in his mouth; and I will be with your mouth and with his mouth, and will teach you what you shall do. 16 He shall speak for you to the people; and he shall be a mouth for you, and you shall be to him as God. 17 And you shall take in your hand this rod, with which you shall do the signs."

The purpose of 4:1–17 parallels that of 3:11 f. The earlier passage (3:11 ff., E) is probably the account, which circulated in the Northern Kingdom, of the effort to equip Moses for the task. This source emphasized two signs: Yahweh's future presence at the mountain of God and the sign of Yahweh's name, given as a means of confirming the validity of Moses' call.

The overarching purpose of 4:1 ff. is to indicate the way in which the Lord counteracted Moses' objections to his call. The fear that men would not believe him was settled by the giving of the signs (vv. 1–9), while the plea that he was not an "eloquent" speaker was countered by giving Aaron as Moses' spokesman (vv.

10–17). Both actions prepared Moses for the task of deliverance.

The Giving of the Signs (1–9). Moses' fear was well founded. After all, he hardly had the best credentials—reared and trained in the court of Pharaoh, a fugitive from Egyptian justice, a sojourner among the Midianites, the husband of a Midianite woman, the father of a son by the same Midianite. Who could have believed his story?

What is that in your hand? Whatever the nature of this experience, its intention is clear: a sign of confirmation concerning the mission of Moses. However, it is important to note that it could be reduplicated by the Egyptian magicians (cf. 7:12). Driver suggests that modern Egyptian serpent-charmers possess unusual power over serpents, and that the practice is alluded to in Psalm 58:5; Jeremiah 8:17; Ecclesiastes 10:11 (cf. Mark 16:18). Probably some such practice constituted the nucleus of the sign described in Exodus 4:2 ff. However, there are elements of the present narrative which go beyond such an explanation. For example, Moses assumedly began with the rod in his hand, probably the shepherd's staff which became the symbol of his authority (cf. 4:17; 7:20); then the rod became a serpent.

The historical nucleus of 4:2 ff. may have consisted in this: Moses (and Aaron, according to 7:10 ff.) was able to perform feats known in the East with regard to serpents. The rod may well have been a serpent made rigid through their power, but which became active when the spell was broken. The narrators have overlaid this historical nucleus with additional material in such way as to equate the rigid serpent with the shepherd's staff belonging to Moses.

Although some aspects of the narrative in its present form may represent additions to the original historical nucleus, the essential purpose of the passage remains clear; and primary attention should be focused upon the revelation of God inherent in the passages. Despite the way in which the passages may have developed layers of added detail over the years, God is present and active in the process and through the literary complex he conveyed an inspired and authoritative revelation of his will: those whom God calls he confirms and equips. Whatever the literary means used to convey the message, this is the essential nucleus of the divine revelation.

As the narrative now appears, the entire transformation, from normalcy to leprous condition and vice versa, was instantaneous. No time element is allowed by the narrative which might possibly be used as a means of interpreting the event as having taken place over a long period of time. One of three possibilities is best suited as an interpretation of the passage: (1) Moses' hand instantaneously passed from normalcy to diseased condition, and back again; (2) Moses experienced the diseased condition which was healed over a period of time, but the time factor has been so compressed by the narrator as to make the experience instantaneous within the narrative; and (3) the account is typical of those narratives which surround the personality of heroic or otherwise significant leaders, especially religious leaders. The details of the account should be sublimated in degree of importance to the revelation of God mediated through the experience; namely, that Moses was uniquely endowed and equipped for his ministry as an agent of God's deliverance.

The third alternative appears fully harmonious with the total nature of the biblical revelation and the relationship of the Lord to the natural order. The second alternative has merit and could well serve as an interpretation of the event which would harmonize the instantaneous change of the leprous hand with what is generally known about the disease. Many sincere individuals would maintain the first alternative, and this may be held with integrity if one accepts a basic presupposition which interprets the natural order as subject to convulsive alteration by men who act as agents of God. Of greater importance is the funda-

mental affirmation of faith that those whom God calls he equips for his task, and that Moses was uniquely endowed and equipped for the Lord's service.

The word sign (*'oth*) (cf. the plagues, 7:17 ff.) is quite often used with regard to objects, events, or experiences whose meaning is not found within themselves but in the interpretation given to them. For example, the word is used of the rainbow (Gen. 9:13), the cord that hung in Rahab's window as a sign indicating her relationship to the spies (Josh. 2:12,18), the stones placed in Jordan as a memorial of God's mighty acts (Josh. 4:6), or the children of Isaiah whose names were significant beyond themselves (Isa. 8:18). Here (v. 9) it is used as a pledge of divine presence, that Moses had actually experienced the meeting with Yahweh.

With regard to the rod-serpent, leprous-normal hand, and water-blood events, Rylaarsdam suggests that while the structure and content may be foreign or strange to us, their point is perennially relevant: the God of the biblical faith is Master of the world he himself has made, and the God who controls even the demons places man under responsibility and calls him to commitment.

The Giving of the Spokesman (4:10–17). Moses' experience with God is characterized by a series of fears: (1) that he is not the person to approach Pharaoh (vv. 11 ff.); (2) that the people will believe neither that the God of their fathers spoke to him nor that he knows the name of the God who met him at the bush (3:13 ff.); (3) that the people will not listen to him or believe that he has a message from God (4:1 ff.); and (4) that he is not an *eloquent* man, that is, a man of words (4: 10 ff.). Each of these fears was in turn answered by Yahweh.

There are numerous points of relationship between the role of Moses and that of a prophet. His call closely parallels the prophetic call—he spoke in Yahweh's name to Pharaoh, and used the prophetic expression, "Thus says the Lord" (5:1; 32:27).

Specifically, prophetic teaching was communicated through him or placed in his mouth (cf. 4:22; 6:6–8; 15:26; 19:3–6; 33:17–19; 34:6–7). Later writers spoke of him as a prophet, although this may be anachronistic (cf. Hos. 12:13; Deut. 18:18). Thus, the Exodus writer's concern to deal with his difficulty in speaking may be related to Moses' prophetic role.

Yahweh's rebuke of Moses reflects two considerations. First, creative power necessary for man's function in a prophetic role is present in Yahweh, and it is implied, although not specifically stated, that it is available to those whom Yahweh calls. The rhetorical question, **Who has made man's mouth? Who makes him dumb, or deaf, or seeing, or blind,** is both an answer to Moses' objection and the foundation for the promise later made to Moses in verse 12. The faculties of both perception (seeing and hearing) and expression (mouth) are ultimately given by God. Second, because it is Yahweh who is uniquely able to equip one for the prophetic role, he **will be with your mouth and teach you what you shall speak.**

Because it is Yahweh who empowers man in the vital areas of the senses—hearing, speaking, seeing—Moses is commanded, **Now therefore go, and I will be with your mouth.** The subject of both verbs is specifically emphasized in the Hebrew text as though to say, "And as for you, *you* go, and I, *I* will be with your mouth."

Yahweh's claim that he will "be with your mouth" uses a verb identical with the one used in giving the name of Yahweh; *'ehyeh* "I will be" (v. 12) being identical with "I am" (3:14). More significant than the words placed in Moses' mouth is the assurance that "I will be" (*'ehyeh*) with your mouth. Indirectly, there is a continuing emphasis upon the presence of God in the life of the believer (cf. 3:12,14). Whatever the historical nature of Moses' response, the narrator used this experience as the means of introducing Aaron to the reader.

Moses hardly needed to be informed that Aaron was a member of the tribe of Levi. Probably, in this particular instance, Levite is a technical term for one who fulfils a priestly role. As such, the term may be older than even the tribe of Levi. The larger purpose of the narrator at this juncture was to introduce the role of the priest into the Exodus narrative.

The rod of God was likely a cane or shepherd's staff used to precipitate "wonders" when utilized by the agent of God's deliverance. This is especially probable in view of its later designation as the "rod of God" (4:20). Later the rod was used in the plagues (7:15,17,20; 9:23; 10:13), the crossing of the sea (14:16), and the giving of the water to Israel in the wilderness (17:5,9). In that part of Exodus stemming from the priestly source the rod is placed in the hands of Aaron (cf. 7:19; 8:5,16–17); but whether utilized by Moses or Aaron, it became the means of precipitating the "wonders" associated with the exodus experience.

(2) Faith Tried in Migration (4:18–26)

18 Moses went back to Jethro his father-in-law and said to him, "Let me go back, I pray, to my kinsmen in Egypt and see whether they are still alive." And Jethro said to Moses, "Go in peace." 19 And the LORD said to Moses in Midian, "Go back to Egypt; for all the men who were seeking your life are dead. 20 So Moses took his wife and his sons and set them on an ass, and went back to the land of Egypt; and in his hand Moses took the rod of God.
21 And the LORD said to Moses, "When you go back to Egypt, see that you do before Pharaoh all the miracles which I have put in your power; but I will harden his heart, so that he will not let the people go. 22 And you shall say to Pharaoh, 'Thus says the LORD, Israel is my first-born son, 23 and I say to you, "Let my son go that he may serve me"; if you refuse to let him go, behold, I will slay your first-born son.' "
24 At a lodging place on the way the LORD met him and sought to kill him. 25 Then Zipporah took a flint and cut off her son's foreskin, and touched Moses' feet with it, and said, "Surely you are a bridegroom of blood to me!" 26 So he let him alone. Then it was that she said, "You are a bridegroom of blood," because of the circumcision.

Facing Separation (vv. 18-20). Like Jacob before him, Moses returned to his father's land with his family. The migration motif within the biblical material is a continual expression of the faith commitment of those who migrate in fulfilment of what they felt to be the overarching purposes of God. While one should not risk ascribing theological significance to every such migration, it is interesting to note the manner in which this motif characterizes the patriarchs, Moses, and the nation Israel in the Old Testament, as well as Joseph and Mary in the New Testament. The life of faith is one of pilgrimage; always *in via.*

Facing Rejection (vv. 21-23). The Hebrew word for miracle (*mopheth*) is used of a special display of God's power (7:3; 11:9; Psalm 105:5; 1 Chron. 16:12) or as a sign or token of a future event, somewhat parallel to *'oth* (cf. 4:8; 1 Kings 13:3,5; Isa. 8:18).

The range of the "extraordinary" is expressed by three Hebrew words: (1) sign (*'oth*), in the sense of a pledge of divine presence and interposition (4:8-9; 7:3; Josh. 24:17); (2) portent or miracle (*mopheth*), as a special display of God's power; (3) wonder (*niphl°oth* or *pele'*), as in Exodus 3:20 and Jeremiah 21:2. It is significant that Moses' action before his own people is a sign (*'oth*), while his deeds before Pharaoh are characterized as miracles (*mopheth*). Widely accepted canons of source criticism ascribe 4:2 ff. to the Southern or "J" source while 4:21 is ascribed to the Northern or "E" source.

While the Hebrew "in your hand" may mean no more than "within your power," it is so reminiscent of the rod of God with which the "miracles" are associated that one is prone to interpret the phrase to imply that the miracles have been placed "in your hand" in the sense that Moses had been given the wonder-working rod of God.

I will harden his heart. Old Testament patterns of thought did not deal with secondary causes standing between the event and God. Thus, in early Israel all action

was attributed to the Lord, although Israel later came to recognize with greater clarity the reality of secondary causes. The pronoun is emphatic, however, and the writer attempted to convey some such ideas as "but I, *I* will harden." The word for harden (*chazaq*) is quite often used within the Old Testament (291 occurrences) with the idea of growing firm, strong, or to strengthen. In the intensive form (used in v. 21) it means to make strong physically (Judg. 16:28), to strengthen the hands of any one, i.e. to sustain or encourage (Judg. 9:24; Isa. 35:3), to make one bold (Deut. 1:38; 2 Sam. 15:5). It is also used with the sense of to make rigid, hard; i.e., perverse, obstinate, harden—the heart of any one (4:21, E; 9:12, P; Josh. 11:20, D; Jer. 5:3). In biblical thought the heart was the center of the will, the seat of volitional action, and did not have the emotional associations of the twentieth century (these were centered in other vital organs). Moses, through divine initiative, recognized before arriving in Egypt that Pharaoh would reject his overtures. Expressed in thought patterns common to the age, this meant that the Lord had hardened the heart or "will" of Pharaoh.

My first-born son. Israel is individualized and spoken of as a son (cf. Hos. 11:1; Jer. 31:9). Often the term is used to express the deep love of God for Israel, or the duties owed to the Father (cf. Hos. 1:10; Isa. 1:2,4; Deut. 14:1; 32:5-6; Jer. 3:14; Isa. 63:8-10).

Facing Adversity (vv. 24-26). This narrative may well be one of the oldest portions of the Bible. This is indicated by the use of the flint knife, the manner in which illness is understood as an attack by the deity, the relation of circumcision to some aspect of marriage (cf. the reference to bridegroom of blood), and the manner in which the attack is repulsed by the symbolic identification of the act of circumcision with Moses. As a statement on the origin of circumcision the passage parallels Genesis 17, although the rite is treated differently in the two passages. In all probability Exodus 4:24–27 is quite ancient and has been so reshaped that some of the original elements are no longer clear.

The statement that the Lord *sought to kill him* represents a common attitude toward severe illness in the ancient world. The phrase has an almost demonic element about it, however, which has led some to suppose that prior to its inclusion within the present work the passage had reference to a demon who sought Moses' life. Later Yahweh was viewed as the principal in the event and not some demonic force. Whether this is correct or not, it is true that the Old Testament often failed to deal with secondary causes, and illness would normally have been traced to the action of the Lord. One is hardly justified in concluding that Yahweh actually attempted to take the life of Moses.

The use of a flint as opposed to a metal object, which would have been in use for centuries prior to this time, is indicative of the ancient origin of circumcision. Circumcising the son was apparently efficacious for Moses, who seemingly was either not circumcised or had not experienced such circumcision as a premarital rite. The statement that Zipporah *touched Moses' feet with it* is probably a euphemistic way of stating that his wife touched Moses' sexual organs with the son's foreskin (cf. Deut. 28:57), thereby symbolically involving Moses in the ritual benefits of circumcision (cf. Isa. 7:20 for an example of the feet as a euphemism for the sexual organs; also Isa. 6:2 may be another illustration).

Since Moses was the father of two sons by this time (cf. 4:20), it is difficult to understand in what sense he could be called a "bridegroom." (The Hebrew word in the text is not the word for "husband," as KJV translates it, but *chathan*, meaning either a daughter's husband or bridegroom, the latter of which is preferable in view of the context. In all probability the statement reflects the manner in which circumcision was originally associated with rites of initiation prior to marriage.)

Circumcision was widely practiced out-side Israel, and in other cultures its significance was at times related to a rite performed at puberty, or more immediately prior to marriage. It is probable that the phrase *bridegroom of blood* is a reflection of this more ancient connotation of circumcision. In this regard, the Hebrew word for "father-in-law" (*chothen*) is directly related to a root which in Arabic signifies "to circumcise." Hence, in one sense the father-in-law was "the circumciser." Moses was not, according to the story, a "blood bridegroom." That is, he had not submitted to circumcision prior to marriage, even though he may have been circumcised earlier according to his own cultural practices. Because he had not experienced circumcision as a premarital rite (i.e., a blood bridegroom) he had incurred the wrath of the deity—Yahweh, according to the present narrator. His wife's action symbolically made him a "bridegroom of blood" and the catastrophe was averted.

Not only does the passage indicate the primitive background of circumcision, it may well be that it had the effect of validating the practice of performing the rite of circumcision early in life rather than during adulthood. Although the account never received significant attention, and the rite described in connection with Abraham (cf. Gen. 17:1 ff.) predominated Israelite thought, Exodus 4:24 remains as a significant statement on the historical background of circumcision.

(3) Faith Tried in Proclamation: The Declaration to the People (4:27–31)

27 The LORD said to Aaron, "Go into the wilderness to meet Moses." So he went, and met him at the mountain of God and kissed him. 28 And Moses told Aaron all the words of the LORD with which he had sent him, and all the signs which he had charged him to do. 29 Then Moses and Aaron went and gathered together all the elders of the people of Israel. 30 And Aaron spoke all the words which the LORD had spoken to Moses, and did the signs in the sight of the people. 31 And the people believed; and when they heard that the LORD had visited the people of Israel and that he had seen their affliction, they bowed their heads and worshiped.

Then Moses and Aaron went and gathered. The verb with which this verse begins in the Hebrew text is singular, third person, masculine: "Then he [Moses] went, and Aaron." This has led some to conclude that originally the passage spoke only of Moses as the one to confront the people, and that the final narrator has introduced Aaron. (Aaron is again introduced following a singular verb related to Moses in 7:12; v. 8, Heb.). However, the second verb in the sentence is plural in Hebrew, "Then they gathered," obviously referring to both Moses and Aaron. Thus, if the passage originally referred only to Moses, a harmonizer has added Aaron and made most of the verbal forms coincide with the introduction of Aaron.

The relationship of Aaron and Moses is too complex to be pursued here, but in all probability the role of Aaron was in the beginning much more insignificant than represented in the present text.

The entire passage (vv. 27–31) is of continuing relevance concerning the providential manner in which God leads differing personalities (vv. 27–28), the faithfulness with which a called person fulfils the divine will through proclaiming the Lord's words. The narrative also suggests the demonstration of tangible proofs of authenticity (vv. 29–30), as well as the positive attitude with which faithful worshipers receive the declared will of God, praising the Lord for what he has done (v. 31).

2. Faith Tested (5:1–21)

This section is best understood as a continuation of the inner struggle of Moses, portrayed so graphically in chapters 3 and 4.

(1) Faith Tested by the Repudiation of Moses' Request (5:1–9)

¹ Afterward Moses and Aaron went to Pharaoh and said, "Thus says the LORD, the God of Israel, 'Let my people go, that they may hold a feast to me in the wilderness.'" ² But Pharaoh said, "Who is the LORD, that I should heed his voice and let Israel go? I do not know the LORD, and moreover I will not let Israel go."

³ Then they said, "The God of the Hebrews has met with us; let us go, we pray, a three days' journey into the wilderness, and sacrifice to the LORD our God, lest he fall upon us with pestilence or with the sword." ⁴ But the king of Egypt said to them, "Moses and Aaron, why do you take the people away from their work? Get to your burdens." ⁵ And Pharaoh said, "Behold, the people of the land are now many and you make them rest from their burdens!" ⁶ The same day Pharaoh commanded the taskmasters of the people and their foremen, ⁷ "You shall no longer give the people straw to make bricks, as heretofore; let them go and gather straw for themselves. ⁸ But the number of bricks which they made heretofore you shall lay upon them, you shall by no means lessen it; for they are idle; therefore they cry, 'Let us go and offer sacrifice to our God.' ⁹ Let heavier work be laid upon the men that they may labor at it and pay no regard to lying words."

The context in which the Old Testament uses the intensive stem of *shalach*, "send forth," is most often one of force and authority. For example, it is used when one divorces a wife (Deut. 22:19,29); to send into exile (Jer. 24:5); to send lions, foxes, pestilence (2 Kings 17:25–26; 2 Kings 24:2; Amos 4:10). It is also used in the sense of "to let go, set free" (Judg. 19:25; Ex. 22:5; 2 Sam. 5:11).

The command in verse 1 stands in marked contrast to the later, strong entreaty "Let us go, we pray" (v. 3). Either the second entreaty was produced by the harsh response of Pharaoh (v. 2) to the initial command (v. 1), or, what is more likely, the statements originated from different sources; the first from the "E" source, and the second from the "J" source. In its present form the entire complex fulfils the original instructions given in 4:23.

Hold a feast is associated with making a pilgrimage or keeping a pilgrim feast. It is used of the feast here suggested by Moses, and the three annual pilgrimages prescribed for Israel (23:14), each of which was celebrated in part by sacred processions and dances. The corresponding word in Arabic means to make a pilgrimage to Mecca. The feast suggested by Moses was likely related to the flock, and possibly held at sheep-shearing time. Later, it was joined with an agricultural feast in which bread was the primary element (cf. 12:1 ff.).

The request of Moses was incredulous. Pharaoh did not know Yahweh. Why should he respond positively to Moses' request? "To know" one's god (God) implied personal, experiential knowledge. Not only did Pharaoh not possess this knowledge of Yahweh, even the Hebrews had only recently been introduced to him. This interplay of Moses versus Pharaoh and Yahweh versus the gods of Egypt is fundamental to an understanding of not only this context but the entire complex of the plagues and the crossing of the sea. If Pharaoh did not know and consequently did not acknowledge the power of Yahweh, Yahweh would respond in such power as to force Pharaoh to acknowledge his priority. Thus, later, the plagues became not only a demonstration to Pharaoh but a triumph of Yahweh, God of Israel, over the gods of Egypt.

(2) Faith Tested by the Retaliation Taken Against the Hebrews (5:10–14)

10 So the taskmasters and the foremen of the people went out and said to the people, "Thus says Pharaoh, 'I will not give you straw. 11 Go yourselves, get your straw wherever you can find it; but your work will not be lessened in the least.'" 12 So the people were scattered abroad throughout all the land of Egypt, to gather stubble for straw. 13 The taskmasters were urgent, saying, "Complete your work, your daily task, as when there was straw." 14 And the foremen of the people of Israel, whom Pharaoh's taskmasters had set over them, were beaten, and were asked, "Why have you not done all your task of making bricks today, as hitherto?"

Taskmasters apparently referred to Egyptian officials in charge of the Hebrew work gangs (cf. 3:7; 5:14), while *the foremen* were Hebrews selected as subordinate officials by the Egyptians (v. 14).

The command that the Hebrews were no longer to be given straw (v. 7) does not mean that the Hebrews made brick without straw. Rather, in addition to making the brick, the Hebrews also had to gather the straw. Despite this increased labor, they were expected to produce the same

number of bricks as during the time the straw was supplied (vv. 8,14).

(3) Faith Tested by the Renunciation of Moses' Leadership by the Hebrews (5:15–21)

15 Then the foremen of the people of Israel came and cried to Pharaoh, "Why do you deal thus with your servants? 16 No straw is given to your servants, yet they say to us, 'Make bricks!' And behold, your servants are beaten; but the fault is in your own people." 17 But he said, "You are idle, you are idle; therefore you say, 'Let us go and sacrifice to the Lord.' 18 Go now, and work; for no straw shall be given you, yet you shall deliver the same number of bricks." 19 The foremen of the people of Israel saw that they were in evil plight, when they said, "You shall by no means lessen your daily number of bricks." 20 They met Moses and Aaron, who were waiting for them, as they came forth from Pharaoh; 21 and they said to them, "The Lord look upon you and judge, because you have made us offensive in the sight of Pharaoh and his servants, and have put a sword in their hand to kill us."

The RSV translation follows the Hebrew text, but the text itself is awkward at this point. The Septuagint translated the phrase, "and you have sinned against your people." The awkward nature of the Hebrew text, plus the fact that it was Pharaoh who was at fault in having originated the decree, strongly suggests that one follow the Septuagint at this point. Thus, verse 16 might well be read: "Behold, your servants are beaten; and you have sinned against your people." In this case "your people" would refer to the Hebrews who, despite their status, considered themselves subjects and under the protection of Pharaoh.

The phrase *The Lord look upon you and judge* is unique to Exodus 5:21, but the expression "the Lord judge between" is found in the context of strife or an oath (cf. Gen. 16:5; 31:53; 1 Sam. 24:12). In view of the context, it would seem that Hebrew foremen called God to *look upon* Moses and Aaron in the negative sense of bringing evil upon them. Whatever its precise signification, the phrase expressed strong hostility. *You have made us offensive.* Literally, the foremen said, "You have caused our scent, or odor, to stink in the eyes of Pharaoh and in the eyes of his servants."

3. Faith Triumphant (5:22—6:1)

22 Then Moses turned again to the LORD and said, "O LORD, why hast thou done evil to this people? Why didst thou ever send me? 23 For since I came to Pharaoh to speak in thy name, he has done evil to this people, and thou hast not delivered thy people at all." 1 But the LORD said to Moses, "Now you shall see what I will do to Pharaoh; for with a strong hand he will send them out, yea, with a strong hand he will drive them out of his land."

The inner struggle of Moses (3:1—6:1) reaches both its climax and its resolution in the conclusion to the Moses-Pharaoh confrontation.[5]

There are times when the depth of faith emerges more forcibly in the questions raised than in the assent given to various bodies of truth. Questioning God does not always have this positive effect, but there are sufficient evidences within the Old Testament to warrant the conclusion that the expression of honest questions gives voice to a faith that is vital (cf. Jer., Hab., and Job). Faced with the extremity of his own need, Moses' first response was to question why God had brought such evil upon the people, and why the Lord had ever sent him.

Why hast thou done evil indicates the manner in which evil was ascribed to the Lord in Old Testament thought. Two points should be noted, however. First, this caused no problem for Old Testament persons, for at this time there was no concept of secondary causes which tended to absolve the Lord, or at least place him twice removed from the actual origin of evil. Whatever happened, the Lord must have done it (cf. Amos 3:6, "Does evil befall a city,

5 Although numerous, very short oral and literary sections stand behind the total complex of material as we now have it, there is a sense in which the entire narrative extending from 3:1—6:1 may be viewed as continuous *within its present literary structure.* Such an emphasis upon continuity within the present literary structure should not obscure the diversity of the passage in terms of its ultimate origins.

unless the Lord has done it?") A comparison of 2 Samuel 24:1 and 1 Chronicles 21:1 is an excellent example of the way in which a later book (Chronicles) removed the Lord from the immediate context of evil attributed to him in an earlier book (Samuel). Second, the word *evil* may also connote calamity, misfortune, or other adversity of such nature (cf. Gen. 43:6; Num. 20:15; Josh. 24:20; 1 Kings 17:20). It does not always connote moral evil. Often it means to "do evil" in the sense of "to do harm."

The reference to Pharaoh's driving *them out of his land* may be no more than a synonymous refrain to *he will send them out.* However, the word drive out (*garash*) is often used of driving out someone with force (cf. 23:28; 1 Sam. 26:19) and may reflect the action described in Exodus 12: 33,39, in which it is stated that Israel was "thrust out of Egypt and could not tarry." One is led to suspect that after experiencing the mighty hand of the Lord, Egypt would be so anxious to be rid of Israel as not only to send them forth (*shalach*) but to thrust (*garash*) them out as one does a hostile people in a time of war.

The pilgrimage of Moses, both in faith and in fact, is so universal in its characteristics as to be the pilgrimage of every man, struggling from his burning bush and scorching desert to the promised land of rest and stability. The pilgrimage from the desert to the cultivated land is the journey of every man. Few are the men who cannot read Exodus 3:1—6:1 and see therein the reflection of their own pilgrimage in faith; its hopes and its fears; its dreams and despairs, its openness and hiddenness, its glory and its futility, its faith and its unbelief, its joy and its sorrow, in essence, the totality of its entire range of experiences. Westermann has well characterized Exodus 3–4 as the "inner struggle of Moses." Borrowing a title from a writer in another discipline, one might well summarize these experiences as the "struggle of the soul," the struggle of man's whole being in the realization of the Lord's purposes.

V. The Manifestation of Lordship over History: Second Account of Moses' Call (6:2—7:13)

Primary motifs of Exodus 3:1—6:1 reappear in the later, more abbreviated narrative of Exodus 6:2—7:13. The self-revelation of the Lord to Moses (6:2–8—3:1 ff.); the declaration to the people and their refusal to hear (6:9–27—4:10 ff.); the choice of Aaron as spokesman for Moses (6:28–7:7—4:10 ff.); and the repudiation of Moses' message by Pharaoh (7:8–13—5:1 ff.). What is the relationship of the passages? The second account (6:2—7:13) may be a supplementary restatement of the first account, a conclusion all but demanded if one presupposes the single authorship of Exodus. Or, the second account may parallel and complement the first narrative, but stem from another source. The latter seems preferable in light of the total evidence.

Accordingly, it is widely accepted that Exodus 6:2—7:13 is an account of the call of Moses and his appearance before Pharaoh which originated in priestly circles. Such a possibility should occasion no greater surprise than did the circulation of parallel accounts of Jesus' life in the Synoptic Gospels.

1. New Insight into Old Truths (6:2–9)

2 And God said to Moses, "I am the LORD. 3 I appeared to Abraham, to Isaac, and to Jacob, as God Almighty, but by my name the LORD I did not make myself known to them. 4 I also established my covenant with them, to give them the land of Canaan, the land in which they dwelt as sojourners. 5 Moreover I have heard the groaning of the people of Israel whom the Egyptians hold in bondage and I have remembered my covenant. 6 Say therefore to the people of Israel, 'I am the LORD, and I will bring you out from under the burdens of the Egyptians, and I will deliver you from their bondage, and I will redeem you with an outstretched arm and with great acts of judgment, 7 and I will take you for my people, and I will be your God; and you shall know that I am the LORD your God, who has brought you out from under the burdens of the Egyptians. 8 And I will bring you into the land which I swore to give to Abraham, to Isaac, and to Jacob; I will give it to you for a possession. I

am the LORD.' " 9 Moses spoke thus to the people of Israel; but they did not listen to Moses, because of their broken spirit and their cruel bondage.

This material should be read in direct parallel with Exodus 3:1–22, especially verses 13 ff., for the two narratives concerning the revelation of the name Yahweh are uniquely complementary. Apparently, the setting of this disclosure of God's personal name is Egypt, whereas the "mountain of God" was the geographical context of the earlier account.

The Name and Nature of God (vv. 2–3). Because God is known by his name and his action, the present passage, also verses 4–9, is extremely important for understanding the nature of God.

And God said to Moses is unique, for not since chapter 3 has the name God appeared in an introduction to a narrative section. This shift from the Lord (*yahweh*) to God *'elohim*) probably marks the introduction of a distinctly new block of material (P).

I am the Lord. This is more than an introductory formula, and should be viewed as parallel to Exodus 3:14. The simplicity of the assertion presupposes familiarity with the name, and there is no repetition of the formula "I will be what I will be" (*'ehyeh 'asher 'ehyeh*) of 3:14.

I appeared . . . as God Almighty ('el shadday). The name for God used here (*'el*) is one of the oldest Semitic designations of God. Although the original meaning of the word is uncertain, Walther Eichrodt suggests that "one can, therefore, choose between 'mighty,' 'Leader' and 'Governor.' It is worth noting that whichever of these meanings we adopt stresses the distance between God and man. In this they are in conformity with a basic characteristic of the Semitic concept of God, namely, that what is of primary importance is not the feeling of kinship with the deity, but fear and trembling in the face of his overwhelming majesty." [6]

6 *Theology of the Old Testament,* tr. J. A. Baker (Philadelphia: Westminster, 1961), I, 179.

Shadday, "Almighty," was most likely directly related to the Assyrian *shadu*, "mountain," and the original connotation was "God of the mountains." It is interesting that the word occurs in inscriptions of Sargon and Asshur-bani-pal as an epithet of Bel and Asshur and as personal names such as *Bel-shadua*, *Marduk-shadua*. Thus, El Shaddai reflects associations between the Hebrews and their Mesopotamian or Canaanite cultural context. The specific meaning of the name is subordinate to the fact that El Shaddai was a primitive name for the God later identified as Yahweh, and was associated by the priestly source with Abraham (cf. Gen. 17:1, the reference probably in the mind of the narrator of Ex. 6:3). There is no attempt within the Old Testament to ascribe theological significance to the meaning of the name per se. "Almighty" is the traditional translation but that this was the primitive meaning is highly questionable.[7]

My name the Lord. This revelation of the name for God (Lord or Yahweh) is the uniquely personal name discussed more fully in 3:14. Only in the earlier passage (3:14) was there any attempt to clarify the meaning of the name. Elsewhere in the Old Testament the name was freely used with no attempt to clarify its meaning. The name means "to be," but "being" in its personal dimensions. For Israel, existence was a concept of relation, "that is to say, it is only real in connection with another existence. God is he who is *with* someone. . . . It is evidently not being that is desired for Yahweh, whose existence was never discussed, but *his effective presence* near the individual or amongst his people." [8]

Although verse 3 states that prior to the

exodus era Yahweh had not been known by the patriarchs, there are pre-exodus contexts in which individuals make use of the name. H. H. Rowley has well summarized this:

"The name is known to Abram (Gen. xv. 2, 8) to Sarai (xvi.2), to Laban (xxiv. 31); it is used by angelic visitors in conversation with Abraham (xviii. 14) and with Lot (xix. 13); and *God is represented as saying 'I am Jehovah'* to Abram (xv. 7) and to Jacob (xxviii. 13). There are even passages which carry the use of this Divine name far back beyond the patriarchs. Gen. iv. 26 states that in the days of Seth, the son of Adam, men began to call on the name of Jehovah, and Gen. iv. 1 says that even before this Jehovah's name was found on the lips of Eve in the moment when she first became a mother." [9] Sources making use of the divine name prior to the exodus era most likely originated in different areas from the source which states that only from the time of Moses was the name Yahweh made known.

The Covenant (vv. 4-5). The promise of a land and its fulfilment summarize the total complex found in Genesis-Joshua. The covenant itself was an old promise, and the only new element in the present passage is the manner in which the covenant's fulfilment was related to the exodus experience.

The Lord's Commitment (vv. 6-8). A commitment as old as the covenant with Abraham received new impetus and power in the assertion that the Lord would lead Israel out of Egypt. An examination of those verbs in which Yahweh is subject and those in which Israel is subject should be helpful.

Seven verbs graphically portrayed what the Lord was about to do for Israel.

First, *I will bring you out from under the burdens of the Egyptians.* The pronoun is emphatic: "And I, I will." The writer underscored the centrality of the Lord's relationship to Israel's deliverance. It was

---

[7] It is interesting that within the Pentateuch the Septuagint translators used a personal expression such as "my God" *"ho theos mou"* or "your God" *"ho theos sou"* to translate *'el shadday* (cf. Gen. 17:1; 28:3; 35:11; 48:3; Ex. 6:3, *theos ōn autōn*).

[8] Edmond Jacob, *Theology of the Old Testament*, trans. Arthur W. Heathcote and Philip J. Allcock (New York: Harper, 1958), p. 52. (Italics are mine.)

[9] *The Growth of the Old Testament*, p. 21.

the Lord who "caused her to go forth."

Second, *I will deliver you* (v. 6). Deliver (*natsal*) is used of delivering prey from the mouth of animals (1 Sam. 17:35; Amos 3:12), also to rescue or recover cities (Judg. 11:26) or wives and property (1 Sam. 30:8,18,22). But its most frequent usage is deliverance from enemies and trouble (cf. 1 Sam. 12:21; Isa. 50:2; Ex. 18:8).

Third, *redeem* (*ga'al*) originally meant to act as kinsman, or do the part of the next of kin. This involved both taking a kinsman's widow (cf. Ruth 2:20; 3:13), redeeming from bondage (Lev. 25:48–49), redeeming a field (Lev. 25:26,33), and fulfilling the role of "avenger of blood" in which case a man's nearest kinsman was obliged to take the life of the deceased person's slayer (cf. Num. 35:19; Deut. 19:6; 2 Sam. 14:11). Thus, the Lord's role as redeemer was parallel to that of a kinsman who set right any wrongs against his relative, or in other ways acted on behalf of his relative. In one sense the Lord is a "near kinsman" committed by the covenant relationship to act on behalf of his "kinsman."

The fourth and fifth phrases, *I will take you for my people* and *I will be your God,* should be understood in the context of the covenant relationship. The phrase "I will be their God, and they shall be my people" is a common covenant expression (cf. Jer. 31:33. Hos. 2:23). The last two phrases are related to the possession of the land promised in the covenant: *I will bring you into the land* and *I will give it to you.* The phrase *which I swore to give* is interesting. The text reads "which I lifted my hand to give" and is the picture of the Lord, lifting his hand as in taking an oath; hence, "I swore."

The action of the Lord falls into three categories: (1) his redemptive activity—bring out, deliver, and redeem; (2) the covenant relationship; and (3) the promise to give to the people a land *for a possession.*

The Response of a Reluctant People (v.

9). The present passage is either a parallel or a supplement to the rejection motif (cf. 5:15 ff.). It seems best to accept it as a parallel by the priestly writer. It may properly be viewed as giving new insight into a motif previously described in the account of the action taken by the Hebrew foremen.

The Hebrew phrase translated *broken spirit* is *miqqotser ruach,* or "on account of their shortness of spirit." The phrase is normally used of reaching the limit of patience or endurance (Judg. 10:16; Mic. 2:7); or utter discouragement (Job 21:4; Judg. 16:16). It is the opposite of the Hebrew word *'arakh,* "long" of spirit, i.e., patient. The word for spirit (*ruach*), when used of the spirit within man, is often used to describe the emotions of courage, anger, impatience or patience, and general disposition. This rests on the basic assumption that *ruach* involves the concept of "vital power," for the spirit is the energizing force and without it one is languid and lifeless (cf. 1 Kings 10:5; 21:5). To be "short of *ruach*" is to be short of "vital power." The cruel oppression which Israel suffered had "shortened her vital energy" to the end that she had become impatient, she had reached the limits of her endurance. The phrase is a graphic portrayal of the futility produced through oppression.

2. New Challenges for Old Loyalties (6:10–13)

10 And the LORD said to Moses, 11 "Go in, tell Pharaoh king of Egypt to let the people of Israel go out of his land." 12 But Moses said to the LORD, "Behold, the people of Israel have not listened to me; how then shall Pharaoh listen to me, who am a man of uncircumcised lips?" 13 But the LORD spoke to Moses and Aaron, and gave them a charge to the people of Israel and to Pharaoh king of Egypt to bring the people of Israel out of the land of Egypt.

The present passage (including 6:28—7:13) is apparently the priestly account of Moses' appearance before Pharaoh. As such it is parallel and complementary to the earlier appearance described in chapters 4 and 5, rather than the record of a different appearance at a time subsequent to the initial repudiation (5:1 ff.). Either Moses appeared before Pharaoh on two occasions (5:1 ff. and 6:28 ff.), or the two appearances are parallel accounts of a single appearance before Pharaoh.

Moses was challenged to proclaim faithfully the Lord's will and word despite circumstances, to combat the open opposition of Pharaoh, to counteract the indifference of the Hebrews, and to demonstrate personal obedience to the will of God despite obstacles and hindrances encountered in the process.

Moses' objection to the Lord's proposal was twofold. First, if his own people had not listened to him, how could anyone expect Pharaoh to listen (v. 12)? If the people of God will not respond to God's word, how can others be expected to do so? Second, Moses claimed to be a *man of uncircumcised lips* (v. 12). The word *uncircumcised* (*'arel*) is an adjective which literally means having a foreskin. It is used of a person who is literally uncircumcised (12:48; Judg. 14:3), but also of character (Jer. 9:25), and as a figurative description of the incapacity to speak (vv. 12,30). Driver suggests that the meaning here involves lips that are closed in, which are not easily opened; closed quite like one who is uncircumcised. He also suggests that uncircumcised of heart (Jer. 9:26; Ezek. 44:7,9) means a heart that is closed as one who is uncircumcised, and the ear is metaphorically in the same condition, and thus hears imperfectly (cf. Jer. 6:10, "their ears are closed," RSV; "their ears are uncircumcised," Heb.). Thus, the present reference to *uncircumcised lips* is best understood against the background of the literal meaning of uncircumcised as being "closed." (Cf. Driver, pp. 45 f.)

Standing as a sequel to the repudiation by Pharaoh (cf. 5:1 ff.), the present directive to Moses concerning his appearance before Pharaoh had the effect of calling Moses back to a task that he may have been tempted to abandon (cf. 5:22 f.). Al-ready rebuffed and repudiated (5:1 ff., JE), Moses was challenged to continue his struggle.

3. New People from Old Tribes (6:14–27)

14 These are the heads of their fathers' houses: the sons of Reuben, the first-born of Israel: Hanoch, Pallu, Hezron, and Carmi; these are the families of Reuben. 15 The sons of Simeon: Jemuel, Jamin, Ohad, Jachin, Zohar, and Shaul, the son of a Canaanite woman; these are the families of Simeon. 16 These are the names of the sons of Levi according to their generations: Gershon, Kohath, and Merari, the years of the life of Levi being a hundred and thirty-seven years. 17 The sons of Gershon: Libni and Shimei, by their families. 18 The sons of Kohath: Amram, Izhar, Hebron, and Uzziel, the years of the life of Kohath being a hundred and thirty-three years. 19 The sons of Merari: Mahli and Mushi. These are the families of the Levites according to their generations. 20 Amram took to wife Jochebed his father's sister and she bore him Aaron and Moses, the years of the life of Amram being one hundred and thirty-seven years. 21 The sons of Izhar: Korah, Nepheg, and Zichri. 22 And the sons of Uzziel: Mishael, Elzaphan, and Sithri. 23 Aaron took to wife Elisheba, the daughter of Amminadab and the sister of Nahshon; and she bore him Nadab, Abihu, Eleazar, and Ithamar. 24 The sons of Korah: Assir, Elkanah, and Abiasaph; these are the families of the Korahites. 25 Eleazar, Aaron's son, took to wife one of the daughters of Putiel; and she bore him Phinehas. These are the heads of the fathers' houses of the Levites by their families. 26 These are the Aaron and Moses to whom the LORD said: "Bring out the people of Israel from the land of Egypt by their hosts." 27 It was they who spoke to Pharaoh king of Egypt about bringing out the people of Israel from Egypt, this Moses and this Aaron.

Exodus 6:2—7:13 is the first major section of material from the priestly source since the introduction in Exodus 1:1 ff., and the first mention of Moses and Aaron by the priestly narrative. Thus, the genealogical table is primarily concerned to introduce Aaron and Moses (an introduction provided in J and E through the material extending from 1:8—6:1), but also to express the continuity between these two and those persons earlier described by the priestly writer (1:1 ff.).

Sons of Israel (Jacob): The "Old Tribes"

of the Descent (vv. 14–16). Jacob's three eldest sons by his first wife, Leah, are first to be cited by the narrator, thus establishing continuity with the individuals involved in the descent into Egypt (cf. 1:1 ff.). It is significant that the narrator deliberately connects Aaron and Moses with the fourth generation from Levi; one of the arguments adduced by those who maintain a short period of time for the sojourn in Egypt.

Leaders for the "New People" of the Exodus (vv. 17–27). The writer's main purpose was to establish the relationship of the new leaders, Aaron and Moses, to the genealogical structure of the Hebrews. Although both Aaron and Moses were cited, Aaron was predominant for the compiler of the genealogy.

What were the purposes of the writer in establishing the genealogical table for Aaron and Moses? First, the writer reflects a concern for Aaron which is best explained against the writer's priestly background. A comparison of the genealogical table clearly reflects his primary purpose, to come as immediately as possible to the descendants of Levi, Kohath, and Amram. Moses is somewhat an aside, for the genealogy runs Levi, Kohath, Amram, Aaron, Eleazer, Phinehas. Although this may reflect no more than the superior age of Aaron, especially does the fact that the writer continues with Aaron's descendants indicate that his primary concern is with Aaron, the father of Israelite priesthood.

Second, the writer sought to establish the credentials of Moses and Aaron for all generations by firmly establishing their organic relationship to the family tree of the Hebrews.

Third, the narrator genealogically related the new leaders for the "new people of God," those coming out of Egypt, with the "old people of God" who were involved in the descent. This genealogical relationship between those who led Israel out of Egypt and the Hebrews who were in the descent has given rise to the thematic title: "new people from old tribes."

4. New Responsibilities for Old Servants (6:28—7:13)

The experience related in this context is either a second appearance of Moses before Pharaoh, or a parallel account of a single appearance. More than likely it parallels the visit earlier described (5:1 ff.). Within the present text it was placed as a sequel to the earlier experience, however, and as such portrayed the manner in which Moses and Aaron, already having served the Lord before the people and Pharaoh (4:27—5:23), were given the added or new responsibility of going again before Pharaoh.

(1) The Renewed Commission of Moses and Pharaoh's Response (6:28—7:7)

28 On the day when the Lord spoke to Moses in the land of Egypt, 29 the Lord said to Moses, "I am the Lord; tell Pharaoh king of Egypt all that I say to you." 30 But Moses said to the Lord, "Behold, I am of uncircumcised lips; how then shall Pharaoh listen to me?" 1 And the Lord said to Moses, "See, I make you as God to Pharaoh; and Aaron your brother shall be your prophet. 2 You shall speak all that I command you; and Aaron your brother shall tell Pharaoh to let the people of Israel go out of his land. 3 But I will harden Pharaoh's heart, and though I multiply my signs and wonders in the land of Egypt, 4 Pharaoh will not listen to you; then I will lay my hand upon Egypt and bring forth my hosts, my people the sons of Israel, out of the land of Egypt by great acts of judgment. 5 And the Egyptians shall know that I am the Lord, when I stretch forth my hand upon Egypt and bring out the people of Israel from among them." 6 And Moses and Aaron did so; they did as the Lord commanded them. 7 Now Moses was eighty years old, and Aaron eighty-three years old, when they spoke to Pharaoh.

The genealogical table has been inserted in such manner as to break the continuity between 6:10 f. and 6:28 ff. Consequently, there is an overlap between the two passages, especially with regard to the command to Moses (6:10,28), and Moses' protest that he is a man of *uncircumcised lips* (6:12,30). The commission is essentially the same: Moses is to appear before Pharaoh and convey to him all that the Lord has spoken concerning the exodus.

The giving of Aaron as a spokesman in 6:28 seems clearly to parallel the earlier event in Exodus 4:14 ff. There is, however, one distinct and interesting difference. Earlier, the Lord indicated, "He [Aaron] shall be a mouth for you, and you shall be to him as God" (4:16, JE). Within the present context the priestly narrator has stated the relationship in such manner that Moses is not God to Aaron, but to Pharaoh. The relationship described in chapter 7 doubtless reflects the veneration of Aaron within the priestly circle. In the earlier source Moses is as God to Aaron (4:16); later this is ameliorated and Moses is *God to Pharaoh* (v. 1). The continuing significance of Moses is clarified, however, in the emphatic use of the pronoun: And you, *you shall speak . . . and Aaron your brother shall tell Pharaoh* (v. 2).

Throughout the book of Exodus three different words are used a total of 19 times when it is said that the Lord would "harden" Pharaoh's heart, or the heart of the people. English translations normally do not clarify this distinction. The present word, *qashah*, appears only once (v. 3). The word means to be hard, severe, or fierce. It is often used of a "stiffened neck" in the sense of obstinancy (cf. 2 Kings 17:14; Jer. 7:26) or of stubbornness (Job 9:4). Psalm 95:8 is a clear illustration of the present meaning: "Harden not your hearts, as at Meribah, as on the day at Massah in the wilderness."

The word most often used of hardening the heart of Pharaoh or the Egyptians is *chazaq*, "to be or grow firm, strong, strengthen." It occurs 12 times—11 referring to Pharaoh and 1 to the Egyptians.[10] Eight of the occurrences are in the priestly source (P) and four in the material from the northern source (E). The southern source (J) never uses *chazaq*. In the intensive stem the word means to make strong physically, to strengthen one's hands, to make firm, or, to make rigid, hard, in the sense

10 Cf. harden, 4:21; 14:4; 14:17; hardened, 7:13; 7:22; 8:19; 9:12; 9:35; 10:20; 10:27; 11:10; 14:17; all making use of some form of the root word *chazaq*.

of perverse, obstinate. Jeremiah used the phrase, "They have made their faces harder than rock" (5:3).

There is a third word, *kabhedh*, used six times, which is translated harden or hardened (cf. 7:14; 8:15,32; 9:7,34; 10:1). It appears only in the material originating in the Southern Kingdom (J) and means to be heavy, weighty, burdensome, honoured. In the causative stem (used consistently in Exodus) it means to make heavy, as a yoke (1 Kings 12:10,14). It also means to make dull, unresponsive, and it is this usage which is implied in the Exodus passages (cf. Isa. 6:10; Zech. 7:11). The phrase "slow of speech and of tongue" (Ex. 4:10) uses the same verb; "heavy of lips and heavy of tongue." Thus, "heavy" (*kabhedh*) may connote an ineffective or unresponsive organ, whether of speech as in the case of Moses, or of heart (motivation) as in the case of Pharaoh.

Heart was the center of volitional decisions in Old Testament thought, not the center of the emotions. Thus, regardless of the verb used to describe the action, the result was essentially the same; Pharaoh's center of volitional decisions was *hardened* (*qashah*), made strong, i.e., stubborn (*chazaq*), or heavy (*kabhedh*).

In this regard it is significant to notice that while in most instances it is stated that the Lord hardened the heart of Pharaoh (cf. 4:21; 7:3), there are passages which state that "Pharaoh hardened his heart" (cf. 8:32; 8:15; 9:34; all from J material, and all use *kabhedh*). Thus within the biblical material itself there is a certain tension. Some elements (E and P) ascribed the hardening to the Lord, while other passages (J) ascribed the hardening to Pharaoh himself.

Later, the purpose of the Lord's having hardened the heart of Pharaoh was clarified; "I have hardened his heart and the heart of his servants, that I may show these signs of mine . . . that you may know that I am the Lord" (10:1 f.). The writer worked with two specific lines of thought to bring about a synthesis: (1) Pharaoh's stubborn attitude produced signs which testified to the lordship of Yahweh; and (2) there was no concept of secondary causes in early Israel, the Lord apparently being responsible for everything. Thus the writer suggests that the purpose of the Lord in hardening Pharaoh's heart was to bring about that type of situation in which the Lord's *signs and wonders* could be revealed in such manner as to testify to his lordship. The writer's action is best understood as the theological interpretation of historical events against the background of an ascription of all action, good or evil, to the sovereign will of God.

As a consequence of the plague experiences, which this conversation is intended to introduce, the Egyptians will *know*, experientially, that the one responsible is the Lord. The phrase *I am the* Lord appears as a simple formula *'ani YHWH*, yet the very simplicity conveys the conviction that the formula conveyed a depth of meaning to those who heard it which escapes those who do not know the original context of the phrase. Especially does it occur in Exodus, Second Isaiah (40—55), and the Holiness Code (Lev. 16—23). Whether it was a formula used in worship, or whatever its contextual origin, *'ani YHWH*, "I am Yahweh," carried a depth of meaning in Israel beyond what it could possibly convey to the modern reader.

When I stretch forth my hand. This probably refers to the stretching forth of the rod. Previously the phrase "I will stretch out my hand" had appeared (3:20). The phrase "stretch forth my hand" expressed the Lord's judgment throughout the history of Israel (cf. 1 Sam. 5:6 ff.; Isa. 9:12,17,21; 10:4; Jer. 6:12; 15:6), the hand being a symbol for might or power (cf. Isa. 50:2; 59:1).

(2) The Revelation of the Sign to Pharaoh (7:8-13)

8 And the Lord said to Moses and Aaron, 9 "When Pharaoh says to you, 'Prove yourselves by working a miracle,' then you shall say to Aaron, 'Take your rod and cast it down before Pharaoh, that it may become a serpent.'" 10 So Moses and Aaron went to Pharaoh and did as the Lord commanded; Aaron cast down his rod before Pharaoh and his servants, and it became a serpent. 11 Then Pharaoh summoned the wise men and the sorcerers; and they also, the magicians of Egypt, did the same by their secret arts. 12 For every man cast down his rod, and they became serpents. But Aaron's rod swallowed up their rods. 13 Still Pharaoh's heart was hardened, and he would not listen to them; as the Lord had said.

The passage illustrates the power of Yahweh over the forces of Egypt, and summarizes the entire power motif present in the plague narratives (7:14 ff.). From the beginning the reader was aware of Yahweh's triumphant power, and it only remained for that power to be recognized by the Egyptians through the medium of the plagues. Thus Exodus 7:8–13 portrays the Lord's sovereign power, a power depicted in greater detail within the plague narrative.

The demonstration of one's legitimacy through the working of a sign was evidently common to the ancient world. See the earlier feats of Joseph (Gen. 40:1 ff.), and the later works of Daniel (2:1 ff.). Both have overtones from wisdom literature.

The English "miracle" is *mopheth*—wonder, sign, portent (cf. 4:8). The significance of the *mopheth* is the fact that it points to a meaning beyond itself. For example, the children of Isaiah were described as "signs and portents in Israel from the Lord of hosts" (Isa. 8:18). Approximately one-third of the usages of *mopheth* refer to a sign or token of a future event, and roughly two-thirds refer to a wonder as a special display of God's power. Within itself the miracle consisted of the change of the rod into the serpent, but beyond itself the miracle bore testimony to the triumphant power of the Lord over Egyptian men and gods. It is this "beyondness" that should be emphasized in miracle.

The word for serpent (*tannin*) is different from the word found in 4:3 (*nachash*). The earlier word (found in the material from the Southern Kingdom) is the customary word for a serpent or snake. The word in 7:9 (*tannin*) means serpent in the sense of "dragon, sea-monster," i.e., large reptiles or sea creatures. In the context it may refer to a crocodile. Did the rod turn to a *nachash* on one occasion and to a *tannin* on another? Did different sources use distinct words for the same type experience? Or, did the priestly narrator refer to the earlier *nachash* as a *tannin* in order to heighten the wonder of the event? One of the latter two possibilities is personally more satisfying, and of the two the final is most likely. Thus, what the earlier source (J) described as a serpent, the later source (P) described as a monster serpent. The alteration positively underscores the growing significance of the event for the faith of Israel and testifies to the writer's conviction that the Lord was sovereign Lord of all the powers of the world. The writer's literary activity was in keeping with practices of the day and would have raised no questions in his own era. Again, his "heightening" of the event by using the word *tannin* rather than the less significant *nachash* is a valid evidence of the narrator's vital faith in the sovereign power of the Lord.

Whatever the precise nature of the wonder performed by Moses and Aaron, the Egyptians reduplicated it. Thus one should interpret "miracle" in verse 9 in such manner as to allow for its reduplication by the Egyptians. The event probably involved serpent-charming, a type of hypnotic trance.

But Aaron's rod swallowed up their rods. One is inclined to ask whether or not *bala'* (swallow) may have a meaning other than the literal. The word consistently means to swallow, although at times in the figurative sense of destruction. Neither do various versions indicate any disagreement with the Hebrew text. The narrator most likely intended to convey the idea that Aaron's rod (i.e., serpent or monster serpent) swallowed the Egyptian serpents. One should read this in light of literature of the period, and recognize that such statements constituted a literary device whereby the writer very cleverly pointed out the superiority of

Aaron's God over the gods of Egypt. An unduly literal reading of the text may possibly see no more than Aaron's serpent (rod) swallowing the Egyptian serpents (rods). Reading the passage against the background of ancient literary devices, one may see reflected in this the affirmation that, despite the power of the Egyptians (who reduplicated the miracle on behalf of their god(s)), the Lord of Israel was triumphant.

Part Two
Yahweh: Lord of Creation
7:14—18:27

With demonstrable power over the forces of Egpyt, sea, and wilderness Yahweh delivered a covenant-destined people from their bondage. How well did the victorious words of Miriam characterize God's total work within the exodus, "Sing to the Lord, for he has triumphed gloriously" (15:21)! The Lord is justly to be praised as one to "reign for ever and ever" (15:18). His lordship is as inclusive as it is certain. He is both Lord of history (1:1—7:14) and Lord of creation (7:14—18:27).

Contrary to Mesopotamian, Egyptian, and Canaanite world views, which saw creation inextricably bound up with the nature of the god or gods, the Hebrews saw nature as the creation of God. Thus, the danger of both pantheism, which equates God and creation, and deism, which suggests that God exists and created the world but thereafter assumed no control over it or the lives of people, was avoided through insisting upon the lordship of God over creation. In total opposition to both ancient and modern concepts of nature, the Old Testament suggests that the natural order was created, is sustained, and will someday be transformed by the Lord.

I. The Plagues as Revelations of Power and Lordship (7:14—11:10; 12:29–40)

The crises popularly described as the "ten plagues" [1] stand at the heart of the

[1] "Plague" occurs only six times in all of Exodus (cf. *Nelson's Complete Concordance of the Revised*

Lord's redemption of Israel. Both the importance of the plagues for biblical faith and the variety of modern attitudes concerning the events demand a preliminary consideration of the nature and character of the experiences.

First, although precise, explanatory details of the plagues may never be successfully delineated, a series of historical catastrophes served as a causative factor for the exodus. In this sense the plagues were firmly grounded in history, as opposed to the view that the plagues were a *de novo* creation within the worshiping community. On the other hand, transmission within the worshiping community has so overlaid the original historical nucleus that the reconstruction of precise historical details is now exceedingly difficult. In this regard general assent is given to the observation that "liturgical usage has given form and heightened theological content to the traditions, though in saying this one must beware of the temptation to assume that the cultus invented the traditions that it celebrated and interpreted." [2]

Second, the plagues are often spoken of under the broad characterization of "the miraculous." It is significant that in each instance they fell into the category of events of nature that might occur in Egypt; events affecting the Nile, disease of animal or man, death, and occurrences within the order of nature such as hail or storm. The writer of Exodus saw the divine energy expressing itself in these events and using them both to achieve the deliverance of Israel and to make God's power known in Egypt and throughout the world (7:4-5; 8:10; 14:14,18; Psalm 77:14-15).

The Egyptians themselves are said to

have duplicated the first two of the events (cf. 7:22; 8:7). Thus, the uniqueness of the plagues may well have rested primarily in their time of occurrence, their locale (often it is stated that the Hebrews did not experience the event), their intensity, and especially their theological interpretation.

Pythian Adams suggests that nature miracles may well be regarded from three perspectives.[3] The *first* he refers to as the "miracle of material coincidence." That is, within the providence of God events occurred at such a time as to meet a particular need. This alone, however, might be described by some as no more than mere chance. As H. H. Rowley incisively points out, however, the prior faith of Moses lifts the events from the realm of mere chance happenings.

"To regard this timely help as a chance coincidence offers no explanation of the return of Moses to Egypt, or the confidence he had known that Yahweh would deliver the people. . . . There was more than the chance coincidence of help in the nick of time. There was also the strange fact that this timely help vindicated the prior faith of a man who profoundly believed that he was the mouthpiece of God." [4]

The *second* element is the "miracle of spiritual coincidence." An inspired interpreter, Moses in this case, interpreted the series of events from the perspective of faith as the expression of the Lord's judgment and saving action.

Third, Adams suggests the "miracle of sacramental coincidence." That is, the event is capable of further elaboration of its spiritual and theological significance. In this regard, the exodus is important not only for its intrinsic significance but for the manner in which it conveyed theological meaning to a later time. For example, within Isaiah 40–55 the return from Exile is consistently interpreted as a "new exodus." Even the Christian community made use of the exodus motif in clarifying the Christian faith.

Standard Version Bible, p. 1489), and the events are perhaps more appropriately described, as in parts of Exodus and Israel's other literature, as signs and wonders in the sense of the marvelous works which bore testimony to God's lordship or sovereign power. Too often "plague" connotes a disease, although Webster suggests its primary meaning as anything that afflicts or troubles, and the verb as to vex; to tease; to harass; to trouble. It is the latter sense that more accurately describes the plagues of Exodus.

[2] J. L. Mihelic and G. E. Wright, "Plagues in Exodus," *The Interpreters Dictionary of the Bible* (Nashville: Abingdon, 1962), K–Q, 822.

[3] *The Call of Israel* (London: Oxford, 1934), pp. 180 f.

[4] *The Faith of Israel* (London: SCM, 1956), p. 42; cf. pp. 40–47.

Such a view of nature miracles insists that the whole of the created order, man and nature, is subject to the providence of God. The events of history are more than the scattered effects of chance happenings. They are the end result of a purposive Will working through the created order, an order subject at every point to the Lord's creative sovereignty.

The plagues are crucial to biblical faith and are appealed to in each section of the canon: Law, Prophets, and Writings. For example, they constituted an integral part of Moses' appeal to Israel (Deut. 4:34; cf. 7:19; 11:3), and Jeremiah reminded seventh-century Israel that the Lord has "shown signs and wonders in the land of Egypt" (32:20). Especially does the Psalter extol the plagues, and this in minute detail. Psalm 78 reviews the exodus events and lists seven of the ten plagues, omitting only plagues 4, 6, and 9—the events concerning the flies, boils, and darkness. Psalm 105 is the second of two psalms that deal historically with the plagues, listing eight of the ten plagues and omitting only plagues 5 and 6, the events of the cattle plague and the boils.

The plagues were consistently interpreted as signs and wonders (translated "miracles" in the RSV). They testified to the power and redemptive action of the Lord (cf. Psalm 78:42), the uniqueness of the Lord's action for his people (Deut. 4:32 ff.), an evidence of the Lord's triumph over Pharaoh and his subsequent ability to conquer other nations through Israel's victory (Deut. 7:17 ff.), or as an evidence that nothing is too hard for the Lord, not even deliverance from a national conqueror (Jer. 32:16 ff.). Thus, the plagues were more than crucial events associated with the exodus from Egypt. They were a continual wellspring for the abiding confidence of succeeding generations in the ability and power of the Lord both to redeem and to deliver.

Fourth, Egyptian views concerning divine presence and the natural world are also important for understanding the full import of the plagues.

First, with regard to the Pharaoh, in many Egyptian texts he is called "the god" or "the good god," and the Egyptians shared with many primitive peoples the belief that their ruler possessed supernatural powers. "There is no doubt that the divinity of Pharaoh was specifically conceived as a sharing of essentials with the god Horus [the great god, lord of heaven], even though the being of the deity was not exhausted by his incarnation in the living ruler of Egypt." [5] The king (Pharaoh) was the source of authority, and his immense power was such that he was deemed capable of sweeping later generations safely into the Beyond.

Second, being essentially rainless, Egypt developed a unique attitude toward the Nile River. For it was the Nile that made life possible in the midst of the wastes of sand and rock, and in the days when the Egyptian language was forming, and before the emergence of formulated theology in Egypt, the Nile River apparently had theological priority over the sun.

Third, despite the original significance of the Nile River, ultimately the sun received theological priority. The significance of the sun for Egyptian thought is reflected in the concept of Rē, the sun god, as supreme god and divine king who was represented with a disk, symbolizing the sun, as his crown. Thus, "the personification of the sun's power, the sun-god, was the supreme god and the creator-god." [6]

Fourth, characteristic of Egyptian theology was a fundamental and pervasive religious awe before all animal life. In this regard Frankfort suggests:

"It would seem that *animals as such* possessed religious significance for the Egyptians. . . . The Egyptian interpreted the nonhuman as superhuman, in particular

[5] Henri Frankfort, *Kingship and the Gods, a Study of Ancient Near Eastern Religion as the Integration of Society & Nature* (Chicago: University, 1948), p. 36. Cf. pp. 52, 54.

[6] John A. Wilson, "Egypt," in *The Intellectual Adventure of Ancient Man*, ed. Frankfort, Wilson, et al (Chicago: University, 1946), p. 35.

when he saw it in animals . . . above all in their static reality. . . . The animals never change, and in this respect especially they would appear to share—in a degree unknown to man—the fundamental nature of creation. . . . Thus animal life would appear superhuman to the Egyptian in that it shared directly, patently, in the static life of the universe. For that reason recognition of the animals' *otherness* would be, for the Egyptian, recognition of the divine." [7]

It is obvious that animals possessed an altogther unique significance for the Egyptians. In Egypt the animal as such, irrespective of its specific nature, possessed religious significance. This significance was so great that not even the mature speculation of later times dispensed with animal forms in plastic or literary images referring to the gods (cf. *ibid.*, p. 9).

These views concerning divine presence and the natural world come into focus in clarifying the conflict between Moses and Pharaoh. While it is correct that the gods of Egypt are mentioned only in Exodus 12:12 ("on all the gods of Egypt I will execute judgments: I am the LORD"), one can hardly read the plague narratives without sensing that this was far more than a struggle between two men, Moses and Pharaoh. If read against the Egyptian view of divine kingship, the unique roles of the Nile River and the sun, and the recognition of the divine in all forms of animal life, the plague narratives take on an entirely different connotation. The conflict involved the most meaningful aspects of life as expressed in Egyptian theology.

Through the plagues Yahweh struck at the heart of Egypt's theological structure. This may or may not have been deliberate. But if it was not deliberate it is a passingly strange coincidence that the plagues involved the basic theological convictions of an Egyptian living during the period of the exodus.

The plagues were grounded in the theological certainty that Yahweh, God of Is-

[7] Henri Frankfort, *Ancient Egyptian Religion* (New York: Harper, 1961), pp. 12–14. Cf. also pp. 15–29.

rael, was sovereign Lord; that history, creation, and man stood beneath his power. Whether as Lord of creation within the exodus narrative or as cosmic Lord of an expanding universe, his sovereignty over creation is a theological certainty.

1. The Pollution of the Nile: The First Plague (7:14–24)

[14] Then the LORD said to Moses, "Pharaoh's heart is hardened, he refuses to let the people go. [15] Go to Pharaoh in the morning, as he is going out to the water; wait for him by the river's brink, and take in your hand the rod which was turned into a serpent. [16] And you shall say to him, 'The LORD, the God of the Hebrews, sent me to you, saying, "Let my people go, that they may serve me in the wilderness; and behold, you have not yet obeyed." [17] Thus says the LORD, "By this you shall know that I am the LORD: behold, I will strike the water that is in the Nile with the rod that is in my hand, and it shall be turned to blood, [18] and the fish in the Nile shall die, and the Nile shall become foul, and the Egyptians will loathe to drink water from the Nile." ' " [19] And the LORD said to Moses, "Say to Aaron, 'Take your rod and stretch out your hand over the waters of Egypt, over their rivers, their canals, and their ponds, and all their pools of water, that they may become blood; and there shall be blood throughout all the land of Egypt, both in vessels of wood and in vessels of stone.' "

[20] Moses and Aaron did as the LORD commanded; in the sight of Pharaoh and in the sight of his servants, he lifted up the rod and struck the water that was in the Nile, and all the water that was in the Nile turned to blood. [21] And the fish in the Nile died; and the Nile became foul, so that the Egyptians could not drink water from the Nile; and there was blood throughout all the land of Egypt. [22] But the magicians of Egypt did the same by their secret arts; so Pharaoh's heart remained hardened, and he would not listen to them; as the LORD said. [23] Pharaoh turned and went into his house; and he did not lay even this to heart. [24] And all the Egyptians dug round about the Nile for water to drink, for they could not drink the water of the Nile.

The first plague narrative speaks with certainty concerning the providential movement of nature and history at the direction of the Lord. It affirms the reality of a purposive Will interwoven into the fabric

of history. The purpose of the plague focused in the recognition that "I am Yahweh" (the Lord). The phrase *'ani YHWH*
is pregnant with meaning and its significance could hardly be overstated.

The phrase occurs 18 times in Exodus
(6:2,6,7,8,29; 7:5,17; 8:22; 10:2; 12:12;
14:4,18; 15:26; 16:12; 20:2; 29:[twice],
beginning with the revelation of the divine
name to Moses in 6:2 ff.

Surveying the whole of O.T. usage, it is
especially pertinent that the primary usages
of the expression occurred during the period
of the Exile, at a time when the competi-
tion between Yahweh and foreign deities
somewhat paralleled the conflict with Pharaoh portrayed in Exodus.

Stauffer suggests that the I-style is firmly
established in the ancient Near East and
cities portions of Babylonian and Egyptian
liturgy. Through the centuries "this form of
self-predication became a common feature
in Near Eastern liturgies. Sometimes names
and attributes are recounted in this style,
sometimes acts, and sometimes both in alternation." [8]

The ego (I) of God is "used for God as
the Subject who can never become an object and before whom all reality, being,
happening and volition is object. This ego
of God will not tolerate any second subject,
any other God." Thus, God is always the
subject. There is no place for another subject, for all else must be object and never
subject. "I Yahweh" is always subject (*ibid.*)

This, then, is the essential meaning of
the phrase, "I am the Lord" (*'ani YHWH*),
wherever it may appear: The will of God is
unlimited and independent of any alien
influence, God always has the first and final
word.

Especially is it relevant to the confidence
expressed by Moses, that Pharaoh will
come to perceive this aspect of the Lord's
nature—Yahweh is subject, and before him
all else is object: "*'ani YHWH* [I am the

---

[8] Ethelbert Stauffer, "EGŌ," in *Theological Dictionary of the New Testament*, ed. Gerhard Kittel; trans.
Geoffrey W. Bromiley (Grand Rapids: Eerdmans,
1966), II, 343.

Lord], and there is no other, besides me
there is no God" (Isa. 45:5).

Martin Noth suggests that "there are
two different detailed descriptions of the
plague, one alongside the other. According
to one the water in the Nile, which is the
source of Egypt's water supply, is made
foul by a sudden, general death of fish
[7:18,21; J], while according to the other
[7:17,19–20,21b–22; E and P] all the
water in the waterways of Egypt is turned
to blood" (pp. 72 f.).

The word translated "blood" (*dam*) is
the common Hebrew word for blood, and
has no other meaning. Hence one faces a
series of possibilities: the water turned to
literal blood, not only in the Nile but every-
place in Egypt (cf. v. 19); blood was used
to describe the reddish color of the water;
or, the term was used in a nonliteral sense
by a later writer stressing the severity of
the event, heightening the historical event
by describing the polluting of the Nile as
"turning to blood." The reality of the event
likely rests in either the second or third
alternatives, with the third probably, although not certainly, the better option. But
many prefer a literal interpretation. Whatever one's specific conclusion, the Lord's
providence is the overarching theme of the
biblical writer. It would be tragic to emphasize the details of the narrative to the
exclusion of the broader, theological purpose.

"Blood" may describe the Nile, discolored by sediment from the south. An objection to this, however, is pertinent. If this
was an annual event, how could it constitute so great a tragedy for Egypt to cause
Pharaoh to respond to Moses' entreaty?
One might suggest that the severity of the
event may have been the deciding factor.
It is interesting to observe that during Jehoram's battle in Moab a rain in Edom
filled the dry stream-bed in Moab with
reddish water which the Moabites thought
was bloody: "And when they rose early in
the morning, and the sun shone upon the
water, the Moabites saw the water opposite them as red as blood. And they said,

'This is blood; the kings have surely fought together, and slain one another" (2 Kings 3:22 f.; cf. 16–23).

Many Old Testament scholars interpret the first plague along these lines, offering substantiating evidence for the discoloration of the Nile. Thus, according to this view, the Nile was discolored at flood time, and the water became foul. Frogs (the second plague) multiplied in the silt, followed by insects (the third and fourth plagues), which in turn produced an epidemic upon cattle and men (the fifth and sixth plagues).

There shall be blood throughout all the land . . . in vessels of wood and in vessels of stone. The word *vessels* does not appear in the Hebrew text. Consequently, Noth suggests that *wood* and *stone* refer to the sap of the trees (wood) and springs of water (stone). This has much to commend it.

Throughout the plague narratives the writer exalted the Lord of Israel through patterns of thought and literary form characteristic of the times when Exodus was written. Divine truth may come in many literary forms within the Bible. Often such literature uses figurative and symbolic language, or places priority upon theological content as opposed to the collection of specific historical details. Thus, ancient literary forms were not always intended to reflect the exactness of modern scientific literature.

Whatever the specific nature of the details, the events could be duplicated. The Egyptians could as legitimately claim credit for the catastrophe as could Aaron or Moses.

The centrality of the Nile for Egyptian life is significant for the first plague. It was the source of life, and was thought to draw its waters from the great subterranean ocean. As such it was a symbol of stability and vitality. For the Nile to succumb to the power of Yahweh reflected his absolute sovereignty. Only the fact that the Egyptians repeated the same event prevented the first plague from reflecting that Yahweh's sovereignty over Egypt was absolute.

It was the writer's intention to say, in his own unique way, that during the initial stages of the encounter neither side immediately prevailed. There is definite movement within the plague narratives, leading from the total lack of response in the first plague to Pharaoh's eventual and climactic capitulation.

2. The Plague of Frogs: The Second Plague (7:25—8:15)

25 Seven days passed after the Lord had struck the Nile.
1 Then the Lord said to Moses, "Go in to Pharaoh and say to him, 'Thus says the Lord, "Let my people go, that they may serve me. 2 But if you refuse to let them go, behold, I will plague all your country with frogs; 3 the Nile shall swarm with frogs which shall come up into your house, and into your bedchamber and on your bed, and into the houses of your servants and of your people, and into your ovens and your kneading bowls; 4 the frogs shall come up on you and on your people and on all your servants." ' " 5 And the Lord said to Moses, "Say to Aaron, 'Stretch out your hand with your rod over the rivers, over the canals, and over the pools, and cause frogs to come upon the land of Egypt!' " 6 So Aaron stretched out his hand over the waters of Egypt; and the frogs came up and covered the land of Egypt. 7 But the magicians did the same by their secret arts, and brought frogs upon the land of Egypt.
8 Then Pharaoh called Moses and Aaron, and said, "Entreat the Lord to take away the frogs from me and from my people; and I will let the people go to sacrifice to the Lord." 9 Moses said to Pharaoh, "Be pleased to command me when I am to entreat, for you and for your servants and for your people, that the frogs be destroyed from you and your houses and be left only in the Nile." 10 And he said, "Tomorrow." Moses said, "Be it as you say, that you may know that there is no one like the Lord our God. 11 The frogs shall depart from you and your houses and your servants and your people; they shall be left only in the Nile." 12 So Moses and Aaron went out from Pharaoh; and Moses cried to the Lord concerning the frogs, as he had agreed with Pharaoh. 13 And the Lord did according to the word of Moses; the frogs died out of the houses and courtyards and out of the fields. 14 And they gathered them together in heaps, and the land stank. 15 But when Pharaoh saw that there was a respite, he hardened his heart, and would not listen to them; as the Lord had said.

The frog was not characteristic of Palestine, and the word appears only in the context of the present passage (cf. Psalms 78:45; 105:30). It was, however, a common natural phenomenon in Egypt with high humidity through the overflowing of the Nile. Within Egyptian mythology the frog was the embodiment of life-giving power.

The emergence of the frogs from the Nile is consonant with a view of modern Egyptians that there is special life-giving power in the slime brought by the Nile. In fact, less than three centuries ago, during a controversy over spontaneous generation, one person suggested that if his opponent disbelieved that life came into being through mud or slime, "let him go to Egypt, and there he will find the fields swarming with mice begot of the mud of Nylus, to the great calamity of the inhabitants" (Wilson, pp. 50 f.). May not such a view, or one comparable, have been present during the time of Moses?

The most distinctive elements in the second plague rest in the timing of the event, both the general time at which it occurred and its appearance and removal in response to the action of Moses and Aaron, and the large number of frogs involved. Yahweh, it is seen, can use the natural elements within the broader purposes of his will.

Contrary to its mythological role as a life-giving power, the frog became the object of a unique pestilence. For the second time, however, the Egyptians duplicated the feat of Aaron and Moses. Thus, the writer underscored the temporary "stand off" in the contest.

The fact that the removal of the plague consisted in the limitation of the frogs to the Nile is significant. For this underscores that the unusual aspect of the plague was not the appearance of the frogs (this was common enough) but their number and their presence throughout the land. The second plague seems to have consisted of the timely appearance of an unusually large number of frogs in regions beyond the Nile, their normal habitat. Also, the death of the frogs, as opposed to the more normal return to the Nile, heightens the unusual nature of the plague.

3. The Plague of Gnats: The Third Plague (8:16–19)

16 Then the Lord said to Moses, "Say to Aaron, 'Stretch out your rod and strike the dust of the earth, that it may become gnats throughout all the land of Egypt.'" 17 And they did so; Aaron stretched out his hand with his rod, and struck the dust of the earth, and there came gnats on man and beast; all the dust of the earth became gnats throughout all the land of Egypt. 18 The magicians tried by their secret arts to bring forth gnats, but they could not. So there were gnats on man and beast. 19 And the magicians said to Pharaoh, "This is the finger of God." But Pharaoh's heart was hardened, and he would not listen to them; as the Lord had said.

The writer may have used dust as the point of beginning because particles of dust so nearly approximated the swarms of insects which plague the land. The word gnats (*ken*) appears only in the present context (cf. also Psalm 105:31) and in Isaiah 51:6 (some feel that Isaiah should be translated in a different manner from the Exodus passage). Hebrew lexicons recognize that the meaning of the word is dubious.

Translators of the King James Version rendered *ken* as "lice," while the Revised Standard Version reads "gnats." Mosquitoes are prevalent in Egypt, especially following the annual inundation of the Nile. The Septuagint translators used the Greek word *skniphes* to translate the Hebrew *ken*. Philo indicated that the *skniphes* was a small insect, "which not only pierced the skin, but also set up intolerable itching, and penetrated the ears and nostrils" (Driver, p. 65). One might well translate the word as mosquito rather than gnat.

All the dust of the earth became gnats throughout all the land. "All" should be read as a literary means of describing the intense numbers involved, not as a literal statement that each particle of dust became an insect on a one-to-one basis. Huge swarms of gnats, or other insects, appear like a cloud of dust. Hence, the descriptive phrase "all the dust of the earth."

For the first time the magicians failed. It is useless to attempt an explanation on the basis that all of the dust had been used (e.g., all of the water had been turned to blood, according to 7:20, but the magicians could reduplicate the feat, turning water to blood). Such an explanation misses the point. The intention of the writer is to suggest that the magicians tried to reduplicate the event but could not do so. Why they could not, the reader is not told; nor does he need to be. The biblical writer had little concern to mention every element of cause and effect. Rather, it was his purpose through this literary device to say that at last the power of the magicians had been surpassed by the representative(s) of Yahweh. The narrative exists in the realm of theological affirmation, not in that of scientific, descriptive detail. The magicians failed, according to biblical thought, not because all dust was gone, but because Yahweh was superior to the gods of Egypt.

This is the finger of God. This expression affirms that the third plague was directly related to the action and purposes of God. It was a divine action (the same phrase, although with a different application, is found in 31:18; Deut. 9:10; Luke 11:20; and, in the plural, in Psalm 8:3). Despite this recognition by the magicians, Pharaoh's *heart was hardened, and he would not listen.*

4. The Plague of Flies: The Fourth Plague (8:20-32)

20 Then the LORD said to Moses, "Rise up early in the morning and wait for Pharaoh, as he goes out to the water, and say to him, 'Thus says the LORD, "Let my people go, that they may serve me. 21 Else, if you will not let my people go, behold, I will send swarms of flies on you and your servants and your people, and into your houses; and the houses of the Egyptians shall be filled with swarms of flies, and also the ground on which they stand. 22 But on that day I will set apart the land of Goshen, where my people dwell, so that no swarms of flies shall be there; that you may know that I

am the LORD in the midst of the earth. 23 Thus I will put a division between my people and your people. By tomorrow shall this sign be." ' " 24 And the LORD did so; there came great swarms of flies into the house of Pharaoh and into his servants' houses, and in all the land of Egypt the land was ruined by reason of the flies.

25 Then Pharaoh called Moses and Aaron, and said, "Go, sacrifice to your God within the land." 26 But Moses said, "It would not be right to do so; for we shall sacrifice to the LORD our God offerings abominable to the Egyptians. If we sacrifice offerings abominable to the Egyptians before their eyes, will they not stone us? 27 We must go three days' journey into the wilderness and sacrifice to the LORD our God as he will command us." 28 So Pharaoh said, "I will let you go, to sacrifice to the LORD your God in the wilderness; only you shall not go very far away. Make entreaty for me." 29 Then Moses said, "Behold, I am going out from you and I will pray to the LORD that the swarms of flies may depart from Pharaoh, from his servants, and from his people, tomorrow; only let not Pharaoh deal falsely again by not letting the people go to sacrifice to the LORD." 30 So Moses went out from Pharaoh and prayed to the LORD. 31 And the LORD did as Moses asked, and removed the swarms of flies from Pharaoh, from his servants, and from his people; not one remained. 32 But Pharaoh hardened his heart this time also, and did not let the people go.

Some suggest that there was a direct, causal relationship between each of the plagues. Finegan, for example, indicates that the pollution of the Nile killed great numbers of fish (cf. Ex. 7:21), which in turn drove the frogs ashore. The masses of dead fish were points of origination for the spread of *Bacillus anthracis* (anthrax), which is carried by insects. The insects, especially the flies of the fourth plague, spread the disease from the dead frogs, causing the plague of cattle and the boils of plagues 5 and 6 (Finegan, pp. 50 ff).

Flies is properly omitted in the King James Version, which translates 'arob as "swarms." The Hebrew word appears a total of nine times, all in contexts related to the plague (cf. 8:21-31; Psalm 78:45; 150:31). The word probably means a swarm, although it may mean a gadfly. Despite the more literal meaning of 'arob as "swarm," there is general agreement that the plague consisted of stinging flies coming in a swarm. Driver suggests that "flies are a common pest in Egypt; swarms are often brought up by the south wind, settling everywhere, filling the houses, irritating men and animals, and often carrying with them the germs of contagious diseases, especially ophthalmia, diphtheria, and (one kind) malignant pustules" (p. 66).

The fact that one half of the plagues were restricted to the Egyptians intensifies the element of wonder in the events. Whatever the explanation for this distinction (Finegan suggests that the flies did not reach the northern area of Goshen, thereby exempting the Israelites from those plagues which may have been associated with the flies), its purpose in the present narrative is to underscore the absolute sovereignty of God. Through natural phenomena Yahweh brings judgment upon his enemies, and the distinction between the two geographical areas is itself a potent "sign" of his sovereignty.

In response to Moses' threat, *great swarms of flies* filled the land. The word *great* (grievous, AV) is based upon the word *kabedh*, rather than the normal word for great (*gadhol*). The word means heavy, something oppressive or burdensome, such as a yoke (1 Kings 12:4,11), famine (Gen. 12:10), or mourning (Gen. 50:11). It is used of a massive, abundant, or numerous people (Num. 20:20), or army (2 Kings 6:14; 18:17). Within Exodus it describes very numerous cattle (12:38), oppressive hail (9:18–24), murrain (9:3), and locusts (10:14). Its purpose is to stress intensity or severity.

Because of the flies *the land was ruined.* "Ruined" is preferable to "corrupted" (KJV), although *shachath* may mean to corrupt or pervert (cf. Gen. 6:12; Prov. 6:32; Ezek. 28:17—these cases refer to moral corruption or the corruption of wisdom). When physical objects are the subject (or object), the primary sense of the word is to destroy: as a vineyard (Jer. 12:10), a city (Gen. 12:10), a temple

(Lam. 2:6), or a crop (Judg. 6:4; Mal. 3:11). Because of their effect upon both man and beast, and the disruption of life generally, the flies destroyed or *ruined* Egypt.

Pharaoh gave permission for the departure from the land, but made two qualifications: they were not to go *far away,* and they (the verb is plural) were to *make entreaty* (pray, or make supplication, 'athar) for Pharaoh. Pharaoh's response marked a significant advance in the conflict and demonstrates the artful manner in which the writer developed a state of tension leading to a fitting climax in the entire release motif.

5. The Pestilence upon the Cattle: The Fifth Plague (9:17)

[1] Then the LORD said to Moses, "Go in to Pharaoh, and say to him, 'Thus says the LORD, the God of the Hebrews, "Let my people go, that they may serve me. [2] For if you refuse to let them go and still hold them, [3] behold, the hand of the LORD will fall with a very severe plague upon your cattle which are in the field, the horses, the asses, the camels, the herds, and the flocks. [4] But the LORD will make a distinction between the cattle of Israel and the cattle of Egypt, so that nothing shall die of all that belongs to the people of Israel." ' " [5] And the LORD set a time, saying, "Tomorrow the LORD will do this thing in the land." [6] And on the morrow the LORD did this thing; all the cattle of the Egyptians died, but of the cattle of the people of Israel not one died. [7] And Pharaoh sent, and behold, not one of the cattle of the Israelites was dead. But the heart of Pharaoh was hardened, and he did not let the people go.

The destruction of Egyptian property marks an advance upon the themes of previous plagues. Cattle plagues were common in Egypt, and not only would such a pestilence have destroyed Egyptian property necessary for life but the sanctity of animals within Egyptian theology and the powerlessness of the Pharaoh to intervene combined to heighten the effect of the plague upon the Egyptians.

"Plague" (*deber*) is used of a plague or pestilence in general (cf. 5:3; 9:15; Lev. 26:25; 2 Sam. 24:13,15; Amos 4:10), or on two occasions of a cattle-plague (v.3; Psalm

78:48), often described as "murrain," a pestilence among cattle (from the Latin *mori*, to die). There seems to be no basis on which one can identify the pestilence, whether anthrax, as some claim, or another disease. All that one can assume with certainty is that the fifth plague describes a possibly infectious but definitely fatal disease of cattle.

The distinction between the cattle of the Egyptians and those of the Hebrews heightens the element of wonder in the plague. Perhaps there were natural explanations of the distinction,[9] but the purpose of the writer is clear. It was the power of God that was ultimately responsible for the distinction between the Egyptians and the Hebrews. When one considers that the Hebrews made no distinction between natural phenomena and the action of God, the possibility that the distinction was produced by natural phenomena is consonant with the biblical writer's purpose.

The fifth plague ended in apparent defeat for the Hebrews. However, in the process, the writer artfully injected the motif of distinction between the Egyptians and the Hebrews to a greater degree than previously. Not only were Egyptian cattle of all various domestic types killed, examination proved that cattle belonging to the Hebrews (and thus in another geographical district) were spared. God not only judged Pharaoh and the gods of Egypt but spared his own people in the process.

6. The Plague of Boils upon Man and Beast: The Sixth Plague (9:8–12)

8 And the LORD said to Moses and Aaron, "Take handfuls of ashes from the kiln, and let Moses throw them toward heaven in the sight of Pharaoh. 9 And it shall become fine dust over all the land of Egypt, and become boils breaking out in sores on man and beast throughout all the land of Egypt." 10 So they took ashes from the kiln, and stood before Pharaoh, and Moses threw them toward

9 Some suggest that the disease was spread from the decomposing frogs to the cattle by the flies of the fourth plague, and the wind blowing from the sea spared Goshen. It is significant that the Hebrews were geographically separated from the Egyptians.

heaven, and it became boils breaking out in sores on man and beast. 11 And the magicians could not stand before Moses because of the boils, for the boils were upon the magicians and upon all the Egyptians. 12 But the LORD hardened the heart of Pharaoh, and he did not listen to them; as the LORD had spoken to Moses.

Take handfuls of ashes . . . and let Moses throw them. The action closely approximates prophetic symbolic action. For example, Ahaijah tore his garment into twelve pieces, depicting the rending of Solomon's kingdom (1 Sam. 15:27–28); Jeremiah's yoke symbolized the bondage to Babylon (27:2–7); Isaiah clothed himself in a captive's garb as a sign of Egypt's captivity by Assyria (Isa. 20:2 ff.). The concept of symbolic action rests on the borderland of sympathetic magic; the belief that through the action of a holy man historical events akin to the actions of the person could be set in motion. These mimetic actions both indicated the future events and effectuated their coming.[10]

The *fine dust* is to become *boils breaking out in sores*. The word for "boil" (*sheᵉchin*), Latin *ulcus*, appears 13 times in the Old Testament. It may occur on man (2 Kings 20:7; Isa. 38:21; Job 2:7); it is possibly leprous (Lev. 13:18–20,23); and in Egypt it appears on both man and beast (vv. 9–11). The contextual usage of the word in Deuteronomy is suggestive concerning the nature of the sixth plague; "The Lord will smite you with the *boils* in Egypt, and with the ulcers and the scurvy and the itch, of which you cannot be healed" (28:27); "The Lord will smite you on the knees and on the legs with grievous *boils* of which you cannot be healed, from the sole of your foot to the crown of your head" (28:35).

Sores, 'abaᵉbuᶜoth, appears only three times, all in the present context (vv. 9–10). The word means blisters, boils, and the Latin counterpart is *pustulae*. Webster defines a pustule as a blister or pimple and suggests that the malignant pustule is char-

10 Cf. V. H. Kooy, "Symbol, Symbolism," in IDB, IV, 474.

acteristic of anthrax. However, one should be cautious in concluding from this that the disease was anthrax, although it may well have been.

The terminology used to describe the ailment identified with the sixth plague suggests a skin eruption of violent nature. If it was not leprous or malignant, it was equally to be feared, and in all probability was deadly.

The malady struck both man ('adam, the generic word for man) and beast. The fact that the previous plague narrative had described the death of all domestic cattle was no problem in either plague narratives six or seven. The failure to reckon with such minute historical details illustrates the primary concern of the writer for the overall theological contribution of the narratives. To major on this apparent inconsistency is to miss the writer's intended purpose.

Not only were the representatives of Pharaoh unable to duplicate the deeds of Moses, Yahweh's ambassador, they were themselves smitten. The writer thus suggested in graphic terms the unlimited power of Yahweh.

The problem with regard to the Lord's action in hardening Pharaoh's heart has often been resolved by pointing out that the Hebrews did not deal with secondary causes. All that transpired ultimately was traceable to God. This is correct, and actions not clearly identifiable with human agency could be ascribed to the Lord (cf. 21:12 f.). Also, actions earlier ascribed to the Lord might be attributed to another origin in later literature. For example, 2 Samuel ascribes the census to the Lord (24:1); but the parallel account in 1 Chronicles, written much later, states that "Satan stood up against Israel, and incited David" (21:1). Also, any direct action which the Lord may have taken was consonant with the character of Pharaoh and operated within the framework of Pharaoh's freedom.

While the above considerations are correct, they tend to obscure the writer's purpose. In suggesting that the Lord hardened Pharaoh's heart the writer expressed his conviction that Yahweh was sovereign Lord. To "psychologize" the statement away is to miss the point. To be sure, fuller understanding of the relationship between the activity of God and human personality now better understood does help one to appreciate how an ancient writer could conceive of the Lord's hardening the heart of an Egyptian pharaoh, even against his will, should the necessity demand. But one should not allow later, scientific understanding to overshadow the writer's theological conviction that Yahweh, Lord of Israel, was also sovereign Lord, even to the point of being directly responsible for Pharaoh's stubbornness.

Walther Eichrodt has clarified the relationship of providence and freedom in Old Testament theology:

"It is not simply that God allows a man to think thus and not otherwise; he is himself also at work within these acts of personal freedom. He causes Absalom to reject the good counsel of Ahitophel, in order to bring evil upon him; [2 Sam. 17.14] he inspires Rehoboam to reject the petitions of the people; [1 Kings 12.15] . . . he hardens the heart of Pharaoh [Ex. 4.21; 7.3; 10.1,27; 14.4,8], of Sihon [Deut. 2.30], and also of the Canaanites as a whole [Josh. 11.20]. . . .

"One will never do justice to the profound grasp of the reality of God which is evinced in these statements by trying to explain them in terms of God's permissive will. This theological dilution both fails in what it sets out to achieve and at the same time stands in danger of making an everyday commonplace out of a distinctive historical phenomenon. In the cases mentioned what is involved is a real act of God, in whose hands men are as clay in the hand of the potter." [11]

Remarkably, this tension between freedom and providence in the Old Testament never led to determinism, depriving man of

[11] *Theology of the Old Testament,* tr. J. A. Baker (Philadelphia: Westminster, 1967), II, 178 (italics are mine); cf. pp. 151–85.

responsibility for his action.

It remains to be said, however, that regardless of either later biblical and theological insight concerning man's freedom and God's action, or clearer psychological understanding of human personality, one should firmly maintain the theological conviction of the writer in stating that the Lord hardened Pharaoh's heart. One should read such an assertion from the historical and theological perspective of the age in which it was written, and not permit more elevated concepts of human personality and divine providence to cancel out the firm assurance of the original writer that the Lord's sovereignty was such that he hardened even the heart of Pharaoh (cf. Rom. 9:17 f.).

The passage is an excellent example of the necessity for putting aside later theological and psychological insights in order to hear what the writer said in the context of his own cultural environment. One might well answer no to the question, "Did Yahweh harden Pharaoh's heart against the king's will?" Yet, despite this answer, based on the fuller revelation of God's nature and human personality, one should allow the Bible to speak the writer's message; a message conditioned by the cultural, psychological, and theological views of his era: God's sovereignty is such that he hardens the heart of an Egyptian Pharaoh, himself a divinized king.

7. The Plague of Hail: The Seventh Plague (9:13–35)

13 Then the LORD said to Moses, "Rise up early in the morning and stand before Pharaoh, and say to him, 'Thus says the LORD, the God of the Hebrews, "Let my people go, that they may serve me. 14 For this time I will send all my plagues upon your heart, and upon your servants and your people, that you may know that there is none like me in all the earth. 15 For by now I could have put forth my hand and struck you and your people with pestilence, and you would have been cut off from the earth; 16 but for this purpose have I let you live, to show you my power, so that my name may be declared throughout all the earth. 17 You are still exalting yourself against my people, and will not let them go. 18 Behold, tomorrow about this time I will cause very heavy hail to fall, such as never has been in Egypt from the day it was founded until now. 19 Now therefore send, get your cattle and all that you have in the field into safe shelter; for the hail shall come down upon every man and beast that is in the field and is not brought home, and they shall die."'" 20 Then he who feared the word of the LORD among the servants of Pharaoh made his slaves and his cattle flee into the houses; 21 but he who did not regard the word of the LORD left his slaves and his cattle in the field.

22 And the LORD said to Moses, "Stretch forth your hand toward heaven, that there may be hail in all the land of Egypt, upon man and beast and every plant of the field, throughout the land of Egypt." 23 Then Moses stretched forth his rod toward heaven; and the LORD sent thunder and hail, and fire ran down to the earth. And the LORD rained hail upon the land of Egypt; 24 there was hail, and fire flashing continually in the midst of the hail, very heavy hail, such as had never been in all the land of Egypt since it became a nation. 25 The hail struck down everything that was in the field throughout all the land of Egypt, both man and beast; and the hail struck down every plant of the field, and shattered every tree of the field. 26 Only in the land of Goshen, where the people of Israel were, there was no hail.

27 Then Pharaoh sent, and called Moses and Aaron, and said to them, "I have sinned this time; the LORD is in the right, and I and my people are in the wrong. 28 Entreat the LORD; for there has been enough of this thunder and hail; I will let you go, and you shall stay no longer." 29 Moses said to him, "As soon as I have gone out of the city, I will stretch out my hands to the LORD; the thunder will cease, and there will be no more hail, that you may know that the earth is the LORD's. 30 But as for you and your servants, I know that you do not yet fear the LORD God." 31 (The flax and the barley were ruined, for the barley was in the ear and the flax was in bud. 32 But the wheat and the spelt were not ruined, for they are late in coming up.) 33 So Moses went out of the city from Pharaoh, and stretched out his hands to the LORD; and the thunder and the hail ceased, and the rain no longer poured upon the earth. 34 But when Pharaoh saw that the rain and the hail and the thunder had ceased, he sinned yet again, and hardened his heart, he and his servants. 35 So the heart of Pharaoh was hardened, and he did not let the people of Israel go; as the LORD had spoken through Moses.

The seventh plague narrative is the longest of the ten, three verses longer than the second longest (the eighth) and 19 verses longer than the shortest narrative (the third).

Plagues (*maggephothay*) means a blow, slaughter, plague, or pestilence. The verb (*nagap*) means to strike or smite. The noun is used but once in the book of Exodus (9:14). Graphically stated, the plague was "a blow" to Egypt. In other contexts the noun is used of a fatal blow (Ezek. 24:16), slaughter in battle (1 Sam. 4:17), and a plague or pestilence as divine judgment (1 Sam. 6:4; Num. 14:37; 25:8), and, more specifically, of wasting of flesh, eyes and tongue (Zech. 14:12,18).

The purpose of the plague, or plagues (v. 14), was the recognition of Yahweh's uniqueness; there is, literally, "an absence of a likeness to me in all the earth" (v. 14).

Hailstorms were common to Canaan, but were quite rare in Egypt. The severity of the storm, the infrequency of such phenomena in Egypt, and the timing of the hailstorm in relationship to Moses' warning combined to create Pharaoh's response. The king's attitude suggests a distinct advance upon responses made to previous plagues. He confessed that he had sinned, that the Lord was in the right, and that he and his people were in the wrong (v. 27). He also appealed to Moses to entreat the Lord for an end to the storm, and, most important, agreed to an unconditional release of the Hebrews, *I will let you go, and you shall stay no longer.*

In response to Pharaoh's entreaty, Moses said that he would stretch out his hands to the Lord. Then, the storm would come to an end. Again, this wonder or miracle is for the purpose of revelation rather than an end in itself: *that you may know that the earth is the Lord's.* Such an assertion, when read against the background of divine kingship and the Egyptian view of the natural world and the gods, suggests an element of triumph. It is not Pharaoh who controls the earth—not even the gods of Egypt. Yahweh, God of Israel, is Lord of creation (Psalm 24:1).

Flax and barley were earlier grains than wheat, and were destroyed. Since the wheat and the spelt (a grain much like, but inferior to, wheat) matured later, the ear of grain had not yet appeared. Hence, although they would have been severely beaten by the hail, the wheat and spelt crops were not destroyed.

From the stage of the various grains at the time of the hailstorm, the storm probably occurred about the middle of January. Such a date would coincide well with an equation of the first plague with the inundation of the Nile (during late summer and early autumn). On this basis, the plagues may have occupied a period approximately eight months long, extending from late summer through early spring.

8. The Plague of Locusts: The Eighth Plague (10:1–20)

¹ Then the Lord said to Moses, "Go in to Pharaoh; for I have hardened his heart and the heart of his servants, that I may show these signs of mine among them, ² and that you may tell in the hearing of your son and of your son's son how I have made sport of the Egyptians and what signs I have done among them; that you may know that I am the Lord."

³ So Moses and Aaron went in to Pharaoh, and said to him, "Thus says the Lord, the God of the Hebrews, 'How long will you refuse to humble yourself before me? Let my people go, that they may serve me. ⁴ For if you refuse to let my people go, behold, tomorrow I will bring locusts into your country, ⁵ and they shall cover the face of the land, so that no one can see the land; and they shall eat what is left to you after the hail, and they shall eat every tree of yours which grows in the field, ⁶ and they shall fill your houses, and the houses of all your servants and of all the Egyptians; as neither your fathers nor your grandfathers have seen, from the day they came on earth to this day.' " Then he turned and went out from Pharaoh.

⁷ And Pharaoh's servants said to him, "How long shall this man be a snare to us? Let the men go, that they may serve the Lord their God; do you not yet understand that Egypt is ruined?" ⁸ So Moses and Aaron were brought back to Pharaoh; and he said to them, "Go, serve the Lord your God; but who are to go?" ⁹ And Moses said, "We will go with our young and our old; we will go with our sons and daughters and with our flocks and herds, for we must hold a feast to the Lord." ¹⁰ And he said to them, "The Lord be with you, if ever I

let you and your little ones go! Look, you have some evil purpose in mind. ¹¹ No! Go, the men among you, and serve the Lord, for that is what you desire." And they were driven out from Pharaoh's presence.

¹² Then the Lord said to Moses, "Stretch out your hand over the land of Egypt for the locusts, that they may come upon the land of Egypt, and eat every plant in the land, all that the hail has left." ¹³ So Moses stretched forth his rod over the land of Egypt, and the Lord brought an east wind upon the land all that day and all that night; and when it was morning the east wind had brought the locusts. ¹⁴ And the locusts came up over all the land of Egypt, and settled on the whole country of Egypt, such a dense swarm of locusts as had never been before, nor ever shall be again. ¹⁵ For they covered the face of the whole land, so that the land was darkened, and they ate all the plants in the land and all the fruit of the trees which the hail had left; not a green thing remained, neither tree nor plant of the field, through all the land of Egypt. ¹⁶ Then Pharaoh called Moses and Aaron in haste, and said, "I have sinned against the Lord your God, and against you. ¹⁷ Now therefore, forgive my sin, I pray you, only this once, and entreat the Lord your God only to remove this death from me." ¹⁸ So he went out from Pharaoh, and entreated the Lord. ¹⁹ And the Lord turned a very strong west wind, which lifted the locusts and drove them into the Red Sea; not a single locust was left in all the country of Egypt. ²⁰ But the Lord hardened Pharaoh's heart, and he did not let the children of Israel go.

Despite the apparent failure of the plague (in the sense that Pharaoh did not release the Hebrews), there are three advances in this plague narrative: (1) Pharaoh's servants have been convinced of Yahweh's power and intercede with Pharaoh; (2) Pharaoh offers to release the Hebrew men prior to the actual occurrence of the plague; and (3) Pharaoh seeks forgiveness. Thus, the writer skilfully maintained the element of tension, while at the same time allowing some progression in the release motif.

9. The Plague of Darkness: The Ninth Plague (10:21–29)

²¹ Then the Lord said to Moses, "Stretch out your hand toward heaven that there may be darkness over the land of Egypt, a darkness to be felt." ²² So Moses stretched out his hand

toward heaven, and there was thick darkness in all the land of Egypt three days; ²³ they did not see one another, nor did any rise from his place for three days; but all the people of Israel had light where they dwelt. ²⁴ Then Pharaoh called Moses, and said, "Go, serve the Lord; your children also may go with you; only let your flocks and your herds remain behind." ²⁵ But Moses said, "You must also let us have sacrifices and burnt offerings, that we may sacrifice to the Lord our God. ²⁶ Our cattle also must go with us; not a hoof shall be left behind, for we must take of them to serve the Lord our God, and we do not know with what we must serve the Lord until we arrive there." ²⁷ But the Lord hardened Pharaoh's heart, and he would not let them go. ²⁸ Then Pharaoh said to him, "Get away from me; take heed to yourself; never see my face again; for in the day you see my face you shall die." ²⁹ Moses said, "As you say! I will not see your face again."

Darkness was a uniquely appropriate plague, for Egyptian theology gave priority to the sun god, Rē, and the Pharaoh was himself the embodiment of that god. For darkness to prevail in the struggle between Moses and Pharaoh struck at the very foundations of Egyptian theology. Thus, it was quite fitting that near the climax of the encounter between Moses and Pharaoh, darkness triumphed over the sun for the space of three days. The word translated *to be felt* may be a figurative way of describing the intensity of the darkness, an expression consonant with contemporary usage; or, a description of a sandstorm. Two evidences argue for the latter possibility. First, the occurrence of such storms during the spring is common to Egypt. The wind normally blows from the north in Egypt (from the Mediterranean Sea), but at times from off the desert to the south, producing an intense sandstorm known as Khamsin.

Second, the fact that people remained within their houses for three days suggests such a storm. It is unlikely that other phenomena would have obscured the sun for so long a time, or would have caused such seclusion. Also, the way in which Goshen was exempted may suggest such a localized storm. All things considered, it appears that the ninth plague is based upon the Khamsin.

Again, distinction was made between the Hebrews and the Egyptians (v. 23). Those acquainted with the spring sandstorms suggest that a times they travel in streaks, leaving parts of the country unscathed. Such an occurrence would well suit the ninth plague narrative.

Moses' response to Pharaoh reflects the manner in which the writer developed his theme. In each narrative Moses was portrayed as holding out for that which Pharaoh would not possibly give in the immediate context. Evidently the writer was deliberately maintaining the tension within the narratives until the climactic and final plague.

10. The Plague of Death: The Tenth Plague (11:1-10; 12:29-42)

¹ The Lord said to Moses, "Yet one plague more I will bring upon Pharaoh and upon Egypt; afterwards he will let you go hence; when he lets you go, he will drive you away completely. ² Speak now in the hearing of the people, that they ask, every man of his neighbor and every woman of her neighbor, jewelry of silver and of gold." ³ And the Lord gave the people favor in the sight of the Egyptians. Moreover, the man Moses was very great in the land of Egypt, in the sight of Pharaoh's servants and in the sight of the people.

⁴ And Moses said, "Thus says the Lord: About midnight I will go forth in the midst of Egypt; ⁵ and all the first-born in the land of Egypt shall die, from the first-born of Pharaoh who sits upon his throne, even to the first-born of the maidservant who is behind the mill; and all the first-born of the cattle. ⁶ And there shall be a great cry throughout all the land of Egypt, such as there has never been, nor ever shall be again. ⁷ But against any of the people of Israel, either man or beast, not a dog shall growl; that you may know that the Lord makes a distinction between the Egyptians and Israel. ⁸ And all these your servants shall come down to me, and bow down to me, saying, 'Get you out, and all the people who follow you.' And after that I will go out." And he went out from Pharaoh in hot anger. ⁹ Then the Lord said to Moses, "Pharaoh will not listen to you; that my wonders may be multiplied in the land of Egypt."

¹⁰ Moses and Aaron did all these wonders before Pharaoh; and the Lord hardened Pharaoh's heart, and he did not let the people of Israel go out of his land.

. . . . .

²⁹ At midnight the Lord smote all the first-born in the land of Egypt, from the first-born of Pharaoh who sat on his throne to the first-born of the captive who was in the dungeon, and all the first-born of the cattle. ³⁰ And Pharaoh rose up in the night, he, and all his servants, and all the Egyptians; and there was a great cry in Egypt, for there was not a house where one was not dead. ³¹ And he summoned Moses and Aaron by night, and said, "Rise up, go forth from among my people, both you and the people of Israel; and go, serve the Lord, as you have said. ³² Take your flocks and your herds, as you have said, and be gone; and bless me also!"

³³ And the Egyptians were urgent with the people, to send them out of the land in haste; for they said, "We are all dead men." ³⁴ So the people took their dough before it was leavened, their kneading bowls being bound up in their mantles on their shoulders. ³⁵ The people of Israel had also done as Moses told them, for they had asked of the Egyptians jewelry of silver and of gold, and clothing; ³⁶ and the Lord had given the people favor in the sight of the Egyptians, so that they let them have what they asked. Thus they despoiled the Egyptians.

³⁷ And the people of Israel journeyed from Rameses to Succoth, about six hundred thousand men on foot, besides women and children. ³⁸ A mixed multitude also went up with them, and very many cattle, both flocks and herds. ³⁹ And they baked unleavened cakes of the dough which they had brought out of Egypt, for it was not leavened, because they were thrust out of Egypt and could not tarry, neither had they prepared for themselves any provisions.

⁴⁰ The time that the people of Israel dwelt in Egypt was four hundred and thirty years. ⁴¹ And at the end of four hundred and thirty years, on that very day, all the hosts of the Lord went out from the land of Egypt. ⁴² It was a night of watching by the Lord, to bring them out of the land of Egypt; so this same night is a night of watching kept to the Lord by all the people of Israel throughout their generations.

The biblical text is printed in the order above rather than according to the RSV sequence, as explained in the following two paragraphs.

The climactic tenth plague is announced in Exodus 11:1-10, but the fulfilment of that threat appears later, in the midst of a complex literary structure (chaps. 12–13). The record of those events which fulfil the threat of death (12:29 ff.) has been surrounded by material concerning Passover (12:1 ff.), unleavened bread (12:14 ff.), and the dedication of the firstborn (13:1 ff.). What was probably at one time a relatively brief unit of material describing both the announcement and the fulfilment of the death plague has been expanded into three chapters (11—13).

Because of the complex literary structure of chapters 12–13, that section describing the fulfilment of the death threat as well as the departure from Egypt (12:29—42) will be lifted from the broader context of Exodus 12-13 and exmained together with Exodus 11:1–10.

The final plague rests upon the action of God, apart from mediation by either Moses or Aaron. By deleting Moses and Aaron from the narrative, the writer, in effect, suggested that the situation had reached such an extremity that the Lord himself intervened more directly. Plague (*nega'*, a stroke, plague, mark) appears only in this context within the book of Exodus. The noun is based upon the verb *naga'*, meaning to touch, reach, and, hence, to strike. It is used of a wound inflicted by a man on man (Deut. 17:8), as a metaphor of a disease (Gen. 12:17), and as a mark. Rather than plague, one might read, "Yet one more blow I will bring upon Pharaoh."

Speak now in the hearing of the people. The narrative reflects the same situation as described in 3:21 f., and the writer may have intended to carry forward the discussion of 3:21 f. in 11:2 ff. The purpose in asking their neighbors for valuable possessions was to profit at the expense of the Egyptians. Such action was viewed as an example of the superior "wisdom" of the Hebrews. The despoiling of the Egyptians probably was a source of delight to Israelites for centuries.

Throughout the plague narratives there occurred a continual erosion of Egyptian rigidity toward Moses (cf. the capitulation of the magicians, 8:18 f.; the acceptance of

Moses' warning, 9:20; the appeal to Pharaoh on behalf of the Hebrews, 10:7). Among both the servants of Pharaoh and the people at large there developed the recognition that Moses was the medium through whom the God of Israel brought the plagues.

About midnight I will go forth . . . and all the first-born in the land of Egypt shall die. The Lord himself was to go through the land as the angel of death (v. 4; cf. 12:23,27). Rylaarsdam suggests that there is a direct relationship between this plague and the belief that each night, according to Egyptian mythology, "the sun fought and overcame the snake, Apophis, who symbolized the hostile darkness. As a god, Pharaoh was the incarnation of the sun, and the hostile darkness was his enemy also. The force of Moses' announcement is that the night is at hand when this customary victory, on which the autonymous existence of Egypt depends, will not take place" (p. 913). Thus, the final plague struck the decisive blow at Egyptian theology. Not only had the Lord overcome the sun in the darkness of the ninth plague, but in the darkness of the night, when the sun usually triumphed over hostile powers, death would smite the firstborn of the Pharaoh at midnight.

The death of the firstborn was of unusal significance, not only because of the extent of the disaster but because the firstborn symbolically stood for the entire offspring.

In seeking to understand the actual event behind the narrative, one might hazard what is clearly to be understood as a hypothesis. In the context of the Moses-Pharaoh struggle, a fatal pestilence struck the Egyptian children and effected the release of the Hebrews. Through years of transmission within Israel the memory of the event was so shaped that the end product, the present narrative, suggests that only the firstborn were involved, and that every firstborn of both man and beast was involved (the passage seems closely related to the whole concept of the dedication of the firstborn).

As the passage stands, it is impossible to find a known malady which would properly fit all circumstances of the narrative. Perhaps one should rest content with the assurance that the providence of God used a fatal pestilence to secure the release of the Hebrews from Egypt.

And he went out from Pharaoh in hot anger. Earlier the writer indicated that Moses would not see Pharaoh again (10:29). Yet, following the address to the people (vv. 2–3), Moses is depicted as leaving Pharaoh's presence (v. 8). Also, the narrative in verses 4 ff. implies that Moses is speaking to Pharaoh (*that you* [singular] *may know; these your* [singular] *servants,* as though Pharaoh is addressed).

The most acceptable solution to the problem appears to be the rearrangement of the chapter. Literary analysis of the chapter indicates that verses 1–3 are E in origin; 4–8, J; and 9–10, P. Also, chapter 10 closes with a section which is J in origin (vv. 28–29). If one rearranges the narrative so that 11:4–8 follows 10:29, material from the same source stands consecutively. Even more important, the passage in 11:4–8, in which Pharaoh is apparently addressed, would then follow a context in which Moses and Pharaoh were engaged in conversation. The rearrangement produces a harmonious context for 11:4–8. Therefore, the following rearrangement is suggested: 10:21–29; 11:4–8; 11:1–4; 11:9–10. The strongest objection to such a rearrangement is the fact that this presupposes that the plague of death came on the night of the day on which Pharaoh repudiated Moses in the ninth plague narrative. Such a rapid response would, however, be quite in keeping with the general character of Moses' departure from Pharaoh.

Pharaoh will not listen to you; that my wonders may be multiplied. This statement is difficult. No request had been made of Pharaoh in the immediately preceding context, and at the conclusion of the last plague the narrative suggests that all possibility of reconciliation had broken down. Thus, the statement may better be treated

as an observation related to the ninth plague rather than to the tenth (such an assertion would be more consonant with the rearrangement suggested above than with the present order of the text). *That my wonders may be multiplied* apparently looks forward to the last plague, death.

Moses and Aaron did all these wonders before Pharaoh. At first glance it would appear that such a summary would more naturally follow the final plague, the tenth. However, several considerations argue for its appropriateness following the ninth plague: (1) Moses and Aaron did not work the final plague; (2) the statement that Pharaoh did not let the people of Israel go could not be applied to the tenth plague; hence the summary is appropriate following the ninth.[12]

The catastrophic death of the firstborn should be read against the earlier affirmation, ". . . if you refuse to let him go, behold, I will slay your first-born son" (4:23). Also, 12:29 is the natural conclusion to 11:8, and could be read profitably immediately after that verse.

In view of Egyptian views on divine kingship, the death of Pharaoh's firstborn was of unique significance. Not only did Pharaoh fail to protect the land and his people (as reflected in the earlier plagues), he could not protect his own firstborn from death—a death initiated, according to Exodus, by Yahweh, God of Israel. The death of the legitimate heir of a "divine king" should indicate clearly the Lord's sovereignty.

One should face realistically the moral problem raised by the assertion that the Lord smote all the firstborn. The total witness of the biblical revelation concerning the nature and character of God suggests that while God may utilize fatal epidemics, or other catastrophes in nature, he hardly

---

[12] Dennis J. McCarthy argues that the plagues really began with the rod-serpent motif (7:8–13) and concluded with the darkness (10:22 ff.) Thus, the death motif is a distinct from either the plague or the sea motif (which stands closer to 7:8–10:27· than to 11–13). Cf. "Plagues and Sea of Reeds: Exodus 5–14", JBL, LXXV, Part II, June, 1966, 137 ff.

goes about slaying children. Thus, either the nature and character of God has changed, or man's comprehension of that nature has enlarged with the fuller appropriation of God's self-revelation.

However one may answer the moral problem,[13] the biblical writer asserts that the providence of God is able to utilize a fatal epidemic; more than this, that "the Lord smote all the first-born." One should read the passage from the theological and cultural perspective of the writer in order for the passage to speak its message: Yahweh, covenant God of Israel, is sovereign Lord—smiting even the heir of a divinized pharaoh.

One should hear the words as they are written; appropriating the message, although recognizing that some presuppositions and conclusions are less than the full expression of God's nature and character. For men can speak the word of God only in the cultural-theological vocabulary and concepts which they possess.

Rather than excising great portions of the Old Testament which do not attain the Christian level, thus forming a canon within the canon, one should hear the words as they come from the writer. The total words convey a message which will be dissolved if the individual statements or words are either removed or rationalized to fit later theologies or ethical concepts.

For example, one may read Exodus

12:29 and feel deeply that in view of the fuller historical revelation of God's nature and character the passage does not describe God's direct slaughter of the Egyptian firstborn, but describes his providential use of a phenomenon produced by a series of secondary causes. He hears the words as they come from the writer, however, recognizing that he must hear the words as a first millennium B.C. person if they are to speak the intended message. He listens for a message that comes in strange sounds, perhaps contradictory to the later and fuller revelation of God; but for a message nonetheless. The words convey a message, without having to be taken individually as either a literal or a full and absolute statement on the eternal nature and character of God.

Such an approach is significant not only for Exodus 12:29 but for the entire Old Testament. It is, in fact, a legitimate hermeneutical principle; and, in the author's judgment, a most rewarding procedure in hearing the word of God in the words of men who spoke in pre-Christian cultural, ethical, and theological words.

And the people of Israel journeyed . . . about six hundred thousand men on foot, besides women and children (12:37). Based on the addition of women and a minimum number of children the total population thus described numbered approximately two million, perhaps two and a half or three. This number seems excessive to many, and its acceptance has been questioned on a number of bases.

For example, it is questionable whether Egypt could have physically kept in subjection a people with 600,000 men. These are assumed, on the basis of later statements, to have been fighting men (cf. Num. 1:45 f.). During his greatest battle, Ramses II utilized only 4 divisions, or a total of 20,000 men. According to the same organizational structure, the Hebrews could have put 120 divisions into battle, or a ratio of 30 Hebrews to each Egyptian. Also, Exodus 1:15 ff. assumes that the number of the Hebrews was such that two midwives could

---

[13] Several suggestions have been given. For example, the Hebrews did not deal with secondary causes, so that whatever happened "God did it." Or, the providence of God is able to utilize phenomena in accord with God's purposes. Again, in earlier phases of religious belief (even in the Old Testament) there is an incomplete moralization of God in prevailing theology (although this was made complete "in the fulness of time"). Yet again, some feel that the Lord directly brought about the death of non-Israelites, whether as judgment upon the people or as the means of realizing his purposes for Israel, or both; thus emphasizing the literal interpretation of the passage. Or, finally, an original historical nucleus (a fatal epidemic) was interpreted as an act of God by the faith community and transmitted among the people for generations. During this time it took on added emphases (restriction to the firstborn, etc.). Each of these cannot be correct, but each is, or has been, maintained with varying degrees of acceptance and cogency.

serve the entire community. Neither Goshen nor Sinai, according to some, could have sustained so large a group as two to two and a half million people. In addition, the problem of moving two million or more persons through the sea, or assemblying them before Sinai, or having them either encamped in a single camp, or follow the line of march described (cf. Num. 2:1–34) would have been exceedingly difficult, if not insuperable. Finally, the spies later reported that the Canaanites were so numerous that the Hebrews could not possibly expect to overcome them (Num. 13, although this could be discounted as an unusually pessimistic report), and, even including the population native to Canaan, the land during and following the conquest was characterized as sparsely settled (cf. Ex. 23:29 ff.). Yet, a population of two or three million Israelites, plus native Canaanites, should have swelled the land to tremendous proportions. Consequently, the number involved in the exodus was in all probability considerably less than six hundred thousand fighting men, "on foot" or the total of two million plus people. All these facts should be faced honestly.

Even so, the biblical text plainly states that 600,000 men were involved in the exodus (and this figure is generally corroborated by Ex. 38:26—603,550 men; Num. 1:46—603,550 men; 11:21—600,000 on foot). If this did not represent the actual number involved in the exodus, how did this number come about?

First, some presuppose a scribal error, whereby 6,000 rather than 600,000 was intended. Such a figure would give a total of approximately 25,000 persons, certainly a much more manageable population. However, the general figure of 600,000 appears in four texts (12:37; 38:26; Num. 1:46; 11:21). Therefore, an error in textual transmission is almost certainly ruled out (although one might presuppose that a scribal error crept into an older source on which the other three passages are dependent, thus leading to an error in all four passages; but this is an exceedingly ten-

uous theory). This view has little to commend it.

Second, some (following the position of W. F. Albright) suggest that the population figures in the Exodus narrative were figures from the census of David (2 Sam. 24). Thus, the figures in Exodus and Numbers would be misplaced census figures. Rather than "misplaced" one might conceive of a later writer superimposing current census figures on an earlier time; either in a mechanical manner, or following the general tendency of a later generation to conceive of former years in terms consonant with its own. The population figure of two to three million is excessively large even for the Davidic era, however, and the misplaced census view does not appear to solve the problem.

Third, the Hebrew word for thousand ('eleph) may also be translated clan or family; "Behold, my clan ['eleph] is the weakest in Manasseh, and I am the least in my family [i.e., my father's house]" (Judg. 6:15). The RSV translates the word as "thousands" in some instances where it refers to tribes or clans. ("Therefore present yourselves before the Lord by your tribes and by your thousands" 1 Sam. 10:19. But verses 20–24, speaking of the fulfilment of that command, speak only of tribes and families). Micah 5:2 (Heb. v. 1) uses the word in the sense of clan, "But you, O Bethlehem Ephrathah, . . . among the clans ['eleph] of Judah." At points the word 'eleph is translated "thousand," in the technical sense of a division comparable to a clan: "the thousands of Israel [i.e., the clans, or divisions], a thousand from each tribe, twelve thousand armed for war" (Num. 31.5; cf. also, Josh. 22:14; 1 Sam. 23:23). 'Eleph was clearly used at times in Israel as a tribal subdivision.

The census lists of Numbers 1 and 26 have been examined in detail by George Mendenhall, who concludes that the 'eleph is a subsection of a tribal group. Such subsections were for the purpose of military service during the period of the Federation, and "the census lists then consists of an enumeration of the number of units . . . into which each tribe is subdivided, and following that, the total number of men to be levied from the tribe." [14] Thus, "the number of the tribe of Simeon was fifty-nine thousand three hundred" (Num. 1:23) does not indicate a total of 59,300 fighting men from the tribe of Simeon. Rather it indicates that there were 59 military units (*'elephim*) with a total of 300 men from Simeon. Dan has sixty-two military units with a total of 700 fighting men available for military service, as opposed to 62,700 fighting men.[15]

Accepting Mendenhall's hypothesis, and based on the census lists of Numbers 1 and 26, there were, during the tribal federation prior to the monarchy, 598 military units with a total of 5,500 fighting men available for military service in all of Israel. Such a view has much to commend it.

Applied to Exodus 12:37, there were about 600 military units (*'elephim*) who went out from Egypt. Thus, the total number leaving Egypt would have been much less than the 600,000 fighting men, and a total population much less than two to two and a half million people.

While it is hazardous to speculate on a specific number as an alternate to the biblical figure, on the basis of a calculated estimate one might assume that there were 2,500 fighting men and a total population of between 12 and 25 thousand people (depending on whether one includes the Leah tribes plus Joseph, or the total twelve-tribe group later known as Israel).

A mixed multitude also went up (12:37). The writer suggests that a mixed group, most likely ethnically unrelated to the Hebrews, also left Egypt under Moses. One

can only speculate that this "mixed multitude" was composed of Egyptians who had married Hebrews (cf. Lev. 24:10; also, Moses' marriage to a non-Hebrew, Num. 12:1 f.), fragments of various ethnic groups who had migrated to Egypt just as had the Hebrews, and prisoners of war employed at forced labor. The verse is significant for understanding the relationship of the Hebrews to other ethnic groups, for rigid separation along ethnic lines was less characteristic in this period of time than is often supposed.

Israel dwelt in Egypt . . . four hundred and thirty years (12:40). This is stated as the period of the sojourn. Genesis 15:13 suggests that Abraham's descendants "will be oppressed for four hundred years." (Cf. Acts 7:6). The Genesis figure is likely a round number, to be treated as synonymous with Exodus 12:40.

On the basis of earlier references and genealogical statements, however, there were but four generations between Jacob and the Exodus. ("They shall come back here [Canaan] in the fourth generation" (Gen. 15:16). The genealogy of Exodus 1:1–13 definitely cites but four generations.[16]

This has led some to suggest that the sojourn was considerably less than 430 years. Perhaps, on the basis of four generations, the sojourn was much nearer 160 years (allowing forty years for the generation). The same problem may be the reason why the Greek translators of Exodus 12:40 suggested that the people of Israel dwelt 430 years in "Egypt *and in Canaan*" rather than simply in Egypt. Since the period from Abraham to Jacob's descent into Egypt is cited as 215 years (cf. Gen. 12:4; 21:5; 25:26; 47:9), the Septuagint translators apparently felt that the sojourn was also 215 years. All of this would suggest a period of less than 430 years for the sojourn.

It was a night of watching (12:42). This

---

[14] "The Census Lists of Numbers 1 and 26" in JBL, LXXVII, Part I, March, 1958, p. 61. Sir Flinders Petrie (1906 and 1923) sought to resolve the problem by suggesting that the *'eleph* was a "tent group."

[15] Dan later sought a place to dwell, and when its men of war were sent forth they numbered only 600 (Judg. 18:11). Although the text does not state that all of Dan's armed men went forth, the nature of the expedition would suggest that they sent their most powerful forces.

[16] Moses' mother was the sister of Kohath, grandson of Levi, thus placing Moses in the fourth generation (6:14–20).

verse is probably an editorial note by the priestly writer to explain why Passover is "a night of watching kept to the Lord by all the people of Israel throughout their generations." Such an observation by later priestly writers does not militate against either the legitimacy or the historicity of the assertion (these must be decided on other bases).

The climactic and final plague closes with the redemption of Israel. Although there is still the crossing of the sea before absolute deliverance can be realized, there is a genuine sense in which the release was effected through the plague of death. The Hebrews have been delivered, and the sea and wilderness deliverances are but further revelations of God's sovereign power.

One might speculate that the plagues at one time constituted a distinct cycle of stories which circulated in Israel, but were fixed at a particular worship center. Later these were joined with the sea motif, which may also have circulated separately from the plague narratives.

It will be helpful at this point to consider the theological significance of the plague narratives.

Six of the ten plague narratives specifically state a primary motive for the plague (7:17; 8:10,22; 9:14,29; 11:7) or in one case for the hardening of Pharaoh's heart (10:2). Only plagues three, five, six, and nine fail to indicate some theological significance related to the plagues. Within the six plague narratives there are eight explanatory, or theological, formulae.

First, the plagues were *revelatory media*. Through these mighty acts, God sought to lead men—both outside and within Israel—to know him. Each of the plagues is interpreted as a means whereby Pharaoh or the Hebrews may *know* the nature and action of Yahweh. On one occasion the word "to see" (*ra'ah*) is used concerning Pharaoh; to show you [lit., to cause you to see] my power (9:16). On two occasions the word declare or recount (*saphar*) "so that my name may be declared throughout all the earth:" (9:16), and so

"that you may *tell* . . . how I have made sport of the Egyptians and what signs I have done among them" (10:2).

Second, *the uniqueness of Yahweh is a primary feature of the theology of the plagues.* Yahweh is the only God, as unique in his living presence and power as in the reality of his existence. Pharaoh experienced in the plagues, and the Hebrews in the hardening of Pharaoh's heart, the realization that "I am Yahweh"; "By this you shall know that I am the Lord (*'ani YHWH*)" (7:17; 10:2).

Much akin to this formula, but distinct from it, is the assertion in connection with the fourth plague that "I am the Lord in the midst of the earth" (8:22). The context underscores the revelation of Yahweh as unique. He is the only subject before whom all else is object; the only real God, in the sense of vital power, in the midst of all the earth.

It is highly significant that of the 167 occurrences of the phrase *'ani YHWH* in the Old Testament, 145, or 86 percent plus occur in books, or sections of books, which are, by all canons of literary criticism, generally associated with either the period of the Exile or the actual exodus. These occurrences are: Exodus, 17; Leviticus (especially the Holiness Code, 17–26), 49; Isaiah 40—66, 15; Ezekiel, 64.[17]

The pattern of usage associates the phrase *'ani YHWH* with a non-Israelite cultural context. The manner in which the phrase characterizes the exodus and the period of the Exile (the return from which is described in Isaiah 40–45 as a "new exodus"), leads to the conclusion that the phrase *'ani YHWH* was a distinct and characteristic assertion of the uniqueness of Yahweh in the presence of other deities. The plague narratives not only speak to us of God but of a unique God, " '*ani YHWH*."

---

[17] The total frequency of occurrence is as follows: Gen., 2; Ex., 17; Lev., 49 (all but 2 in the Holiness Code, 17–26); Num., 5; Deut., 2; Judg., 1; 1 Kings, 2; Psalms, 3; Isa., 15 (all in 40–66, and concentrated in 40–55); Ezekiel, 64; Hosea, 2; Joel, 1; Zech., 1.

Third, *the incomparable nature of Yahweh is a logical implicate of the plagues.* The plague of hail was to create the awareness on the part of Pharaoh that "there is none like me in all the earth" (9:14). Such an emphasis closely parallels the message of Isaiah of the Exile as he described the God of the new exodus (40:18; 44:6–7). Yahweh, the unique God, revealed supremely through his actions in history, is beyond compare. As Miriam later praised him, "Who is like thee, O Lord, among the gods? Who is like thee, majestic in holiness, terrible in glorious deeds, doing wonders?" (15:11). Who, indeed, is like the Lord? He is incomparable.

Fourth, *although mentioned but once, the power of Yahweh is characteristic of each plague* (9:16). Pharaoh is assured that the Lord could much earlier have brought an end to his pretense to power. What then was the Lord's purpose in multiple plagues to Pharaoh, when he could have cut him off from the earth at a moment (9:15)? "For this purpose have I let you live, to show you my power." The sovereign power of Yahweh is a logical implicate of each plague.

Fifth, *the plagues were given to spread the name of Yahweh through the earth.* The name is especially used in the Old Testament as embodying the revealed character of Yahweh (cf. Amos 5:8; 9:6; Jer. 33:2), and at times it is used as a designation of God, specifically Yahweh (cf. Isa. 2:3; Gen. 4:26; Josh. 9:9; Isa. 60:9; Psalm 83:16; Deut. 10:20). In further clarifying why the Lord had brought repeated plagues against the Egyptians rather than cutting them off at once, Israel saw that it was "so that my name may be declared throughout all the earth" (9:16). The wonders of God, miracles, are not an end in themselves. They are a means whereby the name of God may be declared. What God does in wonder, he does to the end that his name may be declared; now as then.

Sixth, *the sovereignty of Yahweh, his lordship over creation, is another theological emphasis of the plagues.* The cessation of the hailstorm was designed that Pharaoh might "know that the earth is the Lord's" (9:29). It is difficult for a person living in the twentieth century to appreciate fully the degree to which the Egyptians, among others, related the natural order to some aspect of the gods. Every aspect of the plague narratives touches in one way or another upon Egyptian theology as it related to the natural order. The triumph of Yahweh in the plagues is indicative of his sovereignty over creation. The earth belongs neither to a divinized king, Pharaoh, nor to the gods of Egypt. Whether in a world dominated by concepts of primitive gods interwoven into creation, or in a modern world with theories of astrophysics and an expanding universe, the earth is the Lord's.

Seventh, *Yahweh, God of Israel, is the deliverer of his people.* When others are smitten, he delivers Israel, "that you may know that the Lord makes a distinction between the Egyptians and Israel" (11:7). One-half of the plagues are specifically said to have exempted the Hebrews (plagues 4, 5, 7, 9, and 10), and some say that the Hebrews were exempt from all of the plagues. Whether or not they escaped all of the plagues, many of the catastrophes did fall exclusively upon the Egyptians, and in the tenth plague it is specifically said that such distinction was directly related to the purposive will of God. He protects and delivers his people.

Eighth, *victory is a characteristic of the plagues.* Especially in the eighth plague Israel specified that the triumph of Yahweh was an implicate of the plague: "I have hardened his heart . . . that you may tell in the hearing of your son and of your son's son how I have made sport of the Egyptians" (10:12). As Israel interpreted the meaning of the hardening of Pharaoh's heart, she saw in this event the revelation of Yahweh's victory and power over the Egyptians, of the way in which he "made sport of the Egyptians."

When the priestly writer interpreted the

events of Passover night, he indicated that through that event the Lord would execute judgments on "all the gods of Egypt" (12:12). Thus, Israel later clearly interpreted the events of the final plague as a time of victory not only over the Pharaoh as a human king but as a time of victory over the gods of Egypt.

In summary, the plagues were theologically significant for the faith of Israel. The theology of the plague narratives assumes that they were revelatory in nature and character; that they revealed a God who was unique, incomparable, powerful, and to be known among the nations through his actions in history. He was the sovereign Lord of creation, who delivered his people in the midst of calamity and who was victorious over all powers hostile to his purposes, even the gods of Egypt. In essence, the plagues demonstrate that Yahweh, God of Israel, is Lord of creation.

II. Cultic Practices of Passover, Unleavened Bread, and Dedication of First-born (12:1—13:16)

To the account of the tenth plague there have been interwoven instructions concerning the Passover (12:1–13,21–28,43–50), unleavened bread (12:14–20; 13:3–10), and the dedication of the firstborn (13:1–2,11–16).

Suceeding generations within the worshiping community associated primary religious observances with the deliverance from Egypt, and by this means the worshiping community expressed the profound conviction that the deliverance was of supreme theological significance. Passover, unleavened bread, and the dedication of the firstborn, each in its own unique way, celebrated the exodus, both reminding worshipers of the past event and recreating the experience in the living present.

1. The Passover 12:1–13,21–28,43–50

The Passover received such unique attention within the worshiping community that the events surrounding it have all but overshadowed the plague narratives which

precede the death of the firstborn. The plague narratives are a distinct literary strain whose purpose is to serve as a setting which enshrines the Passover. In terms of priority, the worshiping community probably began with the Passover tradition and subsequently gathered around that theme the various plague traditions. Throughout the first nine plagues one has the distinct impression that the writer deliberately structured his material with the Passover as the climax. Both his attention to the necessity for a feast and the continued tension between Moses and Pharaoh concerning the release of the Hebrews sustain the suspense of the narratives.

(1) Instructions for the Passover (12:1–13)

¹ The LORD said to Moses and Aaron in the land of Egypt, ² "This month shall be for you the beginning of months; it shall be the first month of the year for you. ³ Tell all the congregation of Israel that on the tenth day of this month they shall take every man a lamb according to their fathers' houses, a lamb for a household; ⁴ and if the household is too small for a lamb, then a man and his neighbor next to his house shall take according to the number of persons; according to what each can eat you shall make your count for the lamb. ⁵ Your lamb shall be without blemish, a male a year old; you shall take it from the sheep or from the goats; ⁶ and you shall keep it until the fourteenth day of this month, when the whole assembly of the congregation of Israel shall kill their lambs in the evening. ⁷ Then they shall take some of the blood, and put it on the two doorposts and the lintel of the houses in which they eat them. ⁸ They shall eat the flesh that night, roasted; with unleavened bread and bitter herbs they shall eat it. ⁹ Do not eat any of it raw or boiled with water, but roasted, its head with its legs and its inner parts. ¹⁰ And you shall let none of it remain until the morning, anything that remains until the morning you shall burn. ¹¹ In this manner you shall eat it: your loins girded, your sandals on your feet, and your staff in your hand; and you shall eat it in haste. It is the LORD's passover. ¹² For I will pass through the land of Egypt that night, and I will smite all the first-born in the land of Egypt, both man and beast; and on all the gods of Egypt I will execute judgments: I am the LORD. ¹³ The blood shall be a sign for you, upon the houses where you are; and when I

see the blood, I will pass over you, and no plague shall fall upon you to destroy you, when I smite the land of Egypt.

The present narrative is priestly in background and appears to reflect the influence of a later era, during which the instructions for observing the Passover were specifically recorded.

These detailed instructions probably stem from as late as the Exile, although fixation in writing at the time of the exile does not militate against the antiquity of the practices.

Any discussion of the Passover should seriously consider the possibility that it was directly related to the feast which Moses wanted to celebrate, and was the basis for his encounters with Pharaoh.[18] Such a celebration may have been a pre-Yahwistic pastoral feast celebrated in the spring.

This month shall be . . . the beginning of months. The Passover was associated with the beginning of the year, during the month Abib, later called Nisan, which is comparable to the period March–April. There are evidences within the Old Testament which point to a time early in Israel when the year perhaps began in the fall (cf. Ex. 23:15; 34:22; 1 Sam. 1:21), and the celebration of New Year in the spring may have been influenced by the Exile and the fact that the Babylonian calendar began in the spring.

On the tenth day. Driver suggests that sanctity was attached to the tenth day. The Day of Atonement was on the tenth day (Lev. 23:27), and in Islam the tenth day of the twelfth month is the day of the great sacrifice associated with the Mecca pilgrimage. (Driver, p. 88).

Originally the blood was smeared upon the doorposts, indicating the domestic nature of the feast. Later, during New Testament times, the blood was manipulated upon the great altar, and the carcass returned to the family, then cooked and eaten at home. Following the final destruc-

tion of the Temple the blood could no longer be offered upon the great altar, and the ceremony lost its sacramental implications. Thus, it became a festival celebrating Israel's freedom. Rylaarsdam suggests that "it has never ceased to awaken Israel's hope for the future; this is indicated by the parting benediction at the Passover table, centuries old and still used today 'Next year in Jerusalem'" (p. 665).

The two doorposts and the lintel. In primitive times the doorposts were uniquely holy, the residence of both good and evil spirits. Arabs later placed images at the threshold to protect their dwellings, and the Old Testament may also reflect the practice: "Behind the door and the doorpost you have set up your symbol" (Isa. 57:8; the total context concerns idolatry). The command that Israel write the commandment "on the doorposts of your house" (Deut. 6:9) may reflect the sanctity of the threshold, as opposed to merely a convenient and public place.

Bitter herbs (maror) appears but five times in the Old Testament; the herbs accompanying the Passover meal (12:8; Num. 9:11); the character of other peoples, "their clusters are bitter" (Deut. 32:32); the bitterness over Jerusalem's fall (Lam. 3:15); or, the bitterness experienced by Job (13:26). The Mishnah, a deposit of Jewish religious and cultural practices in Palestine extending from the earlier half of the second century B.C. to the close of the second century A.D., suggests: "And these are the herbs by [eating] which at Passover a man fulfils his obligation: lettuce, chicory, pepperwort, snakeroot, and dandelion. He fulfils it whether they are fresh or dried, but not if they are pickled, stewed, or cooked."[19] It is exceedingly doubtful that the writer intended merely to suggest an appropriate menu of possible condiments or a salad. The bitter herbs were eaten as a reminder of Israel's

---

18 Cf. Ex. 3:18; 5:1,3,17; 7:16; 8:27 f. Or, cf. the general request that the people be allowed to "serve" the Lord, Ex. 8:1,20,29; 9:1,13; 10:3,7.

19 Pesahim 2:6, *The Mishnah,* trans. Herbert Danby (London: Oxford, 1958), p. 138. Pesahim gives extensive instructions concerning the Passover and is a helpful source for such studies.

bitter experience in Egypt—and succeeding periods of oppression.

The command to roast the animal, as well as the prohibition against boiling, may have originated in Israel's attitude toward the blood or the fat. Most likely, the command rests in reverence for the fat (cf. Lev. 3:17), since ideally, the blood had been removed at the time of slaughter and, in the case of the Passover, manipulated at the threshold.

You shall let none of it remain until morning. As in the case of sacrifices, the command was designed to prevent profanation of the sacrifice. In the event that portions of the sacrifice should be left until morning, despite the prohibition (v. 10), they were to be burned (cf. Lev. 7:15–17).

The brevity of the exodus Passover stood in contrast to the seven-day celebration later observed Pesahim later asked, "Wherein does the Passover of Egypt differ from the Passover of the generations (that followed after)? At the Passover of Egypt the lamb was . . . eaten in haste and during one night; whereas the Passover of the generations (that followed after) continued throughout seven days" (Pesahim 8:5, pp. 148–49).

I will pass through . . . when I see the blood I will pass over you. "Pass through" (*'abar*) is distinct from "pass over" (*pasach*). The festival, Passover (*pesach*), derived its name from the latter verb, meaning to "pass over" (*pasach*). Hence, the English word paschal is used of the paschal lamb, or, in Christian circles, of Easter. The verb *pasach* is used only of the Passover (12:13,23,27), the Elijah narrative ("limping, limped," 1 Kings 18:21,26); and the Lord's deliverance of Jerusalem, "he will protect and deliver it, he will spare [*pasach*] and rescue it" (Isa. 31:5). The basic meaning apparently is to "pass or spring over." The present passage states that the Lord "will pass over you." The phrase *when I smite the land of Egypt* suggests that the writer presupposed no secondary agent through which the Lord

operated. He himself smote Egypt, and as the source of destruction he passed over the Hebrews. Central to the deliverance was the use of the blood as a sign, an indication of Israel's response to the Lord.

(2) Institution of the Passover (12:21–28)

21 Then Moses called all the elders of Israel, and said to them, "Select lambs for yourselves according to your families, and kill the passover lamb. 22 Take a bunch of hyssop and dip it in the blood which is in the basin, and touch the lintel and the two doorposts with the blood which is in the basin; and none of you shall go out of the door of his house until the morning. 23 For the Lord will pass through to slay the Egyptians; and when he sees the blood on the lintel and on the two doorposts, the Lord will pass over the door, and will not allow the destroyer to enter your houses to slay you. 24 You shall observe this rite as an ordinance for you and for your sons for ever. 25 And when you come to the land which the Lord will give you, as he has promised, you shall keep this service. 26 And when your children say to you, 'What do you mean by this service?' 27 you shall say, 'It is the sacrifice of the Lord's passover, for he passed over the houses of the people of Israel in Egypt, when he slew the Egyptians but spared our houses.'" And the people bowed their heads and worshiped.

28 Then the people of Israel went and did so; as the Lord had commanded Moses and Aaron, so they did.

This passage is either parallel to or is continuous with the preceding set of instructions (12:1–13). Many modern commentators and textual students of the Old Testament suggest that the passage is southern in background (J), in contrast to the priestly background of the earlier section (P), and that it has been strongly influenced by the work of those associated with the reform of Josiah and the book of Deuteronomy (D). Although it may be described as the sequel to 12:1–13, the present passage is likely a parallel account of the institution of the Passover festival which circulated in the Southern Kingdom. It is essentially a restatement of the origin of the Passover. At several points it contributes specific details not included in the instructions given to Moses and Aaron.

The Hebrew text suggests only "kill the

passover" (*pasach*). In the RSV "lamb" is an inference. Obviously, the lamb was intended, and the present text merely illustrates the threefold manner in which "passover" (*pesach*) is used in the Old Testament.

First, passover (*pesach*) may apply to the sacrifice of the Passover, including a communion meal, and hence is a type of peace offering (cf. Deut. 16:2, 5–6; 2 Chron. 30:18). Some suggest that the special feature lay in the application of blood to homes to consecrate them (cf. similar Babylonian rite of purification).

Second, passover might apply to the animal victim, as in 12:21 (cf. 2 Chron. 30:15; 35:1,6,11; Ezra (6:20). Third, passover was applied to the festival of the Passover (cf. 34:25; Lev. 23:5; Num. 28:16; Deut. 16:1), observed on the fourteenth day of the first month (Abib), but if this was impossible then on the fourteenth day of the second month (Num. 9:10–12).

Sprinkling with blood was a common means of purification, and the cleansing power of blood in the Old Testament is reflected in C. R. North's statement that the "object of such ritual sprinkling was to neutralize infection or contagion by the person or thing sprinkled." [20] (cf. Lev. 14:7,19,51-52; Num. 19:4). In the present context sprinkling was for the purpose of warding off the plague. Perhaps the text reflects a much earlier practice in which demonic beings were warded off at crucial times in the pastoral community (perhaps at the time of spring lambing, thus involving the whole of a spring, pastoral celebration). Martin Noth suggests that these instructions were "chiefly concerned with the apotropaic [i.e., to ward off evil] smearing of the entrances to the houses with the blood of the sacrificial victims and once again added the prohibition against leaving the houses in view of the nocturnal destruction which is being wrought outside" (p. 97).

Both the lintel and the doorposts were

sacred. In primitive Near Eastern cultures the doorway was the abode of good and evil spirits. E. A. Speiser suggests that demons were "depicted both as benevolent and malevolent, often lurking at the entrance of a building to protect or threaten the occupants. He translates Genesis 4:7, "sin is the demon at the door, whose urge is toward you; yet you can be his master." [21] Such an understanding is directly related to an understanding of the smearing of the blood upon the doorway in the Passover narrative.

Hyssop was a small, bushy plant often used in purification rites. Appearing in only six Old Testament contexts, it was used to sprinkle blood (but only in Ex. 12:22), or other ritual mixtures (Num. 19:18); as an ingredient in ritual cleansing of leprosy (Lev. 14:4,6,49,51-52), or the purification of the unclean (Num. 19:6); and, on one occasion, was associated with the cleansing of sin (Psalm 51:7). It is described as a small plant that "grows out of the wall" (1 Kings 4:33).

The blood which is in the basin. The Hebrew word *saph* may mean either basin or threshold—sill. Translators assume that on 6 occasions it means basin (cf. Ex. 12:22; 2 Sam. 17:28; Zech. 12:2; 1 Kings 7:50; 2 Kings 12:13; Jer. 52:19), and on 24 occasions it means threshold (cf. Judg. 19:27; Isa. 6:4; Zeph. 2:14). Thus 80 percent of the total usages mean threshold. The earliest versions have "threshold" (LXX, *para tēn thuran*). Consequently, and in view of the fact that the Passover was originally a home festival (v 22) *saph* may refer to the threshold rather than to a basin. The animal may have been slain at the threshold. By sprinkling the blood upon the two doorposts and the lintel, the doorway was totally surrounded, insuring protection against demonic or hostile powers. [22]

The Lord will pass over the door, and

20 *The Second Isaiah* (Oxford: Clarendon, 1964), p. 235.

21 "Genesis," *The Anchor Bible* (New York: Doubleday, 1964), pp. 29, 31.

22 Driver supports this view; cf. "Old Problems Reexamined," *Zeitschrift für die Alttestamentliche Wissenschaft* 1968, II, 181: "The blood was poured on the threshold so that it could not be crossed."

will not allow the destroyer to enter your houses to slay you. The earlier instructions suggested that the Lord would "pass over you" (v. 13), whereas here he passes *over the door.* The customary interpretation of this verse affirms that the Lord passed over the household (or, the door), insuring that the plague would not enter the house (such an interpretation is in keeping with verse 13).

However, another interpretation is both possible and highly commendable. Exodus 12:23 states that the Lord will pass over (it could as well be translated "leap over") the door, doorway, or entrance. Then, he will prevent the destroyer from entering "your houses for the purpose of smiting."

Davies summarizes Trumbull as follows: "The Lord will pass over the door-opening . . . and then from within the house prevent the DESTROYER from entering TO SLAY YOU . . . the blood is not apotropaic, i.e. to ward off evil; but it identifies for God the houses of the people where he enters for the covenant meal of the Passover. *The feast is then, as it eventually became, a festival to celebrate a visiting and redeeming God.*" (p. 115. Italics are mine).

Despite the problems raised by 12:13, as well as the traditional interpretation that the Lord "passed over" Israel, the present interpretation fits well the immediate context. For the Lord passed over the door, and possibly into the house. Also, this passage describes the destroyer as though it was some one or thing other than the Lord, a destroyer whom the Lord opposes.

What do you mean by this service? The question-and-answer method of teaching was uniquely characteristic of literature associated with the reform of Josiah, commonly referred to as Deuteronomic literature (cf. Joshua through Kings) because of the priority of Deuteronomy in Josiah's reform. Often children are described as raising a question which the fathers may then answer in the light of God's revelation (cf. 13:14; Josh. 4:6,21; Deut. 6:20). Thus, the questions reflected far more than the in-

quisitive nature of a child. They were a deliberate literary device wherby the Israelite theologian interpreted significant aspects of Israel's history.

(3) Participants in the Passover Festival (12:43–50)

[43] And the LORD said to Moses and Aaron, "This is the ordinance of the passover: no foreigner shall eat of it; [44] but every slave that is bought for money may eat of it after you have circumcised him. [45] No sojourner or hired servant may eat of it. [46] In one house shall it be eaten; you shall not carry forth any of the flesh outside the house; and you shall not break a bone of it. [47] All the congregation of Israel shall keep it. [48] And when a stranger shall sojourn with you and would keep the passover to the LORD, let all his males be circumcised, then he may come near and keep it; he shall be as a native of the land. But no uncircumcised person shall eat of it. [49] There shall be one law for the native and for the stranger who sojourns among you."

[50] Thus did all the people of Israel; as the LORD commanded Moses and Aaron, so they did. [51] And on that very day the LORD brought the people of Israel out of the land of Egypt by their hosts.

The prohibition against breaking the bone may reflect the ancient belief in sympathetic action. Adolphe Lods suggests that "The original reason why it was forbidden to break the bones of the pascal lamb was perhaps the belief that if this were done, the cattle or one of the guests would break a limb during the year."[23] Probably, ancient peoples felt that to break the bone of a sacrificial animal (which in some manner summed up the whole of the flock, the part standing for the whole) would portend evil for the flock during the remainder of the year.

The priestly writer carefully delineated those who could participate in the Passover. At first glance he appears to have distinguished on the basis of the foreigner and the native Israelite. *No foreigner shall eat of it,* nor a *sojourner or hired servant.*

[23] *Israel: From Its Beginnings to the Middle of the Eighth Century,* trans. S. H. Hooke (New York: Knopf, 1953), p. 215.

"Sojourner" (*toshab*) is not the customary word used in the Old Testament (*ger* is the common word, appearing 88 times by actual count). *Toshab* is a late word used in the priestly material, and described a sojourner of a more temporary kind than the *ger*. The **hired servant** most likely described inhabitants of the land (i.e., Canaanites, etc.) who were absorbed into Israelite communities but who did not enter into the mainstream of Israel's covenant life. The three—foreigner, sojourner, and hired servant—were categories associated, but not identified, with Israel through circumcision.

Later, the writer suggested that if a stranger (*ger*, possibly a foreigner who had come to settle on a permanent basis) submitted all of his males to circumcision, and thus identified fully with Israel, he might eat of the Passover (v. 48). Also, *every slave bought for money* (and thus a permanent resident) *may eat of it after you have circumcised him.*

Thus, the distinction between those who might or might not partake of the Passover was grounded in whether or not one was fully identified with Israel through circumcision, not whether one was of "foreign" extraction. Participation was grounded on religious rather than racial or ethnic bases. The foreigner, the temporary sojourner, and the outsider employed as a hired workman, did not identify themselves with Israel. Permanent residents moving in from other areas (the *ger,* or stranger) identified fully by submitting to circumcision, as did the slave "bought for money."

The clause *There shall be one law for the native and for the stranger who sojourns among you* (v. 49) apparently refers to circumcision as a prerequisite to the Passover. Both the *native* (*'ezrach*, a native Israelite—cf. Lev. 23:42; Num. 15:13) and the *stranger* (*ger,* a newcomer with certain conceded but not inherited rights) were to be circumcised prior to participation in the Passover. The priority of circumcision is grounded in the fact that it was the single external sign of the covenant relationship.

2. The Feast of Unleavened Bread
12:14–20; 13:3–10

There are two passages which deal with the feast of unleavened bread. The first appears in the instructions given to Moses and Aaron (12:14–20, often ascribed to the priestly writer). The second appears in Moses' instructions to the people (13:3–10, characterized as J, or southern, in origin). Both passages appear in a context in which the instructions refer to future observance. There is no indication of a feast of unleavened bread during the period of the exodus. Many have concluded that the Passover was a pastoral feast as old as the exodus event but that unleavened bread was an agriculturally related feast from the period of the Canaanite occupation. The manner in which the instructions were given tends to bear this out (Passover was to be observed immediately, unleavened bread was postponed until the time when Israel was in the land).[24]

Within the present context two passages deal with the institution of the feast of unleavened bread. The first (12:14–20, P) is cast in the form of instructions given to Moses and Aaron, while the second is an account of the instructions given to the people by Moses (13:3–10, J or D).

The prohibition of leaven rested in the assumption that it was intrinsically evil, for leaven corrupted other grain. When one considers the yeast working in a loaf of bread, as well as the fermenting of grains and fruit, as in the production of wines and other beverages, it is easy to understand how ancient men saw in the leaven a mysterious, living power. Perhaps as they saw good grain corrupted by contact with fermenting grain they associated leaven with evil. The rationale of the prohibition leads one to conclude that the background for the feast was agricultural.

Later, the prohibition of leaven was associated with the speed which characterized

[24] This coincides with the Mishna's observation that the exodus Passover differed from the later Passover in that only the later Passover was for seven days duration (cf. Pesahim 9:5).

Israel's departure from Egypt (12:34 ff.). Such an explanation probably reflects the effort to provide an acceptable rationale for the inclusion into Israel's worship experience of an agricultural celebration in which leaven was prohibited.

The leaven mentioned throughout the Bible was probably a piece of fermented dough, retained from a previous batch. No other leaven than this sour dough is mentioned in either the Old Testament or the New Testament.[25]

(1) The Lord's Instructions to Moses and Aaron (12:14-20)

14 "This day shall be for you a memorial day, and you shall keep it as a feast to the LORD; throughout your generations you shall observe it as an ordinance for ever. 15 Seven days you shall eat unleavened bread; on the first day you shall put away leaven out of your houses, for if any one eats what is leavened, from the first day until the seventh day, that person shall be cut off from Israel. 16 On the first day you shall hold a holy assembly, and on the seventh day a holy assembly; no work shall be done on those days; but what every one must eat, that only may be prepared by you. 17 And you shall observe the feast of unleavened bread, for on this very day I brought your hosts out of the land of Egypt: therefore you shall observe this day, throughout your generations, as an ordinance for ever. 18 In the first month, on the fourteenth day of the month at evening, you shall eat unleavened bread, and so until the twenty-first day of the month at evening. 19 For seven days no leaven shall be found in your houses; for if any one eats what is leavened, that person shall be cut off from the congregation of Israel, whether he is a sojourner or a native of the land. 20 You shall eat nothing leavened; in all your dwellings you shall eat unleavened bread."

This day shall be for you a memorial day. Day in "memorial day" does not appear in the Hebrew text. Rejecting leaven was intended as a memorial (*zikaron*, a memorial, remembrance). Faith cannot live on memory alone, but it demands celebrations, both to keep alive the reality of the original experience and to create new vitality in the present moment of worship.

25 H. F. Beck, "Leaven," *IDB.*, III, 105.

Unleavened bread appears as the single word *matsah*, without the word for bread (*lechem*). It was normally prepared in the form of bread (*lechem*) or cakes. In addition to this specific feast, unleavened bread was also used at sacrificial meals such as the ritual peace offerings (Lev. 2:4-5), the consecration of priesthood (29:2,23), the peace offering of a Nazirite (Num. 6:15). Unleavened bread occupied a uniquely sacred role in Israel's sacral life, a role dependent upon the removal of "evil" (leaven) from the bread associated with various ceremonial acts.

Not only was unleavened bread to be eaten, but all leaven was removed from the house. Later Judaism was quite specific concerning those items which should be removed:

"These must be removed at Passover: Babylonian porridge, Median beer, Edomite vinegar, and Egyptian Barley-beer, also dyers' pulp, cooks' starch-flour, and writers' paste. R. Eliezer says: Also women's cosmetics. This is the general rule: whatsoever is made from any kind of grain must be removed at passover" (Pesahim 3:1). If as much leavened dough as "an olive's bulk" remained in the cracks of a kneading-trough, this too had to be removed (Pesahim 3:2).

The week of unleavened bread was also to be a "sabbath-week" in that no work was to be done during the seven-day period. Only the preparation of necessary food was permitted (v. 16). Through such cessation from labor during the week, worshipers acknowledged that time uniquely belonged to God. Holy assemblies both opened and closed the week.

Unleavened bread pointed to the actual exodus from Egypt (v. 17), while the Passover in a more restricted sense celebrated the deliverance from the plague of death.

(2) Moses' Instructions to the People (13: 3-10)

3 And Moses said to the people, "Remember this day, in which you came out from Egypt, out of the house of bondage, for by strength of

hand the Lord brought you out from this place; no leavened bread shall be eaten. 4 This day you are to go forth, in the month of Abib. 5 And when the Lord brings you into the land of the Canaanites, the Hittites, the Amorites, the Hivites, and the Jebusites, which he swore to your fathers to give you, a land flowing with milk and honey, you shall keep this service in this month. 6 Seven days you shall eat unleavened bread, and on the seventh day there shall be a feast to the Lord. 7 Unleavened bread shall be eaten for seven days; no leavened bread shall be seen with you, and no leaven shall be seen with you in all your territory. 8 And you shall tell your son on that day, 'It is because of what the Lord did for me when I came out of Egypt.' 9 And it shall be to you as a sign on your hand and as a memorial between your eyes, that the law of the Lord may be in your mouth; for with a strong hand the Lord has brought you out of Egypt. 10 You shall therefore keep this ordinance at its appointed time from year to year.

The biblical writer assumes that Moses gave instructions to the people on the very day that they came out of Egypt. The celebration exalted the fact that the Hebrews came out of Egypt by the strength of the Lord's hand (v. 3). The lordship of Yahweh was central to the interpretation of the deliverance.

No leavened bread shall be eaten. Previously, the command was stated in reverse order, and more positively, "You shall eat unleavened bread" (12:15). Here the command is negative, "you shall not eat that which is leavened" (*chamets*). Leavened bread does not technically mean "bread," but anything which is leavened. The word leavened (*chamets*) is from a verb meaning to be sour (*chomets* was a vinegar; cf. Ruth 2:14; Num. 6:3; Psalm 69:21). Although *chamets* normally referred to bread in the ceremony of worship, it could apply to anything soured or leavened (hence, the extreme attitude toward *chamets* in the Mishna; cf. Pesahim).

In the month Abib. In the previous account the date is given as the "first month" (12:2). Here the technical term of the prexilic era, Abib, is used. During the biblical period three different systems for naming the months were followed: (1) quite

early, and into the early monarchy, the older Canaanite names were used, of which four remain—Abib, Ziv, Ethanim, and Bul; (2) the largest number of biblical references to months uses a system of naming months by their number; and (3) following the Exile some Babylonian names were taken over by transliteration into Jewish usage; Nisan, Sivan, Kislev, Tebet, Shebat, Adar.[26]

Apparently, the feast of unleavend bread was intended only as a later celebration. This statement concerning the initiation of the feast coincides with the belief of some that because of its agricultural nature the feast was native to Canaan and was appropriated as a proper means of celebrating the deliverance of Israel from Egyptian bondage. Should this be true, the relevance of unleavened bread for the faith of Israel would not be impaired. Some of the technical aspects of Israelite worship—especially sites of worship, types of buildings, holy days, to say nothing of the concept of "holy men" such as priests and prophets—had their parallels in other cultures. Baptism is an illustration of a comparable action in the Christian church. Baptism as a physical ceremony was pre-Christian, but when filled with new content and meaning it had a unique and significant role in the faith of the church. So in Israel, there may also have been the adaptation of pre-Israelite forms of worship to the worship life of Israel. Spiritual content, not the source or external form, determines the legitimacy of cultic practices.

Reference to the sign upon the hand was probably metaphorical, although such an expression likely rests in the literal practice of tattoo marks as a means of tribal identification. The *memorial between your eyes* (cf. Deut. 6:8—"frontlets between your eyes") likely referred to a form of headdress or ceremonial dress over the eyes. Both instances likely originated in literal practice in early ancient Near Eastern history, but perhaps by the time of Moses the expres-

26 S. J. DeVries, "Calendar," IDB, I, 483–88.

sions were already understood figuratively rather than literally. The emphasis is clear —men are to keep ever before them the memory of God's action.

With a strong hand. The hand of the Lord is a symbol of his power (cf. 15:6; Deut. 7:19; Isa. 9:12).

3. The Dedication of the Firstborn (13: 1-2,11-16)

The dedication of the firstborn was the final of three cultic observances historically associated with the exodus. Fundamental to its observance was the belief that life was uniquely the gift of God, an altogether fitting premise for a cultic rite associated with Israel's birth-moment.

The practice of dedicating the firstborn of the herd, and possibly man, to the god probably antedated the exodus. From remote antiquity primitive man associated life-giving qualities with the god or gods. Within the faith of Israel the gift of life was uniquely related to the Lord. The inauguration of the ceremony of dedication was appropriately associated with the death of non-Hebraic firstborn, and the deliverance of Hebrew firstborn.

(1) The Lord's Instruction to Moses (13: 1-2)

¹ The LORD said to Moses, ² Consecrate to me all the first-born; whatever is the first to open the womb among the people of Israel, both of man and of beast, is mine."

Consecrate. Consecration involved dedication to God. The direction was positive, for the object dedicated was set apart for the use of God. Too often the practice has been approached negatively and consecration has been understood to mean separation *from* the world. While negative action may be involved in dedication, it is secondary. The primary meaning of the word is that of being set apart, dedicated.

Because God is Creator, all of the herd and its offspring belong to him and share his holiness. Because the herd or flock shared in God's holiness it was "taboo" for

man, he could not appropriate it for himself. Yet, cattle (and produce in the case of the firstfruits) was an imperative need for man's survival. Thus, probably in pre-Israelite times, the practice emerged by which the first of the flock of herd, as well as the grain or the fruit, was offered to the Lord. By the principle of *"pars pro toto,"* the part may stand for the whole. Offering the firstborn symbolized the effectual giving of the entire future offspring, thus leaving succeeding offspring for man's consumption.

The principle by which a part stood for the whole was also applicable to the child. Through the dedication of the firstborn, all succeeding children were also dedicated to the Lord. An examination of laws on dedication of firstborn children reveals that there is no evidence that succeeding children of a marriage were publicly dedicated to the Lord, their dedication apparently having been effected through the dedication of the firstborn.

(2) Instruction Given to the People (13: 11-16)

¹¹ "And when the LORD brings you into the land of the Canaanites, as he swore to you and your fathers, and shall give it to you, ¹² you shall set apart to the LORD all that first opens the womb. All the firstlings of your cattle that are males shall be the LORD's. ¹³ Every firstling of an ass you shall redeem with a lamb, or if you will not redeem it you shall break its neck. Every first-born of man among your sons you shall redeem. ¹⁴ And when in time to come your son asks you, 'What does this mean?' you shall say to him, 'By strength of hand the LORD brought us out of Egypt, from the house of bondage. ¹⁵ For when Pharaoh stubbornly refused to let us go, the LORD slew all the firstborn in the land of Egypt, both the first-born of man and the first-born of cattle. Therefore I sacrifice to the LORD all the males that first open the womb; but all the first-born of my sons I redeem.' ¹⁶ It shall be as a mark on your hand or frontlets between your eyes; for by a strong hand the LORD brought us out of Egypt."

In keeping with the pattern of the two previous celebrations, the Passover and unleavened bread, the essence of the ritual is portrayed as having been given to Moses by the Lord (vv.1–2), while the details for the celebration are set forth in Moses' instructions to the people (vv.11–16).

When the Lord brings you into the land. Apparently, the dedication of the firstborn as a cultic religious observance was not anticipated until Israel was established in the land. The historical origins of the practice, however, may rest in the pastoral conditions long prior to the conquest-settlement. This represents no basic contradiction and may simply indicate that an ancient custom, dedicating the firstborn, was given new meaning in Israel through its association with the deliverance from Egypt. Within Israel dedication was a memorial to the time when God gave life to his people on the night when the Egyptian firstborn died.

Every firstling of an ass. The firstborn male offspring of cattle was the Lord's, probably dedicated to him through sacrifice in early times. Later, firstborn of animals and firstfruits were given to the priest as a part of the priest's livelihood. The ass is specifically exempted from such direct dedication. Probably this was done on the basis that the ass—belonging to the class of animals which do not "part the hoof" and are "unclean" (cf. Lev. 11:1–8; Deut. 14:3–8), or because of its unique holiness for some non-Israelites—was not a proper sacrifice. The latter is more likely, for covenants in the Ancient Near East were at times sealed by slaying an ass. In lieu of offering it to the Lord it could be redeemed by a lamb, which was suitable for dedication (later a price could be paid, Num. 18:15 f.), or it could be put to death by breaking its neck.

Every first-born of man among your sons you shall redeem. The sacrifice of human offspring was prohibited, and provision was made for redemption. The near sacrifice of Isaac (Gen. 22:1 ff.) probably reflects the principle of dedicating the firstborn through child-sacrifice, and one effect of the passage was to legitimatize the offering of an animal as opposed to the primitive act of child-sacrifice (which does occur in the Old Testament, although not as an ap-

proved act of worship).

Paying the redemption price for a child or an unclean animal is probably a late practice, but it is clearly stated: "The firstborn of man you shall redeem, and the firstling of unclean beasts you shall redeem. And their redemption price (at a month old you shall redeem them) you shall fix at five shekels in silver" (Num. 18:15 f.; cf. Ex. 34:20; 13:15).

III. Victory and Freedom Through Yahweh's Lordship (13:17—15:21)

The climactic moment of deliverance from Egypt, was in one sense, the death of the firstborn, following which Pharaoh allowed the Hebrews to leave Egypt. Should this be correct, then the deliverance at the sea was the first of the mighty acts of God within the wilderness theme. Although this view has much to commend it throughout the Old Testament, the actual deliverance is the victory at the sea. The wilderness motif appears following the events at the sea.

1. Victory Through Strategy (13:17—14:4)

17 When Pharaoh let the people go, God did not lead them by way of the land of the Philistines, although that was near; for God said, "Lest the people repent when they see war, and return to Egypt." 18 But God led the people round by the way of the wilderness toward the Red Sea. And the people of Israel went up out of the land of Egypt equipped for battle. 19 And Moses took the bones of Joseph with him; for Joseph had solemnly sworn the people of Israel, saying, "God will visit you; then you must carry my bones with you from here." 20 And they moved on from Succoth, and encamped at Etham, on the edge of the wilderness. 21 And the LORD went before them by day in a pillar of cloud to lead them along the way, and by night in a pillar of fire to give them light, that they might travel by day and by night; 22 the pillar of cloud by day and the pillar of fire by night did not depart from before the people.

1 Then the LORD said to Moses, 2 "Tell the people of Israel to turn back and encamp in front of Pihahiroth, between Migdol and the sea, in front of Baalzephon; you shall encamp over against it, by the sea. 3 For Pharaoh will say of the people of Israel, 'They are entangled

in the land; the wilderness has shut them in.' 4 And I will harden Pharaoh's heart, and he will pursue them and I will get glory over Pharaoh and all his host; and the Egyptians shall know that I am the LORD." And they did so.

Despite the fact that the coastal route, "the way of the Philistines," was much more direct, the Israelites followed a more circuitous route to their destination. There were two reasons for the decision to move southeastward across Sinai rather than along the Mediterranean Sea. First, had Israel followed the coastal route, numerous Egyptian fortifications would have been encountered. This was the traditional route leading to and from Egypt from other regions of the fertile crescent. Second, Moses was apparently instructed, and determined, to lead the people to the "mountain of God" (cf. 3:12). Despite the fact that he had not secured Israel's release soon enough to celebrate the spring festival at the mountain of God (with the result that the feast was celebrated in Egypt), he was apparently determined to bring Israel, however belatedly, to the holy mountain.

But God led the people round by the way of the wilderness toward the Red Sea. The name Red Sea is later than the Hebrew text, which reads yam suph, "sea of reeds." Although English translations consistently translate the phrase "Red Sea," there is no question but that the literal translation of the Hebrew text is "Sea of Reeds." The name itself does not pass judgment upon the location, depth, or other physical factors concerning the sea, however, and one should determine such considerations on bases other than the name.

The phrase yam suph occurs 24 times in the Old Testament: 8 contexts definitely equate it with the Gulf of Aqaba (cf. Num. 14:25; 21:4; 1 Kings 9:26: "King Solomon built a fleet of ships at Ezion-geber, which is near Eloth on the shore of the Red Sea [yam suph], in the land of Edom."); 5 speak of the Sea of Reeds as "behind" the Israelites; 11 refer to it in general terms

without specific identification.

How early the name "Red" was applied to the sea is impossible to determine. By the third century B.C. the Septuagint translated yam suph as eruthran thalassan, Red Sea. Because of the complexity of the issue, neither Red Sea nor Sea of Reeds will be used in this treatment of Exodus. Yam suph will be referred to as "the sea."

The location of the sea should be determined on bases other than the name. It is not likely that the sea is what we know as the Red Sea today. The location of yam suph is most likely (1) the southern edge of Lake Menzaleh, a lake in northern Egypt which may well have been involved, or (2) Lake Timsah, a lake lying midway between the Gulf of Suez and the Mediterranean, or (3) the Gulf of Aqabah.[27]

Since the biblical text indicates that the sea formed a barrier between Egyptian soil and the wilderness it would seem that the sea was either Lake Menzaleh or Lake Timsah. Based upon the location of Succoth (near Lake Timsah), and the fact that after having reached Succoth Israel turned back and encamped some distance to the north "between Migdol and the sea" (v.2), many argue strongly for a northern location, possibly Lake Menzaleh.

Moses took the bones of Joseph. This statement is directly related to the earlier statement that following the death of Joseph, "God will visit you, and bring you up out of this land to the land which he swore to Abraham, to Isaac, and to Jacob" (Gen. 50:24). In this manner the Exodus writer stated his confidence that God fulfils his promises, not only to Joseph personally, but to the whole of Abraham's descendants. God is faithful, dependable.

The Lord went before them by day in

---

27 The author has always had a strong desire to place the site of Sinai to the east of the Gulf of Aqabah in Midian and equate the Gulf of Aqabah with yam suph, but has been unable to justify such a view. However, cf. Eissfeldt, p. 21: "We may therefore believe that the pilgrimage of those who fled from Egypt had as its objective a volcano on the eastern side of the Gulf of Aqaba, or at the northern end of the Red Sea."

a pillar of cloud . . . and by night in a pillar of fire. This reference has been associated with the phenomenon of a volcano, perhaps as far away as Midian. Others interpret the passage as teaching a cloud and a burning fire, both associated with natural phenomena, always before the people. Still others understand the phrase in a metaphorical sense. The passage is a vivid but figurative way of describing the reality of God's presence with his people. This phrase was the writer's way of saying that the Lord leads his people. However one may relate or not relate the expression to physical phenomena, the central truth is that God led Israel in a unique and personal way. The living presence of God is a genuine and vital experience which is expressed in inspired but metaphorical language.

The pillar of cloud by day and the pillar of fire by night did not depart from before the people. God did not abandon Israel, but manifested himself to them throughout the exodus experience. The writer utilized the motif of the abiding cloud and fire to portray the constant presence of God. The external literary form used to express the divine truth was the double figure of the cloud and fire, while the central truth contained within the literary expression was the Lord's abiding presence. The passage speaks of more than a cloud and a fire that did not depart. It speaks of a divine presence that always overshadows God's people in every generation, in every wilderness.

Tell the people of Israel to turn back. Having moved on *from Succoth and encamped at Etham,* Israel turned backward and encamped *in front of Pi-ha-hiroth, between Migdol and the sea, in front of Baal-zephon.* The location of these sites is important for both understanding the line of march followed by Israel and the location of the sea (*yam suph*).

Of the five sites mentioned in connection with Israel's march to the sea, (Succoth, Etham, Pi-ha-hiroth, Migdol, and Baal-zephon), only Succoth and Baal-zephon have

been definitely located. Succoth, according to G. E. Wright, "was situated at the modern Tell el-Maskhutah, about eight and one-half miles east of Pithom in the Wadi Tumilat," [28] roughly midway between the Gulf of Suez and the Mediterranean coast. Thus, after leaving Rameses, the Israelites traveled approximately 32 miles southeastward to Succoth, and from there to the yet unidentified Etham, which lay "on the edge of the wilderness" (v. 20).

For some reason the Israelites at that time then turned backward and traveled northeastward. There they encamped *in front of Pi-ha-hiroth, between Migdol and the sea.* Neither site has been definitely located, although both are mentioned in Egyptian inscriptions. Emil Kraeling suggests that Migdol is "just another name" for Pi-ha-hiroth (*Rand McNally Bible Atlas*). Baal-zephon has been definitely located at the modern Tell Defneh (the Greek Daphne), according to Wright, and Jeremiah was taken there after the fall of Jerusalem and the murder of Gedaliah (Jer. 43:7–9). Such a location is northeastward of Succoth, and quite near Lake Menzaleh (the body of water adjacent to the Mediterranean and the Egyptian coast). Kraeling, Noth, and Davies on the other hand, suggest that Baal-zephon (as well as Migdol) was located on the narrow strip of land dividing the Mediterranean from Lake Sirbonis.[29]

The biblical statement that Israel traveled southward, then turned back northward combines well with the location of Baal-zephon (northward of Succoth), and argues for a northern crossing of the sea. Thus, the sea was probably located to the north of both the Gulf of Suez (traditional site of the crossing) and Lake Timsah (the central site for the crossing of the sea).

[28] *Biblical Archaeology* (Philadelphia: Westminster, 1957), p. 61.

[29] Kraeling, pp. 105 ff.; Noth, p. 110; Davies, p. 122. Kraeling indicates that the Old Testament refers to Migdol as the northernmost point in Egypt (cf. Jer. 44: 1; 46:14; Ezek. 29:10; 30:6). Such a location supports well Kraeling's description of a northern location for the crossing of the sea.

You shall encamp over against it, by the sea. Does the sea refer to the so-called Red Sea, or to the Mediterranean sea? The Hebrew phrase normally translated "Red Sea" (*yam suph*) does not appear, and the reference to "the sea" (*hayyam*) is, according to Noth, the Mediterranean (p. 110). One should not unduly stress the distinction between "the sea" and *yam suph*, however, despite its compatibility with the location of Migdol and Baal-zephon on the Mediterranean coast. Moses' failure to move on into the wilderness when the opportunity seemed at hand made it possible for Pharaoh to overtake the Israelites before the sea (*yam suph*). The entire paragraph (vv. 1-4) revolves around the premise that Israel's turning northward was the means of the Lord's exaltation over the Egyptians.

2. Victory Through Yahweh's Support of Israel (14:5-20)

In addition to the overall strategy which governed Israel's line of march, victory also came through the more direct support of Yahweh.

(1) Egyptian Might in Pursuit of Israel (14:5-9)

5 When the king of Egypt was told that the people had fled, the mind of Pharaoh and his servants was changed toward the people, and they said, "What is this we have done, that we have let Israel go from serving us?" 6 So he made ready his chariot and took his army with him, 7 and took six hundred picked chariots and all the other chariots of Egypt with officers over all of them. 8 And the LORD hardened the heart of Pharaoh king of Egypt and he pursued the people of Israel as they went forth defiantly. 9 The Egyptians pursued them, all Pharaoh's horses and chariots and his horsemen and his army, and overtook them encamped at the sea, by Pihahiroth, in front of Baalzephon.

The writer used Pharaoh's vacillation to maintain the suspense and tension of the deliverance theme. Pharaoh's indecision with regard to Israel's release leads the reader to look for that fuller and ultimate deliverance of Israel.

The vacillation theme is once again in-

jected into the narratives, for, as had happened on previous occasions, Pharaoh reached a decision during the heat of crisis which he repudiated in the calm of later circumstances (cf. the plague narratives: 8:8, 13 f.; 9:27, 34 ff.). Thus, the contest between the Lord and Pharaoh had not been ultimately settled, despite the response of Pharaoh following the night of death (cf. 12:31 ff.).

Just as the response and vacillation of Pharaoh in the plague narratives maintained the suspense of the plagues, causing one to look forward to the final plague, so, here, the vacillation of Pharaoh was utilized by the writer to maintain suspense and tension until the final revelation of the Lord's redemptive power in the act of deliverance at the sea.

(2) Promise of the Lord's Salvation (14: 10-18)

10 When Pharaoh drew near, the people of Israel lifted up their eyes, and behold, the Egyptians were marching after them; and they were in great fear. And the people of Israel cried out to the LORD; 11 and they said to Moses, "Is it because there are no graves in Egypt that you have taken us away to die in the wilderness? What have you done to us, in bringing us out of Egypt? 12 Is not this what we said to you in Egypt, 'Let us alone and let us serve the Egyptians'? For it would have been better for us to serve the Egyptians than to die in the wilderness." 13 And Moses said to the people, "Fear not, stand firm, and see the salvation of the LORD, which he will work for you today; for the Egyptians whom you see today, you shall never see again. 14 The LORD will fight for you, and you have only to be still." 15 The LORD said to Moses, "Why do you cry to me? Tell the people of Israel to go forward. 16 Lift up your rod, and stretch out your hand over the sea and divide it, that the people of Israel may go on dry ground through the sea. 17 And I will harden the hearts of the Egyptians so that they shall go in after them, and I will get glory over Pharaoh and all his host, his chariots, and his horsemen. 18 And the Egyptians shall know that I am the LORD, when I have gotten glory over Pharaoh, his chariots, and his horsemen."

Moses' response to Israel's despair was stated in three verbs, each in its own way either commanding or entreating Israel to a particular course of action (v. 13). *Fear not, stand firm, and see the salvation of the Lord, which he will work.* The form in which the phrase *fear not* was written stressed the element of exhortation or urgency on the part of Moses. The verbal form is not an imperative, but it does make a very strong appeal. "Fear not" is a frequent biblical appeal (Gen. 26:24; 50:19; Num. 14:9; Deut. 1:21; Isa. 40:9; 41:10).

Stand firm translates a Hebrew verb which means to set or station oneself, to take one's stand. It is used of taking one's position (2:4; Hab. 2:1), to take one's stand to fight (1 Sam. 17:16; Psalm 2:2; Jer. 46:4), and also of standing quiet and passive to see the deliverance of the Lord (cf. 1 Sam. 12:7, 16; 2 Chron. 20:17).

The call to *see the salvation* is an imperative form of a verb meaning to see or behold with the eye. It is the common verb, *ra'ah.*

"Salvation" in the Old Testament is most often associated with deliverance from an enemy, illness, death, or other calamity. It should be noted, however, that such physical deliverance was never abstracted from spiritual overtones, for it was the Lord who delivered.

The picture of the Lord fighting the battles of his people is a common Old Testament motif (cf. Psalm 35:1; Neh. 4:20; Isa. 30:32). A most graphic picture is found in Isaiah of the Exile, "I have trodden the wine press alone . . . so my own arm brought me victory" (Isa. 63:3–5). Such anthropomorphic expressions convey the legitimate conviction that the Lord delivers his people.

The Lord's deliverance demanded trust which expressed itself in quietude. The word translated *be still* (*charash*) basically means to be silent, dumb, or speechless. In the particular verbal form in which it appears in this verse, it means to be silent (cf. Judg. 18:19; Gen. 24:21; 34:5; 2 Sam. 13:20). The vast majority of usages means to be quiet. In the context of verse 14 the word may be a call to Israel to stop complaining rather than *to be still.* One might well paraphrase the verse, "And you, you have only to stop complaining."

The Lord rebuked the empty cry of Israel, devoid of action, by calling upon them to go forward. "To go forward" is from a verb meaning to pull out or up; hence (from pulling up tent pegs) to set out, or depart (Gen. 46:1; Josh. 3:14; Num. 33:8). The verb means to set out on a journey or march (Gen. 12:9; Ex. 17:1). Thus the Lord called on Israel to do more than "go forward." The call was to pull up their tent pegs and set out on the journey to which the Lord called them.

As in the later crossing of the Jordan (there are many direct parallels between the two which raise the question of the relationship of the one to the other), the deliverance of the people follows their direct action in moving forward (cf. Josh. 3:13).

As opposed to the plague narratives, in which Aaron played a quite significant part (often wielding the rod, 7:19, or his hand, 8:5), Aaron is not directly involved in the wonder at the sea.

Although no statement was made at this juncture concerning precisely how the sea was to be divided, other than that Moses was to stretch out his rod, the fact that the same writer later explained the division of the sea in terms of a secondary medium suggests that division was to be accomplished through some secondary means. When the writer later described the stretching out of Moses' hand over the sea he suggested that "the Lord drove the sea back by a strong east wind" (14:21). There are two important points to recognize: the event came at a time of crisis and in response to faith; and by the biblical writer's own statement the waters did not divide apart from some action within the realm of nature.

I will harden the hearts of the Egyptians. This is the only instance in which the Egyptians, apart from Pharaoh, are included in the process of God's hardening the heart (in other instances the Lord hardened the heart of Pharaoh and his servants; cf. 9:34; 10:1).

(3) The Angel of God Providing for Israel (14:19–20)

19 Then the angel of God who went before the host of Israel moved and went behind them; and the pillar of cloud moved from before them and stood behind them, 20 coming between the host of Egypt and the host of Israel. And there was the cloud and the darkness; and the night passed without one coming near the other all night.

The term *angel of God* is unusual in that "angel of the Lord" predominates in Old Testament literature. "Angel of God" also appears in Genesis 21:17; 31:11; Judges 6:20; 13:6,9; 2 Samuel 14:17,20. These are normally ascribed to the E source. The same concept is involved, however, regardless of whether the term is angel of the Lord or angel of God. This is borne out by a comparison of those passages where the two phrases are used interchangeably (cf. Judg. 6:12, "angel of the Lord," and v. 20, "angel of God," Judg. 13:3, "angel of the Lord," and v. 9, "angel of God").

The angel of God (or the angel of the Lord) was a theophany (an appearance of God) in which the presence of God was an evident reality. This is the same concept associated with the call of Moses; "The angel of the Lord appeared to him in a flame of fire" (3:2). The angel of the Lord is often associated with fire (cf. Judg. 13:20), and it is interesting that the presence of God symbolized by fire in J (13:21) was in E associated with the angel of God (14:19). Whatever one's conclusion concerning the reality of angels and the precise nature of that which Israel may or may not have physically seen in the exodus, this is clear: God was present as a living reality, and by means of his divine providence led Israel in her deliverance.

In some way the writer conceived of the angel of God and the pillar of cloud as related one to the other. When the angel of God went behind Israel, so did the cloud. The purpose of this movement seems to

have been that of protecting the Israelites by obscuring them from the sight of the Egyptians, *coming between the host of Egypt and the host of Israel. And there was the cloud and the darkness.*

The night passed without one coming near the other. This translation presupposes that because of the darkness neither side drew near the other ("and this one did not draw near to this one all the night"). Rather than "the night passed" (RSV follows the Septuagint rather than the Hebrew text), however, the Hebrew text has a verb translated, "and it caused the night to be light" (Psalm 139:10). The verb *'or* means to be or become light, and appears in this context in a causative stem—to cause to be light or to light.

Thus, the Hebrew text indicates that the cloud caused the night to be light. Such a phenomenon would be in keeping with the pillar of cloud and the pillar of fire said to have been before the Israelites in Exodus 13:21. If the cloud and fire were associated with a volcano, perhaps as far away as Midian (an attractive thesis but incapable of specific validation), then the Hebrew text may reflect the tradition that the night was lit by the fiery presence. The Septuagint translators used an entirely different word (*dielthen,* from *dierchomai,* to go through; hence, of time, pass or elapse): "and the night passed."

However one may deal with the Septuagint evidence, the Hebrew text is clear: the cloud lit the night (night is preceded by the sign of the direct object). It is quite likely that this phenomenon is related to the pillar of fire in Exodus 13:21. Following the victory at *yam suph* the Egyptians were never again a threat to Israel during the exodus-conquest period. Of all the redemptive acts in Exodus, this is the climactic moment of deliverance and salvation.

3. Deliverance at the Sea (14:21–25)

21 Then Moses stretched out his hand over the sea; and the LORD drove the sea back by a strong east wind all night, and made the sea dry land, and the waters were divided. 22 And

the people of Israel went into the midst of the sea on dry ground, the waters being a wall to them on their right hand and on their left. 23 The Egyptians pursued, and went in after them into the midst of the sea, all Pharaoh's horses, his chariots, and his horsemen. 24 And in the morning watch the LORD in the pillar of fire and of cloud looked down upon the host of the Egyptians, and discomfited the host of the Egyptians, 25 clogging their chariot wheels so that they drove heavily; and the Egyptians said, "Let us flee from before Israel; for the LORD fights for them against the Egyptians."

The sea was always foreboding to the Israelites, and Israelite men seldom, if ever, went down to the sea in ships. Even when Israel possessed a navy of sorts under Solomon, Phoenicians sailed them (cf. 1 Kings 9:26 ff.). Against the background of her Mesopotamian origins, Israel always looked with awe upon the sea.

The sea was a symbol of chaos, if not evil, in the literature of the Ancient Near East; a chaos monster to be conquered. In the Babylonian epic of creation, for example, Apsu and Tiamat, male and female primordial sources of the gods, were principles of water (salt and sweet) who were vanquished by the gods (Ea vanquished Apsu, and Marduk destroyed Tiamat). Thus, from primitive times in the ancient world there was a basic conflict between the waters of chaos and the gods of light. Each spring, for example, Marduk, god of light, was championed in the Babylonian New Year Festival as the victor over the waters of chaos.

The conquest of the sea and chaos is reminiscent of Genesis 1:1 ff., and may also appear in the Lord's victory over the sea (yam suph) in the exodus narratives. In fact, later Old Testament thought related the conquest of the sea in Exodus to the slaying of the chaos monster. (Cf. Isa. 51:9-10; Psalm 74:13-14; Ezek. 29:3.) These examples show that in later literature writers saw in the conquest of the sea overtones of the Lord's conflict with the forces of chaos. (Cf. Hab. 3:13-15, which associates the crushing of a possible sea creature with the triumph over the sea.)

The crossing of the sea was more than a means of escape for the Israelites. It was also reminiscent of the Lord's conquest of chaos. Victory over the sea, symbol of chaos, is but another testimony to the absolute lordship of Yahweh.

The writer (J) described the Lord's action through a natural medium, the east wind which, according to him, drove back the sea and made the seabed dry. The east wind appears 19 times in the Old Testament and consistently indicates a destructive agent (cf. Gen. 41:6; Psalm 48:7; Jer. 18:17; Ezek. 19:12; et al.), or a mystery (Job 38:24). It is a phenomenon uniquely related to the Lord, "the east wind, the wind of the Lord, shall come" (Hos. 13:15). The phrase "west wind" occurs only once (Ex. 10:19). God brought the west wind to blow away the locusts blown into the country by the east wind. The west wind was the prevailing wind in Israel, while the east wind, blowing in from the desert with devastating effect, occurred sporadically (primarily, spring and fall). For this reason the east wind became a symbol of destruction, and because of its sporadic appearance was uniquely related to the Lord. Thus, the phrase east wind was used in Exodus because of the fierce windstorms which blew into Israel from the east, plus the fact that the east wind was especially related to the direct control and action of the Lord.

Two statements on the division of the sea are apparently interwoven into the narrative. One (P) suggests that the sea was both divided and closed in response to Moses' outstretched hand. The other (J) injects the east wind as the natural force used by the Lord in the fulfilment of his purposes, despite the inherent question of how men could have walked into a wind strong enough to part the sea. The two sources are complementary, not contradictory. The earlier source includes the natural element, the strong east wind. The later source is no longer concerned with the natural source and is only interested in indicating that the division of the sea was an action in response to the faith of God's servant Moses. Both emphases are needed and have been interwoven into the present narrative. Even the earlier source has minimal concern for the natural force, and was certainly not attempting to give a "natural explanation" for the division of the sea. Its author was as thoroughly convinced of the "miraculous" nature of the event as was the priestly writer who ascribed the event to the outstretched hand of Moses.

Actually, it is impossible to reconstruct the physical details related to the crossing of the sea. We now possess in Exodus a theological interpretation of those events, as opposed to a minute account of the physical details, but there is a consistent emphasis upon the fact that God delivered Israel through a concrete happening within space and time.

Among the explanations given concerning the crossing of the sea are the following. (1) Based upon Exodus 14:21, the Lord used a strong east wind to blast a passage through the sea, leaving a wall of water to the left and right. The major objection to this rest is the difficulty Hebrews would have faced marching directly into the face of a wind so severe as to divide a sea. (2) Others feel that a strong wind blew back the waters at the head of a gulf, Israel passed through, and when the Egyptians attempted the same passage the waters returned. This has the same objection as the former. (3) Some feel that a seismic disturbance, related to volcanic activity in Midian, produced a recession of the waters, near the head of a gulf or lake, through which Israel passed safely. Then, at the precise moment, Egypt attempted to do the same thing, and a tidal wave destroyed them. (4) Still others say that Israel passed through the upper part of the gulf at low tide, and Egypt was caught in the return of the tide.

Personally, I know of no completely acceptable, natural explanation for the crossing of the sea, although the Lord probably utilized some aspect of the natural order. In evaluating the narrative, Noth suggests

that the recovery of physical details is impossible: "In any case J is clearly speaking here of a divine miracle; and it is extremely questionable whether it is appropriate to look for a 'natural' parallel for the events he describes and thus seek to explain the whole 'naturally'" (p. 116). Later, he adds, "Everywhere we have simply variants of the single theme of the destruction of the Egyptians in 'the sea.' This fact of the saving of Israel through the destruction of an Egyptian chariot force in 'the sea' forms the historical basis of the tradition" (p. 118).

The Hebrew for *dry land* consistently means dry land, or dry ground. It is used of the crossing of the sea, the crossing of Jordan (Josh. 4:22), of dry land as opposed to the sea at creation (Gen. 1:9–10), of the shore (Jonah 1:13; 2:10), and in a figurative sense of needy Israel, to be refreshed by the Spirit of the Lord.

4. Destruction in the Sea (14:26–29)

26 Then the LORD said to Moses, "Stretch out your hand over the sea, that the water may come back upon the Egyptians, upon their chariots, and upon their horsemen." 27 So Moses stretched forth his hand over the sea, and the sea returned to its wonted flow when the morning appeared; and the Egyptians fled into it, and the LORD routed the Egyptians in the midst of the sea. 28 The waters returned and covered the chariots and the horsemen and all the host of Pharaoh that had followed them into the sea; not so much as one of them remained. 29 But the people of Israel walked on dry ground through the sea, the waters being a wall to them on their right hand and on their left.

There is no reference to the abating of the wind, but in view of the ascription of the opening of the sea to the wind in verse 21*b* one would assume that the wind ceased. It may well be, however, that the priestly writer saw both the opening and closing of the sea as totally related to the wonder-working rod of Moses (cf. 14:16). This emphasis upon the supernatural would be in keeping with the tendency of the priestly writer to speak of God's action in such manner.

5. Dedication in Response to the Lord's Victory (14:30–31)

30 Thus the LORD saved Israel that day from the hand of the Egyptians; and Israel saw the Egyptians dead upon the seashore. 31 And Israel saw the great work which the LORD did against the Egyptians, and the people feared the LORD; and they believed in the LORD and in his servant Moses.

Whatever one's conclusions concerning the physical media which may have been involved in the fulfilment of the exodus, this phrase is central: *the Lord saved Israel*. This is a theological interpretation of events, grounded in the conviction that the Lord acts redemptively within the framework of history. There is no legitimate basis on which one should deny the possibility of a deliverance of Israel from Egyptian power by a series of physical crises comparable to those described in Exodus. Nor is there always a rational basis upon which one can prove the reality of the deliverance. At this juncture one stands within the realm of faith, and listens as a precursor to one's own faith affirms that the Lord *saved* (with all the rich overtones of that word) his people from Egyptian bondage. This is salvation-history.

The response of Israel to the death of the Egyptians was twofold. First, they feared the Lord. Fear (*yare'*) within the Old Testament denotes the common human emotion, akin to terror, (cf. Judg. 7:3; cf. Gen. 3:10), but it developed a reverential quality of awe in its associations with God. In the latter sense it came to connote reverence (cf. Gen. 42:18; Ex. 18:21; Job 1:1,8–9).

Second, having come to fear the Lord, Israel then *believed in the Lord and in his servant Moses*. *'Aman* means to confirm or support. In the causative stem it means to stand firm, or to trust, to believe (cf. Isa. 7:9; 43:10; Jer. 40:14). The basic meaning of "believe" is to lean upon someone or something for support; to depend upon. Through the experience at the sea, Israel learned to depend upon both the Lord and his servant. The experience was not only

an act of deliverance but a lesson in dependence upon the Lord and his servant. The act of God confirmed Moses as God's servant in the eyes of the people.

6. Victory in Retrospect (15:1–21)

The songs of Moses and Miriam comprise a study of victory in retrospect. Those present at the passage through the sea, as well as later generations, looked back upon the victory and praised God for his deliverance.

The Song of Miriam (vv. 20–21) is the essence of Israel's praise of God for his deliverance. Often the song is acknowledged to have been chronologically contemporary with the victory at the sea. As such, it is one of the older literary passages of the Old Testament. The Song of Moses (vv. 1–19), on the other hand, is frequently understood as having reached its present form at a time following the conquest, although Josephus ascribed the song to Moses (*Antiquities*, 16, 4). Such an assumption is based partially upon the belief that verses 13–16 presuppose the pilgrimage in the desert as an accomplished fact and that verse 17 speaks, however indirectly, of worship in Jerusalem.[30] If this analysis is correct, then 15:1–19 is chronologically later than 15:20–21, and the Song of Miriam actually served as a prototype in miniature for the Song of Moses.

Thus, the Song of Moses is a further elaboration of the Song of Miriam, in which Israel praised the Lord for his wonderful, redemptive action. Whether one assumes that Moses actually led Israel in singing the song as 15:1 suggests, or that inspired men at a time later than Solomon led Israel so to praise the Lord, the theological content is the same.

(1) The Song of Moses (15:1–19)

1 Then Moses and the people of Israel sang this song to the LORD, saying,
"I will sing to the LORD, for he has triumphed gloriously;

30 Noth, however, feels that v. 17 may mean the whole of the land, p. 126.

the horse and his rider he has thrown into
the sea.
2 The Lord is my strength and my song,
and he has become my salvation;
this is my God, and I will praise him,
my father's God, and I will exalt him.
3 The Lord is a man of war;
the Lord is his name.

4 "Pharaoh's chariots and his host he cast into
the sea;
and his picked officers are sunk in the Red
Sea.
5 The floods cover them;
they went down into the depths like a
stone.
6 Thy right hand, O Lord, glorious in power,
thy right hand, O Lord, shatters the
enemy.
7 In the greatness of thy majesty thou over-
throwest thy adversaries;
thou sendest forth thy fury, it consumes
them like stubble.
8 At the blast of thy nostrils the waters piled
up,
the floods stood up in a heap;
the deeps congealed in the heart of the
sea.
9 The enemy said, 'I will pursue, I will overtake,
I will divide the spoil, my desire shall
have its fill of them.
I will draw my sword, my hand shall destroy them.'
10 Thou didst blow with thy wind, the sea
covered them;
they sank as lead in the mighty waters.

11 "Who is like thee, O Lord, among the gods?
Who is like thee, majestic in holiness,
terrible in glorious deeds, doing wonders?
12 Thou didst stretch out thy right hand,
the earth swallowed them.

13 "Thou hast led in thy steadfast love the
people whom thou hast redeemed,
thou hast guided them by thy strength
to thy holy abode.
14 The peoples have heard, they tremble;
pangs have seized on the inhabitants of
Philistia.
15 Now are the chiefs of Edom dismayed;
the leaders of Moab, trembling seizes
them;
all the inhabitants of Canaan have melted
away.
16 Terror and dread fall upon them;
because of the greatness of thy arm, they
are still as a stone,
till thy people, O Lord, pass by,

till the people pass by whom thou hast
purchased.
17 Thou wilt bring them in, and plant them
on thy own mountain,
the place, O Lord, which thou hast made
for thy abode,
the sanctuary, O Lord, which thy hands
have established.
18 The Lord will reign for ever and ever."
19 For when the horses of Pharaoh with his
chariots and his horsemen went into the sea,
the Lord brought back the waters of the sea
upon them; but the people of Israel walked on
dry ground in the midst of the sea.

Regardless of its precise date of composition, the Song of Moses was probably
used at some time as a hymn in Israel's
worship, quite likely in association with the
Passover. Through this medium Israel
praised the Lord for the wonder of his
redemptive action in the victory at the sea.
Through its consistent use in worship, the
hymn reminded succeeding generations
that the Lord was a redeemer God.

Claus Westermann has suggestively
pointed out that the word "to thank" is not
in biblical Hebrew, and that "thanksgiving"
is a relatively modern development.[31] Those
places where "thank" appears in English
translations, "bless" or "praise" would be a
more appropriate rendering of the Hebrew
verbs. The hymn in Israelite poetry conveys
the element of praise, under which "thanksgiving" was subsumed.

In praise, God is the subject—*"Thou
has done"* or *"Thou art."* In thinking, man
is the subject—*"I thank you."* Praising ele-
vates the one praised, thanking leaves him
in the same position. Praise exalts God,
ascribing to him both adoration and honor
in response to his action. Westermann suggests that "where a worshipper in the
Psalms says, 'I will praise the Lord . . . ,'
he does not mean, 'I will be thankful to
God,' but, 'I will respond to him for what
he has done for me' " (p. 29). Such an
emphasis is quite appropriate to the nature
of this passage.

There are three primary emphases

31 *The Praise of God in the Psalms,* trans. Keith R.
Crim (Richmond: John Knox, 1965), p. 25.

within the Song of Moses, plus a summary explanation in prose.

First, *the hymn praises God for his mighty deeds* (15:1–3). The song (*shir*) was a common poetic form in Israel, and Eissfeldt suggests that it was "accompanied by instrumental music (Gen. xxxi,27; Amos vi,5; Isa. xxiii,16; xxx,29), and the verb *to sing* which corresponds to the noun is mentioned in association with dancing (I Sam. xviii,6; Ps. lxxxvii,7)." [32]

The songs of Israel dealt with a wide variety of topics: songs of work and harvest (Judg. 9:27; 21:21; Num. 21:17–18; Isa. 9:3; 16:10); drinking songs (Amos 6:4–6; Isa. 5:11–13); songs of marriage and love (Song of Songs 1:7–8,9–17; 2:8–14); watchman's songs (Isa. 21:11–12; 52:8–9); mocking songs and funeral dirges (Isa. 23:15–16; Num. 21:27–30; Jer. 9:19); royal songs and victory songs (2 Sam. 23:1–7; Psalm 22:4; Ex. 15:20–21; Judg. 11:34); as well as cultic songs which included royal songs (Psalms 2, 18, 20, 72); hymns (Ex. 15:21; Psalms 98, 100, 110); accession songs (Psalms 47, 93); songs of lamentation (Psalms 44, 60, 74); trust (Psalms 4, 11, 125); and thanksgiving (Psalms 30, 136) (*ibid.*, pp. 88–124). The Song of Moses is a victory song with strong hymnic qualities.

Israel's praise fell into two categories: declarative, declaring how God had acted, and descriptive, describing who God is (Westermann, p. 34). Israel praised the Lord for his redemptive action, declaring that he destroyed the Egyptians in the sea, thereby delivering Isarel (v. 1). The declarative nature of Israel's praise was characteristic of the hymn, for "the Hymn is the song which extols the glory and the greatness of Yahweh as it is revealed in nature and history, and particularly in Israel's history" (Eissfeldt, pp. 105 f.).

The praise of verses 2–3 is descriptive, asserting what God is like or who God is.

The Lord is my strength and my song. This phrase was taken up and used in the

worship life of Israel. The psalmist used the phrase (Psalm 118:14), as did Isaiah (12:2). "The Lord is my song" evidently means that the Lord is the subject of the song, or the cause of rejoicing. The word for song (*zimrah*) in verse 2 is distinct from "I will sing" (*shir*), in verse 1, but the two are parallel in thought if not synonymous.

For the first time in Exodus the writer used the abbreviation *yah* rather than the full name for the Lord (Yahweh).

He has become my salvation. The word translated "salvation" may mean welfare or prosperity (cf. Job 30:15), deliverance (2 Sam. 10:11), salvation by God from external evils but often with added spiritual overtones (cf. Isa. 33:2; 52:7,10; 59:11), or victory (1 Sam. 14:45; Isa. 26:18). Within the present context salvation has reference to the victory wrought by the Lord for his people over the Egyptians (cf. Hab. 3:8; Psalm 20:6, where *yeshu'ah*, "salvation," is translated quite properly as "victory" in the RSV). Because the word is uniquely associated with the activity of the Lord, it has spiritual overtones which should not be dismissed.

My father's God. The phrase may be no more than a case of synonymous parallelism, underscoring the previous affirmation —"this is my God." However, the phrase is identical with "God of my father" (*'elohey 'abi*) associated with the patriarchs (cf. Gen. 31:5,42; 32:9), and felt by some to suggest a distinct manifestation of God (i.e., the name "God of my father" or "God of your father" refers to God as worshiped by the patriarchs). In the unique revelation to Moses the Lord identified himself by saying, "I am the God of your father" (Ex. 3:6). Also, the phrase appears later, "The God of my father was my help" (18:4). It may well be that the present affirmation is an attempt to equate the redeemer God of exodus with the ancestral God of the patriarchs.

Second, the song *proclaims God's mighty deeds in the victory at the sea* (15:4–12). The drowning of Pharaoh's officers *sunk*

[32] *The Old Testament: An Introduction,* trans. Peter R. Ackroyd (New York: Harper, 1965), p. 87.

in the Red Sea by the floods is ascribed to the right hand of the Lord. The right hand was a symbol of might and power in Old Testament thought. The right hand was used in conveying the father's blessing (Gen. 48:17), and the right side of sacrifices or persons is specifically referred to in sacrificial and other cultic rites (cf. Lev. 7:32; 8:23; 14:14 *et al*). The expression is uniquely characteristic of the Psalter, where the phrase occurs over 20 times— "mighty victories by his right hand" (20:6); "Thy right hand is filled with victory" (48: 10); "The right hand of the Lord does valiantly, the right hand of the Lord is exalted" (118:15 f.).

In the greatness of thy majesty. Majesty (*ga'on*) basically means exaltation. When used of nations, it may refer to national exaltation through wealth, power, or magnificence of buildings (cf. Ezek. 32:12; Isa. 13:11,19), but it is used of God's exaltation, or majesty (Isa. 24:14; Job 37:4).

The destruction of the Lord's adversaries (v. 7) is related to the storm, *At the blast of thy nostrils the waters piled up.* "Blast" is a translation of the common word for wind (*ruach*), and the writer apparently sought to convey the idea that the wind of the Lord was instrumental in the crossing of the sea. This is in keeping with the central role that the thunderstorm played in Old Testament thought (cf. Psalm 77:16–19).

The reference to *the deeps congealed in the heart of the sea* reflects the ancient belief that the great subterranean ocean (*tehom*) was connected with the sea. Thus, the congealing (from *qapha'*, to thicken, condense, congeal; cf. Job 10:10) of the great deep shut off the supply of water for the seas. Such action is the opposite of the flood narrative, when "all the fountains of the great deep burst forth" (Gen. 7:11). The writer used a common belief of the day to indicate that the Lord closed off the water of the sea—dried it up, as it were—for the purpose of delivering Israel. The pre-scientific view that a great subterranean ocean supplied the seas with water should

not be allowed to obscure the legitimate emphasis that the Lord is ultimately in control of all seas.

In response to the proclamation of God's redemptive action at the sea, the song declares the incomparable nature of the Lord (vv. 11–12).

Who is like thee, O Lord, among the gods? The common word for God is *'elohim*. Although it may apply to a non-Israelite god such as Dagon (1 Sam. 5:7), Chemosh (Judg. 11:24), or Baal (1 Kings 18:25), the preponderant usage refers to the true God, the God of Israel. *'El*, the plural of which (*'elim*) appears in verse 11, also means God. Most often it refers to the one and only God, the God of Israel (of approximately 245 occurrences 217 refer to the true God). *'El* and *'elim* may also refer to men of might and rank (Ezek. 31:11; 2 Kings 24:15), angels (Psalm 29:1; 89:6), and the gods of the nations (Dan. 11:36; Ex. 15:11), as well as idols (Isa. 43:10; 44:10,15,17).

The song probably means that there is no god like the Lord among all the gods of the nations. In keeping with common patterns of thought, the Old Testament often spoke of other gods as though they actually existed. In fact, the Old Testament mentions these "other gods" 63 times.

Who is like thee, majestic in holiness? The verb translated "majestic" (*'adar*) is found only in 15:7,11 and Isaiah 33:21. In the Niphal participle (15:6,11) it means to be majestic or glorious. The word literally means to be wide, great; to be high, noble. Hence, majestic connotes the idea of exaltation. The adjective *'adir* is used of the majesty of the sea (15:10; Psalm 93:4), a ship (Isa. 33:21), a tree (Ezek. 17:23); but also of kings (Psalm 136:18), nations (Ezek. 32:18), and gods (1 Sam. 4:8). The Lord's majesty exceeds that of the towering tree, the ship triumphantly sailing the seas, or the regal and proud king reigning over a nation.

The holiness of God refers to his distinction over against man, his "otherness." The word *qadhash* first meant to be separate;

and, from man's point of view, holiness basically means separation to God. Or, from another perspective, it means that God is separate, "other than man," although not unapproachable. Only later in the development of the word was it associated with righteousness and moral overtones. Within the present context the writer does not praise God's "perfection" or moral nature as much as he praises him because God is distinct and separate, beyond compare. Thus, in praising the redemptive activity of God at the exodus, the writer stressed God's holiness in its primal meaning of separation, uniqueness, distinction, and exaltation.

There is, however, another possible meaning of the phrase *majestic in holiness* which, although based upon an alternate textual witness, should be considered. Septuagint translators translated the phrase, "Who is like you, glorified (from *doxazo*, to clothe with splendor, glorify) among the holy ones?" In Old Testament thought the holy ones were conceived of as inhabitants of the divine court (cf. Job 1:6 ff. for the concept of a divine court). Job mentions them (5:1; 15:15). Zechariah foresaw the time when "the Lord your God will come, and all the holy ones with him" (14:5; cf. also Dan. 8:13).

Accepting this emendation of the Hebrew text by the Greek text, one might read verse as follows: "Who is like thee, O Lord, among the gods? Who is like thee, majestic among the holy ones?" The psalmist used a comparable analogy: "For who in the skies can be compared to the Lord? Who among the heavenly beings [literally, sons of god] is like the Lord, a God feared in the council of the holy ones?" (89:6 f.). The parallelism of thought within the verse would be well balanced, and this emendation-interpretation has much to commend it.

Terrible in glorious deeds. The word terrible may convey an improper connotation of the word *nora'*. In English, the word is often used colloquially as very bad, unpleasant, or disagreeable. Hence, "terrible"

may connote for some an improper concept concerning the meaning of God in verse 11. The Niphal usage of the verb *yare'* means to be fearful, dreadful—to cause astonishment and awe of the Lord himself; to inspire reverence, godly fear and awe. The writer sought to convey the idea that God was one whose glorious deeds were awe-inspiring, causing fear (in the biblical sense of fear).

The earth swallowed them. This may reflect the Old Testament belief that Sheol, being beneath the earth, swallowed the Egyptians. The concept of the earth's "swallowing up" occurs on several occasions in the Old Testament (cf. Num. 16:30 ff.; Deut. 11:6; Psalm 106:17).

Third, *the song states the ultimate purpose of God's mighty deeds*: the establishment of his people upon a land of their own (15:13–19).

The redemptive action of God was accompanied by a "steadfast love" which led the redeemed into the realization of the Lord's purposes (v. 13).

Steadfast love (*chesedh*) is one of the most meaningful words within the covenant community. It signifies the Lord's "covenant-love," a love that might well be conveyed in the term "loyal-love." It is that quality of love within the covenant which prompts loyalty and devotion. The word is used of man's action as often as it is of God's, and is most commonly translated "kindness." Such extreme emphasis upon "kindness" does not do justice to the richness of meaning within the word. For example, Norman Snaith has distinguished between *'ahab* and *'ahabah* as "election love," that quality of love which prompts the initiation of the covenant, and *chesedh* as "covenant love," the love *within* the covenant which prompts loyalty and other actions appropriate to the covenant. He has established beyond question, in the judgment of many, the distinctly covenantal nature of *chesedh* (*The Distinctive Ideas of the Old Testament*). In the vast majority of instances, if not every instance, the word connotes a loyalty within the covenant which prompts action consonant with covenant faith. When used of God, *chesedh* suggests his lovingkindness in responding to the needs of his people within the covenant. This may express itself in redemption from enemies and troubles (Gen. 19:19; Jer. 31:3), the preservation of life from death (Psalms 6:5; 86:13; Job 10:12), the quickening of spiritual life (Psalms 109:26; 119:41,76), redemption from sin (Psalms 25:7; 51:1), and in keeping the covenants with Abraham, Moses, and Israel (Deut. 7:9,12; 1 Kings 8:23).

The God who redeems manifests that quality of "loyal-love" which brings to fulfilment within the life of the redeemed those purposes which the Lord intended for them at the moment of redemption. The Lord's love is a faithful love.

The people whom thou hast redeemed. Redeem (*ga'al*) means either to "redeem" or to "act as a kinsman." In the latter instance it refers to the nearest of kin who vindicates his deceased relative (cf. the blood feud and the "avenger of blood," Num. 35:19 ff.; Deut. 19:6 ff.), takes his kinsman's widow to rear children under the family name (Ruth 3:13), redeems property sold by a poorer relative (Lev. 25:25), or generally acts to maintain the right and integrity of his kinsman, and thus his own family name.

Items consecrated at the shrine could on some occasions be redeemed by the payment of an assessed value (Lev. 27:13 ff.). Especially, however, did the word come to be applied to the Lord's redemptive action: whether of individuals from death (Psalm 103:4) or orphans (Prov. 23:10–11), but especially Israel from Egyptian bondage (Psalm 74:2; 77:15) and from exile (Isa. 43:1; cf. the Lord is *go'el*, "redeemer," Isa. 41:14). God acts on man's behalf as would his nearest kinsman; vindicates his name, and delivers him from adversity.

Thou hast guided them . . . to thy holy abode. Within the Old Testament the Lord's abode is most often thought of as Zion, and especially the Temple. However,

in the present context the writer may well have conceived of Canaan-Israel itself as the Lord's abode. The song thus not only celebrates the Lord's leadership of Israel into the land following the exodus, but indirectly underscores the fulfilment of the promise long made to the patriarchs. The theme of promise and fulfilment concerning the land is central to all of the Hexateuch (Genesis–Judges).

This section (vv. 14–16) presupposes the pilgrimage in the desert as an accomplished fact. It is either a forecast of possible reaction or a description written following the response of the nations. The latter choice seems preferable. "Philistia" is described first (v. 14), perhaps because of the abortive effort of the Israelites to enter the land at Kadesh-Barnea (cf. Num. 13–14; Deut. 1:19–46), or simply because the Philistines represented the most significant group on the Mediterranean coast (reference to established Philistines at this time would be anachronistic, for Philistines did not settle in "Philistia" until approximately 1188 B.C. and following). Edom and Moab are then mentioned (v. 15), probably because they were encountered as Moses led Israel to the west of the Jordan-Aqabah rift prior to entrance into the land of Canaan (cf. Num. 20:14 ff.). Finally, as the Hebrews entered the land of Canaan, *all the inhabitants of Canaan have melted away* (v. 15).

The writer made clear that their response was due to *the greatness of thy arm.* In this manner he underscored God's redemptive action as a continuing reality. There is a sense in which the conquest-settlement narrative is a unified exposition of the continuing revelation of the Lord's redemption.

The people . . . thou hast purchased. "Purchase" (*qanah*) literally means to get, acquire. It is used of Eve and Cain (Gen. 4:1), and of God as victoriously redeeming his people (Isa. 11:11; Psalms 74:2; 78:52–55). It is often used of buying (Deut. 28:68; Isa. 24:2). "Purchase" (*qanah*), "ransom" (*padhah*), (Deut. 7:8; Mic. 6:4; Psalm 78:42), "redeem" (*ga'al*),

(Psalm 74:2; Isa. 43:1), and "know" (*yadha'*, Amos 3:2; Hos. 13:5) are all graphically used in describing the redemptive deliverance of Israel.

The realization of the Lord's purposes is clearly stated in the declaration, *Thou wilt bring them in, and plant them on thy own mountain.* The references to *thy own mountain, thy abode,* and *the sanctuary . . . which thy hands have established* more likely than not refer to Jerusalem, although Martin Noth may be correct in indicating that "we are not to understand the word 'sanctuary' in v. 17*b* as a single holy place, which would compel us to think of Jerusalem, but we are to see the whole land, because it is the possession of Yahweh and the 'abode of God,' as a holy realm" (p. 126).

In either instance, the intent of the writer is the same: The Lord brought his purposes to realization by establishing his people in their own land.

"The Lord will reign for ever and ever." The proclamation of the Lord's kingship and perpetual sovereignty is a fitting climax to the song. The lordship of Yahweh is appropriately set in the context of his victory at the sea. The kingship of Yahweh is an Old Testament theme found in 1 Samuel 8:7; Psalms 47:8; 93:1; 96:10; 97:1; 99:1; 146:10; Isaiah 24:23; 52:7; Ezekiel 20:33; Micah 4:7. As stated earlier, Exodus may be understood as a proclamation of Yahweh's lordship. He is Lord of history, creation, man, and worship. The theme, "The Lord will reign for ever and ever," is the continuing hope of the covenant community, the old and the new.

(2) The Song of Miriam (15:20-21)

20 Then Miriam, the prophetess, the sister of Aaron, took a timbrel in her hand; and all the women went out after her with timbrels and dancing. 21 And Miriam sang to them:
"Sing to the Lord, for he has triumphed gloriously;
the horse and his rider he has thrown into the sea."

The religious dance was a common means of praise in Israel. David danced before the Lord (2 Sam. 6:14 ff.), and the psalmist calls upon the worshipers to "Praise him with timbrel and dance" (150:4), "Let them praise his name with dancing" (149:3). Seemingly, dancers constituted a group that stood alongside the singers within Israelite worship. "Singers and dancers alike say, 'All my springs are in you'" (Psalm 87:7).

Verse 20 serves as a prose introduction to the song, written in poetic form, in verse 21.

Sing to the Lord. The Song of Miriam is quite brief, and ancient. It was the point of beginning for the later Song of Moses (15:1).

The phrase *triumphed gloriously* translates *ga'oh ga'ah,* a phrase using a construction peculiarly designed to emphasize the intensity of the Lord's victory. The root meaning of the word is "rise up," and its usage is limited to five occurrences in the Old Testament: waters rising up (Ezek. 47:5); plants growing up (Job 8:11); one's head lifted up (Job 10:16); and the present reference to the lifting up of Yahweh in triumph (15:21). The word is not the normal means of expressing victory in the sense of *smiting* one's enemy. The Septuagint translates the phrase *endoxos gar dedoxastai,* "glorious, for he shall be glorified," thus emphasizing glory rather than victory. This may well be correct. The Lord is high, *ga'ah,* in the sense that the victory exalts him. In this regard the ASV suggests in a footnote that the phrase might be translated "for he is highly exalted." This has much to commend it.

James Muilenburg, commenting on Miriam's Song, suggests that "the Lord God of Israel had shown himself to be the Lord of history and had determined the direction in which Israel's life in the world was to move" (p. 54).

IV. Providential Care Through the Wilderness (15:22—18:27)

The wilderness narrative of Exodus 15:22–18:27 is but one element within the larger complex of material dealing with the wilderness-conquest motif. The Sinai narrative (Ex. 19:1–Num. 10:16) is both preceded and followed by an emphasis upon the wilderness era prior to the conquest, and Exodus 15:22–18:27 should be read with Numbers 10:17 to Joshua 24:33 as an integral part of a larger but single literary complex describing the wilderness-conquest epoch.

The central theme of the wilderness narratives in Exodus is the preservation of Israel through Yahweh's lordship. As Claus Westermann observes, "It is not preservation, however, that is due to the sustenance that continually comes from the soil or is the result of stable and orderly institutions. It is rather preservation due to a series of miracles concerned with elementary needs of human existence: hunger, thirst, and despair."[33]

Israel's movement through the wilderness is pointedly described by three usages of the verb *nasa'*, meaning to set out on a journey (cf. 15:22; 16:1; 17:1). Following these three catchwords the wilderness narratives may be divided into three periods of encampment at Marah and Elim (15:22–27), the wilderness of Sin (16:1–36), and Rephidim (17:1–18:27); successively characterized by the basic needs of thirst, hunger, and despair.

1. Thirst: Bitter Waters of Marah (15:22–27)

22 Then Moses led Israel onward from the Red Sea, and they went into the wilderness of Shur; they went three days in the wilderness and found no water. 23 When they came to Marah, they could not drink the water of Marah because it was bitter; therefore it was named Marah. 24 And the people murmured against Moses, saying, "What shall we drink?" 25 And he cried to the LORD; and the LORD showed him a tree, and he threw it into the water, and the water became sweet.

There the LORD made for them a statute and an ordinance and there he proved them, 26 saying, "If you will diligently hearken to the voice of the LORD your God, and do that which

is right in his eyes, and give heed to his commandments and keep all his statutes, I will put none of the diseases upon you which I put upon the Egyptians; for I am the LORD, your healer."

27 Then they came to Elim, where there were twelve springs of water and seventy palm trees; and they encamped there by the water.

Deliverance at Mara (vv. 22–26). The adjective *mar*, bitter, bitterness, is used of water (v. 23), food (Prov. 27:7), and wormwood (Prov. 5:4), but it is most often used in a figurative manner of the bitterness of soul, death, etc. Because of the springs of bitterness (*mar*) the site was known as *marah* (Marah). Martin Noth suggests that later Israelites "knew of a waterhole whose name 'Marah' indicated that the water of the spring must be 'bitter,' just as there were similar 'bitter' springs in the salty ground of the wilderness; this one, however, was sweet, because it had been made sweet at the time of Israel's Exodus from Egypt" (p. 129).

The murmuring of Israel against Moses and the Lord is a theme common to the wilderness narratives. The specific word "murmur" (*lun*) occurs only in Exodus 15, 16, and 17; Numbers 14, 16, and 17; Joshua 9:18, thereby limiting the murmuring tradition to the wilderness era. Two distinct attitudes toward the wilderness era are present within the Old Testament. One exalts the wilderness era as the ideal period of communion between the Lord and his people (cf. Hos. 2:14 f.; Jer. 2:2 f.), while the other interprets the wilderness as a time of murmuring against the Lord and a rejection of his counsel (cf. Ezek. 20:13). One might also contrast Psalm 105:41 ff. and Psalm 106:13–33. The complexity of the problem has led to several special studies, and some feel that the murmuring tradition is a late development, related to the period of the early monarchy.[34] The murmuring tradition underscores the fact that

---

[33] *Handbook to the Old Testament,* trans. and ed. Robert H. Boyd (Minneapolis: Augsburg, 1967), p. 60.

[34] Cf. Simon DeVries, "The Origin of the Murmuring Tradition," JBL., LXXXVII, March 1968, 51 ff. George W. Coates, *Rebellion in the Wilderness: The Murmuring Motif in the Wilderness Traditions of the Old Testament* (Nashville: Abingdon, 1968).

"Israel did not follow the way of the Exodus from Egypt by free choice (cf. 14. 11 f.) but followed the guidance of their God with which they were not completely happy from the very beginning (cf. 5. 20 ff.), so that God's universal plan of salvation might be carried out even against the will of Israel (cf. Gen. 12:1–3)" (Noth, p. 129). In this regard, among Coates' conclusions is the assumption that "a form-critical study of the relevant texts reveals that the murmuring motif is not designed to express a disgruntled complaint. Quite the contrary, it describes an open rebellion. The act of murmuring which, if unresolved, demands loss of office, due punishment, and perhaps death" (p. 249).

The ability to counteract the pollution of the water may have come to Moses during his exile in this general area (cf. 2:15 ff.). Apparently, the tree possessed purifying qualities, and the Lord utilized the created order for the fulfilment of his own purposes. The latent energies of the world came to life under the responsible direction of a man committed to the will of God, and Israel was delivered.

Israel's legal corpus is normally associated with Sinai, but as early as Marah the Lord gave *a statute* (*choq*) *and an ordinance* (*mishpat*). It is impossible to determine precisely what this was, and no record has been preserved of any legislation associated with Marah. Whatever the precise nature of the legislation, its purpose was to "prove" or "test" Israel.

The use of *healer* as an appellative for the Lord appears unique at first glance, but it is a rather frequent Old Testament emphasis. The word is used once of Egyptian physicians (Gen. 50:2), but it is quite often used as a figure of the Lord, as one who heals his people. This often involves the restoration of his favor, and, at times, forgiveness (cf. Hos. 6:1; Isa. 57:18; Psalm 30:2).

Arrival at Elim (*v. 27*). The next stage on the journey toward Sinai was Elim, where for the first time Israel found a source of fresh water. Traditionally it has been located approximately 63 miles from Suez. Some who locate Sinai east of Aqabah equate Elim with Elath, at the head of the Gulf of Aqabah.[35] The name '*eylim* is related to '*el* (God), and may indicate that the site was a holy place for a considerable period of time. Both the fresh water and the grove of trees would have conveyed sanctity to such a place.

2. Hunger: The Provision of Quail and Manna (16:1–36)

The second elementary human need which threatened Israel was physical hunger, a need which was met through the Lord's provision of quail and manna.

(1) Murmuring against the Lord's leaders (16:1–3)

¹ They set out from Elim, and all the congregation of the people of Israel came to the wilderness of Sin, which is between Elim and Sinai, on the fifteenth day of the second month after they had departed from the land of Egypt. ² And the whole congregation of the people of Israel murmured against Moses and Aaron in the wilderness, ³ and said to them, "Would that we had died by the hand of the LORD in the land of Egypt, when we sat by the fleshpots and ate bread to the full; for you have brought us out into this wilderness to kill this whole assembly with hunger."

Confronted with the threat of hunger, the whole of the congregation of Israel turned against Moses and Aaron. The use of the word *congregation* reflects basic terminology of the later Israelite period.

Death with the Egyptians at the hand of the Lord (apparently on the night of the death plague) would have been preferable to starvation in the wilderness. Unable to forget the pots filled with flesh and the unlimited consumption of bread, Israel preferred death under those conditions than freedom without such provisions in the wilderness.

---

[35] In this regard, it is interesting to note that Numbers states, "they set out from Elim, and encamped by the Red Sea [*yam suph*]" (33:10), and that the Old Testament refers to the Gulf of Aqabah as *yam suph*.

One might observe that Israel was equally distraught and disgruntled with circumstances in Egypt (cf. 2:23 ff.). Characteristically, the attitude of the people toward Moses and Aaron fluctuated with changing fortunes—believing in them when the sea was crossed (14:13), repudiating and murmuring against them as adversity replaced benediction.

(2) Moses' Mediatorial Office (16:4–12)

4 Then the LORD said to Moses, "Behold, I will rain bread from heaven for you; and the people shall go out and gather a day's portion every day, that I may prove them, whether they will walk in my law or not. 5 On the sixth day, when they prepare what they bring in, it will be twice as much as they gather daily." 6 So Moses and Aaron said to all the people of Israel, "At evening you shall know that it was the LORD who brought you out of the land of Egypt, 7 and in the morning you shall see the glory of the LORD, because he has heard your murmurings against the LORD. For what are we, that you murmur against us?" 8 And Moses said, "When the LORD gives you in the evening flesh to eat and in the morning bread to the full, because the LORD has heard your murmurings which you murmur against him—what are we? Your murmurings are not against us but against the LORD."
9 And Moses said to Aaron, "Say to the whole congregation of the people of Israel, 'Come near before the LORD, for he has heard your murmurings.'" 10 And as Aaron spoke to the whole congregation of the people of Israel, they looked toward the wilderness, and behold, the glory of the LORD appeared in the cloud. 11 And the LORD said to Moses, 12 "I have heard the murmurings of the people of Israel; say to them, 'At twilight you shall eat flesh, and in the morning you shall be filled with bread; then you shall know that I am the LORD your God.'"

I will rain bread from heaven for you. God was enthroned above the heavens, and "heaven" meant the expanse between earth and the firmament, i.e., the solid-appearing vault of heaven (Gen. 1:6 f.). However, the reference does indicate that *bread* would come from an unexpected source. Later, the manna was associated with the dew (which fell from heaven, according to biblical thought), an association which

may explain the reference "bread from heaven."

Prove (*nasah*) means only to test or try with the intent of determining between two opposing alternatives (cf. Judg. 6:39). It does not have the negative associations often associated with test or tempt. The purpose of the test was to determine whether or not Israel would walk in the Lord's instruction (*torah*, often translated law, but embracing a wider range of meaning than a legal code of law). The daily provision of manna was later reflected in the New Testament prayer, "Give us this day our daily bread" (Matt. 6:11) and the worshiper's inherent willingness to trust God to provide from one day to the next.

Following verse 5 one might well insert verses 9–12 to stand prior to verses 6–8, as suggested by Driver, who justified such an alteration on the assumption that "the message given to the people (vv. 6–8) *precedes* the command to deliver it (vv. 9–12)." Such an alteration is commendable, not only on Driver's suggestion that the giving of the message to the people precedes the command to deliver it as the passage now stands, but also because of the manner in which verses 6–8 are clarified when verses 9–12 are read between verses 4–5 and 6–8. This alteration is followed in the present discussion.

Say to the whole congregation. The people are directed to look *toward the wilderness,* from whence they would behold *the glory of the Lord* in the cloud. Perhaps there was an actual phenomenon in or beyond the wilderness, associated with fire; or, the call to look eastward (i.e., toward the wilderness) was a call to behold the angel of the Lord.

At evening you shall know that it was the Lord. The miraculous provision of meat, destined to come at twilight, would refute the conclusion, which may well have arisen, that the deliverance at the sea was not necessarily the Lord's work. Thus, the provision of the quail tended to confirm the prior redemptive activity of the Lord.

(3) *Manna and Quail for a Hungry People* (*16:13–21*)

13 In the evening quails came up and covered the camp; and in the morning dew lay round about the camp. 14 And when the dew had gone up, there was on the face of the wilderness a fine, flake-like thing, fine as hoarfrost on the ground. 15 When the people of Israel saw it, they said to one another, "What is it?" For they did not know what it was. And Moses said to them, "It is the bread which the LORD has given you to eat. 16 This is what the LORD has commanded: 'Gather of it, every man of you, as much as he can eat; you shall take an omer apiece, according to the number of the persons whom each of you has in his tent.' " 17 And the people of Israel did so; they gathered, some more, some less. 18 But when they measured it with an omer, he that gathered much had nothing over, and he that gathered little had no lack; each gathered according to what he could eat. 19 And Moses said to them, "Let no man leave any of it till the morning." 20 But they did not listen to Moses; some left part of it till the morning, and it bred worms and became foul; and Moses was angry with them. 21 Morning by morning they gathered it, each as much as he could eat; but when the sun grew hot, it melted.

Although the provision of food took the form of both quail and manna, the narrative is primarily concerned with the manna. The account concerning the quail utilizes only 10 words, while the manna narrative extends over the entire 22 verses remaining in the chapter.

Why so little space on this subject, and so much attention to the manna? Could it be that the use of bread in Israel's later cultic life has so influenced the writer that he has given unusual attention to the manna, which was a bread substitute? In all probability the concern of the writer for the manna probably rests in some such worship-centered interest.

Quail (*selaw*) is probably a non-Hebraic loan word, and, apart from the present passage, occurs only in Numbers 11:31-32; and Psalm 105:40. According to McCullough, "Quails in the Mediterranean area winter in Africa and migrate northward in vast flocks in the spring. . . . This is an exhausting flight and is done in stages.

When the birds alight to refresh themselves, they are easily caught. Presumably it was a cloud of migrating quails that came down on the Hebrew encampment" (IDB, III, 973).

The book of Numbers also describes a comparable provision of food by the Lord, and specifically states that "there went forth a wind from the Lord, and it brought quails from the sea, and let them fall beside the camp" (Num. 11:31).

Apparently, migratory birds provided the food promised by the Lord through Moses. This was interpreted, and properly so, as the Lord's providential deliverance. In this regard, it is significant that according to Exodus there was but the single appearance of the quail. In contrast with this, the manna was apparently characteristic of the peninsula, for the Israelites ate it during the entire time they were in the wilderness (cf. 16:35). In the providential appearance of migratory birds, one can again see the lordship of Yahweh over the created order.[36]

The indefinite description underscores Israel's lack of acquaintance with manna. Upon seeing it for the first time, the people asked, *What is it?* (*man hu'*). Through popular etymology the question *man hu* ("What is it?") was equated with the name manna. Thus, the name manna means, "What is it?" [37]

Moses answered the question by suggesting that the manna was the bread which the Lord had given Israel. Although

---

36 The prior faith of Moses, and his announcement of deliverance to the people (16:6 ff.) lifts the appearance of the migratory birds from the category of chance happening into the realm of providential action. In this regard it is entirely possible that in view of Moses' exile among the Midianites and his presence near the mountain of God, he may have known of both the migratory birds and the manna. If so, this would not detract from the providential timing of the miracle. It would, in fact, underscore the providential preparation of Moses during his exile.

37 It should be noted, however, that from a technical point of view such an etymological relationship is questionable, and one can no longer give a technical etymological explanation of manna.

described as bread, it was more precisely a bread substitute.

What was manna, and how was it given to Israel in the wilderness? First, what does the narrative itself suggest? (1) It came during the night and could not be collected until the dew was gone in the morning, suggesting that the manna was dissolved by the dew, and not necessarily produced by it (v. 13). (2) When collected it was quite *fine* and *flake-like* (v. 14). (3) It was geographically limited to the Sinai peninsula, for Israel apparently had not heard of it before (v. 15), and ate it only as long as they were in the wilderness (v. 35). (4) It was susceptible to rapid spoilage, and could not be kept from day to day (v. 20). (5) When exposed to the sun it melted (v. 21). (6) It was white in color and sweet in taste (v. 31).

Second, are there phenomena associated with the Sinai peninsula which meet these general descriptions?

Josephus indicated that manna was still available in the Sinai peninsula during his time,[38] and modern geographers and explorers confirm that a residue which resembles the description of biblical manna is still collected in the same geographical area. The manna of the modern era is the sweet secretion of the tamarisk. Following rainy periods the bush produces a type of manna from the size of a pinhead to a pea. At the peak of the season Mihelic suggests that a "steady worker may collect over half a pound (kilogram) per day" (IDB, III, 260). A fresh supply appears each night and must be gathered the next day before the sun melts it.

There is no indication that manna of the postbiblical era could have been used as bread itself, and contemporary manna fulfils a role comparable to honey (although when collected it is in a solid or semisolid state).

Mihelic concludes his essay by suggesting that "on the basis of these findings,

manna production is a biological phenomenon of the dry deserts and steppes. The liquid honeydew excretions of a number of cicadas, plant lice, and scale insects speedily solidify by rapid evaporation. From remote time the resulting sticky and often granular masses have been collected and called manna."

Despite the many similarities between manna of the more recent era and the period of the exodus, there are numerous characteristics of the exodus phenomenon which remain unexplained.

In summation, one faces one of several conclusions, among which are: (1) Biblical manna was totally different from anything ever associated with the Sinai peninsula, and the more recent phenomenon described as manna reflects solely external similarities. (2) Biblical manna was essentially the same phenomenon as more recent manna but had unique, miraculous characteristics. (3) Biblical manna was for all practical purposes identical with that of the modern era; the unique aspects of the biblical account are the result of later theological and literary expansions of the original historical event.

Whatever one's conclusion, it is clear from the biblical record that in the moment of Israel's need for food, the Lord providentially answered that need. How this was accomplished is of secondary importance. Driver has well suggested that "the narrative is to be taken as a signal and beautiful illustration of the great truth of God's *ever-sustaining providence*: He supplies His people with food, cares for them in their needs, and He makes the food which He gives them the vehicle of spiritual lessons."

(4) Manna for the Sabbath (16:22–30)

22 On the sixth day they gathered twice as much bread, two omers apiece; and when all the leaders of the congregation came and told Moses, 23 he said to them, "This is what the LORD has commanded: 'Tomorrow is a day of solemn rest, a holy sabbath to the LORD; bake what you will bake and boil what you will boil, and all that is left over lay by to be kept till

---

[38] "Even now, in all that place, this manna comes down in rain." *Antiquities*, III.7.

the morning.' " 24 So they laid it by till the morning, as Moses bade them; and it did not become foul, and there were no worms in it. 25 Moses said, "Eat it today, for today is a sabbath to the LORD; today you will not find it in the field. 26 Six days you shall gather it; but on the seventh day, which is a sabbath, there will be none." 27 On the seventh day some of the people went out to gather, and they found none. 28 And the LORD said to Moses, "How long do you refuse to keep my commandments and my laws? 29 See! The LORD has given you the sabbath, therefore on the sixth day he gives you bread for two days; remain every man of you in his place, let no man go out of his place on the seventh day." 30 So the people rested on the seventh day.

(5) Israel's Memory of the Miracle of the Manna (16:31–36)

31 Now the house of Israel called its name manna; it was like coriander seed, white, and the taste of it was like wafers made with honey. 32 And Moses said, "This is what the LORD has commanded: 'Let an omer of it be kept throughout your generations, that they may see the bread with which I fed you in the wilderness, when I brought you out of the land of Egypt.' " 33 And Moses said to Aaron, "Take a jar, and put an omer of manna in it, and place it before the LORD, to be kept throughout your generations." 34 As the LORD commanded Moses, so Aaron placed it before the testimony, to be kept. 35 And the people of Israel ate the manna forty years, till they came to a habitable land; they ate the manna, till they came to the border of the land of Canaan. 36 (An omer is the tenth part of an ephah.)

This passage gives every evidence of having been a later Israelite memory of the manna. Strangely enough, there is no attention at all given to the quails. The manna overshadowed the quail in its significance for the faith of Israel, and only the manna was preserved as a memorial.

Now the house of Israel called its name manna. The name *manna* (*man*) had earlier been related to the question, "What is it?" (v. 15), and the present explanation may well be a later summary of the experience. The manna is described as though the writer may still have been familiar with the phenomenon. *Coriander* appears only in verse 31 and Numbers 11:7, and its root meaning is dubious. *Coriander seed* are about the size of a peppercorn; the seed-

like, strong-smelling fruit is used in cooking for flavoring and in medicine.

A jar with *an omer* of manna was to *be kept* so that future generations could see how the Lord had provided for Israel in the exodus. The statement that *Aaron placed it before the Testimony, to be kept* is likely anachronistic, since the testimony "before the Lord" was at least post-Sinaitic in origin. The passage was apparently written at a time when the sanctuary was part of Israel's worship life.

An omer is the tenth part of an ephah. The omer (24 dry quarts) is mentioned only in connection with the manna, and elsewhere "the tenth part of an ephah" is the characteristic expression. *Omer* is probably an ancient term handed down with the story of the manna. For this reason an explanatory note was added, explaining to the reader what an omer contained. This tends to indicate a late date of composition for the passage, or that the verse is a later explanatory addition. One would assume that those associated with the exodus would have been acquainted with an omer.

In summary, the whole of the quail-manna experience was a means of underscoring Israel's dependence upon the Lord and his ability and willingness to provide for the needs of his people. Deuteronomy interpreted the experience as a time of spiritual discipline: "And he humbled you and let you hunger and fed you with manna, which you did not know, nor did your fathers know; that he might make you know that man does not live by bread alone, but that man lives by everything that proceeds out of the mouth of the Lord" (8:3). Much later, Jesus responded to the manna experience cited by the Jews, and claimed that he was the true bread which came "down from heaven" (John 6:58).

3. Despair: The Frustration of National Enemies and Domestic Problems (17:1—18:27)

The suggestion that the wilderness narratives are concerned with the Lord's action in preserving his people, and that the final elemental need with which the narrative deals is that of human despair in the face of insuperable odds is stimulating and commendable.

Within the present narratives there are three primary emphases: (1) water from the rock, which may well be associated with the earlier water narrative; (2) the battle with the Amalekites; and, (3) the visit of Jethro and his counsel concerning the domestic problems faced by Moses and Israel.

(1) Water from the Rock (17:1-7)

¹ All the congregation of the people of Israel moved on from the wilderness of Sin by stages, according to the commandment of the LORD, and camped at Rephidim; but there was no water for the people to drink. ² Therefore the people found fault with Moses, and said, "Give us water to drink." And Moses said to them, "Why do you find fault with me? Why do you put the LORD to the proof?" ³ But the people thirsted there for water, and the people murmured against Moses, and said, "Why did you bring us up out of Egypt, to kill us and our children and our cattle with thirst?" ⁴ So Moses cried to the LORD, "What shall I do with this people? They are almost ready to stone me." ⁵ And the LORD said to Moses, "Pass on before the people, taking with you some of the elders of Israel; and take in your hand the rod with which you struck the Nile, and go. ⁶ Behold, I will stand before you there on the rock at Horeb; and you shall strike the rock, and water shall come out of it, that the people may drink." And Moses did so, in the sight of the elders of Israel. ⁷ And he called the name of the place Massah and Meribah, because of the faultfinding of the children of Israel, and because they put the LORD to the proof by saying, "Is the LORD among us or not?"

Westermann suggests that the water miracle should be included with 15:22 ff. and Numbers 20:1-13. In keeping with their former attitude of skepticism and distrust, the children of Israel used the lack of water as an occasion to murmur against Moses and, in so doing, against the Lord.

All the congregation . . . moved on . . . by stages. The phrase *by stages* may mean no more than that they moved from one encampment to the other on the line of march (stage, *nasa'*, means a pulling up, hence, a journey, and came to mean a station, stage, or journey by stages; cf. also Num. 10:12; Deut. 10:11). However, the Septuagint understood the Hebrew text to mean that they set forth according to their various divisions, or camps (*kata parembolas autōn; parembolē* may mean a company of soldiers, Gen. 32:2).

In order to facilitate the movement of the group, smaller units may have made their way to the next stage, Rephidim. Finding no water at **Rephidim,** the people apparently blamed Moses. The phrase *found fault with (wayyareb)* translates a verb (*rib*) meaning to strive or contend, from which the nouns "strife" and "dispute" originate. The verb is commonly used of the lawsuit motif in the Old Testament, and also of one who makes a complaint. Cognate languages use related words to express the connotation of agitate, cry or shout, quarrel noisily, shouting and clamor.

Moses interpreted Israel's quarrel with him as a quarrel with the Lord. In what may have been intended as a rebuff, he used the same word which the Lord had formerly used of Israel, "that I may prove (*nasah*) them" (16:4). Israel reversed the process; rather than being tested by the Lord, they put him to the test.

The writer's strong emphasis upon the rebellious attitude in the wilderness may reflect a later desire to justify the superiority of Jerusalem and the Davidic covenant following the division of the kingdom. The writer's point is, simply stated, that from the beginning there was rebellion; rebellion which invalidated the later cult of the Northern Kingdom and at the same time validated the Davidic covenant and superior role of Jerusalem (cf. Coats, p. 251).

Whatever one's attitude toward the nature of the event, the ultimate objective is the same: God provided water for his people in time of need. Some perhaps believe that Moses struck a solid rock that had never contained water, and water flowed from the rock. Others are equally convinced that Moses smote a water-bearing rock and opened up a previously closed spring for the people (a feat that some say has been reduplicated in the modern era; i.e., finding water by striking open a rock which sealed off a spring). Still others may agree with Noth that "the spring of Meribah gushed from a rock in a way which so surprised those who went there that they could only think that at one time the rock had been made to produce water in a miraculous way" (p. 140). God is again revealed as the source of life-giving water, a theme ultimately taken on into the New Testament assertion that Jesus was the Water of life (cf. John 4:10 ff.).

And he called the name of the place Massah and Meribah. Because of Israel's murmuring, Moses called the site "Proof and Contention." *Massah* is related to Israel's putting the Lord to the test (*naṣah*) and *Meribah* comes from *rib,* their arguing with Moses.

Israel's question concerning whether or not the Lord was with them doubtless rested upon the failure to find water. More significant than the provision of water for thirsty people was the demonstration that the Lord was with his people. This is the ultimate significance of the story: God never abandons his people, but grants to them life-giving water. "The Lord is among his people!"

(2) External Enemies: The Battle with the Amalekites (17:8–16)

8 Then came Amalek and fought with Israel at Rephidim. 9 And Moses said to Joshua, "Choose for us men, and go out, fight with Amalek; tomorrow I will stand on the top of the hill with the rod of God in my hand." 10 So Joshua did as Moses told him, and fought with Amalek; and Moses, Aaron, and Hur went up to the top of the hill. 11 Whenever Moses held up his hand, Israel prevailed; and whenever he lowered his hand, Amalek prevailed. 12 But Moses' hands grew weary; so they took a stone and put it under him, and he sat upon it, and Aaron and Hur held up his hands, one on one side, and the other on the other side; so his hands were steady until the going down of the sun. 13 And Joshua mowed down Amalek and his people with the edge of the sword.
14 And the LORD said to Moses, "Write this

as a memorial in a book and recite it in the ears of Joshua, that I will utterly blot out the remembrance of Amalek from under heaven." 15 And Moses built an altar and called the name of it, The LORD is my banner, 16 saying, "A hand upon the banner of the LORD! The LORD will have war with Amalek from generation to generation."

Amalekite origins reach back to the patriarchal era, and Amalek himself is said to have been a grandson of Esau (Gen. 36:12). The tribe was nomadic and ranged over the Sinai peninsula. They are mentioned at least 25 times in the Old Testament, and in order to clarify any discussion of the tribe one should categorize their contacts with Israel into periods of the exodus (Num. 13–14); conquest (Judges 3); monarchy (1 Samuel 14:48). Amalek is mentioned 22 times, and, again, one should carefully distinguish the chronological periods, whether the early era (Gen. 36:12); the exodus (17:8 ff.; Num. 24:20; Deut. 25:17,19); or that of the monarchy (1 Sam. 15:2 ff.).

In keeping with ancient patterns of thought, the writer probably interpreted Moses' conduct as a type of symbolic action in which Moses' action was directly responsible for the release of divine power. One might interpret the passage to mean that as long as Israelite warriors saw Moses giving the battle signal they prevailed, but that when he weakened they, too, failed. In all probability, however, the original writer saw a much more mysterious force at work. So one is confronted with the same difficult issue he had in appraising the precise role of Moses' staff in the working of the plagues or the crossing of the sea. The reader is introduced to Joshua, a second Moses, who would eventually lead Israel through the period of the conquest. Aaron and Hur became traditional examples of those who lend support to a leader. They *held up his hands . . . so his hands were steady until the going down of the sun.*

For the first time in Exodus Moses was instructed to commit material to writing. The Hebrew text uses the definite article, "the book." The material committed to writing dealt with the threat to *utterly blot out the remembrance of Amalek.* Writing material *in a book* was designed to confirm the threat or promise when it later came to pass. In all probability the material reflects the conflict between Israel and the Amalekites during the time of the monarchy, and was not limited to the wilderness period (cf. 1 Sam. 14:48; 15:1 ff.).

The name of the altar, *The Lord is my banner* (YHWH *niṣi*), may refer to the Lord as a rallying point for Israel. *Neṣ* (hence, *niṣi*) meant a standard or an ensign, such as a battle flag; hence, a sign. One wonders whether the *neṣ* may not refer to Moses' rod, held aloft as a battle standard or ensign. Ancient armies often assembled around pictures or symbols of their god; and, although orthodox Israel's cult was imageless, this verse may represent a sign of divine presence.

The Lord will have war with Amalek from generation to generation. The writer intended to convey a portent of the hostility which existed between Israel and the Amalekites throughout the period of wilderness, conquest, and monarchy. The phrase may well represent the statement of one who had already witnessed such conflict.

(3) Domestic Problems: The Visit of Jethro (18:1–27)

¹ Jethro, the priest of Midian, Moses' father-in-law, heard of all that God had done for Moses and for Israel his people, how the Lord had brought Israel out of Egypt. ² Now Jethro, Moses' father-in-law, had taken Zipporah, Moses' wife, after he had sent her away, ³ and her two sons, of whom the name of the one was Gershom (for he said, "I have been a sojourner in a foreign land"), ⁴ and the name of the other, Eliezer (for he said, "The God of my father was my help, and delivered me from the sword of Pharaoh"). ⁵ And Jethro, Moses' father-in-law, came with his sons and his wife to Moses in the wilderness where he was encamped at the mountain of God. ⁶ And when one told Moses, "Lo, your father-in-law Jethro is coming to you with your wife and her two sons with her," ⁷ Moses went out to meet his father-in-law, and did obeisance and kissed

him; and they asked each other of their welfare, and went into the tent. ⁸ Then Moses told his father-in-law all that the Lord had done to Pharaoh and to the Egyptians for Israel's sake, all the hardship that had come upon them in the way, and how the Lord had delivered them. ⁹ And Jethro rejoiced for all the good which the Lord had done to Israel, in that he had delivered them out of the hand of the Egyptians.

¹⁰ And Jethro said, "Blessed be the Lord, who has delivered you out of the hand of the Egyptians and out of the hand of Pharaoh. ¹¹ Now I know that the Lord is greater than all gods, because he delivered the people from under the hand of the Egyptians, when they dealt arrogantly with them." ¹² And Jethro, Moses' father-in-law, offered a burnt offering and sacrifices to God; and Aaron came with all the elders of Israel to eat bread with Moses' father-in-law before God.

¹³ On the morrow Moses sat to judge the people, and the people stood about Moses from morning till evening. ¹⁴ When Moses' father-in-law saw all that he was doing for the people, he said, "What is this that you are doing for the people? Why do you sit alone, and all the people stand about you from morning till evening?" ¹⁵ And Moses said to his father-in-law, "Because the people come to me to inquire of God; ¹⁶ when they have a dispute, they come to me and I decide between a man and his neighbor, and I make them know the statutes of God and his decisions." ¹⁷ Moses' father-in-law said to him, "What you are doing is not good. ¹⁸ You and the people with you will wear yourselves out, for the thing is too heavy for you; you are not able to perform it alone. ¹⁹ Listen now to my voice; I will give you counsel, and God be with you! You shall represent the people before God, and bring their cases to God; ²⁰ and you shall teach them the statutes and the decisions, and make them know the way in which they must walk and what they must do. ²¹ Moreover choose able men from all the people, such as fear God, men who are trustworthy and who hate a bribe; and place such men over the people as rulers of thousands, of hundreds, of fifties, and of tens. ²² And let them judge the people at all times; every great matter they shall bring to you, but any small matter they shall decide themselves; so it will be easier for you, and they will bear the burden with you. ²³ If you do this, and God so commands you, then you will be able to endure, and all this people also will go to their place in peace."

²⁴ So Moses gave heed to the voice of his father-in-law and did all that he had said. ²⁵ Moses chose able men out of all Israel, and made them heads over the people, rulers of

thousands, of hundreds, of fifties, and of tens. ²⁶ And they judged the people at all times; hard cases they brought to Moses, but any small matter they decided themselves. ²⁷ Then Moses let his father-in-law depart, and he went his way to his own country.

The visit of Jethro revolved around two basic areas of concern, the one related to the other. First, Jethro heard of the Lord's victorious deeds on behalf of Israel, and, having expressed renewed confidence in the Lord, led in a cultic ceremony. Second, and possibly related to Jethro's cultic role, since the dispensing of decisions was originally a sacral act, Jethro advised Moses to adopt a better method of dispensing justice.

Prior to the cultic ceremony, however, Jethro reunited Moses with his wife and sons, and heard of the Lord's mighty deeds (vv. 1–9).

The oldest form of the text may have contained only "Moses' father-in-law," and the insertion of "Jethro" may be a later attempt toward clarification. Moses' father-in-law is referred to in a variety of ways: "Jethro his father-in-law" (4:18 + 9 times, all E), "Hobab the father-in-law of Moses" (Judg. 4:11; cf. Num. 10:29), and Moses' wife and sisters-in-law returned "to their father Reuel" (2:18, J). Hicks suggests the following possibilities:

"(a) All three names may refer to the same person; (b) Reuel may be a tribal rather than personal appellation; (c) Hobab may be Moses' brother-in-law; (d) Hobab and Jethro may designate the father-in-law, with Reuel as Hobab's father (and being a gloss at Exod. 2:18). The last is widely accepted" (IDB, IV, 54).

And Jethro said, "Blessed be the Lord. . . . Now I know that the Lord is greater than all gods." Such a reference may mean that Jethro for the first time acknowledged the Lord, or that Jethro's previous relationship with the Lord was confirmed by his mighty action. The fact that he later offered sacrifices to God (apparently taking the leading role) would tend to confirm the second possibility, although it does not de-

mand such an interpretation. Although Moses had known the God of his fathers from early childhood, through the teaching of his parents, it was only after his original contact with the Midianites that he came to know God as the Lord YHWH (cf. 2:15b ff.). Consequently, some feel that Jethro and the Midianites (or Kenites) were the mediators of the name Yahweh, bearing it from Hebrews in the south of Judah to Moses. Such a view is possible, but hardly the only explanation for Moses' unique apprehension of the name YHWH.

Jethro's recognition that the Lord was *greater than all gods* reflected the common view of the day. Thus, far from detracting from the Lord by associating him with other gods, Jethro's statement represented a genuine commitment of life to the Lord. (Cf. Psalms 77:13; 86:8 for a comparable biblical view of the Lord as sovereign over other gods.)

Apparently, Jethro officiated as priest at the ceremony. Some, who object to the idea of a "non-Israelite" officiating, insist that Jethro offered sacrifices only as a worshiper. It would seem, however, that Jethro did officiate, and, in this capacity, gave evidence of religious associations between the Midianites and the Israelites (to whom the Midianites were related through Keturah; cf. Gen. 25:1 ff.; 1 Chron. 1:32).

The statement that Aaron and the elders of Israel came to Jethro strengthens the view that Jethro officiated. The meal was likely a communal meal eaten before God or a means of establishing community between the two groups. Moses was not mentioned as a participant in the communal meal, but if the purpose of the meal was to seal relationships between the Israelites and the Midianites, this would explain why it was unnecessary for Moses to share in the meal. He had already been initiated into Midianite fellowship during the period of his exile and sojourn in Midian.

Following the worship ceremony (vv. 10–12), Jethro counseled Moses concerning a more acceptable method of administering justice (vv. 13–24).

Moses is here introduced in the role of *shophet,* judge.

The many-faceted ministry of Moses led Walther Eichrodt to suggest that "it is characteristic of Moses that it should be impossible to classify him in any of the ordinary categories applicable to a leader of a nation; he is neither a king, nor a commander of an army, nor a tribal chieftain, nor a priest, nor an inspired seer and medicine man. To some extent he belongs to all these categories; but none of them adequately explains his position. . . . *It is precisely the secret of this man's greatness that he unites in himself gifts not normally found in combination,* and is therefore, able to work with lasting effect in the most diverse fields." [39]

The two actions, inquiring of God and settling a dispute, are probably related, if not synonymous. *Darash* may mean to tread in the sense of resorting to a place (Deut. 12:5). In the vast majority of the cases it came to mean seeking, consulting, or inquiring of the Lord, although it also had other related meanings (to inquire, investigate, demand). *Dispute* translates *dabar,* which most often means word. *Dabar* came to be used in a very general way of any matter or affair about which one speaks: business (1 Sam. 21:8), acts (1 Kings 11:41), affair (as, the affair of Uriah, 1 Kings 15:5), events (Gen. 15:1), or a cause or case for judicial investigation (cf. 18:16; 22:8–9; 24:14). Hence, the word *dabar* is in this instance rather colorless. It suggests no connotation of strife or dispute as such, but referred to anything that arose between people. One would, however, assume that such decisions were argumentative in nature.

There were four characteristics for men who would share judicial responsibility with Moses. First, they were to be *able men.* Able (*chayil*) most often means strength, usually physical. It is used of mighty men of valor, heroic men (cf. Josh.

[39] *Theology of the Old Testament,* I, 289 f. Italics are mine.

1:14; Judg. 6:12; 1 Kings 11:28), and also of a force or army (14:4, 9, 17, 28). The word also connotes ability or efficiency, often involving moral worth (Prov. 12:4; 31:10; Ruth 3:11). However, of 244 usages in the Old Testament only 13 refer to "ability," 30 refer to wealth, and all others refer to strength and to a force or army.

Septuagint translators understood the word to mean strong, mighty, or powerful (*dunatos*). Either heroic men, or men of strength, is a good translation.

Second, men to whom authority is delegated must be those who *fear God,* a phrase fraught with overtones of reverence, awe, wonder, dedication, religious commitment.

Third, men chosen are to be *trustworthy* (literally, men of truth). '*Emeth* means firmness, faithfulness, or truth. It is used of reliability, as a "sure way" (Gen. 24:48); stability or continuance (Isa. 39:8; Esther 9:30; Jer. 33:6); faithfulness or reliability (Neh. 7:2; 1 Kings 2:4). Basically, "dependability" sums up the essence of its meaning. The noun ('*emeth*) came from the verb '*aman,* meaning confirm or support. Derivatives of the verb are foster father (Num. 11:12), foster mother (Ruth 4:16), pillars or supporters of the door (2 Kings 18:16). The verb came to mean "believe" in the sense of depend upon. Hence, whoever or whatever is '*emeth* is dependable. You can lean upon him for support, as the door does upon the doorpost or a child upon its foster parent.

Fourth, the final prerequisite for those to assist Moses was the repudiation of the bribe. The dishonest judge and witness were constant sources of irritation in Israel, and they were the special object of prophetic wrath. Moses' assistants must *hate a bribe.* Such abhorrence of the bribe may reflect an actual situation much later than Moses, in the settled community where the problem of bribery and judicial injustice had become realities.

The authority with which Jethro spoke for God, *And God so commands you,* suggests that he occupied a special role in the Midianite-Israelite structure which gave to him the power to speak in this manner to Moses.

Moses' character is reflected in both his willingness to accept the counsel of another religious leader in implementing a new approach to governing the people, and his delegation of authority to responsible men within the community.

Initially, all judicial matters were religious in the sense that a religious leader had to determine the will of God in particular cases. As cases were heard, however, there grew up a body of "case law" (comparable to the Book of the Covenant, 21–23). Minor judges decided cases on the basis of precedent, while major decisions, especially those involving a new area of decision, were given to the central religious leader who determined the will of God through oracle, lot, or other technical means.

The present passage may represent the first separation between the religious and secular areas of judicial life, although one should never distinguish between "sacred" and "secular" to the same degree in biblical as in modern thought.

The whole literary complex extending from Exodus 7:14—18:27 may be summarized under the theme, "Yahweh, Lord of Creation." The whole of the created order is subservient to the providential reality of the Lord. The plagues were more than chance happenings, they were one segment of the purposive will of God. Phenomena of the created order coincided with the need of Israel in such manner as to confirm the prior faith of Moses in the power of the Lord to deliver his people. Each plague struck at some aspect of Egyptian divinized power, and the struggle reflected in the plagues was not simply that of Moses and the king of Egypt but that of Yahweh, Lord of Israel, and the gods of Egypt present in Pharaoh and represented by the various magicians of Egypt.

The sea, ancient symbol of chaos and a power unto itself according to the thought patterns of many ancient peoples, yielded to the sovereign power of the Lord. For not only did the victory at the sea utterly destroy Egyptian divinized power in the person of Pharaoh but the sea itself was conquered, and ever after that moment Israel sang of the kingship of Yahweh and his victory over the sea.

The wilderness, abode of unknown and hostile powers antagonistic to the ordered life of man, was no less subservient to the power of the Lord. It is highly significant that it was in the wilderness that the Lord manifested his providential deliverance of Israel by preserving them from the elemental human needs of thirst, hunger, and despair. For the wilderness, somewhat like the sea, was an area foreign to the gods of settled lands.

Thus, Yahweh is sovereign Lord of the created order. He triumphed over the gods of Egypt and their nature-oriented manifestations. The sea yielded to his sovereign power, as did the wilderness. Indeed the whole of the created order rests beneath his lordship. Just as he is Lord of history (1:1—7:13), so is he Lord of creation (7:14—18:27). The redemptive Lord of the exodus is sovereign Lord of all.

Part Three
Yahweh: Lord of Man
19:1—24:14

The Exodus narrative at this point portrays Yahweh as sovereign Lord over the life of man (19:1—24:14). Both the nature of the covenant relationship and the authoritative character of the law underscore Yahweh's lordship.

All of Exodus 1—18 is preparatory to the events described in 19—24, and the Sinai narrative (19:1—24:14; 32:1—34:35) is the climatic point of the entire book. All before Sinai is prelude; all that follows is postlude. Here is the mountain of God, so often mentioned as the object of Moses' dream. Especially is Sinai the scene of the sealing of the covenant and the establishment of a continuing relationship between Yahweh and the Hebrews. Upon the basis of the covenant sealed at Sinai and affirmed at Shechem the isolated tribes of the preconquest period were forged into the semblance of a union that later became a nation.

I. Yahweh: The Holy One of Israel (19:1-25)

In all probability the narrative now imbedded in chapter 19 was often used in the worship life of Israel, both in the Northern and Southern kingdoms. The historical acts of God associated with the faith of Israel were often recreated in worship, and the central act of lawgiving and covenant must surely have been crucial in the annual religious festivals. Thus, the present call to prepare for the appearance of the Lord may have been used as men of later generations prepared to receive a comparable theophany or appearance of God.

1. The Call to Covenant Life (19:1-9a)

¹ On the third new moon after the people of Israel had gone forth out of the land of Egypt, on that day they came into the wilderness of Sinai. ² And when they set out from Rephidim and came into the wilderness of Sinai, they encamped in the wilderness; and there Israel encamped before the mountain. ³ And Moses went up to God, and the LORD called to him out of the mountain, saying, "Thus you shall say to the house of Jacob, and tell the people of Israel: ⁴ You have seen what I did to the Egyptians, and how I bore you on eagles' wings and brought you to myself. ⁵ Now therefore, if you will obey my voice and keep my covenant, you shall be my own possession among all peoples; for all the earth is mine, ⁶ and you shall be to me a kingdom of priests and a holy nation. These are the words which you shall speak to the children of Israel."
⁷ So Moses came and called the elders of the people, and set before them all these words which the LORD had commanded him. ⁸ And all the people answered together and said, "All that the LORD has spoken we will do." And Moses reported the words of the people to the LORD. ⁹ And the LORD said to Moses, "Lo, I am coming to you in a thick cloud, that the people may hear when I speak with you, and may also believe you for ever."

The essential content here is an invitation to meet the Lord at Sinai, to obey his

voice, and to enter into covenant relationship with him (cf. vv. 4 f.). Thus, this paragraph summarizes well the whole of chapters 19—24; meeting Yahweh (19), the law of God (20—23), and the sealing of the covenant (24).

Obey my voice may point toward 20.1, "And God spoke all these words." Keeping the covenant suggests the covenant stipulations in legal form found in Exodus 21:1 ff. (i.e., the whole of the Book of the Covenant, 20:22—23:33). To "keep" (*shamar*) means to keep or have charge of, as a garden (Gen. 2:15), the ark (1 Sam. 7:1), or property in trust (22:7); to keep or retain, as in storing up food (Gen. 41:35); to meet one's obligations or discharge an office (Num. 3:7–10); but also, as in this context, to keep the Lord's covenant (cf. Deut. 29:9; 1 Kings 11:11).

The phrase *kingdom of priests and a holy nation* appears only in this context (cf. Isa. 61:6; 1 Peter 2:5,9). Those who are faithful to the Lord enter into a positional and functional relationship with him. They attain the position of men dedicated supremely to the Lord, and they function as those who mediate the covenant life.

The Lord's promise is not far from the later declaration of Moses, "Would that all the Lord's people were prophets" (Num. 11:29). The promise to Israel concerning a universal priesthood is closely related to the concept of the priesthood of the believer: every man within the covenant community is a priest before God.

On the other hand, while the above interpretation is possible, the writer may have meant no more than that Israel was to become a people uniquely dedicated to the Lord. Both "kingdom of priests" and "holy nation" may stand in synonymous parallelism to the former promise that Israel would be "my own possession."

All that the Lord has spoken we will do. Israel's response so directly parallels that of Exodus 24:3,7 as to cause one to conclude that all of 19:1–7 is a portrait in miniature of the larger complex of events described in 19—24. The phrase sounds as though it may have been a cultic response to stipulations set before the people during a time of worship. The specific phrase, however, is limited to 19:7; 24:3,7. It does not occur in cultic passages such as the Psalms or other portions of the Law or the Prophets. Ezekiel used almost the same phrase, however, as a means of underscoring the Lord's certain fulfilment of particular actions: "I the Lord have spoken, and I will do it" (17:24).

Numerous areas of the Old Testament describe God's presence through a nature theophany (Ex. 19:16 ff.; Judg. 5:4 ff.; 1 Sam. 12:17 ff.), but some psalms are especially graphic in their theophanic descriptions (cf. 18:7 ff.; 29:1 ff.). That the mysterious forces of storm, fire, and earthquake were equated with the presence of God should occasion no surprise. One would expect ancient men to equate the powerful and the mysterious with the divine to a degree seldom approximated in a scientifically oriented age.

The Lord revealed himself to ancient Israelites in keeping with their own patterns of thought, as, in this instance, the belief that God was present in the storm and fire.

In viewing ancient media of revelation one would do well to remember that the validity of revelation does not depend upon the media used. Legitimate revelation may come through a succession of physical and psychically conditioned media which are part of the temporary thought processes of a culture, without adversely affecting the validity of the revelation.

2. Consecration Preparatory to Meeting the Lord (19:9b–15)

Then Moses told the words of the people to the LORD. 10 And the LORD said to Moses, "Go to the people and consecrate them today and tomorrow, and let them wash their garments, 11 and be ready by the third day; for on the third day the LORD will come down upon Mount Sinai in the sight of all the people. 12 And you shall set bounds for the people round about, saying, 'Take heed that you do not go up into the mountain or touch the border of it; whoever touches the mountain shall be put to death; 13 no hand shall touch him, but he shall be stoned or shot; whether beast or man, he shall not live.' When the trumpet sounds a long blast, they shall come up to the mountain." 14 So Moses went down from the mountain to the people, and consecrated the people; and they washed their garments. 15 And he said to the people, "Be ready by the third day; do not go near a woman."

Ancient men lived in a world dominated by the sacred. Some objects were holy, characterized by "mana," the mysterious and positive divine force within sacred objects, sites, and persons. Others were equally holy, but were "taboo." As objects or persons dedicated to god(s), they possessed mysterious negative forces. One sought always to appropriate the positive forces of holiness, that which was "mana." On the other hand, one dared not appropriate that which was "taboo." To violate the holiness of the god(s) was to risk disaster, perhaps death. Against such a background as this the consecration of Israel at Sinai may best be understood.

"Consecrate" translates the verb *qadhash*, related to the noun *qodhesh*, "apartness, sacredness," and the adjective *qadhosh*, "sacred, holy." The root meaning of all the forms is that of separation or withdrawal. That this may involve withdrawal from the world of the profane or common does not negate the fact that the direction of the word is positive. Hence contemporary understandings of "holiness" which stress separation from the world may miss the biblical emphasis. Biblically, holiness on the part of man involves dedication *to* God. The direction is always positive. When used of God, *qdsh* suggests the "otherness" of God. He is God and not man —an entirely different essence as well as being.

Consecration was at times effected through anointing with oil or blood (cf. Lev. 8:30), the sacrifice of an appropriate animal(s) (29:10 ff.; Lev. 12:6 ff.), and on occasions by washings of the body (cf. 29:4; Lev. 1:9), or, as in the case of purifying lepers, by shaving one's hair (Lev.

14:8 ff.). In view of the time required for the consecration of Israel at Sinai (two days, i.e., "today and tomorrow"), dietary considerations were perhaps involved. Abstinence from sexual intercourse was also enjoined (19:15). Even garments were to be washed (v. 10), a practice in keeping with the general custom of washing one's garments in order to purify oneself (cf. Lev. 11:25,28,40; 14:8-9; 15:5-8; 17:15).

Those who violated the holiness of the restricted area were to be put to death by stone or arrow in order that no human hand would touch the one who had violated the Lord's holiness. Because the offender had shared the negative aspects of holiness (taboo), no one was to touch him, lest he be affected by the offender's condition. Later Israelites believed that evil was contagious, but that holiness was not (cf. Hag. 2:11 ff.). Hence, the command was likely grounded in the belief that if the man was not "unclean," he at least possessed negative qualities detrimental to those who might come in contact with him.

Do not go near a woman. Sexual abstinence was apparently a part of one's purification rite. For example, when David asked for bread from the priest Ahimelech at Nob, Ahimelech agreed to allow David's men to participate in the holiness of the bread, "if only the young men have kept themselves from women" (1 Sam. 21:4; cf. 2 Sam. 11:6 ff). David's answer illustrates the consecration of men involved in a holy war; "Of a truth women have been kept from us as always when I go on an expedition; the vessels of the young men are holy, even when it is a common journey; how much more today will their vessels be holy?" (1 Sam. 21:5).

3. The Coming of the Lord (19:16-25)

16 On the morning of the third day there were thunders and lightnings, and a thick cloud upon the mountain, and a very loud trumpet blast, so that all the people who were in the camp trembled. 17 Then Moses brought the people out of the camp to meet God; and they took their stand at the foot of the mountain. 18 And Mount Sinai was wrapped in

smoke, because the LORD descended upon it in fire; and the smoke of it went up like the smoke of a kiln, and the whole mountain quaked greatly. 19 And as the sound of the trumpet grew louder and louder, Moses spoke, and God answered him in thunder. 20 And the LORD came down upon Mount Sinai, to the top of the mountain; and the LORD called Moses to the top of the mountain, and Moses went up. 21 And the LORD said to Moses, "Go down and warn the people, lest they break through to the LORD to gaze and many of them perish. 22 And also let the priests who come near to the LORD consecrate themselves, lest the LORD break out upon them." 23 And Moses said to the LORD, "The people cannot come up to Mount Sinai; for thou thyself didst charge us, saying, 'Set bounds about the mountain, and consecrate it.' " 24 And the LORD said to him, "Go down, and come up bringing Aaron with you; but do not let the priests and the people break through to come up to the LORD, lest he break out against them." 25 So Moses went down to the people and told them.

Anyone who speaks of the coming of God must do so in keeping with the cultural patterns of thought in which he shares. The very real and personal appearance of the Lord is described in verses 16 ff. against the background of cultural patterns of thought consonant with the second millennium B.C. Drawing on the storm and fire theophanies, the writer portrayed the Lord's appearance in a thunderstorm. Perhaps the narrative reflects a double emphasis upon storm theophany, embracing cloud, thunder, and lightning (vv. 16,19, E), and the earthquake as a theophanic appearance of the Lord (v. 18, J). It could not be emphasized too strongly, however that, despite the transient nature of the thought patterns, the revelation of God was legitimate, personal, and effectual in the sense that it was the focal point of Israel's personal commitment to the Lord within the framework of the covenant.

And a very loud trumpet blast. The *thunders and lightnings, and a thick cloud* were followed by the sounding of the shophar (RSV, trumpet). Was the trumpet part of the natural phenomena, some type of blasting noise associated with storm or volcano? Or, was an actual trumpet used to assemble the people? The word for trumpet (shophar) in this verse is distinct from trumpet (*yovel*) in verse 13. The shophar is mentioned almost twice as often as the *yovel* (72 vs. 27 instances), although the two are synonymous in Joshua 6:5. The shophar of verse 16 probably was a musical instrument, synonymous with *yovel* of verse 13.

The trumpet was used at times in later Israel in connection with worship (cf. Joel 2:15; Psalms 47:5; 81:3; 98:6; 150:3; 2 Chron. 15:14), and the awesome silence following the blast of the trumpet may have signified the theophanic presence of the Lord in worship; "God has gone up with a shout, the Lord with the sound of a trumpet" (Psalm 47:5).

And Mount Sinai was wrapped in smoke. Numerous scholars believe that Sinai was volcanic, and that the description of Exodus 19 depicts an active volcano. However, the writer may well have used metaphorical language drawn from volcanic terminology to describe the awesome experience.

Throughout chapter 19 the writer(s) probably used metaphors drawn from various nature theophanies, but did not attempt to describe actual seismic or meteorological conditions.

The sound of the trumpet grew louder and louder. This statement suggests that the purpose of the trumpet was more than a means of calling Israel to assemble before the mountain. In some way it appears to be directly related to the revelation of God. If it did not depict some aspect of the natural order, then it probably is related to the sound of the trumpet, announcing the theophany of Yahweh during worship. It may be that the loud, intermittent blasts on the trumpet announced the appearance of the Lord in the worship center, and that the present statement is a reflection of later cultic usage. At the climax of the blasting of the shophar the Lord spoke to Moses.

God answered him in thunder. The word for thunder (*qol*) is identical with the word for voice. Thunder is the voice of God. Since *qol* is also translated thunder in numerous contexts (cf. Ex. 9:23 ff.; 1 Sam.

12:17; Job 28:26), and in view of the storm motif in Exodus 19, the translation "thunder" is preferable here in verse 19. On occasions, however, translators render *qol* as the Lord's voice (cf. Gen. 22:18; 26:5; Ex. 5:2; 15:26; 19:5). Also, within Israel there was the belief that the Lord spoke the Decalogue so that Israel could hear: "The Lord spoke with you face to face at the mountain, out of the midst of the fire" (Deut. 5:4; cf. Ex. 20:1 f.). It is possible to translate the phrase in verse 19 as ". . . God answered him by voice."[1]

The nineteenth chapter of Exodus is a significant and relevant biblical statement dealing with the Lord's call to covenant life, challenging man to respond in such manner to the revelation of God as to become the Lord's unique possession, "a kingdom of priests and a holy nation" (19:6). Man cannot approach God apart from a covenant-mediator (vv. 7–9a), but under his leadership man may so consecrate himself that he can experience the presence of God (vv. 9b–15). Once man has responded in faith to the invitation to covenant life, and has consecrated himself in keeping with the Lord's instructions, then the Lord breaks into his life, confronting him against the background of his cultural patterns of thought, and, most of all, disclosing his will through a personal meeting with the covenant-mediator (vv. 16–25).

II. The Decalogue: Foundation for Covenant Life (20:1–21)

The genius of Israel's existence was her commitment to the Lord, and the covenant which sealed that commitment was the cohesive force that held together the disparate elements of the early confederacy. The earliest organization of the tribes was a religious federation based upon a common allegiance to the Lord, centered

---

1 When one considers that v. 19 is generally ascribed to E, and that the Elohistic narrative does not begin again until 20:1 ff., the tentative suggestion that *qol* should read "voice" is strengthened. Reading *qol* as voice, the E narrative indicates that "God answered him by voice" (v. 19), "and God spoke all these words" (20:1).

around a central sanctuary.

Central to the Sinai covenant were the stipulations known popularly as the Ten Commandments, or, more properly, the Decalogue ("ten words").[2]

The Decalogue contains those principles which were to govern the relationship between Israel and the Lord and which became, in time, the foundation for other legislation incorporated into the covenant community. As stipulations which set forth the obligations of Israel toward God within the covenant, the Decalogue was the foundation of covenant life. It was not the means to achieving the covenant, for the covenant was an expression of God's grace. But the law served as a net cast over Israel, insuring that she was within the bounds of covenant fellowship. Finally, later laws within Israel were the outworking of principles inherent in the Decalogue.

1. The Worth and the Worship of God (20:1–11)

1 And God spoke all these words, saying,
2 "I am the LORD your God, who brought you out of the land of Egypt, out of the house of bondage.
3 "You shall have no other gods before me.
4 "You shall not make for yourself a graven image, or any likeness of anything that is in heaven above, or that is in the earth beneath, or that is in the water under the earth; 5 you shall not bow down to them or serve them; for I the LORD your God am a jealous God, visiting the iniquity of the fathers upon the children to the third and the fourth generation of those who hate me, 6 but showing steadfast love to thousands of those who love me and keep my commandments.
7 "You shall not take the name of the LORD your God in vain; for the LORD will not hold him guiltless who takes his name in vain.
8 "Remember the sabbath day, to keep it holy. 9 Six days you shall labor, and do all your work; 10 but the seventh day is a sabbath to the LORD your God; in it you shall not do any work, you, or your son, or your daughter, your man-

---

2 The covenant stipulations are known in the Old Testament as (1) the "ten words," hence decalogue, from *deka logous* (Deut. 10:4; cf. Deut. 4:13; Ex. 34:28); (2) "the testimony" (Ex. 25:16), and (3) "the covenant" (Ex. 34:28; Deut. 4:13; 9:9). They were ten "words" in the sense of concepts, principles, or declarations of the Lord's will.

servant, or your maidservant, or your cattle, or the sojourner who is within your gates; 11 for in six days the LORD made heaven and earth, the sea, and all that is in them, and rested the seventh day; therefore the LORD blessed the sabbath day and hallowed it.

The worth and the worship of God constitute the vertical dimensions of the Decalogue. The worth of God focuses in the uniqueness of God—the stipulation that there is but one who may be worshiped in the community of faith, Yahweh—the Lord (v. 3). The worship of God is grounded in the worth of God, and the second through the fourth obligations stipulate that the right God is to be worshiped in the right manner (vv. 4–11).

Preamble (vv. 1–2). A careful examination of the material preceding and following 20:1–17 reveals the manner in which the Decalogue "sits loosely" in its present literary context. The fear of Israel, so graphically portrayed in chapter 19, is introduced again in 20:18, with the result that the deletion of 20:1–17 would not interrupt the flow of the narrative.

The suggestion that the Decalogue may have had a separate literary history is considerably strengthened by the realization that the Decalogue appears again in Deuteronomy (cf. 5:6 ff.). Although the ten stipulations (coinciding, perhaps, with the ten fingers) are identical in major emphases, there are certain differences in the elaboration attached to certain of the separate forms (cf. vv. 4,5,10 especially). These differences do not alter the basic meaning of the commandments, but they do suggest that the commandments have had a separate literary history during which they tended to circulate and to develop emphases unique to a particular locale or era within the history of Israel.

I am the Lord your God. In keeping with the format of covenant agreements in the ancient Near East, Israel's covenant with the Lord began with a preamble which identified the author of the covenant. Notice that the Lord alone was mentioned. The covenant was made solely by the Lord and was not a joint covenant between Israel and the Lord, as between equals. The covenant originated in the lordship of Yahweh over the life of man. He is Lord, and his sovereignty was the source of the covenant.

Who brought you out of the land of Egypt. In the suzerainty treaties of the ancient Near East great attention was placed upon the beneficient deeds of the king toward the vassal. Thus, it is not surprising that the Sinai covenant was predicated upon this historical prologue describing God's redemptive activity. This statement is fundamental to numerous aspects of Israelite thought and worship. The exodus was Israel's key to her self-understanding as a people, her concept of the redeemer God, the theocentric conception of history, as well as her continuing life of worship.

So fundamental is this verse for many, that within Judaism it is counted as the first of the commandments. Verses 3 and 4 are then reckoned as the second commandment, so that the total number remains ten.[3]

The Uniqueness of Yahweh (v. 3). Israel was to give neither allegiance nor worship to any other god. Often understood to mean that there is only one God, the first stipulation insists, rather, that among all the gods of the ancient Near East, the Lord was supreme in the worship of Israel. This does not mean that Israel could worship other gods as long as the Lord remained at the apex of her theistic structure. The commandment passes over the other gods of the ancient world in silence, and comes to

[3] The total number of ten commandments is unquestioned. Since there is no means of distinguishing the separate commandments in the biblical text, however, the division of the biblical material into ten commandments has been the subject of extensive debate. In addition to the division within Judaism, Roman and Lutheran churches, following Augustine, combine verses 3 and 4 into a single commandment, but divide verse 17 into two commandments in order to retain the tenfold division. The arrangement with which most readers are acquainted was recognized by ancient Jewish writers, Philo and Josephus, Origen and the early Christian church, the later Greek church, and the reformed churches generally.

the point of true significance in its insistence that Israel shall worship no other gods.

There did come the time when Israel affirmed that not only should one worship only the Lord, but that he alone existed; all other gods were illusions (Isa. 45:5; 46:1 f.). Although there may have been keenly sensitive persons throughout the history of Israel (i.e., from the time of the exodus) who themselves were monotheistic, true monotheism was apprehended on the larger scale much later in Israel's faith experience.

The word from the Lord (v. 3) took religious commitment for granted. There were no atheists in the Ancient Near East; gods abounded on every hand. At Sinai Israel's initial decision was identical with the later question posed at the covenant renewal ceremony; "And if you be unwilling to serve the Lord, choose this day whom you will serve (Josh. 24:15; cf. 1 Kings 18:21).

Contemporary man faces essentially the same decision posed by the first of the covenant stipulations, although in a form modified by the differences between the cultural context of the Sinai covenant and his own situation in life.

The Means of Revelation (vv. 4-6). Ancient worshipers knew that in many cases the god was more cosmic than local, but the idol remained a means of revelation, and through it the vital forces of the god(s) were available for the worshiper.

In opposition to revelation through the idol, God's revelation focused in the word. Hence, within the Old Testament the "word" and the "name" came to convey the reality of God's presence. The Lord reveals himself through his word, and his presence is made known as he causes his "name" to dwell in a particular place (cf. Deut. 12:5 ff.), as men praise the "name" of Yahweh (Psalm 61:8), or as men otherwise worship in the "name" of Yahweh (cf. Psalms 48:10; 72:17; 74:7; 96:8).

Thus, the stipulation deals with the hidden manner in which the Lord's revelation comes in both history and worship (cf. Deut. 4:15 ff.). Men always seek a concrete manifestation, an idol, which can be controlled and manipulated as the means of revelation. But this cannot be. The Lord's revelation was through word: living and active, mysterious and susceptible to certain fluidity.

The biblical writer saw the universe in terms of three stories: the heaven above, the earth, and the world beneath. Nothing from any of these areas, the total of the created order, is to be used as an idol for the Lord's worship. The prohibition was never designed to include general art work, but was a polemic against the manner in which the idols were interpreted as revelations of the deities. (Note, for example, the highly decorative art work of both the tabernacle and the Temple). In English, "jealous" connotes a certain pettiness which is not characteristic of the biblical word. The adjective "jealous" (*qana'*) is used only of the Lord (cf. 34:14; Deut. 5:9). The word connotes zeal or ardor, and one might say that God is zealous.

One is always tempted to objectify God in such manner as to become guilty of idolatry. But the revelation of God is living and active, and often there is a radical discontinuity between the inbreak of God as living word and the concretized form of previous understandings of his nature and will. Many men still cling to a medium of revelation that is mechanical and rigid.

Too often, "We fear a word from God, a gospel that is like new wine, fermenting and expanding, discontent, and unable to remain in old forms. We want a word from God that is stabilized so that we can handle it and control it. But when the word of God ceases to be living, active, fermenting in the heat of its own movement, and at times bursting old wineskins or tearing new patches off old garments, it will no longer be God's word but man's word that we confront." [4]

[4] Roy L. Honeycutt, *These Ten Words* (Nashville: Broadman Press, 1966), pp. 35 f.

With regard to the extended length of this particular stipulation, it should be observed that originally each of the covenant stipulations, or commandments, was probably exceedingly brief, much like forms 1, 6,7,8. The elaboration of the commandment is doubtless later than the original statement, and it is now impossible to reconstruct the original form of each commandment. The stronger arguments for this position include the points of difference between identical commandments in chapter 20 and Deuteronomy 5. To the original, pithy saying there was added commentary or hortatory material either explaining the command or appealing to the reader/listener to obey. It is this added commentary and homiletical material which contains divergent emphases in the two forms of the commandments.

Protecting the Lord's Name (v. 7). If the Lord reveals himself essentially in his word, and thus appears before men through his word as opposed to an idol (as suggested in the second commandment), then it is logical to anticipate a unique veneration of the Lord's name within Israel. This was the intent and purpose of the third covenant stipulation.

The name in biblical thought summed up the essence of a person, compressing one's whole being into one, articulated form (cf. the manner in which the names for the prophets graphically summarized their ministries and/or personalities). Names in Israel were often consonant with some unique characteristic, and on occasion, as in the case of Jacob, could be changed in keeping with some basic change of character or personality on the part of the individual (cf. the change of Jacob to Israel, Gen. 32:27 f.). This was no less true of God than of man, and the name of God expressed the particular connotation of God for the name-giver.

In vain. The interpretation of this stipulation hinges upon the meaning of the single word "vain" (*shawe'*). The word means emptiness, nothingness, or vanity, in the sense of being ineffective or lacking in purpose; emptiness of speech, and hence that which is false, whether of prophecy (Ezek. 12:24), or speech (Isa. 59:4); and worthlessness of conduct.

When one considers that what the idol was to the noncovenantal person the Name was to the covenant member, the conviction is intensified that the third commandment had a cultic setting. The word *shawe'* most likely carried evil connotations which went far beyond the limited concept of falsehood. Von Rad correctly suggests that it may have had magical connotations and cites S. Mowinckel that "even in Israel people were at times liable to use Jahweh's name for sinister purposes dangerous to the community." [5]

The fact that the command appears at the center of those exhortations which sought to guarantee the proper worship of the Lord gives added weight to an interpretation of the commandment which stresses the negative use of the name in worship. The strong probability is that the writer sought to prohibit a semimagical or magical use of the Lord's name.

Beyond the improper manipulation of the Lord's name in worship, his name could be profaned by falseswearing (Lev. 19:12) or by abandoning the worship of the Lord (cf. Lev. 18:21; 20:3). Thus, in the broader sense, any action which denied the centrality of the Lord's revelation through his word and name was to take his name "in vain."

The third of the covenant stipulations deals forthrightly with the continual tendency of men to manipulate the name of God, using it for their own ends and robbing it of intrinsic meaning. Members of the covenant community are warned against paganizing their faith by perverting it into no more than a restructured magic by which God may be coerced into fulfilling the worshiper's will.

Sanctifying the Sabbath (vv. 8–11). What was the principle inherent within the sanctity of the seventh day, and its rela-

tionship to the covenant? The principle of *pars pro toto* (the part may stand for the whole) was significant for several Old Testament practices. For example, first fruits were dedicated to the Lord in the belief that the whole of the crop was compressed into the first offering. In the giving of the part, the whole was also being offered up to God. The same was true of the sacrifice of the firstborn animal, or the dedication of the firstborn of men. Future offspring were symbolically compressed into the animal sacrificed or the child dedicated. Even part of the people could stand or act for the whole family or nation, as in the case of Aachan (Josh. 7:1 ff.) or the Suffering Servant (Isa. 53:1 ff.).

The same principle was probably inherent in the sabbath. The whole of the week was symbolically compressed into the one day and dedicated to the Lord. By refraining from his own efforts on that day, man effectually recognized divine ownership. Thus, all time belonged to God, as did the whole of the creation. Just as all of the grain, grapes, flock, herd, fruit, etc., belonged to him, and man acknowledged this by sacrificing a part of the whole in lieu of the whole, so in the case of the sabbath. Man "sanctified" a part of the week, and in so doing acknowledged that in reality the whole was the Lord's. Rest allowed the whole of creation to return to its primal condition with the Lord.

The essential meaning of the fourth stipulation is clear, whether in verses 8 ff. or Deuteronomy 5:12 ff. There are, however, numerous points of difference between the commentary section of the commandment as it appears in Exodus and Deuteronomy. First, Exodus begins, "Remember" (*zakhar*, v. 8); Deuteronomy, "Observe" (*shamar*, guard, or keep, 5:12).

Second, Deuteronomy makes additions not found in Exodus. Following the exhortation to "keep it holy," the Deuteronomist adds "as the Lord your God commanded you." Also, following the prohibition of work, the Deuteronomist adds "your ox, or your ass," which has no counterpart in the

[5] *Old Testament Theology,* p. 183.

Exodus form of the command.

Third, Exodus appeals to Israel to keep the sabbath holy because of the creative activity of the Lord (v. 11) but makes no mention of the exodus. Deuteronomy, on the other hand, appeals on the basis that "you were a servant in the land of Egypt" (5:15). The minor additions present in Deuteronomy do not alter the meaning of the commandment, but they do reflect an added emphasis upon the legal nature of the command, and either the humanitarian concern for one's animals or the conviction that on the sabbath day all creation should return to its primal condition, animals included (a highly probable interpretation).

The sanctity of one day in seven continues to embody the Christian's understanding of the essential sanctity of all time, and the conviction that man is the recipient of time through God's grace. Rewarding observance of the stipulation is grounded in an act of free will in which one consecrates one day in seven as a symbol of the consecration of all his time.

2. Other Men Have Rights, Too (20:12–17)

12 "Honor your father and your mother, that your days may be long in the land which the LORD your God gives you.
13 "You shall not kill.
14 "You shall not commit adultery.
15 "You shall not steal.
16 "You shall not bear false witness against your neighbor.
17 "You shall not covet your neighbor's house; you shall not covet your neighbor's wife, or his manservant, or his maidservant, or his ox, or his ass, or anything that is your neighbor's."

The horizontal dimension of the covenant sought to protect the rights of those who were joined within the covenant community. Rather than insisting on the rights of the individual, the stipulations made clear that the larger community had every right to expect certain qualities of conduct from those who entered upon the covenant life.

The negative form of the commandments actually gave greater freedom to the individual than would have a series of positive injunctions. As Mendenhall and others have demonstrated, prohibitions define only the area that is not permitted, leaving all other realms of action free. By thus leaving all other action to the self-determination of the people, under the spirit of the covenant, the covenant stipulations actually assured for Israel a degree of freedom which is seldom recognized.

Honor Within the Home (v. 12). The covenant stipulations were addressed to adult, male members of the community, for both women and children were recipients of the covenant only as they were related to the husband-father. Thus, verse 12 was far more than an exhortation to preadolescent children. It was an obligation imposed by covenant stipulation upon mature members of the community.

The verb "honor" (*kabed*) is directly related to the noun translated both honor and glory. Throughout the Old Testament the "glory of God" (*kabod*) described the nature and presence of God (cf. Ex. 33:18; 1 Kings 8:11; Isa. 6:3). Children, therefore, were expected to manifest honor toward parents and glory to God; glory and honor are identical.

Septuagint translators of this passage used the verb *timao* rather than *doxa* (glory). In nonbiblical Greek *timao* was used of the honor rendered to superiors, of men to gods, and of men to their elders, rulers, or guests. In the New Testament *timao* described the value fixed on Christ (Matt. 27:9). Other New Testament contexts use the noun in the sense of a "valuing" (Acts 4:34; 1 Cor. 6:20). Thus, the Septuagint used a word for "honor" which meant the value of a person or object. Following the influence of the Septuagint, one might paraphrase the statement, "You shall value, or treasure, your father and your mother."

The absolute seriousness of the command is reflected in the ascription of the death penalty in cases of extreme parental abuse (cf. 21:15,17; Lev. 20:9; Deut.

21:18 ff.). Concerning this practice, however, one should distinguish between the cultural practice of the day (the death penalty for disrespect to one's parents) and the ultimate will of God (parents are to be honored, and disrespect is to be disciplined within the context of God's revelation).

The Right to Life (*v. 13*). Among ancient peoples the mysterious and the holy were closely linked, and the more mysterious an object the more likely that it would be treated as holy and therefore associated with the realm of the gods. This was especially true of life; blood was holy for Old Testament men because they understood it to contain the life (Lev. 17:11). Life came to be interpreted as the unique gift of God, and upon this premise the covenant stipulated that only God could say yes or no to the life of man. Members of the covenant community were protected from the threat of death at the hands of an individual. Only the community had the right to take the life of covenant members, but this right was asserted quite clearly in the numerous cases involving the death penalty in Israelite law. The command prohibits an individual from taking the life of a covenant member, but it makes no judgment upon community action. Therefore the passage makes no judgment upon capital punishment (it is clearly provided in Israel's corpus of law) or war (the holy war is specifically described in Deuteronomy).

Elsewhere in the Old Testament the prohibition of murder was clearly related to the fact that man was created in the image of God (cf. Gen. 9:6). His life was entitled, therefore, to unique respect within the created order. Jesus took this commandment and expanded it to include human dignity in its larger dimensions (cf. Matt. 5:21–22), and the concept that all men are made in God's image is foundational for Jesus' statement that whatever one does to another individual within the covenant, he has at that same time done to the Lord (cf. Matt. 25:31 ff.).

The verb *kill* (*ratsach*) is quite often used of murder, killing with premeditation

(20:13; Josh. 4:2; Jer. 7:9; 1 Kings 21:19), but it is also frequently used of involuntary manslaughter (cf. Deut. 4:42; 19:3,4,6; Num. 35:6,11; Josh. 20:3,5,6). Hence, its usage is divided between premeditated murder, involuntary manslaughter, and the permissible execution of an individual by a near kinsman who avenges the death of his relative (cf. Num. 35:27,30).

The suggestion has been made that the commandment does not prohibit killing in the more general sense (*haragh*), but only in the restricted sense of *ratsach*. It is much sounder, however, to conclude that there was no essential distinction between the words with regard to premeditated murder, involuntary or voluntary manslaughter, the execution of an individual, or death in battle.

Within the cultural and religious context in which the command was given, it sought to take life and death out of the hands of the individual and insure that the prerogative of life or death would remain with God, mediated through the covenant people. The community on necessary occasions would discern the will of God and then declare war or the death penalty. Life, then, was a sacred trust to the community within the bonds of the covenant. Such a principle expresses itself in the negative assertion that on the individual level one should not take the life of another. More positively, the community is also responsible for the good of the individual, and community actions as well as attitudes should be consonant with the dignity and worth of every constituent member as an individual made in God's image.

Protecting the Home (*v. 14*). Within the context of Old Testament cultural patterns, adultery involved extramarital sexual relations between a male Israelite, whether married or single, and the wife of a fellow Israelite. The man was considered the aggressor, as in the phrase, "If a man commits adultery with the wife of his neighbor, both the adulterer and the adulteress shall be put to death" (Lev. 20:10). The Old Testament would hardly agree with Webster's full definition of adultery: "sexual intercourse between a married man and a woman not his wife, or between a married woman and a man not her husband." It is doubtful that the Old Testament would have viewed sexual intercourse between a married man and a woman as adultery, unless the woman was married.[6]

Adultery was primarily a crime against the husband of the woman involved, rather than the woman herself. Legal sections of the Old Testament concerning sexual violations were grounded in the protection of the man's rights and gave little consideration to the wrong done the assaulted woman. For example, in the case of the assault of a betrothed virgin, the death penalty was passed (Deut. 22:22–25), but if the virgin was not betrothed, the death sentence was not passed. Thus, the severity of the penalty rested in the violation of the man to whom the virgin was betrothed, not the virgin herself. Should one violate a virgin not betrothed to a man, a fine (indemnification) was paid to the father. The father had been wronged, for the assault of his daughter jeopardized the possibility of her future marriage, to say nothing of the loss of dowry.

In keeping with his application of the spirit of Old Testament law to a new situation, Jesus went beyond the literal meaning of the commandment and dealt with the whole range of man's thoughts, especially lust (Matt. 5:27 f.). Recognizing that lust is self-destructive, Jesus called men to a purity of heart equal to, or exceeding, purity of life.

Freedom from Theft (v. 15). "You shall not steal" has been most often interpreted as a reference to general theft and as such suggests the positive principle that within the covenant community men have the right to be free from anxiety concerning the ap-

propriation of their property. The verb *steal* (*ganav*) is often used in this literal sense (cf. 22:7) as a prohibition of general theft.

In addition to this more widely accepted interpretation, there is also the strong possibility that the unnamed object of the theft may have been a man, and the commandment may have originally referred to manstealing; an action clearly prohibited in Israel (cf. 21:16). Two evidences support such a view. First, the commandment appears in a context dealing with basic human rights. Second, the final commandment dealt specifically with the problem of taking the property of another, for it is highly probable that "covet" meant to do so with the view of appropriating the object involved.

The Right to Expect the Truth (v. 16). Whether the ninth covenant stipulation involved the more general aspects of daily life or the limited and technical area of the law court, truth of word is fundamental to the command. Those who live within the covenant community have the right to expect the truth from others within the community.

The verb *bear* (*'anah*) in the Old Testament literally meant to answer or respond. Of a total of 316 occurrences, however, 22 are to "testify" in the more restricted sense of responding as a witness (cf. Mal. 2:12; 1 Sam. 12:3; 2 Sam. 1:16). This underscores the possibility that the context of the ninth command was the court of law.

Freedom from Envy (v. 17). "Covet" (*chamadh*) in all probability denoted not only the improper thought with regard to another's property but the overt attempt to take that property.

An examination of the Old Testament usage of covet (*chamadh*) generally confirms this position. For example, "Neither shall any man desire your land, when you go up to appear before the Lord your God three times in the year" (34:24) guarantees an Israelite that while he has gone up to

---

[6] The accepted role of the prostitute and the concubine in early Israel, as well as the possible relationship to a slave or other non-Israelite servant, suggests that the commandment under consideration did not, in its setting, reflect the Christian concept.

the Lord (i.e., to Jerusalem) during the three annual festivals no one will take his property—not that no one will covet in the sense of desiring. One might also compare passages in which the word covet is immediately followed in a parallel passage by the description of the taking of an object: "You shall not covet the silver or the gold that is on them, or take it for yourselves" (Deut. 7:25), or, "When I saw among the spoil . . . I coveted them, and took them" (Josh. 7:21; cf. also, Mic. 2:2).

House summed up all that belonged to one's neighbor, as opposed to his dwelling; including his *wife, or his manservant, or his maidservant, or his ox, or his ass, or anything that is your neighbor's.* The fact that a man's wife was counted among his property should not obscure the noble role of a godly woman in Israelite thought (cf. Prov. 31:10 ff.), despite her generally secondary position in society.

Exodus and Deuteronomy differ considerably in the form of the final command, without adversely affecting the central meaning of the stipulation. For example, Exodus states the all-inclusive term house, and then lists the possessions in order of importance. Deuteronomy placed the wife first, in a separate category, and began the commandment, "Neither shall you covet your neighbor's wife" (Deut. 5:21). Then, the deuteronomist continued by citing the all-inclusive term house and those persons and objects which might be more appropriately described as property than could one's wife: "and you shall not desire your neighbor's house, his field, or his manservant, or his maidservant, his ox, or his ass, or anything that is your neighbor's." Deuteronomy also mentions "field" while Exodus does not, and uses two verbs to describe desire; the first identical with the verb in Exodus, the second, not found in Exodus, meaning to "desire" (*'awah*). Despite these variations, the essential meaning of the final obligation of covenant life is the same, whether in the form found in Exodus or Deuteronomy.

3. Israel's Fear Before the Lord (20:18–20)

[18] Now when all the people perceived the thunderings and the lightnings and the sound of the trumpet and the mountain smoking, the people were afraid and trembled; and they stood afar off, [19] and said to Moses, "You speak to us, and we will hear; but let not God speak to us, lest we die." [20] And Moses said to the people, "Do not fear; for God has come to prove you, and that the fear of him may be before your eyes, that you may not sin."

As the narrative is now arranged, the people apparently had already heard the declaration of the ten covenant obligations (20:1 ff.). Their request was therefore related to the Lord's future declaration(s). One would assume that God's speech took the form of phenomena associated with Sinai, or that this statement is a literary means of describing the revelation of the Lord's will to Israel. One need not necessarily conceive of these words as spoken in a particular language, audible to the physical ear—though some persons hold to a literal interpretation. The words may, however, well have been spoken at Sinai by a covenant-mediator representing God—Moses in all probability. Later the commandments may have been spoken in a worship context by a covenant-mediator who spoke for God within the cult.

Those parts of the narrative which portray God as speaking in audible tones to an assembled people are best understood as anthropomorphic. The revelation was unmistakably clear and precise, but the medium whereby the "ten words" were shared is not so clearly delineated.

Verse 21 characterizes the relationship between the people, Moses, and the Lord during the remainder of the theophanic appearance. The people stand *afar off*, keeping a respectful distance from the "Holy One of Israel." As covenant-mediator *Moses drew near to the thick cloud where God was* (v. 21). Finally, the Lord spoke the remainder of the laws on Sinai to Moses, who then shared them with the people. The verse graphically portrays the mediatorial office of Moses, and the manner in which the Lord's revelation came to Israel through the personality of Moses.

III. The Book of the Covenant: Legislation Guarding the Covenant Relationship (20:21—23:33)

Because it contains the legal corpus integral to the outworking of the covenant at Sinai, Exodus 20:22—23:33 is commonly referred to as the Book of the Covenant. The actual phrase appears in the narrative describing the sealing of the covenant between the Lord and Israel (24:4,7).

The laws within the Book of the Covenant were largely the result of case laws, based upon judicial practices and technically classified as "casuistic." Casuistic laws began with a particular case, either stated or presupposed. For example, "When a man sells" (21:7), or, "Whoever strikes his father" (21:15), or, "If a man delivers to his neighbor" (22:10). Casuistic laws probably reflected both the primitive laws common to the ancient world [7] and also the decisions handed down from as early as the period of the exodus-conquest. "Apodictic" laws, on the other hand, are best illustrated by the categorical imperatives and prohibitions such as the Decalogue's "thou shalt not." Israelite law was a mixture of apodictic and casuistic law.

Suggestions for the date of the covenant code, or Book of the Covenant, have traveled almost a complete circle. Prior to the advent of modern literary criticism the legislation was ascribed to Moses, almost without exception. The advent of the scientific era of higher criticism witnessed the emerging conclusion that written codes of law prior to the eighth-century prophets would have been impossible, and many placed the actual legislation later than that period. Today, however, there is a growing awareness that, while Moses may not have been responsible for all legislation, nor was

all legislation dated during his general era, Israel's legal corpus had Mosaic roots. For example, Walther Eichrodt suggests that "serious consideration has had to be given once more to the possibility of a written codification of the law in the time of Moses, and either *the Decalogue* of Ex. 20:1 alone or the Decalogue and *the Book of the Covenant* (Ex. 20–23) together have been derived from Moses himself." [8]

Mendenhall supports this in his appraisal: "The laws of the Covenant Code reflect the customs, morality, and religious obligations of the Israelite community . . . before the monarchy. . . . Since it exhibits just that mixture of case law and apodictic law . . . which we find in covenants from the Hittite sources, and in Mesopotamian codes as well, *any study which assumes that it is a later artificial composite from originally independent literary sources may be assigned rather to rational ingenuity than to historical fact*" (p. 14, italics are mine).

Before considering the Book of the Covenant in detail, it remains only to indicate the relationship between that code and the Decalogue. Simply stated, the Decalogue consisted of principles which found concrete expression within the Book of the Covenant. The Decalogue expressed the obligations imposed upon covenant members by the Lord. The Book of the Covenant contains the specific legislation, with appropriate punishment, designed to guarantee that the Decalogue would be implemented. By so guaranteeing the implementation of the Decalogue, the community averted the divine wrath associated with the violation of the Decalogue. The Book of the Covenant was the legal instrument for guarding the covenant relationship.

1. Cultic Laws (20:21–26)

[21] And the people stood afar off, while Moses drew near to the thick darkness where God was. [22] And the LORD said to Moses, "Thus you shall say to the people of Israel: 'You have

---

[7] At least half a dozen Ancient Near Eastern Law codes, prior to the time of Moses, have been discovered.

[8] *Theology of the Old Testament*, trans. J. A. Baker (Philadelphia: Westminster, 1961), I, 70 f.

seen for yourselves that I have talked with you from heaven. 23 You shall not make gods of silver to be with me, nor shall you make for yourselves gods of gold. 24 An altar of earth you shall make for me and sacrifice on it your burnt offerings and your peace offerings, your sheep and your oxen; in every place where I cause my name to be remembered I will come to you and bless you. 25 And if you make me an altar of stone, you shall not build it of hewn stones; for if you wield your tool upon it you profane it. 26 And you shall not go up by steps to my altar, that your nakedness be not exposed on it.'

The entire narrative has numerous marks of antiquity about it; the primitive altar, the abhorence of a tool upon the stone, the simplicity of the sacrifices offered (there are only two mentioned), as well as the fact that the passage makes no reference to the priests and addresses Israelites as ascending the steps of the altar.

Preference for an earthen altar reflects the primitive or seminomadic era, prior to the conquest or even the exodus, when stone was not widely used. The condition that no tool could be used in shaping the stone was in keeping with the assumption that the holiness of the natural object was destroyed by shaping it with a man-made tool (cf. the Nazarite vow and the prohibition against cutting the hair).

Nakedness is a common Old Testament euphimism for sexual organs, as the phrase "to look on another's nakedness" suggests; "None of you shall approach any one near of kin to him to uncover nakedness" (Lev. 18:6). The prohibition concerning ascending the steps of the altar was grounded in the concept of the holy more than in a sense of modesty or propriety. The mystery of life and its relationship to the organ of generation gave to the sexual parts an unusual state of holiness. This concept of the holy is foundational for the practice of circumcision, as well as the ancient custom of the patriarchial era concerning taking an oath; "And Abraham said to his servant . . . 'Put your hand under my thigh, and I will make you swear by the Lord'" (Gen. 24:2–3).

2. Civil and Criminal Laws (21:1—22:17)

Laws within Israel were so uniquely related to the Lord that it may be misleading to speak of "civil" law. This passage, however, is concerned with a series of laws which deal with noncultic decisions.

(1) Laws Concerning Hebrew Slaves (21: 1–11)

1 "Now these are the ordinances which you shall set before them. 2 When you buy a Hebrew slave, he shall serve six years, and in the seventh he shall go out free, for nothing. 3 If he comes in single, he shall go out single; if he comes in married, then his wife shall go out with him. 4 If his master gives him a wife and she bears him sons or daughters, the wife and her children shall be her master's and he shall go out alone. 5 But if the slave plainly says, 'I love my master, my wife, and my children; I will not go out free,' 6 then his master shall bring him to God, and he shall bring him to the door or the doorpost; and his master shall bore his ear through with an awl; and he shall serve him for life.

7 "When a man sells his daugher as a slave, she shall not go out as the male slaves do. 8 If she does not please her master, who has designated her for himself, then he shall let her be redeemed; he shall have no right to sell her to a foreign people, since he has dealt faithlessly with her. 9 If he designates her for his son, he shall deal with her as with a daughter. 10 If he takes another wife to himself, he shall not diminish her food, her clothing, or her marital rights. 11 And if he does not do these three things for her, she shall go out for nothing, without payment of money.

Although either stealing a man or possession of a stolen man (21:16) was prohibited, slaves acquired through accepted means such as war or indebtedness were held in Israel. It is significant that Israel provided legal safeguards for the slave, as for the free population.

Protecting the Home (vv. 1–6). "Ordinances" (*mishpatim*) were the decisions, most often handed down by the judge (*shophet*), and cataloged for the guidance of succeeding generations. The *mishpatim* were probably intended as principles to give guidance in making later decisions, as opposed to a code of law. Therefore, the law codes in Israel were not exhaustive in the sense of attempting to set forth every decision. Rather, they set forth selected illustrative decisions for the guidance of those charged with legal decisions. Within the Old Testament, latitude was given the judge (who may have been a king, or someone other than an actual judge) as he sought to determine the will of God concerning the issue at hand. The codes of law were for his guidance, therefore, as opposed to an exhaustive listing of all legislation.[9]

Hebrew slave. Hebrews could be sold into slavery by their parents (21:7), or could be taken in order to satisfy a debt (cf. 2 Kings 4:1 ff.).

Bring him to God and *the doorpost* are synonymous, suggesting that the entrance to the house was sacred—the special dwelling place of the household god into whose household the slave was entering.

The larger purpose of this particular collection of *mishpatim* was the protection of the home, a right to which even the slave was entitled. His marriage was protected in that if he entered slavehood married, he could not be separated from his wife when he was freed (v. 3).

Protecting the Female Slave (21:7–11). "Slave" (*'amah*) may mean a maidservant in the literal sense, but was also applied to a concubine (Gen. 20:17), and was specifically used of Hagar, Sarah's maid (Gen. 16:2). The reference to *marital rights* is a circumlocution describing the woman's right to proper sexual life with her husband-owner. *Marital rights* is a single word, *'onathah,* defined as "cohabitation."

Because of the secondary and often un-

9 This view of the law codes is espoused by Mendenhall and is significant not only for understanding the nature of Israelite law codes but for the role of Scripture as well. Some view Scripture as an exhaustive listing of specific laws or exhortations, much like a code of law. Scripture, however, in many instances illustrates principles for man's guidance in making decisions. For example, there are concrete situations today which were unknown in the biblical era. Yet, the Bible sets forth illustrations of the will of God for a comparable, but not identical, situation which suggest the present course of action most likely to be the will of God.

protected role of women in the ancient world, it is of unique significance that the Old Testament gave specific guidance to Israelite jurists who made decisions concerning the *'amah,* the female slave. Such specific compassion for those normally outside the area of direct concern is one mark of the deep moral content which characterizes Israelite law.

(2) Capital Offenses (21:12–17)

12 "Whoever strikes a man so that he dies shall be put to death. 13 But if he did not lie in wait for him, but God let him fall into his hand, then I will appoint for you a place to which he may flee. 14 But if a man wilfully attacks another to kill him treacherously, you shall take him from my altar, that he may die.

15 "Whoever strikes his father or his mother shall be put to death.

16 "Whoever steals a man, whether he sells him or is found in possession of him, shall be put to death.

17 "Whoever curses his father or his mother shall be put to death.

Premeditated Murder (vv. 12–14). Classification of striking a man "so that he dies" as premeditated murder is based upon the fact that although verse 13 provides a place of refuge for involuntary homicide, no refuge was anticipated for this action.

God let him fall into his hand. This is the biblical way of saying that the death was not planned. Since the Bible does not deal with secondary causes, "chance happenings," anything which man did not specifically plan must have been caused by God's action.

A place to which he may flee. In cases of accidental death, the slayer might flee to a city of refuge until it could be established whether or not the slaying was deliberate. Such refuge protected the slayer from being put to death by the slain person's nearest of kin, a common Old Testament practice (cf. Num. 35:10 ff.; Deut. 19:1 ff.; Josh. 20:1 ff. for a summary of the regulations concerning the cities of refuge).

You shall take him from my altar. The altar of God was a place of refuge, and those who claimed its protection were safe.

The right of sanctuary was denied to premeditated murderers.

Striking a Parent (v. 15). Later legislation corroborated this by calling for the death penalty of an incorrigible child (cf. Deut. 21:18 ff.). The Code of Hammurabi, however, specified only that "if a son has struck his father, they shall cut off his hand" (#195).

The passage is a good example of the manner in which an interpreter of the Bible should distinguish between a temporary, cultural practice (putting a child to death for smiting a parent) and the divine word (order and respect are to be maintained in the home).

Stealing a Man (v. 16). Deuteronomy reaffirmed this principle of verse 16 and in so doing clarified the person as "one of his brethren, the people of Israel" (24:7). Both in ancient Greece and Rome selling a free-born citizen was punishable by death, and the Code of Hammurabi provided a stipulation comparable to the covenant code of Exodus.

Cursing a Parent (v. 17). According to thought patterns of the ancient world the curse was a potent and effective means of releasing hostile, and perhaps demonic, forces upon an individual, not simply a parallel to modern profanity (cf. Deut. 27:15–16). The practice closely approximates "voodoo" and was practiced widely in the ancient Near East, on both the individual and the national level (nations were also cursed, as, for example, in the execration texts from Egypt). Both the blessing and the curse were understood as possessing objective reality with the inherent power necessary to bring about their own fulfilment. (For the most positive concept of God's word, cf. Isa. 55:10 f.) Any person who released evil forces upon his parents was to be executed.

(3) Bodily Injury: Noncapital Crimes Involving Blows and Wounds (21:18–32)

18 "When men quarrel and one strikes the other with a stone or with his fist and the man does not die but keeps his bed, 19 then if the man rises again and walks abroad with his staff, he that struck him shall be clear; only he shall pay for the loss of his time, and shall have him thoroughly healed.

20 "When a man strikes his slave, male or female, with a rod and the slave dies under his hand, he shall be punished. 21 But if the slave survives a day or two, he is not to be punished; for the slave is his money.

22 "When men strive together, and hurt a woman with child, so that there is a miscarriage, and yet no harm follows, the one who hurt her shall be fined, according as the woman's husband shall lay upon him; and he shall pay as the judges determine. 23 If any harm follows, then you shall give life for life, 24 eye for eye, tooth for tooth, hand for hand, foot for foot, 25 burn for burn, wound for wound, stripe for stripe.

26 "When a man strikes the eye of his slave, male or female, and destroys it, he shall let the slave go free for the eye's sake. 27 If he knocks out the tooth of his slave, male or female, he shall let the slave go free for the tooth's sake.

28 "When an ox gores a man or a woman to death, the ox shall be stoned, and its flesh shall not be eaten; but the owner of the ox shall be clear. 29 But if the ox has been accustomed to gore in the past, and its owner has been warned but has not kept it in, and it kills a man or a woman, the ox shall be stoned, and its owner also shall be put to death. 30 If a ransom is laid on him, then he shall give for the redemption of his life whatever is laid upon him. 31 If it gores a man's son or daughter, he shall be dealt with according to this same rule. 32 If the ox gores a slave, male or female, the owner shall give to their master thirty shekels of silver, and the ox shall be stoned.

Succeeding jurists doubtless faced numerous specific decisions not found in this section, but through the succinct examples cited here they were more likely to arrive at a just decision in keeping with the spirit of the specific legislation.

Blows Between Israelite Men (vv. 18–20). The Code of Hammurabi provided that "if a seignior has struck a (nother) seignior in a brawl and has inflicted an injury on him, that seignior shall swear, 'I did not strike him deliberately [lit. "while I was aware of it"]'; and he shall also pay for the physician" (#206).

The close similarity between Exodus 21:12–27 and the Code of Hammurabi,

195–214, plus the general similarity of
other sections of Exodus with that code as
well as other codes of the ancient world,
such as the Hittite code, suggest that Israel
drew from a common background of legal
jurisprudence shared throughout much of
the ancient Near East.

Beating a Slave (*vv. 20–21*). One might
take the phrase *naqom yinnagem* to mean
surely he (i.e., the slave) will be avenged.
The word punish is *naqam*—to avenge or
take vengeance—and if the owner is the
subject, could be translated, "he will surely
suffer vengeance." The probability is that
vengeance was to be taken on the owner
by the clan of the deceased slave (who
may well have been a Hebrew slave), or
by the assessing of a penalty by the proper
official in the community.

Should the slave live a day or two this
should indicate that the master did not
unduly beat the slave. Severe beatings
were apparently accepted as normal. Since
the slave "was his money" in the sense of
belonging to the master, the owner could
do with him as he pleased. Distinction between the two cases may be based on
voluntary and involuntary homicide.

Not even the life of a slave could be
taken with impunity. The passage does reflect a distinction between a free man and
a slave in that an intentional and fatal
beating of a free man was punishable by
death (v. 12). In the case of the slave,
however, the law makes only the vague
statement that vengeance would be taken.

Injury During Pregnancy (*vv. 22–25*).
Injury to a woman during pregnancy, resulting in miscarriage, was satisfied by an appropriate fine, suggested by the husband and
paid under the supervision of the judges.

The *lex talionis*, "eye for an eye," was
given for the guidance of the judges in
making decisions where judgment was to
be commensurate with the nature of the
injury. The law of retaliation does not serve
as the basis for personal action, not even
according to the Old Testament code.
Rather than reflecting the negative characteristics often ascribed to it, the law of retal-

iation made these positive contributions.
First, it insured that within the judicial
system individuals, such as the pregnant
woman in this instance, would be protected
in that the punishment would be made to
suit the offense. Second, the law of retaliation limited judgment so that it would not
be out of proportion to the nature of the
crime—more excessive than necessary.

The Code of Hammurabi dealt extensively with the matter of miscarriage produced by a blow:

"209: If a seignior struck a (nother)
seignior's daughter and has caused her to
have a miscarriage, he shall pay ten shekels
of silver for her fetus.

210: If that woman has died, they shall
put his daughter to death.

211: If by a blow he has caused a com-
moner's daughter to have a miscarriage, he
shall pay five shekels of silver.

212: If that woman died, he shall pay
one-third mina of silver." [10]

Physical Abuse of Slaves (*vv. 26–27*).
The loss of an eye or tooth through the
abuse of an owner justified the release of
the slave. In other legislation of the ancient Near East indemnification was made,
not freedom. Among the Hittites, for example, "If anyone blinds a male or female
slave or knocks out his/her teeth, he shall
give ten shekels of silver and pledge his
estate as security."

An Ox That Gores (*vv. 28–32*). Throughout the ancient Near East there was an
assumed responsibility on the part of an
owner toward his ox, as well as the distinction between accidental goring and injury
by an animal known to be dangerous. The
Code of Hammurabi provided that "250: If
an ox, when it was walking along the
street, gored a seignior to death, that case
is not subject to claim. 251: If a seignior's
ox was a gorer and his city council made it
known to him that it was a gorer, but he
did not pad its horns or tie up his ox, and
that ox gored to death a member of the

10 All citations of Ancient Near Eastern laws are
from *Ancient Near Eastern Texts*, ed. James B. Pritchard (Princeton: University, 1950).

aristocracy, he shall give one half mina of silver. 252: If it was a seignior's slave, he shall give one-third mina of silver."

(4) Property Rights: Compensation and Indemnification (21:33—22:17)

33 "When a man leaves a pit open, or when a man digs a pit and does not cover it, and an ox or an ass falls into it, 34 the owner of the pit shall make it good; he shall give money to its owner, and the dead beast shall be his.

35 "When one man's ox hurts another's, so that it dies, then they shall sell the live ox and divide the price of it; and the dead beast also they shall divide. 36 Or if it is known that the ox has been accustomed to gore in the past, and its owner has not kept it in, he shall pay ox for ox, and the dead beast shall be his.

1 "If a man steals an ox or a sheep, and kills it or sells it, he shall pay five oxen for an ox, and four sheep for a sheep.° He shall make restitution; if he has nothing, then he shall be sold for his theft. 4 If the stolen beast is found alive in his possession, whether it is an ox or an ass or a sheep, he shall pay double.

2 "If a thief is found breaking in, and is struck so that he dies, there shall be no blood-guilt for him; 3 but if the sun has risen upon him, there shall be bloodguilt for him.

5 When a man causes a field or vineyard to be grazed over, or lets his beast loose and it feeds in another man's field, he shall make restitution from the best in his own field and in his own vineyard.

6 "When fire breaks out and catches in thorns so that the stacked grain or the standing grain or the field is consumed, he that kindled the fire shall make full restitution.

7 "If a man delivers to his neighbor money or goods to keep, and it is stolen out of the man's house, then, if the thief is found, he shall pay double. 8 If the thief is not found, the owner of the house shall come near to God, to show whether or not he has put his hand to his neighbor's goods.

9 "For every breach of trust, whether it is for ox, for ass, for sheep, for clothing, or for any kind of lost thing, of which one says, 'This is it,' the case of both parties shall come before God; he whom God shall condemn shall pay double to his neighbor.

10 "If a man delivers to his neighbor an ass or an ox or a sheep or any beast to keep, and it dies or is hurt or is driven away, without any one seeing it, 11 an oath by the LORD shall be between them both to see whether he has not put his hand to his neighbor's property; and

° Restoring the second half of verse 3 with 4 to their place immediately following verse 1.

the owner shall accept the oath, and he shall not make restitution. 12 But if it is stolen from him, he shall make restitution to its owner. 13 If it is torn by beasts, let him bring it as evidence; he shall make restitution for what has been torn.

14 "If a man borrows anything of his neighbor, and it is hurt or dies, the owner not being with it, he shall not make full restitution. 15 If the owner was with it, he shall not make restitution; if it was hired, it came for its hire.

16 "If a man seduces a virgin who is not betrothed, and lies with her, he shall give the marriage present for her, and make her his wife. 17 If her father utterly refuses to give her to him, he shall pay money equivalent to the marriage present for virgins.

The principle of indemnification represented an advance upon retaliatory action taken among some groups. There is no provision in Old Testament law for bodily mutilation, as the Assyrian laws provided. Should one be unable to make financial indemnification, according to Old Testament law he could be sold into slavery, but his life was spared.

Negligence and Property Loss (v. 33). The principle of personal liability with regard to property loss is fundamental to this law. Upon the basis of this principle other specific cases within Israel were likely settled—the code making no attempt to cover every possible case.

Liability for the Action of One's Property (vv. 35–36). Such laws were common to the ancient Near East, and as early as the Code of Eshnunna (1850 B.C.) the matter of responsibility for dangerous animals or property was dealt with: a dog that was mad but not kept in (#56), or a wall threatening to fall but not strengthened (#58). In all the ancient Near East, successive cultures from as early as the second millennium B.C., and probably much earlier, assumed that an owner was directly liable for damages precipitated through his own property.

Cattle and Sheep Stealing (22:1). Despite the severity of the penalty, it is an advance upon other laws of the ancient world which called for the death penalty in the case of property theft. The Code of

Hammurabi specified that "7: If a seignior stole either an ox or a sheep or an ass or a pig or a boat, if it belonged to the church (or) if it belonged to the state, he shall make thirty-fold restitution; if it belonged to a private citizen, he shall make good ten-fold. If the thief does not have sufficient to make restitution, he shall be put to death."

Since verse 4 deals with the same issue, and apparently was misplaced in the Hebrew text, the RSV places verse 4 following verse 1.

Distinctions of Homicide (vv. 2–3). One who slew a thief at night was guiltless, but should one slay a thief breaking in during the day the slayer was guilty. The inherent principle is of fundamental importance: human life is of greater value than human property.

Abuse of Another's Field or Vineyard (v. 5). Either the deliberate or the unintentional grazing of another person's field or vineyard was to be compensated for by giving the best of one's own field or vineyard to the offended party.

Responsibility for Fire (v. 6). Personal judgment for one's irresponsibility or carelessness is clearly underscored.

Money or Goods Held in Trust (vv. 7–8). Laws 120–125 of the Code of Hammurabi all deal with property left in trust with another, indicating that this may have been a common problem for the ancient world.

Disputed Ownership of Property Left in Trust (v. 9). The command is distinct from verse 7, which deals with property stolen by a thief.

Responsibilities of Shepherds and Herdsmen (vv. 10–13). Shepherds and herdsmen held the animals of others according to these principles: (1) animals which were unintentionally hurt, killed, or driven away were not charged to the account of the keeper—assuming that the herdsman took an oath before God; (2) should an animal be stolen, *restitution* was made on a two to one basis—shepherds are paid to prevent theft; (3) in the case of animals torn by beast, the shepherd could bring the remains of the beast, thus proving he had not misappropriated the animal and paid no restitution (cf. Amos 3:12).

Damaging Borrowed Property (vv. 14–15). Three principles governed borrowing *anything of his neighbor:* (1) borrowed property unaccompanied by the owner must be compensated for in case of damage; (2) property accompanied by the owner, although borrowed by another, was not liable to compensation—the owner should look out for it, even if it was borrowed; (3) if property was rented (hired) damages were not paid—the owner assumed some risk when he rented the object—*it came for its hire.*

Seduction of a Virgin (vv. 16–17). The appearance of laws regulating the violation of virgins in a section of laws on property rights may appear strange to contemporary readers. A man's family was, however, his property; although it is exceedingly doubtful that a father looked upon children as no more than property. But they were objects of value, and in case of debt could be sold.

A virgin daughter represented dowry money to the father—a source of income no longer available in the event that a virgin was violated. In keeping with Old Testament patterns of thought, the law sought to protect the father's property rights. There was no attempt to protect the rights of the virgin who had been violated (who, under modern concepts, would be an object of concern).

Normally, the person who violated the daughter was to marry her, paying *the marriage present.* Should the father disapprove of the marriage, the money equivalent to the marriage present was to be paid (Deut. 22:29 specified 50 shekels of silver). Notice that priority is given to the marriage present, and marriage itself was left somewhat to the option of the girl's father.

3. Moral and Religious Laws (22:18—23:19)

The designation "Moral and Religious Laws" should not be understood to infer that previous laws were unconcerned with either morality or religion. Rather, the present body of material was uniquely concerned with issues related to personal morality and ethics, plus religious practices.

(1) Capital Offenses (22:18-20)

18 "You shall not permit a sorceress to live.
19 "Whoever lies with a beast shall be put to death.
20 "Whoever sacrifices to any god, save to the LORD only, shall be utterly destroyed.

Three laws concerned with religious practice and personal morality are cited in verses 18-20, and in each instance violation is punishable by capital punishment.

The Sorceress (v. 18). Sorcery, the appeal to supernatural powers on the basis of magical technique, was specifically prohibited in Israelite law, although it continued as a practice within Israel through much of her history (cf. Isa. 8:19; Mic. 5:12; Mal. 3:5). It was commonly practiced among other nations (cf. Ex. 7:11; Isa. 47:9,12; Dan. 2:2). All efforts to contact supernatural powers through magical techniques were a repudiation of biblical faith.

The Prohibition of Bestiality (v. 19). Sodomy, defined by Webster as any sexual intercourse regarded as abnormal, as between persons of the same sex, especially males, or between a person and an animal, was an object of continual denunciation within biblical literature (cf. Lev. 18:22; 20:13); and the wages of homosexuality could not be used in the payment of any vow made to God (cf. Deut. 23:18). As in the present verse, the Old Testament also condemned sexual intercourse between a person and an animal, described herein as bestiality, the practice of a bestial act (cf. Lev. 20:15 f.).

The Prohibition of Apostasy (v. 20). The phrase *shall be utterly destroyed* translates the Hebrew verb "he shall be put to the ban," i.e., he shall be exterminated. The verb *charam* had religious overtones, and meant to "ban, devote, exterminate." Whatever was holy to a non-Israelite was *cherem* (just as objects dedicated to the God of Israel were *qodhesh*). Thus, objects or persons hostile to the Israelite theocracy were destroyed (*charam*). It is significant that Exodus 22:20 uses *charam*, for it conveyed religious overtones absent in common words for kill or slaughter.

(2) Ethical and Moral Responsibility (22: 21-28)

21 "You shall not wrong a stranger or oppress him, for you were strangers in the land of Egypt. 22 You shall not afflict any widow or orphan. 23 If you do afflict them, and they cry out to me, I will surely hear their cry; 24 and my wrath will burn, and I will kill you with the sword, and your wives shall become widows, and your children fatherless.
25 "If you lend money to any of my people with you who is poor, you shall not be to him as a creditor, and you shall not exact interest from him. 26 If ever you take your neighbor's garment in pledge, you shall restore it to him before the sun goes down; 27 for that is his only covering, it is his mantle for his body; in what else shall he sleep? And if he cries to me, I will hear, for I am compassionate.
28 "You shall not revile God, nor curse a ruler of your people.

Israelite law was concerned with one's ethical and moral responsibility, especially as it related to strangers and other helpless individuals, the poor of the land, as well as one's attitude toward God and his representatives.

Responsibility for the Helpless (vv. 21-24). The covenant community is characterized by a sympathetic identification with the unfortunate. Remembering that once they knew the same condition, Israelites were challenged to respond to the helpless with thoughtful consideration.

Compassion for the Poor (vv. 25-27). Human need was met with a spirit of godly piety which expressed itself in the willingness to care for the less fortunate without personal recompense. Later, Nehemiah condemned the Israelite community for their exploitation of less fortunate brothers who had borrowed money in order to meet taxes and buy food during a famine (Neh. 5:3-10).

While this statement on interest should hardly serve as a permanent principle in modern banking circles, it should represent the spirit of compassion with which the community of faith seeks to minister to the needs of the less fortunate poor. The self-assertion of God, *for I am compassionate* (v. 27), is adequate ground and encouragement for compassion as a primary evidence of God's presence within the community of faith.

Honoring God and His Representative (v. 28). Noth is probably correct in his suggestion that the *nasi'* was "the representative of the twelve tribes on the occasions when all Israel is gathered together" (p. 187).

The fact that *nasi'* stands in parallel construction with God, suggests that verse 28 dealt not with two separate actions, reviling God and cursing a ruler; but with a single action: repudiating God's representative, an action which repudiated God.

(3) Religious (Cultic) Regulations (22: 29–31)

29 "You shall not delay to offer from the fulness of your harvest and from the outflow of your presses.

"The first-born of your sons you shall give to me. 30 You shall do likewise with your oxen and with your sheep: seven days it shall be with its dam; on the eighth day you shall give it to me.

31 "You shall be men consecrated to me; therefore you shall not eat any flesh that is torn by beasts in the field; you shall cast it to the dogs.

Inserted at this juncture are three cultic regulations dealing with offerings of the harvest (v. 29a), firstborn (vv. 29b–30), and the prohibition against eating flesh killed by beasts in the field (v. 31).

Offerings of the Harvest (v. 29). The *fulness of your harvest* likely refers both to grain and grape (cf. Deut. 22:9 where fulness is translated "yield of the vineyard"). *Outflow of your presses* would then refer to the olive oil out of the press.

Offering the Firstborn (vv. 29b–30). Later, in Israel the redemption price of the firstborn of man was given to the priest as part of his livelihood (cf. Num. 18:15),

and the flesh of the firstborn animal was eaten by the priestly family (Num. 18: 17 f.).

Contaminated Flesh (v. 31). The prohibition against eating the flesh of an animal torn by beasts in the field rested in the commonly accepted veneration of blood, and the attendant belief concerning the manner in which an animal's blood was to be handled preparatory to human consumption of the flesh.

(4) Justice and Duty Toward One's Enemy 23:1–9

1 "You shall not utter a false report. You shall not join hands with a wicked man, to be a malicious witness. 2 You shall not follow a multitude to do evil; nor shall you bear witness in a suit, turning aside after a multitude so as to pervert justice; 3 nor shall you be partial to a poor man in his suit.

4 "If you meet your enemy's ox or his ass going astray, you shall bring it back to him. 5 If you see the ass of one who hates you lying under its burden, you shall refrain from leaving him with it, you shall help him to lift it up.

6 "You shall not pervert the justice due to your poor in his suit. 7 Keep far from a false charge, and do not slay the innocent and righteous, for I will not acquit the wicked. 8 And you shall take no bribe, for a bribe blinds the officials, and subverts the cause of those who are in the right.

9 "You shall not oppress a stranger; you know the heart of a stranger, for you were strangers in the land of Egypt.

Last among the moral and religious laws in this section of the covenant code are those emphases concerned with the principle of justice, and the statement of one's duty toward an enemy.

Five Principles of Justice (vv. 1–3). The negative particle appears five times in these three verses, marking five principles which should guide members of the covenant community in maintaining justice.

Duty to One's Enemy (vv. 4–5). The meaning is quite clear; one is not to allow personal animosity to destroy one's willingness to be of assistance in a time of need.

Justice for the Poor (vv. 6–8). In an effort to protect the poor, the innocent, and the righteous (all of which may be synonymous), there are two specific warnings to the people of God. (1) Do not falsely charge an individual, for to do so would be to *slay the innocent and righteous*. (2) Reject a bribe, for a bribe subverts to the cause of those who are in the right by blinding the eyes of officials. For those who do such things, the writer warns, the Lord will not acquit the wicked, referring apparently to those who falsely accuse the poor as the "wicked." Throughout its legal system the covenant community made every effort to guarantee justice to its members.

Concern for the Stranger (v. 9). See comment 22:21.

(5) Laws Governing Religious Institutions and Practices 23:10-19

10 "For six years you shall sow your land and gather in its yield; 11 but the seventh year you shall let it rest and lie fallow, that the poor of your people may eat; and what they leave the wild beasts may eat. You shall do likewise with your vineyard, and with your olive orchard. 12 "Six days you shall do your work, but on the seventh day you shall rest; that your ox and your ass may have rest, and the son of your bondmaid, and the alien, may be refreshed. 13 Take heed to all that I have said to you; and make no mention of the names of other gods, nor let such be heard out of your mouth. 14 "Three times in the year you shall keep a feast to me. 15 You shall keep the feast of unleavened bread; as I commanded you, you shall eat unleavened bread for seven days at the appointed time in the month of Abib, for in it you came out of Egypt. None shall appear before me empty-handed. 16 You shall keep the feast of harvest, of the first fruits of your labor, of what you sow in the field. You shall keep the feast of ingathering at the end of the year, when you gather in from the field the fruit of your labor. 17 Three times in the year shall all your males appear before the LORD GOD. 18 "You shall not offer the blood of my sacrifice with leavened bread, or let the fat of my feast remain until the morning. 19 "The first of the first fruits of your ground you shall bring into the house of the LORD your God.

"You shall not boil a kid in its mother's milk.

Inserted at this point are laws related to the sabbatical year, the sabbath, the three annual feasts, plus a brief collection of ritual stipulations.

Sabbatical Year (vv. 10-11). This stipulation was grounded in the biblical view of divine ownership. The land belonged to God, and man used it as a steward, ultimately responsible to God.

Observing the Sabbath, and Devotion to God (vv. 12-13). Both the land and time belong to God, and there is a decided attempt to return to creation, in both time and the unfettered condition of man and beast.

Take heed might be translated "*guard yourself.*" The name was an especially vital means of indicating one's relationship to a god; to call on his name, worship his name, etc. Hence, the admonition in verse 13 centered in *make no mention of the names of other gods*.

The Great Feasts of Israel (vv. 14-17). The three great feasts of Israel were identified in the covenant code as (1) the feast of unleavened bread, verse 15; (2) the feast of harvest, verse 16; and (3) the feast of ingathering, verse 16b. Unleavened bread combined with the Passover and was celebrated on 14-21 Nisan, or March-April (cf. Lev. 23:4 ff.; Num. 28:16 ff.; Deut. 16:1 ff.). The *feast of harvest* (v. 16) was a one-day festival, celebrated early in the third month, May-June, on the fiftieth day after the offering of the barley sheaf at the feast of unleavened bread,[11] hence, the later name Pentecost, from *pentekonia*, fifty (cf. Lev. 23:15 ff.; Num. 28:26 ff.; Deut. 16: 9 ff.). The *feast of ingathering* was later known as the feast of booths and, even more commonly, as the Feast of Tabernacles. It was celebrated for seven days, beginning on the fifteenth day of the seventh month, September-October. It recalled the wandering in the wilderness, and was an adaptation of an ancient vintage festival (cf. Lev. 23:33 ff.; Num. 29:12 ff.; Deut. 16:13 ff.). The second and third feasts were clearly related to harvest seasons for grain and grapes, but unleavened bread, although agrarian in origin, was not a harvest festival. On the occasion of each of

[11] J. C. Rylaarsdam, "Feasts and Fasts," IDB, II. 263.

the three feasts "all your males appear before the Lord God" (v. 17).

Ritual Instructions (vv. 18–19). Four laws on ritual conduct concludes the section of the code dealing with religious observances.

Leaven and Fat (v. 18). Both blood and fat were holy (cf. Lev. 3:17).

First Fruits (v. 19a). The whole of the crop was symbolically represented in the first fruits, and the presentation of the first portion of the new crop to the Lord effectually offered the whole of the crop.

Prohibition of Pagan Practices (v. 19b). The interpretation of this rather strange prohibition against boiling a kid in its mother's milk illustrates the manner in which archaeological discovery illuminated Ancient Near Eastern cultural practices. Older commentaries often related the prohibition to the possible sanctity of milk (comparable to that of blood), the use of sour milk in preparing the meal (which was in turn related to leaven), or even suggested that such a practice indicated contempt for the relationship between parent and young. Following the discovery and interpretation of the Ras Shamra literature, dating to approximately the fourteenth century B.C., this verse quite often has been interpreted as the prohibition of a Canaanite ritual in which a kid was boiled in its mother's milk: "Over the fire seven times the sacrificers cook a kid in milk (?) (and) mint (?) in butter and over the cauldron seven times fresh water (?) is poured." [12]

4. Promises and Instruction for Entry into the Promised Land (23:20–33)

20 "Behold, I send an angel before you, to guard you on the way and to bring you to the place which I have prepared. 21 Give heed to him and hearken to his voice, do not rebel against him, for he will not pardon your transgression; for my name is in him.
22 "But if you hearken attentively to his voice and do all that I say, then I will be an

---

12 "Shachar and Shalim," 1:14, in G. R. Driver, *Canaanite Myths and Legends* (Edinburgh: T. & T. Clark, 1956), p. 121.

enemy to your enemies and an adversary to your adversaries.
23 "When my angel goes before you, and brings you in to the Amorites, and the Hittites, and the Perizzites, and the Canaanites, the Hivites, and the Jebusites, and I blot them out, 24 you shall not bow down to their gods, nor serve them, nor do according to their works, but you shall utterly overthrow them and break their pillars in pieces. 25 You shall serve the LORD your God, and I will bless your bread and your water; and I will take sickness away from the midst of you. 26 None shall cast her young or be barren in your land; I will fulfil the number of your days. 27 I will send my terror before you, and will throw into confusion all the people against whom you shall come, and I will make all your enemies turn their backs to you. 28 And I will send hornets before you, which shall drive out Hivite, Canaanite, and Hittite from before you. 29 I will not drive them out from before you in one year, lest the land become desolate and the wild beasts multiply against you. 30 Little by little I will drive them out from before you, until you are increased and possess the land. 31 And I will set your bounds from the Red Sea to the sea of the Philistines, and from the wilderness to the Euphrates; for I will deliver the inhabitants of the land into your hand, and you shall drive them out before you. 32 You shall make no covenant with them or with their gods. 33 They shall not dwell in your land, lest they make you sin against me; for if you serve their gods, it will surely be a snare to you."

The concluding section of the Book of the Covenant bears all of the marks of a farewell address. As opposed to laws, it contains promises and exhortations, as well as warnings, concerning the journey into the promised land. The Lord will send his angel before Israel, and will become an enemy to all of Israel's adversaries. Israel has only to respond positively to the Lord's leadership and the conquest will become a reality.

Experiencing the Lord's Leadership (vv. 20–21). However one may interpret the angel whom the Lord promised to send, the intent of the passage is clear: the Lord guides in his own way those who follow his will. *Angel* means messenger, and one is tempted to interpret the passage to mean that the Lord promised to send a "leader," who would be the Lord's messenger, or angel. The suggestion may be correct that the reference was to the ark which went before the tribes, bore the revelation of God, and symbolized the presence of God.

In keeping with the patterns of thought contemporary to the time of the passage, *angel* probably referred to an intermediary; one who appeared as a nonhuman figure to lead God's people (cf. the angel of God's leadership at the sea, 14:19 ff.). On the other hand, is it not possible that, despite the fact that individuals contemporary with the origin of the account believed in the literal, physical reality of angels, one may legitimately understand the verse as a genuine and profound means of asserting the reality of Divine Providence, without insisting upon the physical reality of angels?

The Lord's Identification with Israel (v. 22). The Lord fulfilled the role of Israel's warrior-god, fighting her battles through plague, hail, storm, and earthquake. The very human description of the Lord as an *enemy* or *adversary* should be understood against the background of cultural patterns of thought contemporary to the time of the conquest, and should not be allowed to obscure the later and broader understanding that the Lord was not restricted to a single people. In the case of the conquest, however, the providence of God did operate in such fashion that the land became Israel's, leading successive interpreters to portray the Lord as an enemy and an adversary to all those who stood between the tribes and the Promised Land.

Conquest and Settlement of the Land (vv. 23–33). "Hornets" is am ambiguous term, but one might interpret it as a plague, a calamitous storm such as those which precipitated victories during the conquest (cf. Josh. 10:11 ff.; Judg. 5:1 ff.), or a military expedition by an external nation or seminomadic group. Only two other contexts use the word "hornet" (cf. Josh. 24:12; Deut. 7:20).

The whole of the passage is closely related to Deuteronomic thought, especially that of the holy war. The implication that

had the Lord not allowed the inhabitants to be driven out *little by little* the land would have become desolate and the wild beasts would have multiplied against Israel indirectly suggests that the number of the incoming Israelites was considerably smaller than the two and a half million population often presupposed on the basis of six hundred thousand fighting men (cf. 12:37).

IV. Ratification of the Covenant (24:1–14)

The ceremony of ratification for the Sinai covenant revolved around two primary emphases: the meal, shared between the elders of Israel before the Lord (vv. 1–2,9–11); the sealing the covenant through sprinkling the people with blood (vv. 3–8).

1. The Vision and the Communal Meal (24:1–2,9–11)

¹ And he said to Moses, "Come up to the LORD, you and Aaron, Nadab, and Abihu, and seventy of the elders of Israel, and worship afar off. ² Moses alone shall come near to the LORD; but the others shall not come near, and the people shall not come up with him."

. . . . .

⁹ Then Moses and Aaron, Nadab, and Abihu, and seventy of the elders of Israel went up, ¹⁰ and they saw the God of Israel; and there was under his feet as it were a pavement of sapphire stone, like the very heaven for clearness. ¹¹ And he did not lay his hand on the chief men of the people of Israel; they beheld God, and ate and drank.

To have eaten with one's enemy would have been inconceivable, and the common meal presupposed a psychic community between participants. As Pedersen suggests, "Nothing was so well suited to unite souls and strengthen the covenant as a meal which gathered relatives and friends around the common food in a communal spirit. The meal of such a fellowship confirmed and strengthened the peace, the harmony on which all joint life was dependent" (p. 334). For this reason the communal meal was a primary means of sealing a covenant.

Upon ascending the mountain *they saw the God of Israel. Saw* is the common word for seeing with the physical eye (*ra'ah*), while *beheld* (v. 11) is the customary word for seeing as in a vision (*chazah*). The sapphire was a sky blue, semiprecious stone, which may suggest some relationship between gazing up into the sapphire-blue sky, described by the biblical writer as "a pavement of sapphire stone," and a vision of heaven.

The nature of the larger context would suggest that the meal was directly related to the confirmation of the covenant. Such an exalted spiritual experience was hardly the place for a "common" meal, especially when one considers the sanctity of the mountain reflected in Exodus 19. Considering all aspects of the issue, it appears thoroughly plausible that verse 11 was intended as the description of a covenant meal which constituted at least one element in the ratification of the covenant.

2. A Covenant Sealed with Blood (24:3–8)

³ Moses came **and told the people all the words of the LORD and all the ordinances; and all the people answered with one voice, and said, "All the words which the LORD has spoken we will do."** ⁴ **And Moses wrote all the words of the LORD. And he rose early in the morning, and built an altar at the foot of the mountain, and twelve pillars, according to the twelve tribes of Israel.** ⁵ **And he sent young men of the people of Israel, who offered burnt offerings and sacrificed peace offerings of oxen to the LORD.** ⁶ **And Moses took half of the blood and put it in basins, and half of the blood he threw against the altar.** ⁷ **Then he took the book of the covenant, and read it in the hearing of the people; and they said, "All that the LORD has spoken we will do, and we will be obedient."** ⁸ **And Moses took the blood and threw it upon the people, and said, "Behold the blood of the covenant which the LORD has made with you in accordance with all these words."**

Many feel that the *words* refer to the ten words (20:3–17), a thesis with much to commend it but devoid of absolute confirmation. Should this hypothesis be correct, then the Book of the Covenant was placed between the Decalogue and the ratification of the covenant at a time subsequent to the Sinai-Kadesh sojourn.

In all probability the Decalogue, in its primal form, derives from Moses himself, and served as the basic stipulations for the Sinai covenant. The Book of the Covenant, on the other hand, was a later compilation, although certainly no later than the eighth century, and much more likely to be placed in the period of the tribal confederacy or early monarchy.

Reading the words and affirming obedience was probably an ancient practice long related to the Book of the Covenant, and was repeated through much of Israel's history as Israelites of succeeding generations reaffirmed their loyalty in a covenant renewal ceremony (cf. Josh. 24:1 ff.).

Throwing the blood **upon the people** symbolically identified them with the sacrificial offering, and through this brought them into union with God. The effectual result of the symbolic act was to seal the affirmation of loyalty by a bond of union between the people and God.

Behold the blood of the covenant. The history of the covenant does not end at Sinai, but should be pursued throughout the history of Israel, both old and new. One should consider, for example, Jeremiah's hope of a new covenant (31:31 ff.), and Jesus' "blood of the covenant, which is poured out for many" (Matt. 26:28).

3. Confirmation Through Writing (24:12–14)

¹² **The LORD said to Moses, "Come up to me on the mountain, and wait there; and I will give you the tables of stone, with the law and the commandment, which I have written for their instruction."** ¹³ **So Moses rose with his servant Joshua, and Moses went up into the mountain of God.** ¹⁴ **And he said to the elders, "Tarry here for us, until we come to you again; and, behold, Aaron and Hur are with you; whoever has a cause, let him go to them."**

Although the covenant stipulations were given orally (cf. 20:1 ff.; Deut. 4:10 ff.), at the conclusion of the ceremony of ratification the Lord promised to give Moses tables of stone upon which the stipulations were written. Commitment to writing apparently served both to confirm the oral pronouncement and to preserve the stipulations as a binding covenant for future generations. The inscription of the stipulations and their storage before God closely paralleled the same element in ancient Near Eastern treaty covenants.

Which I have written should be interpreted in a manner consonant with Exodus 31:18. The phrase underscores the divine source and authority of the ten words but should not be taken in an unduly literal manner concerning the actual method followed in inscribing the commandments.

This entire passage should be read in conjunction with 32:1 ff., which is the immediate sequel to 24:12–14.

Part Four
Yahweh: Lord of Worship
24:15—40:38

Yahweh's lordship is further reflected in each of the several areas of cultic legislation designed to prescribe the essential content of Israel's worship.

I. Priestly Ordinances for the Sanctuary and Ministry (24:15—31:18)

This complex of priestly legislation was set within the context of the Sinai experience, although not all of it presupposes Moses' presence on the mountain. As one studies the priestly legislation, he may well discern the emergence of practices and institutions later than the Sinai era which have been set into this original context by the editors of the literary material.

That Yahweh is sovereign Lord of worship is the underlying premise of the legislation. In both the authoritative nature of the instructions for the life of Israel and the manner in which the Lord is exalted in holiness and majesty through various aspects of both the tabernacle and the priesthood, the writer presupposes that Yahweh is Lord of worship.

1. Revelation of the Lord's Purposes to Moses (24:15–18)

15 Then Moses went up on the mountain, and the cloud covered the mountain. 16 The glory of the Lord settled on Mount Sinai, and the cloud covered it six days; and on the seventh day he called to Moses out of the midst of the cloud. 17 Now the appearance of the glory of the Lord was like a devouring fire on the top of the mountain in the sight of the people of Israel. 18 And Moses entered the cloud, and went up on the mountain. And Moses was on the mountain forty days and forty nights.

Upon ascending the mountain, Moses did not have immediate access to the Lord but waited for six days before the Lord spoke to him on the seventh day. Such an arrangement reflects the priestly writer's concern both to systematize events and to relate them to a sacral order.

Forty days and forty nights may be a round number for a long period of time rather than precisely forty twelve-hour days and twelve-hour nights. Moses was on the mountain so long that the people felt that he had deserted them (cf. 32:1 ff.).

2. The Tabernacle (25:1—27:21)

Biblical interpretation passed through an era of extreme typological and Christological emphases in which the tabernacle was interpreted almost exclusively as a type of Christ. That there were legitimate principles concerning the nature of God inherent within the structure of the tabernacle, as well as the priest's dress and functions, is gladly recognized. One should, however, be exceedingly cautious not to tear the Scripture from its historical and theological context, and force it to serve an end for which it was never intended.

(1) Contributions for the Sanctuary (25: 1–9)

1 The Lord said to Moses, 2 "Speak to the people of Israel, that they take for me an offering; from every man whose heart makes him willing you shall receive the offering for me. 3 And this is the offering which you shall receive from them: gold, silver, and bronze, 4 blue and purple and scarlet stuff and fine twined linen, goats' hair, 5 tanned rams' skins, goatskins, acacia wood, 6 oil for the lamps, spices for the anointing oil and for the fragrant incense, 7 onyx stones, and stones for setting, for the ephod and for the breastpiece. 8 And let

them make me a sanctuary, that I may dwell in their midst. [9] According to all that I show you concerning the pattern of the tabernacle, and of all its furniture, so you shall make it.

If the God who met Israel at Sinai was to go with them, a proper dwelling must be provided, *that I may dwell in their midst* (v. 8). The *sanctuary* (*miqdosh*, v. 8) means a holy place, but is variously referred to throughout the Old Testament. On occasion it was called the "tent of meeting" (33:7; Num. 11:16), "the tent" (1 Kings 2:28 ff.; 1 Chron. 9:23), "tabernacle," (26:1, literally, "a dwelling"), or "tabernacle of the testimony" (38:21; cf. Num. 9:15). Detailed analysis of the narratives reveals a dual tradition concerning (1) a rather simple tent of meeting and (2) the elaborate picture of the tabernacle found in other portions of the biblical narratives. The reason given for the sanctuary, *that I may dwell* (*shakan*), uses a verb from which the word tabernacle (*mishkan*) was derived.

The command to make all things *concerning the pattern* (v. 9) reflects the common ancient view that the earthly dwelling of the god(s), or God, is the counterpart to the heavenly archetype. As Eliade suggests, "an object or an act becomes real only insofar as it imitates or repeats an archetype. Thus, reality is acquired solely through repetition or participation; everything which lacks an exemplary model is 'meaningless,' i.e., it lacks reality."[1]

(2) *The Furnishings Within the Tabernacle* (25:10–40)

Predominant in the thought of the writer were the furnishings within the tabernacle as opposed to the tabernacle itself, the courtyard, or the furnishings of the courtyard. Perhaps it was for this reason that he listed first the ark, then the table for the bread of the Presence, followed by the golden lampstand.

[1] Mircea Eliade, *The Myth of the Eternal Return*, trans. Willard R. Trask (London: Routledge & Kegan Paul, 1955), p. 34.

a. *The Ark* (25:10–22)

[10] "They shall make an ark of acacia wood; two cubits and a half shall be its length, a cubit and a half its breadth, and a cubit and a half its height. [11] And you shall overlay it with pure gold, within and without shall you overlay it, and you shall make upon it a molding of gold round about. [12] And you shall cast four rings of gold for it and put them on its four feet, two rings on the one side of it, and two rings on the other side of it. [13] You shall make poles of acacia wood, and overlay them with gold. [14] And you shall put the poles into the rings on the sides of the ark, to carry the ark by them. [15] The poles shall remain in the rings of the ark; they shall not be taken from it. [16] And you shall put into the ark the testimony which I shall give you. [17] Then you shall make a mercy seat of pure gold; two cubits and a half shall be its length, and a cubit and a half its breadth. [18] And you shall make two cherubim of gold; of hammered work shall you make them, on the two ends of the mercy seat. [19] Make one cherub on the one end, and one cherub on the other end; of one piece with the mercy seat shall you make the cherubim on its two ends. [20] The cherubim shall spread out their wings above, overshadowing the mercy seat with their wings, their faces one to another; toward the mercy seat shall the faces of the cherubim be. [21] And you shall put the mercy seat on the top of the ark; and in the ark you shall put the testimony that I shall give you. [22] There I will meet with you, and from above the mercy seat, from between the two cherubim that are upon the ark of the testimony, I will speak with you of all that I will give you in commandment for the people of Israel.

The *ark* (*'aron*) was a rectangular chest 27 inches wide, 45 inches long, and 27 inches deep,[2] but should not be confused with the word for either Noah's ark or Moses' ark, basket (Gen. 6:14 and Ex. 2:3 use *tebah*, probably an Egyptian loan word, meaning a vessel). It was overlaid both inside and outside with gold, and fitted with a molding of gold which could well have served as a rim for the cover, although it might also have been a decorative band extending around the box. Each of the cult objects was fitted with rings and poles

[2] A cubit, the distance from one's elbow to the tip of the middle finger, was approximately 18 inches; the "span" was half a cubit, and the "handbreadth" was one-sixth a cubit. Cf. Noth, p. 204.

which enabled the objects to be transported without allowing men to touch holy objects.

Exodus mentions only *the testimony* (i.e., the Decalogue) within the ark, and the earliest functional use of the ark may have been that of a depository for the covenant stipulations. This functional purpose was soon overshadowed by the theological interpretation of the ark as a portable throne for the Lord.

The covering was known as the *mercy seat* or the "cover" (*kapporeth* could mean either), and was constructed of solid gold, 45 inches long and 27 inches wide, no depth being specified. On opposite ends of the mercy seat, *two cherubim* were to be constructed of solid *gold,* and of one piece with the mercy seat, their outstretched wings overshadowing the mercy seat. Their faces were to be *toward the mercy seat,* probably bowed in adoration and humility before the presence of the Lord.

The cherubim were winged creatures, probably with human faces and animal bodies. Figures of this type were common to the Ancient Near East, especially as attendants associated with religious sites. The *cherubim* were likely earthly counterparts to heavenly beings which ancient persons associated with the gods, or God.

Although *kapporeth* (v. 17) may be translated "cover," the RSV is likely correct in the assumption that more was connoted by the word than merely a lid for the ark; hence, the translation "mercy seat." The verb *kipper* means to cover over, figuratively, to pacify, or to make propitiation (although some argue that it means to "wipe away," cf. McNeile, *op. cit.,* pp. 160, 209). Each year, on the Day of Atonement (*yom kippur,* i.e., "day of covering over") the high priest entered into the holy of holies and brought the blood to atone for Israel's sin. Herrmann suggests that "the *kapporeth* cannot be regarded merely as a cover over the ark. According to Ex. 25:21 it is to be put above the chest as the tables of the Law are put in it. According to passages like Ex. 26:34; 35:12; 39:35 it is

no part of the ark. It is called 'the *kapporeth* that is over the ark of the law' (Ex. 30:6; Num. 7:89); never is it the *kapporeth* of the ark . . . the LXX calls it *'ilasterion epithema,* an atoning headpiece. After that it simply has *'ilasterion,* which can mean a means or place of expiation." [3]

The ark was primary for Israelite worship, for it was there that the Lord promised to meet Moses (*you* of v. 22 is singular). It was probably used widely in general worship, and in the era of the Temple it was to this religious object that the priest drew near once a year to offer atonement. The ark conveyed a double meaning for the faith of Israel; revelation through the ten words within the ark, and expiation, or atonement, through the blood upon *the mercy seat* which stood over the ark. The whole of the ark, chest and covering, symbolized for Israel the Lord's presence, assuring Israel of the Lord's revelation and his provision for atonement.

b. The Table (25:23–30)

23 "And you shall make a table of acacia wood; two cubits shall be its length, a cubit its breadth, and a cubit and a half its height. 24 You shall overlay it with pure gold, and make a molding of gold around it. 25 And you shall make around it a frame a handbreadth wide, and a molding of gold around the frame. 26 And you shall make for it four rings of gold, and fasten the rings to the four corners at its four legs. 27 Close to the frame the rings shall lie, as holders for the poles to carry the table. 28 You shall make the poles of acacia wood, and overlay them with gold, and the table shall be carried with these. 29 And you shall make its plates and dishes for incense, and its flagons and bowls with which to pour libations; of pure gold you shall make them. 30 And you shall set the bread of the Presence on the table before me always.

A *table,* 36 inches long, 18 inches wide, and 27 inches tall, was to be built for the purpose of holding the bread of the Presence, as well as the utensils used in offering incense and drink offerings (v. 29). The

---

[3] Herrmann, *'ilasterion, Theological Dictionary of the New Testament,* ed. Gerhard Kittel, trans. and ed. Geoffrey W. Bromiley (Grand Rapids: Eerdmans, 1967), III, 319.

table was overlaid with pure gold with *a molding of gold around it*, perhaps a raised, decorative piece on the edge of the table's top. *A frame a handbreadth* (about 3 inches) *wide*, extended around the legs, and *rings of gold* were attached *to the four corners* of the frame, at some distance from the top of the table. The *plates* were perhaps used to transport the bread of the Presence, while the dishes were for incense offerings (cf. 30:1) and the *flagons and bowls* were for drink offerings (cf. 2 Kings 16:13; Hosea 9:4).

Although the Lord was not present in the bread, the bread acknowledged the presence and providence of the Lord. The bread was known as "continual bread" (Num. 4:7), and, as one might anticipate, "holy bread" (1 Sam. 21:4 ff.), and was arranged in two rows of six loaves each (Lev. 24:6). In New Testament times the old bread was eaten by the priests who participated in exchanging the new bread for the old (cf. Menahoth 11:7).

c. The Lampstand—Menorah (25:31–40)

31 "And you shall make a lampstand of pure gold. The base and the shaft of the lampstand shall be made of hammered work; its cups, its capitals, and its flowers shall be of one piece with it; 32 and there shall be six branches going out of its sides, three branches of the lampstand out of one side of it and three branches of the lampstand out of the other side of it; 33 three cups made like almonds, each with capital and flower, on one branch, and three cups made like almonds, each with capital and flower, on the other branch—so for the six branches going out of the lampstand; 34 and on the lampstand itself four cups made like almonds, with their capitals and flowers, 35 and a capital of one piece with it under each pair of the six branches going out from the lampstand. 36 Their capitals and their branches shall be of one piece with it, the whole of it one piece of hammered work of pure gold. 37 And you shall make the seven lamps for it; and the lamps shall be set up so as to give light upon the space in front of it. 38 Its snuffers and their trays shall be of pure gold. 39 Of a talent of pure gold shall it be made, with all these utensils. 40 And see that you make them after the pattern for them, which is being shown you on the mountain.

The shape of the lampstand, plus the *almonds, each with capital and flower* (i.e., calyx and petals), suggest that the lampstand typified a tree. If so, this may reflect the reverence for sacred trees, although the religious conception attached to the lamp in Israel was vastly different from the general reverence of the sacred tree. The tree of life was known in pre-Israelite times, and the lampstand may have combined the concept of life inherent in both the tree of life and light, which was universally associated with life.

The lampstand served three purposes: (1) functional, for it gave light to an otherwise dark place; (2) aesthetic, lending "glory and beauty" to the holy place, for which there is a proper and continuing need; and (3) symbolic, conveying the concept of life through both the tree of life and light.

Ultimately the menorah (lampstand) became a unique Judaistic symbol for both the home and the worship center. By the time of New Testament Judaism, extinguishing the *menorah* was a symbol of disaster. Although the lamp of the tabernacle may not have been precisely like that of Herod's Temple, it may well have resembled the excellent portrayal of the seven-branched candelabra of Herod's Temple which appears on the Arch of Titus in Rome.

(3) Architecture (26:1–37)

The tabernacle encompassed a rectangular area 15 by 45 feet (10 cubits by 30 cubits), and was 15 feet high. The structure was in turn divided so that there were two rooms; the rear room 15 by 15 (the most holy place, or the holy of holies), and the entrance room, 15 by 30 (the holy place).

a. Dimensions of the Tabernacle (26:1–6)

1 "Moreover you shall make the tabernacle with ten curtains of fine twined linen and blue and purple and scarlet stuff; with cherubim skilfully worked shall you make them. 2 The length of each curtain shall be twenty-eight

cubits, and the breadth of each curtain four cubits; all the curtains shall have one measure. 3 Five curtains shall be coupled to one another; and the other five curtains shall be coupled to one another. 4 And you shall make loops of blue on the edge of the outmost curtain in the first set; and likewise you shall make loops on the edge of the outmost curtain in the second set. 5 Fifty loops you shall make on the one curtain, and fifty loops you shall make on the edge of the curtain that is in the second set; the loops shall be opposite one another. 6 And you shall make fifty clasps of gold, and couple the curtains one to the other with the clasps, that the tabernacle may be one whole.

Although the curtains described in verses 1–6 were so extensive that they had the size and appearance of a rectangular tent, they were not designed as an outer covering, and were in turn covered by the tent described in 26:7 ff. If the framework of the tabernacle was of open construction, as it probably was, then the curtains formed a beautiful and symbolic wall with decorative work comparable to the cherubim carved in the walls of the Temple (cf. 1 Kings 6:29).

b. The Tent and the Covering (26:7–14)

7 "You shall also make curtains of goats' hair for a tent over the tabernacle; eleven curtains shall you make. 8 The length of each curtain shall be thirty cubits, and the breadth of each curtain four cubits; the eleven curtains shall have the same measure. 9 And you shall couple five curtains by themselves, and six curtains by themselves, and the sixth curtain you shall double over at the front of the tent. 10 And you shall make fifty loops on the edge of the curtain that is outmost in one set, and fifty loops on the edge of the curtain which is outmost in the second set.
11 "And you shall make fifty clasps of bronze, and put the clasps into the loops, and couple the tent together that it may be one whole. 12 And the part that remains of the curtains of the tent, the half curtain that remains, shall hang over the back of the tabernacle. 13 And the cubit on the one side, and the cubit on the other side, of what remains in the length of the curtains of the tent shall hang over the sides of the tabernacle, on this side and that side, to cover it. 14 And you shall make for the tent a covering of tanned rams' skins and goatskins.

A rectangular tent made of *goats' hair* was prepared and fitted to the tabernacle frame. Like the inner curtain, it was con-

structed of separate sections, joined into two large panels.

The two sections of the tent were to be joined with *fifty clasps of bronze* (v. 11), as opposed to the clasps of gold for the inner curtain (v. 6), the outer covering not requiring metal so precious as the curtain which touched the holy area. The plan for the tabernacle embodied a consistent movement from the more valuable to the less valuable products as one moved from the most holy place to the holy place and to the outer area. Thus, the nature of the material used was in direct relationship to the degree of holiness involved in adjoining areas.

The final stage in preparing the fabric for the tabernacle was the preparation of a protective cover. The RSV translation suggests a single covering: *make for the tent a covering of tanned rams' skins and goatskins* (v. 14), as though the tent was constructed of two separate materials. The Hebrew text supports the possibility of two separate objects: "And you shall make a covering for the tent, red skins of rams, and a covering (of) skins of sealskins above." The "sealskin" (ASV), translated "badger" in the KJV, and "goatskins" in the RSV, is a word (*tachash*) which probably referred to a dugong, an animal of the Indian Ocean also called a sea cow. The word may also be translated porpoise; hence porpoise skins. Rather than two separate coverings, however, the verse most likely refers to a single protective covering made of red rams' skins along the three sides, but with water-repellent skins such as the word *tachash* connotes above. The Hebrew text specifically states that the skins of the sea animals should be "above." The ASV translation supports such a position; "And thou shalt make a covering for the tent of rams' skins dyed red, and a covering of sealskins above" (v. 14, but cf. "fine leather," T.J.B.).

c. The Wooden Framework (26:15–25)

15 "And you shall make upright frames for the tabernacle of acacia wood. 16 Ten cubits shall be the length of a frame, and a cubit and

a half the breadth of each frame. [17] There shall be two tenons in each frame, for fitting together; so shall you do for all the frames of the tabernacle. [18] You shall make the frames for the tabernacle: twenty frames for the south side; [19] and forty bases of silver you shall make under the twenty frames, two bases under one frame for its two tenons, and two bases under another frame for its two tenons; [20] and for the second side of the tabernacle, on the north side twenty frames, [21] and their forty bases of silver, two bases under one frame, and two bases under another frame; [22] and for the rear of the tabernacle westward you shall make six frames. [23] And you shall make two frames for corners of the tabernacle in the rear; [24] they shall be separate beneath, but joined at the top, at the first ring; thus shall it be with both of them; they shall form the two corners. [25] And there shall be eight frames, with their bases of silver, sixteen bases; two bases under one frame, and two bases under another frame.

The fabric of the tabernacle was supported by a wooden frame, constructed in such manner as to be dismantled for transport. Crucial to the understanding of the construction is the meaning of *qerashim*, translated as "boards" in both the KJV and the ASV, but as "frames" in the RSV. Except for its reference to the deck of a ship in Ezekiel 27:6, *qeresh*, of which *qerashim* is the plural, always appears in the context of the tabernacle.

Most commentators of this century have followed the leadership of A. R. S. Kennedy, whose work appeared in Hastings *Dictionary of the Bible*, and have assumed that the word connoted a frame rather than a solid board. The frames were 15 feet high and 27 inches wide (v. 16). They were constructed of two parallel pieces of narrow material, probably joined at top, middle, and bottom. The lower end of the frames formed tenons (v. 16 f.) which fit into bases so constructed as to receive them. Such open construction permitted the inner curtain of fine material and woven cherubim to be seen from within the tabernacle, which would have been impossible had the frames been solid. Since the inner curtain was covered by the tent, neither could the curtains have been seen from the outside. Thus, only if the frames

were open could the inner curtain have been seen, and if they were not designed to be seen, why the beautiful and intricate work expended on the curtains?

d. Supporting Bars for the Frames (26: 26–30)

[26] "And you shall make bars of acacia wood, five for the frames of the one side of the tabernacle, [27] and five bars for the frames of the other side of the tabernacle, and five bars for the frames of the side of the tabernacle at the rear westward. [28] The middle bar, halfway up the frames, shall pass through from end to end. [29] You shall overlay the frames with gold, and shall make their rings of gold for holders for the bars; and you shall overlay the bars with gold. [30] And you shall erect the tabernacle according to the plan for it which has been shown you on the mountain.

In order to tie the frames together, rings were attached to the frames at the top, bottom, and middle, and **bars of acacia wood**, overlaid with gold (vv. 26–27), were then inserted through the rings. The middle bars were as long as the section they held together; the side walls being 45 feet, and the rear wall 15 feet. The top and bottom bars ran only half the distance of the walls they supported (v. 28). Consequently each wall required *five bars;* one for the middle rings which ran the length of the wall, two for the top, and two for the bottom.

This frame construction rather than the customary tent with poles and supporting ropes has led some to conclude that the tabernacle reflected a style of construction better associated with settled than with nomadic life; that the narrative reflects a reading back into the text of the Temple in Jerusalem. Although this is not necessarily the case, the frame construction in all probability did originate in a cultural context other than the desert. This does not necessarily presuppose a reading back into the text of a later construction, however, and may actually reflect a pattern of construction older than Israel. For example, the same word translated "frames" or "boards," *qerashim*, is used in Ugaritic literature to describe the dwelling of 'El at the head of the rivers. 'El's throne room was likely a trellis pavilion,[4] and, although the duplication of a word does not prove a direct borrowing of architectural form, the framework of the tabernacle was certainly more at home in Canaanite cultural circles than in nomadic society.

e. The Veil of the Holy Place (26:31–35)

31 "And you shall make a veil of blue and purple and scarlet stuff and fine twined linen; in skilled work shall it be made, with cherubim; 32 and you shall hang it upon four pillars of acacia overlaid with gold, with hooks of gold, upon four bases of silver. 33 And you shall hang the veil from the clasps, and bring the ark of the testimony in thither within the veil; and the veil shall separate for you the holy place from the most holy. 34 You shall put the mercy seat upon the ark of the testimony in the most holy place. 35 And you shall set the table outside the veil, and the lampstand on the south side of the tabernacle opposite the table; and you shall put the table on the north side.

A *veil*, constructed of the same material and woven with the same design as the curtain, divided the rectangular tent into two rooms. It was suspended by hooks on four pillars of acacia wood overlaid with gold, and separated the tabernacle into *the holy place*, which one entered immediately upon coming into the tabernacle, and *the most holy* place (holy of holies) at the rear of the tabernacle. The *mercy seat* was to be placed *upon the ark of the testimony* (notice the way in which they are treated as separate functional items, the ark simply being the place where the mercy seat rested) and placed *in the most holy place* (v. 34). In the holy place, *outside the veil, the lampstand* was *on the south side* (left) and *the table* was *on the north side* (right). No mention was made of an altar of incense (cf. 30:1 ff.).

f. The Screen for the Door (26:36–37)

36 "And you shall make a screen for the door of the tent, of blue and purple and scarlet stuff and fine twined linen, embroidered with needlework. 37 And you shall make for the screen

---

[4] Frank Cross, "The Tabernacle," *Biblical Archaeologist*, X, 3, 1947, p. 62.

five pillars of acacia, and overlay them with gold; their hooks shall be of gold, and you shall cast five bases of bronze for them.

The *screen for the door* to the tabernacle was made of the same fine material as the veil and the curtain, but the screen was *embroidered with needlework* rather than the cherubim which appeared on the curtains and the veil. Apparently the cherubim were uniquely associated with the deity. As the bases of bronze rather than silver served to distinguish between the holiness of the inner sanctuary and the screen doorway, so the cherubim appeared only on the walls, roof, or veil within the sanctuary. The screen was suspended from *five pillars of acacia* wood, set in bronze bases. The screen completed the construction of the tabernacle, and the often-used sketch by A. R. S. Kennedy clearly suggests the primary characteristics of the tabernacle.

(4) The Tabernacle Court (27:1–21)

Specific instructions were given for preparing the altar, the wall of the court, and the oil for the lamp—which seems strangely out of place in a context discussing the courtyard.

a. The Altar (27:1–8)

1 "You shall make the altar of acacia wood, five cubits long and five cubits broad; the altar shall be square, and its height shall be three cubits. 2 And you shall make horns for it on its four corners; its horns shall be of one piece with it, and you shall overlay it with bronze. 3 You shall make pots for it to receive its ashes, and shovels and basins and forks and firepans; all its utensils you shall make of bronze. 4 You shall also make for it a grating, a network of bronze; and upon the net you shall make four bronze rings at its four corners. 5 And you shall set it under the ledge of the altar so that the net shall extend half way down the altar. 6 And you shall make poles for the altar, poles of acacia wood, and overlay them with bronze; 7 and the poles shall be put through the rings, so that the poles shall be upon the two sides of the altar, when it is carried. 8 You shall make it hollow, with boards; as it has been shown you on the mountain, so shall it be made.

The *altar* was *of acacia wood* overlaid with bronze, and measured 4½ feet high and 7½ feet by 7½ feet across the top. It was apparently hollow, and may have been filled with earth when in use. There is no suggestion that it was so filled, however, but without some such provision the wood would not likely have withstood the fire of the sacrifice (earth would also conform to the ancient altar law of 20:24). The *horns* of the altar were projections *on its four corners,* and were uniquely holy. An individual could lay hold upon the horns and thus claim refuge from those who sought his life (cf. 1 Kings 1:50 f.; 2:28). The origin of the horns is uncertain, but may have been related to the horns of an animal, the functional purpose of holding parts of the sacrificial animal, or sanctity common to the four corners of an object.

The lower half of the altar was covered by a bronze *grating,* probably extending completely around the altar, for it had *four bronze rings at its four corners,* used to transport the altar (vv. 4,7).

Midway of the altar's sides there was a ledge which extended to the ground. It probably served the utilitarian purpose of holding various equipment associated with the sacrifice (cf. v. 3). The suggestion that the ledge served as a step from which the priest could offer the sacrifice is hardly correct, for the altar was only 4½ feet tall, and the ledge midway would have placed the sacrifice 2¼ feet above the priest's feet, an awkward position to say the least.

b. The Wall of the Court (27:9–19)

9 "You shall make the court of the tabernacle. On the south side the court shall have hangings of fine twined linen a hundred cubits long for one side; 10 their pillars shall be twenty and their bases twenty, of bronze, but the hooks of the pillars and their fillets shall be of silver. 11 And likewise for its length on the north side there shall be hangings a hundred cubits long, their pillars twenty and their bases twenty, of bronze, but the hooks of the pillars and their fillets shall be of silver. 12 And for the breadth of the court on the west side there shall be hangings for fifty cubits, with ten pillars and ten bases. 13 The breadth of the court on the front to the east shall be fifty cubits. 14 The hangings for the one side of the gate shall be fifteen cubits, with three pillars and three bases. 15 On the other side the hangings shall be fifteen cubits, with three pillars and three bases. 16 For the gate of the court there shall be a screen twenty cubits long, of blue and purple and scarlet stuff and fine twined linen, embroidered with needlework; it shall have four pillars and with them four bases. 17 All the pillars around the court shall be filleted with silver; their hooks shall be of silver, and their bases of bronze. 18 The length of the court shall be a hundred cubits, the breadth fifty, and the height five cubits, with hangings of fine twined linen and bases of bronze. 19 All the utensils of the tabernacle for every use, and all its pegs and all the pegs of the court, shall be of bronze.

The wall of the courtyard was a series of curtains 7½ feet high which encompassed a rectangular area 75 feet wide and 150 feet long. The courtyard was oriented toward the east, with the gate facing eastward. On both the north and south sides of the wall curtains 150 feet in length were suspended from twenty pillars set in bronze bases. The use of bronze, in contrast to the silver bases for the tabernacle, reflects the threefold division concerning the sanctity of the tabernacle complex: (1) the most holy place (2) the holy place, and (3) the court. The pillars were *filleted with silver* (vv. 17,11), i.e., inlaid with silver rings for decoration, and had a silver capital, or design, on top the pillar (cf. 38:17). The curtain on the west wall was 75 feet long and was suspended from ten pillars (v. 12). The east wall was not completely enclosed, but had a curtain 22½ feet long, set on three pillars extending from the corner of the south wall, and a comparable curtain extending 22½ feet from the corner of the north wall. This left a gate in the east wall which was thirty feet wide, woven of *blue and purple and scarlet stuff and fine twined linen, embroidered with needlework* (v. 16), suspended from four pillars.

The probable intention of the relationship of the number of the pillars to the length of various walls was to create a design in which the wall panels were broken into sections 7½ feet square (the wall being 7½ feet tall). Thus, the 150 feet on the north and south walls were divided into 20 sections, each 7½ feet wide; as was the 75-foot long rear wall with its 10 pillars, and the 2 small walls by the gate, each 22½ feet long with 3 pillars.

c. Oil for the Lamp (27:20–21)

20 "And you shall command the people of Israel that they bring to you pure beaten olive oil for the light, that a lamp may be set up to burn continually. 21 In the tent of meeting, outside the veil which is before the testimony, Aaron and his sons shall tend it from evening to morning before the LORD. It shall be a statute for ever to be observed throughout their generations by the people of Israel.

The sanctity of the holy place demanded the purest of oil for the lamp that burned within the holy place; hence, the *command* in verse 20. The natural meaning of *continually* suggests that the light was never to go out; a practice confirmed in Judaism. It more probably refers, however, to the order, *It shall be a statute for ever* (v. 21).

The whole of the tabernacle complex underscored the Lord's continuing presence. Not only was he present on Sinai, but with his people wherever they might go. His presence was mobile rather than static, and he was continually with his people. Although his holiness demanded obedient and reverential conduct, he was not unapproachable. Those who entered his court first faced the central object of the courtyard, the altar, and made offerings of forgiveness and communion. Later (30:1 ff.) a laver for ritual washing was placed between the altar and the holy place, providing for the cleansing of all priests who approached God. Within the holy place the bread of the Presence constantly reminded Israel of the Lord's presence and sustaining power. The lamp spread the light of life within the holy place, and the cherubim from three walls and the ceiling symbolized his heavenly court.

Within the most holy place, the ark proclaimed the Lord's revelation, and the mercy seat atop the ark was the site for the atonement of Israel's sin. Finally, at the conclusion of the long journey from the courtyard altar, the Lord himself dwelt above the mercy seat, between the cherubim. Although not every person could make the full journey from altar to the Presence, the priests made the journey on behalf of Israel, and each Israelite felt himself individually borne into the presence of God. The way of Israel was the way of the symbol—leading from altar, laver, bread, lamp, incense, law, and atonement, to ultimate presence with the Lord.

3. The Priestly Vestments (28:1–43)

The priestly garments, like the tabernacle, were rich in symbolism but not unduly typological.

(1) Introduction and Summary of Priestly Vestments (28:1–4)

1 "Then bring near to you Aaron your brother, and his sons with him, from among the people of Israel, to serve me as priests—Aaron and Aaron's sons, Nadab and Abihu, Eleazar and Ithamar. 2 And you shall make holy garments for Aaron your brother, for glory and for beauty. 3 And you shall speak to all who have ability, whom I have endowed with an able mind, that they make Aaron's garments to consecrate him for my priesthood. 4 These are the garments which they shall make: a breastpiece, an ephod, a robe, a coat of checker work, a turban, and a girdle; they shall make holy garments for Aaron your brother and his sons to serve me as priests.

Basic to the entire concept of priestly dress was the principle that one's clothing must be clean, pure, or holy before one could approach a holy God. The garments are *for glory and for beauty* (v. 2), symbolizing the burning presence of God.

The garments were constructed by those *whom I have endowed with an able mind* (v. 3), or, better, "whom I have filled with a spirit of wisdom." This description was more than an assessment of the several abilities of the workmen. It suggests that man's ability is related to the gift of God, and that the garments were made according to a divine pattern.

The equipment described, however, was for Aaron, the high priest, and was not duplicated for each of the priests. Their garments were less impressive, and are described in verses 40 ff. The royal nature of Aaron's regalia is suggestive of the postexilic period when, in the absence of a king, the high priest became a semiroyal figure.

(2) The Ephod (28:5–14)

5 "They shall receive gold, blue and purple and scarlet stuff, and fine twined linen. 6 And they shall make the ephod of gold, of blue and purple and scarlet stuff, and of fine twined linen, skilfully worked. 7 It shall have two shoulder-pieces attached to its two edges, that it may be joined together. 8 And the skilfully woven band upon it, to gird it on, shall be of the same workmanship and materials, of gold, blue and purple and scarlet stuff, and fine twined linen. 9 And you shall take two onyx stones, and engrave on them the names of the sons of Israel, 10 six of their names on the one stone, and the names of the remaining six on the other stone, in the order of their birth. 11 As a jeweler engraves signets, so shall you engrave the two stones with the names of the sons of Israel; you shall enclose them in settings of gold filigree. 12 And you shall set the two stones upon the shoulder-pieces of the ephod, as stones of remembrance for the sons of Israel; and Aaron shall bear their names before the LORD upon his two shoulders for remembrance. 13 And you shall make settings of gold filigree, 14 and two chains of pure gold, twisted like cords; and you shall attach the corded chains to the settings.

The *ephod* described here was a vest-like garment, beautifully made *of gold, of blue and purple and scarlet stuff, and of fine twined linen* (v. 5), and suspended by shoulder straps. Other passages in the Old Testament suggest that the ephod may have been an image, for Gideon made an ephod of gold, weighing possibly as much as 1,700 shekels (cf. Judg. 8:26 ff.; Hos. 3:4). When David went to Nob he found the sword of Goliath "wrapped in a cloth behind the ephod" (1 Sam. 21:9). Samuel, however, was girded with a linen ephod (1 Sam. 2:18), as was David when he brought the ark to Jerusalem (2 Sam. 6:14). The ephod is clearly a garment in the present passage, however, and it is possible that references to the ephod as an image were based upon the vest-like outer covering of the image.

On each of the *two shoulder-pieces,* craftsmen fixed an onyx stone, inscribed with the twelve *names of the sons of Israel,* arranged *in the order of their birth.* The *onyx* was a precious stone with a luster nearly like wax, and often banded with alternating black and milk-white, or red banded with white. In primitive eras jewels were probably used as amulets, affording the wearer whatever potency inherent within the precious jewel. This was not the function of the jewels associated with the ephod, however, for they were specifically called *stones of remembrance* (v. 12). As the priest ministered before the Lord he continually bore his people with him— a noble ideal, whatever the age or circumstance.

(3) The Breastpiece of Judgment (28: 15–30)

15 "And you shall make a breastpiece of judgment, in skilled work; like the work of the ephod you shall make it; of gold, blue and purple and scarlet stuff, and fine twined linen shall you make it. 16 It shall be square and double, a span its length and a span its breadth. 17 And you shall set in it four rows of stones. A row of sardius, topaz, and carbuncle shall be the first row; 18 and the second row an emerald, a sapphire, and a diamond; 19 and the third row a jacinth, an agate, and an amethyst; 20 and the fourth row a beryl, an onyx, and a jasper; they shall be set in gold filigree. 21 There shall be twelve stones with their names according to the names of the sons of Israel; they shall be like signets, each engraved with its name, for the twelve tribes. 22 And you shall make for the breastpiece twisted chains like cords, of pure gold; 23 and you shall make for the breastpiece two rings of gold, and put the two rings on the two edges of the breastpiece. 24 And you shall put the two cords of gold in the two rings at the edges of the breastpiece; 25 the two ends of the two cords you shall attach to the two settings of filigree, and so attach it in front to the shoulder-pieces of the ephod. 26 And you shall make two rings of gold, and put them at the two ends of the breastpiece, on its inside edge next to the ephod. 27 And you shall make two rings of gold, and attach them in front to the lower part of the two shoulder-pieces of the ephod, at its joining above the skilfully woven band of the ephod. 28 And they shall bind the breastpiece by its rings to the rings of the ephod with

a lace of blue, that it may lie upon the skilfully woven band of the ephod, and that the breast-piece shall not come loose from the ephod. ²⁹ So Aaron shall bear the names of the sons of Israel in the breastpiece of judgment upon his heart, when he goes into the holy place, to bring them to continual remembrance before the Lord. ³⁰ And in the breastpiece of judgment you shall put the Urim and the Thummim, and they shall be upon Aaron's heart, when he goes in before the Lord; thus Aaron shall bear the judgment of the people of Israel upon his heart before the Lord continually.

The *breastpiece of judgment* was so called because it contained the sacred lots (v. 30) by which decisions were reached and judgment given. The *breastpiece* was a pouch, 9 inches square, covered with *four rows of stones,* three stones to the row, symbolizing *the twelve tribes* of Israel. The function of the stones was identical with those on the ephod (v. 29), and the present description is probably chronologi-cally later than the ephod description. The *breastpiece* was attached with golden rings *to the shoulder-pieces of the ephod* (vv. 24 ff.), so that the sacred pouch was worn across the chest; hence the name "breast-piece." The primary function of the sacred pouch was to serve as a container for *the Urim and the Thummim* (v. 30), and the reference to their role as a means of bear-ing Israel in remembrance before God is probably secondary, although nonetheless of considerable significance.

The Urim and the Thummim were the sacred lots used to transmit revelation from the Lord. Whatever the derivation of the names and however the objects may have been used, they apparently could only give yes and no answers (cf. 1 Sam. 14:38 ff.).

(4) The Priestly Robe (28:31–35)

³¹ "And you shall make the robe of the ephod all of blue. ³² It shall have in it an opening for the head, with a woven binding around the opening, like the opening in a garment, that it may not be torn. ³³ On its skirts you shall make pomegranates of blue and purple and scarlet stuff, around its skirts, with bells of gold between them, ³⁴ a golden bell and a pomegranate, a golden bell and a pome-granate, round about on the skirts of the robe.

³⁵ And it shall be upon Aaron when he minis-ters, and its sound shall be heard when he goes into the holy place before the Lord, and when he comes out, lest he die.

The robe was a blue, sleeveless garment, of one piece, fitted with an opening with a woven binding for the head. Around the skirt there were alternating *pomegranates of blue and purple and scarlet with bells of gold between them.* The pomegranate was one of several fruits mentioned in de-scribing the Promised Land (cf. Deut. 8:8; Num. 20:5). It was a bright red, orange-size fruit, and in ancient art and religion was a symbol of fertility. It is by no means clear that its role on the priest's garment was related to fertility, however; it was probably simply decorative.

One primary function of the robe was to announce the entrance of the priest as he came to minister. The phrase *lest he die* (v. 35), rather than referring to death by demons, as some suggest, assumes that should one enter the Lord's presence sud-denly, unannounced by the tinkling of the bells, he would die for having violated the holiness of God. Although highly anthropo-morphic in nature, the passage vividly por-trays the extreme efforts taken in ancient Israel to magnify the Lord's holiness. The bells also allowed worshipers to hear the priest as he moved about in his service within the tabernacle.

(5) The Engraved Talisman of the Turban (28:36–38)

³⁶ "And you shall make a plate of pure gold, and engrave on it, like the engraving of a signet, 'Holy to the Lord.' ³⁷ And you shall fasten it on the turban by a lace of blue; it shall be on the front of the turban. ³⁸ It shall be upon Aaron's forehead, and Aaron shall take upon himself any guilt incurred in the holy offering which the people of Israel hallow as their holy gifts; it shall always be upon his forehead, that they may be accepted before the Lord.

The priest wore *a turban of fine linen* (v. 39), and on this a gold plate, or talis-man, proclaiming *Holy to the Lord* (v. 36). The high priest, entering nearer to the Lord's presence than any other, was uniquely holy, and the engraved plate worn above his forehead (reminiscent of the "frontlets between your eyes," Deut. 6:8) identified Aaron as the holy representative of his people before God. The primary function of the talisman, however, was to make possible the acceptance of the people before God in cases of ritual infractions.

The direct relationship between the golden talisman and the acceptance of the people is clearly stated, *that they may be accepted before the Lord* (v. 39). Thus, Aaron was constantly reminded of the sanctity of his own office, and the responsibility he bore on behalf of his people.

(6) The Coat and Turban (28:39)

39 "And you shall weave the coat in checker work of fine linen, and you shall make a turban of fine linen, and you shall make a girdle embroidered with needlework.

The coat, probably resembling a dressing gown, was of fine linen, a cool and treasured material. The reference to *checker work* suggests the alternation of colors in the warp and woof of the material, or, possibly, a quilted or other raised pattern of the same color. Except for Ezekiel 21:26, "turban" is used only of the priestly attire. It was probably folded many times around the head—the Talmud suggests that it contained 16 cubits, or 24 feet, of material. The word girdle is completely misleading for contemporary society. The girdle (*'abnet*) was a sash worn around a robe or coat (cf. Isa. 22:21).

(7) Garments for the Priests (28:40–43)

40 "And for Aaron's sons you shall make coats and girdles and caps; you shall make them for glory and beauty. 41 And you shall put them upon Aaron your brother, and upon his sons with him, and shall anoint them and ordain them and consecrate them, that they may serve me as priests. 42 And you shall make for them linen breeches to cover their naked flesh; from the loins to the thighs they shall reach; 43 and they shall be upon Aaron, and upon his sons, when they go into the tent of meeting, or when they come near the altar to

minister in the holy place; lest they bring guilt upon themselves and die. This shall be a perpetual statute for him and for his descendants after him.

For Aaron's sons, Nadab, Abihu, Eleazar, and Ithamar, the craftsmen were to make coats, sashes, and caps *for glory and beauty* (v. 40). The simplicity of these garments stood in marked contrast to the extensive regalia of the high priest, which was so ornate in character.

Three words characterized the inauguration of the priests: *anoint, ordain,* and *consecrate.* Anointing with oil symbolically identified the person with God, anointing being directly related to the holiness of the fat (the olive oil, literally, was the "fat of the olive"). Sacred sites were anointed, as were religious objects generally (cf. the altar, 29:35–37), including the shields during the time of Solomon. Especially did anointing come to characterize the setting apart of kings, and, later, priests, to the service of God.

Ordain translates the phrase *umille'tha 'eth-yadam,* "and you shall fill their hand," perhaps in the sense of filling the priest's hand with a sacrifice. To ordain a priest was to fill his hand with the work of his ministry—an apt and continuing description of ordination. Since the hand was a symbol of power, however, the phrase may equally as well refer to endowing the priest with the power necessary to function in his office.

Consecrate is the common word (*qadhash* meaning to set apart for the service of God. The inauguration of the priests thus included: (1) identification with God through anointing; (2) filling his hand for the task; and (3) setting him apart to the service of God.

The primary purpose of the *linen breeches* (v. 42) was to cover the sexual organs of the priests while they ministered before the Lord. Such breeches were not normally worn in Israel, and the present provisions reflect a problem comparable to the prohibition against going up the steps of an altar, "that your nakedness be not exposed on it" (20:26). In both passages far more than either modesty or propriety was involved, for the problem reflected ancient and very basic attitudes toward holiness, especially protecting the holiness of God. The breeches were specifically provided for Aaron as well as his sons (cf. vv. 42 f.).

4. Consecration of the Priests (29:1–46)

Consecration of the priests involved: ceremonial washing, robing, and anointing and the offering of three sacrifices on behalf of the priests. For he who would minister before God must first experience within his own life the experiences through which he seeks to lead others.

(1) Purification, Robing, and Anointing (29:1–9)

1 "Now this is what you shall do to them to consecrate them, that they may serve me as priests. Take one young bull and two rams without blemish, 2 and unleavened bread, unleavened cakes mixed with oil, and unleavened wafers spread with oil. You shall make them of fine wheat flour. 3 And you shall put them in one basket and bring them in the basket, and bring the bull and the two rams. 4 You shall bring Aaron and his sons to the door of the tent of meeting, and wash them with water. 5 And you shall take the garments, and put on Aaron the coat and the robe of the ephod, and the ephod, and the breastpiece, and gird him with the skilfully woven band of the ephod; 6 and you shall set the turban on his head, and put the holy crown upon the turban. 7 And you shall take the anointing oil, and pour it on his head and anoint him. 8 Then you shall bring his sons, and put coats on them, 9 and you shall gird them with girdles and bind caps on them; and the priesthood shall be theirs by a perpetual statute. Thus you shall ordain Aaron and his sons.

Ritual washings were common to the Old Testament, and continued into the Judaistic and Christian eras. Such lustrations probably formed the background of "baptism" as practiced among the Essenes and the Qumran community, as well as the baptism of John. Thus, they stand as the ultimate background for Christian baptism, despite the transformation of meaning which

accompanied the Christian adaptation of lustrations. It is highly significant that the first step in ordination involved the symbolic washing away of whatever was "unclean" and might, therefore, corrupt the "holy things" associated with the priestly ministry (cf. the laver, and, later, the "bronze sea" in the temple).

(2) The Sin Offering for the Priests (29: 10–14)

10 "Then you shall bring the bull before the tent of meeting. Aaron and his sons shall lay their hands upon the head of the bull, 11 and you shall kill the bull before the LORD, at the door of the tent of meeting, 12 and shall take part of the blood of the bull and put it upon the horns of the altar with your finger, and the rest of the blood you shall pour out at the base of the altar. 13 And you shall take all the fat that covers the entrails, and the appendage of the liver, and the two kidneys with the fat that is on them, and burn them upon the altar. 14 But the flesh of the bull, and its skin, and its dung, you shall burn with fire outside the camp; it is a sin offering.

The sin offering (cf. Lev. 4:1 ff.) was a sacrifice of expiation which effectually secured forgiveness. The holy parts of the animal were offered to God (vv. 12 f.), and the remainder of the animal was taken outside the camp and burned (v. 14). The offerants placed their hands upon the sacrificial animal; either identifying the animal as theirs and their life with that of the animal, or transferring their sin to the sacrifice (v. 10). The fact that the animal was taken outside the camp and burned suggests that the animal had taken the sin of the offerants upon itself, and was therefore unclean and thus inappropriate for offering on the altar. Neither could it properly be consumed by either priest or people. The "unclean" nature of the sacrificial carcass strongly suggests the transference of "uncleanness" from the offerer to the animal. Some of the blood was placed on the four corners of the altar—the "horns"—and the remainder dashed at the base of the altar. Thus, the life of the animal and those identified with it were released to God. The fat plus the limited central organs were burned upon the altar, and thus were offered up to God; the fat, like the blood, being especially holy (cf. Lev. 3:17, which links the two). Purification and dedication were the primary purposes of the sin offering.

(3) The Burnt Offering (29:15–18)

15 "Then you shall take one of the rams, and Aaron and his sons shall lay their hands upon the head of the ram, 16 and you shall slaughter the ram, and shall take its blood and throw it against the altar round about. 17 Then you shall cut the ram into pieces, and wash its entrails and its legs, and put them with its pieces and its head, 18 and burn the whole ram upon the altar; it is a burnt offering to the LORD; it is a pleasing odor, an offering by fire to the LORD.

Within Israel's developed sacrificial system the *burnt offering* was a sacrifice offered to make atonement (cf. Lev. 1:4). Burning the entire animal on the altar, in contrast with the use of only selected portions, suggests the possibility that the sacrifice conveyed the complete giving of the worshiper to the Lord. Through laying their hands upon the sacrificial animal (v. 15), worshipers effectually identified themselves with the animal, and in the upward ascent of the smoke of the sacrifice the worshipers themselves were offered to God. The "wholeness" of the burnt offering properly symbolized the complete giving of oneself to the Lord, and was, therefore, wholly appropriate for the sacrifice prior to the act of ordination.

(4) The Peace Offering—the Ram of Ordination (29:19–34)

19 "You shall take the other ram; and Aaron and his sons shall lay their hands upon the head of the ram, 20 and you shall kill the ram, and take part of its blood and put it upon the tip of the right ear of Aaron and upon the tips of the right ears of his sons, and upon the thumbs of their right hands, and upon the great toes of their right feet, and throw the rest of the blood against the altar round about. 21 Then you shall take part of the blood that is on the altar, and of the anointing oil, and sprinkle it upon Aaron and his garments, and upon his sons and his sons' garments with him;

and he and his garments shall be holy, and his sons and his sons' garments with him.

22 "You shall also take the fat of the ram, and the fat tail, and the fat that covers the entrails, and the appendage of the liver, and the two kidneys with the fat that is on them, and the right thigh (for it is a ram of ordination), 23 and one loaf of bread, and one cake of bread with oil, and one wafer, out of the basket of unleavened bread that is before the LORD; 24 and you shall put all these in the hands of Aaron and in the hands of his sons, and wave them for a wave offering before the LORD. 25 Then you shall take them from their hands, and burn them on the altar in addition to the burnt offering, as a pleasing odor before the LORD; it is an offering by fire to the LORD.

26 "And you shall take the breast of the ram of Aaron's ordination and wave it for a wave offering before the LORD; and it shall be your portion. 27 And you shall consecrate the breast of the wave offering, and the thigh of the priests' portion, which is waved, and which is offered from the ram of ordination, since it is for Aaron and for his sons. 28 It shall be for Aaron and his sons as a perpetual due from the people of Israel, for it is the priests' portion to be offered by the people of Israel from their peace offerings; it is their offering to the LORD.

29 "The holy garments of Aaron shall be for his sons after him, to be anointed in them and ordained in them. 30 The son who is priest in his place shall wear them seven days, when he comes into the tent of meeting to minister in the holy place.

31 "You shall take the ram of ordination, and boil its flesh in a holy place; 32 and Aaron and his sons shall eat the flesh of the ram and the bread that is in the basket, at the door of the tent of meeting. 33 They shall eat those things with which atonement was made, to ordain and consecrate them, but an outsider shall not eat of them, because they are holy. 34 And if any of the flesh for the ordination, or of the bread, remain until the morning, then you shall burn the remainder with fire; it shall not be eaten, because it is holy.

The third offering is more fully described than the previous two, and was identified, quite appropriately, as the *ram of ordination*. It was uniquely associated with the ritual of installation; while the previous two sacrifices were offered on other occasions and for persons other than priests.

Sanctified by Blood (vv. 19–21). Although some of the blood was manipulated on the altar (v. 20b), the blood from the ram of ordination was used primarily to bring Aaron and his sons into a unique state of holiness. The blood of the victim was applied to the right side of the priests, to those parts of the body especially appropriate to their ministry.

While the two earlier sacrifices removed contagion, "uncleanness," or sin, through their atoning power, the present sacrifice regenerated the life of the worshipers by infusing them with a state of holiness. Both Aaron and his sons thus entered into a special state of holiness, unlike that of other worshipers; and they, alone, were permitted immediate access to God.

The Wave Offering (vv. 22–25). The wave offering was so-called because of the manner in which the officiating priest moved the sacrifice toward the altar and back again (as opposed to a right to left motion). Since most of the wave offerings were given to the priests, the back-and-forth movement of the offering may suggest the symbolic giving of the offering to God, and its subsequent gift by God to the priest.

Sharing the Peace Offering (vv. 26–28). The breast and right thigh of the ram were given to the priests, as expected in view of the fact that the priesthood received its sustenance from the sacrifices and other offerings. Leviticus further clarified this practice and suggests that the breast was given to "Aaron and his sons," i.e., the priests generally, but that the right thigh was specifically designated for the individual priest who offered the sacrifice (7:31 f.).

Future Use of Ceremonial Regalia (vv. 29–30). Successors to the office of high priest, possibly in the postexilic era, were instructed to wear the traditional regalia of the high priest for a period of seven days upon first entering the office (v. 30).

The Communion Meal (vv. 31–34). To share a meal in the ancient world was a unique symbol of fellowship, and the act of eating the sacrificial animal in particular kinds of offerings stressed the communion which had been established between the offerer(s) and the Lord. The statement that Aaron and his sons ate the flesh of the ram and the bread *at the door of the tent of meeting* (v. 32) suggests that it was a meal deliberately related to the Lord's presence. Thus, the total effect of the ram of ordination was to underscore the communion which existed between the priestly ministrants and the Lord, a quality of communion which ideally ought to characterize all who minister "before the Lord."

(5) Sanctifying the Altar (29:35–37)

35 "Thus you shall do to Aaron and to his sons, according to all that I have commanded you; through seven days shall you ordain them, 36 and every day you shall offer a bull as a sin offering for atonement. Also you shall offer a sin offering for the altar, when you make atonement for it, and shall anoint it, to consecrate it. 37 Seven days you shall make atonement for the altar, and consecrate it, and the altar shall be most holy; whatever touches the altar shall become holy.

The seven-day period of time allotted for the ceremonial installation of the priests is of unique importance. Numerology ascribes a special sanctity to the number 7, and the seven-day period suggests idea of sanctity, and also of completeness. Based upon the principle that the whole may be compressed into the part, the seven-day ritual sanctified all of the priest's time. All of his days were symbolically and ritually compressed into the holy week, then effectually dedicated to the Lord.

The altar was also uniquely dedicated to the Lord. A sin offering was made on behalf of the altar, perhaps reflecting a primitive conception whereby inanimate objects could be filled with "good" and "evil"— perhaps good and evil spirits. Whatever the basis, the altar was "forgiven" and then anointed. The unclean was put away by the offering of atonement, and "the holy" infused the altar through the act of anointing with holy oil. At the conclusion the altar was so uniquely holy that whatever touched it became holy, and thus acceptable to the Lord.

(6) Morning and Evening Sacrifices (29: 38-46)

[38] "Now this is what you shall offer upon the altar: two lambs a year old day by day continually. [39] One lamb you shall offer in the morning, and the other lamb you shall offer in the evening; [40] and with the first lamb a tenth measure of fine flour mingled with a fourth of a hin of beaten oil, and a fourth of a hin of wine for a libation. [41] And the other lamb you shall offer in the evening, and shall offer with it a cereal offering and its libation, as in the morning, for a pleasing odor, an offering by fire to the LORD. [42] It shall be a continual burnt offering throughout your generations at the door of the tent of meeting before the LORD, where I will meet with you, to speak there to you. [43] There I will meet with the people of Israel, and it shall be sanctified by my glory; [44] I will consecrate the tent of meeting and the altar; Aaron also and his sons I will consecrate, to serve me as priests. [45] And I will dwell among the people of Israel, and will be their God. [46] And they shall know that I am the LORD their God, who brought them forth out of the land of Egypt that I might dwell among them; I am the LORD their God.

At the door to the tent of meeting, where the Lord promised both to meet with Israel and speak to them, sacrifices were to be offered throughout her history (cf. 2 Kings 16:15; Neh. 10:33; Ezra 9:4; Ezek. 46:13 f.).

The phrases associated with the closing instructions are uniquely related to the covenant: *I . . . will be their God* (v. 45), and *they shall know that I am the Lord* (*'ani YHWH*).

5. Additional Instructions (30:1-38)

After specific instructions concerning the ordination of the priests, there follows in chapter 30 a miscellaneous collection of additional instructions related to the worship center. These may have come from a time chronologically later than the material cited in previous chapters; likely as late as the exile. If so, this would have been in keeping with the strong probability that the tabernacle was probably much simpler in earlier times than the minute details of Exodus 25 suggest.

(1) The Altar of Incense (30:1-10)

[1] "You shall make an altar to burn incense upon; of acacia wood shall you make it. [2] A cubit shall be its length, and a cubit its breadth; it shall be square, and two cubits shall be its height; its horns shall be of one piece with it. [3] And you shall overlay it with pure gold, its top and its sides round about and its horns; and you shall make for it a molding of gold round about. [4] And two golden rings shall you make for it; under its molding on two opposite sides of it shall you make them, and they shall be holders for poles with which to carry it. [5] You shall make the poles of acacia wood, and overlay them with gold. [6] And you shall put it before the veil that is by the ark of the testimony, before the mercy seat that is over the testimony, where I will meet with you. [7] And Aaron shall burn fragrant incense on it; every morning when he dresses the lamps he shall burn it, [8] and when Aaron sets up the lamps in the evening, he shall burn it, a perpetual incense before the LORD throughout your generations. [9] You shall offer no unholy incense thereon, nor burnt offering, nor cereal offering; and you shall pour no libation thereon. [10] Aaron shall make atonement upon its horns once a year; with the blood of the sin offering of atonement he shall make atonement for it once in the year throughout your generations; it is most holy to the LORD."

The altar was 36 inches tall, 18 inches square, overlaid with gold, and fitted with a molding, possibly as a ledge for the top, or, more likely, a decorative piece extending around the altar.

Incense was offered on the altar every morning when the high priest, Aaron, dressed the lamps, and again in the evening when Aaron set up the lamps (suggesting that the lamps were burned only at night). The most likely background of the incense was the thundercloud often associated with the theophany, and especially the "pillar of cloud" which was so characteristic of the exodus. One wonders whether the "cloud" of 40:34 may not have been the cloud of incense, and that "whenever the cloud was taken up" refers to the manner in which smoke at times rose directly into the atmosphere, as opposed to those occasions when it tended to hover at ground level.

(2) The Poll Tax (30:11–16)

11 The LORD said to Moses, 12 "When you take the census of the people of Israel, then each shall give a ransom for himself to the LORD when you number them, that there be no plague among them when you number them. 13 Each who is numbered in the census shall give this: half a shekel according to the shekel of the sanctuary (the shekel is twenty gerahs), half a shekel as an offering to the LORD. 14 Every one who is numbered in the census, from twenty years old and upward, shall give the LORD's offering. 15 The rich shall not give more, and the poor shall not give less, than the half shekel, when you give the LORD's offering to make atonement for yourselves. 16 And you shall take the atonement money from the people of Israel, and shall appoint it for the service of the tent of meeting; that it may bring the people of Israel to remembrance before the LORD, so as to make atonement for yourselves."

The "poll tax," so called because it was a tax on each poll (literally, head), was levied upon every person in the census who was above twenty years of age. The levy amounted to *half a shekel according to the shekel of the sanctuary* (v. 13). Coins were not introduced until late in the history of Israel, and the shekel referred to was a unit of weight.

A census acquired the kind of knowledge which was the restricted province of God (cf. the Davidic census and the problems connected with it, 2 Sam. 24:1 ff.; 1 Chron. 21:1 ff.). Hence, the tax was used to offer atonement, lest a plague smite the people for their having presumed upon an area normally restricted to God (vv. 11 ff.). Fundamental to the entire passage, therefore, is the evil nature of a census, grounded in the mysterious connotation of knowing the full number of a people (which is somewhat comparable to knowing the name of an individual). More important for the ultimate life of Israel, however, it was the basis for establishing a systematic means of supporting the priestly ministry.

(3) The Laver for Washing (30:17–21)

17 The LORD said to Moses, 18 "You shall also make a laver of bronze, with its base of bronze, for washing. And you shall put it between the tent of meeting and the altar, and you shall put water in it, 19 with which Aaron and his sons shall wash their hands and their feet. 20 When they go into the tent of meeting, or when they come near the altar to minister, to burn an offering by fire to the LORD, they shall wash with water, lest they die. 21 They shall wash their hands and their feet, lest they die: it shall be a statute for ever to them, even to him and to his descendants throughout their generations."

The *laver of bronze*, like the altar of incense, was not listed in the earlier chapters which dealt with tabernacle equipment (cf. 25:1 ff; 27:1 ff.). Contrary to all previous items of equipment, no specific dimensions were given for the laver. Its function was ceremonial and symbolized the purification of the priests prior to participation in their ministry. In contrast to washing the entire body in the ordination, the priests washed only *their hands and their feet*: their hands because they handled holy items, their feet because they walked in sacred ways. The phrase *lest they die* (v. 21) suggests that failing to wash violated the holiness of God.

(4) The Anointing Oil (30:22–33)

22 Moreover, the LORD said to Moses, 23 "Take the finest spices: of liquid myrrh five hundred shekels, and of sweet-smelling cinnamon half as much, that is, two hundred and fifty, and of aromatic cane two hundred and fifty, 24 and of cassia five hundred, according to the shekel of the sanctuary, and of olive oil a hin; 25 and you shall make of these a sacred anointing oil blended as by the perfumer; a holy anointing oil it shall be. 26 And you shall anoint with it the tent of meeting and the ark of the testimony, 27 and the table and all its utensils, and the lampstand and its utensils, and the altar of incense, 28 and the altar of burnt offering with all its utensils and the laver and its base; 29 you shall consecrate them, that they may be most holy; whatever touches them will become holy. 30 And you shall anoint Aaron and his sons, and consecrate them, that they may serve me as priests. 31 And you shall say to the people of Israel, 'This shall be my holy anointing oil throughout your generations. 32 It shall not be poured upon the bodies of ordinary men, and you shall make no other like it in composition; it is holy, and it shall be holy

to you. 33 Whoever compounds any like it or whoever puts any of it on an outsider shall be cut off from his people.' "

The anointing oil was a blend of myrrh, cinnamon, aromatic cane, cassia, and olive oil. *Myrrh* was an important ingredient in perfumes, while *cassia* was an aromatic bark. Both are used to describe the fragrance of the king's robes: "Your robes are all fragrant with myrrh and aloes and cassia" (Psalm 45:8). Although one cannot determine the precise weight of *the shekel of the sanctuary* (v. 24), the shekel has generally been reckoned to weigh 0.403 ounces, while the *hin* (v. 24) was a unit of measure equal to about 1 gallon. Hence, the anointing oil specified by the recipe in verses 22 ff. would have approximated 37.78+ pounds, plus the weight of the 1 gallon of olive oil. In view of the large amount prepared, this was probably intended to suffice for the foreseeable future: *This shall be my holy anointing oil throughout your generations.*

Anointing *the tent of meeting* and the objects associated with it effectually brought them into relationship with God, and as a consequence they appropriated the holiness associated with God (v. 29). Anointing was a symbolic means of identifying persons or objects as uniquely set apart to the service of God. For the ancient person, however, anointing was viewed in a much more literal fashion, and anointed objects were thought to have appropriated the mysterious power associated with the god(s), God. This unique aspect of holiness is related to the prohibition against making such oil for personal use (v. 33).

(5) Incense for the Altar (30:34–38)

34 And the LORD said to Moses, "Take sweet spices, stacte, and onycha, and galbanum, sweet spices with pure frankincense (of each shall there be an equal part), 35 and make an incense blended as by the perfumer, seasoned with salt, pure and holy; 36 and you shall beat some of it very small, and put part of it before the testimony in the tent of meeting where I shall meet with you; it shall be for you most holy. 37 And the incense which you shall make

according to its composition, you shall not make for yourselves; it shall be for you holy to the LORD. 38 Whoever makes any like it to use as perfume shall be cut off from his people."

The incense for the altar was composed of fragrant spices often associated with perfume. *Stacte* is a transliteration of the Greek *stactē* (Vulgate, *stacte*), and literally meant that which drips. One cannot be more specific than to suggest that it was a resin or oil, probably quite fragrant. *Onycha* is a mollusk which emits a highly aromatic odor when burned. It has been gathered until recent years in the Near East and used as an ingredient in perfume as well as a principle component for incense in India (Driver). *Galbanum* (LXX, *chalbanē*) was the resin of a plant, and, according to some, was used medicinally and was burned to ward off insects. *Frankincense* was a fragrant gum resin, which exuded from slits cut into trees. It was in milky form when gathered, and the adjective *pure* (v. 34) probably suggests that the more refined form of frankincense was intended. When burned, frankincense emitted a balsalm-like odor. Gold and frankincense are coupled in such fashion as to suggest that frankincense was quite valuable (cf. Isa. 60:6; Matt. 2:11). The tree belongs to the genus *Boswelliana*, found today mostly in regions of Africa but in ancient times South Arabia was most prominent as the source of frankincense (cf. Jer. 6:20; Isa. 60:6).

6. Provisions for Construction of the Worship Center and Its Cult Objects (31:1–17)

(1) Workmen for the Tabernacle (31:1–11)

1 The LORD said to Moses, 2 "See, I have called by name Bezalel the son of Uri, son of Hur, of the tribe of Judah: 3 and I have filled him with the Spirit of God, with ability and intelligence, with knowledge and all craftsmanship, 4 to devise artistic designs, to work in gold, silver, and bronze, 5 in cutting stones for setting, and in carving wood, for work in every craft. 6 And behold, I have anointed with him

Oholiab, the son of Ahisamach, of the tribe of Dan; and I have given to all able men ability, that they may make all that I have commanded you: 7 the tent of meeting, and the ark of the testimony, and the mercy seat that is thereon, and all the furnishings of the tent, 8 the table and its utensils, and the pure lampstand with all its utensils, and the altar of incense, 9 and the altar of burnt offering with all its utensils, and the laver and its base, 10 and the finely worked garments, the holy garments for Aaron the priest and the garments of his sons, for their service as priests, 11 and the anointing oil and the fragrant incense for the holy place. According to all that I have commanded you they shall do."

The name *Bezalel* means "in the shadow of God," i.e., in God's protection, while *Oholiab* meant "father's tent." In keeping with biblical patterns of thought, Bezalel's skill was directly related to *the Spirit of God.* Spirit in its most basic meaning was an energizing force or power which gave life and vitality. The spirit of a man was related to courage, anger, impatience or patience, inner disposition, or other characteristics such as a prophetic spirit or a spirit of deep sleep. The Spirit of God, however (94 of 378 uses of *ruach* as spirit refer to God's Spirit), was the energizing force which inspired the ecstatic state of prophecy in early Israel (Num. 11:17 ff.; 1 Sam. 10:6,10), and in later times impelled prophets to utter instruction or warnings (cf. Num. 24:2; 2 Sam. 23:2; Isa. 2; 48:16; 61:1 ff.). It was the Spirit of God that imparted executive and warlike power in ancient Israel (Judg. 3:10, *et al*), and that later came to rest upon the anointed king (Isa. 11:2). In later Israel the Spirit of God endowed men with technical skills, as in the present context, as well as understanding (Job 32:8).

(2) Keeping the Sabbath (31:12-17)

12 And the LORD said to Moses, 13 "Say to the people of Israel, 'You shall keep my sabbaths, for this is a sign between me and you throughout your generations, that you may know that I, the LORD, sanctify you. 14 You shall keep the sabbath, because it is holy for you; every one who profanes it shall be put to death; whoever does any work on it, that soul shall be cut off

from among his people. 15 Six days shall work be done, but the seventh day is a sabbath of solemn rest, holy to the LORD; whoever does any work on the sabbath day shall be put to death. 16 Therefore the people of Israel shall keep the sabbath, observing the sabbath throughout their generations, as a perpetual covenant. 17 It is a sign for ever between me and the people of Israel that in six days the LORD made heaven and earth, and on the seventh day he rested, and was refreshed.' "

Because the sabbath was a sign indicating Israel's relationship to the Lord, the people were to observe it perpetually (vv. 12 ff.). Violation of the sabbath incurred the death penalty (v. 15), although there are no records of death penalties having been administered for sabbath violation.

7. The Giving of the Written Testimony (31:18)

18 And he gave to Moses, when he had made an end of speaking with him upon Mount Sinai, the two tables of the testimony, tables of stone, written with the finger of God.

This verse serves as the transition between the priestly legislation dealing with the tabernacle and the priests (chaps. 25—31) and the case of apostasy and renewal of the covenant (chaps. 32—34). As such, it could equally as well be treated as the introduction to 32—34.

The two tables of stone contained the "ten words" or the "testimony," as described in verse 18. The written form of the testimony stands in marked contrast to the oral form of the preceding material (25—31).

There is no reasonable basis for questioning the statement that Moses wrote ten basic "stipulations," or words, on stone tablets during the time of the experience at Sinai. In view of what is now known concerning literary activity of the second and third millennia B.C., those who would repudiate such a view would be hard pressed for rational evidence to the contrary.

Written with the finger of God suggests the divine source and authority of the Decalogue. An experience during the plagues substantiates the probability of such an interpretation, for when the Egyptian magicians found themselves unable to duplicate the third plague, they conceded, "This is the finger of God" (8:19).

Hence, far from suggesting that God chiseled the Decalogue into the tables of stone apart from human mediation, the phrase *written with the finger of God* suggests the absolute authority of the Decalogue. Later, the phrase was used in the New Testament in a comparable manner, "But if it is by the finger of God that I cast out demons" (Luke 11:20).

II. Apostasy and Renewal of the Covenant (32:1—34:35)

Exodus 32—34 continues the theme of the Sinai narrative (19—24) and is an excellent study in rebellion and apostasy, restoration of the Lord's purposes, and the renewal of covenant life. Despite the diversity of origin and composite literary structure which characterize the narrative, there is an overarching and unifying theme which binds the three chapters together in their present form.

1. Rebellion: The Sin of the Golden Calf (32:1–35)

The present narrative reflects tremendous similarity between Jeroboam I and Aaron, as well as the sacred bulls of the two eras.

Although there was an original act of apostasy involving calf worship, Exodus 32 was probably used in the course of its literary development as a polemic against the practices inaugurated by Jeroboam I (although calf worship, so-called, may have been in vogue prior to his time).

(1) The Act of Apostasy (32:1–6)

¹ When the people saw that Moses delayed to come down from the mountain, the people gathered themselves together to Aaron, and said to him, "Up, make us gods, who shall go before us; as for this Moses, the man who brought us up out of the land of Egypt, we do not know what has become of him." ² And Aaron said to them, "Take off the rings of gold which are in the ears of your wives, your sons, and your daughters, and bring them to me." ³ So all the people took off the rings of gold which were in their ears, and brought them to Aaron. ⁴ And he received the gold at their hand, and fashioned it with a graving tool, and made a molten calf; and they said, "These are your gods, O Israel, who brought you up out of the land of Egypt!" ⁵ When Aaron saw this, he built an altar before it; and Aaron made proclamation and said, "Tomorrow shall be a feast to the LORD." ⁶ And they rose up early on the morrow, and offered burnt offerings and brought peace offerings; and the people sat down to eat and drink, and rose up to play.

The fashioning of a golden calf reflects the almost universal equation of the bull with vigor and strength in the Ancient Near East. Israel probably utilized a common symbol of vitality to represent the Lord, and it is improbable that the text suggests the reversion to Egyptian gods. Living animals, not idols, were worshiped in Egypt—to say nothing of the improbability of choosing an Egyptian deity as an Israelite national god. The bull is often associated with Canaanite Baalism, and it may well be that Israel had come into contact with the bull image through her common Semitic heritage.

The plural reference, *These are your gods . . . who brought you up out of the land of Egypt!* might very well be interpreted to mean that the revelation of Yahweh mediated through Moses was temporarily abandoned in favor of previous god(s), of whom the bull was the representative. Although the references to the plural "gods" in verses 1 and 4 do suggest the idea of a revelation other than through the Lord, the fact that the feast with its offerings was specifically related to the Lord (vv. 5 f.) links the molten calf to the Lord's worship.

The plural *gods* is almost identical with 1 Kings 12:28, and probably reflects the period in the literary history of the text when a strong polemic was directed against the religious practices of the Northern Kingdom.

Israel's apostasy consisted primarily in the violation of the second covenant stipulation: making a graven image of an animal and worshiping the Lord under that guise. Added to this, however, was their faithlessness and impatience in abandoning Moses for the *gods, who shall go before us,* substituting a created image for living personality as the media of divine revelation. Finally, their apostasy was apparently accompanied by improper personal and moral conduct associated with their worship: *and rose up to play* (v. 6). The verb translated *to play* suggests sexual orgies which accompanied fertility rites, especially in Canaanite Baalism. The same verb, *tsachaq*, is used here as in Genesis 26:8; "Abimelech . . . looked out of a window and saw Isaac *fondling* Rebekah his wife."

(2) Tension Between Judgment and Mercy (32:7-14)

Verses 7-8 might well be read immediately preceeding verses 15-24, and verses 9-14 placed prior to verses 25-35. Such a rearrangement would take into consideration the literary sources of the various elements, while at the same time smoothing out the somewhat awkward transition at verse 9.

(3) Judgment Threatened (32:7-10)

⁷ And the LORD said to Moses, "Go down; for your people, whom you brought up out of the land of Egypt, have corrupted themselves; ⁸ they have turned aside quickly out of the way which I commanded them; they have made for themselves a molten calf, and have worshiped it and sacrificed to it, and said, 'These are your gods, O Israel, who brought you up out of the land of Egypt!'" ⁹ And the LORD said to Moses, "I have seen this people, and behold, it is a stiff-necked people; ¹⁰ now therefore let me alone, that my wrath may burn hot against them and I may consume them; but of you I will make a great nation."

The Lord's response to Moses stands in marked contrast to earlier affirmations such as, "I am the Lord your God, who brought you out of the land of Egypt" (20:2). Following Israel's conduct at Sinai the Lord described Israel as *your people* (Moses'), *whom you brought up out of the land of Egypt.* This may well have been a deliberate effort at repudiation, akin to the breaking of the tablets of testimony (v. 19); they are not the people whom the Lord brought up, but whom Moses brought up.

Israel's apostasy was threefold. *First,* they had corrupted themselves (*shachath*). The Hebrew verb means to go to ruin, and is used of that which is marred, spoiled, or morally corrupt. It is used to characterize the world of Noah's day (Gen. 6:12). *Second,* Israel had **turned aside quickly** (*sur,* meaning to turn aside or depart, but often used of turning aside from the Lord, as in Judges 2:17; Deuteronomy 9:12), *Third,* Israel not only made *a molten calf,* but *worshiped it and sacrificed to it, and said, "These are your gods, O Israel."* However Aaron or other leaders may have understood the relationship between the golden calf and the Lord, the people themselves worshiped the calf and offered sacrifices to it. Attempting to synchronize revealed religion and cultural forms of her era, Israel failed to maintain the distinctive emphases of Mosaic Yahwism, and thus fell error to the fault of confusing an aid to worship with the object of worship.

Of you I will make a great nation is reminiscent of Abraham's call (Gen. 12:1 ff.), and suggests the possibility that the Lord will begin again and build a people from Moses as he had intended to build from Abraham.

(4) Judgment Tempered (32:11-14)

¹¹ But Moses besought the LORD his God, and said, "O LORD, why does thy wrath burn hot against thy people, whom thou hast brought forth out of the land of Egypt with great power and with a mighty hand? ¹² Why should the Egyptians say, 'With evil intent did he bring them forth, to slay them in the mountains, and to consume them from the face of the earth'? Turn from thy fierce wrath, and repent of this evil against thy people. ¹³ Remember Abraham, Isaac, and Israel, thy servants, to whom thou didst swear by thine own self, and didst say to them, 'I will multiply your descendants as the stars of heaven, and all this land that I have promised I will give to your descendants, and they shall inherit it for ever.'" ¹⁴ And the LORD repented of the evil which he thought to do to his people.

Moses' request as well as the Lord's response may raise problems for some. *And the Lord repented of the evil which he thought to do to his people.* What does it mean for the Lord to repent? The customary Old Testament word for "repentance" is *nacham,* meaning to be sorry, moved to pity, have compassion, and, hence, to be sorry, suffer grief, repent of one's own doings. The verb is also translated comfort or console: "Thy rod and thy staff, they comfort me" (Psalm 23:4). All meanings of the verb connote an inner mental and/or emotional attitude related to sorrow or consolation. Of 26 occurrences of "repent" cited in the RSV, *nacham* occurs 21 times (in the 5 other cases the Hebrew verb *shub,* to turn, or return, is used). "Repented" occurs 11 times in the RSV, translating *nacham* 8 times and *shub* 3 times. *Shub* literally means to turn back or return, and in a majority of those instances when the RSV translates it as either "repent" or "repented" one could equally as well translate it "return," as, "*Return* [rather than repent] and turn away from your idols" (Ezek. 14:6). A turning of one's life in its external dimensions is rather clearly the connotation of *shub.* The two terms, *nacham* and *shub,* are closely related but hardly synonymous. Repentance of its fullest sense is an inward attitude of regret or sorrow (*nacham*) leading to an external change or "turning" (*shub*).

Of 35 occurrences of *nacham,* 30 refer to God as subject and only 5 to man's motion. For God to *repent* (*nacham*) suggests that he changes his mind or intention in accord with his righteous purposes and takes action commensurate with that purpose: "Then I will repent of the good which I had intended to do to it" (Jer. 18:10).

(5) Moses, Covenant Mediator (32:15–35)

15 And Moses turned, and went down from the mountain with the two tables of the testimony in his hands, tables that were written on both sides; on the one side and on the other were they written. 16 And the tables were the

work of God, and the writing was the writing of God, graven upon the tables. 17 When Joshua heard the noise of the people as they shouted, he said to Moses, "There is a noise of war in the camp." 18 But he said, "It is not the sound of shouting for victory, or the sound of the cry of defeat, but the sound of singing that I hear." 19 And as soon as he came near the camp and saw the calf and the dancing, Moses' anger burned hot, and he threw the tables out of his hands and broke them at the foot of the mountain. 20 And he took the calf which they had made, and burnt it with fire, and ground it to powder, and scattered it upon the water, and made the people of Israel drink it.

21 And Moses said to Aaron, "What did this people do to you that you have brought a great sin upon them?" 22 And Aaron said, "Let not the anger of my lord burn hot; you know the people, that they are set on evil. 23 For they said to me, 'Make us gods, who shall go before us; as for this Moses, the man who brought us up out of the land of Egypt, we do not know what has become of him.' 24 And I said to them, 'Let any who have gold take it off'; so they gave it to me, and I threw it into the fire, and there came out this calf."

25 And when Moses saw that the people had broken loose (for Aaron had let them break loose, to their shame among their enemies), 26 then Moses stood in the gate of the camp, and said, "Who is on the LORD's side? Come to me." And all the sons of Levi gathered themselves together to him. 27 And he said to them, "Thus says the LORD God of Israel, 'Put every man his sword on his side, and go to and fro from gate to gate throughout the camp, and slay every man his brother, and every man his companion, and every man his neighbor.'" 28 And the sons of Levi did according to the word of Moses; and there fell of the people that day about three thousand men. 29 And Moses said, "Today you have ordained yourselves for the service of the LORD, each one at the cost of his son and of his brother, that he may bestow a blessing upon you this day."

30 On the morrow Moses said to the people, "You have sinned a great sin. And now I will go up to the LORD; perhaps I can make atonement for your sin." 31 So Moses returned to the LORD and said, "Alas, this people have sinned a great sin; they have made for themselves gods of gold. 32 But now, if thou wilt forgive their sin—and if not, blot me, I pray thee, out of thy book which thou hast written." 33 But the LORD said to Moses, "Whoever has sinned against me, him will I blot out of my book. 34 But now go, lead the people to the place of which I have spoken to you; behold, my angel shall go before you. Nevertheless, in the day when I visit, I will visit their sin upon them."

35 And the LORD sent a plague upon the people, because they made the calf which Aaron made.

Throughout the Sinai narrative Moses is portrayed as the covenant mediator who initiates the meeting with the Lord (19:3 ff.), mediates the covenant stipulations (20:1–17; 18 ff.), leads in the inauguration of the covenant on behalf of the people (24:2 ff.), receives the priestly legislation (24:15 ff.), and intercedes on behalf of his people (32:15 ff.). In all probability one confronts in the picture of Moses as covenant mediator not only a historical tradition of the role of Moses in the Sinai experience but a continuing office in Israel. Succeeding generations probably witnessed the emergence of a "covenant mediator" who proclaimed the word of God in public worship, and led in the covenant renewal ceremony, which was probably annually reenacted. Kraus argues cogently for the permanency of such an office and suggests: "Although it is difficult to prove from Deut. xviii. 15 ff. that there was a succession in the office of the prophetic mediator, we must at least raise the question whether there are traces in the Old Testament of a continuity in Mosaic prophecy." [5]

The office of covenant mediator was probably permanently established in Israel following the Sinai events, and the principle of mediation is inherent in the vocation of religious leadership.

Annulment of the Covenant (vv. 15–29). The Decalogue is graphically referred to at this juncture as the *tables of the testimony,* a term quite often used of the ten words as the solemn charge of the Lord (cf. 31:18; 39:35; Josh. 4:16). The uniqueness of the testimony is suggested in that the tables were written on both sides while the common practice was to write on only one side. They were characterized as *the work of God.* The phrase *the writing was the writing of God, graven upon the tables* might be taken to mean that the Lord

wrote the words without human mediation, the writing was itself distinct from the form which prevailed at the time, or, more likely, the words bore the authority of God; they were uniquely his writing. The passage should be interpreted in light of Exodus 31:18, and the intention of the writer, far from suggesting that the words were "graven" apart from human agency, was to underscore the divine source and authoritative nature of the revelation mediated through Moses and committed to writing by him.

Whether the breaking of the two tables of testimony was due solely to Moses' anger or whether there was a specific annulment of the covenant is difficult to determine. Admittedly, *Moses' anger burned hot,* but it is questionable whether one should interpret the breaking of the tables as the result of an uncontrolled outburst of anger. The larger purpose of the narrative most likely suggests the annulment of the covenant.

Moses' action in grinding the calf to powder and, after having mixed it with water, causing the people to drink the mixture closely resembles the ancient ordeal in which one was forced to drink a strange mixture, with one's innocence or guilt determined by whether or not he reacted physically to the drink (cf. the law or ordeal of jealousy, Num. 5:5 ff.). Guilt was apparently easily established in the present case, however, and making the people drink the mixture probably reflected the belief that those guilty would suffer some type of plague, of which verse 35 may be reminiscent.

A Rationale for Aaron's Action (vv. 21–24). In a section which Noth suggests is a later addition to the narrative, the writer sought to explain why Aaron responded as he did to the rebellion. Are verses 21–24 a serious effort to place the blame upon the people, or are they a tongue-in-cheek ridicule of Aaron? Both sides may be argued cogently, but Moses' question seems more nearly designed to chasten than to acquire information: *What did this people do to*

---

[5] Hans-Joachim Kraus, *Worship in Israel: A Cultic History of the Old Testament,* trans. Geoffrey Buswell (Oxford: Basil Blackwell, 1966), pp. 110 f.

you that you have brought a great sin upon them? The record suggests that the people did no more than ask, and Aaron responded. Again, is verse 22 a serious evaluation of the people, as it may well be, or is it Aaron's shallow and ineffective means of evading responsibility? Finally, was Aaron really so uninvolved in the apostasy as to suggest that he merely threw the gold *into the fire, and there came out this calf.* May it not be that these verses were designed to portray the essential weakness of Aaron, as over against Moses, "man of God," and that this may have been used as a strong polemic against Jeroboam I, who apparently paralleled much of Aaron's action?

Explaining a Ministry (vv. 25–29). The overarching purpose of the writer is to offer an explanation for the Levitical ministry—a ministry that transcended all tribal and family loyalties. In view of ancient practices with regard to slaughtering others "in the name of the Lord," there is nothing at all improbable in the suggestion that some such significant number of persons was actually slain at a time early in the desert period.

The phrase, *Today you have ordained yourselves,* is the writer's way of suggesting that ordination was an act of supreme loyalty and dedication in which men chose fidelity to the Lord above that of family, clan, or tribe.

Moses Interceding for Israel (vv. 30–34). By placing the personal pronoun separately, the writer underscored Israel's sin: "And *you, you* have sinned a great sin." Consequently Moses suggests, hopefully but not certainly (*'ulay* usually expresses a hope, as in Gen. 27:12; Jer. 20:10, but also a fear or doubt as in Gen. 27:12; Job 1:5), that he may be able to "make atonement" (a common word for covering over, to pacify, propitiate; hence, to atone, the same root word from which the "mercy seat" is derived).

Moses' request that should the Lord not forgive the sin of Israel he *blot* Moses *out of the book* presupposes a book of life in which the names of the living are written (cf. Psalm 69:28; Isa. 4:3, "everyone who has been recorded for life in Jerusalem"). At this early date one should hardly presuppose a book of "eternal life," as some interpret Revelation 20:12 ff. The reference to drinking the mixture in verses 19 ff., Moses' offer to give his life for the life of Israel, and the plague of verse 35 should be read in concert.

The Lord's reponse to Moses clearly enunciates the principle of individual responsibility: *Whoever has sinned against me, him will I blot out of my book;* a principle in keeping with the clear prophetic emphasis of Jeremiah and Ezekiel (cf. Jer. 31:29 ff. and Ezek. 18:1 ff.).[6]

The reference to the plague in verse 35 is vague and without chronological detail, but it was probably interpreted as a direct consequence of Israel's sin: *because they made the calf which Aaron made.* Possibly, it was the consequence of the potion they had to drink. Moses' offer to give his own life for the life of his people apparently failed, for every man must stand responsible for himself. Not even Moses could bear the guilt of Israel, and the covenant community waited for a new Moses of another covenant to do what the old Moses could not do.

2. Restoration: The Promise of God's Presence (33:1-23)

The theme of the Lord's presence unifies all of chapter 33 and is directly related to the departure mentioned in 32:34a. Although some of the material likely consists of later additions (cf. "Now Moses used to" v. 7 ff.), each paragraph is related to the theme of the Lord's presence. His presence is forfeited by conduct such as that at Sinai, secured by renewal and recommitment, guaranteed by the tent of meeting where the Lord comes to meet Moses, experienced in the assurance that the Lord's

---

6 The primary emphasis of Ezekiel is upon individual responsibility, and the phrase "the soul that sins shall die" is concerned not so much with retribution as with individual responsibility.

"presence will go with you," and shared with Moses as he participates in the hidden glory of the Lord.

(1) The Withdrawal of God (33:1–3)

[1] The LORD said to Moses, "Depart, go up hence, you and the people whom you have brought up out of the land of Egypt, to the land of which I swore to Abraham, Isaac, and Jacob, saying, 'To your descendants I will give it.' [2] And I will send an angel before you, and I will drive out the Canaanites, the Amorites, the Hittites, the Perizzites, the Hivites, and the Jebusites. [3] Go up to a land flowing with milk and honey; but I will not go up among you, lest I consume you in the way, for you are a stiff-necked people."

"I will not go up among you, lest I consume you" is an anthropomorphic suggestion that the Lord's anger was such that he could not restrain himself, and that if he did go up he would destroy Israel because of her apostasy.

(2) Renewal and Recommitment (33:4–6)

[4] When the people heard these evil tidings, they mourned; and no man put on his ornaments. [5] For the LORD had said to Moses, "Say to the people of Israel, 'You are a stiff-necked people; if for a single moment I should go up among you, I would consume you. So now put off your ornaments from you, that I may know what to do with you.' " [6] Therefore the people of Israel stripped themselves of their ornaments, from Mount Horeb onward.

Was the removal of the ornaments a sign of perpetual grief, or did the act have more significant meaning? May it not be that the *ornaments* were religious medallions of one type or another? The experience under Jacob at Bethel suggests that this may be the case, for when the patriarch led the people in recommitment to the Lord, the people gave him "all the foreign gods that they had, and the rings that were in their ears; and Jacob hid them under the oak which was near Shechem" (Gen. 35:4). Seemingly, the rings were in some way associated with foreign gods, and putting away the rings was related to dedication to the Lord. The entire golden calf episode may have represented a reversion to gods known during another era, and the removal of ornaments may have paralleled the action under Jacob.

The likelihood of this possibility is strengthened by the fact that putting away the ornaments was a precondition to the nature of the Lord's response: *that I may know what to do with you* (v. 5).

(3) The Tent of Meeting (33:7–11)

[7] Now Moses used to take the tent and pitch it outside the camp, far off from the camp; and he called it the tent of meeting. And every one who sought the LORD would go out to the tent of meeting, which was outside the camp. [8] Whenever Moses went out to the tent, all the people rose up, and every man stood at his tent door, and looked after Moses, until he had gone into the tent. [9] When Moses entered the tent, the pillar of cloud would descend and stand at the door of the tent, and the LORD would speak with Moses. [10] And when all the people saw the pillar of cloud standing at the door of the tent, all the people would rise up and worship, every man at his tent door. [11] Thus the LORD used to speak to Moses face to face, as a man speaks to his friend. When Moses turned again into the camp, his servant Joshua the son of Nun, a young man, did not depart from the tent.

The narrative on the tent of meeting was introduced at this juncture because of the thematic emphasis upon the Lord's presence. The *tent of meeting* was a simple tent and stood in marked contrast to the tabernacle.

Some scholars suggest that originally the tent of meeting and the ark were separate objects, signifying the presence of God,[7] and that the two were brought together at a later time and served as the prototype for the tabernacle. *Face to face, as a man speaks to his friend* is a figurative way of expressing the reality and depth of communion between Moses and the Lord.

[7] Cf. Gerhard von Rad, "The Tent and the Ark," *The Problem of the Hexateuch and Other Essays,* pp. 103 ff. Murray Newman, *The People of the Covenant* (Nashville: Abingdon, 1962), pp. 55 ff.

(4) The Promise of God's Presence (33:12–16)

12 Moses said to the LORD, "See, thou sayest to me, 'Bring up this people'; but thou hast not let me know whom thou wilt send with me. Yet thou hast said, 'I know you by name, and you have also found favor in my sight.' 13 Now therefore, I pray thee, if I have found favor in thy sight, show me now thy ways, that I may know thee and find favor in thy sight. Consider too that this nation is thy people." 14 And he said, "My presence will go with you, and I will give you rest." 15 And he said to him, "If thy presence will not go with me, do not carry us up from here. 16 For how shall it be known that I have found favor in thy sight, I and thy people? Is it not in thy going with us, so that we are distinct, I and thy people, from all other people that are upon the face of the earth?"

The primary concern of this unit of material is the question, "How can the Lord be present with his people beyond Sinai?" The passage fails to reckon with the tent of meeting, suggesting the possibility that verses 7–11 (E) originated in a separate area from verses 12–16 (J).

Moses' response to the Lord's command suggests an objection to the promise of "an angel" (33:2; cf. 32:34) as vague and undefined. Moses desired concrete assurance concerning who was to lead Israel through the unknown areas beyond Sinai. The request reflected several incisive and legitimate relationships: the Lord knows Moses by name, implying a unique relationship inherent in the sharing of one's name; Moses had found favor (i.e., has found acceptance, cf. Gen. 6:8; 18:3; 2 Sam. 15:25) with God; the nation *is thy people,* and thus has legitimate claim upon the national God; and, finally, it is only in the unique presence of God that Israel is *distinct* from other nations.

My presence will go with you might more literally be translated "my face will go and I will give you rest." The "face of God" is a term for the self-manifestation of God which in earlier times probably was conceived in concrete fashion. In paganism the expression may have originated in the literal face of the idol, although it later connoted a more spiritual concept, even in non-Israelite circles (cf. the *pn b'l,* "the face of Baal"). Since God was conceived as enthroned above the ark, between the cherubim, 33:14 very probably reflects the role of the ark as the mediating instrument for the presence of God. When Israel did set out from Sinai it was the ark that went before them (Num. 10:33 ff.).

The "face of God" also came to be used in a metaphorical sense of God's gracious presence, and often appeared in Israel's worship (Psalm 24:6; 1 Chron. 21:30). In polytheistic structures, lesser gods could express various aspects of the deity's nature, while maintaining the distance between the god and worshipers. In Israel, expressions such as the face of God, his name, and the angel of the Lord, were media which maintained the separate nature of God while mediating aspects of his nature to man.

Despite the veiled nature of the language, the "face of God" expressed the personal activity of God as he providentially led Israel. Eichrodt suggests that "it is almost impossible not to conclude that we have here another *form of self-manifestation of the transcendent God,* by means of which his presence is at the same time made tolerable to men and guaranteed to them" (p. 38; cf. pp. 35 ff.) The promise represents a definite advance upon the gift of the angel to lead Israel (32:34; 33:2), for the Lord's "face" will go with Israel to give them rest.

The phrase *I will give you rest* is related to a biblical concept often ignored or overlooked; the rest for God's people. (Cf. von Rad, pp. 94 ff.) Although the Old Testament promised rest is not wholly eschatological, but is related more directly to the life of the people in the land, this rest is ultimately a gift "which Israel will find only by a wholly personal entering into its God" and contains latent elements of expectation (cf. Deut. 12:9 ff.; 15:19; Josh. 21:43 ff.; 1 Kings 8:56; Psalm 95:11). As von Rad suggests: "The deuteronomist . . . believes in a situation in which the people of God find rest with God, just as a woman finds rest with her husband (Ruth 1:9); and this deuteronomic presentation of 'rest' bears witness to the same God whose voice we hear in the New Testament" (p. 100; cf. Heb. 3:7 ff.).

The promise of rest, perhaps best understood as "wholeness," can be appreciated only by those who know that they are always *in via*, on the way, to use von Rad's phrase, "in a sense which affects him to the very core of his being." But to those who are the pilgrims, the wanderers, those who are always caught up *in via*, there is the promise of rest, wholeness, or unhindered communion; and that rest is not wholly eschatological but contemporary while maintaining its forward thrust. We are in God and "at rest," but there remains a rest for God's people. The promise to Moses is that God's face will lead men to that rest in which the hope of unhindered communion and wholeness will become a reality.

(5) The Hidden Glory (33:17–23)

17 And the LORD said to Moses, "This very thing that you have spoken I will do; for you have found favor in my sight, and I know you by name." **18** Moses said, "I pray thee, show me thy glory." **19** And he said, "I will make all my goodness pass before you, and will proclaim before you my name 'The LORD'; and I will be gracious to whom I will be gracious, and will show mercy on whom I will show mercy. **20** But," he said, "you cannot see my face; for man shall not see me and live." **21** And the LORD said, "Behold, there is a place by me where you shall stand upon the rock; **22** and while my glory passes by I will put you in a cleft of the rock, and I will cover you with my hand until I have passed by; **23** then I will take away my hand, and you shall see my back; but my face shall not be seen."

Because the Lord knows Moses by name, suggesting a full sharing of personality, and because Moses has found acceptance (*favor*) before the Lord, the Lord agrees to do the *very thing you have spoken*—go with the people so that the distinctiveness of Israel may be guaranteed (v. 16). Pressing beyond this response, however, Moses prays that the Lord will *show me thy glory.*

The "glory of God" was related to the "face of God," for in response to Moses' request that he see the Lord's glory, the Lord reminds him, *you cannot see my face*, using face as a synonym for glory. Moses apparently desired to apprehend the full nature of God, to see his glory (the burning presence of God) or his face. To see the face is to see the whole of the person, and the Old Testament at times uses the phrase to describe common meetings of men in life, as in the meeting of Jacob and Esau, "and afterwards I shall see his face" (Gen. 32:20).

In a wide variety of ways the Lord does reveal himself: his goodness that passes before an individual, the revelation of his personal name, suggesting the inmost disclosure of himself, to say nothing of the consistent revelation of his grace and mercy (v. 19). Despite such self-disclosures of the divine presence, however, "you cannot see my face; for man shall not see me and live" (v. 20). To behold God face to face is to know him absolutely, to exhaust the depth of his being, to remove the last vestige of mystery from the being of God. To attempt to embrace the full nature of God is to forget that there is a hiddenness about the nature of God which we ignore at our own peril.

In a highly figurative but equally valid manner the Lord proposed a solution to Moses' desire to know him fully. Those who interpret this passage literally are likely to thwart its message of splendor and wonder. To understand this in other than poetic or figurative thought patterns fails altogether to understand the meaning of the writer. The passage is concerned with more than a God who has a physical hand large enough to cover the mouth of a cave in the rock, a mere giant of a God. Rather, the writer is concerned to suggest that man never sees God face to face, never apprehends God fully; that God is always the God of the beyond.

Rather than a source of discouragement, however, the limitless nature of God is a wellspring of constant hope and challenge for those who are willing to stand upon the rock and follow newer and fuller vistas; content always to behold his back, never realizing the unfinished quest of seeing him face to face—at least not now. Whatever one may experience or know about God, there is always more to be experienced and known. For this reason the Lord's glory is a hidden glory, and for this reason man's quest is unending.

3. Renewal: The Restoration of the Covenant (34:1-35)

Within the context of the present arrangement of the text the renewal of the covenant described in chapter 34 replaces the covenant broken by the apostasy of Israel (32:1 ff.). Many regard the chapter as the oldest written record of the covenant at Sinai.

(1) The Lord's Instructions and Moses' Entreaty (34:1-9)

¹ The LORD said to Moses, "Cut two tables of stone like the first; and I will write upon the tables the words that were on the first tables, which you broke. ² Be ready in the morning, and come up in the morning to Mount Sinai, and present yourself there to me on the top of the mountain. ³ No man shall come up with you, and let no man be seen throughout all the mountain; let no flocks or herds feed before that mountain." ⁴ So Moses cut two tables of stone like the first; and he rose early in the morning and went up on Mount Sinai, as the LORD had commanded him, and took in his hand two tables of stone. ⁵ And the LORD descended in the cloud and stood with him there, and proclaimed the name of the LORD. ⁶ The LORD passed before him, and proclaimed, "The LORD, the LORD, a God merciful and gracious, slow to anger, and abounding in steadfast love and faithfulness, ⁷ keeping steadfast love for thousands, forgiving iniquity and transgression and sin, but who will by no means clear the guilty, visiting the iniquity of the fathers upon the children and the children's children, to the third and the fourth generation." ⁸ And Moses made haste to bow his head toward the earth, and worshiped. ⁹ And he said, "If now I have found favor in thy sight, O LORD, let the Lord, I pray thee, go in the midst of us, although it is a stiff-necked people; and pardon our iniquity and our sin, and take us for thy inheritance."

Examination of 34:1 ff. and the previous covenant described in 20:1 ff.; 24:1 ff. causes one to conclude that the relationship between the two is much more complex than is suggested in the view that chapter 34 is simply a replacement of the broken covenant. For example, the content of the covenant in 34:10 ff. is certainly different from that of the previous covenant. Either the Lord changed the covenant stipulations subsequent to the apostasy, which is unlikely, or chapter 34:1 ff. describes totally different content for the same covenant relationship.

A suggestive hypothesis is offered by the literary analysis of the two accounts. It is highly probable that there are two distinct accounts of the Sinai covenant, one in chapter 34 (J) the other in 20:1 ff. and major portions of 24:1 ff. (E). The two accounts are complementary, the one illuminating the other, and arose in separate geographical areas as well as distinct chronological eras. They were left to stand separately because each makes significant contributions to Old Testament religion and theology. One should not be adopted as "authentic" at the expense of the other. In fact, to follow this route is completely to misunderstand the nature of the Old Testament as a body of ancient literature. The most viable solution to the problem, therefore, appears to be the assumption that 34:1 ff. is the account of the covenant which circulated in the Southern Kingdom from a very early period of time. In the main, Exodus 20:1 ff. and 24:1 ff. came from the Northern Kingdom, and is a younger account of the Sinai covenant that is 34:1 ff.

(2) Another Covenant (34:10-28)

¹⁰ And he said, "Behold, I make a covenant. Before all your people I will do marvels, such as have not been wrought in all the earth or in any nation; and all the people among whom you are shall see the work of the LORD; for it is a terrible thing that I will do with you. ¹¹ "Observe what I command you this day. Behold, I will drive out before you the Amorites, the Canaanites, the Hittites, the Perizzites, the Hivites, and the Jebusites. ¹² Take heed to

yourself, lest you make a covenant with the inhabitants of the land whither you go, lest it become a snare in the midst of you. ¹³ You shall tear down their altars, and break their pillars, and cut down their Asherim ¹⁴ (for you shall worship no other god, for the LORD, whose name is Jealous, is a jealous God), ¹⁵ lest you make a covenant with the inhabitants of the land, and when they play the harlot after their gods and sacrifice to their gods and one invites you, you eat of his sacrifice, ¹⁶ and you take of their daughters for your sons, and their daughters play the harlot after their gods and make your sons play the harlot after their gods.

¹⁷ "You shall make for yourself no molten gods.

¹⁸ "The feast of unleavened bread you shall keep. Seven days you shall eat unleavened bread, as I commanded you, at the time appointed in the month Abib; for in the month Abib you came out from Egypt. ¹⁹ All that opens the womb is mine, all your male cattle, the firstlings of cow and sheep. ²⁰ The firstling of an ass you shall redeem with a lamb, or if you will not redeem it you shall break its neck. All the first-born of your sons you shall redeem. And none shall appear before me empty.

²¹ "Six days you shall work, but on the seventh day you shall rest; in plowing time and in harvest you shall rest. ²² And you shall observe the feast of weeks, the first fruits of wheat harvest, and the feast of ingathering at the year's end. ²³ Three times in the year shall all your males appear before the LORD God, the God of Israel. ²⁴ For I will cast out nations before you, and enlarge your borders; neither shall any man desire your land, when you go up to appear before the LORD your God three times in the year.

²⁵ "You shall not offer the blood of my sacrifice with leaven; neither shall the sacrifice of the feast of the passover be left until the morning. ²⁶ The first of the first fruits of your ground you shall bring to the house of the LORD your God. You shall not boil a kid in its mother's milk."

²⁷ And the LORD said to Moses, "Write these words; in accordance with these words I have made a covenant with you and with Israel." ²⁸ And he was there with the LORD forty days and forty nights; he neither ate bread nor drank water. And he wrote upon the tables the words of the covenant, the ten commandments.

The account of this covenant should be read in conjunction with 20:1 ff.; 24:1 ff.

Statement of Covenant and Purpose (v. 10). "Behold I make a covenant." Exodus 34:1 ff. is thought by many to have been the oldest account of the Sinaitic covenant, and is certainly more detailed in terms of covenant requirements than the account in 24:1 ff. Three phrases characterize the wonderful nature of the Lord's purposes for Israel. The Lord will do "marvels" (*niphla'-oth*), a word which H. Wheeler Robinson characterizes as "nearer to the etymology of our English word 'miracle,' though not to its implication in our usage of a sharp division between natural and supernatural." [8]

The word describes the wonderful acts of the Lord in judgment and redemption (cf. Judg. 6:13; Jer. 21:2; Psalm 26:7). Second, nations will *see the work of the Lord* reflected in the life of Israel as the Lord manifests himself through her. Finally, the Lord's action *is a terrible thing*, although not terrible in the popular connotation of the word. "Terrible" (*nora'*, from *yare'*) most often means to cause astonishment, whether of the Lord himself (15:11; Psalm 47:2) or of the Lord's doings (as in the present verse, plus Psalm 66:3, 5). It is in the sense of that which inspires reverence, godly fear, or awe that the word is used here in verse 10.

Obligations of the Covenant (vv. 11–16). The unifying purpose of verses 11–16 is the maintenance of covenant faith. The phrase *lest you* occurs three times and suggests the priority of dedication to the Lord. No covenant is to be made *with the inhabitants of the land,* their religious shrines are to be put to the ban, and marriage is prohibited—all to the end that Israel may maintain purity of worship. Even the initial promise to drive out the inhabitants may have been related to religious purity—the expulsion of present occupants of the land serving to provide a context wholesome to the maintenance of religious purity.

The entire appeal for religious purity is grounded in the affirmation, parenthetically inserted into the text, that *the Lord, whose name is Jealous, is a jealous God.*

---

[8] *Inspiration and Revelation in the Old Testament* (Oxford: Clarendon, 1950), p. 37.

The first meaning suggested for "jealous" in English is "suspicious; apprehensive of rivalry," although the word does have the denotation of "demanding exclusive loyalty; as, the Lord is a *jealous* God." It is this latter denotation which is inherent within the name "Jealous" as the Lord's name. The adjective "jealous" (*qana'*) is used only of God in the Old Testament (cf. 20:5; Deut. 4:24; 6:15) and has none of the pettiness often associated with the word. One might substitute "zealous" for "jealous," although this is unnecessary if one remembers that "jealous" is associated with the Lord's demand for exclusive service.

There is a distinct and obvious parallel between the detailed comments concerning the absolute priority of the Lord over all other gods (vv. 11–16) and the first of the ten words, or Decalogue: "You shall have no other gods before me" (20:3). Whether the present text may be a more primitive and detailed statement upon which the concise commandment is based is debatable. But the possibility that this may be the case is intriguing.

No Molten Gods (v. 17). Although the specific formulation of the second commandment (Ex. 20:4 ff.) and the present prohibition of molten gods is quite distinct, the general intent of the two passages is identical. Exodus 20:4 uses the word *pesel*, "idol, image" (cf. Deut. 4:16 ff.; Judg. 18:31; Isa. 48:5), while Exodus 34:17 uses *massekhah*, a "molten image." The *massekhah* was molten (from *nasak*, to "pour out," hence, *massekhah* might mean either a libation or molten metal). The construction of a *pesel*, graven image, on the other hand, is graphically described by Isaiah as having been made from wood (44:14 ff.), possibly overlaid with precious metal (cf. Jer. 10:3 f.). The specific prohibition of the "molten god" may be directly related to the construction of the molten calf of gold (32:1 ff.). During the period of the monarchy the prohibition may have served as an especially vehement polemic against the use of the calves in the worship of the Northern Kingdom.

Remembering Deliverance from Egypt (vv. 18–20). Israel was to observe those feasts and ritual practices associated with the deliverance from Egypt. The feast of unleavened bread, inaugurated as a reminder of the deliverance out of Egypt (cf. 12:14–20), was viewed as of such importance as to stand alongside the commandments concerning the priority of the Lord (vv. 11–16) and the prohibition of molten gods (v. 17). In addition, the firstborn, *all that opens the womb,* was to be offered to the Lord as a constant reminder of the Lord's action in slaying the firstborn of Egypt and his deliverance of Israel's firstborn (13:11–16). The firstborn of acceptable animals were to be sacrificed, an ass could be redeemed or put to death by breaking its neck (was its blood nonsacral?), and the firstborn of man was to be redeemed.

Observing Holy Days (vv. 21–28). Two types of holy days were marked as of singular importance for Israel's future worship; the weekly day of rest, and those periodic feast days occurring on a cyclical basis during the agricultural year. The sabbath commandment was peculiarly related to an agrarian society and was to be observed even in the busy seasons of plowing and harvest (v. 21). All males were to appear before the Lord on three occasions during the year, the limitation to male members apparently reflecting the fact that the covenant was made with men (females were within the covenant relationship solely because of their identification with the male).

The statement of the three annual feasts is a duplication of the laws given in 23:14–17. The *feast of weeks* (cf. Deut. 16:9 ff. for a fuller explanation) was synonymous with the feast of unleavened bread, associated with the Passover. The *first fruits of wheat harvest* came fifty days after the feast of unleavened bread and was known later as Pentecost. The *feast of ingathering* came in the fall, was probably related to the grape harvest, and was later known as the feast of tabernacles (cf. 23:14–17).

The statement of the holy days stands in

the same relationship to the present series of covenant stipulations as the fourth commandment stands to the larger covenant stipulations of Exodus 20. The additional emphasis upon the festivals, as compared with the single emphasis on the sabbath in Exodus 20, is indicative of the ritual interests of the author of Exodus 34.

Four warnings, largely repetitions of instructions previously given, are injected concerning the proper offering of one's sacrifice. The fact that each law had been stated previously suggests that the present listing is probably a parallel collection, although it is impossible to determine chronological priority.

The laws (literally "words") given in chapter 34 are said to have been the basis of the covenant which the Lord made with Israel (v. 27). The forty-day motif again is introduced (cf. 24:18), but the present description associates a period of fasting with the reception of the law (v. 28).

The relationship between the present collection of stipulations and the "ten words" of Exodus 20 is complex. Are the "words of the covenant" (v. 28*b*) identical with the words of verse 27, *in accordance with these words I have made a covenant?* Or, does verse 28*b* refer to the words of Exodus 20, which were said to have been on the tables broken by Moses? The most acceptable solution appears to be the assumption that the words of the covenant which Moses wrote on the tables (v. 28) were those stipulations given in 34:10–26.

If this premise is correct, then the material in 34:10–26, represents a decalogue other than the Decalogue of Exodus 20. Despite the similarities, there are greater points of dissimilarity than similarity between the two. Rather than two parallel statements of the same law, one confronts two separate expressions of covenant stipulations. Each had its place within the faith of Israel, and one would be in error to adjudge one legitimate and the other false. Both gave needed guidance for the worship life of Israel (34:1 ff.) as well as the personal conduct of covenant members

(20:1 ff.).

Because of the distinct emphases of the two decalogues, the first, Exodus 20, is often referred to as the "ethical decalogue," while Exodus 34 is characterized as the "ritual decalogue." Perhaps the terminology is unfortunate, but the distinction is legitimate. Exodus 34:10–26 is closely related to Exodus 23:14–19, and also has affinities with Exodus 20:2 ff., but it is better to view them as distinct decalogues.[9]

(3) The Transformation of Moses (34:29–35)

[29] When Moses came down from Mount Sinai, with the two tables of the testimony in his hand as he came down from the mountain, Moses did not know that the skin of his face shone because he had been talking with God. [30] And when Aaron and all the people of Israel saw Moses, behold, the skin of his face shone, and they were afraid to come near him. [31] But Moses called to them; and Aaron and all the leaders of the congregation returned to him, and Moses talked with them. [32] And afterward all the people of Israel came near, and he gave them in commandment all that the Lord had spoken with him in Mount Sinai. [33] And when Moses had finished speaking with them, he put a veil on his face; [34] but whenever Moses went in before the Lord to speak with him, he took the veil off, until he came out; and when he came out, and told the people of Israel what he was commanded, [35] the people of Israel saw the face of Moses, that the skin of Moses' face shone; and Moses would put the veil upon his face again, until he went in to speak with him.

The essential purpose of the writer was to suggest that Moses lived in such communion with God that he came to reflect the glory of God. The statement that *the skin of his face shone because he had been talking with God* reflects the relationship between the glory of God and the burning, fiery presence. The word translated "shone" (*qaran*) is not the normal word for "shine"

---

9 Noth, p. 265. Goethe was the first person in modern times to see a decalogue in Exodus 34, although he had been preceded by a Greek writer of the fifth century. Morgenstern isolates five decalogues in the Old Testament. Cf. H. H. Rowley, *Moses and the Decalogue* (Manchester: University Press, 1951), p. 89. Rowley's work is exceedingly helpful and profitable.

and the verb is used only in Exodus 34:29,30,35; Psalm 69:31. The verb is a denominative from *qeren*, "horn," and literally means to send out horns (cf. Psalm 69:31). From the context of 34:29 ff., however, the translation "shone" (i.e., to send out rays, as horns) is quite acceptable. The rarity of the word plus the clear meaning of *qeren* as "horn" led older translators (cf. Jerome) to speak of a "horned" Moses. Davies, Driver, and Noth all refer to the representation of Moses with horns in pictorial arts, the most famous of which is that of Michael Angelo.

The reference to the **Veil** may reflect an era when priests wore a veil (although there is no such item cited in the extensive listings of the priestly regalia). Non-Israelite priests, especially in Egypt, wore masks which were cast in the image of the deity and thus identified the priest and the god. It may well have been that Moses did wear a veil when addressing the people (this the biblical text does state, cf. vv. 34 f.), and the present narrative may have served as an explanation concerning why this was necessary.

Probably intended as a vivid and picturesque manner of expressing Moses' relationship to the Lord, the light associated with Moses' face is both a vivid portrayal of the transforming power of divine communion and a meaningful testimony to the role of Moses within the faith of Israel.

The narrative was doubtless recounted in oral form long before it assumed its present literary structure, and, beyond the Old Testament era, was still a vital emphasis in the New Testament (cf. 2 Cor. 3:13). The original purpose of the story may have been, as Noth suggests, to explain why Moses wore a veil when he came out to speak to the people. The ultimate purpose of the narrative, however, is its testimony to the reflective glory of God in the life of the "man of God." It is enshrined within the Old Testament as a testimony to the possibility of so living in God's presence as to share his glory—to become like one's object of communion and contemplation.

III. Fulfilling the Lord's Command (35: 1—40:38)

That which was stated as a command in 24:15—31:18 is presented as a report in 35:1—40:38, for the latter section records the fulfilment of the commands previously stated in the instructions given to Moses. With few exceptions, therefore, the material in 35:1—40:38 makes no new contribution to an understanding of Israel's worship. The passage under consideration may best be examined by reading it in parallel with its counterpart in the earlier portion of Exodus. For this reason, except in those passages which make contributions not found in Exodus 24—31, the Scripture will be printed without comment.

The narrative describes the preparations for building, construction of the tabernacle, equipment for the tabernacle, the priestly vestments, the completion and erection of the tabernacle, and the account of the glory of God filling the tabernacle.

1. Preparation for the Fulfilment of the Lord's Instructions (35:1—36:7)

(1) The Sabbath Rest (35:1–3)

¹ Moses assembled all the congregation of the people of Israel, and said to them, "These are the things which the LORD has commanded you to do. ² Six days shall work be done, but on the seventh day you shall have a holy sabbath of solemn rest to the LORD; whoever does any work on it shall be put to death; ³ you shall kindle no fire in all your habitations on the sabbath day."

(2) Moses' Call for the Offering (35:4–9)

⁴ Moses said to all the congregation of the people of Israel, "This is the thing which the LORD has commanded. ⁵ Take from among you an offering to the LORD; whoever is of a generous heart, let him bring the LORD's offering: gold, silver, and bronze; ⁶ blue and purple and scarlet stuff and fine twined linen; goats' hair, ⁷ tanned rams' skins, and goatskins; acacia wood, ⁸ oil for the light, spices for the anointing oil and for the fragrant incense, ⁹ and onyx stones and stones for setting, for the ephod and for the breastpiece.

(3) Laborers for the Task (35:10–19)

10 "And let every able man among you come and make all that the LORD has commanded: the tabernacle, 11 its tent and its covering, its hooks and its frames, its bars, its pillars, and its bases; 12 the ark with its poles, the mercy seat, and the veil of the screen; 13 the table with its poles and all its utensils, and the bread of the Presence; 14 the lampstand also for the light, with its utensils and its lamps, and the oil for the light; 15 and the altar of incense, with its poles, and the anointing oil and the fragrant incense, and the screen for the door, at the door of the tabernacle; 16 the altar of burnt offering, with its grating of bronze, its poles, and all its utensils, the laver and its base; 17 the hangings of the court, its pillars and its bases, and the screen for the gate of the court; 18 the pegs of the tabernacle and the pegs of the court, and their cords; 19 the finely wrought garments for ministering in the holy place, the holy garments for Aaron the priest, and the garments of his sons, for their service as priests."

(4) Responding to the Call for Offerings (35:20–29)

20 Then all the congregation of the people of Israel departed from the presence of Moses. 21 And they came, every one whose heart stirred him, and every one whose spirit moved him, and brought the LORD's offering to be used for the tent of meeting, and for all its service, and for the holy garments. 22 So they came, both men and women; all who were of a willing heart brought brooches and earrings and signet rings and armlets, all sorts of gold objects, every man dedicating an offering of gold to the LORD. 23 And every man with whom was found blue or purple or scarlet stuff or fine linen or goats' hair or tanned rams' skins or goatskins, brought them. 24 Every one who could make an offering of silver or bronze brought it as the LORD's offering; and every man with whom was found acacia wood of any use in the work, brought it. 25 And all women who had ability spun with their hands, and brought what they had spun in blue and purple and scarlet stuff and fine twined linen; 26 all the women whose hearts were moved with ability spun the goats' hair. 27 And the leaders brought onyx stones and stones to be set, for the ephod and for the breastpiece, 28 and spices and oil for the light, and for the anointing oil, and for the fragrant incense. 29 All the men and women, the people of Israel, whose heart moved them to bring anything for the work which the LORD had commanded by Moses to be done, brought it as their freewill offering to the LORD.

(5) Craftsmen for the Sanctuary (35:30–36:7)

30 And Moses said to the people of Israel, "See, the LORD has called by name Bezalel the son of Uri, son of Hur, of the tribe of Judah; 31 and he has filled him with the Spirit of God, with ability, with intelligence, with knowledge, and with all craftsmanship, 32 to devise artistic designs, to work in gold and silver and bronze, 33 in cutting stones for setting, and in carving wood, for work in every skilled craft. 34 And he has inspired him to teach, both him and Oholiab the son of Ahisamach of the tribe of Dan. 35 He has filled them with ability to do every sort of work done by a craftsman or by a designer or by an embroiderer in blue and purple and scarlet stuff and fine twined linen, or by a weaver—by any sort of workman or skilled designer. 1 Bezalel and Oholiab and every able man in whom the LORD has put ability and intelligence to know how to do any work in the construction of the sanctuary shall work in accordance with all that the LORD has commanded."

2 And Moses called Bezalel and Oholiab and every able man in whose mind the LORD had put ability, every one whose heart stirred him up to come to do the work; 3 and they received from Moses all the freewill offering which the people of Israel had brought for doing the work on the sanctuary. They still kept bringing him freewill offerings every morning, 4 so that all the able men who were doing every sort of task on the sanctuary came, each from the task that he was doing, 5 and said to Moses, "The people bring much more than enough for doing the work which the LORD has commanded us to do." 6 So Moses gave command, and word was proclaimed throughout the camp, "Let neither man nor woman do anything more for the offering for the sanctuary." So the people were restrained from bringing; 7 for the stuff they had was sufficient to do all the work, and more.

2. Building the Tabernacle (36:8–38)

The erection of so elaborate a building complex at this stage in Israel's history has long been the object of extensive debate. During the late nineteenth and early twentieth centuries it was common to find Old Testament scholars who argued that the picture of the tabernacle was an idealization based on the later Temple, and that Israel did not have the complex portable dwelling in her early years. Others, equally as vehemently, argued that the construction of such an elaborate complex was not impossible, despite the staggering amount of material required or the transportation problem associated with so large and heavy a burden.

In more recent years, others identified the tabernacle with the tent of David's time, suggesting that "by the time of David, the costly materials, the elaborate design, the skilled labor and the advanced theology of the Tabernacle, not to mention its necessity as the home of the ark, are all present" (Davies, p. 200).

In all probability the tabernacle should be traced to the period of the twelve-tribe federation at Shechem, and probably nearer the period immediately prior to the monarchy, if not the era of David himself. This does not mean that there was no sanctuary from the period of Sinai and Kadesh-Barnea. There was a sanctuary, but most probably in its earliest form it was much more like the tent of meeting, described as the place where the Lord came down to meet with Moses (33:7 ff.).

Later, the ark may have been associated with the tent of meeting, and within the tent there was added a succession of worship objects, including the table and the lampstand.

One probably confronts in Exodus 35:1—40:38, therefore, an idealized picture which has superimposed upon the absolute beginnings of the tabernacle the fully developed tabernacle—a reality which did not come into being until quite late. This composite and idealized picture drew together (1) the simple "tent of meeting"; (2) the sanctuary of the premonarchial confederacy; (3) David's tent; and (4) the Solomonic Temple. Despite this, however, one is on exceedingly tenuous ground in failing to take seriously the presence of a tent of meeting with cult objects from as early as the Sinai experience.

(1) Making the Curtains (36:8–9)

8 And all the able men among the workmen made the tabernacle with ten curtains; they were made of fine twined linen and blue and purple and scarlet stuff, with cherubim skilfully worked. 9 The length of each curtain was twenty-eight cubits, and the breadth of each curtain four cubits; all the curtains had the same measure.

(2) Joining the Curtains for the Tabernacle (36:10–13)

10 And he coupled five curtains to one another, and the other five curtains he coupled to one another. 11 And he made loops of blue on the edge of the outmost curtain of the first set; likewise he made them on the edge of the outmost curtain of the second set; 12 he made fifty loops on the one curtain, and he made fifty loops on the edge of the curtain that was in the second set; the loops were opposite one another. 13 And he made fifty clasps of gold, and coupled the curtains one to the other with clasps; so the tabernacle was one whole.

(3) The Tent for Covering the Tabernacle (36:14–19)

14 He also made curtains of goats' hair for a tent over the tabernacle; he made eleven curtains. 15 The length of each curtain was thirty cubits, and the breadth of each curtain four cubits; the eleven curtains had the same measure. 16 He coupled five curtains by themselves, and six curtains by themselves. 17 And he made fifty loops on the edge of the outmost curtain of the one set, and fifty loops on the edge of the other connecting curtain. 18 And he made fifty clasps of bronze to couple the tent together that it might be one whole. 19 And he made for the tent a covering of tanned rams' skins and goatskins.

(4) The Frames for the Tabernacle (36:20–30)

20 Then he made the upright frames for the tabernacle of acacia wood. 21 Ten cubits was the length of a frame, and a cubit and a half the breadth of each frame. 22 Each frame had two tenons, for fitting together; he did this for all the frames of the tabernacle. 23 The frames for the tabernacle he made thus: twenty frames for the south side; 24 and he made forty bases of silver under the twenty frames, two bases under one frame for its two tenons, and two bases under another frame for its two tenons. 25 And for the second side of the tabernacle, on the north side, he made twenty frames 26 and their forty bases of silver, two bases under one frame and two bases under another frame. 27 And for the rear of the tabernacle westward he made six frames. 28 And he made two

frames for corners of the tabernacle in the rear. [29] And they were separate beneath, but joined at the top, at the first ring; he made two of them thus, for the two corners. [30] There were eight frames with their bases of silver: sixteen bases, under every frame two bases.

(5) Supporting Bars (36:31–34)

[31] And he made bars of acacia wood, five for the frames of the one side of the tabernacle, [32] and five bars for the frames of the other side of the tabernacle, and five bars for the frames of the tabernacle at the rear westward. [33] And he made the middle bar to pass through from end to end halfway up the frames. [34] And he overlaid the frames with gold, and made their rings of gold for holders for the bars, and overlaid the bars with gold.

(6) The Veil and the Screen (36:35–38)

[35] And he made the veil of blue and purple and scarlet stuff and fine twined linen; with cherubim skilfully worked he made it. [36] And for it he made four pillars of acacia, and overlaid them with gold; their hooks were of gold, and he cast for them four bases of silver. [37] He also made a screen for the door of the tent, of blue and purple and scarlet stuff and fine twined linen, embroidered with needlework; [38] and its five pillars with their hooks. He overlaid their capitals, and their fillets were of gold, but their five bases were of bronze.

3. Equipment for the Tabernacle (37:1— 38:31)

In rapid succession each item of equipment for the tabernacle is described, the construction (37:1—38:31) following the instructions (25:10—38; 27:1 ff.; 30:1 ff.) quite precisely.

(1) The Ark (37:1–9)

[1] Bezalel made the ark of acacia wood; two cubits and a half was its length, a cubit and a half its breadth, and a cubit and a half its height. [2] And he overlaid it with pure gold within and without, and made a molding of gold around it. [3] And he cast for it four rings of gold for its four corners, two rings on its one side and two rings on its other side. [4] And he made poles of acacia wood, and overlaid them with gold, [5] and put the poles into the rings on the sides of the ark, to carry the ark. [6] And he made a mercy seat of pure gold; two cubits and a half was its length, and a cubit and a half its breadth. [7] And he made two cherubim of hammered gold; on the two ends of the mercy seat he made them, [8] one cherub on the end, and one cherub on the other end; of one piece with the mercy seat he made the cherubim on its two ends. [9] The cherubim spread out their wings above, overshadowing the mercy seat with their wings, with their faces one to another; toward the mercy seat were the faces of the cherubim.

(2) The Table for the Presence Bread (37:10–16)

[10] He also made the table of acacia wood; two cubits was its length, a cubit its breadth, and a cubit and a half its height; [11] and he overlaid it with pure gold, and made a molding of gold around it. [12] And he made around it a frame a handbreadth wide, and made a molding of gold around the frame. [13] He cast for it four rings of gold, and fastened the rings to the four corners at its four legs. [14] Close to the frame were the rings, as holders for the poles to carry the table. [15] He made the poles of acacia wood to carry the table, and overlaid them with gold. [16] And he made the vessels of pure gold which were to be upon the table, its plates and dishes for incense, and its bowls and flagons with which to pour libations.

(3) The Lampstand (37:17–24)

[17] He also made the lampstand of pure gold. The base and the shaft of the lampstand were made of hammered work; its cups, its capitals, and its flowers were of one piece with it. [18] And there were six branches going out of its sides, three branches of the lampstand out of one side of it and three branches of the lampstand out of the other side of it; [19] three cups made like almonds, each with capital and flower, on one branch, and three cups made like almonds, each with capital and flower, on the other branch—so for the six branches going out of the lampstand. [20] And on the lampstand itself were four cups made like almonds, with their capitals and flowers, [21] and a capital of one piece with it under each pair of the six branches going out of it. [22] Their capitals and their branches were of one piece with it; the whole of it was one piece of hammered work of pure gold. [23] And he made its seven lamps and its snuffers and its trays of pure gold. [24] He made it and all its utensils of a talent of pure gold.

(4) The Altar of Incense (37:25–28)

[25] He made the altar of incense of acacia wood; its length was a cubit, and its breadth was a cubit; it was square, and two cubits was

its height; its horns were of one piece with it. [26] He overlaid it with pure gold, its top, and its sides round about, and its horns; and he made a molding of gold round about it, [27] and made two rings of gold on it under its molding, on two opposite sides of it, as holders for the poles with which to carry it. [28] And he made the poles of acacia wood, and overlaid them with gold.

(5) The Anointing Oil and the Incense (37:29)

[29] He made the holy anointing oil also, and the pure fragrant incense, blended as by the perfumer.

(6) The Bronze Altar of Burnt Offering (38:1-7)

[1] He made the altar of burnt offering also of acacia wood; five cubits was its length, and five cubits its breadth; it was square, and three cubits was its height. [2] He made horns for it on its four corners; its horns were of one piece with it, and he overlaid it with bronze. [3] And he made all the utensils of the altar, the pots, the shovels, the basins, the forks, and the firepans: all its utensils he made of bronze. [4] And he made for the altar a grating, a network of bronze, under its ledge, extending halfway down. [5] He cast four rings on the four corners of the bronze grating as holders for the poles; [6] he made the poles of acacia wood, and overlaid them with bronze. [7] And he put the poles through the rings on the sides of the altar, to carry it with them; he made it hollow, with boards.

(7) The Laver of Bronze (38:8)

[8] And he made the laver of bronze and its base of bronze, from the mirrors of the ministering women who ministered at the door of the tent of meeting.

The writer adds that the basin was constructed from the mirrors of the women who "ministered at the door of the tent of meeting"—an anachronism, since there was no tent of meeting before which they could minister, if one follows the present scheme literally. There is no reference during this era to women who ministered at the door of the tent, but during the premonarchical era there were "women who served at the entrance to the tent of meeting" (1 Sam. 2:22).

McNeile suggests that "what sort of service the writer intends to describe is uncertain. Driver (1 S.) thinks that they were engaged in menial offices; Dillmann and Strack would add dancing and singing. Peritz (JBL xvii, 145 f.) believes that they did more than that, and lays stress on the fact that zaba' is used (in Num.) of the service of the Levites. He also contends that the service of women must have been an ancient custom, and renders 'which had served'" (p. 234).

(8) The Tabernacle Court (38:9-20)

[9] And he made the court; for the south side the hangings of the court were of fine twined linen, a hundred cubits; [10] their pillars were twenty and their bases twenty, of bronze, but the hooks of the pillars and their fillets were of silver. [11] And for the north side a hundred cubits, their pillars twenty, their bases twenty, of bronze, but the hooks of the pillars and their fillets were of silver. [12] And for the west side were hangings of fifty cubits, their pillars ten, and their sockets ten; the hooks of the pillars and their fillets were of silver. [13] And for the front to the east, fifty cubits. [14] The hangings for one side of the gate were fifteen cubits, with three pillars and three bases. [15] And so for the other side; on this hand and that hand by the gate of the court were hangings of fifteen cubits, with three pillars and three bases. [16] All the hangings round about the court were of fine twined linen. [17] And the bases for the pillars were of bronze, but the hooks of the pillars and their fillets were of silver; the overlaying of their capitals was also of silver, and all the pillars of the court were filleted with silver. [18] And the screen for the gate of the court was embroidered with needlework in blue and purple and scarlet stuff and fine twined linen; it was twenty cubits long and five cubits high in its breadth, corresponding to the hangings of the court. [19] And their pillars were four; their four bases were of bronze, their hooks of silver, and the overlaying of their capitals and their fillets of silver. [20] And all the pegs for the tabernacle and for the court round about were of bronze.

(9) Summary of the Offerings and Work (38:21-31)

[21] This is the sum of the things for the tabernacle, the tabernacle of the testimony, as they were counted at the commandment of Moses, for the work of the Levites under the

direction of Ithamar the son of Aaron the priest. 22 Bezalel the son of Uri, son of Hur, of the tribe of Judah, made all that the LORD commanded Moses; 23 And with him was Oholiab the son of Ahisamach, of the tribe of Dan, a craftsman and designer and embroiderer in blue and purple and scarlet stuff and fine twined linen.

24 All the gold that was used for the work, in all the construction of the sanctuary, the gold from the offering, was twenty-nine talents and seven hundred and thirty shekels, by the shekel of the sanctuary. 25 And the silver from those of the congregation who were numbered was a hundred talents and a thousand seven hundred and seventy-five shekels, by the shekel of the sanctuary: 26 a beka a head (that is, half a shekel, by the shekel of the sanctuary), for every one who was numbered in the census, from twenty years old and upward, for six hundred and three thousand, five hundred and fifty men. 27 The hundred talents of silver were for casting the bases of the sanctuary, and the bases of the veil; a hundred bases for the hundred talents, a talent for a base. 28 And of the thousand seven hundred and seventy-five shekels he made hooks for the pillars, and overlaid their capitals and made fillets for them. 29 And the bronze that was contributed was seventy talents, and two thousand and four hundred shekels; 30 with it he made the bases for the door of the tent of meeting, the bronze altar and the bronze grating for it and all the utensils of the altar, 31 the bases round about the court, and the bases of the gate of the court, all the pegs of the tabernacle, and all the pegs round about the court.

The following summary of work and the weight of the metals used completes the record of the tabernacle's construction.

The Work on the Tabernacle (vv. 21–23). The tabernacle is referred to as the *tabernacle of the testimony* because of the primacy of the ten words contained in the ark. The place of worship was one of revelation as well as praise. The summary describes the threefold division of work concerning the tabernacle: (1) Moses, who gave the Lord's commandment; (2) Ithamar, son of Aaron, under whom the Levites, who made use of the tabernacle, served; and (3) Bezalel and his associate Oholiab who executed the skilled work on the tabernacle.

The Weight of Metal Used (vv. 24–31). The gold, silver, and bronze used in the

construction of the tabernacle and its fittings are summarized by weight, the weight being given in shekels and talents. The talent weighted approximately 75.6 pounds (the precise calculation of weights being tenuous), and the shekel .403 ounce, with 3,000 shekels to the talent.[10] Calculated on this basis, there were 2,206.88 pounds of gold, 7,604.7 pounds of silver, and 5,352.45 pounds of bronze, or a total of 15,164.03 pounds or slightly more than 7½ tons of metal.

The writer calculated the amount of silver used on the basis of one-half shekel poll tax for each of 603,550 men, which yielded a total of 301,750 shekels, or 100 talents (figured at 3,000 shekels to the talent) plus an additional 1,750 shekels (cf. v. 25). No account was taken of silver which may have been contributed apart from the tax. Contrary to its use in constructing the tabernacle, however, Exodus 30:11 ff. presupposes that the poll tax was for the continual maintenance of the sanctuary service (v. 16 says, "appoint it for the service of the tent of meeting"), not for construction purposes.

The total weight of the metals given here doubtless would have precipitated a considerable problem in transportation, to say nothing of a slave people possessing precious metals in such quantities. According to the book of Numbers, the entire tabernacle complex—court, tabernacle, and attendant equipment—was transported on 6 covered wagons drawn by 12 oxen, 2 oxen to the wagon (7:1 ff.). In addition, the frames, bars, pillars, bases, and other accessories were placed in the charge of Merari (Num. 3:33 ff.), who was given 4 wagons and 8 oxen to handle the equipment (Num. 7:8). By these figures one would assume that each wagon held an average of approximately 2 tons of metal alone, to say nothing of the weight of the hundreds of pieces of bars and frames, plus attendant equipment, and was drawn by 2

[10] If the shekel of the sanctuary was heavier than the normal shekel, then the above weights may be as much as 20 percent less than some calculations.

oxen! In fact, the load carried was probably much lighter, for the tabernacle was probably less complex than described by the priestly writer.

4. The Priestly Dress (39:1–31)

The writer duplicated the previous instructions given through Moses concerning the priestly apparel, making an almost word for word repetition of the previous narrative (cf. 28:1 ff.).

(1) Fulfilling the Lord's Command (39:1)

¹ And of the blue and purple and scarlet stuff they made finely wrought garments, for ministering in the holy place; they made the holy garments for Aaron; as the LORD had commanded Moses.

(2) The Ephod 39:2–7

² And he made the ephod of gold, blue and purple and scarlet stuff, and fine twined linen. ³ And gold leaf was hammered out and cut into threads to work into the blue and purple and the scarlet stuff, and into the fine twined linen, in skilled design. ⁴ They made for the ephod shoulder-pieces, joined to it at its two edges. ⁵ And the skilfully woven band upon it, to gird it on, was of the same materials and workmanship, of gold, blue and purple and scarlet stuff, and fine twined linen; as the LORD had commanded Moses.

⁶ The onyx stones were prepared, enclosed in settings of gold filigree and engraved like the engravings of a signet, according to the names of the sons of Israel. ⁷ And he set them on the shoulder-pieces of the ephod, to be stones of remembrance for the sons of Israel; as the LORD had commanded Moses.

(3) The Breastpiece of Judgment 39:8–21

⁸ He made the breastpiece, in skilled work, like the work of the ephod, of gold, blue and purple and scarlet stuff, and fine twined linen. ⁹ It was square; the breastpiece was made double, a span its length and a span its breadth when doubled. ¹⁰ And they set in it four rows of stones. A row of sardius, topaz, and carbuncle was the first row; ¹¹ and the second row, an emerald, a sapphire, and a diamond; ¹² and the third row, a jacinth, an agate, and an amethyst; ¹³ and the fourth row, a beryl, an onyx, and a jasper; they were enclosed in settings of gold filigree. ¹⁴ There were twelve stones with their names according to the names of the sons of Israel; they were like signets, each engraved with its name, for the twelve tribes. ¹⁵ And they made on the breastpiece twisted chains like cords, of pure gold; ¹⁶ and they made two settings of gold filigree and two gold rings, and put the two rings on the two edges of the breastpiece; ¹⁷ and they put the two cords of gold in the two rings at the edges of the breastpiece. ¹⁸ Two ends of the two cords they had attached to the two settings of filigree; thus they attached it in front to the shoulder-pieces of the ephod. ¹⁹ Then they made two rings of gold, and put them at the two ends of the breastpiece, on its inside edge next to the ephod. ²⁰ And they made two rings of gold, and attached them in front to the lower part of the two shoulder-pieces of the ephod, at its joining above the skilfully woven band of the ephod. ²¹ And they bound the breastpiece by its rings to the rings of the ephod with a lace of blue, so that it should lie upon the skilfully woven band of the ephod, and that the breastpiece should not come loose from the ephod; as the LORD had commanded Moses.

(4) The Robe of the Ephod 39:22–26

²² He also made the robe of the ephod woven all of blue; ²³ and the opening of the robe in it was like the opening in a garment, with a binding around the opening, that it might not be torn. ²⁴ On the skirts of the robe they made pomegranates of blue and purple and scarlet stuff and fine twined linen. ²⁵ They also made bells of pure gold, and put the bells between the pomegranates upon the skirts of the robe round about, between the pomegranates; ²⁶ a bell and a pomegranate, a bell and a pomegranate round about upon the skirts of the robe for ministering; as the LORD had commanded Moses.

The present passage suggests only *and the opening of the robe . . . was like the opening in a garment, with a binding around the opening,* while the instructions specifically suggested that the ephod was to have "an opening for the head" (28:32). If the robe was worn over the breastpiece of judgment, which was attached to the ephod, how did the priest have access to the urim and thummim (contained in the judgment pouch)? May it not be that the vague reference to an opening in verse 23 suggests an opening larger than merely a space for inserting the head? Could the robe possibly have had a slit extending low enough below the neck to give access to the breastpiece of judgment?

(5) The Garments for Aaron's Sons (39:27-29)

27 They also made the coats, woven of fine linen, for Aaron and his sons, 28 and the turban of fine linen, and the caps of fine linen, and the linen breeches of fine twined linen, 29 and the girdle of fine twined linen and of blue and purple and scarlet stuff, embroidered with needlework; as the LORD had commanded Moses.

(6) The Gold Talisman (39:30-31)

30 And they made the plate of the holy crown of pure gold, and wrote upon it an inscription, like the engraving of a signet, "Holy to the LORD." 31 And they tied to it a lace of blue, to fasten it on the turban above; as the LORD had commanded Moses.

Although the instruction passage specified only a "plate of pure gold," the fulfilment passage further characterized the plate as *the plate of the holy crown.* Since the golden plate was tied to the turban with a *lace of blue,* it was hardly a crown in the traditional connotation of the word, and one should interpret the present passage in the same manner as 28:36 f.

5. The Completion and Erection of the Tabernacle (39:32—40:33)

Following the construction of the tabernacle and its furnishings under the leadership of Bezalel, Moses erected the tabernacle. The implication of the narrative is that Moses did this alone, an almost superhuman feat if the tabernacle described in 35—40 existed in full form at Sinai. One might conclude that the passage means that Moses gave leadership to others in raising the tabernacle. The metal alone weighed 7½ tons, according to the priestly narrative, and this alone—to say nothing of the frames, tabernacle, tent, and covering —would cause one to suppose that Moses simply took the lead in erecting the tabernacle, or that what he erected was less complex than the building described in Exodus.

(1) Presentation to Moses (39:32-43)

32 Thus all the work of the tabernacle of the tent of meeting was finished; and the people of Israel had done according to all that the LORD had commanded Moses; so had they done. 33 And they brought the tabernacle to Moses, the tent and all its utensils, its hooks, its frames, its bars, its pillars, and its bases; 34 the covering of tanned rams' skins and goatskins, and the veil of the screen; 35 the ark of the testimony with its poles and the mercy seat; 36 the table with all its utensils, and the bread of the Presence; 37 the lampstand of pure gold and its lamps with the lamps set and all its utensils, and the oil for the light; 38 the golden altar, the anointing oil and the fragrant incense, and the screen for the door of the tent; 39 the bronze altar, and its grating of bronze, its poles, and all its utensils; the laver and its base; 40 the hangings of the court, its pillars, and its bases, and the screen for the gate of the court, its cords, and its pegs; and all the utensils for the service of the tabernacle, for the tent of meeting; 41 the finely worked garments for ministering in the holy place, the holy garments for Aaron the priest, and the garments of his sons to serve as priests. 42 According to all that the LORD had commanded Moses, so the people of Israel had done all the work. 43 And Moses saw all the work, and behold, they had done it; as the LORD had commanded, so had they done it. And Moses blessed them.

The reference to the *tabernacle of the tent of meeting* may represent the blending of the more simple concept of the tent of meeting, described in 33:7-11, with the more complicated tabernacle of a later era, probably during the period immediately prior to the construction of the Temple. The lengthy narrative (vv. 32-43) is a catalog of those items which were constructed. More than this, however, the catalog is an evidence of the faithfulness of Israel to the revealed will of God, a faithfulness which was doubtless appealed to in succeeding generations.

(2) The Lord's Instructions Concerning the Erection of the Tabernacle (40:1-15)

1 The LORD said to Moses, 2 "On the first day of the first month you shall erect the tabernacle of the tent of meeting. 3 And you shall put in it the ark of the testimony, and you shall screen the ark with the veil. 4 And you shall bring in

the table, and set its arrangements in order; and you shall bring in the lampstand, and set up its lamps. 5 And you shall put the golden altar for incense before the ark of the testimony, and set up the screen for the door of the tabernacle. 6 You shall set the altar of burnt offering before the door of the tabernacle of the tent of meeting, 7 and place the laver between the tent of meeting and the altar, and put water in it. 8 And you shall set up the court round about, and hang up the screen for the gate of the court. 9 Then you shall take the anointing oil, and anoint the tabernacle and all that is in it, and consecrate it and all its furniture; and it shall become holy. 10 You shall also anoint the altar of burnt offering and all its utensils, and consecrate the altar; and the altar shall be most holy. 11 You shall also anoint the laver and its base, and consecrate it. 12 Then you shall bring Aaron and his sons to the door of the tent of meeting, and shall wash them with water, 13 and put upon Aaron the holy garments, and you shall anoint him and consecrate him, that he may serve me as priest. 14 You shall bring his sons also and put coats on them, 15 and anoint them, as you anointed their father, that they may serve me as priests: and their anointing shall admit them to a perpetual priesthood throughout their generations."

Following the placement of the tabernacle and its equipment, Moses was to anoint the entire tabernacle, plus all attendant equipment, thereby symbolizing their consecration or setting apart to the service of God (vv. 9–11). Then, Aaron and his sons were to be brought to the door of the tent, washed with water, garbed, and consecrated through anointment (vv. 12–15). Thus, the entire tabernacle complex, including its personnel, was dedicated to the Lord's service.

(3) Erecting the Tabernacle and Placing the Equipment (40:16–33)

16 Thus did Moses; according to all that the LORD commanded him, so he did. 17 And in the first month in the second year, on the first day of the month, the tabernacle was erected. 18 Moses erected the tabernacle; he laid its bases, and set up its frames, and put in its poles, and raised up its pillars; 19 and he spread the tent over the tabernacle, and put the covering of the tent over it, as the LORD had commanded Moses. 20 And he took the testimony and put it into the ark, and put the poles on the ark, and set the mercy seat above on the ark; 21 and he brought the ark into the tabernacle, and set up the veil of the screen, and screened the ark of the testimony; as the LORD had commanded Moses. 22 And he put the table in the tent of meeting, on the north side of the tabernacle, outside the veil, 23 and set the bread in order on it before the LORD; as the LORD had commanded Moses. 24 And he put the lampstand in the tent of meeting, opposite the table on the south side of the tabernacle, 25 and set up the lamps before the LORD; as the LORD had commanded Moses. 26 And he put the golden altar in the tent of meeting before the veil, 27 and burnt fragrant incense upon it; as the LORD had commanded Moses. 28 And he put in place the screen for the door of the tabernacle. 29 And he set the altar of burnt offering at the door of the tabernacle of the tent of meeting, and offered upon it the burnt offering and the cereal offering; as the LORD had commanded Moses. 30 And he set the laver between the tent of meeting and the altar, and put water in it for washing, 31 with which Moses and Aaron and his sons washed their hands and their feet; 32 when they went into the tent of meeting, and when they approached the altar, they washed; as the LORD commanded Moses. 33 And he erected the court round the tabernacle and the altar, and set up the screen of the gate of the court. So Moses finished the work.

In keeping with the practice of the priestly stratum of material throughout the book of Exodus, the instructions (40:1–15) are followed by a narrative describing the fulfilment of those instructions (40:16–33). The repetitious nature of this procedure is prone to obscure the conceptual principle which led the priestly writer to arrange his material in a consistent pattern of instruction and fulfilment (this pattern extends throughout Exodus). By developing his narrative around this repetitious pattern, the priestly writer suggests that the earlier work of Moses in Egypt and the wilderness, as well as the construction of the tabernacle, followed a divine plan. Thus, the twofold pattern of instruction-fulfilment stresses the conformity of Israel's sacral life to a divine archetype.

The only new item of information is the elaboration concerning the purpose of *the laver*. The priests washed both their hands and feet before either entering the tabernacle or ministering at the altar. Thus, their feet were ritually cleansed prior to stepping into the holy precincts of the tabernacle just as their hands were cleansed before offering the Lord's sacrifice. One entered a holy place without shoes (cf. 3:5, "put off your shoes from your feet").

So Moses finished the work. One cannot read these words without speculating on the sense of fulfilment that must have characterized Moses, despite the precise nature of the tabernacle, the number of the people involved in the exodus, or other technical problems. In the space of approximately two years he had returned from Egypt to this same mountain, secured the freedom of his people, witnessed their mighty deliverance at the sea and in the wilderness, mediated the covenant and its stipulations, and now had secured a portable sanctuary that guaranteed the Lord's continuing presence beyond Sinai. When Moses was initially called of God he requested some sign of validation, but received only the vague and indefinite assurance that "when you have brought forth the people out of Egypt, you shall serve God upon this mountain" (Ex. 3:12).

Now the sign was fulfilled, and the formative elments of tribal solidarity had begun to emerge in the gathering of a people around a central sanctuary. Although there were yet other journeys to begin and further trials ahead, there was nonetheless a note of finality in the editor's words, "So Moses finished the work." How desirable that this might be said of every called person!

6. The Glory of God Fills the Tabernacle (40:34–38)

34 Then the cloud covered the tent of meeting, and the glory of the Lord filled the tabernacle. 35 And Moses was not able to enter the tent of meeting, because the cloud abode upon it, and the glory of the Lord filled the tabernacle. 36 Throughout all their journeys, whenever the cloud was taken up from over the tabernacle, the people of Israel would go onward; 37 but if the cloud was not taken up, then they did not go onward till the day that it was taken up. 38 For throughout all their journeys the cloud of the Lord was upon the tabernacle by day, and fire was in it by night, in the sight of all the house of Israel.

As though to place a stamp of divine approval upon the work of Moses and his people, the glory of God filled the tabernacle, not only assuring Israel of the Lord's continuing presence, but guaranteeing them that the Lord approved of what had been done. The experience is, of course, closely paralleled by the glory of God filling the Temple in the Solomonic era (cf. 1 Kings 8:11).

By the time the present narrative was written, Israel had come to understand the cloud as an unusual phenomenon which at times filled the tabernacle and on other occasions rose above the tent. When the cloud settled in and around the tent, Israel remained at rest from her journeying, but she moved forward when the cloud rose over the tabernacle. In addition, fire was in it by night, probably symbolizing the glory of God, his burning, fiery presence.

Behind the present narrative stand the incense and the lampstand; the cloud of incense smoke symbolizing the Lord's presence by day, and the light of the lampstand (which was apparently tended only at night) signifying his presence by night. With the passage of time, successive generations idealized and heightened the incense and lampstand until in later times the incense had become a cloud, and the light of the lamp had become a fire, unrelated to the lampstand. This idealization by later generations should not obscure the fact that the Lord's presence was a reality for Israel of both the early and latter stages, and that his reality was unrelated to the specific nature of the cloud and fire. It is altogether feasible that the smoke above the tabernacle did serve as an omen concerning the movement of Israel. The incense may have been burned and the smoke observed as a deliberate means of receiving an oracle or omen from the Lord. When the incense smoke settled about the tent, Israel remained at rest, but when it arose heavenward she also moved. This would have been wholly in keeping with contemporary cultural patterns of thought. Also, the fire in the lampstand forever symbolized the burning presence of God, so much so that in much later times for the light to go out in the sanctuary was a portent of catastrophe. Above all, however, one should see beyond the physical phenomena to the reality of God's presence in the midst of Israel, a reality symbolized in smoke and fire.

Thus, the purpose in building the tabernacle *of the tent of meeting* was realized. The Lord God who met Israel at Sinai would not be left behind on the mountain abode. He would accompany Israel wherever she went, enshrined as he was above the cherubim within the most holy place of the tabernacle. God always abides with his covenant people, never abandoning them to the chaos of wilderness.